Spring 6 Recipes

A Problem-Solution Approach to Spring Framework

Fifth Edition

Marten Deinum
Daniel Rubio
Josh Long

Apress®

Spring 6 Recipes: A Problem-Solution Approach to Spring Framework

Marten Deinum
Meppel, Drenthe, The Netherlands

Josh Long
Canyon Country, CA, USA

Daniel Rubio
Ensenada, Baja California, Mexico

ISBN-13 (pbk): 978-1-4842-8648-7
https://doi.org/10.1007/978-1-4842-8649-4

ISBN-13 (electronic): 978-1-4842-8649-4

Managing Director, Apress Media LLC: Welmoed Spahr
Acquisitions Editor: Steve Anglin
Development Editor: Laura Berendson
Coordinating Editor: Mark Powers

Cover designed by eStudioCalamar

Cover image by Yoksel Zok on Unsplash (www.unsplash.com)

Distributed to the book trade worldwide by Apress Media, LLC, 1 New York Plaza, New York, NY 10004, U.S.A. Phone 1-800-SPRINGER, fax (201) 348-4505, e-mail orders-ny@springer-sbm.com, or visit www.springeronline.com. Apress Media, LLC is a California LLC and the sole member (owner) is Springer Science + Business Media Finance Inc (SSBM Finance Inc). SSBM Finance Inc is a **Delaware** corporation.

For information on translations, please e-mail booktranslations@springernature.com; for reprint, paperback, or audio rights, please e-mail bookpermissions@springernature.com.

Apress titles may be purchased in bulk for academic, corporate, or promotional use. eBook versions and licenses are also available for most titles. For more information, reference our Print and eBook Bulk Sales web page at http://www.apress.com/bulk-sales.

Any source code or other supplementary material referenced by the author in this book is available to readers on GitHub (https://github.com/Apress). For more detailed information, please visit http://www.apress.com/source-code.

Printed on acid-free paper

Table of Contents

About the Authors

Marten Deinum is a submitter on the open source Spring Framework project. He is also a Java/software consultant working for Conspect. He has developed and architected software, primarily in Java, for small and large companies. He is an enthusiastic open source user and longtime fan, user, and advocate of the Spring Framework. He has held a number of positions including software engineer, development lead, coach, and Java and Spring trainer.

Daniel Rubio has more than 10 years of experience in enterprise and web-based software and is currently the founder and technical lead at MashupSoft.com. He has authored several books for Apress. Daniel's expertise lies in Java, Spring, Python, Django, JavaScript/CSS, and HTML.

Josh Long is the Spring developer advocate at Pivotal. Josh is a Java champion, the author of five books (including O'Reilly's upcoming *Cloud Native Java*) and three best-selling training videos (including "*Building Microservices* with Spring Boot" with Phil Webb), and an open source contributor (Spring Boot, Spring Integration, Spring Cloud, Activiti, and Vaadin).

About the Technical Reviewer

Manuel Jordan Elera is an autodidactic developer and researcher who enjoys learning new technologies for his own experiments and creating new integrations. Manuel won the 2013 Springy Award–Community Champion and Spring Champion. In his little free time, he reads the Bible and composes music on his guitar. Manuel is known as dr_pompeii. He has tech-reviewed numerous books, including *Pro Spring MVC with WebFlux* (Apress, 2020), *Pro Spring Boot 2* (Apress, 2019), *Rapid Java Persistence and Microservices* (Apress, 2019), *Java Language Features* (Apress, 2018), *Spring Boot 2 Recipes* (Apress, 2018), and *Java APIs, Extensions and Libraries* (Apress, 2018). You can read his detailed tutorials on Spring technologies and contact him through his blog at www.manueljordanelera.blogspot.com. You can follow Manuel on his Twitter account, @dr_pompeii.

Acknowledgments

The acknowledgments are probably the hardest thing to write in a book. It is impossible to name everyone personally that I want to thank, and I will forget someone. For that, I want to apologize beforehand.

Although this is the seventh book I have written, I couldn't have done it without the great team at Apress. Special thanks to Mark Powers for keeping me focused and on schedule and Steve Anglin for giving me the opportunity to write this update and for sticking with me even when I couldn't keep my schedule due to personal circumstances. I thank Manuel Jordan, without whose comments and suggestions this book would never have become what it is now.

Thanks to my family and friends for the times they had to miss me and to my dive team for all the dives and trips I missed.

Last but definitely not the least, I thank my wife, Djoke Deinum, and daughters, Geeske and Sietske, for their endless support, love, and dedication, despite the long evenings and sacrificed weekends and holidays to finish the book. Without your support, I probably would have abandoned the endeavor long ago.

—Marten Deinum

Introduction

The Spring Framework is still growing. It has always been about choice. Java EE focused on a few technologies, largely to the detriment of alternative, better solutions. When the Spring Framework debuted, few would have agreed that Java EE represented the best-in-breed architectures of the day. Spring debuted to great fanfare, because it sought to simplify Java EE. Each release since has marked the introduction of new features designed to both simplify and enable solutions.

With version 2.0 and newer, the Spring Framework started targeting multiple platforms. The framework provided services on top of existing platforms, as always, but was decoupled from the underlying platform wherever possible. Java EE is still a major reference point, but it's not the only target. Additionally, the Spring Framework runs on different cloud environments. Frameworks built on top of Spring have emerged to support application integration, batch processing, messaging, and much more. Version 6 of the Spring Framework is a major upgrade; the baseline was raised to Java 17. Spring 5 introduced Spring WebFlux, a reactive programming web framework; Spring 6 broadens the effort to reactive database access with R2DBC and further improvements in the reactive programming paradigm. Spring 6 also adds native support for AOT (Ahead of Time) compilation with GraalVM. Finally, the move from Java EE to Jakarta EE was also done in Spring 6, which targets newer APIs and is also a breaking change.

This is the fifth edition of this superb recipe book, and it covers the updated framework, describing the new features and explaining the different configuration options.

It was impossible to describe every project in the Spring ecosystem, so we had to decide what to keep, what to add, and what to update. This was a hard decision, but we think we have included the most important content.

Who This Book Is For

This book is for Java developers who want to simplify their architecture and solve problems outside the scope of the Jakarta EE platform. If you are already using Spring in your projects, the more advanced chapters discuss newer technologies that you might not know about already. If you are new to the framework, this book will get you started in no time.

This book assumes you have some familiarity with Java and an IDE of some sort. While it is possible, and indeed useful, to use Java exclusively with client applications, Java's largest community lives in the enterprise space, and that, too, is where you'll see these technologies deliver the most benefit. Thus, some familiarity with basic enterprise programming concepts such as the Servlet API is assumed.

How This Book Is Structured

Chapter 1, "Spring Core Tasks," gives a general overview of the Spring Framework, including how to set it up, what it is, and how it's used.

Chapter 2, "Spring MVC," covers web-based application development using the Spring Web MVC framework.

Chapter 3, "Spring MVC: REST Services," introduces Spring's support for RESTful web services.

Chapter 4, "Spring WebFlux," introduces reactive programming for the Web.

Chapter 5, "Spring Security," provides an overview of the Spring Security project to help you better secure your application.

Chapter 6, "Data Access," discusses how to use Spring to talk to datastores using APIs such as Java Database Connectivity (JDBC), Hibernate/JPA, and R2DBC.

Chapter 7, "Spring Transaction Management," introduces the concepts behind Spring's robust transaction management facilities.

Chapter 8, "Spring Batch," introduces the Spring Batch framework, which provides a way to model solutions traditionally considered the domain of mainframes.

Chapter 9, "Spring Data Access with NoSQL," introduces multiple Spring Data portfolio projects, covering different NoSQL technologies.

Chapter 10, "Spring Java Enterprise Services and Remoting Technologies," introduces you to JMX support, scheduling, email support, and various facilities, including the Spring Web Services (Spring-WS) project.

Chapter 11, "Spring Messaging," discusses using Spring with message-oriented middleware through JMS and RabbitMQ and the simplifying Spring abstractions.

Chapter 12, "Spring Integration," discusses using the Spring Integration framework to integrate disparate services and data.

Chapter 13, "Spring Testing," discusses unit testing with the Spring Framework.

Chapter 14, "Caching," introduces the Spring Caching abstraction, including how to configure it and how to transparently add caching to your application.

Conventions

Sometimes when we want you to pay particular attention to a part within a code example, we will make the font **bold**. Please note that the bold doesn't necessarily reflect a code change from the previous version.

In cases when a code line is too long to fit the page's width, we will break it with a code continuation character. Please note that when you enter the code, you have to concatenate the line without any spaces.

Prerequisites

Because the Java programming language is platform independent, you are free to choose any supported operating system. However, some of the examples in this book use platform-specific paths. Translate them as necessary to your operating system's format before typing the examples.

To make the most of this book, install Java Development Kit (JDK) version 19 or higher. You should have a Java IDE installed to make development easier. For this book, the sample code is Gradle-based. If you're running Eclipse and install the Gradle plugin, you can open the same code in Eclipse, and the CLASSPATH and dependencies will be filled in by the Gradle metadata.

If you're using Eclipse, you might prefer Spring Tools 4, as it comes preloaded with the plugins you'll need to be productive with the Spring Framework in Eclipse. If you use IntelliJ IDEA, you need to enable the Gradle and Groovy plugins.

As the code is based on Gradle, you will need to install Gradle (version 7.5 or up) **or** use the provided Gradle Wrapper script to download the needed Gradle version. You can build each recipe with `gradle build` or `../../gradlew build` (to use the Gradle Wrapper).

To make it easier, the project(s) also has some scripts that can launch Docker containers; if you want to use those, you will need to have Docker preinstalled on your computer.

Downloading the Code

The source code for this book is available for download at `github.com/apress-spring-6-recipes-5e`. The source code is organized by chapters, each of which includes one or more independent examples.

Contacting the Authors

We always welcome your questions and feedback regarding the contents of this book. You can contact Marten Deinum at `marten@deinum.biz`.

CHAPTER 1

■ ■ ■

Spring Core Tasks

In this chapter, you'll learn about the core tasks associated with Spring. At the heart of the Spring Framework is the Spring Inversion of Control (IoC) container. The IoC container is used to manage and configure POJOs or Plain Old Java Objects. Because one of the primary appeals of the Spring Framework is to build Java applications with POJOs, many of Spring's core tasks involve managing and configuring POJOs in the IoC container.

So whether you plan to use the Spring Framework for web applications, enterprise integration, or some other type of project, working with POJOss and the IoC container is one of the first steps you need to take to work with the Spring Framework. The majority of the recipes in this chapter cover tasks that you'll use throughout the book and on a daily basis to develop Spring applications.

ⓘ The term "bean" is used interchangeably with a POJO instance both in the book and the Spring documentation. Both refer to an object instance created from a Java class. The term "component" is used interchangeably with a POJO class both in the book and the Spring documentation. Both refer to the actual Java class from which object instances are created.

1-1. Using Java Config to Configure POJOs

Problem

You want to manage POJOs with annotations with Spring's IoC container.

Solution

Design a POJO class. Next, create a Java Config class with the @Configuration and @Bean annotations to configure POJO instance values or set up Java components with @Component, @Repository, @Service, or @Controller annotations to later create POJO instance values. Next, instantiate the Spring IoC container to scan for Java classes with annotations. The POJO instances or bean instances then become accessible to put together as part of an application.

© Marten Deinum, Daniel Rubio, Josh Long 2023
M. Deinum et al., *Spring 6 Recipes*, https://doi.org/10.1007/978-1-4842-8649-4_1

How It Works

Suppose you're going to develop an application to generate sequence numbers and that you are also going to need many series of sequence numbers for different purposes. Each sequence will have its own prefix, suffix, and initial value. So you have to create and maintain multiple generator instances for the application.

Create a Class to Be Instantiated as a Bean

In accordance with the requirements, you create a Sequence class that has three properties—prefix, suffix, and initial. You also create a private field counter to store the numeric value of each generator. Each time you call the nextValue() method on a generator instance, you get the last sequence number with the prefix and suffix joined.

Sequence class

```
package com.apress.spring6recipes.sequence;

import java.util.concurrent.atomic.AtomicInteger;

public class Sequence {

  private final AtomicInteger counter = new AtomicInteger();
  private String prefix;
  private String suffix;

  public void setPrefix(String prefix) {
    this.prefix = prefix;
  }

  public void setSuffix(String suffix) {
    this.suffix = suffix;
  }

  public void setInitial(int initial) {
    this.counter.set(initial);
  }

  public String nextValue() {
    return prefix + counter.getAndIncrement() + suffix;
  }
}
```

Create Java Config with @Configuration and @Bean to Create POJOs

To define instances of a POJO class in the Spring IoC container, you can create a Java Config class with instantiation values. A Java Config class with a POJO or bean definition would look like the following.

SequenceConfiguration

```
package com.apress.spring6recipes.sequence.config;

import org.springframework.context.annotation.Bean;
import org.springframework.context.annotation.Configuration;

import com.apress.spring6recipes.sequence.Sequence;

@Configuration
public class SequenceConfiguration {

  @Bean
  public Sequence sequence() {
    var seqgen = new Sequence();
    seqgen.setPrefix("30");
    seqgen.setSuffix("A");
    seqgen.setInitial(100000);
    return seqgen;
  }
}
```

Notice the SequenceConfiguration class is decorated with the @Configuration annotation. This tells Spring it's a configuration class. When Spring encounters a class with the @Configuration annotation, it looks for bean instance definitions in the class, which are Java methods decorated with the @Bean annotation. The Java methods create and return a bean instance.

Any method definitions decorated with the @Bean annotation generate a bean name based on the method name. Alternatively, you can explicitly specify the bean name in the @Bean annotation with the name attribute (e.g., @Bean(name="mys1") makes the bean available as mys1; if you explicitly specify the bean name, the method name is ignored for purposes of bean creation).

Instantiate the Spring IoC Container to Scan for Annotations

You have to instantiate the Spring IoC container to scan for Java classes that contain annotations. In doing so, Spring detects @Configuration and @Bean annotations, so you can later get bean instances from the IoC container itself.

Spring provides two types of IoC container implementations. The basic one is called bean factory. The more advanced one is called application context, which is compatible with the bean factory. Note the configuration files for these two types of IoC containers are identical.

The application context provides more advanced features than the bean factory while keeping the basic features compatible. Therefore, we strongly recommend using the application context for every application unless the resources of an application are restricted (such as when running Spring for an applet or a mobile device). The interfaces for the bean factory and the application context are BeanFactory and ApplicationContext, respectively. The ApplicationContext interface is a subinterface of BeanFactory for maintaining compatibility.

Since ApplicationContext is an interface, you have to instantiate an implementation of it. Spring has several application context implementations. We recommend you use AnnotationConfigApplicationContext, which is the newest and most flexible implementation. With this class you can load the Java Config file:

```
var context = new AnnotationConfigApplicationContext(SequenceConfiguration.class);
```

Once the application context is instantiated, the object reference—in this case context—provides an entry point to access the POJO instances or beans.

Get POJO Instances or Beans from the IoC Container

To get a declared bean from a bean factory or an application context, you use the getBean() method and pass in the unique bean name. The return type of the getBean() method is java.lang.Object, so you have to cast it to its actual type before using it:

```
var generator = (Sequence) context.getBean("sequence");
```

The getBean() method also supports another variation where you can provide the bean class name to avoid making the cast:

```
var generator = context.getBean("sequence", Sequence.class);
```

Or if there is only a single bean, you could omit the bean name:

```
var generator = context.getBean(Sequence.class);
```

Once you reach this step, you can use the POJO or bean just like any object created using a constructor outside of Spring.

A Main class to run the sequence application would be the following.

Main.java for running the sequence generator application

```
package com.apress.spring6recipes.sequence;

import com.apress.spring6recipes.sequence.config.SequenceConfiguration;

import org.springframework.context.annotation.AnnotationConfigApplicationContext;

public class Main {

  public static void main(String[] args) {

    var cfg = SequenceConfiguration.class;
    try (var ctx = new AnnotationConfigApplicationContext(cfg)) {
      var generator = ctx.getBean(Sequence.class);
      System.out.println(generator.nextValue());
      System.out.println(generator.nextValue());
    }
  }
}
```

If everything is available in the Java classpath (Sequence class and the Spring JAR dependencies), you should see the following output, along with some logging messages:

```
30100000A
30100001A
```

Create a POJO Class with the @Component Annotation to Create Beans with DAO

Up to this point, the Spring bean instantiations have been done hard-coding the values in a Java Config class. This was the preferred approach to simplify the Spring examples.

However, the POJO instantiation process for most applications is done from either a database or user input. So now it's time to move forward and use a more real-world scenario. For this section, we'll use a domain class and a Data Access Object (DAO) class to create POJOs. You still won't need to set up a database—we'll actually hard-code values in the DAO class—but familiarizing yourself with this type of application structure is important since it's the basis for most real-world applications and future recipes.

Suppose you are asked to develop a sequence generator application like the one you did in the last section. We'll need to modify the class structure slightly to accommodate a domain class and DAO pattern. First, create a domain class Sequence containing the id, prefix, and suffix properties.

Modified Sequence class

```java
package com.apress.spring6recipes.sequence;

public class Sequence {

    private final String id;
    private final String prefix;
    private final String suffix;

    public Sequence(String id, String prefix, String suffix) {
        this.id = id;
        this.prefix = prefix;
        this.suffix = suffix;
    }

    public String getId() {
        return id;
    }

    public String getPrefix() {
        return prefix;
    }

    public String getSuffix() {
        return suffix;
    }
}
```

Then, you create an interface for the Data Access Object (DAO), which is responsible for accessing data from the database. The getSequence() method loads a POJO or Sequence object from a database table by its ID, while the getNextValue() method retrieves the next value of a particular database sequence.

SequenceDao interface

```
package com.apress.spring6recipes.sequence;

public interface SequenceDao {

  Sequence getSequence(String sequenceId);
  int getNextValue(String sequenceId);
}
```

In a production application, you would implement this DAO interface to use a data access technology. But to simplify this example, we'll implement a DAO with hard-coded values in a map to store the sequence instances and values.

Map-based implementation of the SequenceDao interface

```
package com.apress.spring6recipes.sequence;

import org.springframework.stereotype.Component;

import java.util.Map;
import java.util.concurrent.ConcurrentHashMap;
import java.util.concurrent.atomic.AtomicInteger;

@Component("sequenceDao")
class SimpleSequenceDao implements SequenceDao {

  private final Map<String, Sequence> sequences = new ConcurrentHashMap<>();
  private final Map<String, AtomicInteger> values = new ConcurrentHashMap<>();

  SimpleSequenceDao() {
    sequences.put("IT", new Sequence("IT", "30", "A"));
    values.put("IT", new AtomicInteger(10000));
  }

  @Override
  public Sequence getSequence(String sequenceId) {
    return sequences.get(sequenceId);
  }

  @Override
  public int getNextValue(String sequenceId) {
    var value = values.get(sequenceId);
    return value.getAndIncrement();
  }
}
```

Observe how the SimpleSequenceDao class is decorated with the @Component("sequenceDao") annotation. This marks the class so Spring can create a bean for it. The value inside the @Component annotation defines the bean instance id, in this case sequenceDao. If no bean value name is provided in the @Component annotation, by default the bean name is assigned as the uncapitalized non-qualified class name. (e.g., for the SimpleSequenceDao class, the default bean name would be simpleSequenceDao).

A call to the getSequence method returns the value of the given sequenceID. And a call to the getNextValue method creates a new value based on the value of the given sequenceID and returns the new value.

@COMPONENT, @REPOSITORY, @SERVICE, OR @CONTROLLER?

POJOs are classified in application layers. In Spring these layers are three: persistence, service, and presentation. @Component is a general-purpose annotation to decorate POJOs for Spring detection, whereas @Repository, @Service, and @Controller are specializations of @Component for more specific cases of POJOs associated with the persistence, service, and presentation layers.

If you're unsure about a POJO's purpose, you can decorate it with the @Component annotation. However, it's better to use the specialization annotations where possible, because these provide extra facilities based on a POJO's purpose (e.g., @Repository causes exceptions to be wrapped up as DataAccessExceptions, which makes debugging easier).

Instantiate the Spring IoC Container with Filters to Scan for Annotations

By default, Spring detects all classes decorated with @Configuration, @Component, @Repository, @Service, and @Controller annotations, among others. You can customize the scan process to include one or more include/exclude filters. This is helpful when a Java package has dozens or hundreds of classes. For certain Spring application contexts, it can be necessary to exclude or include POJOs with certain annotations.

 Scanning every package class can slow down the startup process unnecessarily.

Spring supports four types of filter expressions. The annotation and assignable types are to specify an annotation type and a class/interface for filtering. The regex and aspectj types allow you to specify a regular expression and an AspectJ pointcut expression for matching the classes. You can also disable the default filters with the use-default-filters attribute.

For example, the following component scan includes all classes in the com.apress.spring6recipes. sequence whose name contains the word Dao or Service and excludes the classes with the @Controller annotation:

```
@ComponentScan(
  includeFilters = {
    @ComponentScan.Filter(
      type = FilterType.REGEX,
      pattern = {
        "com.apress.spring6recipes.sequence.*Dao",
        "com.apress.spring6recipes.sequence.*Service"})},
```

```
excludeFilters = {
    @ComponentScan.Filter(
        type = FilterType.ANNOTATION,
        classes = {org.springframework.stereotype.Controller.class})})
```

When applying include filters to detect all classes whose name contains the word Dao or Service, even classes that don't have annotations are auto-detected.

Get POJO Instances or Beans from the IoC Container

Then, you can test the preceding components with the following Main class:

Main.java for running the application

```
package com.apress.spring6recipes.sequence;

import org.springframework.context.annotation.AnnotationConfigApplicationContext;

public class Main {

  public static void main(String[] args) {

    var basePackages = "com.apress.spring6recipes.sequence";
    try (var context = new AnnotationConfigApplicationContext(basePackages)) {

      var sequenceDao = context.getBean(SequenceDao.class);
      System.out.println(sequenceDao.getNextValue("IT"));
      System.out.println(sequenceDao.getNextValue("IT"));
    }
  }
}
```

1-2. Create POJOs by Invoking a Constructor

Problem

You would like to create a POJO instance or bean in the Spring IoC container by invoking its constructor, which is the most common and direct way of creating beans. It is equivalent to using the new operator to create objects in Java.

Solution

Define a POJO class with a constructor or constructors. Next, create a Java Config class to configure POJO instance values with constructors for the Spring IoC container. Next, instantiate the Spring IoC container to scan for Java classes with annotations. The POJO instances or bean instances become accessible to put together as part of an application.

How It Works

Suppose you're going to develop a shop application to sell products online. First of all, you create the Product class, which has several properties, such as the product name and price. As there are many types of products in your shop, you make the Product class abstract to extend it for different product subclasses.

Product base class

```
package com.apress.spring6recipes.shop;

public abstract class Product {

  private final String name;
  private final double price;

  public Product(String name, double price) {
    this.name = name;
    this.price = price;
  }

  public String getName() {
    return name;
  }

  public double getPrice() {
    return price;
  }

  @Override
  public String toString() {
    return String.format("%s: name=%s, price=$%.2f",
            getClass().getSimpleName(), name, price);
  }
}
```

Create the POJO Classes with Constructors

Then you create two product subclasses, Battery and Disc. Each of them has its own properties.

Battery class

```
package com.apress.spring6recipes.shop;

public class Battery extends Product {

  private final boolean rechargeable;

  public Battery(String name, double price, boolean rechargeable) {
    super(name, price);
    this.rechargeable = rechargeable;
  }
```

9

```java
  public boolean isRechargeable() {
    return rechargeable;
  }

  @Override
  public String toString() {
    var msg = super.toString() + ", rechargeable=%b";
    return String.format(msg, this.rechargeable);
  }
}
```

Disc class

```java
package com.apress.spring6recipes.shop;

public class Disc extends Product {

  private final int capacity;

  public Disc(String name, double price, int capacity) {
    super(name, price);
    this.capacity = capacity;
  }

  public int getCapacity() {
    return capacity;
  }

  @Override
  public String toString() {
    var msg = super.toString() + ", capacity=%dMB";
    return String.format(msg, this.capacity);
  }
}
```

Create Java Config for Your POJOs

To define instances of a class in the Spring IoC container, you have to create a configuration class with instantiation values. A configuration class with bean definitions made by invoking constructors would look like the following.

Configuration for the shop application

```java
package com.apress.spring6recipes.shop.config;

import org.springframework.context.annotation.Bean;
import org.springframework.context.annotation.Configuration;

import com.apress.spring6recipes.shop.Disc;
import com.apress.spring6recipes.shop.Battery;
import com.apress.spring6recipes.shop.Product;
```

```java
@Configuration
public class ShopConfiguration {

  @Bean
  public Product aaa() {
    return new Battery("AAA", 2.5, true);
  }

  @Bean
  public Product cdrw() {
    return new Disc("CD-RW", 1.5, 700);
  }
}
```

Next, you can write the following class to test your products by retrieving them from the Spring IoC container.

Main.java for running the application

```java
package com.apress.spring6recipes.shop;

import org.springframework.context.annotation.AnnotationConfigApplicationContext;

import com.apress.spring6recipes.shop.config.ShopConfiguration;

public class Main {

  public static void main(String[] args) {
    var cfg = ShopConfiguration.class;
    try (var ctx = new AnnotationConfigApplicationContext(cfg)) {
      var aaa = ctx.getBean("aaa", Product.class);
      var cdrw = ctx.getBean("cdrw", Product.class);
      System.out.println(aaa);
      System.out.println(cdrw);
    }
  }
}
```

1-3. Use POJO References and Autowiring to Interact with Other POJOs

Problem

The beans that make up an application often need to collaborate with each other to complete the application's functions. You want to use annotations to use references and autowiring.

Solution

For instances defined in a configuration class, you can use standard Java code to create references between beans. To autowire references, you can mark a field, a setter method, a constructor, or even an arbitrary method with the @Autowired annotation.

How It Works

Reference POJOs in a Java Config Class

When bean instances are defined in a configuration class—as illustrated in Recipes 1-1 and Recipe 1-2—references are straightforward to use because everything is Java code. Take, for example, when a bean property references another bean:

```
package com.apress.spring6recipes.sequence.config;

import org.springframework.context.annotation.Bean;
import org.springframework.context.annotation.Configuration;

import com.apress.spring6recipes.sequence.PrefixGenerator;
import com.apress.spring6recipes.sequence.DatePrefixGenerator;
import com.apress.spring6recipes.sequence.Sequence;

@Configuration
public class SequenceConfiguration {

  @Bean
  public DatePrefixGenerator datePrefixGenerator() {
    return new DatePrefixGenerator("yyyyMMdd");
  }

  @Bean
  public Sequence sequenceGenerator(PrefixGenerator prefixGenerator) {
    var generator = new Sequence("A", 100000);
    generator.setPrefixGenerator(prefixGenerator);
    return generator;
  }
}
```

The prefixGenerator property of the Sequence class is an instance of a DatePrefixGenerator bean.

The first bean declaration creates a DatePrefixGenerator bean. By convention, the bean becomes accessible with the bean name datePrefixGenerator (i.e., the method name). But since the bean instantiation logic is also a standard Java method, the bean is also accessible by making a standard Java call. When the prefixGenerator property is set—in the second bean, via a setter—a standard Java call is made to the method datePrefixGenerator() to reference the bean.

Autowire POJO Fields with the @Autowired Annotation

Next, let's use autowiring on the SequenceDao field of the DAO SimpleSequenceDao class introduced in the second part of Recipe 1-1. We'll add a service class to the application to illustrate autowiring with the DAO class.

A service class to generate service objects is another real-world application best practice, which acts as a façade to access DAO objects—instead of accessing DAO objects directly. Internally, the service object interacts with the DAO to handle the sequence generation requests:

```
package com.apress.spring6recipes.sequence;

import org.springframework.beans.factory.annotation.Autowired;
import org.springframework.stereotype.Service;

@Service
public class SequenceService {

  @Autowired
  private SequenceDao sequenceDao;

  public String generate(String sequenceId) {
    var sequence = sequenceDao.getSequence(sequenceId);
    var value = sequenceDao.getNextValue(sequenceId);
    return sequence.prefix() + value + sequence.suffix();
  }
}
```

The SequenceService class is decorated with the @Service annotation. This allows Spring to detect the class. Because the @Service annotation has no name, the default bean name is sequenceService, which is based on the class name.

The SequenceDao field of the SequenceService class is decorated with the @Autowired annotation. This allows Spring to autowire the field with the sequenceDao bean (i.e., the SimpleSequenceDao class).

The @Autowired annotation can also be applied to a field of an array type to have Spring autowire all the matching beans. For example, you can annotate a PrefixGenerator[] field with @Autowired. Then, Spring will autowire all the beans whose type is compatible with PrefixGenerator at one time:

```
package com.apress.spring6recipes.sequence;

import org.springframework.beans.factory.annotation.Autowired;

public class Sequence {

  @Autowired
  private PrefixGenerator[] prefixGenerators;
  ...
}
```

If you have multiple beans whose type is compatible with the PrefixGenerator defined in the IoC container, they will be added to the prefixGenerators array automatically.

In a similar way, you can apply the @Autowired annotation to a type-safe collection. Spring can read the type information of this collection and autowire all the beans whose type is compatible:

```
package com.apress.spring6recipes.sequence;

import org.springframework.beans.factory.annotation.Autowired;

public class Sequence {

    @Autowired
    private List<PrefixGenerator> prefixGenerators;
    ...
}
```

If Spring notices that the @Autowired annotation is applied to a type-safe java.util.Map with a String as the key type, it will add all the beans of the compatible type, with the bean names as the keys, to this map:

```
package com.apress.spring6recipes.sequence;

import org.springframework.beans.factory.annotation.Autowired;

public class Sequence {

    @Autowired
    private Map<String, PrefixGenerator> prefixGenerators;
    ...
}
```

ℹ️   Using @Autowired on fields is not the recommended practice. The rule of thumb is to use constructor injection for required fields and setter injection for optional fields.

Autowire Methods and Constructors with the @Autowired Annotation and Make Autowiring Optional

The @Autowired annotation can also be applied directly to a method of a class (generally a setter method). As an example, you can annotate the setter method of the prefixGenerator property with @Autowired. Then, Spring attempts to wire a bean whose type is compatible with prefixGenerator:

```
package com.apress.spring6recipes.sequence;

import org.springframework.beans.factory.annotation.Autowired;

public class Sequence {
    ...
```

```
@Autowired
public void setPrefixGenerator(PrefixGenerator prefixGenerator) {
    this.prefixGenerator = prefixGenerator;
}
}
```

By default, all the properties with @Autowired are required. When Spring can't find a matching bean to wire, it will throw an exception. If you want a certain property to be optional, you can use the required attribute of @Autowired and set it false. Then, when Spring can't find a matching bean, it will leave this property unset:

```
package com.apress.spring6recipes.sequence;

import org.springframework.beans.factory.annotation.Autowired;

public class Sequence {
    ...
    @Autowired(required=false)
    public void setPrefixGenerator(PrefixGenerator prefixGenerator) {
        this.prefixGenerator = prefixGenerator;
    }
}
```

Another option is to use java.util.Optional, which in turn, as the name implies, makes it optional. You can then either set the value detected, or you can provide a default instance using orElseGet. Using java.util.Optional will also make the injection lazy; the dependency won't be retrieved until the dependency needs to be retrieved, that is, when using Optional.get and so on. The use of java.util. Optional is also available for field or constructor injection:

```
package com.apress.spring6recipes.sequence;

import org.springframework.beans.factory.annotation.Autowired;

public class Sequence {
    ...
    @Autowired
    public void setPrefixGenerator(Optional<PrefixGenerator> prefixGenerator) {
        this.prefixGenerator = prefixGenerator.orElse(null);
    }
}
```

Instead of Optional you could also use the org.springframework.beans.factory.ObjectProvider, an interface from Spring that allows you to optionally get the bean. Its getIfUnique() method will act like the Optional.orElse. It will only return an instance if there is one and only one; if there are none or more, it will return null. The ObjectProvider has multiple methods to obtain one or more instances of the bean, depending on the need. This is very useful in configuration classes when building a library, framework, or plugin-based system:

```
package com.apress.spring6recipes.sequence;

import org.springframework.beans.factory.ObjectProvider;
import org.springframework.beans.factory.annotation.Autowired;
```

```
public class Sequence {
    ...
    @Autowired
    public void setPrefixGenerator(ObjectProvider<PrefixGenerator>
    prefixGeneratorProvider) {
        this.prefixGenerator = prefixGeneratorProvider.getIfUnique();
    }
}
```

You may also apply the @Autowired annotation to a method with an arbitrary name and an arbitrary number of arguments, and, in that case, Spring attempts to wire a bean with the compatible type for each of the method arguments:

```
package com.apress.spring6recipes.sequence;

import org.springframework.beans.factory.annotation.Autowired;

public class Sequence {
    ...
    @Autowired
    public void myOwnCustomInjectionName(PrefixGenerator prefixGenerator) {
        this.prefixGenerator = prefixGenerator;
    }
}
```

And finally you may also apply the @Autowired annotation to a constructor that you want to be used for autowiring. The constructor can have any number of arguments, and Spring will attempt to wire a bean with the compatible type for each of the constructor arguments:

```
@Service
public class SequenceService {

    private final SequenceDao sequenceDao;

    @Autowired
    public SequenceService(SequenceDao sequenceDao) {
        this.sequenceDao=sequenceDao;
    }

    public String generate(String sequenceId) {
        var sequence = sequenceDao.getSequence(sequenceId);
        var value = sequenceDao.getNextValue(sequenceId);
        return sequence.getPrefix() + value + sequence.getSuffix();
    }
}
```

💡 If you only have a single constructor, Spring will automatically use that constructor for autowiring. In that case you can omit the @Autowired annotation.

Resolve Autowire Ambiguity with the @Primary and @Qualifier Annotations

By default, autowiring by type will not work when there is more than one bean with the compatible type in the IoC container and the property isn't a group type (e.g., array, list, map), as illustrated previously. However, there are two workarounds to autowiring by type if there's more than one bean of the same type, the @Primary annotation and the @Qualifier annotation.

Resolve Autowire Ambiguity with the `@Primary` Annotation

Spring allows you to specify a candidate bean by type decorating the candidate with the @Primary annotation. The @Primary annotation gives preference to a bean when multiple candidates are qualified to autowire a single-valued dependency:

```
package com.apress.spring6recipes.sequence;
import org.springframework.context.annotation.Primary;
import org.springframework.stereotype.Component;


@Component
@Primary
public class DatePrefixGenerator implements PrefixGenerator {
```

Notice the preceding class implements the PrefixGenerator interface and is decorated with the @Primary annotation. If you attempted to autowire a bean with a PrefixGenerator type, even if Spring had more than one bean instance with the same PrefixGenerator type, Spring would autowire the DatePrefixGenerator because it's marked with the @Primary annotation.

Resolve Autowire Ambiguity with the `@Qualifier` Annotation

Spring also allows you to specify a candidate bean by type providing its name in the @Qualifier annotation:

```
package com.apress.spring6recipes.sequence;

import org.springframework.beans.factory.annotation.Autowired;
import org.springframework.beans.factory.annotation.Qualifier;

public class Sequence {

  @Autowired
  @Qualifier("datePrefixGenerator")
  private PrefixGenerator prefixGenerator;
}
```

Once you've done this, Spring attempts to find a bean with that name in the IoC container and wire it into the property.

The @Qualifier annotation can also be applied to a method argument for autowiring:

```
package com.apress.spring6recipes.sequence;

import org.springframework.beans.factory.annotation.Autowired;
import org.springframework.beans.factory.annotation.Qualifier;
```

```
import java.util.concurrent.atomic.AtomicInteger;

public class Sequence {

private PrefixGenerator prefixGenerator;

  @Autowired
  public void setPrefixGenerator(
          @Qualifier("datePrefixGenerator") PrefixGenerator prefixGenerator) {
    this.prefixGenerator = prefixGenerator;
  }
}
```

If you want to autowire bean properties by name, you can annotate a setter method, a constructor, or a field with the JSR-250 @Resource annotation described in the next recipe.

Resolve POJO References from Multiple Locations

As an application grows, it can become difficult to manage every POJO in a single Java configuration class. A common practice is to separate POJOs into multiple Java configuration classes according to their functionalities. When you create multiple Java configuration classes, obtaining references and autowiring POJOs that are defined in different classes aren't as straightforward as when everything is in a single Java configuration class.

One approach is to initialize the application context with the location of each Java configuration class. In this manner, the POJOs for each Java configuration class are loaded into the context, and references and autowiring between POJOs are possible:

```
var cfg = new Class[] { PrefixConfiguration.class, SequenceConfiguration.class };
var context = new AnnotationConfigApplicationContext(cfg);
```

Another alternative is to use the @Import annotation so Spring makes the beans from one configuration file available in another:

```
package com.apress.spring6recipes.sequence.config;

import com.apress.spring6recipes.sequence.PrefixGenerator;
import com.apress.spring6recipes.sequence.Sequence;
import org.springframework.context.annotation.Bean;
import org.springframework.context.annotation.Configuration;
import org.springframework.context.annotation.Import;

@Configuration
@Import(PrefixConfiguration.class)
public class SequenceConfiguration {

  @Bean
  public Sequence sequence(PrefixGenerator prefixGenerator) {
    return new Sequence(prefixGenerator, "A", 100000);
  }
}
```

The sequence bean requires to set a prefixGenerator bean. But notice no prefixGenerator bean is defined in the Java configuration class. The prefixGenerator bean is defined in a separate Java configuration class PrefixConfiguration. With the @Import(PrefixConfiguration.class) annotation, Spring brings all the POJOs in the Java configuration class into the scope of the current application context. With the POJOs from PrefixConfiguration in scope, we can autowire them as we did before through @Autowired or as here as a method parameter for a @Bean method.

1-4. Autowire POJOs with the @Resource and @Inject Annotations

Problem

You want to use the Java standard @Resource and @Inject annotations to reference POJOs via autowiring, instead of the Spring-specific @Autowired annotation.

Solution

JSR-250 or Common Annotations for the Java platform defines the @Resource annotation to autowire POJO references by name. JSR-330 or Standard Annotations for injection defines the @Inject annotation to autowire POJO references by type.

How It Works

The @Autowired annotation described in the previous recipe belongs to the Spring Framework, specifically to the org.springframework.beans.factory.annotation package. This means it can only be used in the context of the Spring Framework.

Soon after Spring added support for the @Autowired annotation, the Java language itself standardized various annotations to fulfill the same purpose of the @Autowired annotation. These annotations are @Resource, which belongs to the jakarta.annotation package, and @Inject, which belongs to the jakarta.inject package.

Autowire POJOs with the @Resource Annotation

By default, the @Resource annotation works like Spring's @Autowired annotation and attempts to autowire by type. For example, the following POJO attribute is decorated with the @Resource annotation, and so Spring attempts to locate a POJO that matches the PrefixGenerator type:

```
package com.apress.spring6recipes.sequence;

import jakarta.annotation.Resource;

public class Sequence {

    @Resource
    private PrefixGenerator prefixGenerator;
    ...
}
```

However, unlike the @Autowired annotation that requires the @Qualifier annotation to autowire a POJO by name, the @Resource ambiguity is eliminated if more than one POJO type of the same kind exists. Essentially, the @Resource annotation provides the same functionality as putting together the @Autowired annotation and @Qualifier annotation.

Autowire POJOs with the @Inject Annotation

The @Inject annotation also attempts to autowire by type, like the @Resource and @Autowired annotations. For example, the following POJO attribute is decorated with the @Inject annotation, and so Spring attempts to locate a POJO that matches the PrefixGenerator type:

```
package com.apress.spring6recipes.sequence;

import jakarta.inject.Inject;

public class Sequence {

    @Inject
    private PrefixGenerator prefixGenerator;
    ...
}
```

But just like the @Resource and @Autowired annotations, a different approach has to be used to match POJOs by name or avoid ambiguity if more than one POJO type of the same kind exists. The first step to do autowiring by name with the @Inject annotation is to create a custom annotation to identify both the POJO injection class and POJO injection point:

```
package com.apress.spring6recipes.sequence;

import java.lang.annotation.Documented;
import java.lang.annotation.ElementType;
import java.lang.annotation.Retention;
import java.lang.annotation.RetentionPolicy;
import java.lang.annotation.Target;

import jakarta.inject.Qualifier;

@Qualifier
@Target({ElementType.TYPE, ElementType.FIELD, ElementType.PARAMETER})
@Documented
@Retention(RetentionPolicy.RUNTIME)
public @interface DatePrefixAnnotation {
}
```

Notice the custom annotation makes use of the @Qualifier annotation. This annotation is different from the one used with Spring's @Qualifier annotation, as this last class belongs to the same Java package as the @Inject annotation (i.e., jakarta.inject).

Once the custom annotation is done, it's necessary to decorate the POJO injection class that generates the bean instance, which in this case is the DatePrefixGenerator class:

```
package com.apress.spring6recipes.sequence;
...
@DatePrefixAnnotation
public class DatePrefixGenerator implements PrefixGenerator {
...
}
```

Finally, the POJO attribute or injection point is decorated with the same custom annotation to qualify the POJO and eliminate any ambiguity:

```
package com.apress.spring6recipes.sequence;

import jakarta.inject.Inject;

public class Sequence {

    @Inject @DataPrefixAnnotation
    private PrefixGenerator prefixGenerator;
    ...
}
```

@AUTOWIRED, @RESOURCE, OR @INJECT ?

As you've seen in Recipes 1-3 and 1-4, the three annotations @Autowired, @Resource, and @Inject can achieve the same result. The @Autowired annotation is a Spring-based solution, whereas the @Resource and @Inject annotations are Java standard (i.e., JSR)–based solutions. If you're going to do name-based autowiring, the @Resource annotation offers the simplest syntax. For autowiring by class type, all three annotations are as straightforward to use because all three require a single annotation.

1-5. Set a POJO's Scope with the @Scope Annotation

Problem

When you declare a POJO instance with an annotation like @Component, you are actually defining a template for bean creation, not an actual bean instance. When a bean is requested by the getBean() method or a reference from other beans, Spring decides which bean instance should be returned according to the bean scope. Sometimes, you have to set an appropriate scope for a bean other than the default scope.

Solution

A bean's scope is set with the @Scope annotation. By default, Spring creates exactly one instance for each bean declared in the IoC container, and this instance is shared in the scope of the entire IoC container. This unique bean instance is returned for all subsequent getBean() calls and bean references. This scope is called singleton, which is the default scope of all beans. Table 1-1 lists all valid bean scopes in Spring.

Table 1-1. *Valid Bean Scopes in Spring*

Scope	Description
singleton	Creates a single bean instance per Spring IoC container
prototype	Creates a new bean instance each time when requested
request	Creates a single bean instance per HTTP request, only valid in the context of a web application
session	Creates a single bean instance per HTTP session, only valid in the context of a web application
application	Similar to singleton but will register the bean in the ServletContext to be shared among multiple servlets
websocket	Stores the reference to the bean in the websocket-related session attributes

How It Works

To demonstrate the concept of bean scope, let's consider a shopping cart example in a shopping application. First, you create the ShoppingCart class as follows:

```
package com.apress.spring6recipes.shop;

import org.springframework.stereotype.Component;

import java.util.ArrayList;
import java.util.Collections;
import java.util.List;

@Component
public class ShoppingCart {

  private final List<Product> items = new ArrayList<>();

  public void addItem(Product item) {
    this.items.add(item);
  }

  public List<Product> getItems() {
    return Collections.unmodifiableList(this.items);
  }
}
```

Then you declare the product beans in a Java Config file so they can later be added to the shopping cart:

```
package com.apress.spring6recipes.shop.config;

import org.springframework.context.annotation.Bean;
import org.springframework.context.annotation.ComponentScan;
import org.springframework.context.annotation.Configuration;
```

```
import com.apress.spring6recipes.shop.Disc;
import com.apress.spring6recipes.shop.Battery;
import com.apress.spring6recipes.shop.Product;

@Configuration
@ComponentScan("com.apress.spring6recipes.shop")
public class ShopConfiguration {

  @Bean
  public Product aaa() {
    return new Battery("AAA", 2.5, true);
  }

  @Bean
  public Product cdrw() {
    return new Disc("CD-RW", 1.5, 700);
  }

  @Bean
  public Product dvdrw() {
    return new Disc("DVD-RW", 3.0, 4900);
  }
}
```

Once you do this, you can define a Main class to test the shopping cart by adding some products to it. Suppose there are two customers navigating in your shop at the same time. The first one gets a shopping cart by the getBean() method and adds two products to it. Then, the second customer also gets a shopping cart by the getBean() method and adds another product to it.

```
package com.apress.spring6recipes.shop;

import com.apress.spring6recipes.shop.config.ShopConfiguration;
import org.springframework.context.annotation.AnnotationConfigApplicationContext;

public class Main {

  public static void main(String[] args) {
    var cfg = ShopConfiguration.class;
    try (var context = new AnnotationConfigApplicationContext(cfg)) {

      var aaa = context.getBean("aaa", Product.class);
      var cdrw = context.getBean("cdrw", Product.class);
      var dvdrw = context.getBean("dvdrw", Product.class);

      var cart1 = context.getBean(ShoppingCart.class);
      cart1.addItem(aaa);
      cart1.addItem(cdrw);
      System.out.println("Shopping cart 1 contains " + cart1.getItems());
```

```
        var cart2 = context.getBean(ShoppingCart.class);
        cart2.addItem(dvdrw);
        System.out.println("Shopping cart 2 contains " + cart2.getItems());
    }
  }
}
```

As a result of the preceding bean declaration, you can see that the two customers get the same shopping cart instance:

```
Shopping cart 1 contains [AAA 2.5, CD-RW 1.5]
Shopping cart 2 contains [AAA 2.5, CD-RW 1.5, DVD-RW 3.0]
```

This is because Spring's default bean scope is singleton. This means Spring creates exactly one shopping cart instance per IoC container.

In your shop application, you expect each customer to get a different shopping cart instance when the getBean() method is called. To ensure this behavior, the scope of the shoppingCart bean needs to be set to prototype. Then Spring creates a new bean instance for each getBean() method call:

```
package com.apress.spring6recipes.shop;

import java.util.ArrayList;
import java.util.Collections;
import java.util.List;

import org.springframework.context.annotation.Scope;
import org.springframework.stereotype.Component;

@Component
@Scope("prototype")
public class ShoppingCart {
}
```

Now if you run the Main class again, you can see the two customers get a different shopping cart instance:

```
Shopping cart 1 contains [AAA 2.5, CD-RW 1.5]
Shopping cart 2 contains [DVD-RW 3.0]
```

1-6. Use Data from External Resources (Text Files, XML Files, Properties Files, or Image Files)

Problem

Sometimes, applications need to read external resources (e.g., text files, XML files, properties files, or image files) from different locations (e.g., a file system, classpath, or URL). Usually, you have to deal with different APIs for loading resources from different locations.

Solution

Spring offers the @PropertySource annotation as a facility to load the contents of a properties file (i.e., key-value pairs) to set up bean properties.

Spring also has a resource loader mechanism, which provides a unified Resource interface to retrieve any type of external resource by a resource path. You can specify different prefixes for this path to load resources from different locations with the @Value annotation. To load a resource from a file system, you use the file prefix. To load a resource from the classpath, you use the classpath prefix. You can also specify a URL in the resource path.

How It Works

To read the contents of a properties file (i.e., key-value pairs) to set up bean properties, you can use Spring's @PropertySource annotation with PropertySourcesPlaceholderConfigurer. If you want to read the contents of any file, you can use Spring's Resource mechanism decorated with the @Value annotation.

Use Properties File Data to Set Up POJO Instantiation Values

Let's assume you have a series of values in a properties file you want to access to set up bean properties. Typically this can be the configuration properties of a database or some other application values composed of key-value pairs. For example, take the following key-value pairs stored in a file called discounts.properties:

```
specialcustomer.discount=0.1
summer.discount=0.15
endofyear.discount=0.2
```

 To read properties files for the purpose of internationalization (i18n), see the next recipe.

To make the contents of the discounts.properties file accessible to set up other beans, you can use the @PropertySource annotation to convert the key-value pairs into a bean inside a Java Config class:

```
package com.apress.spring6recipes.shop.config;

import org.springframework.beans.factory.annotation.Value;
import org.springframework.context.annotation.Bean;
import org.springframework.context.annotation.ComponentScan;
import org.springframework.context.annotation.Configuration;
import org.springframework.context.annotation.PropertySource;
import org.springframework.context.support.PropertySourcesPlaceholderConfigurer;

import com.apress.spring6recipes.shop.Disc;
import com.apress.spring6recipes.shop.Battery;
import com.apress.spring6recipes.shop.Product;
```

```
@Configuration
@PropertySource("classpath:discounts.properties")
@ComponentScan("com.apress.spring6recipes.shop")
public class ShopConfiguration {

  @Value("${endofyear.discount:0}")
  private double specialEndofyearDiscountField;

  @Bean
  public static PropertySourcesPlaceholderConfigurer pspc() {
    return new PropertySourcesPlaceholderConfigurer();
  }

  @Bean
  public Product dvdrw() {
    return new Disc("DVD-RW", 1.5, 4700, specialEndofyearDiscountField);
  }
}
```

You define a @PropertySource annotation with a value of classpath:discounts.properties to decorate the Java Config class. The classpath: prefix tells Spring to look for the discounts.properties file in the Java classpath.

Once you define the @PropertySource annotation to load the properties file, you also need to define a PropertySourcesPlaceholderConfigurer bean with the @Bean annotation. Spring automatically wires the @PropertySource discounts.properties file so its properties become accessible as bean properties.

Next, you need to define Java variables to take values from the discounts.properties file. To define the Java variable values with these values, you make use of the @Value annotation with a placeholder expression.

The syntax is @Value("${key:default_value}"). A search is done for the key value in all the loaded application properties. If a matching key is found in the properties file, the corresponding value is assigned to the bean property. If no matching key is found in the loaded application properties, the default_value is assigned to the bean property (the part after the semicolon in the value expression).

Once a Java variable is set with a discount value, you can use it to set up bean instances for a bean's discount property.

If you want to use properties file data for a different purpose than setting up bean properties, you should use Spring's Resource mechanism, which is described next.

Use Data from Any External Resource File for Use in a POJO

Suppose you want to display a banner at the startup of an application. The banner is made up of the following characters and stored in a text file called banner.txt. This file can be put in the classpath of your application:

```
*************************
*  Welcome to My Shop!  *
*************************
```

Next, let's write a BannerLoader POJO class to load the banner and output it to the console:

```java
package com.apress.spring6recipes.shop;

import jakarta.annotation.PostConstruct;
import org.springframework.core.io.Resource;

import java.io.IOException;
import java.nio.charset.StandardCharsets;
import java.nio.file.Files;
import java.nio.file.Path;

public class BannerLoader {

  private final Resource banner;

  public BannerLoader(Resource banner) {
    this.banner = banner;
  }

  @PostConstruct
  public void showBanner() throws IOException {
    var path = Path.of(banner.getURI());
    try (var lines = Files.lines(path, StandardCharsets.UTF_8)) {
      lines.forEachOrdered(System.out::println);
    }
  }
}
```

Notice the POJO banner field is a Spring Resource type. The field value will be populated through constructor injection when the bean instance is created—to be explained shortly. The showBanner method makes a call to the getURI() method to retrieve the java.net.URI from the Resource. Once you have this URI, you can use Java NIO to read the content and print it to the console.

Also notice the showBanner() method is decorated with the @PostConstruct annotation. Because you want to show the banner at startup, you use this annotation to tell Spring to invoke the method automatically after creation. This guarantees the showBanner() method is one of the first methods to be run by the application and therefore ensures the banner appears at the outset.

Next, the POJO BannerLoader needs to be initialized as an instance. In addition, the banner field of the BannerLoader also needs to be injected. So let's create a Java Config class for these tasks:

```java
package com.apress.spring6recipes.shop.config;

import org.springframework.beans.factory.annotation.Value;
import org.springframework.context.annotation.Bean;
import org.springframework.context.annotation.ComponentScan;
import org.springframework.context.annotation.Configuration;
import org.springframework.context.annotation.PropertySource;
import org.springframework.context.support.PropertySourcesPlaceholderConfigurer;
import org.springframework.core.io.Resource;

import com.apress.spring6recipes.shop.BannerLoader;
import com.apress.spring6recipes.shop.Battery;
```

```
import com.apress.spring6recipes.shop.Disc;
import com.apress.spring6recipes.shop.Product;

@Configuration
@PropertySource("classpath:discounts.properties")
@ComponentScan("com.apress.spring6recipes.shop")
public class ShopConfiguration {

  @Value("classpath:banner.txt")
  private Resource banner;

  @Bean
  public BannerLoader bannerLoader() {
    return new BannerLoader(banner);
  }
}
```

See how the banner property is decorated with the @Value("classpath:banner.txt") annotation. This tells Spring to search for the banner.txt file in the classpath and inject it. Spring uses the preregistered property editor ResourceEditor to convert the file definition into a Resource object before injecting it into the bean.

Once the banner property is injected, it's assigned to the BannerLoader bean instance through constructor injection.

Because the banner file is located in the Java classpath, the resource path starts with the classpath: prefix. The preceding resource path specifies a resource in the relative path of the file system. You can specify an absolute path as well:

```
file:c:/shop/banner.txt
```

When a resource is located in Java's classpath, you have to use the classpath prefix. If there's no path information presented, it will be loaded from the root of the classpath:

```
classpath:banner.txt
```

If the resource is located in a particular package, you can specify the absolute path from the classpath root:

```
classpath:com/apress/spring6recipes/shop/banner.txt
```

Besides support to load from a file system path or the classpath, a resource can also be loaded by specifying a URL:

```
http://springrecipes.apress.com/shop/banner.txt
```

Since the bean class uses the @PostConstruct annotation on the showBanner() method, the banner is sent to output when the IoC container is set up. Because of this, there's no need to tinker with an application's context or explicitly call the bean to output the banner. However, sometimes it can be necessary to access an external resource to interact with an application's context. Now suppose you want to display a legend at the end of an application. The legend is made up of the discounts previously described in the discounts.properties file. To access the contents of the properties file, you can also leverage Spring's Resource mechanism.

Next, let's use Spring's Resource mechanism, but this time directly inside an application's Main class to output a legend when the application finishes:

```
package com.apress.spring6recipes.shop;

import org.springframework.context.annotation.AnnotationConfigApplicationContext;
import org.springframework.core.io.ClassPathResource;
import org.springframework.core.io.support.PropertiesLoaderUtils;

import com.apress.spring6recipes.shop.config.ShopConfiguration;

public class Main {

  public static void main(String[] args) throws Exception {

    var resource = new ClassPathResource("discounts.properties");
    var props = PropertiesLoaderUtils.loadProperties(resource);
    System.out.println("And don't forget our discounts!");
    System.out.println(props);
  }
}
```

Spring's ClassPathResource class is used to access the discounts.properties file, which casts the file's contents into a Resource object. Next, the Resource object is processed into a Properties object with Spring's PropertiesLoaderUtils class. Finally, the contents of the Properties object are sent to the console as the final output of the application.

Because the legend file (i.e., discounts.properties) is located in the Java classpath, the resource is accessed with Spring's ClassPathResource class. If the external resource were in a file system path, the resource would be loaded with Spring's FileSystemResource:

```
var resource = new FileSystemResource("c:/shop/banner.txt")
```

If the external resource were at a URL, the resource would be loaded with Spring's UrlResource:

```
var resource = new UrlResource("https://www.apress.com/")
```

1-7. Resolve I18N Text Messages for Different Locales in Properties Files

Problem

You want an application to support internationalization (I18N) via annotations.

Solution

MessageSource is an interface that defines several methods for resolving messages in resource bundles. ResourceBundleMessageSource is the most common MessageSource implementation that resolves messages from resource bundles for different locales. After you declare a ResourceBundleMessageSource POJO, you can use the @Bean annotation in a Java Config file to make the I18N data available in an application.

How It Works

As an example, create the following resource bundle, messages_en_US.properties, for the English language in the United States. Resource bundles are loaded from the root of the classpath, so ensure they're available in the Java classpath. Place the following key-value pairs in the file:

```
alert.checkout=A shopping cart has been checked out.
alert.inventory.checkout=A shopping cart with {0} has been checked out at {1}.
```

To resolve messages from resource bundles, let's create a Java Config file with a ReloadableResourceBundleMessageSource bean:

```
package com.apress.spring6recipes.shop.config;

import org.springframework.context.annotation.Bean;
import org.springframework.context.annotation.Configuration;
import org.springframework.context.support.ReloadableResourceBundleMessageSource;

@Configuration
public class ShopConfiguration {

  @Bean
  public ReloadableResourceBundleMessageSource messageSource() {
    var messageSource = new ReloadableResourceBundleMessageSource();
    messageSource.setBasenames("classpath:messages");
    messageSource.setCacheSeconds(1);
    return messageSource;
  }
}
```

The bean instance must have the name messageSource for the application context to detect it. Inside the bean definition, you declare a String list via the setBasenames method to locate bundles for the ResourceBundleMessageSource. In this case, we just specify the default convention to look up files located in the Java classpath that start with messages. In addition, the setCacheSeconds method sets a value to 1 to avoid reading stale messages. Note that a refresh attempt first checks the last modified timestamp of the properties file before actually reloading it; so if files don't change, the setCacheSeconds interval can be set rather low, as refresh attempts aren't actually reloaded.

For this MessageSource definition, if you look up a text message for the United States locale, whose preferred language is English, the resource bundle messages_en_US.properties is considered first. If there's no such resource bundle or the message can't be found, then a messages_en.properties file that matches the language is considered. If a resource bundle still can't be found, the default messages.properties for all locales is chosen. For more information on resource bundle loading, you can refer to the Javadoc of the java.util.ResourceBundle class.

Next, you can configure the application context to resolve messages with the getMessage() method. The first argument is the key corresponding to the message, and the third is the target locale:

```
package com.apress.spring6recipes.shop;

import com.apress.spring6recipes.shop.config.ShopConfiguration;
import org.springframework.context.annotation.AnnotationConfigApplicationContext;

import java.time.LocalDateTime;
import java.util.Locale;

public class Main {

  private static final String MSG = "The I18N message for %s is: %s%n";

  public static void main(String[] args) {

    var cfg = ShopConfiguration.class;
    try (var context = new AnnotationConfigApplicationContext(cfg)) {

      var alert = context.getMessage("alert.checkout", null, Locale.US);
      var alert_inventory = context.getMessage("alert.inventory.checkout",
          new Object[] { "[DVD-RW 3.0]", LocalDateTime.now() }, Locale.US);

      System.out.printf(MSG, "alert.checkout", alert);
      System.out.printf(MSG, "alert.inventory.checkout", alert_inventory);
    }
  }
}
```

The second argument of the getMessage() method is an array of message parameters. In the first String statement, the value is null. In the second String statement, an object array to fill in the message parameters is used.

In the Main class, you can resolve text messages because you can access the application context directly. But for a bean to resolve text messages, you have to inject a MessageSource implementation into the bean that needs to resolve text messages. Let's implement a Cashier class for the shopping application that illustrates how to resolve messages:

```
package com.apress.spring6recipes.shop;
...
@Component
public class Cashier {

    @Autowired
    private MessageSource messageSource;

    public void checkout(ShoppingCart cart) throws IOException {
        var alert = messageSource.getMessage("alert.inventory.checkout",
            new Object[] { cart.getItems(), new Date() }, Locale.US);
        System.out.println(alert);
    }
}
```

Notice the POJO `messageSource` field is a Spring `MessageSource` type. The field is annotated with the @Autowired annotation, so it's populated through injection when the bean instance is created. Then the checkout method can access the `messageSource` field, which gives the bean access to the `getMessage` method to gain access to text messages based on I18N criteria.

1-8. Customize POJO Initialization and Destruction with Annotations

Problem

Some POJOs have to perform certain types of initialization tasks before they're used. These tasks can include opening a file, opening a network/database connection, allocating memory, and so on. In addition, these same POJOs also have to perform the corresponding destruction tasks at the end of their life cycle. Therefore, sometimes it's necessary to customize bean initialization and destruction in the Spring IoC container.

Solution

Spring can recognize initialization and destruction callback methods by setting the `initMethod` and `destroyMethod` attributes of a @Bean definition in a Java Config class. Or Spring can also recognize initialization and destruction callback methods if POJO methods are decorated with the @PostConstruct and @PreDestroy annotations, respectively. Spring can also delay the creation of a bean up until the point it's required—a process called lazy initialization—with the @Lazy annotation. Spring can also ensure the initialization of certain beans before others with the @DependsOn annotation.

How It Works

Define Methods to Run Before POJO Initialization and Destruction with @Bean

Let's take the case of the shopping application and consider an example involving a checkout function. Let's modify the `Cashier` class to record a shopping cart's products and the checkout time to a text file:

```
package com.apress.spring6recipes.shop;

import java.io.BufferedWriter;
import java.io.IOException;
import java.nio.charset.StandardCharsets;
import java.nio.file.Files;
import java.nio.file.Path;
import java.nio.file.StandardOpenOption;
import java.time.LocalDateTime;

public class Cashier {
```

```
private final String filename;
private final String path;
private BufferedWriter writer;

public Cashier(String filename, String path) {
  this.filename = filename;
  this.path = path;
}

public void openFile() throws IOException {
  var checkoutPath = Path.of(path, filename + ".txt");
  if (Files.notExists(checkoutPath.getParent())) {
    Files.createDirectories(checkoutPath.getParent());
  }
  this.writer = Files.newBufferedWriter(checkoutPath, StandardCharsets.UTF_8,
        StandardOpenOption.CREATE, StandardOpenOption.APPEND);
}

public void checkout(ShoppingCart cart) throws IOException {
  writer.write(LocalDateTime.now() + "\t" + cart.getItems() + "\r\n");
  writer.flush();
}

public void closeFile() throws IOException {
  writer.close();
}
}
```

In the Cashier class, the openFile() method first verifies if the target directory and the file to write the data exist. It then opens the text file in the specified system path and assigns it to the writer field. Then each time the checkout() method is called, the date and cart items are appended to the text file. Finally, the closeFile() method closes the file to release its system resources.

Next, let's explore how this bean definition has to be set up in a Java Config class, in order to execute the openFile() method just before the bean is created and the closeFile() method just before it's destroyed:

```
@Bean(initMethod = "openFile", destroyMethod = "closeFile")
public Cashier cashier() {
  var path = System.getProperty("java.io.tmpdir") + "/cashier";
  return new Cashier("checkout", path);
}
```

Notice the POJO's initialization and destruction tasks are defined with the initMethod and destroyMethod attributes of a @Bean annotation. With these two attributes set in the bean declaration, when the Cashier class is created, it first triggers the openFile() method—verifying if the target directory and the file to write the data exist, as well as opening the file to append records—and when the bean is destroyed, it triggers the closeFile() method, ensuring the file reference is closed to release system resources.

Define Methods to Run Before POJO Initialization and Destruction with @PostConstruct and @PreDestroy

Another alternative if you'll define POJO instances outside a Java Config class (e.g., with the @Component annotation) is to use the @PostConstruct and @PreDestroy annotations directly in the POJO class:

```
package com.apress.spring6recipes.shop;

import jakarta.annotation.PostConstruct;
import jakarta.annotation.PreDestroy;

import java.nio.charset.StandardCharsets;
import java.nio.file.Files;
import java.nio.file.Paths;

import java.nio.file.StandardOpenOption;

public class Cashier {

    @PostConstruct
    public void openFile() throws IOException {

        var checkoutPath = Paths.get(path, filename + ".txt");
        if (Files.notExists(checkoutPath.getParent())) {
            Files.createDirectories(checkoutPath.getParent());
        }
        this.writer = Files.newBufferedWriter(checkoutPath, StandardCharsets.UTF_8,
                StandardOpenOption.CREATE, StandardOpenOption.APPEND);
    }

    @PreDestroy
    public void closeFile() throws IOException {
        writer.close();
    }
}
```

The openFile() method is decorated with the @PostConstruct annotation, which tells Spring to execute the method right after a bean is constructed. The closeFile() method is decorated with the @PreDestroy annotation, which tells Spring to execute the method right before a bean is destroyed.

Define Lazy Initialization for POJOs with @Lazy

By default, Spring performs eager initialization on all POJOs. This means POJOs are initialized at startup. In certain circumstances though, it can be convenient to delay the POJO initialization process until a bean is required. Delaying the initialization is called "lazy initialization."

Lazy initialization helps limit resource consumption peaks at startup and save overall system resources. Lazy initialization can be particularly relevant for POJOs that perform heavyweight operations (e.g., network connections, file operations). To mark a bean with lazy initialization, you decorate a bean with the @Lazy annotation:

```
package com.apress.spring6recipes.shop;

import org.springframework.context.annotation.Lazy;
import org.springframework.context.annotation.Scope;
import org.springframework.stereotype.Component;

@Component
@Scope("prototype")
@Lazy
public class ShoppingCart {
```

In the preceding declaration, because the POJO is decorated with the @Lazy annotation, if the POJO is never required by the application or referenced by another POJO, it's never instantiated.

ℹ️   The @Lazy annotation can also be used on a field or constructor together with @Autowired to have the injection done lazily.

Define Initialization of POJOs Before Other POJOs with @DependsOn

As an application's number of POJOs grows, so does the number of POJO initializations. This can create race conditions if POJOs reference one another and are spread out in different Java configuration classes. What happens if bean "C" requires the logic in bean "B" and bean "F"? If bean "C" is detected first and Spring hasn't initialized bean "B" and bean "F," you'll get an error, which can be hard to detect. To ensure that certain POJOs are initialized before other POJOs and to get a more descriptive error in case of a failed initialization process, Spring offers the @DependsOn annotation. The @DependsOn annotation ensures a given bean is initialized before another bean:

```
package com.apress.spring6recipes.sequence.config;

import org.springframework.context.annotation.Bean;
import org.springframework.context.annotation.Configuration;
import org.springframework.context.annotation.DependsOn;

import com.apress.spring6recipes.sequence.Sequence;

@Configuration
public class SequenceConfiguration {

  @Bean
  @DependsOn("datePrefixGenerator")
  public Sequence sequenceGenerator() {
    return new Sequence("A", 100000);
  }
}
```

In the preceding snippet, the declaration @DependsOn("datePrefixGenerator") ensures the datePrefixGenerator bean is created before the sequenceGenerator bean.

1-9. Create Post-processors to Validate and Modify POJOs

Problem

You want to apply tasks to all bean instances or specific types of instances during construction to validate or modify bean properties according to particular criteria.

Solution

A bean post-processor allows bean processing before and after the initialization callback method (i.e., the one assigned to the initMethod attribute of the @Bean annotation or the method decorated with the @PostConstruct annotation). The main characteristic of a bean post-processor is that it processes all the bean instances in the IoC container, not just a single bean instance. Typically, bean post-processors are used to check the validity of bean properties, alter bean properties according to particular criteria, or apply certain tasks to all bean instances.

How It Works

Suppose you want to audit the creation of every bean. You may want to do this to debug an application, verify the properties of every bean, or some other scenario. A bean post-processor is an ideal choice to implement this feature, because you don't have to modify any preexisting POJO code.

Create a POJO to Process Every Bean Instance

To write a bean post-processor, a class has to implement BeanPostProcessor. When Spring detects a bean that implements this class, it applies the postProcessBeforeInitialization() and postProcessAfterInitialization() methods to all bean instances managed by Spring. You can implement any logic you wish in these methods, to either inspect, modify, or verify the status of a bean:

```
package com.apress.spring6recipes.shop;

import org.springframework.beans.BeansException;
import org.springframework.beans.factory.config.BeanPostProcessor;
import org.springframework.stereotype.Component;

@Component
public class AuditCheckBeanPostProcessor implements BeanPostProcessor {

    @Override
    public Object postProcessBeforeInitialization(Object bean, String beanName)
            throws BeansException {
        var msg = "In AuditCheckBeanPostProcessor.postProcessBeforeInitialization, processing
        bean type: %s%n";
        System.out.printf(msg, bean.getClass().getName());
        return bean;
    }

    @Override
    public Object postProcessAfterInitialization(Object bean, String beanName)
```

```
        throws BeansException {
    return bean;
  }
}
```

Notice the postProcessBeforeInitialization() and postProcessAfterInitialization() methods must return the original bean instance even if you don't do anything in the method.

To register a bean post-processor in an application context, annotate the class with the @Component annotation. The application context is able to detect which bean implements the BeanPostProcessor interface and register it to process all other bean instances in the container.

Create a POJO to Process Selected Bean Instances

During bean construction, the Spring IoC container passes all the bean instances to the bean post-processor one by one. This means if you only want to apply a bean post-processor to certain types of beans, you must filter the beans by checking their instance type. This allows you to apply logic more selectively across beans.

Suppose you now want to apply a bean post-processor but just to Product bean instances. The following example is another bean post-processor that does just this:

```
package com.apress.spring6recipes.shop;

import org.springframework.beans.BeansException;
import org.springframework.beans.factory.config.BeanPostProcessor;

public class ProductCheckBeanPostProcessor implements BeanPostProcessor {

  private static final String MSG =
          "In ProductCheckBeanPostProcessor.%s, processing Product: %s%n";

  public Object postProcessBeforeInitialization(Object bean, String beanName)
          throws BeansException {
    if (bean instanceof Product product) {
      var productName = product.getName();
      System.out.printf(MSG, "postProcessBeforeInitialization", productName);
    }
    return bean;
  }

  public Object postProcessAfterInitialization(Object bean, String beanName)
          throws BeansException {
    if (bean instanceof Product product) {
      var productName = product.getName();
      System.out.printf(MSG, "postProcessAfterInitialization", productName);
    }
    return bean;
  }
}
```

Both the postProcessBeforeInitialization() and postProcessAfterInitialization() methods must return an instance of the bean being processed. However, this also means you can even replace the original bean instance with a brand-new instance in your bean post-processor.

1-10. Create POJOs with a Factory (Static Method, Instance Method, Spring's FactoryBean)

Problem

You want to create a POJO instance in the Spring IoC container by invoking a static factory method or instance factory method. The purpose of this approach is to encapsulate the object creation process either in a static method or in a method of another object instance, respectively. The client who requests an object can simply make a call to this method without knowing about the creation details. You want to create a POJO instance in the Spring IoC container using Spring's factory bean. A factory bean is a bean that serves as a factory for creating other beans within the IoC container. Conceptually, a factory bean is very similar to a factory method, but it's a Spring-specific bean that can be identified by the Spring IoC container during bean construction.

Solution

To create a POJO by invoking a static factory method inside a @Bean definition of a Java configuration class, you use standard Java syntax to call the static factory method. To create a POJO by invoking an instance factory method inside a @Bean definition of a Java configuration class, you create a POJO to instantiate the factory values and another POJO to act as a façade to access the factory.

As a convenience, Spring provides an abstract template class called `AbstractFactoryBean` to extend Spring's `FactoryBean` interface.

How It Works

Create POJOs by Invoking a Static Factory Method

For example, you can write the following `createProduct` static factory method to create a product from a predefined product ID. According to the product ID, this method decides which concrete product class to instantiate. If there is no product matching this ID, it throws an `IllegalArgumentException`:

```
package com.apress.spring6recipes.shop;

public class ProductCreator {

  public static Product createProduct(String productId) {
    return switch (productId) {
      case "aaa" -> new Battery("AAA", 2.5, true);
      case "cdrw" -> new Disc("CD-RW", 1.5, 700);
      case "dvdrw" -> new Disc("DVD-RW", 3.0, 4700);
      default -> {
        var msg = "Unknown product '" + productId + "'";
        throw new IllegalArgumentException(msg);
      }
    };
  }
}
```

To create a POJO with a static factory method inside a @Bean definition of a Java configuration class, you use regular Java syntax to call the factory method:

```
package com.apress.spring6recipes.shop.config;

import org.springframework.context.annotation.Bean;
import org.springframework.context.annotation.ComponentScan;
import org.springframework.context.annotation.Configuration;

import com.apress.spring6recipes.shop.Product;
import com.apress.spring6recipes.shop.ProductCreator;

@Configuration
@ComponentScan("com.apress.spring6recipes.shop")
public class ShopConfiguration {

  @Bean
  public Product aaa() {
    return ProductCreator.createProduct("aaa");
  }

  @Bean
  public Product cdrw() {
    return ProductCreator.createProduct("cdrw");
  }

  @Bean
  public Product dvdrw() {
    return ProductCreator.createProduct("dvdrw");
  }
}
```

Create POJOs by Invoking an Instance Factory Method

For example, you can write the following ProductCreator class by using a configurable map to store predefined products. The createProduct() instance factory method finds a product by looking up the supplied productId in the map. If there is no product matching this ID, it will throw an IllegalArgumentException:

```
package com.apress.spring6recipes.shop;

import java.util.Map;

public class ProductCreator {

  private final Map<String, Product> products;

  public ProductCreator(Map<String, Product> products) {
    this.products = products;
  }
```

```
  public Product createProduct(String productId) {
    Product product = products.get(productId);
    if (product != null) {
      return product;
    }
    var msg = "Unknown product '" + productId + "'";
    throw new IllegalArgumentException(msg);
  }
}
```

To create products from this ProductCreator, you first declare a @Bean to instantiate the factory values. Next, you declare a second bean to act as a façade to access the factory. Finally, you can call the factory and execute the createProduct() method in to instantiate other beans:

```
package com.apress.spring6recipes.shop.config;

import com.apress.spring6recipes.shop.Battery;
import com.apress.spring6recipes.shop.Disc;
import com.apress.spring6recipes.shop.Product;
import com.apress.spring6recipes.shop.ProductCreator;
import org.springframework.context.annotation.Bean;
import org.springframework.context.annotation.ComponentScan;
import org.springframework.context.annotation.Configuration;

import java.util.Map;

@Configuration
@ComponentScan("com.apress.spring6recipes.shop")
public class ShopConfiguration {

  @Bean
  public ProductCreator productCreatorFactory() {

    var products = Map.of(
      "aaa", new Battery("AAA", 2.5, true),
      "cdrw", new Disc("CD-RW", 1.5, 700),
      "dvdrw", new Disc("DVD-RW", 3.0, 4700));
    return new ProductCreator(products);
  }

  @Bean
  public Product aaa(ProductCreator productCreator) {
    return productCreator.createProduct("aaa");
  }

  @Bean
  public Product cdrw(ProductCreator productCreator) {
    return productCreator.createProduct("cdrw");
  }
```

```
@Bean
public Product dvdrw(ProductCreator productCreator) {
    return productCreator.createProduct("dvdrw");
}
}
```

Create POJOs Using Spring's Factory Bean

Although you'll seldom have to write custom factory beans, you may find it helpful to understand their internal mechanisms through an example. For example, you can write a factory bean for creating a product with a discount applied to the price. It accepts a product property and a discount property to apply the discount to the product and return it as a new bean:

```
package com.apress.spring6recipes.shop;

import org.springframework.beans.factory.config.AbstractFactoryBean;

public class DiscountFactoryBean extends AbstractFactoryBean<Product> {

    private Product product;
    private double discount;

    public void setProduct(Product product) {
        this.product = product;
    }

    public void setDiscount(double discount) {
        this.discount = discount;
    }

    @Override
    public Class<?> getObjectType() {
        return product.getClass();
    }

    @Override
    protected Product createInstance() throws Exception {
        product.setPrice(product.getPrice() * (1 - discount));
        return product;
    }
}
```

By extending the AbstractFactoryBean class, the factory bean can simply override the createInstance() method to create the target bean instance. In addition, you have to return the target bean's type in the getObjectType() method for the autowiring feature to work properly.

Next, you can declare product instances using a regular @Bean annotation to apply DiscountFactoryBean:

```
package com.apress.spring6recipes.shop.config;

import org.springframework.context.annotation.Bean;
import org.springframework.context.annotation.ComponentScan;
import org.springframework.context.annotation.Configuration;

import com.apress.spring6recipes.shop.Battery;
import com.apress.spring6recipes.shop.DiscountFactoryBean;
import com.apress.spring6recipes.shop.Disc;

@Configuration
@ComponentScan("com.apress.spring6recipes.shop")
public class ShopConfiguration {

  @Bean
  public Battery aaa() {
    return new Battery("AAA", 2.5, true);
  }

  @Bean
  public Disc cdrw() {
    return new Disc("CD-RW", 1.5, 700);
  }

  @Bean
  public Disc dvdrw() {
    return new Disc("DVD-RW", 3.0, 4700);
  }

  @Bean
  public DiscountFactoryBean discountFactoryBeanAAA(Battery aaa) {
    var factory = new DiscountFactoryBean();
    factory.setProduct(aaa);
    factory.setDiscount(0.2);
    return factory;
  }

  @Bean
  public DiscountFactoryBean discountFactoryBeanCDRW(Disc cdrw) {
    var factory = new DiscountFactoryBean();
    factory.setProduct(cdrw);
    factory.setDiscount(0.1);
    return factory;
  }

  @Bean
  public DiscountFactoryBean discountFactoryBeanDVDRW(Disc dvdrw) {
    var factory = new DiscountFactoryBean();
```

```
        factory.setProduct(dvdrw);
        factory.setDiscount(0.1);
        return factory;
    }
}
```

1-11. Use Spring Environments and Profiles to Load Different Sets of POJOs

Problem

You want to use the same set of POJO instances or beans but with different instantiation values for different application scenarios (e.g., "production," "development," and "testing").

Solution

Create multiple Java configuration classes and group POJO instances or beans into each of these classes. Assign a profile name to the Java configuration class with the @Profile annotation based on the purpose of the group. Get the environment for an application's context and set the profile to load a specific group of POJOs.

How It Works

POJO instantiation values can vary depending on different application scenarios. For example, a common scenario can occur when an application goes from development to testing and on to production. In each of these scenarios, the properties for certain beans can vary slightly to accommodate environment changes (e.g., database username/password, file paths, etc.).

You can create multiple Java configuration classes each with different POJOs (e.g., ShopConfigurationGlobal, ShopConfigurationSpr, and ShopConfigurationSumWin). And in the application context, only load a given configuration class file based on the scenario. Beans without a @Profile annotation are always loaded as they aren't bound to a certain profile.

Create Java Configuration Classes with the @Profile Annotation

Let's create multiple Java configuration classes with the @Profile annotation for the shopping application presented in previous recipes:

```
package com.apress.spring6recipes.shop.config;

import com.apress.spring6recipes.shop.Cashier;
import org.springframework.context.annotation.Bean;
import org.springframework.context.annotation.ComponentScan;
import org.springframework.context.annotation.Configuration;

@Configuration
@ComponentScan("com.apress.spring6recipes.shop")
public class ShopConfigurationGlobal {
```

```java
  @Bean(initMethod = "openFile", destroyMethod = "closeFile")
  public Cashier cashier() {
    var path = System.getProperty("java.io.tmpdir") + "/cashier";
    return new Cashier("checkout", path);
  }
}


package com.apress.spring6recipes.shop.config;

import org.springframework.context.annotation.Bean;
import org.springframework.context.annotation.Configuration;
import org.springframework.context.annotation.Profile;

import com.apress.spring6recipes.shop.Battery;
import com.apress.spring6recipes.shop.Disc;
import com.apress.spring6recipes.shop.Product;

@Configuration
@Profile({ "summer", "winter" })
public class ShopConfigurationSumWin {

  @Bean
  public Product aaa() {
    return new Battery("AAA", 2.0, true);
  }

  @Bean
  public Product cdrw() {
    return new Disc("CD-RW", 1.0, 700);
  }

  @Bean
  public Product dvdrw() {
    return new Disc("DVD-RW", 2.5, 4700);
  }
}


package com.apress.spring6recipes.shop.config;

import com.apress.spring6recipes.shop.Battery;
import com.apress.spring6recipes.shop.Disc;
import com.apress.spring6recipes.shop.Product;
import org.springframework.context.annotation.Bean;
import org.springframework.context.annotation.Configuration;
import org.springframework.context.annotation.Profile;

@Configuration
@Profile("autumn")
public class ShopConfigurationAut {
```

```
@Bean
public Product aaa() {
  return new Battery("AAA", 2.5, true);
}

@Bean
public Product cdrw() {
  return new Disc("CD-RW", 1.5, 700);
}

@Bean
public Product dvdrw() {
  return new Disc("DVD-RW", 3.0, 4700);
}
}
```

```
package com.apress.spring6recipes.shop.config;

import org.springframework.context.annotation.Bean;
import org.springframework.context.annotation.Configuration;
import org.springframework.context.annotation.Profile;

import com.apress.spring6recipes.shop.Battery;
import com.apress.spring6recipes.shop.Disc;
import com.apress.spring6recipes.shop.Product;

@Configuration
@Profile("spring")
public class ShopConfigurationSpr {

  @Bean
  public Product aaa() {
    return new Battery("AAA", 2.5, true);
  }

  @Bean
  public Product cdrw() {
    return new Disc("CD-RW", 1.5, 700);
  }

  @Bean
  public Product dvdrw() {
    return new Disc("DVD-RW", 3.0, 4700);
  }
}
```

The @Profile annotation decorates the entire Java configuration class, so all the @Bean instances belong to the same profile. To assign a @Profile name, you just place the name inside "". Notice it's also possible to assign multiple @Profile names using a comma-separated value (CSV) syntax surrounded by {} (e.g., {"summer","winter"}). The ShopConfigurationGlobal doesn't have the @Profile annotation as that is our main configuration class, which will detect the other @Configuration classes.

Load Profiles into Environments

To load the beans from a certain profile into an application, you need to activate a profile. You can load multiple profiles at a time, and it's also possible to load profiles programmatically, through a Java runtime flag, or even as an initialization parameter of a web archive (WAR) file.

To load profiles programmatically (i.e., via the application context), you get the context environment from where you can load profiles via the setActiveProfiles() method:

```
var context = new AnnotationConfigApplicationContext();
context.getEnvironment().setActiveProfiles("winter");
context.register(ShopConfigurationGlobal.class);
context.refresh();
```

It's also possible to indicate which Spring profile to load via a Java runtime flag. In this manner, you can pass the following runtime flag to load all beans that belong to the global and winter profiles:

```
-Dspring.profiles.active=winter
```

Set a Default Profile

To avoid the possibility of errors because no profiles are loaded into an application, you can define default profiles. Default profiles are only used when Spring can't detect any active profiles—defined using any of the previous methods: programmatically, via a Java runtime flag, or via a web application initialization parameter.

To set up default profiles, you can also use any of the three methods to set up active profiles. Programmatically, you use the method setDefaultProfiles() instead of setActiveProfiles(), and via a Java runtime flag or web application initialization parameter, you can use the spring.profiles.default parameter instead of spring.profiles.active.

1-12. Making POJOs Aware of Spring's IoC Container Resources

Problem

Even though a well-designed component should not have direct dependencies on Spring's IoC container, sometimes it's necessary for beans to be aware of the container's resources.

Solution

Your beans can be aware of the Spring IoC container's resources by implementing certain "aware" interfaces. The most common ones are shown in Table 1-2. Spring injects the corresponding resources to beans that implement these interfaces via the setter methods defined in these interfaces.

Table 1-2. Common Aware Interfaces in Spring

Aware Interface	Target Resource Type
BeanNameAware	The bean name of its instances configured in the IoC container
BeanFactoryAware	The current bean factory, through which you can invoke the container's services
ApplicationContextAware	The current application context, through which you can invoke the container's services
MessageSourceAware	A message source, through which you can resolve text messages
ApplicationEventPublisherAware	An application event publisher, through which you can publish application events
ResourceLoaderAware	A resource loader, through which you can load external resources
EnvironmentAware	The org.springframework.core.env.Environment instance associated with the ApplicationContext
EmbeddedValueResolverAware	The StringValueResolver to be used for resolving embedded values (i.e., Spring value expressions)
LoadTimeWeaverAware	The LoadTimeWeaver instance used when load-time weaving (LTW) is enabled
ApplicationStartupAware	The org.springframework.core.metrics.ApplicationStartup associated with the ApplicationContext

ℹ️ The ApplicationContext interface in fact extends the MessageSource, ApplicationEventPublisher, and ResourcePatternResolver interfaces, so you only need to be aware of the application context to access all these services. However, the best practice is to choose an aware interface with minimum scope that can satisfy your requirement.

The setter methods in the aware interfaces are called by Spring after the bean properties have been set, but before the initialization callback methods are called, as illustrated in the following list:

- Create the bean instance either by a constructor or by a factory method.

- Set the values and bean references to the bean properties.

- Call the setter methods defined in the aware interfaces.

- Pass the bean instance to the postProcessBeforeInitialization() method of each bean post-processor.

- Call the initialization callback methods.

- Pass the bean instance to the postProcessAfterInitialization() method of each bean post-processor.

- The bean is ready to be used.

- When the container is shut down, call the destruction callback methods.

Keep in mind that once a bean implements an aware interface, it is bound to Spring and won't work properly outside the Spring IoC container. So consider carefully whether it's necessary to implement such proprietary interfaces.

ℹ️ With the newer versions of Spring, it is not strictly necessary to implement the aware interfaces. You could also use @Autowired to get, for instance, access to the ApplicationContext. However, if you are writing a framework/library, it might be better to implement the interfaces.

How It Works

For example, you can make the shopping application's POJO instances of the Cashier class aware of their corresponding bean name by implementing the BeanNameAware interface. By implementing the interface, Spring automatically injects the bean name into the POJO instance. In addition to implementing the interface, you also need to add the necessary setter method to handle the bean name:

```
package com.apress.spring6recipes.shop;

import org.springframework.beans.factory.BeanNameAware;

public class Cashier implements BeanNameAware {

    private final String path;
    private String fileName;
    @Override
    public void setBeanName(String name) {
        this.fileName = name;
    }
}
```

When the bean name is injected, you can use the value to do a related POJO task that requires the bean name. For example, you could use the value to set the filename to record a cashier's checkout data. In this way, you can erase the configuration of the fileName constructor argument:

```
@Bean(initMethod = "openFile", destroyMethod = "closeFile")
public Cashier cashier() {
    var path = System.getProperty("java.io.tmpdir") + "cashier";
    var cashier = new Cashier(path);
    return c1;
}
```

1-13. Aspect-Oriented Programming with Annotations

Problem

You want to use aspect-orientated programming (AOP) with Spring and AspectJ.

Solution

You define an aspect by decorating a Java class with the @Aspect annotation. Each of the methods in a class can be become an advice with another annotation. You can use five types of advice annotations: @Before, @After, @AfterReturning, @AfterThrowing, and @Around. These annotations are provided by AspectJ and can be used to define aspects for use within a Spring application.

To enable annotation support in the Spring IoC container, you have to add @EnableAspectJAutoProxy to one of your configuration classes. To apply AOP Spring creates proxies, and by default it creates JDK dynamic proxies, which are interface based. For cases in which interfaces are not available or not used in an application's design, it's possible to create proxies by relying on CGLIB. To enable CGLIB, you need to set the attribute proxyTargetClass=true on the @EnableAspectJAutoProxy annotation.

How It Works

To support aspect-oriented programming with annotations, Spring uses the same annotations as AspectJ, using a library supplied by AspectJ for pointcut parsing and matching, although the AOP runtime is still pure Spring AOP and there is no dependency on the AspectJ compiler or weaver.

To illustrate the enablement of aspect-oriented programming with annotations, we'll use the following calculator interfaces to define a set of sample POJOs:

```
package com.apress.spring6recipes.calculator;

public interface ArithmeticCalculator {

  double add(double a, double b);
  double sub(double a, double b);
  double mul(double a, double b);
  double div(double a, double b);
}
```

```
package com.apress.spring6recipes.calculator;

public interface UnitCalculator {

  double kilogramToPound(double kilogram);
  double kilometerToMile(double kilometer);
}
```

Next, let's create POJO classes for each interface with println statements to know when each method is executed:

```
package com.apress.spring6recipes.calculator;

import org.springframework.stereotype.Component;

@Component
class StandardArithmeticCalculator implements ArithmeticCalculator {
```

```java
  @Override
  public double add(double a, double b) {
    var result = a + b;
    System.out.printf("%f + %f = %f%n", a, b, result);
    return result;
  }

  @Override
  public double sub(double a, double b) {
    var result = a - b;
    System.out.printf("%f - %f = %f%n", a, b, result);
    return result;
  }

  @Override
  public double mul(double a, double b) {
    var result = a * b;
    System.out.printf("%f * %f = %f%n", a, b, result);
    return result;
  }

  @Override
  public double div(double a, double b) {
    if (b == 0) {
      throw new IllegalArgumentException("Division by zero");
    }
    var result = a / b;
    System.out.printf("%f / %f = %f%n", a, b, result);
    return result;
  }
}


package com.apress.spring6recipes.calculator;

import org.springframework.stereotype.Component;

@Component
class StandardUnitCalculator implements UnitCalculator {

  @Override
  public double kilogramToPound(double kg) {
    var pound = kg * 2.2;
    System.out.printf("%f kilogram = %f pound%n", kg, pound);
    return pound;
  }

  @Override
  public double kilometerToMile(double km) {
    var mile = km * 0.62;
```

```
System.out.printf("%f kilometer = %f mile%n", km, mile);
    return mile;
  }
}
```

Note that each POJO implementation is decorated with the @Component annotation to create bean instances.

Declare Aspects, Advices, and Pointcuts

An aspect is a Java class that modularizes a set of concerns (e.g., logging or transaction management) that cuts across multiple types and objects. Java classes that modularize such concerns are decorated with the @Aspect annotation. In AOP terminology, aspects are also complemented by advices, which in themselves have pointcuts. An advice is a simple Java method with one of the advice annotations. AspectJ supports five types of advice annotations: @Before, @After, @AfterReturning, @AfterThrowing, and @Around. On the other hand, a pointcut is an expression that looks for types and objects on which to apply the aspect's advices.

Aspect with the @Before Advice

To create a before advice to handle crosscutting concerns before particular program execution points, you use the @Before annotation and include the pointcut expression as the annotation value:

```
package com.apress.spring6recipes.calculator;

import org.aspectj.lang.annotation.Aspect;
import org.aspectj.lang.annotation.Before;
import org.slf4j.Logger;
import org.slf4j.LoggerFactory;
import org.springframework.stereotype.Component;

@Aspect
@Component
public class CalculatorLoggingAspect {

    private final Logger log = LoggerFactory.getLogger(this.getClass());

    @Before("execution(* ArithmeticCalculator.add(..))")
    public void logBefore() {
        log.info("The method add() begins");
    }
}
```

This pointcut expression matches the add() method execution of the ArithmeticCalculator interface. The preceding wildcard in this expression matches any modifier (public, protected, and private) and any return type. The two dots in the argument list match any number of arguments.

ⓘ   For the preceding aspect to work (i.e., output its message), you need to set up logging. The following `logback.xml` can be used for Logback. The recipe itself uses the SLF4J simple logger and provides a default configuration for logging.

Sample Logback configuration

```xml
<?xml version="1.0" encoding="UTF-8"?>
<configuration>

    <appender name="STDOUT" class="ch.qos.logback.core.ConsoleAppender">
        <layout class="ch.qos.logback.classic.PatternLayout">
            <Pattern>%d [%15.15t] %-5p %30.30c - %m%n</Pattern>
        </layout>
    </appender>

    <root level="INFO">
        <appender-ref ref="STDOUT" />
    </root>

</configuration>
```

ⓘ   The @Aspect annotation is not sufficient for auto-detection in the classpath. Therefore, you need to add a separate @Component annotation for the POJO to be detected.

Next, you create a Spring configuration to scan all POJOs, including the POJO calculator implementation and aspect, as well as include the @EnableAspectJAutoProxy annotation:

```java
package com.apress.spring6recipes.calculator;

import org.springframework.context.annotation.ComponentScan;
import org.springframework.context.annotation.Configuration;
import org.springframework.context.annotation.EnableAspectJAutoProxy;

@Configuration
@EnableAspectJAutoProxy
@ComponentScan
public class CalculatorConfiguration { }
```

And as the last step, you can test the aspect with the following Main class:

```java
package com.apress.spring6recipes.calculator;

import org.springframework.context.annotation.AnnotationConfigApplicationContext;

public class Main {
```

```
public static void main(String[] args) {
    var cfg = CalculatorConfiguration.class;
    try (var context = new AnnotationConfigApplicationContext(cfg)) {

        var arithmeticCalculator = context.getBean(ArithmeticCalculator.class);
        arithmeticCalculator.add(1, 2);
        arithmeticCalculator.sub(4, 3);
        arithmeticCalculator.mul(2, 3);
        arithmeticCalculator.div(4, 2);

        var unitCalculator = context.getBean(UnitCalculator.class);
        unitCalculator.kilogramToPound(10);
        unitCalculator.kilometerToMile(5);
    }
}
}
```

The execution points matched by a pointcut are called join points. In this term, a pointcut is an expression to match a set of join points, while an advice is the action to take at a particular join point.

For your advice to access the details of the current join point, you can declare an argument of type JoinPoint in your advice method. Then, you can get access to join point details such as the method name and argument values. Now, you can expand your pointcut to match all methods by changing the class name and method name to wildcards:

```
package com.apress.spring6recipes.calculator;

import org.aspectj.lang.JoinPoint;
import org.aspectj.lang.annotation.Aspect;
import org.aspectj.lang.annotation.Before;
import org.slf4j.Logger;
import org.slf4j.LoggerFactory;
import org.springframework.stereotype.Component;

import java.util.Arrays;

@Aspect
@Component
public class CalculatorLoggingAspect {

    private Logger log = LoggerFactory.getLogger(this.getClass());

    @Before("execution(* *.*(..))")
    public void logBefore(JoinPoint joinPoint) {
        var name = joinPoint.getSignature().getName();
        var args = Arrays.toString(joinPoint.getArgs());
        log.info("The method {}() begins with {} ", name , args);
    }
}
```

Aspect with the @After Advice

An after advice is represented by a method annotated with @After and is executed after a join point finishes, whenever it returns a result or throws an exception abnormally. The following after advice logs the calculator method ending:

```
package com.apress.spring6recipes.calculator;

import org.aspectj.lang.JoinPoint;
import org.aspectj.lang.annotation.After;
import org.aspectj.lang.annotation.Aspect;
import org.slf4j.Logger;
import org.slf4j.LoggerFactory;
import org.springframework.stereotype.Component;

import java.util.Arrays;

@Aspect
@Component
public class CalculatorLoggingAspect {

  private Logger log = LoggerFactory.getLogger(this.getClass());

  @After("execution(* *.*(..))")
  public void logAfter(JoinPoint joinPoint) {
    var name = joinPoint.getSignature().getName();
    log.info("The method {}() ends", name);
  }
}
```

Aspect with the @AfterReturning Advice

An after advice is executed regardless of whether a join point returns normally or throws an exception. If you would like to perform logging only when a join point returns, you should replace the after advice with an after returning advice:

```
package com.apress.spring6recipes.calculator;

import org.aspectj.lang.JoinPoint;
import org.aspectj.lang.annotation.AfterReturning;
import org.aspectj.lang.annotation.Aspect;
import org.slf4j.Logger;
import org.slf4j.LoggerFactory;
import org.springframework.stereotype.Component;

@Aspect
@Component
public class CalculatorLoggingAspect {
```

```
    @AfterReturning("execution(* *.*(..))")
    public void logAfterReturning(JoinPoint joinPoint) {
        var name = joinPoint.getSignature().getName();
        log.info("The method {}() has ended.", name);
    }
}
```

In an after returning advice, you can get access to the return value of a join point by adding a returning attribute to the @AfterReturning annotation. The value of this attribute should be the argument name of this advice method for the return value to pass in. Then, you have to add an argument to the advice method signature with this name. At runtime, Spring AOP will pass in the return value through this argument. Also note that the original pointcut expression needs to be presented in the pointcut attribute instead:

```
package com.apress.spring6recipes.calculator;

import org.aspectj.lang.JoinPoint;
import org.aspectj.lang.annotation.AfterReturning;
import org.aspectj.lang.annotation.Aspect;
import org.slf4j.Logger;
import org.slf4j.LoggerFactory;
import org.springframework.stereotype.Component;

import java.util.Arrays;

@Aspect
@Component
public class CalculatorLoggingAspect {

    private Logger log = LoggerFactory.getLogger(this.getClass());

    @AfterReturning(
            pointcut = "execution(* *.*(..))",
            returning = "result")
    public void logAfterReturning(JoinPoint joinPoint, Object result) {
        var name = joinPoint.getSignature().getName();
        log.info("The method {}() ends with {}", name, result);
    }
}
```

Aspect with the @AfterThrowing Advice

An after throwing advice is executed only when an exception is thrown by a join point:

```
package com.apress.spring6recipes.calculator;

import org.aspectj.lang.JoinPoint;
import org.aspectj.lang.annotation.AfterThrowing;
import org.aspectj.lang.annotation.Aspect;
import org.slf4j.Logger;
import org.slf4j.LoggerFactory;
import org.springframework.stereotype.Component;
```

```java
@Aspect
@Component
public class CalculatorLoggingAspect {

    private final Logger log = LoggerFactory.getLogger(this.getClass());

    @AfterThrowing("execution(* *.*(..))")
    public void logAfterThrowing(JoinPoint joinPoint) {
        var name = joinPoint.getSignature().getName();
        log.error("An exception has been thrown in {}()", name);
    }
}
```

Similarly, the exception thrown by the join point can be accessed by adding a throwing attribute to the @AfterThrowing annotation. The type Throwable is the superclass of all errors and exceptions in the Java language. So the following advice will catch any of the errors and exceptions thrown by the join points:

```java
package com.apress.spring6recipes.calculator;

import org.aspectj.lang.JoinPoint;
import org.aspectj.lang.annotation.AfterThrowing;
import org.aspectj.lang.annotation.Aspect;
import org.slf4j.Logger;
import org.slf4j.LoggerFactory;
import org.springframework.stereotype.Component;

@Aspect
@Compoonent
public class CalculatorLoggingAspect {

    private final Logger log = LoggerFactory.getLogger(this.getClass());

    @AfterThrowing(
        pointcut = "execution(* *.*(..))",
        throwing = "ex")
    public void logAfterThrowing(JoinPoint joinPoint, Throwable ex) {
        var name = joinPoint.getSignature().getName();
        log.error("An exception {} has been thrown in {}()", ex, name);
    }
}
```

However, if you are interested in one particular type of exception only, you can declare it as the argument type of the exception. Then your advice will be executed only when exceptions of compatible type (i.e., this type and its subtypes) are thrown:

```java
package com.apress.spring6recipes.calculator;

import org.aspectj.lang.JoinPoint;
import org.aspectj.lang.annotation.AfterThrowing;
import org.aspectj.lang.annotation.Aspect;
import org.slf4j.Logger;
```

```
import org.slf4j.LoggerFactory;
import org.springframework.stereotype.Component;

import java.util.Arrays;

@Aspect
@Component
public class CalculatorLoggingAspect {

  private final Logger log = LoggerFactory.getLogger(this.getClass());

  @AfterThrowing(
          pointcut = "execution(* *.*(..))",
          throwing = "ex")
  public void logAfterThrowing(JoinPoint joinPoint, IllegalArgumentException ex) {
    var args = Arrays.toString(joinPoint.getArgs());
    var name = joinPoint.getSignature().getName();
    log.error("Illegal argument {} in {}()", args, name);
  }
}
```

Aspect with the @Around Advice

The last type of advice is an around advice. It is the most powerful of all the advice types. It gains full control of a join point, so you can combine all the actions of the preceding advices into one single advice. You can even control when, and whether, to proceed with the original join point execution.

The following around advice is the combination of the before, after returning, and after throwing advices you created before. Note that for an around advice, the argument type of the join point must be ProceedingJoinPoint. It's a subinterface of JoinPoint that allows you to control when to proceed with the original join point. To continue the process, you need to call the proceed() method on the ProceedingJoinPoint:

```
package com.apress.spring6recipes.calculator;

import org.aspectj.lang.ProceedingJoinPoint;
import org.aspectj.lang.annotation.Around;
import org.aspectj.lang.annotation.Aspect;
import org.slf4j.Logger;
import org.slf4j.LoggerFactory;
import org.springframework.stereotype.Component;

import java.util.Arrays;

@Aspect
@Component
public class CalculatorLoggingAspect {

  private final Logger log = LoggerFactory.getLogger(this.getClass());

  @Around("execution(* *.*(..))")
```

```
public Object logAround(ProceedingJoinPoint joinPoint) throws Throwable {
  var name = joinPoint.getSignature().getName();
  var args = Arrays.toString(joinPoint.getArgs());
  log.info("The method {}() begins with {}.", name, args);
  try {
    var result = joinPoint.proceed();
    log.info("The method {}() ends with {}.", name, result);
    return result;
  }
  catch (IllegalArgumentException ex) {
    log.error("Illegal argument {} in {}()", args, name);
    throw ex;
  }
}
}
```

The around advice type is very powerful and flexible in that you can even alter the original argument values and change the final return value. You must use this type of advice with great care, as the call to proceed with the original join point may easily be forgotten.

A best practice in choosing an advice type is to use the least powerful one that can satisfy your requirements.

1-14. Accessing the Join Point Information

Problem

In AOP, an advice is applied to different program execution points, which are called join points. For an advice to take the correct action, it often requires detailed information about join points.

Solution

An advice can access the current join point information by declaring an argument of type org.aspectj.lang. JoinPoint in the advice method signature.

How It Works

For example, you can access the join point information through the following advice. The information includes the join point kind (only method execution in Spring AOP), the method signature (declaring type and method name), and the argument values, as well as the target object and proxy object:

```
package com.apress.spring6recipes.calculator;

import org.aspectj.lang.JoinPoint;
import org.aspectj.lang.annotation.Aspect;
import org.aspectj.lang.annotation.Before;
```

```
import org.slf4j.Logger;
import org.slf4j.LoggerFactory;
import org.springframework.stereotype.Component;

import java.util.Arrays;

@Aspect
@Component
public class CalculatorLoggingAspect {

    private final Logger log = LoggerFactory.getLogger(this.getClass());

    @Before("execution(* *.*(..))")
    public void logJoinPoint(JoinPoint jp) {
        log.info("Join point kind : {}", jp.getKind());
        log.info("Signature declaring type : {}", jp.getSignature().getDeclaringTypeName());
        log.info("Signature name : {}", jp.getSignature().getName());
        log.info("Arguments : {}", Arrays.toString(jp.getArgs()));
        log.info("Target class : {}", jp.getTarget().getClass().getName());
        log.info("This class : {}", jp.getThis().getClass().getName());
    }
}
```

The original bean that was wrapped by a proxy is called the target object, while the proxy object is called the this object. They can be accessed by the join point's getTarget() and getThis() methods. From the following outputs, you can see that the classes of these two objects are not the same:

```
Join point kind : method-execution
Signature declaring type : com.apress.spring6recipes.calculator.ArithmeticCalculator
Signature name : add
Arguments : [1.0, 2.0]
Target class : com.apress.spring6recipes.calculator.StandardArithmeticCalculator
This class : com.sun.proxy.$Proxy6
```

1-15. Specifying Aspect Precedence with the @Order Annotation

Problem

When there's more than one aspect applied to the same join point, the precedence of the aspects is undefined unless you have explicitly specified it.

Solution

The precedence of aspects can be specified either by implementing the Ordered interface or by using the @ Order annotation.

How It Works

Suppose you have written another aspect to validate the calculator arguments. There's only one before advice in this aspect:

```
package com.apress.spring6recipes.calculator;

import org.aspectj.lang.JoinPoint;
import org.aspectj.lang.annotation.Aspect;
import org.aspectj.lang.annotation.Before;

import org.springframework.stereotype.Component;

@Aspect
@Component
public class CalculatorValidationAspect {

    @Before("execution(* *.*(double, double))")
    public void validateBefore(JoinPoint joinPoint) {
        for (var arg : joinPoint.getArgs()) {
            validate((Double) arg);
        }
    }

    private void validate(double a) {
        if (a < 0) {
            throw new IllegalArgumentException("Positive numbers only");
        }
    }
}
```

If you apply this aspect and the previous one, you can't guarantee which one is applied first. To guarantee that one aspect is applied before another, you need to specify precedence. To specify precedence, you have to make both aspects implement the Ordered interface or use the @Order annotation.

If you decide to implement the Ordered interface, the lower value returned by the getOrder method represents higher priority. So if you prefer the validation aspect to be applied first, it should return a value lower than the logging aspect:

```
package com.apress.spring6recipes.calculator;

import org.springframework.core.Ordered;

@Aspect
@Component
public class CalculatorValidationAspect implements Ordered {

  @Override
  public int getOrder() {
    return 0;
  }
}
```

Another way to specify precedence is through the @Order annotation. The order number should be presented in the annotation value:

```
package com.apress.spring6recipes.calculator;

import org.springframework.core.annotation.Order;

@Aspect
@Component
@Order(0)
public class CalculatorValidationAspect {
}
```

1-16. Reuse Aspect Pointcut Definitions

Problem

When writing aspects, you can directly embed a pointcut expression in an advice annotation. You want to use the same pointcut expression in multiple advices without embedding it multiple times.

Solution

You can use the @Pointcut annotation to define a pointcut independently to be reused in multiple advices.

How It Works

In an aspect, a pointcut can be declared as a simple method with the @Pointcut annotation. The method body of a pointcut is usually empty, as it is unreasonable to mix a pointcut definition with application logic. The access modifier of a pointcut method controls the visibility of this pointcut as well. Other advices can refer to this pointcut by the method name:

```
package com.apress.spring6recipes.calculator;

import org.aspectj.lang.annotation.Pointcut;
@Aspect
@Component
public class CalculatorLoggingAspect {

    @Pointcut("execution(* *.*(..))")
    private void loggingOperation() {}

    @Before("loggingOperation()")
    public void logBefore(JoinPoint joinPoint) {
    }

    @After("loggingOperation()")
    public void logAfter(JoinPoint joinPoint) {
    }
```

```
@AfterReturning(
        pointcut = "loggingOperation()",
        returning = "result")
public void logAfterReturning(JoinPoint joinPoint, Object result) {
}

@AfterThrowing(
        pointcut = "loggingOperation()",
        throwing = "ex")
public void logAfterThrowing(JoinPoint joinPoint, IllegalArgumentException ex) {
}

@Around("loggingOperation()")
public Object logAround(ProceedingJoinPoint joinPoint) throws Throwable {
}
}
```

Usually, if your pointcuts are shared between multiple aspects, it is better to centralize them in a common class. In this case, they must be declared as public:

```
package com.apress.spring6recipes.calculator;

import org.aspectj.lang.annotation.Aspect;
import org.aspectj.lang.annotation.Pointcut;

@Aspect
public class CalculatorPointcuts {

  @Pointcut("execution(* *.*(..))")
  public void loggingOperation() {}
}
```

When you refer to this pointcut, you have to include the class name as well. If the class is not located in the same package as the aspect, you have to include the package name also:

```
package com.apress.spring6recipes.calculator;

@Aspect
@Component
public class CalculatorLoggingAspect {

  @Before("com.apress.spring6recipes.calculator.CalculatorPointcuts.loggingOperation()")
  public void logBefore(JoinPoint joinPoint) {
  }

  @After("com.apress.spring6recipes.calculator.CalculatorPointcuts.loggingOperation()")
  public void logAfter(JoinPoint joinPoint) {
  }
```

```
@AfterReturning(
        pointcut = "com.apress.spring6recipes.calculator.CalculatorPointcuts.
        loggingOperation()",
        returning = "result")
public void logAfterReturning(JoinPoint joinPoint, Object result) {
}

@AfterThrowing(
        pointcut = "com.apress.spring6recipes.calculator.CalculatorPointcuts.
        loggingOperation()",
        throwing = "ex")
public void logAfterThrowing(JoinPoint joinPoint, IllegalArgumentException ex) {
}

@Around("com.apress.spring6recipes.calculator.CalculatorPointcuts.loggingOperation()")
public Object logAround(ProceedingJoinPoint joinPoint) throws Throwable {
}
}
```

1-17. Writing AspectJ Pointcut Expressions

Problem

Crosscutting concerns can happen at different program execution points, which are called join points.
Because of the variety of join points, you need a powerful expression language (EL) to help match them.

Solution

The AspectJ pointcut language is a powerful expression language that can match various kinds of join points.
However, Spring AOP only supports method execution join points for beans declared in its IoC container.
For this reason, only those pointcut expressions supported by Spring AOP are presented in this recipe. For
a full description of the AspectJ pointcut language, please refer to the AspectJ programming guide available
on AspectJ's website (www.eclipse.org/aspectj/). Spring AOP makes use of the AspectJ pointcut language
for its pointcut definition and interprets the pointcut expressions at runtime by using a library provided
by AspectJ. When writing AspectJ pointcut expressions for Spring AOP, you must keep in mind that Spring
AOP only supports method execution join points for the beans in its IoC container. If you use a pointcut
expression out of this scope, an IllegalArgumentException is thrown.

How It Works

Method Signature Patterns

The most typical pointcut expressions are used to match a number of methods by their signatures. For
example, the following pointcut expression matches all of the methods declared in the ArithmeticCalculator
interface. The initial wildcard matches methods with any modifier (public, protected, and private) and
any return type. The two dots in the argument list match any number of arguments:

```
execution(* com.apress.spring6recipes.calculator.ArithmeticCalculator.*(..))
```

You can omit the package name if the target class or interface is located in the same package as the aspect:

```
execution(* ArithmeticCalculator.*(..))
```

The following pointcut expression matches all the public methods declared in the ArithmeticCalculator interface:

```
execution(public * ArithmeticCalculator.*(..))
```

You can also restrict the method return type. For example, the following pointcut matches the methods that return a double number:

```
execution(public double ArithmeticCalculator.*(..))
```

The argument list of the methods can also be restricted. For example, the following pointcut matches the methods whose first argument is of primitive double type. The two dots then match any number of following arguments:

```
execution(public double ArithmeticCalculator.*(double, ..))
```

Or you can specify all the argument types in the method signature for the pointcut to match:

```
execution(public double ArithmeticCalculator.*(double, double))
```

Although the AspectJ pointcut language is powerful in matching various join points, sometimes, you may not be able to find any common characteristics (e.g., modifiers, return types, method name patterns, or arguments) for the methods you would like to match. In such cases, you can consider providing a custom annotation for them. For instance, you can define the following marker annotation. This annotation can be applied to both the method level and type level:

```java
package com.apress.spring6recipes.calculator;

import java.lang.annotation.Documented;
import java.lang.annotation.ElementType;
import java.lang.annotation.Retention;
import java.lang.annotation.RetentionPolicy;
import java.lang.annotation.Target;

@Target({ ElementType.METHOD, ElementType.TYPE })
@Retention(RetentionPolicy.RUNTIME)
@Documented
public @interface LoggingRequired { }
```

Next, you can annotate all methods that require logging with this annotation or the class itself to apply the behavior to all methods. Note that the annotations must be added to the implementation class but not the interface, as they will not be inherited:

```
package com.apress.spring6recipes.calculator;

import org.springframework.stereotype.Component;

@Component
@LoggingRequired
class StandardArithmeticCalculator implements ArithmeticCalculator {
}
```

Then you can write a pointcut expression to match a class or methods with the @LoggingRequired annotation using the @annotation keyword on the @Pointcut annotation:

```
package com.apress.spring6recipes.calculator;

import org.aspectj.lang.annotation.Pointcut;

public class CalculatorPointcuts {

  @Pointcut("@annotation(com.apress.spring6recipes.calculator.LoggingRequired)")
  public void loggingOperation() {
  }
}
```

Type Signature Patterns

Another kind of pointcut expressions matches all join points within certain types. When applied to Spring AOP, the scope of these pointcuts will be narrowed to matching all method executions within the types. For example, the following pointcut matches all the method execution join points within the com.apress. spring6recipes.calculator package:

```
within(com.apress.spring6recipes.calculator.*)
```

To match the join points within a package and its subpackage, you have to add one more dot before the wildcard:

```
within(com.apress.spring6recipes.calculator..*)
```

The following pointcut expression matches the method execution join points within a particular class:

```
within(com.apress.spring6recipes.calculator.StandardArithmeticCalculator)
```

Again, if the target class is located in the same package as this aspect, the package name can be omitted:

```
within(StandardArithmeticCalculator)
```

You can match the method execution join points within all classes that implement the ArithmeticCalculator interface by adding a plus symbol:

```
within(ArithmeticCalculator+)
```

The custom annotation @LoggingRequired can be applied to the class or method level as illustrated previously:

```
package com.apress.spring6recipes.calculator;

@LoggingRequired
public class StandardArithmeticCalculator implements ArithmeticCalculator {}
```

And then you can match the join points within the class or methods that have been annotated with @LoggingRequired using the @within keyword on the @Pointcut annotation:

```
@Pointcut("@within(com.apress.spring6recipes.calculator.LoggingRequired)")
public void loggingOperation() {}
```

ℹ️   You might have noticed the `within` and `@within` and `@annotation`. For several pointcut expressions, there is a keyword with and without a leading @. The difference is that the one without the @ is a regular AspectJ expression and applies to package and class names that match. The one with the @ applies to annotations. So if you want to match something in a class annotated with a certain annotation, you have to use `@within`; if you want to match a class, you have to use `within`.

Combining Pointcut Expressions

In AspectJ, pointcut expressions can be combined with the operators && (and), || (or), and ! (not). For example, the following pointcut matches the join points within classes that implement either the ArithmeticCalculator or UnitCalculator interface:

```
within(ArithmeticCalculator+) || within(UnitCalculator+)
```

The operands of these operators can be any pointcut expressions or references to other pointcuts:

```
package com.apress.spring6recipes.calculator;

import org.aspectj.lang.annotation.Pointcut;

public class CalculatorPointcuts {

  @Pointcut("within(com.apress.spring6recipes.calculator.ArithmeticCalculator+)")
  public void arithmeticOperation() {}

  @Pointcut("within(com.apress.spring6recipes.calculator.UnitCalculator+)")
  public void unitOperation() {}

  @Pointcut("arithmeticOperation() || unitOperation()")
  public void loggingOperation() {}
}
```

Declaring Pointcut Parameters

One way to access join point information is by reflection (i.e., via an argument of type org.aspectj.lang. JoinPoint in the advice method). Besides, you can access join point information in a declarative way by using some kinds of special pointcut expressions. For example, the expressions target() and args() capture the target object and argument values of the current join point and expose them as pointcut parameters. These parameters are passed to your advice method via arguments of the same name:

```
package com.apress.spring6recipes.calculator;

import org.aspectj.lang.annotation.Aspect;
import org.aspectj.lang.annotation.Before;
import org.springframework.stereotype.Component;

@Aspect
@Component
public class CalculatorLoggingAspect {

  @Before("execution(* *.*(..)) && target(target) && args(a,b)")
  public void logParameter(Object target, double a, double b) {
    log.info("Target class : {}" , target.getClass().getName());
    log.info("Arguments : {},{}", a , b);
  }
}
```

When declaring an independent pointcut that exposes parameters, you have to include them in the argument list of the pointcut method as well:

```
package com.apress.spring6recipes.calculator;

import org.aspectj.lang.annotation.Pointcut;

public class CalculatorPointcuts {

  @Pointcut("execution(* *.*(..)) && target(target) && args(a,b)")
  public void parameterPointcut(Object target, double a, double b) {}
}
```

Any advice that refers to this parameterized pointcut can access the pointcut parameters via method arguments of the same name:

```
package com.apress.spring6recipes.calculator;

import org.aspectj.lang.annotation.Aspect;
import org.aspectj.lang.annotation.Before;
import org.springframework.stereotype.Component;

@Aspect
@Component
public class CalculatorLoggingAspect {
```

```
@Before("com.apress.spring6recipes.calculator.CalculatorPointcuts.
parameterPointcut(target, a, b)")
public void logParameter(Object target, double a, double b) {
  log.info("Target class : {}" , target.getClass().getName());
  log.info("Arguments : {},{}", a , b);
}
}
```

1-18. AOP Introductions for POJOs

Problem

Sometimes, you may have a group of classes that share a common behavior. In OOP, they must extend the same base class or implement the same interface. This issue is actually a crosscutting concern that can be modularized with AOP. In addition, the single inheritance mechanism of Java only allows a class to extend one base class at most. So you cannot inherit behaviors from multiple implementation classes at the same time.

Solution

An introduction is a special type of advice in AOP. It allows objects to implement an interface dynamically by providing an implementation class for that interface. It seems as if objects extend an implementation class at runtime. Moreover, you are able to introduce multiple interfaces with multiple implementation classes to your objects at the same time. This can achieve the same effect as multiple inheritance.

How It Works

Suppose you have two interfaces, MaxCalculator and MinCalculator, to define the max() and min() operations:

```
package com.apress.spring6recipes.calculator;

public interface MaxCalculator {

  double max(double a, double b);
}
```

```
package com.apress.spring6recipes.calculator;

public interface MinCalculator {

  double min(double a, double b);
}
```

Then you have an implementation for each interface with print statements to let you know when the methods are executed:

```java
package com.apress.spring6recipes.calculator;

public class SimpleMaxCalculator implements MaxCalculator {

  @Override
  public double max(double a, double b) {
    var result = Math.max(a, b);
    System.out.printf("max(%f,%f) = %f%n", a,b, result);
    return result;
  }
}
```

```java
package com.apress.spring6recipes.calculator;

public class SimpleMinCalculator implements MinCalculator {

  @Override
  public double min(double a, double b) {
    var result = Math.min(a, b);
    System.out.printf("min(%f,%f) = %f%n", a, b, result);
    return result;
  }
}
```

Now, suppose you would like StandardArithmeticCalculator to perform the max() and min() calculations also. As the Java language supports single inheritance only, it is not possible for the StandardArithmeticCalculator class to extend both the SimpleMaxCalculator and SimpleMinCalculator classes at the same time. The only possible way is to extend either class (e.g., SimpleMaxCalculator) and implement another interface (e.g., MinCalculator), either by copying the implementation code or delegating the handling to the actual implementation class. In either case, you have to repeat the method declarations.

With an introduction, you can make StandardArithmeticCalculator dynamically implement both the MaxCalculator and MinCalculator interfaces by using the implementation classes SimpleMaxCalculator and SimpleMinCalculator. It has the same effect as multiple inheritance from SimpleMaxCalculator and SimpleMinCalculator. The idea behind an introduction is that you needn't modify the StandardArithmeticCalculator class to introduce new methods. That means you can introduce methods to your existing classes even without source code available.

You may wonder how an introduction can do that in Spring AOP. The answer is a dynamic proxy. As you may recall, you can specify a group of interfaces for a dynamic proxy to implement. An introduction works by adding an interface (e.g., MaxCalculator) to the dynamic proxy. When the methods declared in this interface are called on the proxy object, the proxy will delegate the calls to the back-end implementation class (e.g., SimpleMaxCalculator).

Introductions, like advices, must be declared within an aspect. You may create a new aspect or reuse an existing aspect for this purpose. In this aspect, you can declare an introduction by annotating an arbitrary field with the @DeclareParents annotation:

```
package com.apress.spring6recipes.calculator;

import org.aspectj.lang.annotation.Aspect;
import org.aspectj.lang.annotation.DeclareParents;
import org.springframework.stereotype.Component;

@Aspect
@Component
public class CalculatorIntroduction {

  @DeclareParents(
      value = "com.apress.spring6recipes.calculator.StandardArithmeticCalculator",
      defaultImpl = SimpleMaxCalculator.class)
  public MaxCalculator maxCalculator;

  @DeclareParents(
      value = "com.apress.spring6recipes.calculator.StandardArithmeticCalculator",
      defaultImpl = SimpleMinCalculator.class)
  public MinCalculator minCalculator;

}
```

The value attribute of the @DeclareParents annotation type indicates which classes are the targets for this introduction. The interface to introduce is determined by the type of the annotated field. Finally, the implementation class used for this new interface is specified in the defaultImpl attribute.

Through these two introductions, you can dynamically introduce a couple of interfaces to the StandardArithmeticCalculator class. Actually, you can specify an AspectJ type-matching expression in the value attribute of the @DeclareParents annotation to introduce an interface to multiple classes.

As you have introduced both the MaxCalculator and MinCalculator interfaces to your arithmetic calculator, you can cast it to the corresponding interface to perform the max() and min() calculations:

```
package com.apress.spring6recipes.calculator;

import org.springframework.context.annotation.AnnotationConfigApplicationContext;

public class Main {

  public static void main(String[] args) {

    var cfg = CalculatorConfiguration.class;
    try (var context = new AnnotationConfigApplicationContext(cfg)) {

      var maxCalculator = (MaxCalculator) arithmeticCalculator;
      maxCalculator.max(1,2);
```

```
    var minCalculator = (MinCalculator)arithmeticCalculator;
    minCalculator.min( 1, 2);
  }
}
```

ℹ️   You could also do context.getBean(MaxCalculator.class); to obtain a reference to the calculator and do the calculations. This sample is to show that the same bean now implements multiple interfaces and that AOP is used to invoke the actual implementing method.

1-19. Introduce States to Your POJOs with AOP

Problem

Sometimes, you may want to add new states to a group of existing objects to keep track of their usage, such as the calling count, the last modified date, and so on. It should not be a solution if all the objects have the same base class. However, it's difficult to add such states to different classes if they are not in the same class hierarchy.

Solution

You can introduce a new interface to your objects with an implementation class that holds the state field. Then, you can write another advice to change the state according to a particular condition.

How It Works

Suppose you would like to keep track of the calling count of each calculator object. Since there is no field for storing the counter value in the original calculator classes, you need to introduce one with Spring AOP. First, let's create an interface for the operations of a counter:

```
package com.apress.spring6recipes.calculator;

public interface Counter {

  void increase();
  int getCount();
}
```

Next, just write a simple implementation class for this interface. This class has a counter field for storing the counter value:

```
package com.apress.spring6recipes.calculator;

import java.util.concurrent.atomic.AtomicInteger;

public class SimpleCounter implements Counter {

  private final AtomicInteger counter = new AtomicInteger();
```

```
  @Override
  public void increase() {
    counter.incrementAndGet();
  }

  @Override
  public int getCount() {
    return counter.get();
  }
}
```

To introduce the Counter interface to all your calculator objects with SimpleCounter as the implementation, you can write the following introduction with a type-matching expression that matches all the calculator implementations:

```
package com.apress.spring6recipes.calculator;

import org.aspectj.lang.annotation.Aspect;
import org.aspectj.lang.annotation.DeclareParents;
import org.springframework.stereotype.Component;

@Aspect
@Component
public class CalculatorIntroduction {

  @DeclareParents(
      value = "com.apress.spring6recipes.calculator.Standard*Calculator",
      defaultImpl = SimpleCounter.class)
  public Counter counter;
}
```

This introduction introduces SimpleCounter to each of your calculator objects. However, it's still not enough to keep track of the calling count. You have to increase the counter value each time a calculator method is called. You can write an after advice for this purpose. Note that you must get the this object but not the target object, as only the proxy object implements the Counter interface:

```
package com.apress.spring6recipes.calculator;

import org.aspectj.lang.annotation.After;
import org.aspectj.lang.annotation.Aspect;
import org.springframework.stereotype.Component;

@Aspect
@Component
public class CalculatorIntroduction {

  @After("execution(* com.apress.spring6recipes.calculator.*Calculator.*(..))
  && this(counter)")
  public void increaseCount(Counter counter) {
    counter.increase();
  }
}
```

In the Main class, you can output the counter value for each of the calculator objects by casting them into the Counter type:

```
package com.apress.spring6recipes.calculator;

import org.springframework.context.annotation.AnnotationConfigApplicationContext;

public class Main {

  public static void main(String[] args) {
    var cfg = CalculatorConfiguration.class;
    try (var context = new AnnotationConfigApplicationContext(cfg)) {
      var arithmeticCalculator = context.getBean(ArithmeticCalculator.class);
      arithmeticCalculator.add(1, 2);
      arithmeticCalculator.sub(4, 3);
      arithmeticCalculator.mul(2, 3);
      arithmeticCalculator.div(4, 2);

      var unitCalculator = context.getBean(UnitCalculator.class);
      unitCalculator.kilogramToPound(10);
      unitCalculator.kilometerToMile(5);

      var maxCalculator = (MaxCalculator) arithmeticCalculator;
      maxCalculator.max(1,2);

      var minCalculator = (MinCalculator)arithmeticCalculator;
      minCalculator.min( 1, 2);

      var arithmeticCounter = (Counter) arithmeticCalculator;
      System.out.println(arithmeticCounter.getCount());

      var unitCounter = (Counter) unitCalculator;
      System.out.println(unitCounter.getCount());
    }
  }
}
```

1-20. Load-Time Weaving AspectJ Aspects in Spring

Problem

The Spring AOP framework supports only limited types of AspectJ pointcuts and allows aspects to apply to beans declared in the IoC container. If you want to use additional pointcut types or apply your aspects to objects created outside the Spring IoC container, you have to use the AspectJ framework in your Spring application.

Solution

Weaving is the process of applying aspects to your target objects. With Spring AOP, weaving happens at runtime through dynamic proxies. In contrast, the AspectJ framework supports both compile-time and load-time weaving.

AspectJ compile-time weaving is done through a special AspectJ compiler called ajc. It can weave aspects into your Java source files and output woven binary class files. It can also weave aspects into your compiled class files or JAR files. This process is known as post-compile-time weaving. You can perform compile-time and post-compile-time weaving for your classes before declaring them in the Spring IoC container. Spring is not involved in the weaving process at all. For more information on compile-time and post-compile-time weaving, please refer to the AspectJ documentation.

AspectJ load-time weaving (also known as LTW) happens when the target classes are loaded into the JVM by a class loader. For a class to be woven, a special class loader is required to enhance the bytecode of the target class. Both AspectJ and Spring provide load-time weavers to add load-time weaving capability to the class loader. You need only simple configurations to enable these load-time weavers.

How It Works

To understand the AspectJ load-time weaving process in a Spring application, let's consider a calculator for complex numbers. First, you create the Complex record to represent complex numbers:

```
package com.apress.spring6recipes.calculator;

public record Complex(int real, int imaginary) {

  @Override
  public String toString() {
    return "(" + real + " + " + imaginary + "i)";
  }
}
```

Next, you define an interface for the operations on complex numbers. For simplicity's sake, only add() and sub() are supported:

```
package com.apress.spring6recipes.calculator;

public interface ComplexCalculator {

  Complex add(Complex a, Complex b);
  Complex sub(Complex a, Complex b);
}
```

The implementation code for this interface is as follows. Each time, you return a new complex object as the result:

```
package com.apress.spring6recipes.calculator;

import org.springframework.stereotype.Component;

@Component
class StandardComplexCalculator implements ComplexCalculator {
```

```
@Override
public Complex add(Complex a, Complex b) {
  var result = new Complex(a.real() + b.real(), a.imaginary() + b.imaginary());
  System.out.printf("%s + %s = %s%n", a, b, result);
  return result;
}

@Override
public Complex sub(Complex a, Complex b) {
  var result = new Complex(a.real() - b.real(), a.imaginary() - b.imaginary());
  System.out.printf("%s - %s = %s%n", a, b, result);
  return result;
}
}
```

Now, you can test this complex number calculator with the following code in the Main class:

```
package com.apress.spring6recipes.calculator;

import org.springframework.context.annotation.AnnotationConfigApplicationContext;

public class Main {

  public static void main(String[] args) {

    var cfg = CalculatorConfiguration.class;
    try (var ctx = new AnnotationConfigApplicationContext(cfg)) {
      var complexCalculator = ctx.getBean( ComplexCalculator.class);

      complexCalculator.add(new Complex(1, 2), new Complex(2, 3));
      complexCalculator.sub(new Complex(5, 8), new Complex(2, 3));
    }
  }
}
```

So far, the complex calculator is working fine. However, you may want to improve the performance of the calculator by caching complex number objects. As caching is a well-known crosscutting concern, you can modularize it with an aspect:

```
package com.apress.spring6recipes.calculator;

import org.aspectj.lang.ProceedingJoinPoint;
import org.aspectj.lang.annotation.Around;
import org.aspectj.lang.annotation.Aspect;

import java.util.Map;
import java.util.concurrent.ConcurrentHashMap;

@Aspect
public class ComplexCachingAspect {

  private final Map<String, Complex> cache = new ConcurrentHashMap<>();
```

```
@Around("call(public com.apress.spring6recipes.calculator.Complex.new(int, int)) &&
args(a,b)")
public Object cacheAround(ProceedingJoinPoint pjp, int a, int b) throws Throwable {
  var key = a + "," + b;
  return cache.compute(key, (key1, val) -> checkCacheOrCalculate(pjp, key1, val));
}

private Complex checkCacheOrCalculate(ProceedingJoinPoint pjp, String key, Complex
current) {
  if (current == null) {
    try {
      System.out.println("Cache MISS for (" + key + ")");
      return (Complex) pjp.proceed();
    } catch (Throwable ex) {
      throw new IllegalStateException(ex);
    }
  } else {
    System.out.println("Cache HIT for (" + key + ")");
    return current;
  }
}
}
```

In this aspect, you cache the complex objects in a map with their real and imaginary values as keys. Then, the most suitable time to look up the cache is when a complex object is created by invoking the constructor. You use the AspectJ pointcut expression call to capture the join points of calling the Complex(int,int) constructor.

Next, you need an around advice to alter the return value. If a complex object of the same value is found in the cache, you return it to the caller directly. Otherwise, you proceed with the original constructor invocation to create a new complex object. Before you return it to the caller, you cache it in the map for subsequent usages.

The call pointcut is not supported by Spring AOP, so if you attempt to let Spring scan the pointcut annotation, you'll get the error "unsupported pointcut primitive call."

Because this type of pointcut is not supported by Spring AOP, you have to use the AspectJ framework to apply this aspect. The configuration of the AspectJ framework is done through a file named aop.xml in the META-INF directory in the classpath root:

```
<!DOCTYPE aspectj PUBLIC "-//AspectJ//DTD//EN"
        "http://www.eclipse.org/aspectj/dtd/aspectj.dtd">

<aspectj>
  <weaver options="-verbose">
    <include within="com.apress.spring6recipes.calculator.*"/>
  </weaver>

  <aspects>
    <aspect name="com.apress.spring6recipes.calculator.ComplexCachingAspect"/>
  </aspects>
</aspectj>
```

In this AspectJ configuration file, you have to specify the aspects and which classes you want your aspects to weave in. Here, you specify weaving ComplexCachingAspect into all the classes in the com. apress.spring6recipes.calculator package.

Finally, to make this load-time weaving, you need to run the application in one of two ways as described in the next sections.

Load-Time Weaving by the AspectJ Weaver

AspectJ provides a load-time weaving agent to enable load-time weaving. You need only to add a VM argument to the command that runs your application. Then your classes will get woven when they are loaded into the JVM:

```
java --add-opens java.base/java.lang=ALL-UNNAMED -javaagent:lib/aspectjweaver-1.9.19.jar -jar recipe_1_20_ii-6.0.0-all.jar
```

> ℹ The -add-opens is needed due to changes in the JDK and AspectJ not having found a solution, yet, to work around that.

If you run your application with the preceding argument, you will get the following output and cache status. The AspectJ agent advises all calls to the Complex(int,int) constructor:

```
Cache MISS for (1,2)
Cache MISS for (2,3)
Cache MISS for (3,5)
(1 + 2i) + (2 + 3i) = (3 + 5i)
Cache MISS for (5,8)
Cache HIT for (2,3)
Cache HIT for (3,5)
(5 + 8i) - (2 + 3i) = (3 + 5i)
```

Load-Time Weaving by the Spring Load-Time Weaver

Spring has several load-time weavers for different runtime environments. To turn on a suitable load-time weaver for your Spring application, you need to add @EnableLoadTimeWeaving to the configuration.

Spring will be able to detect the most suitable load-time weaver for your runtime environment. Some Java EE application servers have class loaders that support the Spring load-time weaver mechanism, so there's no need to specify a Java agent in their startup commands. However, for a simple Java application, you still require a weaving agent provided by Spring to enable load-time weaving. You have to specify the Spring agent in the VM argument of the startup command:

```
java --add-opens java.base/java.lang=ALL-UNNAMED -javaagent:lib/spring-instrument-6.0.3.jar -jar recipe_1_20_ii-6.0.0-all.jar
```

If you run your application, you will get the following output and cache status:

```
Cache MISS for (3,5)
(1 + 2i) + (2 + 3i) = (3 + 5i)
Cache HIT for (3,5)
(5 + 8i) - (2 + 3i) = (3 + 5i)
```

This is because the Spring agent advises only the Complex(int,int) constructor calls made by beans declared in the Spring IoC container. As the complex operands are created in the Main class, the Spring agent will not advise their constructor calls.

ℹ️ When using a standalone configuration, it might be a bit tricky to get load-time weaving with the instrumentation to work. This is due to component scanning picking up classes very early in the process, even before load-time weaving is enabled by Spring. To work around this, you can enable load-time weaving very early in the process by using an ApplicationInitializer and call this before refreshing the ApplicationContext:

```
package com.apress.spring6recipes.calculator;

import org.springframework.context.ApplicationContextInitializer;
import org.springframework.context.annotation.AnnotationConfigApplicationContext;
import org.springframework.context.weaving.AspectJWeavingEnabler;
import org.springframework.context.weaving.DefaultContextLoadTimeWeaver;

public class LoadTimeWeaverApplicationContextInitializer
        implements ApplicationContextInitializer<AnnotationConfigApplicationContext> {
  @Override
  public void initialize(AnnotationConfigApplicationContext applicationContext) {
    var beanClassLoader = applicationContext.getBeanFactory().getBeanClassLoader();
    var ltw = new DefaultContextLoadTimeWeaver(beanClassLoader);
    AspectJWeavingEnabler.enableAspectJWeaving(ltw, beanClassLoader);
  }
}
```

This will, before the context has been fully started, enable load-time weaving for the class loaders in play. See the provided Main class in the sources on how to use and enable this initializer.

1-21. Configuring Aspects in Spring

Problem

Aspects used in the AspectJ framework are instantiated by the AspectJ framework itself. Therefore, you have to retrieve the aspect instances from the AspectJ framework to configure them.

Solution

Each AspectJ aspect provides a factory class `Aspects` that has a static factory method called `aspectOf()`, which allows you to access the current aspect instance. In the Spring IoC container, you can declare a bean created by this factory method by calling `Aspects.aspectOf(ComplexCachingAspect.class)`.

How It Works

For instance, you can allow the cache map of `ComplexCachingAspect` to be preconfigured via a setter method:

```
package com.apress.spring6recipes.calculator;
import org.aspectj.lang.annotation.Aspect;

import java.util.Map;
import java.util.concurrent.ConcurrentHashMap;

@Aspect
public class ComplexCachingAspect {

  private final Map<String, Complex> cache = new ConcurrentHashMap<>();

  public void setCache(Map<String, Complex> cache) {
    this.cache.clear();
    this.cache.putAll(cache);
  }
}
```

To configure the aspect, create a @Bean-annotated method that calls the aforementioned factory method `Aspects.aspectOf`. This will give you the instance of the aspect. This instance can in turn be configured:

```
package com.apress.spring6recipes.calculator;

import org.aspectj.lang.Aspects;
import org.springframework.context.annotation.Bean;
import org.springframework.context.annotation.ComponentScan;
import org.springframework.context.annotation.Configuration;

import java.util.concurrent.ConcurrentHashMap;

@Configuration
@ComponentScan
public class CalculatorConfiguration {

  @Bean
  public ComplexCachingAspect complexCachingAspect() {

    var cache = new ConcurrentHashMap<String, Complex>();
    cache.put("2,3", new Complex(2, 3));
    cache.put("3,5", new Complex(3, 5));
```

```
  var complexCachingAspect = Aspects.aspectOf(ComplexCachingAspect.class);
  complexCachingAspect.setCache(cache);
  return complexCachingAspect;
 }
}
```

To run the application, you use AspectJ's weaver:

```
java -javaagent:lib/aspectjweaver-1.9.19.jar -jar recipe_1_21-6.0.0-all.jar
```

1-22. Inject POJOs into Domain Objects with AOP

Problem

Beans declared in the Spring IoC container can wire themselves to one another through Spring's dependency injection capability. However, objects created outside the Spring IoC container cannot wire themselves to Spring beans via configuration. You have to perform the wiring manually with programming code.

Solution

Objects created outside the Spring IoC container are usually domain objects. They are often created using the new operator or from the results of database queries. To inject a Spring bean into domain objects created outside Spring, you need the help of AOP. Actually, the injection of Spring beans is also a kind of crosscutting concern. As the domain objects are not created by Spring, you cannot use Spring AOP for injection. Spring supplies an AspectJ aspect specialized for this purpose. You can enable this aspect in the AspectJ framework.

How It Works

Suppose you have a global formatter to format complex numbers. This formatter accepts a pattern for formatting and uses the standard @Component annotation to instantiate a POJO:

```
package com.apress.spring6recipes.calculator;

import org.springframework.stereotype.Component;

@Component
public class ComplexFormatter {

  private String pattern = "(a + bi)";

  public void setPattern(String pattern) {
    this.pattern = pattern;
  }

  public String format(Complex complex) {
    return pattern
```

```
            .replaceAll("a", Integer.toString(complex.real()))
            .replaceAll("b", Integer.toString(complex.imaginary())));
  }
}
```

In the Complex class, you want to use this formatter in the toString() method to convert a complex number into a string. It exposes a setter method for ComplexFormatter.

However, because Complex objects are not instantiated by the Spring IoC container, they cannot be configured for dependency injection in the regular manner. Spring includes AnnotationBeanConfigurerAspect in its aspect library to configure the dependencies of any objects, even if they were not created by the Spring IoC container.

First of all, you have to annotate your object type with the @Configurable annotation to declare that this type of object is configurable:

```
package com.apress.spring6recipes.calculator;

import org.springframework.beans.factory.annotation.Autowired;
import org.springframework.beans.factory.annotation.Configurable;
import org.springframework.context.annotation.Scope;
import org.springframework.stereotype.Component;

@Configurable
@Component
@Scope("prototype")
public class Complex {

  private final int real;
  private final int imaginary;
  private ComplexFormatter formatter;

  public Complex(int real, int imaginary) {
    this.real = real;
    this.imaginary = imaginary;
  }

  public int imaginary() {
    return imaginary;
  }

  public int real() {
    return real;
  }

  @Autowired
  public void setFormatter(ComplexFormatter formatter) {
    this.formatter = formatter;
  }
}
```

```
@Override
public String toString() {
  return formatter.format(this);
}
}
```

In addition to the @Configurable annotation, you decorate the POJO with the standard @Component, @Scope, and @Autowired annotations so the bean gets its standard Spring behaviors. However, the @Configurable annotation is the most important configuration piece, and for it Spring defines a convenient annotation @EnableSpringConfigured for you to enable the mentioned aspect. You need to add this annotation next to the @EnableLoadTimeWeaving annotation, as the @Configurable will work only with either load-time or compile-time weaving:

```
package com.apress.spring6recipes.calculator;

import org.springframework.context.annotation.Bean;
import org.springframework.context.annotation.ComponentScan;
import org.springframework.context.annotation.Configuration;
import org.springframework.context.annotation.EnableLoadTimeWeaving;
import org.springframework.context.annotation.aspectj.EnableSpringConfigured;
import org.springframework.context.weaving.AspectJWeavingEnabler;

@Configuration
@EnableSpringConfigured
@EnableLoadTimeWeaving
@ComponentScan
public class CalculatorConfiguration {

  @Bean
  public static AspectJWeavingEnabler aspectJWeavingEnabler() {
    return new AspectJWeavingEnabler();
  }

}
```

When a class with the @Configurable annotation is instantiated, the aspect will look for a prototype-scoped bean definition whose type is the same as this class. Then, it will configure the new instances according to this bean definition. If there are properties declared in the bean definition, the new instances will also have the same properties set by the aspect.

Finally, to run the application, you weave the aspect into your classes at load time with the AspectJ agent:

```
java -javaagent:lib/aspectjweaver-1.9.19.jar -jar recipe_1_21-6.0.0-all.jar
```

1-23. Concurrency with Spring and TaskExecutors

Problem

You want to build a threaded, concurrent program with Spring but don't know what approach to use, since there's no standard approach.

Solution

Use Spring's TaskExecutor abstraction. This abstraction provides numerous implementations for many environments, including basic Java SE Executor implementations, the CommonJ WorkManager implementations, and custom implementations.

In Spring all the implementations are unified and can be cast to Java SE's Executor interface too.

How It Works

Threading is a difficult issue, which can be particularly tedious to implement using standard threading in the Java SE environment. Concurrency is another important aspect of server-side components but has little to no standardization in the enterprise Java space. In fact some parts of the Java Enterprise Edition specifications forbid the explicit creation and manipulation of threads.

In the Java SE landscape, many options have been introduced over the years to deal with threading and concurrency. First, there was the standard java.lang.Thread support present since day one and Java Development Kit (JDK) 1.0. Java 1.3 saw the introduction of java.util.TimerTask to support doing some sort of work periodically. Java 5 debuted the java.util.concurrent package, as well as a reworked hierarchy for building thread pools, oriented around the java.util.concurrent.Executor. Java 19 introduced, in preview, the notion of virtual threads and structured concurrent programming.

The application programming interface (API) for Executor is simple:

```
package java.util.concurrent;

public interface Executor {
    void execute(Runnable command);
}
```

ExecutorService, a subinterface, provides more functionality for managing threads and provides support to raise events to threads, such as shutdown(). There are several implementations that have shipped with the JDK since Java SE 5.0. Many of them are available via static factory methods in the java.util.concurrent package. What follows are several examples using Java SE classes.

The ExecutorService class provides a submit() method, which returns a Future<T> object. An instance of Future<T> can be used to track the progress of a thread that's usually executing asynchronously. You can call Future.isDone() or Future.isCancelled() to determine whether the job is finished or cancelled, respectively. When you use the ExecutorService and submit() inside a Runnable instance whose run method has no return type, calling get() on the returned Future returns null or the value specified on submission:

```
Runnable task = new Runnable(){
  public void run(){
    try{
        Thread.sleep( 1000 * 60 ) ;
        System.out.println("Done sleeping for a minute, returning! " );
    } catch (Exception ex) { /* ... */ }
  }
};

var executorService  = Executors.newCachedThreadPool() ;

if(executorService.submit(task, Boolean.TRUE).get().equals( Boolean.TRUE ))
    System.out.println( "Job has finished!");
```

With this background information, we can explore some of the characteristics of the various implementations. For example, the following is a class designed to mark the passage of time using Runnable:

```
package com.apress.spring6recipes.executors;

import com.apress.spring6recipes.utils.Utils;

import java.time.LocalDate;
import java.util.concurrent.TimeUnit;

public class DemonstrationRunnable implements Runnable {

  @Override
  public void run() {
    Utils.sleep(1, TimeUnit.SECONDS);

    System.out.printf("Hello at %s from %s%n",
            LocalDate.now(), Thread.currentThread().getName());
  }
}
```

You'll use the same instance when you explore Java SE Executors and Spring's TaskExecutor support:

```
package com.apress.spring6recipes.executors;

import java.time.LocalDateTime;
import java.time.format.DateTimeFormatter;
import java.util.concurrent.Executors;
import java.util.concurrent.TimeUnit;

public class ExecutorsDemo {

  public static void main(String[] args) throws Throwable {
    var task = new DemonstrationRunnable();
    // will create a pool of threads and attempt to
    // reuse previously created ones if possible
    try (var cachedThreadPoolExecutorService = Executors.newCachedThreadPool()) {
      if (cachedThreadPoolExecutorService.submit(task).get() == null)
        printStatus(cachedThreadPoolExecutorService);
    }

    // limits how many new threads are created, queueing the rest
    try (var fixedThreadPool = Executors.newFixedThreadPool(100)) {
      if (fixedThreadPool.submit(task).get() == null)
        printStatus(fixedThreadPool);
    }

    // doesn't use more than one thread at a time
    try (var singleThreadExecutorService = Executors.newSingleThreadExecutor()) {
      if (singleThreadExecutorService.submit(task).get() == null)
        printStatus(singleThreadExecutorService);
    }
```

```
  // support sending a job with a known result
  try (var es = Executors.newCachedThreadPool()) {
    if (es.submit(task, Boolean.TRUE).get().equals(Boolean.TRUE))
      System.out.println("Job has finished!");
  }

  // Create a Virtual Thread per Launched task
  try (var vt = Executors.newVirtualThreadPerTaskExecutor()) {
    if (vt.submit(task).get() == null) {
      printStatus(vt);
    }
  }

  // mimic TimerTask
  try (var scheduledThreadExecutorService = Executors.newScheduledThreadPool(10)) {
    if (scheduledThreadExecutorService.schedule(task, 30, TimeUnit.SECONDS).get() == null)
      printStatus(scheduledThreadExecutorService);

    // this doesn't stop until it encounters
    // an exception or its cancel()ed
    scheduledThreadExecutorService.scheduleAtFixedRate(task, 0, 5, TimeUnit.SECONDS);
  }

}

static void printStatus(Object executor) {
  var type = executor.getClass().getSimpleName();
  var datetime = LocalDateTime.now();
  System.out.printf("The %s has succeeded at %s%n", type, datetime.
  format(DateTimeFormatter.ISO_DATE_TIME));
}

}
```

If you use the submit() method version of the ExecutorService that accepts Callable<T>, then submit() returns whatever was returned from the main call() method in Callable. The interface for Callable is the following:

```
package java.util.concurrent;

@FunctionalInterface
public interface Callable<V> {
    V call() throws Exception;
}
```

In the Jakarta EE landscape, different approaches for solving these sorts of problems have been created, since Java EE by design restricts the handling of threads.

Quartz (a job scheduling framework) was among the first solutions to fill this thread feature gap with a solution that provided scheduling and concurrency. JEE Connector Architecture (JCA) 1.5 is another specification that provides a primitive type of gateway for integration functionality and supports ad hoc concurrency. JCA components are notified about incoming messages and respond concurrently. JCA 1.5 provides a primitive, limited enterprise service bus (ESB)—similar to integration features, without nearly as much of the finesse of something like SpringSource's Spring Integration framework.

The requirement for concurrency wasn't lost on application server vendors, though. Many other initiatives came to the forefront. For example, in 2003, IBM and BEA jointly created the Timer and Work Manager API, which eventually became JSR-237 and was then merged with JSR-236 to focus on how to implement concurrency in a managed environment. The Service Data Object (SDO) Specification, JSR-235, also had a similar solution. In addition, open source implementations of the CommonJ API have sprung up in recent years to achieve the same solution.

The issue is that there's no portable, standard, simple way of controlling threads and providing concurrency for components in a managed environment, similar to the case of Java SE solutions.

Spring provides a unified solution via the `org.springframework.core.task.TaskExecutor` interface. The `TaskExecutor` abstraction extends `java.util.concurrent.Executor`.

In fact, the `TaskExecutor` interface is used quite a bit internally in the Spring Framework. For example, for Spring Quartz integration (which supports threading) and the message-driven POJO (MDP) container support, there's wide use of TaskExecutor:

```
package org.springframework.core.task;

import java.util.concurrent.Executor;

@FunctionalInterface
public interface TaskExecutor extends Executor {
  void execute(Runnable task);
}
```

In some places, the various solutions mirror the functionality provided by the core JDK options. In others, they're quite unique and provide integrations with other frameworks such as with CommonJ WorkManager. These integrations usually take the form of a class that can exist in the target framework but that you can manipulate just like any other TaskExecutor abstraction.

Although there's support for adapting an existing Java SE Executor or ExecutorService as a `TaskExecutor`, this isn't so important in Spring because the base class for `TaskExecutor` is an `Executor`, anyway. In this way, the `TaskExecutor` in Spring bridges the gap between various solutions on Java EE and Java SE.

Next, let's see a simple example of the `TaskExecutor`, using the same `Runnable` defined previously. The client for the code is a simple Spring POJO, into which you've injected various instances of `TaskExecutor` with the sole aim of submitting `Runnable`:

```
package com.apress.spring6recipes.executors;

import jakarta.annotation.PostConstruct;
import org.springframework.beans.factory.annotation.Autowired;
import org.springframework.context.annotation.AnnotationConfigApplicationContext;
import org.springframework.core.task.SimpleAsyncTaskExecutor;
import org.springframework.core.task.SyncTaskExecutor;
import org.springframework.core.task.support.TaskExecutorAdapter;
import org.springframework.scheduling.concurrent.ConcurrentTaskExecutor;
import org.springframework.scheduling.concurrent.ThreadPoolTaskExecutor;
import org.springframework.stereotype.Component;

@Component
public class SpringExecutorsDemo {
```

```
@Autowired
private SimpleAsyncTaskExecutor asyncTaskExecutor;

@Autowired
private SyncTaskExecutor syncTaskExecutor;

@Autowired
private TaskExecutorAdapter taskExecutorAdapter;

@Autowired
private ThreadPoolTaskExecutor threadPoolTaskExecutor;

@Autowired
private DemonstrationRunnable task;

@Autowired
private ConcurrentTaskExecutor virtualThreadsTaskExecutor;

@PostConstruct
public void submitJobs() {
  syncTaskExecutor.execute(task);
  taskExecutorAdapter.submit(task);
  asyncTaskExecutor.submit(task);

  for (int i = 0 ; i < 500; i++) {
    virtualThreadsTaskExecutor.submit(task);
  }

  for (int i = 0; i < 500; i++) {
    threadPoolTaskExecutor.submit(task);
  }
}

public static void main(String[] args) {
  var cfg = ExecutorsConfiguration.class;
  try (var ctx = new AnnotationConfigApplicationContext(cfg)) {}
}
}
```

The application context demonstrates the creation of these various TaskExecutor implementations. Most are so simple that you could create them manually. Only in one case do you delegate to a factory bean to automatically trigger the execution:

```
package com.apress.spring6recipes.executors;

import org.springframework.context.annotation.Bean;
import org.springframework.context.annotation.ComponentScan;
import org.springframework.context.annotation.Configuration;
import org.springframework.core.task.SimpleAsyncTaskExecutor;
import org.springframework.core.task.SyncTaskExecutor;
import org.springframework.core.task.support.TaskExecutorAdapter;
```

```
import org.springframework.scheduling.concurrent.ConcurrentTaskExecutor;
import org.springframework.scheduling.concurrent.ScheduledExecutorFactoryBean;
import org.springframework.scheduling.concurrent.ScheduledExecutorTask;
import org.springframework.scheduling.concurrent.ThreadPoolTaskExecutor;

import java.util.concurrent.Executors;

@Configuration
@ComponentScan
public class ExecutorsConfiguration {

  @Bean
  public TaskExecutorAdapter taskExecutorAdapter() {
    return new TaskExecutorAdapter(Executors.newCachedThreadPool());
  }

  @Bean
  public SimpleAsyncTaskExecutor simpleAsyncTaskExecutor() {
    return new SimpleAsyncTaskExecutor();
  }

  @Bean
  public SyncTaskExecutor syncTaskExecutor() {
    return new SyncTaskExecutor();
  }

  @Bean
  public ScheduledExecutorFactoryBean scheduledExecutorFactoryBean(ScheduledExecutorTask
  scheduledExecutorTask) {
    var scheduledExecutorFactoryBean = new ScheduledExecutorFactoryBean();
    scheduledExecutorFactoryBean.setScheduledExecutorTasks(scheduledExecutorTask);
    return scheduledExecutorFactoryBean;
  }

  @Bean
  public ScheduledExecutorTask scheduledExecutorTask(Runnable runnable) {
    var scheduledExecutorTask = new ScheduledExecutorTask();
    scheduledExecutorTask.setPeriod(50);
    scheduledExecutorTask.setRunnable(runnable);
    return scheduledExecutorTask;
  }

  @Bean
  public ThreadPoolTaskExecutor threadPoolTaskExecutor() {
    var taskExecutor = new ThreadPoolTaskExecutor();
    taskExecutor.setCorePoolSize(50);
    taskExecutor.setMaxPoolSize(100);
    taskExecutor.setAllowCoreThreadTimeOut(true);
    taskExecutor.setWaitForTasksToCompleteOnShutdown(true);
    return taskExecutor;
  }
```

```
@Bean
public ConcurrentTaskExecutor virtualThreadsTaskExecutor() {
  var virtualThreadsExecutor = Executors.newVirtualThreadPerTaskExecutor();
  return new ConcurrentTaskExecutor(virtualThreadsExecutor);
}
}
```

The preceding code shows different implementations of the TaskExecutor interface. The first bean, the TaskExecutorAdapter instance, is a simple wrapper around a java.util.concurrence.Executors instance so you can deal with it in terms of the Spring TaskExecutor interface. You use Spring here to configure an instance of an Executor and pass it in as the constructor argument.

SimpleAsyncTaskExecutor provides a new Thread for each submitted job. It does no thread pooling or reuse. Each job submitted runs asynchronously in a thread.

SyncTaskExecutor is the simplest of the implementations of TaskExecutor. Submission of a job is synchronous and tantamount to launching a Thread, running it, and then using join() to connect it immediately. It's effectively the same as manually invoking the run() method in the calling thread, skipping threading altogether.

ScheduledExecutorFactoryBean automatically triggers jobs defined as ScheduledExecutorTask beans. You can specify a list of ScheduledExecutorTask instances to trigger multiple jobs simultaneously. A ScheduledExecutorTask instance can accept a period to space out the execution of tasks.

The ThreadPoolTaskExecutor is a full-on thread pool implementation built on java.util.concurrent. ThreadPoolExecutor.

The final example shows how to utilize the new virtual threads in your application. You can wrap the Executor created with Executors.newVirtualThreadPerTaskExecutor() with a TaskExecutorAdapter, which will adapt it to the TaskExecutor interface. Another option is to wrap it with a ConcurrentTaskExecutor to achieve the same result.

The jakarta.enterprise.concurrent package was added, specifically the ManagedExecutorService. An instance of this ManagedExecutorService must be provided by JEE9-compliant servers. If you want to use this mechanism with Spring TaskExecutor support, you can configure a DefaultManagedTaskExecutor, which will try to detect the default ManagedExecutorService (as mentioned by the specification), or you can explicitly configure it.

The TaskExecutor support provides a powerful way to access scheduling services on an application server via a unified interface. If you're looking for more robust (albeit much more heavyweight) support that can be deployed on any app server (e.g., Tomcat and Jetty), you might consider Spring's Quartz support.

1-24. Communicate Application Events Between POJOs

Problem

In a typical communication between POJOs, the sender has to locate the receiver to call a method on it. In this case, the sender POJO must be aware of the receiver component. This kind of communication is direct and simple, but the sender and receiver POJOs are tightly coupled.

When using an IoC container, POJOs can communicate by interface rather than by implementation. This communication model helps reduce coupling. However, it is only efficient when a sender component has to communicate with one receiver. When a sender needs to communicate with multiple receivers, it has to call the receivers one by one.

Solution

Spring's application context supports event-based communication between its beans. In the event-based communication model, the sender POJO just publishes an event without knowing who the receiver is, since there can actually be more than one receiver. Also, the receiver doesn't necessarily know who is publishing the event. It can listen to multiple events from different senders at the same time. In this way, the sender and receiver components are loosely coupled.

Traditionally, to listen for events, a bean has to implement the ApplicationListener interface and specify the type of events it wants to be notified about by specifying the type parameter, that is, Ap plicationListener<CheckoutEvent>. Listeners of this kind can only listen to events that extend from ApplicationEvent as that is the type signature of the ApplicationListener interface.

To publish an event, a bean needs access to the ApplicationEventPublisher and for sending an event needs to call the publishEvent method. To get access to the ApplicationEventPublisher, a class can either implement ApplicationEventPublisherAware or use @Autowired on a field of type ApplicationEventPublisher.

How It Works

Define Events Using ApplicationEvent

The first step of enabling event-based communication is to define the event. Suppose you would like a cashier bean to publish a CheckoutEvent after the shopping cart is checked out. This event includes a checkout time property:

```java
package com.apress.spring6recipes.shop;

import org.springframework.context.ApplicationEvent;

import java.time.LocalDateTime;

@SuppressWarnings("serial")
public class CheckoutEvent extends ApplicationEvent {

  private final ShoppingCart cart;
  private final LocalDateTime time;

  public CheckoutEvent(ShoppingCart cart, LocalDateTime time) {
    super(cart);
    this.cart = cart;
    this.time = time;
  }

  public ShoppingCart getCart() {
    return cart;
  }

  public LocalDateTime getTime() {
    return this.time;
  }
}
```

Publish Events

To publish an event, you just create an event instance and make a call to the publishEvent()
method of an application event publisher, which becomes accessible by implementing the
ApplicationEventPublisherAware interface:

```
package com.apress.spring6recipes.shop;

import org.springframework.context.ApplicationEventPublisher;
import org.springframework.context.ApplicationEventPublisherAware;

import java.time.LocalDateTime;

public class Cashier implements ApplicationEventPublisherAware {

  private ApplicationEventPublisher applicationEventPublisher;

  @Override
  public void setApplicationEventPublisher(ApplicationEventPublisher aep) {
    this.applicationEventPublisher = aep;
  }

  public void checkout(ShoppingCart cart) {
    var event = new CheckoutEvent(cart, LocalDateTime.now());
    applicationEventPublisher.publishEvent(event);
  }
}
```

Or you could simply autowire it on a field property or constructor argument:

```
package com.apress.spring6recipes.shop;

import org.springframework.context.ApplicationEventPublisher;
import org.springframework.stereotype.Component;

@Component
public class Cashier {

  private final ApplicationEventPublisher applicationEventPublisher;

  public Cashier(ApplicationEventPublisher applicationEventPublisher) {
    this.applicationEventPublisher = applicationEventPublisher;
  }
}
```

Listen to Events

Any bean defined in the application context that implements the ApplicationListener interface is notified
of all events that match the type parameter (this way you could listen for a certain group of events like
ApplicationContextEvent):

```
package com.apress.spring6recipes.shop;

import org.springframework.context.ApplicationListener;
import org.springframework.stereotype.Component;

@Component
public class CheckoutListener implements ApplicationListener<CheckoutEvent> {

  @Override
  public void onApplicationEvent(CheckoutEvent event) {
    // Do anything you like with the checkout time
    System.out.printf("Checkout event [%s]%n", event.getTime());
  }
}
```

You can also create event listeners using the @EventListener annotation instead of implementing the ApplicationListener interface:

```
package com.apress.spring6recipes.shop;

import org.springframework.context.event.EventListener;
import org.springframework.stereotype.Component;

@Component
public class CheckoutListener {

  @EventListener
  public void onApplicationEvent(CheckoutEvent event) {
    // Do anything you like with the checkout time
    System.out.printf("Checkout event [%s]%n", event.getTime());
  }
}
```

Next, you have to register the listener in the application context to listen for all events. The registration is as simple as declaring a bean instance of this listener or letting component scanning detect it. The application context recognizes the beans that implement the ApplicationListener interface and the beans that have methods annotated with @EventListener and notifies them of each event they are interested in.

Using @EventListener has another nice feature, and that is that the events don't have to extend ApplicationEvent anymore. This way your events don't rely on Spring Framework classes but are plain POJOs again:

```
package com.apress.spring6recipes.shop;

import java.time.LocalDateTime;

public class CheckoutEvent {

  private final ShoppingCart cart;
  private final LocalDateTime time;
```

```java
public CheckoutEvent(ShoppingCart cart, LocalDateTime time) {
  this.cart = cart;
  this.time = time;
}

public ShoppingCart getCart() {
  return this.cart;
}

public LocalDateTime getTime() {
  return time;
}
}
```

> **ⓘ** Finally, remember the application context itself also publishes container events such as
> `ContextClosedEvent`, `ContextRefreshedEvent`, and `RequestHandledEvent`. If any beans want to be
> notified of these events, they can implement the `ApplicationListener` interface.

1-25. Create and Register Beans in a Functional Way

Problem

Since Java 8 it is possible to do some functional programming in Java. Newer versions of Java have improved
on it, and it has become a common practice to use things like lambdas and method references in our day-
to-day Java programming. Now you would also like to use this with Spring to create your configuration files
instead of annotations.

Solution

The Spring `GenericApplicationContext`, which serves as a base class for many of the `ApplicationContext`
implementations, provides the `registerBean` method in several variations. The most interesting, and useful,
ones are the ones that take either a `Supplier` or a `BeanDefinitionCustomizer` argument. Those can be used
to register beans into the context and have them participate in the container and bean life cycles or be used
as dependencies for other beans.

How It Works

Let's take the code from Recipes 1-1 and Recipe 1-3 and rewrite that in a more functional style.

Create a Simple Bean in a Functional Way

To register a bean, you need to create an instance of an `ApplicationContext`. Here we can use the same
`AnnotationConfigApplicationContext` as we did before, but without any configuration. Next, we call the
`registerBean` method to register a bean of a certain type (first argument) and then provide the `Supplier`
that will eventually create the bean.

When you are finished with registering the beans, you need to call refresh on the context, and it will create all the bean instances it needs:

```
package com.apress.spring6recipes.sequence;

import org.springframework.context.annotation.AnnotationConfigApplicationContext;

public class Main {

  public static void main(String[] args) {

    try (var ctx = new AnnotationConfigApplicationContext()) {
      ctx.registerBean(Sequence.class, () -> new Sequence("30", "A", 10000));
      ctx.refresh();
      var generator = ctx.getBean(Sequence.class);
      System.out.println(generator.nextValue());
      System.out.println(generator.nextValue());
    }
  }
}
```

Create Multiple Beans with Dependencies in a Functional Way

Before we only registered a single bean without any references to other beans. To get references to other beans, you can access the ApplicationContext and call getBean or better getBeanProvider (see also Recipe 1-3) to get the optional bean or list of beans depending on your needs.

We still need to create the ApplicationContext type we want to use and call the registerBean methods for both beans. The registration for the Sequence is now a bit more complex as we need to obtain the reference to the bean we need. For this we use the getBeanProvider method, which returns an ObjectProvider (see Recipe 1-3) that we can use to get the reference (or references) we need:

```
package com.apress.spring6recipes.sequence;

import org.springframework.context.annotation.AnnotationConfigApplicationContext;

public class Main {

  public static void main(String[] args) {

    try (var ctx = new AnnotationConfigApplicationContext()) {
      ctx.registerBean(PrefixGenerator.class, () ->
            new DatePrefixGenerator("yyyyMMdd"));
      ctx.registerBean(Sequence.class, () -> {
        var seq = new Sequence("A", 100000);
        ctx.getBeanProvider(PrefixGenerator.class)
              .ifUnique(seq::setPrefixGenerator);
        return seq;
      });
      ctx.refresh();
```

```
    var generator = ctx.getBean(Sequence.class);
    System.out.println(generator.getSequence());
    System.out.println(generator.getSequence());
  }
 }
}
```

Modify the BeanDefinition for a Functionally Registered Bean

Up until now we plainly registered beans. But what about defining a bean as primary or changing the scope, order, etc.? For this we can pass in a BeanDefinitionCustomizer (or multiple as it is a varargs) to modify the, eventually, created BeanDefinition. The BeanDefinition is the recipe that is used to create the bean and holds things like the scope of the bean, if it is the primary bean, etc. See Table 1-3 for a list of properties that can be set.

Table 1-3. Properties of BeanDefinition

Property	Description
autowireCandidate	If this bean should be used in autowiring scenarios or not. The default is true.
dependsOn	Names of the beans this one depends on, same as @DependsOn.
description	Additional description for the bean.
destroyMethodName	Method name to be used as a destruction callback when the ApplicationContext is closed and stopped. Similar to @PreDestroy on a method.
initMethodName	Method name to be used as an initialization callback when the ApplicationContext is started. Similar to @PostConstruct on a method.
lazyInit	Should the bean be lazily created, that is, on first use. The default is false.
primary	Is this bean the primary bean to use when multiples are found. The default is true.
scope	The name of the scope of the bean, same as @Scope.

Let's add a BeanDefinitionCustomizer that makes the Sequence bean both lazy and have a prototype scope. Create a class SequenceBeanDefinitionCustomizer, which modifies the BeanDefinition to set lazyInit to true and the scope to prototype:

```
package com.apress.spring6recipes.sequence;

import org.springframework.beans.factory.config.BeanDefinition;
import org.springframework.beans.factory.config.BeanDefinitionCustomizer;
import org.springframework.context.annotation.AnnotationConfigApplicationContext;

public class Main {

  public static void main(String[] args) {

    try (var ctx = new AnnotationConfigApplicationContext()) {
      ctx.registerBean(PrefixGenerator.class, () ->
            new DatePrefixGenerator("yyyyMMdd"));
```

95

```
ctx.registerBean(Sequence.class, () -> {
    var seq = new Sequence("A", 100000);
    ctx.getBeanProvider(PrefixGenerator.class)
            .ifUnique(seq::setPrefixGenerator);
    return seq;
}, new SequenceBeanDefinitionCustomizer());
ctx.refresh();

var generator = ctx.getBean(Sequence.class);
System.out.println(generator.getSequence());
System.out.println(generator.getSequence());
    }
  }
}

class SequenceBeanDefinitionCustomizer implements BeanDefinitionCustomizer {

    @Override
    public void customize(BeanDefinition bd) {
        bd.setScope(BeanDefinition.SCOPE_PROTOTYPE);
        bd.setLazyInit(true);
    }
}
```

💡 For clarity the code for the customizer has been written as a class. However, it could have been another lambda as well.

1-26. Summary

In this chapter, you learned about Spring's core tasks. You learned how Spring supports the @Configuration and @Bean annotations to instantiate POJOs via a Java Config class. You also learned how to use the @Component annotation to administer POJOs with Spring. In addition, you learned about the @Repository, @Service, and @Controller annotations, which provide more specific behavior than the @Component annotation.

You also learned how to reference POJOs from other POJOs, as well as how to use the @Autowired annotation, which can automatically associate POJOs by either type or name. In addition, you also explored how the standard @Resource and @Inject annotations work to reference POJOs via autowiring, instead of using the Spring-specific @Autowired annotation.

You then learned how to set a Spring POJO's scope with the @Scope annotation. You also learned how Spring can read external resources and use this data in the context of POJO configuration and creation using the @PropertySource and @Value annotations. In addition, you learned how Spring supports different languages in POJOs through the use of i18n resource bundles.

Next, you learned how to customize the initialization and destruction of POJOs with the initmethod and destroyMethod attributes of a @Bean annotation, as well as the @PostConstruct and @PreDestroy annotations. In addition, you learned how to do lazy initialization with the @Lazy annotation and define initialization dependencies with the @DependsOn annotation.

You then learned about Spring post-processors to validate and modify POJO values. Next, you explored how to work with Spring environments and profiles to load different sets of POJOs, including how to use the @Profile annotation.

Next, you explored aspect-oriented programming in the context of Spring and learned how to create aspects, pointcuts, and advices. This included the use of the @Aspect annotation, as well as the @Before, @After, @AfterReturning, @AfterThrowing, and @Around annotations.

Next, you learned how to access AOP join point information and apply it to different program execution points. And then you learned how to specify aspect precedence with the @Order annotation, followed by how to reuse aspect pointcut definition.

In this chapter, you also learned how to write AspectJ pointcut expressions, as well as how to apply the concept of AOP "introductions" so a POJO can inherit behaviors from multiple implementation classes at the same time. You also learned how to introduce states to POJOs with AOP, as well as how to apply the technique of load-time weaving.

You also learned how to configure AspectJ aspects in Spring, how to inject POJOs into domain objects, as well as how to deal with concurrency with Spring and TaskExecutors and, last but not least, how to create, publish, and listen to events in Spring.

Finally, we had a look at the functional bean registration API available on the GenericApplicationContext and its subclasses.

CHAPTER 2

■ ■ ■

Spring MVC

MVC is an important module of the Spring Framework. It builds on the powerful Spring IoC container and makes extensive use of the container features to simplify its configuration.

Model-view-controller (MVC) is a common design pattern in UI design. It decouples business logic from UIs by separating the roles of model, view, and controller in an application. *Models* are responsible for encapsulating application data for views to present. *Views* should only present this data, without including any business logic. *Controllers* are responsible for receiving requests from users and invoking back-end services for business processing. After processing, back-end services may return some data for views to present. Controllers collect this data and prepare models for views to present. The core idea of the MVC pattern is to separate business logic from UIs to allow them to change independently without affecting each other.

In a Spring MVC application, models usually consist of objects that are processed by the service layer and persisted by the persistence layer. Views are usually templates written as Java Server Pages, Thymeleaf or FreeMarker (to name a few). However, it's also possible to define views as PDF files, Excel files, or RESTful web services.

Upon finishing this chapter, you will be able to develop Java web applications using Spring MVC. You will also understand Spring MVC's common controller and view types, including what has become the de facto use of annotations for creating controllers. Moreover, you will understand the basic principles of Spring MVC, which will serve as the foundations for more advanced topics covered in the upcoming chapters. For a full in-depth explanation of Spring MVC and its reactive counterpart, Spring WebFlux, we recommend *Pro Spring MVC with WebFlux* (Apress, 2021).

💡 To run the code from these recipes, you can run `gradle build`, and it will build a WAR file for deployment on a Jakarta EE server. However, running `gradle docker` will create a Docker container with an embedded Tomcat and a deployed application. Using `gradle dockerRun` will launch the container that afterward is accessible through `http://localhost:8080`. To be able to do this, it is required to have Docker installed.

2-1. Developing a Simple Web Application with Spring MVC

Problem

You want to develop a simple web application with Spring MVC to learn the basic concepts and configurations of this framework.

Solution

The central component of Spring MVC is a front controller. In the simplest Spring MVC application, this controller is the only servlet you need to configure in a Java web deployment descriptor (i.e., the ServletContainerInitializer). A Spring MVC controller—often referred to as a DispatcherServlet–acts as the front controller of the Spring MVC framework, and every web request must go through it so that it can manage the entire request handling process.

When a web request is sent to a Spring MVC application, a controller first receives the request. Then it organizes the different components configured in Spring's web application context or annotations present in the controller itself, all needed to handle the request. Figure 2-1 shows the primary flow of request handling in Spring MVC.

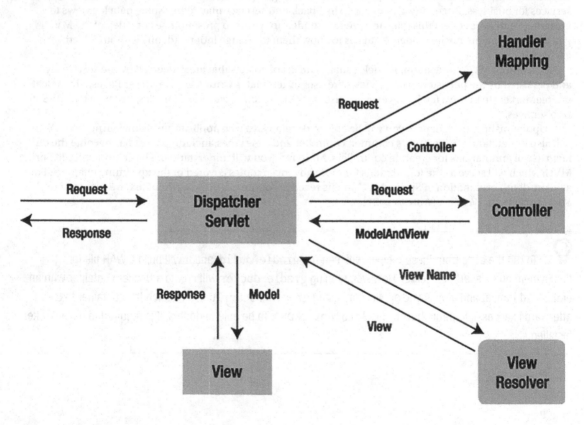

Figure 2-1. *Primary flow of request handling in Spring MVC*

To define a controller class in Spring, a class has to be marked with the @Controller or @RestController annotation.

When a @Controller-annotated class (i.e., a controller class) receives a request, it looks for an appropriate handler method to handle the request. This requires that a controller class map each request to a handler method by one or more handler mappings. In order to do so, a controller class's methods are decorated with the @RequestMapping annotation, making them handler methods.

The signature for these handler methods—as you can expect from any standard class—is open ended. You can specify an arbitrary name for a handler method and define a variety of method arguments. Equally, a handler method can return any of a series of values (e.g., string or void), depending on the application logic it fulfills. As the book progresses, you will encounter the various method arguments that can be used in handler methods using the @RequestMapping annotation. The following is a, partial, list of valid argument types, just to give you an idea:

- HttpServletRequest or HttpServletResponse

- Request parameters of arbitrary type, annotated with @RequestParam

- Request attributes of arbitrary type, annotated with @RequestAttribute

- Model attributes of arbitrary type, annotated with @ModelAttribute

- Cookie values included in an incoming request, annotated with @CookieValue

- Map or ModelMap, for the handler method to add attributes to the model

- Errors or BindingResult, for the handler method to access the binding and validation result for the command object

- SessionStatus, for the handler method to notify its completion of session processing

Once the controller class has picked an appropriate handler method, it invokes the handler method's logic with the request. Usually, a controller's logic invokes back-end services to handle the request. In addition, a handler method's logic is likely to add or remove information to or from the numerous input arguments (e.g., HttpServletRequest, Map, Errors, or SessionStatus) that will form part of the ongoing Spring MVC flow.

After a handler method has finished processing the request, it delegates control to a view, which is represented as the handler method's return value. To provide a flexible approach, a handler method's return value doesn't represent a view's implementation (e.g., user.jsp or report.pdf) but rather a logical view (e.g., user or report)—note the lack of file extension.

A handler method's return value can be either a String—representing a logical view name—or void, in which case a default logical view name is determined on the basis of a handler method's or controller's name.

In order to pass information from a controller to a view, it's irrelevant that a handler method returns a logical view name—String or a void—since the handler method input arguments will be available to a view. For example, if a handler method takes Map and SessionStatus objects as input parameters—modifying their contents inside the handler method's logic—these same objects will be accessible to the view returned by the handler method.

When the controller class receives a view, it resolves the logical view name into a specific view implementation (e.g., user.jsp, todos.html, or report.pdf) by means of a view resolver. A view resolver is a bean configured in the web application context that implements the ViewResolver interface. Its responsibility is to return a specific view implementation (HTML, JSP, PDF, or others) for a logical view name.

Once the controller class has resolved a view name into a view implementation, per the view implementation's design, it renders the objects (e.g., HttpServletRequest, Map, Errors, or SessionStatus) passed by the controller's handler method. The view's responsibility is to display the objects added in the handler method's logic to the user.

How It Works

Suppose you are going to develop a court reservation system for a sports center. The UI of this application is web-based so that users can make online reservations. You want to develop this application using Spring MVC. First of all, you create the following domain classes:

```
package com.apress.spring6recipes.court.domain;

import java.time.LocalDate;

public class Reservation {

  private String courtName;
  private LocalDate date;
  private int hour;
  private Player player;
  private SportType sportType;

  public Reservation() { }

  public Reservation(String courtName, LocalDate date, int hour, Player player,
                     SportType sportType) {
    this.courtName = courtName;
    this.date = date;
    this.hour = hour;
    this.player = player;
    this.sportType = sportType;
  }

  public String getCourtName() {
    return courtName;
  }

  public void setCourtName(String courtName) {
    this.courtName = courtName;
  }

  public LocalDate getDate() {
    return date;
  }

  public void setDate(LocalDate date) {
    this.date = date;
  }
```

```java
  public int getHour() {
    return hour;
  }

  public void setHour(int hour) {
    this.hour = hour;
  }

  public Player getPlayer() {
    return player;
  }

  public void setPlayer(Player player) {
    this.player = player;
  }

  public SportType getSportType() {
    return sportType;
  }

  public void setSportType(SportType sportType) {
    this.sportType = sportType;
  }
}

package com.apress.spring6recipes.court.domain;

public class Player {

  private String name;
  private String phone;

  public Player() {
  }

  public Player(String name) {
    this.name = name;
  }

  public String getName() {
    return name;
  }

  public void setName(String name) {
    this.name = name;
  }

  public String getPhone() {
    return phone;
  }
```

```
  public void setPhone(String phone) {
    this.phone = phone;
  }
}

package com.apress.spring6recipes.court.domain;

public class SportType {

  private int id;
  private String name;

  public SportType() {}

  public SportType(int id, String name) {
    this.id = id;
    this.name = name;
  }

  public int getId() {
    return id;
  }

  public void setId(int id) {
    this.id = id;
  }

  public String getName() {
    return name;
  }

  public void setName(String name) {
    this.name = name;
  }

}
```

Then you define the following service interface in the `service` subpackage to provide reservations to the presentation layer:

```
package com.apress.spring6recipes.court.service;

import com.apress.spring6recipes.court.domain.Reservation;
import java.util.List;

public interface ReservationService {

  List<Reservation> query(String courtName);
}
```

In a production application, you should implement this interface with some form of persistence. But for simplicity's sake, you can store the reservation records in memory and hard-code several reservations for testing purposes:

```
package com.apress.spring6recipes.court.service;

import com.apress.spring6recipes.court.domain.Reservation;
import java.util.List;

@Service
class InMemoryReservationService implements ReservationService {

  private final List<Reservation> reservations =
    Collections.synchronizedList(new ArrayList<>());

  public InMemoryReservationService() {

    var roger = new Player("Roger");
    var james = new Player("James");
    var date = LocalDate.of(2022, 10, 18);
    reservations.add(new Reservation("Tennis #1", date, 16, roger, TENNIS));
    reservations.add(new Reservation("Tennis #2", date, 20, james, TENNIS));
  }

  @Override
  public List<Reservation> query(String courtName) {
    return this.reservations.stream()
            .filter( (r) -> StringUtils.startsWithIgnoreCase(r.getCourtName(), courtName))
            .collect(Collectors.toList());
  }
}
```

Setting Up a Spring MVC Application

Next, you need to create a Spring MVC application layout. In general, a web application developed with Spring MVC is set up in the same way as a standard Java web application, except that you have to add a couple of configuration files and required libraries specific to Spring MVC.

The Jakarta EE specification defines the valid directory structure of a Java web application made up of a web archive or WAR file. For example, you have to provide a web deployment descriptor in the WEB-INF root or one or more classes implementing ServletContainerInitializer. The class files and JAR files for this web application should be put in the WEB-INF/classes and WEB-INF/lib directories, respectively.

For the court reservation system, create the following directory structure. Note that the highlighted files are Spring-specific configuration files.

ℹ️   To develop a web application with Spring MVC, you have to add all the normal Spring dependencies (see Chapter 1 for more information) as well as the Spring Web and Spring MVC dependencies to your CLASSPATH. If you are using Maven, add the following dependencies to your Maven project:

```
<dependency>
  <groupId>org.springframework</groupId>
  <artifactId>spring-webmvc</artifactId>
  <version>6.0.3</version>
</dependency>
```

Or add the following dependencies when using Gradle:

```
dependencies {
  implementation "org.springframework:spring-webmvc:6.0.3"
}
```

The files outside the WEB-INF directory are directly accessible to users via URLs, so the CSS files and image files must be put there. When using Spring MVC, the JSP files act as templates. They are read by the framework for generating dynamic content, so the JSP files should be put inside the WEB-INF directory to prevent direct access to them. However, some application servers don't allow the files inside WEB-INF to be read by a web application internally. In that case, you can only put them outside the WEB-INF directory.

Creating the Configuration Files

The web deployment descriptor (web.xml or ServletContainerInitializer) is the essential configuration file for a Java web application. In this file, you define the servlets for your application and how web requests are mapped to them. For a Spring MVC application, you only have to define a single DispatcherServlet instance that acts as the front controller for Spring MVC, although you are allowed to define more than one if required.

In large applications, it can be convenient to use multiple DispatcherServlet instances. This allows DispatcherServlet instances to be designated to specific URLs, making code management easier and letting individual team members work on an application's logic without getting in each other's way:

```
package com.apress.spring6recipes.court.web;

import com.apress.spring6recipes.court.config.CourtConfiguration;
import jakarta.servlet.ServletContainerInitializer;
import jakarta.servlet.ServletContext;
import jakarta.servlet.ServletException;

import org.springframework.web.context.support.AnnotationConfigWebApplicationContext;
import org.springframework.web.servlet.DispatcherServlet;

import java.util.Set;

public class CourtServletContainerInitializer implements ServletContainerInitializer {

  public static final String MSG = "Starting Court Web Application";
```

```
@Override
public void onStartup(Set<Class<?>> c, ServletContext ctx) throws ServletException {

    ctx.log(MSG);

    var applicationContext = new AnnotationConfigWebApplicationContext();
    applicationContext.register(CourtConfiguration.class);

    var dispatcherServlet = new DispatcherServlet(applicationContext);

    var courtRegistration = ctx.addServlet("court", dispatcherServlet);
    courtRegistration.addMapping("/");
    courtRegistration.setLoadOnStartup(1);
  }
}
```

In this CourtServletContainerInitializer, you define a servlet of type DispatcherServlet. This is the core servlet class in Spring MVC that receives web requests and dispatches them to appropriate handlers. You set this servlet's name to court and map all URLs using a / (slash), with the slash representing the root directory. Note that the URL pattern can be set to more granular patterns. In larger applications it can make more sense to delegate patterns among various servlets, but for simplicity all URLs in the application are delegated to the single court servlet.

To have the CourtServletContainerInitializer detected, you also have to add a file named jakarta. servlet.ServletContainerInitializer into the META-INF/services directory. The content of the file should be the full name of the CourtServletContainerInitializer. This file is loaded by the servlet container and used to bootstrap the application:

```
com.apress.spring6recipes.court.web.CourtServletContainerInitializer
```

Finally, add the CourtConfiguration class, which is a very simple @Configuration class:

```
package com.apress.spring6recipes.court.config;

import org.springframework.context.annotation.Bean;
import org.springframework.context.annotation.ComponentScan;
import org.springframework.context.annotation.Configuration;
import org.springframework.web.servlet.config.annotation.EnableWebMvc;
import org.springframework.web.servlet.view.InternalResourceViewResolver;

@Configuration
@ComponentScan("com.apress.spring6recipes.court")
@EnableWebMvc
public class CourtConfiguration {
}
```

It defines a @ComponentScan annotation, which will scan the com.apress.spring6recipes. court package (and subpackages) and register all the detected beans (in this case the InMemoryReservationService and the yet-to-be-created @Controller-annotated classes). It also specifies the @EnableWebMvc annotation indicating we want to configure Spring MVC. The @EnableWebMvc does some additional setup for the Spring MVC application (although the DispatcherServlet itself has some defaults as well) and allows modification of its configuration through the use of WebMvcConfigurer instances (see the next recipes for information on that).

Creating Spring MVC Controllers

An annotation-based controller class can be an arbitrary class that doesn't implement a particular interface or extend a particular base class. You can annotate it with the @Controller annotation. There can be one or more handler methods defined in a controller to handle single or multiple actions. The signature of the handler methods is flexible enough to accept a range of arguments.

The @RequestMapping annotation can be applied to the class level or the method level. The first mapping strategy is to map a particular URL pattern to a controller class and then a particular HTTP method to each handler method:

```
package com.apress.spring6recipes.court.web;

import org.springframework.stereotype.Controller;
import org.springframework.ui.Model;
import org.springframework.web.bind.annotation.RequestMapping;
import org.springframework.web.bind.annotation.RequestMethod;

import java.time.LocalDate;

@Controller
@RequestMapping("/welcome")
public class WelcomeController {

  @RequestMapping(method = RequestMethod.GET)
  public String welcome(Model model) {
    model.addAttribute("today", LocalDate.now());
    return "/WEB-INF/jsp/welcome.jsp";
  }
}
```

This controller creates a java.time.LocalDate object to retrieve the current date and then adds it to the input Model object as an attribute so the target view can display it.

Since you've already activated annotation scanning on the com.apress.spring6recipes.court package, the annotations for the controller class are detected upon deployment.

The @Controller annotation defines the class as a Spring MVC controller. The @RequestMapping annotation is more interesting since it contains properties and can be declared at the class or handler method level. The first value used in this class—("/welcome")—is used to specify the URL on which the controller is actionable, meaning any request received on the /welcome URL is attended by the WelcomeController class.

Once a request is attended by the controller class, it delegates the call to the default HTTP GET handler method declared in the controller. The reason for this behavior is that every initial request made on a URL is of the HTTP GET kind. So when the controller attends a request on the /welcome URL, it subsequently delegates to the default HTTP GET handler method for processing.

The annotation @RequestMapping(method = RequestMethod.GET) is used to decorate the welcome method as the controller's default HTTP GET handler method. It's worth mentioning that if no default HTTP GET handler method is declared, a ServletException is thrown, hence the importance of a Spring MVC controller having at a minimum a URL route and default HTTP GET handler method.

Another variation to this approach can be declaring both values—URL route and default HTTP GET handler method—in the @RequestMapping annotation used at the method level. This declaration is illustrated next:

```
package com.apress.spring6recipes.court.web;

import org.springframework.stereotype.Controller;
import org.springframework.ui.Model;
import org.springframework.web.bind.annotation.RequestMapping;
import org.springframework.web.bind.annotation.RequestMethod;

import java.time.LocalDate;

@Controller
public class WelcomeController {

  @RequestMapping(path = "/welcome", method = RequestMethod.GET)
  public String welcome(Model model) {
    model.addAttribute("today", LocalDate.now());
    return "/WEB-INF/jsp/welcome.jsp";
  }
}
```

This last declaration is equivalent to the earlier one. The path (or value) attribute indicates the URL to which the handler method is mapped, and the method attribute defines the handler method as the controller's default HTTP GET method. Finally, there are also some convenient annotations like @GetMapping, @PostMapping, etc. to minimize the configuration. The following mapping will do the same as the earlier mentioned declarations:

```
package com.apress.spring6recipes.court.web;

import org.springframework.stereotype.Controller;
import org.springframework.ui.Model;
import org.springframework.web.bind.annotation.GetMapping;

import java.time.LocalDate;

@Controller
public class WelcomeController {

  @GetMapping("/welcome")
  public String welcome(Model model) {
    model.addAttribute("today", LocalDate.now());
    return "/WEB-INF/jsp/welcome.jsp";
  }
}
```

The @GetMapping makes the class a bit shorter and maybe easier to read.

This last controller illustrates the basic principles of Spring MVC. However, a typical controller may invoke back-end services for business processing. For example, you can create a controller for querying reservations of a particular court as follows:

```
package com.apress.spring6recipes.court.web;

import com.apress.spring6recipes.court.domain.Reservation;
import com.apress.spring6recipes.court.service.ReservationService;
import org.springframework.stereotype.Controller;
import org.springframework.ui.Model;
import org.springframework.web.bind.annotation.GetMapping;
import org.springframework.web.bind.annotation.PostMapping;
import org.springframework.web.bind.annotation.RequestMapping;
import org.springframework.web.bind.annotation.RequestParam;

@Controller
@RequestMapping("/reservationQuery")
public class ReservationQueryController {

  private final ReservationService reservationService;

  public ReservationQueryController(ReservationService reservationService) {
    this.reservationService = reservationService;
  }

  @GetMapping
  public void setupForm() {}

  @PostMapping
  public String sumbitForm(@RequestParam("courtName") String courtName, Model model) {
    var reservations = java.util.Collections.<Reservation>emptyList();
    if (courtName != null) {
      reservations = reservationService.query(courtName);
    }
    model.addAttribute("reservations", reservations);
    return "/WEB-INF/jsp/reservationQuery.jsp";
  }
}
```

As outlined earlier, the controller then looks for a default HTTP GET handler method. Since the public void setupForm() method is assigned the necessary @RequestMapping annotation for this purpose, it's called next.

Unlike the previous default HTTP GET handler method, notice that this method has no input parameters, has no logic, and has a void return value. This means two things. By having no input parameters and no logic, a view only displays data hard-coded in the implementation template (e.g., JSP), since no data is being added by the controller. By having a void return value, a default view name based on the request URL is used. Therefore, since the requesting URL is /reservationQuery, a return view named reservationQuery is assumed.

The remaining handler method is decorated with the @PostMapping annotation. At first sight, having two handler methods with only the class-level /reservationQuery URL statement can be confusing, but it's really simple. One method is invoked when HTTP GET requests are made on the /reservationQuery URL and the other when HTTP POST requests are made on the same URL.

The majority of requests in web applications are of the HTTP GET kind, whereas requests of the HTTP POST kind are generally made when a user submits an HTML form. So revealing more of the application's view (which we will describe shortly), one method is called when the HTML form is initially loaded (i.e., HTTP GET), whereas the other is called when the HTML form is submitted (i.e., HTTP POST).

Looking closer at the HTTP POST default handler method, notice the two input parameters. First is the @RequestParam("courtName") String courtName declaration, used to extract a request parameter named courtName. In this case, the HTTP POST request comes in the form /reservationQuery?courtName =<value>. This declaration makes said value available in the method under the variable named courtName. Second, the Model declaration is used to define an object in which to pass data onto the returning view.

The logic executed by the handler method consists of using the controller's reservationService to perform a query using the courtName variable. The results obtained from this query are assigned to the Model object that will later become available to the returning view for display.

Finally, note that the method returns a view named reservationQuery. This method could have also returned void, just like the default HTTP GET, and have been assigned to the same reservationQuery default view on account of the requesting URL. Both approaches are identical.

Now that you are aware of how Spring MVC controllers are constituted, it's time to explore the views to which a controller's handler methods delegate their results.

Creating JSP Views

Spring MVC supports many types of views for different presentation technologies. These include JSPs, HTML, PDF, Excel worksheets (XLS), XML, JSON (JavaScript Object Notation), Atom and RSS feeds, JasperReports, and other third-party view implementations.

In a Spring MVC application, views are most written in a template language; the default available with a Jakarta EE server is the JSP templates written with JSTL. When the DispatcherServlet receives a view name returned from a handler, it resolves the logical view name into a view implementation for rendering (see also Recipe 2-6). For example, you can configure the InternalResourceViewResolver bean, in this case in the CourtConfiguration, of a web application's context to resolve view names into JSP files in the /WEB-INF/jsp/ directory:

```
@Bean
public InternalResourceViewResolver internalResourceViewResolver() {
  var viewResolver = new InternalResourceViewResolver();
  viewResolver.setPrefix("/WEB-INF/jsp/");
  viewResolver.setSuffix(".jsp");
  return viewResolver;
}
```

By using this last configuration, a logical view named reservationQuery is delegated to a view implementation located at /WEB-INF/jsp/reservationQuery.jsp. Knowing this you can create the following JSP template for the welcome controller, naming it welcome.jsp and putting it in the /WEB-INF/jsp/ directory:

```
<!DOCTYPE html>
<html>
<head>
    <title>Welcome</title>
</head>
```

```
<body>
<h2>Welcome to Court Reservation System</h2>
Today is ${today}.
</body>
</html>
```

Next, you can create another JSP template for the reservation query controller and name it reservationQuery.jsp to match the view name:

```
<!DOCTYPE html>
<%@ taglib prefix="c" uri="http://java.sun.com/jsp/jstl/core" %>
<html>
<head>
  <title>Reservation Query</title>
</head>

<body>
<div>
  <form method="post">
    <label for="courtName">Court Name</label>
    <input type="text" name="courtName" value="${courtName}"/>
    <input type="submit" value="Query"/>
  </form>
</div>
<div>
  <table style="border: 1px black;">
    <tr>
      <th>Court Name</th>
      <th>Date</th>
      <th>Hour</th>
      <th>Player</th>
    </tr>
    <c:forEach items="${reservations}" var="reservation">
      <tr>
        <td>${reservation.courtName}</td>
        <td>${reservation.date}</td>
        <td>${reservation.hour}</td>
        <td>${reservation.player.name}</td>
      </tr>
    </c:forEach>
  </table>
</div>
</body>
</html>
```

In this JSP template, you include a form for users to input the court name they want to query and then use the <c:forEach> tag to loop the reservations model attribute to generate the result table.

Deploying the Web Application

In a web application's development process, we strongly recommend installing a local Jakarta EE application server that comes with a web container for testing and debugging purposes. For the sake of easy configuration and deployment, we have chosen Apache Tomcat 10.1.x as the web container.

The deployment directory for this web container is located under the webapps directory. By default, Tomcat listens on port 8080 and deploys applications onto a context by the same name of an application WAR. Therefore, if you package the application in a WAR named court.war, the welcome controller and the reservation query controller can be accessed through the following URLs:

```
http://localhost:8080/court/welcome
http://localhost:8080/court/reservationQuery
```

♀ The project can also create a Docker container with the app: run ../../gradlew build docker to get a container with Tomcat and the application. You can then start a Docker container to test the application (../../gradlew dockerRun or manually start it with Docker yourself).

Bootstrap the Application Using a WebApplicationInitializer

In the previous section, you created a CourtServletContainerInitializer together with a file in META-INF/services to bootstrap the application.

Instead of implementing our own, we are now going to leverage the convenient Spring implementation: the SpringServletContainerInitializer. This class is an implementation of the ServletContainerInitializer interface and scans the classpath for implementations of a WebApplicationInitializer interface. Luckily, Spring provides some convenience implementations of this interface, which you can leverage for the application. One of them is the AbstractAnnotationConfigDispatcherServletInitializer:

```
package com.apress.spring6recipes.court.web;

import com.apress.spring6recipes.court.config.CourtConfiguration;
import org.springframework.web.servlet.support.
AbstractAnnotationConfigDispatcherServletInitializer;

public class CourtWebApplicationInitializer
        extends AbstractAnnotationConfigDispatcherServletInitializer {

  @Override
  protected Class<?>[] getRootConfigClasses() {
    return null;
  }

  @Override
  protected Class<?>[] getServletConfigClasses() {
    return new Class<?>[] { CourtConfiguration.class };
  }
```

```
@Override
protected String[] getServletMappings() {
    return new String[] { "/" };
}
}
```

The newly introduced CourtWebApplicationInitializer already creates a DispatcherServlet, so the only thing you need to do is to configure the mappings in the getServletMappings method and the configuration classes you want to load in the getServletConfigClasses. Next to the servlet, there is also another component being created, optionally, which is the ContextLoaderListener; this is a ServletContextListener, which also creates an ApplicationContext that will be used as a parent ApplicationContext for the DispatcherServlet. This is very convenient if you have multiple servlets needing access to the same beans (services, data sources, etc.).

2-2. Mapping Requests with @RequestMapping

Problem

When DispatcherServlet receives a web request, it attempts to dispatch requests to the various controller classes that have been declared with the @Controller annotation. The dispatching process depends on the various @RequestMapping annotations declared in a controller class and its handler methods. You want to define a strategy for mapping requests using the @RequestMapping annotation.

Solution

In a Spring MVC application, web requests are mapped to handlers by one or more @RequestMapping annotations declared in controller classes.

Handler mappings match URLs according to their paths relative to the context path (i.e., the web application context's deployed path) and the servlet path (i.e., the path mapped to DispatcherServlet). So, for example, in the URL http://localhost:8080/court/welcome, the path to match is /welcome, as the context path is /court and there's no servlet path—recall the servlet path declared as / in the CourtWebApplicationInitializer.

How It Works

Mapping Requests by Method

The simplest strategy for using @RequestMapping annotations is to decorate the handler methods directly. For this strategy to work, you have to declare each handler method with the @RequestMapping annotation containing a URL pattern. If a handler's @RequestMapping annotation matches a request's URL, DispatcherServlet dispatches the request to this handler for it to handle the request:

```
package com.apress.spring6recipes.court.web;

import com.apress.spring6recipes.court.domain.Member;
import com.apress.spring6recipes.court.service.MemberService;
import org.springframework.stereotype.Controller;
import org.springframework.ui.Model;
import org.springframework.web.bind.annotation.RequestMapping;
```

```java
import org.springframework.web.bind.annotation.RequestMethod;
import org.springframework.web.bind.annotation.RequestParam;

@Controller
public class MemberController {

  private MemberService memberService;

  public MemberController(MemberService memberService) {
    this.memberService = memberService;
  }

  @RequestMapping("/member/add")
  public String addMember(Model model) {
    model.addAttribute("member", new Member());
    model.addAttribute("guests", memberService.list());
    return "memberList";
  }

  @RequestMapping(value = { "/member/remove", "/member/delete" },
                  method = RequestMethod.GET)
  public String removeMember(@RequestParam("memberName") String memberName) {
    memberService.remove(memberName);
    return "redirect:";
  }
}
```

This last listing illustrates how each handler method is mapped to a particular URL using the @RequestMapping annotation. The second handler method illustrates the assignment of multiple URLs, so both /member/remove and /member/delete trigger the execution of the handler method. When no method is given, it will match all incoming HTTP method types (GET, POST, PUT, etc.); this can be narrowed down by specifying the method to use for mapping.

Mapping Requests by Class

The @RequestMapping annotation can also be used to decorate a controller class. This allows handler methods to either forgo the use of @RequestMapping annotations, as illustrated in the ReservationQueryController in Recipe 2-1, or use finer-grained URLs with their own @RequestMapping annotation. For broader URL matching, the @RequestMapping annotation also supports the use of wildcards (i.e., *).

The following listing illustrates the use of URL wildcards in a @RequestMapping annotation, as well as finer-grained URL matching on @RequestMapping annotations for handler methods:

```java
package com.apress.spring6recipes.court.web;

import com.apress.spring6recipes.court.domain.Member;
import com.apress.spring6recipes.court.service.MemberService;
import org.springframework.stereotype.Controller;
import org.springframework.ui.Model;
import org.springframework.web.bind.annotation.PathVariable;
import org.springframework.web.bind.annotation.RequestMapping;
import org.springframework.web.bind.annotation.RequestMethod;
```

```
import org.springframework.web.bind.annotation.RequestParam;

@Controller
@RequestMapping("/member/*")
public class MemberController {

  private MemberService memberService;

  public MemberController(MemberService memberService) {
    this.memberService = memberService;
  }

  @RequestMapping("/add")
  public String addMember(Model model) {
    model.addAttribute("member", new Member());
    model.addAttribute("guests", memberService.list());
    return "memberList";
  }

  @RequestMapping(path = { "/remove", "/delete" }, method = RequestMethod.GET)
  public String removeMember(@RequestParam("memberName") String memberName) {
    memberService.remove(memberName);
    return "redirect:";
  }

  @RequestMapping("/display/{member}")
  public String displayMember(@PathVariable("member") String member, Model model) {
    model.addAttribute("member", memberService.find(member).orElse(null));
    return "member";
  }

  @RequestMapping
  public void memberList() {}

  public void memberLogic(String memberName) {}

}
```

Note the class-level @RequestMapping annotation uses a URL wildcard: /member/*. This in turn delegates all requests under the /member/ URL to the controller's handler methods.

The first two handler methods make use of the @RequestMapping annotation. The addMember() method is invoked when an HTTP GET request is made on the /member/add URL, whereas the removeMember() method is invoked when an HTTP GET request is made on either the /member/remove or /member/delete URL.

The third handler method uses the special notation {path_variable} to specify its @RequestMapping value. By doing so, a value present in the URL can be passed as input to the handler method. Notice the handler method declares @PathVariable("member") String member. In this manner, if a request is received in the form member/display/jdoe, the handler method has access to the member variable with a jdoe value. This is mainly a facility that allows you to avoid tinkering with a handler's request object and an approach that is especially helpful when you design RESTful web services.

The fourth handler method also uses the @RequestMapping annotation, but in this case lacks a URL value. Since the class level uses the /member/* URL wildcard, this handler method is executed as a catch-all. So any URL request (e.g., /member/abcdefg or /member/randomroute) triggers this method. Note the void return value that in turn makes the handler method default to a view by its name (i.e., memberList).

The last method—memberLogic—lacks any @RequestMapping annotations; this means the method is a utility for the class and has no influence on Spring MVC.

Mapping Requests by HTTP Request Type

By default, @RequestMapping annotations handle all types of incoming requests. It is however, in most cases, not wanted that the same method is executed for both a GET and POST request. To differentiate on HTTP request, it's necessary to specify the type explicitly in the @RequestMapping annotation as follows:

```
@RequestMapping(value= "processUser", method = RequestMethod.POST)
public String submitForm(@ModelAttribute("member") Member member,
                         BindingResult result, Model model) {
}
```

The extent to which you require specifying a handler method's HTTP type depends on what is interacting with a controller and how. For the most part, web browsers perform the bulk of their operations using HTTP GET and HTTP POST requests. However, other devices or applications (e.g., RESTful web services) may require support for other HTTP request types. In all, there are nine different HTTP request types: HEAD, GET, POST, PUT, DELETE, PATCH, TRACE, OPTIONS, and CONNECT. However, support for handling all these request types goes beyond the scope of an MVC controller, since a web server and the requesting party need to support such HTTP request types. Considering the majority of HTTP requests are of the GET or POST kind, you will rarely if ever require implementing support for these additional HTTP request types.

For the most commonly used request methods, Spring MVC provides specialized annotations.

Request Method to Annotation Mapping

Request Method	Annotation
POST	@PostMapping
GET	@GetMapping
DELETE	@DeleteMapping
PUT	@PutMapping
PATCH	@PatchMapping

These convenience annotations are all specialized @RequestMapping annotations and make writing request handling methods a bit more compact:

```
@PostMapping("processUser")
public String submitForm(@ModelAttribute("member") Member member,
                         BindingResult result, Model model) {
}
```

WHERE ARE THE URL EXTENSIONS LIKE .HTML AND .JSP?

You might have noticed that in all the URLs specified in @RequestMapping annotations, there was no trace of a file extension like .html or .jsp. This is good practice in accordance with MVC design, even though it's not widely adopted.

A controller should not be tied to any type of extension that is indicative of a view technology, like HTML or JSP. This is why controllers return logical views and also why matching URLs should be declared without extensions.

In an age where it's common to have applications serve the same content in different formats, such as XML, JSON, PDF, or XLS (Excel), it should be left to a view resolver to inspect the extension provided in a request—if any—and determine which view technology to use.

In this short introduction, you've seen how a resolver is configured in an MVC's configuration class to map logical views to JSP files, all without ever using a URL file extension like .jsp.

In later recipes, you will learn how Spring MVC uses this same non-extension URL approach to serve content using different view technologies.

2-3. Intercepting Requests with Handler Interceptors

Problem

Servlet filters defined by the Servlet API can pre-handle and post-handle every web request before and after it's handled by a servlet. You want to configure something with similar functions as filters in Spring's web application context to take advantage of the container features.

Moreover, sometimes you may want to pre-handle and post-handle web requests that are handled by Spring MVC handlers and manipulate the model attributes returned by these handlers before they are passed to the views.

Solution

Spring MVC allows you to intercept web requests for pre-handling and post-handling through handler interceptors. Handler interceptors are configured in Spring's web application context, so they can make use of any container features and refer to any beans declared in the container. A handler interceptor can be registered for particular URL mappings, so it only intercepts requests mapped to certain URLs.

Each handler interceptor must implement the HandlerInterceptor interface, which contains three callback methods for you to implement: preHandle(), postHandle(), and afterCompletion(). You only need to implement the callback methods you are going to need. The first and second methods are called before and after a request is handled by a handler. The second method also allows you to get access to the returned ModelAndView object, so you can manipulate the model attributes in it. The last method is called after the completion of all request processing (i.e., after the view has been rendered).

How It Works

Suppose you are going to measure each web request's handling time by each request handler and allow the views to show this time to the user. You can create a custom handler interceptor for this purpose:

```
package com.apress.spring6recipes.court.web;

import jakarta.servlet.http.HttpServletRequest;
import jakarta.servlet.http.HttpServletResponse;

import org.springframework.util.StopWatch;
import org.springframework.web.servlet.HandlerInterceptor;
import org.springframework.web.servlet.ModelAndView;

public class MeasurementInterceptor implements HandlerInterceptor {

  private static final String NAME = "MeasurementInterceptor.TIMER";

  @Override
  public boolean preHandle(HttpServletRequest request, HttpServletResponse response,
                           Object handler) {
    var sw = new StopWatch();
    sw.start();
    request.setAttribute(NAME, sw);
    return true;
  }

  @Override
  public void postHandle(HttpServletRequest request, HttpServletResponse response,
                         Object handler, ModelAndView modelAndView) {
    var timer = (StopWatch) request.getAttribute(NAME);
    timer.stop();
    modelAndView.addObject("processingTime", timer.getTotalTimeMillis());
  }
}
```

In the preHandle() method of this interceptor, you create a StopWatch and start it and save it to a request attribute. This method should return true, allowing DispatcherServlet to proceed with request handling. Otherwise, DispatcherServlet assumes that this method has already handled the request, so DispatcherServlet returns the response to the user directly. Then, in the postHandle() method, you retrieve the StopWatch, stop it, and get the total processing time.

To register an interceptor, you need to use the WebMvcConfigurer. This is an interface with several callback methods used by the Spring Web MVC configuration to do some specific setup. You can either implement this on your existing CourtConfiguration or provide a separate configuration class for this. Either way you need to override the addInterceptors method. The method gives you access to the InterceptorRegistry, which you can use to add interceptors:

```
package com.apress.spring6recipes.court.config;

import com.apress.spring6recipes.court.web.MeasurementInterceptor;
import org.springframework.context.annotation.Bean;
```

119

```
import org.springframework.context.annotation.Configuration;
import org.springframework.web.servlet.config.annotation.InterceptorRegistry;
import org.springframework.web.servlet.config.annotation.WebMvcConfigurer;

@Configuration
public class InterceptorConfiguration implements WebMvcConfigurer {

  @Override
  public void addInterceptors(InterceptorRegistry registry) {
    registry.addInterceptor(measurementInterceptor());
  }

  @Bean
  public MeasurementInterceptor measurementInterceptor() {
    return new MeasurementInterceptor();
  }
}
```

Now you can show this time in welcome.jsp to verify this interceptor's functionality. As WelcomeController doesn't have much to do, you may likely see that the handling time is 0 milliseconds. If this is the case, you may add a sleep statement to this class to see a longer handling time:

```
<!DOCTYPE html>
<html>
<head>
  <title>Welcome</title>
</head>

<body>
<h2>Welcome to Court Reservation System</h2>
Today is ${today}.
<hr/>
Processing time : ${processingTime}ms.
</body>
</html>
```

By default HandlerInterceptors apply to all @Controllers. However, sometimes you want to discriminate on which controllers interceptors are applied. The namespace and the Java-based configuration allow for interceptors to be mapped to particular URLs. It is only a matter of configuration. The following is the Java configuration of this:

```
package com.apress.spring6recipes.court.config;

import com.apress.spring6recipes.court.web.ExtensionInterceptor;
import com.apress.spring6recipes.court.web.MeasurementInterceptor;
import org.springframework.context.annotation.Bean;
import org.springframework.context.annotation.Configuration;
import org.springframework.web.servlet.config.annotation.InterceptorRegistry;
import org.springframework.web.servlet.config.annotation.WebMvcConfigurer;
```

```
@Configuration
public class InterceptorConfiguration implements WebMvcConfigurer {

    @Override
    public void addInterceptors(InterceptorRegistry registry) {
        registry.addInterceptor(measurementInterceptor());
        registry.addInterceptor(summaryReportInterceptor())
                .addPathPatterns("/reservationSummary*");
    }

    @Bean
    public MeasurementInterceptor measurementInterceptor() {
        return new MeasurementInterceptor();
    }

    @Bean
    public ExtensionInterceptor summaryReportInterceptor() {
        return new ExtensionInterceptor(cnm);
    }
}
```

First, there is the addition of the interceptor bean summaryReportInterceptor. The structure of the backing class for this bean is identical to that of the measurementInterceptor (i.e., it implements the HandlerInterceptor interface). However, this interceptor performs logic that should be restricted to a particular controller that is mapped to the /reservationSummary URI. When registering an interceptor, we can specify which URLs it maps to; by default this takes an ANT-style expression. We pass this pattern into the addPathPatterns method. There is also an excludePathPatterns method, which you can use to exclude the interceptor for certain URLs.

2-4. Resolving User Locales

Problem

In order for your web application to support internationalization, you have to identify each user's preferred locale and display contents according to this locale.

Solution

In a Spring MVC application, a user's locale is identified by a locale resolver, which has to implement the LocaleResolver interface. Spring MVC comes with several LocaleResolver implementations for you to resolve locales by different criteria. Alternatively, you may create your own custom locale resolver by implementing this interface.

You can define a locale resolver by registering a bean of type LocaleResolver in the web application context. You must set the bean name of the locale resolver to localeResolver for DispatcherServlet to auto-detect. Note that you can register only one locale resolver per DispatcherServlet.

How It Works

Resolving Locales by an HTTP Request Header

The default locale resolver used by Spring is `AcceptHeaderLocaleResolver`. It resolves locales by inspecting the accept-language header of an HTTP request. This header is set by a user's web browser according to the locale setting of the underlying operating system. Note that this locale resolver cannot change a user's locale because it is unable to modify the locale setting of the user's operating system.

Resolving Locales by a Session Attribute

Another option of resolving locales is by `SessionLocaleResolver`. It resolves locales by inspecting a predefined attribute in a user's session. If the session attribute doesn't exist, this locale resolver determines the default locale from the accept-language HTTP header:

```
@Bean
public LocaleResolver localeResolver () {
    var localeResolver = new SessionLocaleResolver();
    localeResolver.setDefaultLocale(Locale.of("en"));
    return localeResolver;
}
```

You can set the `defaultLocale` property for this resolver in case the session attribute doesn't exist. Note that this locale resolver is able to change a user's locale by altering the session attribute that stores the locale.

Resolving Locales by a Cookie

You can also use `CookieLocaleResolver` to resolve locales by inspecting a cookie in a user's browser. If the cookie doesn't exist, this locale resolver determines the default locale from the accept-language HTTP header:

```
@Bean
public LocaleResolver localeResolver() {
    return new CookieLocaleResolver();
}
```

The cookie used by this locale resolver can be customized by providing the name of the cookie through the constructor. The `cookieMaxAge` property indicates how many seconds this cookie should be persisted; the preferred usage is to pass a `Duration` (as done in the sample). The value `-1` indicates that this cookie will be invalid after the browser is closed:

```
@Bean
public LocaleResolver localeResolver() {
    var cookieLocaleResolver = new CookieLocaleResolver("language");
    cookieLocaleResolver.setCookieMaxAge(Duration.ofHours(1));
    cookieLocaleResolver.setDefaultLocale(Locale.of("en"));
    return cookieLocaleResolver;
}
```

You can also set the defaultLocale property for this resolver in case the cookie doesn't exist in a user's browser. This locale resolver is able to change a user's locale by altering the cookie that stores the locale.

Changing a User's Locale

In addition to changing a user's locale by calling LocaleResolver.setLocale() explicitly, you can also apply LocaleChangeInterceptor to your handler mappings. This interceptor detects if a special parameter is present in the current HTTP request. The parameter name can be customized with the paramName property of this interceptor. If such a parameter is present in the current request, this interceptor changes the user's locale according to the parameter value:

```
package com.apress.spring6recipes.court.config;

import org.springframework.context.annotation.Bean;
import org.springframework.context.annotation.Configuration;
import org.springframework.web.servlet.config.annotation.InterceptorRegistry;
import org.springframework.web.servlet.config.annotation.WebMvcConfigurer;
import org.springframework.web.servlet.i18n.CookieLocaleResolver;
import org.springframework.web.servlet.i18n.LocaleChangeInterceptor;

import java.time.Duration;
import java.util.Locale;

@Configuration
public class I18NConfiguration implements WebMvcConfigurer {

  @Override
  public void addInterceptors(InterceptorRegistry registry) {
    registry.addInterceptor(localeChangeInterceptor());
  }

  @Bean
  public LocaleChangeInterceptor localeChangeInterceptor() {
    var localeChangeInterceptor = new LocaleChangeInterceptor();
    localeChangeInterceptor.setParamName("language");
    return localeChangeInterceptor;
  }

  @Bean
  public CookieLocaleResolver localeResolver() {
    var cookieLocaleResolver = new CookieLocaleResolver("language");
    cookieLocaleResolver.setCookieMaxAge(Duration.ofHours(1));
    cookieLocaleResolver.setDefaultLocale(Locale.of("en"));
    return cookieLocaleResolver;
  }

}
```

Now a user's locale can be changed by any URLs with the language parameter. For example, the following two URLs change the user's locale to English for the United States and to German, respectively:

```
http://localhost:8080/court/welcome?language=en_US
http://localhost:8080/court/welcome?language=de
```

Then you can show the HTTP response object's locale in welcome.jsp to verify the locale interceptor's configuration:

```
<!DOCTYPE html>
<html>
<head>
  <title>Welcome</title>
</head>

<body>
<h2>Welcome to Court Reservation System</h2>
Today is ${today}.

<hr/>
Processing time : ${processingTime}ms.

<br/>
Locale : ${pageContext.response.locale}
</body>
</html>
```

2-5. Externalizing Locale-Sensitive Text Messages

Problem

When developing an internationalized web application, you have to display your web pages in a user's preferred locale. You don't want to create different versions of the same page for different locales.

Solution

To avoid creating different versions of a page for different locales, you should make your web page independent of the locale by externalizing locale-sensitive text messages. Spring is able to resolve text messages for you by using a message source, which has to implement the MessageSource interface. Then your JSP files can use the <spring:message> tag, defined in Spring's tag library, to resolve a message given the code.

How It Works

You can define a message source by registering a bean of type MessageSource in the web application context. You must set the bean name of the message source to messageSource for DispatcherServlet to auto-detect. Note that you can register only one message source per DispatcherServlet. The

ResourceBundleMessageSource implementation resolves messages from different resource bundles for different locales. For example, you can register it in WebConfiguration to load resource bundles whose base name is messages:

```
@Bean
public MessageSource messageSource() {
  var messageSource = new ResourceBundleMessageSource();
  messageSource.setBasename("messages");
  return messageSource;
}
```

Then you create two resource bundles, messages.properties and messages_de.properties, to store messages for the default and German locales. These resource bundles should be put in the root of the classpath. In the project the proper place is the src/main/resources folder:

```
welcome.title=Welcome
welcome.message=Welcome to Court Reservation System

welcome.title=Willkommen
welcome.message=Willkommen zum Spielplatz-Reservierungssystem
```

Now, in a JSP file such as welcome.jsp, you can use the <spring:message> tag to resolve a message given the code. This tag automatically resolves the message according to a user's current locale. Note that this tag is defined in Spring's tag library, so you have to declare it at the top of your JSP file:

```
<%@ taglib prefix="fmt" uri="http://java.sun.com/jsp/jstl/fmt" %>
<%@ taglib prefix="spring" uri="http://www.springframework.org/tags" %>
<html>
<head>
    <title><spring:message code="welcome.title" text="Welcome"/></title>
</head>

<body>
<h2><spring:message code="welcome.message"
                    text="Welcome to Court Reservation System"/></h2>
Today is ${today}.
<hr/>
Processing time : ${processingTime}ms.
<br/>
Locale : ${pageContext.response.locale}
</body>
</html>
```

In <spring:message>, you can specify the default text to output when a message for the given code cannot be resolved.

2-6. Resolving Views by Names

Problem

After a handler has finished handling a request, it returns a logical view name. In this case the DispatcherServlet has to delegate control to a view template so the information is rendered. You want to define a strategy for DispatcherServlet to resolve views by their logical names.

Solution

In a Spring MVC application, views are resolved by one or more view resolver beans declared in the web application context. These beans have to implement the ViewResolver interface for DispatcherServlet to auto-detect them. Spring MVC comes with several ViewResolver implementations for you to resolve views using different strategies.

How It Works

Resolving Views Based on a Template's Name and Location

The basic strategy of resolving views is to map them to a template's name and location directly. The view resolver InternalResourceViewResolver maps each view name to an application's directory by means of a prefix and a suffix declaration. To register InternalResourceViewResolver, you can declare a bean of this type in the web application context:

```
package com.apress.spring6recipes.court.config;

import org.springframework.context.annotation.Bean;
import org.springframework.context.annotation.Configuration;
import org.springframework.web.servlet.view.InternalResourceViewResolver;

@Configuration
public class ViewResolverConfiguration {

  @Bean
  public InternalResourceViewResolver internalResourceViewResolver() {
    var viewResolver = new InternalResourceViewResolver();
    viewResolver.setPrefix("/WEB-INF/jsp/");
    viewResolver.setSuffix(".jsp");
    return viewResolver;
  }
}
```

For example, InternalResourceViewResolver resolves the view names welcome and reservationQuery in the following way:

```
welcome --> /WEB-INF/jsp/welcome.jsp
reservationQuery --> /WEB-INF/jsp/reservationQuery.jsp
```

The type of the resolved views can be specified by the viewClass property. By default, InternalResourceViewResolver resolves view names into view objects of type JstlView if the JSTL library (i.e., jstl.jar) is present in the classpath. So you can omit the viewClass property if your views are JSP templates with JSTL tags.

InternalResourceViewResolver is simple, but it can only resolve internal resource views that can be forwarded by the Servlet API's RequestDispatcher (e.g., an internal JSP file or a servlet). As for other view types supported by Spring MVC, you have to resolve them using other ViewResolver implementations. Spring itself has support for the following technologies.

Table 2-1. *Supported View Technologies*

View Technology	ViewResolver
FreeMarker	org.springframework.web.servlet.view.freemarker.FreeMarkerViewResolver
Groovy markup	org.springframework.web.servlet.view.groovy.GroovyMarkupViewResolver
Script template (JSR-223)	org.springframework.web.servlet.view.script.ScriptTemplateViewResolver
XSLT	org.springframework.web.servlet.view.xslt.XsltViewResolver
Bean name	org.springframework.web.servlet.view.BeanNameViewResolver

With the BeanNameViewResolver it is possible to define views in your configuration and have them resolved by this ViewResolver. That way you can add support for PDF, Excel, Atom, and RSS as well.

Using the ViewResolverRegistry to Register ViewResolvers

Instead of manually adding a bean and configuring it, another option is to use the ViewResolverRegistry to register one or more ViewResolvers. The benefit of this is that for the out-of-the-box supported technologies (see Table 2-1), there are some factory methods on there that help with the configuration. This saves you from the burden to know which specific ViewResolver to use:

```
package com.apress.spring6recipes.court.config;

import org.springframework.context.annotation.Configuration;
import org.springframework.web.servlet.config.annotation.ViewResolverRegistry;
import org.springframework.web.servlet.config.annotation.WebMvcConfigurer;

@Configuration
public class ViewResolverConfiguration implements WebMvcConfigurer {

  @Override
  public void configureViewResolvers(ViewResolverRegistry registry) {
    registry.jsp()
            .prefix("/WEB-INF/jsp/")
            .suffix(".jsp");
  }
}
```

The Redirect Prefix

If you have `InternalResourceViewResolver` configured in your web application context (actually any `UrlBasedViewResolver` supports the `redirect:` prefix), it can resolve redirect views by using the `redirect:` prefix in the view name. Then the rest of the view name is treated as the redirect URL. For example, the view name `redirect:welcome` triggers a redirect to the relative URL welcome. You may also specify an absolute URL in the view name.

2-7. Views and Content Negotiation

Problem

You are relying on extensionless URLs in your controllers—welcome and not `welcome.html` or `welcome.pdf`. You want to devise a strategy so the correct content and type are returned for all requests.

Solution

When a request is received for a web application, it contains a series of properties that allow the processing framework, in this case Spring MVC, to determine the correct content and type to return to the requesting party. The default strategies supported by Spring are listed in Table 2-2.

Table 2-2. *Content Negotiation Strategies*

Strategy	Description	Enabled by default	Property
HTTP Accept header	Inspects the `Accept` header of the HTTP request to determine the media type to use	Yes	`ignoreAcceptHeader`
File/URL extension	Uses the extension (`.pdf`, `.html`, etc.) to determine the media type	No	`favorPathExtension`
Parameter	Uses a parameter in the request to determine the media type	No	`favorParameter`

For example, if a request is made to a URL in the form `/reservationSummary.xml`, a controller is capable of inspecting the extension and delegating it to a logical view representing an XML view. However, the possibility can arise for a request to be made to a URL in the form `/reservationSummary`. Should this request be delegated to an XML view or an HTML view? Or perhaps some other type of view? It's impossible to tell through the URL. But instead of deciding on a default view for such requests, a request can be inspected for its HTTP Accept header to decide what type of view is more appropriate.

Inspecting HTTP Accept headers in a controller can be a messy process. So Spring MVC supports the inspection of headers through the `ContentNegotiatingViewResolver`, allowing view delegation to be made based on either a URL file extension or HTTP Accept header value.

How It Works

The first thing you need to realize about Spring MVC content negotiation is that it's configured as a resolver, just like those illustrated in Recipe 2-6. The Spring MVC content negotiating resolver is based on the ContentNegotiatingViewResolver class. But before we describe how it works, we will illustrate how to configure and integrate it with other resolvers:

```
package com.apress.spring6recipes.court.config;

import org.springframework.context.annotation.Configuration;
import org.springframework.http.MediaType;
import org.springframework.web.servlet.config.annotation.ContentNegotiationConfigurer;
import org.springframework.web.servlet.config.annotation.ViewResolverRegistry;
import org.springframework.web.servlet.config.annotation.WebMvcConfigurer;

@Configuration
public class ViewResolverConfiguration implements WebMvcConfigurer {

  @Override
  public void configureContentNegotiation(ContentNegotiationConfigurer configurer) {
    configurer.mediaType("html", MediaType.TEXT_HTML);
    configurer.mediaType("xls", MediaType.valueOf("application/vnd.ms-excel"));
    configurer.mediaType("pdf", MediaType.APPLICATION_PDF);
    configurer.mediaType("xml", MediaType.APPLICATION_XML);
    configurer.mediaType("json", MediaType.APPLICATION_JSON);
    configurer.favorPathExtension(true);
  }

  @Override
  public void configureViewResolvers(ViewResolverRegistry registry) {
    registry.enableContentNegotiation();
    registry.jsp("/WEB-INF/jsp/", ".jsp");
  }
}
```

First of all we need to configure content negotiation. The default configuration adds a ContentNegotiationManager, which can be configured by overriding the configureContentNegotiation method. Through the mediaType method, we can add the media types that are supported to the ContentNegotiationManager. We also enable path extensions as those are disabled by default.

⚠ favorPathExtension is deprecated and will eventually be removed from Spring MVC. This is because extensionless URLs are preferred together with using the Accept header to determine what type of content to return.

To enable the ContentNegotiatingViewResolver, you also need to override the configureViewResolvers method and call the enableContentNegotiation method. This will set up the ContentNegotiatingViewResolver to have the highest priority among all resolvers, which is necessary to make the content negotiating resolver work. The reason for this resolver having the highest priority is that it does not resolve views themselves, but rather delegates them to other view resolvers (which it automatically detects). Since a resolver that does not resolve views can be confusing, we will elaborate with an example.

Let's assume a controller receives a request for /reservationSummary.xml. Once the handler method finishes, it sends control to a logical view named reservation. At this point Spring MVC resolvers come into play, the first of which is the ContentNegotiatingViewResolver, since it has the highest priority.

The ContentNegotiatingViewResolver first determines the media type for a request based on the following criteria:

If path extensions are enabled, it checks a request path extension (e.g., .html, .xml, or .pdf) against the default media types (e.g., text/html) specified by the mediaTypes map in the configuration of the ContentNegotiationManager bean. If a request path has an extension but no match can be found in the default mediaTypes section, attempt is made to determine an extension's media type using FileTypeMap belonging to JavaBeans Activation Framework. If no extension is present in a request path, the HTTP Accept header of the request is used. For the case of a request made on /reservationSummary.xml, the media type is determined in step 1 to be application/xml. However, for a request made on a URL like /reservationSummary, the media type is not determined until step 3.

The HTTP Accept header contains values like Accept: text/html or Accept: application/pdf; these values help the resolver determine the media type a requester is expecting, given that no extension is present in the requesting URL.

At this juncture, the ContentNegotiatingViewResolver has a media type and logical view named reservation. Based on this information, an iteration is performed over the remaining resolvers—based on their order—to determine what view best matches the logical name based on the detected media type.

This process allows you to have multiple logical views with the same name, each supporting a different media type (e.g., HTML, PDF, or XLS), with ContentNegotiatingViewResolver resolving which is the best match. In such cases a controller's design is further simplified, since it won't be necessary to hard-code the logical view necessary to create a certain media type (e.g., pdfReservation, xlsReservation, or htmlReservation), but instead a single view (e.g., reservation), letting the ContentNegotiatingViewResolver determine the best match.

A series of outcomes for this process can be the following:

- The media type is determined to be application/pdf. If the resolver with the highest priority (lower order) contains a mapping to a logical view named reservation, but such a view does not support the application/pdf type, no match occurs—the lookup process continues onto the remaining resolvers.

- The media type is determined to be application/pdf. The resolver with the highest priority (lower order) containing a mapping to a logical view named reservation and having support for application/pdf is matched.

- The media type is determined to be text/html. There are four resolvers with a logical view named reservation, but the views mapped to the two resolvers with highest priority do not support text/html. It's the remaining resolver containing a mapping for a view named reservation that supports text/html that is matched.

This search process for views automatically takes place on all the resolvers configured in an application. It's also possible to configure—within the ContentNegotiatingViewResolver bean—default views and resolvers, in case you don't want to fall back on configurations made outside the ContentNegotiatingViewResolver.

Recipe 2-11 will illustrate a controller that relies on the ContentNegotiatingViewResolver to determine an application's views.

2-8. Mapping Exceptions to Views

Problem

When an unknown exception occurs, your application server usually displays the evil exception stack trace to the user. Your users have nothing to do with this stack trace and complain that your application is not user-friendly. Moreover, it's also a potential security risk, as you may expose the internal method call hierarchy to users. Though a web application's web.xml can be configured to display friendly JSP pages in case an HTTP error or class exception occurs, Spring MVC supports a more robust approach to managing views for class exceptions.

Solution

In a Spring MVC application, you can register one or more exception resolver beans in the web application context to resolve uncaught exceptions. These beans have to implement the HandlerExceptionResolver interface for DispatcherServlet to auto-detect them. Spring MVC comes with a simple exception resolver for you to map each category of exceptions to a view.

How It Works

Suppose your reservation service throws the following exception due to a reservation not being available:

```
package com.apress.spring6recipes.court.service;

import java.time.LocalDate;

public class ReservationNotAvailableException extends RuntimeException {

    public static final long serialVersionUID = 1L;

    private final String courtName;
    private final LocalDate date;
    private final int hour;

    public ReservationNotAvailableException(String courtName, LocalDate date, int hour) {
        this.courtName = courtName;
        this.date = date;
        this.hour = hour;
    }

    public String getCourtName() {
        return courtName;
    }

    public LocalDate getDate() {
        return date;
    }
```

```
public int getHour() {
  return hour;
}
}
```

To resolve uncaught exceptions, you can write your custom exception resolver by implementing the HandlerExceptionResolver interface. Usually, you'll want to map different categories of exceptions into different error pages. Spring MVC comes with the exception resolver SimpleMappingExceptionResolver for you to configure the exception mappings in the web application context. For example, you can register the following exception resolver in your configuration:

```
package com.apress.spring6recipes.court.config;

import com.apress.spring6recipes.court.service.ReservationNotAvailableException;
import org.springframework.context.annotation.Bean;
import org.springframework.context.annotation.Configuration;
import org.springframework.web.servlet.HandlerExceptionResolver;
import org.springframework.web.servlet.config.annotation.WebMvcConfigurer;
import org.springframework.web.servlet.handler.SimpleMappingExceptionResolver;

import java.util.List;
import java.util.Properties;

@Configuration
public class ErrorHandlingConfiguration implements WebMvcConfigurer {

  @Override
  public void configureHandlerExceptionResolvers(List<HandlerExceptionResolver> resolvers) {
    resolvers.add(handlerExceptionResolver());
  }

  @Bean
  public HandlerExceptionResolver handlerExceptionResolver() {
    var mappings = new Properties();
    mappings.setProperty(ReservationNotAvailableException.class.getName(),
    "reservationNotAvailable");

    var resolver = new SimpleMappingExceptionResolver();
    resolver.setExceptionMappings(mappings);
    resolver.setDefaultErrorView("error");
    return resolver;
  }
}
```

In this exception resolver, you define the logical view name reservationNotAvailable for ReservationNotAvailableException. You can add any number of exception classes using the exceptionMappings property, all the way down to the more general exception class java.lang.Exception. In this manner, depending on the type of class exception, a user is served a view in accordance with the exception.

The property defaultErrorView is used to define a default view named error, used in case an exception class not mapped in the exceptionMappings element is raised.

Addressing the corresponding views, if the InternalResourceViewResolver is configured in your web application context, the following reservationNotAvailable.jsp page is shown in case of a reservation not being available:

```
<%@ taglib prefix="fmt" uri="http://java.sun.com/jsp/jstl/fmt" %>

<html>
<head>
    <title>Reservation Not Available</title>
</head>

<body>
Your reservation for ${exception.courtName} is not available on ${exception.date} at
${exception.hour}:00.
</body>
</html>
```

In an error page, the exception instance can be accessed by the variable ${exception}, so you can show the user more details on this exception.

It's a good practice to define a default error page for any unknown exceptions. You can use the property defaultErrorView to define a default view or map a page to the key java.lang.Exception as the last entry of the mapping, so it will be shown if no other entry has been matched before. Then you can create this view's JSP— error.jsp—as follows:

```
<html>
<head>
    <title>Error</title>
</head>

<body>
An error has occurred. Please contact our administrator for details.
</body>
</html>
```

Mapping Exceptions Using @ExceptionHandler

Instead of configuring a HandlerExceptionResolver, we can also annotate a method with @ExceptionHandler. It works in a similar way as the @RequestMapping annotation:

```
@Controller
@RequestMapping("/reservationForm")
public class ReservationFormController {

  @ExceptionHandler(ReservationNotAvailableException.class)
  public String handle(ReservationNotAvailableException ex) {
    return "reservationNotAvailable";
  }
```

```
@ExceptionHandler
public String handleDefault(Exception e) {
  return "error";
}
}
```

We have here two methods annotated with @ExceptionHandler. The first is for handling the specific ReservationNotAvailableException; the second is the general (catch-all) exception handling method. You also don't have to specify a HandlerExceptionResolver in the WebConfiguration anymore.

Methods annotated with @ExceptionHandler can have a variety of return types (like the @RequestMapping methods). Here we just return the name of the view that needs to be rendered, but we could also have returned a ModelAndView, a View, etc.

Although using @ExceptionHandler-annotated methods is very powerful and flexible, there is a drawback when you put them in controllers. Those methods will only work for the controller they are defined in, so if we have an exception occurring in another controller (for instance, the WelcomeController), these methods won't be called. Generic exception handling methods have to be moved to a separate class, and that class has to be annotated with @ControllerAdvice:

```
package com.apress.spring6recipes.court.web;

import com.apress.spring6recipes.court.service.ReservationNotAvailableException;
import org.springframework.web.bind.annotation.ControllerAdvice;
import org.springframework.web.bind.annotation.ExceptionHandler;

@ControllerAdvice
public class ExceptionHandlingAdvice {

  @ExceptionHandler(ReservationNotAvailableException.class)
  public String handle(ReservationNotAvailableException ex) {
    return "reservationNotAvailable";
  }

  @ExceptionHandler
  public String handleDefault(Exception ex) {
    return "error";
  }
}
```

This class will apply to all controllers in the application context, hence the name @ControllerAdvice.

2-9. Handling Forms with Controllers

Problem

In a web application, you often have to deal with forms. A form controller has to show a form to a user and also handle the form submission. Form handling can be a complex and variable task.

Solution

When a user interacts with a form, it requires support for two operations from a controller. First, when a form is initially requested, it asks the controller to show a form by an HTTP GET request that renders the form view to the user. Then when the form is submitted, an HTTP POST request is made to handle things like validation and business processing for the data present in the form. If the form is handled successfully, it renders the success view to the user. Otherwise, it renders the form view again with errors.

How It Works

Suppose you want to allow a user to make a court reservation by filling out a form. To give you a better idea of the data handled by a controller, we will introduce the controller's view (i.e., the form) first.

Creating a Form's Views

Let's create the form view `reservationForm.jsp`. The form relies on Spring's form tag library, as this simplifies a form's data binding, the display of error messages, and the redisplay of original values entered by the user in case of errors:

```
<%@ taglib prefix="form" uri="http://www.springframework.org/tags/form" %>

<html>
<head>
    <title>Reservation Form</title>
    <style>
        .error {
            color: #ff0000;
            font-weight: bold;
        }
    </style>
</head>

<body>
<form:form method="post" modelAttribute="reservation">
    <form:errors path="*" cssClass="error"/>
    <table>
        <tr>
            <td>Court Name</td>
            <td><form:input path="courtName"/></td>
            <td><form:errors path="courtName" cssClass="error"/></td>
        </tr>
        <tr>
            <td>Date</td>
            <td><form:input path="date"/></td>
            <td><form:errors path="date" cssClass="error"/></td>
        </tr>
```

```
        <tr>
            <td>Hour</td>
            <td><form:input path="hour"/></td>
            <td><form:errors path="hour" cssClass="error"/></td>
        </tr>
        <tr>
            <td colspan="3"><input type="submit"/></td>
        </tr>
    </table>
</form:form>
</body>
</html>
```

The Spring `<form:form>` declares two attributes: the `method="post"` attribute used to indicate a form performs an HTTP POST request upon submission and the `modelAttribute="reservation"` attribute used to indicate the form data is bound to a model named reservation. The first attribute should be familiar to you since it's used on most HTML forms. The second attribute will become clearer once we describe the controller that handles the form.

Bear in mind the `<form:form>` tag is rendered into a standard HTML before it's sent to a user, so it's not that the `modelAttribute="reservation"` is of use to a browser; the attribute is used as a facility to generate the actual HTML form.

Next, you can find the `<form:errors>` tag, used to define a location in which to place errors in case a form does not meet the rules set forth by a controller. The attribute `path="*"` is used to indicate the display of all errors—given the wildcard *—whereas the attribute `cssClass="error"` is used to indicate a CSS formatting class to display the errors.

Next, you can find the form's various `<form:input>` tags accompanied by another set of corresponding `<form:errors>` tags. These tags make use of the attribute path to indicate the form's fields, which in this case are `courtName`, `date`, and `hour`.

The `<form:input>` tags are bound to properties corresponding to the `modelAttribute` by using the `path` attribute. They show the user the original value of the field, which will either be the bound property value or the value rejected due to a binding error. They must be used inside the `<form:form>` tag, which defines a form that binds to the `modelAttribute` by its name.

Finally, you can find the standard HTML tag `<input type="submit" />` that generates a "Submit" button and triggers the sending of data to the server, followed by the `</form:form>` tag that closes out the form. In case the form and its data are processed correctly, you need to create a success view to notify the user of a successful reservation. The `reservationSuccess.jsp` illustrated next serves this purpose:

```
<html>
<head>
    <title>Reservation Success</title>
</head>

<body>
Your reservation has been made successfully.
</body>
</html>
```

It's also possible for errors to occur due to invalid values being submitted in a form. For example, if the date is not in a valid format or an alphabetic character is presented for the hour, the controller is designed to reject such field values. The controller will then generate a list of selective error codes for each error to be returned to the form view, values that are placed inside the `<form:errors>` tag.

For example, for an invalid value input in the date field, the following error codes are generated by a controller:

```
typeMismatch.command.date
typeMismatch.date
typeMismatch.java.time.LocalDate
typeMismatch
```

If you have a ResourceBundleMessageSource defined, you can include the following error messages in your resource bundle for the appropriate locale (e.g., messages.properties for the default locale):

```
typeMismatch.date=Invalid date format
typeMismatch.hour=Invalid hour format
```

The corresponding error codes and their values are what is returned to a user if a failure occurs processing form data.

Now that you know the structure of the views involved with a form, as well as the data handled by it, let's take a look at the logic that handles the submitted data (i.e., the reservation) in a form.

Creating a Form's Service Processing

This is not the controller but rather the service used by the controller to process the form's data. First, define a make() method in the ReservationService interface:

```
package com.apress.spring6recipes.court.service;

import com.apress.spring6recipes.court.domain.Reservation;

public interface ReservationService {

  void make(Reservation reservation) throws ReservationNotAvailableException;
}
```

Then you implement this make() method by adding a Reservation item to the list that stores the reservations. You throw a ReservationNotAvailableException in case of a duplicate reservation:

```
package com.apress.spring6recipes.court.service;
@Service
class InMemoryReservationService implements ReservationService {

  private final List<Reservation> reservations =
    Collections.synchronizedList(new ArrayList<>());

  @Override
  public void make(Reservation res) throws ReservationNotAvailableException {
    long cnt = reservations.stream()
            .filter((r) -> Objects.equals(r.getCourtName(), res.getCourtName()))
            .filter((r) -> Objects.equals(r.getDate(), res.getDate()))
            .filter((r) -> r.getHour() == res.getHour()).count();
```

```
  if (cnt > 0) {
    throw new ReservationNotAvailableException(res.getCourtName(), res.getDate(),
        res.getHour());
  } else {
    reservations.add(res);
  }
 }
}
```

Now that you have a better understanding of the two elements that interact with a controller—a form's views and the reservation service class—let's create a controller to handle the court reservation form.

Creating a Form's Controller

A controller used to handle forms makes use of practically the same annotations you've already used in the previous recipes. So let's get right to the code:

```java
package com.apress.spring6recipes.court.web;

import com.apress.spring6recipes.court.domain.Reservation;
import com.apress.spring6recipes.court.service.ReservationService;
import org.springframework.stereotype.Controller;
import org.springframework.ui.Model;
import org.springframework.web.bind.annotation.GetMapping;
import org.springframework.web.bind.annotation.ModelAttribute;
import org.springframework.web.bind.annotation.PostMapping;
import org.springframework.web.bind.annotation.RequestMapping;
import org.springframework.web.bind.annotation.SessionAttributes;

@Controller
@RequestMapping("/reservationForm")
@SessionAttributes("reservation")
public class ReservationFormController {

  private final ReservationService reservationService;

  public ReservationFormController(ReservationService reservationService) {
    this.reservationService = reservationService;
  }

  @GetMapping
  public String setupForm(Model model) {
    var reservation = new Reservation();
    model.addAttribute("reservation", reservation);
    return "reservationForm";
  }
```

```
@PostMapping
public String submitForm(@ModelAttribute("reservation") Reservation reservation) {
    reservationService.make(reservation);
    return "redirect:reservationSuccess";
}
}
```

The controller starts by using the standard @Controller annotation, as well as the @RequestMapping annotation that allows access to the controller through the following URL:

http://localhost:8080/court/reservationForm

When you enter this URL in your browser, it will send an HTTP GET request to your web application. This in turn triggers the execution of the setupForm method, which is designated to attend to this type of request based on its @RequestMapping annotation.

The setupForm method defines a Model object as an input parameter, which serves to send model data to the view (i.e., the form). Inside the handler method, an empty Reservation object is created that is added as an attribute to the controller's Model object. Then the controller returns the execution flow to the reservationForm view, which in this case is resolved to reservationForm.jsp (i.e., the form).

The most important aspect of this last method is the addition of an empty Reservation object. If you analyze the form reservationForm.jsp, you will notice the <form:form> tag declares an attribute modelAttribute="reservation". This means that upon rendering the view, the form expects an object named reservation to be available, which is achieved by placing it inside the handler method's Model. In fact, further inspection reveals that the path values for each <form:input> tag correspond to the field names belonging to the Reservation object. Since the form is being loaded for the first time, it should be evident that an empty Reservation object is expected.

Another aspect that is vital to describe prior to analyzing the other controller handler method is the @SessionAttributes("reservation") annotation—declared at the top of the controller class. Since it's possible for a form to contain errors, it can be an inconvenience to lose whatever valid data was already provided by a user on every subsequent submission. To solve this problem, the @SessionAttributes is used to save a reservation field to a user's session, so that any future reference to the reservation field is in fact made on the same reference, whether a form is submitted twice or more times. This is also the reason only a single Reservation object is created and assigned to the reservation field in the entire controller. Once the empty Reservation object is created—inside the HTTP GET handler method—all actions are made on the same object, since it's assigned to a user's session.

Now let's turn our attention to submitting the form for the first time. After you have filled in the form fields, submitting the form triggers an HTTP POST request that in turn invokes the submitForm method—on account of this method's @RequestMapping value. The input fields declared for the submitForm method are three. The @ModelAttribute("reservation") Reservation reservation used to reference the reservation object. The BindingResult object that contains newly submitted data by the user. And the SessionStatus object used in case it's necessary to access a user's session.

At this juncture, the handler method doesn't incorporate validation or perform access to a user's session, which is the purpose of the BindingResult object and SessionStatus object—I will describe and incorporate them shortly.

The only operation performed by the handler method is reservationService.make(reservation);. This operation invokes the reservation service using the current state of the reservation object. Generally, controller objects are first validated prior to performing this type of operation on them. Finally, note the handler method returns a view named redirect:reservationSuccess. The actual name of the view in this case is reservationSuccess, which is resolved to the reservationSuccess.jsp page you created earlier.

The redirect: prefix in the view name is used to avoid a problem known as duplicate form submission.

When you refresh the web page in the form success view, the form you just submitted is resubmitted again. To avoid this problem, you can apply the post/redirect/get design pattern, which recommends redirecting to another URL after a form submission is handled successfully, instead of returning an HTML page directly. This is the purpose of prefixing a view name with redirect:.

Initializing a Model Attribute Object and Pre-populating a Form with Values

The form is designed to let users make reservations. However, if you analyze the Reservation domain class, you will note the form is still missing two fields in order to create a complete reservation object. One of these fields is the player field, which corresponds to a Player object. Per the Player class definition, a Player object has both name and phone fields.

So can the player field be incorporated into a form view and controller? Let's analyze the form view first:

```
<tr>
    <td>Player Name</td>
    <td><form:input path="player.name"/></td>
    <td><form:errors path="player.name" cssClass="error"/></td>
</tr>
<tr>
    <td>Player Phone</td>
    <td><form:input path="player.phone"/></td>
    <td><form:errors path="player.phone" cssClass="error"/></td>
</tr>
```

Using a straightforward approach, you add two additional <form:input> tags used to represent the Player object's fields. Though these form declarations are simple, you also need to perform modifications to the controller. Recall that by using <form:input> tags, a view expects to have access to model objects passed by the controller that match the path value for <form:input> tags.

Though the controller's HTTP GET handler method returns an empty reservation Reservation to this last view, the player property is null, so it causes an exception when rendering the form. To solve this problem, you have to initialize an empty Player object and assign it to the Reservation object returned to the view:

```
@GetMapping
public String setupForm(@RequestParam(required = false, value = "username")
                        String username, Model model) {
    var reservation = new Reservation();
    reservation.setPlayer(new Player(username));
    model.addAttribute("reservation", reservation);
    return "reservationForm";
}
```

In this case, after creating the empty Reservation object, the setPlayer method is used to assign it an empty Player object. Further, note that the creation of the Player object relies on the username value. This particular value is obtained from the @RequestParam input value, which was also added to the handler method. By doing so, the Player object can be created with a specific username value passed in as a request parameter, resulting in the username form field being pre-populated with this value.

So, for example, let's say a request to the form is made in the following manner:

```
http://localhost:8080/court/reservationForm?username=Roger
```

This allows the handler method to extract the username parameter to create the Player object, in turn pre-populating the form's username form field with a Roger value. It's worth noting that the @RequestParam annotation for the username parameter uses the property required=false; this allows a form request to be processed even if such a request parameter is not present.

Providing Form Reference Data

When a form controller is requested to render the form view, it may have some types of reference data to provide to the form (e.g., the items to display in an HTML selection). Now suppose you want to allow a user to select the sport type when reserving a court—which is the final unaccounted field for the Reservation class:

```
<tr>
    <td>Sport Type</td>
    <td>
        <form:select path="sportType" items="${sportTypes}"
                      itemValue="id" itemLabel="name"/>
    </td>
    <td><form:errors path="sportType" cssClass="error"/></td>
</tr>
```

The <form:select> tag provides a way to generate a drop-down list of values passed to the view by the controller. Thus, the form represents the sportType field as a set of HTML <select> elements, instead of the previous open-ended fields—<input>—that require a user to introduce text values.

Next, let's take a look at how the controller assigns the sportType field as a model attribute. The process is a little different than the previous fields.

First, let's define the getAllSportTypes() method in the ReservationService interface for retrieving all available sport types:

```
package com.apress.spring6recipes.court.service;

import com.apress.spring6recipes.court.domain.SportType;
import java.util.List;

public interface ReservationService {

  List<SportType> getAllSportTypes();
}
```

Then you can implement this method by returning a hard-coded list:

```
package com.apress.spring6recipes.court.service;

import com.apress.spring6recipes.court.domain.SportType;
import java.util.List;

@Service
class InMemoryReservationService implements ReservationService {

  private static final SportType TENNIS = new SportType(1, "Tennis");
  private static final SportType SOCCER = new SportType(2, "Soccer");
```

```
  @Override
  public List<SportType> getAllSportTypes() {
    return List.of(TENNIS, SOCCER);
  }
}
```

Now that you have an implementation that returns a hard-coded list of SportType objects, let's take a look at how the controller associates this list for it to be returned to the form view:

```
package com.apress.spring6recipes.court.web;

import com.apress.spring6recipes.court.domain.Player;
import com.apress.spring6recipes.court.domain.Reservation;
import com.apress.spring6recipes.court.domain.SportType;
import com.apress.spring6recipes.court.service.ReservationService;
import org.springframework.stereotype.Controller;
import org.springframework.ui.Model;
import org.springframework.web.bind.annotation.GetMapping;
import org.springframework.web.bind.annotation.RequestMapping;
import org.springframework.web.bind.annotation.RequestParam;
import org.springframework.web.bind.annotation.SessionAttributes;

import java.util.List;

@Controller
@RequestMapping("/reservationForm")
@SessionAttributes("reservation")
public class ReservationFormController {

  private final ReservationService reservationService;

  public ReservationFormController(ReservationService reservationService) {
    this.reservationService = reservationService;
  }

  @ModelAttribute("sportTypes")
  public List<SportType> populateSportTypes() {
    return reservationService.getAllSportTypes();
  }

  @GetMapping
  public String setupForm(@RequestParam(required = false, value = "username")
                          String username, Model model) {
    var reservation = new Reservation();
    reservation.setPlayer(new Player(username));
    model.addAttribute("reservation", reservation);
    return "reservationForm";
  }
}
```

Notice that the setupForm handler method charged with returning the empty Reservation object to the form view remains unchanged.

The new addition and what is responsible for passing a SportType list as a model attribute to the form view is the method decorated with the @ModelAttribute("sportTypes") annotation. The @ModelAttribute annotation is used to define global model attributes, available to any returning view used in handler methods, in the same way a handler method declares a Model object as an input parameter and assigns attributes that can be accessed in the returning view.

Since the method decorated with the @ModelAttribute("sportTypes") annotation has a return type of List<SportType> and makes a call to reservationService.getAllSportTypes(), the hard-coded TENNIS and SOCCER SportType objects are assigned to the model attribute named sportTypes. This last model attribute is used in the form view to populate a drop-down list (i.e., <form: select> tag).

Binding Properties of Custom Types

When a form is submitted, a controller binds the form field values to the model object's properties of the same name, in this case a Reservation object. However, for properties of custom types, a controller is not able to convert them unless you specify the corresponding property editors for them.

For example, the sport type selection field only submits the selected sport type ID—as this is the way HTML <select> fields operate. Therefore, you have to convert this ID into a SportType object with a property editor. First of all, you require the getSportType() method in ReservationService to retrieve a SportType object by its ID:

```
package com.apress.spring6recipes.court.service;

import com.apress.spring6recipes.court.domain.SportType;

public interface ReservationService {

  SportType getSportType(int sportTypeId);
}
```

For testing purposes, you can implement this method with a switch/case statement:

```
package com.apress.spring6recipes.court.service;

import com.apress.spring6recipes.court.domain.SportType;
import org.springframework.stereotype.Service;
import java.util.List;

@Service
class InMemoryReservationService implements ReservationService {

  private static final SportType TENNIS = new SportType(1, "Tennis");
  private static final SportType SOCCER = new SportType(2, "Soccer");

  @Override
  public SportType getSportType(int sportTypeId) {
    return switch (sportTypeId) {
      case 1 -> TENNIS;
```

```
      case 2 -> SOCCER;
      default -> null;
  };
 }
}
```

Then you create the SportTypeConverter class to convert a sport type ID into a SportType object. This converter requires ReservationService to perform the lookup:

```
package com.apress.spring6recipes.court.domain;

import com.apress.spring6recipes.court.service.ReservationService;
import org.springframework.core.convert.converter.Converter;
import org.springframework.stereotype.Component;

@Component
public class SportTypeConverter implements Converter<String, SportType> {

  private final ReservationService reservationService;

  public SportTypeConverter(ReservationService reservationService) {
    this.reservationService = reservationService;
  }

  @Override
  public SportType convert(String source) {
    var sportTypeId = Integer.parseInt(source);
    return reservationService.getSportType(sportTypeId);
  }
}
```

Now that you have the supporting SportTypeConverter class required to bind form properties to a custom class like SportType, you need to associate it with the controller. For this purpose, we can use the addFormatters method from the WebMvcConfigurer.

By overriding this method in your configuration class, custom types can be associated with a controller. This includes the SportTypeConverter class and other custom types like Date. Though we didn't mention the date field earlier, it suffers from the same problem as the sport type selection field. A user introduces date fields as text values. In order for the controller to assign these text values to the Reservation object's date fields, this requires the date fields be associated with a Date object. Given the Date class is part of the Java language, it won't be necessary to create a special class like SportTypeConverter for this purpose. The Spring Framework already includes a custom class for this purpose.

Knowing you need to bind the SportTypeConverter class to the underlying controller, the following listing illustrates the modifications to the configuration class:

```
package com.apress.spring6recipes.court.config;

import com.apress.spring6recipes.court.domain.SportTypeConverter;
import org.springframework.context.annotation.ComponentScan;
import org.springframework.context.annotation.Configuration;
import org.springframework.format.FormatterRegistry;
import org.springframework.web.servlet.config.annotation.EnableWebMvc;
```

```
import org.springframework.web.servlet.config.annotation.WebMvcConfigurer;

@Configuration
@ComponentScan("com.apress.spring6recipes.court")
@EnableWebMvc
public class CourtConfiguration implements WebMvcConfigurer {

  private final SportTypeConverter sportTypeConverter;

  public CourtConfiguration(SportTypeConverter sportTypeConverter) {
    this.sportTypeConverter = sportTypeConverter;
  }

  @Override
  public void addFormatters(FormatterRegistry registry) {
    registry.addConverter(sportTypeConverter);
  }
}
```

The only field for this last class corresponds to sportTypeConverter, used to access the application's SportTypeConverter bean. Next, you can find the addFormatters method used to bind the SportTypeConverter class. The method belongs to the FormatterRegistry object, which is passed as an input parameter to the addFormatters method. By using this approach, every annotation-based controller (i.e., classes using the @Controller annotation) can have access to the same custom converters and formatters in their handler methods.

Validating Form Data

When a form is submitted, it's standard practice to validate the data provided by a user before a submission is successful. Spring MVC supports validation by means of a validator object that implements the Validator interface. You can write the following validator to check if the required form fields are filled and if the reservation hour is valid on holidays and weekdays:

```
package com.apress.spring6recipes.court.domain;

import org.springframework.stereotype.Component;
import org.springframework.validation.Errors;
import org.springframework.validation.ValidationUtils;
import org.springframework.validation.Validator;

import java.time.DayOfWeek;

@Component
public class ReservationValidator implements Validator {

  @Override
  public boolean supports(Class<?> clazz) {
    return Reservation.class.isAssignableFrom(clazz);
  }
```

```
@Override
public void validate(Object target, Errors errors) {
  ValidationUtils.rejectIfEmptyOrWhitespace(errors, "courtName", "required.courtName",
  "Court name is required.");
  ValidationUtils.rejectIfEmpty(errors, "date", "required.date", "Date is required.");
  ValidationUtils.rejectIfEmpty(errors, "hour", "required.hour", "Hour is required.");
  ValidationUtils.rejectIfEmptyOrWhitespace(errors, "player.name", "required.playerName",
          "Player name is required.");
  ValidationUtils.rejectIfEmpty(errors, "sportType", "required.sportType", "Sport type is
  required.");

  var reservation = (Reservation) target;
  var date = reservation.getDate();
  var hour = reservation.getHour();
  if (date != null) {
    if (date.getDayOfWeek() == DayOfWeek.SUNDAY) {
      if (hour < 8 || hour > 22) {
        errors.reject("invalid.holidayHour", "Invalid holiday hour.");
      }
    } else {
      if (hour < 9 || hour > 21) {
        errors.reject("invalid.weekdayHour", "Invalid weekday hour.");
      }
    }
  }
}
}
```

In this validator, you use utility methods such as rejectIfEmptyOrWhitespace() and rejectIfEmpty() in the ValidationUtils class to validate the required form fields. If any of these form fields is empty, these methods will create a field error and bind it to the field. The second argument of these methods is the property name, while the third and fourth are the error code and default error message.

You also check whether the reservation hour is valid on holidays and weekdays. In case of invalidity, you should use the reject() method to create an object error to be bound to the reservation object, not to a field.

Since the validator class is annotated with the @Component annotation, Spring attempts to instantiate the class as a bean in accordance with the class name, in this case reservationValidator.

Since validators may create errors during validation, you should define messages for the error codes for displaying to the user. If you have ResourceBundleMessageSource defined, you can include the following error messages in your resource bundle for the appropriate locale (e.g., messages.properties for the default locale):

```
required.courtName=Court name is required
required.date=Date is required
required.hour=Hour is required
required.playerName=Player name is required
required.sportType=Sport type is required
invalid.holidayHour=Invalid holiday hour
invalid.weekdayHour=Invalid weekday hour
```

To apply this validator, you need to perform the following modification to your controller:

```
package com.apress.spring6recipes.court.web;

import com.apress.spring6recipes.court.domain.Reservation;
import com.apress.spring6recipes.court.domain.ReservationValidator;
import org.springframework.stereotype.Controller;
import org.springframework.ui.Model;
import org.springframework.validation.BindingResult;
import org.springframework.validation.annotation.Validated;
import org.springframework.web.bind.WebDataBinder;
import org.springframework.web.bind.annotation.GetMapping;
import org.springframework.web.bind.annotation.InitBinder;
import org.springframework.web.bind.annotation.ModelAttribute;
import org.springframework.web.bind.annotation.PostMapping;
import org.springframework.web.bind.annotation.RequestMapping;
import org.springframework.web.bind.annotation.RequestParam;
import org.springframework.web.bind.annotation.SessionAttributes;
import org.springframework.web.bind.support.SessionStatus;

import java.util.List;

@Controller
@RequestMapping("/reservationForm")
public class ReservationFormController {

  private final ReservationService reservationService;
  private final ReservationValidator reservationValidator;

  public ReservationFormController(ReservationService reservationService,
                                   ReservationValidator reservationValidator) {
    this.reservationService = reservationService;
    this.reservationValidator = reservationValidator;
  }

  @PostMapping
  public String submitForm(@ModelAttribute("reservation") @Validated
                           Reservation reservation, BindingResult result,
                           SessionStatus status) {
    if (result.hasErrors()) {
      return "reservationForm";
    } else {
      reservationService.make(reservation);
      return "redirect:reservationSuccess";
    }
  }

  @InitBinder
  public void initBinder(WebDataBinder binder) {
    binder.setValidator(reservationValidator);
  }
}
```

The first addition to the controller is the ReservationValidator field that gives the controller access to an instance of the validator bean.

The next modification takes place in the HTTP POST handler method, which is always called when a user submits a form. Next to the @ModelAttribute annotation, there is now a @Validated annotation; this annotation triggers validation of the object. After the validation, the parameter BindingResult object contains the results for the validation process. So next, a conditional based on the value of result. hasErrors() is made. If the validation class detects errors, this value is true.

In case errors are detected in the validation process, the handler method returns the view reservationForm, which corresponds to the same form so that a user can resubmit information. In case no errors are detected in the validation process, a call is made to perform the reservation— reservationService.make(reservation);—followed by a redirection to the success view reservationSuccess.

The registration of the validator is done in the @InitBinder-annotated method. The validator is set on the WebDataBinder so that it can be used after binding. To register the validator, one needs to use the setValidator method. You can also register multiple validators using the addValidators method; this method takes a varargs argument for one or more Validator instances.

ⓘ The WebDataBinder can also be used to register additional PropertyEditor, Converter, and Formatter instances for type conversion. This can be used instead of registering global PropertyEditors, Converters, or Formatters.

Expiring a Controller's Session Data

In order to support the possibility of a form being submitted multiple times and not losing data provided by a user in between submissions, the controller relies on the use of the @SessionAttributes annotation. By doing so, a reference to the reservation field represented as a Reservation object is saved between requests.

However, once a form is submitted successfully and a reservation is made, there is no point in keeping the Reservation object in a user's session. In fact, if a user revisits the form within a short period of time, there is a possibility remnants of this old Reservation object emerge if not removed.

Values assigned using the @SessionAttributes annotation can be removed using the SessionStatus object, an object that can be passed as an input parameter to handler methods. The following listing illustrates how to expire the controller's session data:

```
package com.apress.spring6recipes.court.web;
import com.apress.spring6recipes.court.domain.ReservationValidator;
import org.springframework.stereotype.Controller;
import org.springframework.ui.Model;
import org.springframework.validation.BindingResult;
import org.springframework.validation.annotation.Validated;
import org.springframework.web.bind.WebDataBinder;
import org.springframework.web.bind.annotation.GetMapping;
import org.springframework.web.bind.annotation.InitBinder;
import org.springframework.web.bind.annotation.ModelAttribute;
import org.springframework.web.bind.annotation.PostMapping;
import org.springframework.web.bind.annotation.RequestMapping;
import org.springframework.web.bind.annotation.RequestParam;
import org.springframework.web.bind.annotation.SessionAttributes;
```

```
import org.springframework.web.bind.support.SessionStatus;

import java.util.List;

@Controller
@RequestMapping("/reservationForm")
@SessionAttributes("reservation")
public class ReservationFormController {

  private final ReservationService reservationService;
  private final ReservationValidator reservationValidator;

  public ReservationFormController(ReservationService reservationService,
                                   ReservationValidator reservationValidator) {
    this.reservationService = reservationService;
    this.reservationValidator = reservationValidator;
  }
  }

  @PostMapping
  public String submitForm(@ModelAttribute("reservation") @Validated
                           Reservation reservation, BindingResult result,
                           SessionStatus status) {
    if (result.hasErrors()) {
      return "reservationForm";
    } else {
      reservationService.make(reservation);
      status.setComplete();
      return "redirect:reservationSuccess";
    }
  }

  @InitBinder
  public void initBinder(WebDataBinder binder) {
    binder.setValidator(reservationValidator);
  }
}
```

Once the handler method performs the reservation by calling reservationService.make(reservation); and right before a user is redirected to a success page, it becomes an ideal time to expire a controller's session data. This is done by calling the setComplete() method on the SessionStatus object. It's that simple.

2-10. Bean Validation with Annotations (Jakarta Bean Validation API)

Problem

You want to validate Java beans in a web application using annotations based on the Jakarta Bean Validation API.

Solution

Bean Validation is a specification whose objective is to standardize the validation of Java beans through annotations.

In the previous examples, you saw how the Spring Framework supports an ad hoc technique for validating beans. This requires you to extend one of the Spring Framework's classes to create a validator class for a particular type of Java bean.

The objective of the standard is to use annotations directly in a Java bean class. This allows validation rules to be specified directly in the code they are intended to validate, instead of creating validation rules in separate classes—just like you did earlier using a Spring Framework class.

How It Works

The first thing you need to do is decorate a Java bean with the necessary annotations. To use them one needs to have both the API and an implementation of that API in the classpath. Most commonly used is the Hibernate Validator project, which is also the reference implementation of this API.

Gradle dependencies for Jakarta Bean Validation

```
implementation group: 'jakarta.validation', name: 'jakarta.validation-api', version: '3.0.2'
runtimeOnly group: 'org.hibernate.validator', name: 'hibernate-validator', version:
'8.0.0.Final'
```

Maven dependencies for Jakarta Bean Validation

```
<dependency>
  <groupId>jakarta.validation</groupId>
  <artifactId>jakarta.validation-api</artifactId>
  <version>3.0.2</version>
<dependency>
<dependency>
  <groupId>org.hibernate.validation</groupId>
  <artifactId>hibernate-validator</artifactId>
  <version>8.0.0.Final</version>
  <scope>runtime</scope>
<dependency>
```

The following listing illustrates (part of) the Reservation domain class used in the court reservation application decorated with Jakarta Bean Validation annotations:

```
package com.apress.spring6recipes.court.domain;

import jakarta.validation.Valid;
import jakarta.validation.constraints.Max;
import jakarta.validation.constraints.Min;
import jakarta.validation.constraints.NotNull;
import jakarta.validation.constraints.Size;

import java.time.LocalDate;
```

```
public class Reservation {

  @NotNull
  @Size(min = 4)
  private String courtName;

  @NotNull
  private LocalDate date;

  @Min(8)
  @Max(22)
  private int hour;

  @Valid
  private Player player;

  @NotNull
  private SportType sportType;
}
```

The courtName field is assigned two annotations: the @NotNull annotation, which indicates that a field cannot be null, and the @Size annotation used to indicate a field has to have a minimum of four characters.

The date and sportType fields are annotated with @NotNull as those are required.

The hour field is annotated with @Min and @Max because those are the lower and upper limits of the hour field.

Both the fields in the Player domain class are annotated with @NotNull; to also trigger validation of the related object, we have annotated it with @Valid.

Now that you know how a Java bean class is decorated with annotations belonging to Jakarta Bean Validation, let's take a look at how these validator annotations are enforced in a controller:

```
package com.apress.spring6recipes.court.web;
import jakarta.validation.Valid;
import org.springframework.stereotype.Controller;
import org.springframework.ui.Model;
import org.springframework.validation.BindingResult;
import org.springframework.web.bind.annotation.GetMapping;
import org.springframework.web.bind.annotation.ModelAttribute;
import org.springframework.web.bind.annotation.PostMapping;
import org.springframework.web.bind.annotation.RequestMapping;
import org.springframework.web.bind.annotation.RequestParam;
import org.springframework.web.bind.annotation.SessionAttributes;
import org.springframework.web.bind.support.SessionStatus;
@Controller
@RequestMapping("/reservationForm")
@SessionAttributes("reservation")
public class ReservationFormController {

  private final ReservationService reservationService;

  public ReservationFormController(ReservationService reservationService) {
    this.reservationService = reservationService;
  }
```

```
@PostMapping
public String submitForm(@ModelAttribute("reservation") @Valid
                         Reservation reservation, BindingResult result,
                         SessionStatus status) {
  if (result.hasErrors()) {
    return "reservationForm";
  } else {
    reservationService.make(reservation);
    status.setComplete();
    return "redirect:reservationSuccess";
  }
 }
}
```

The controller is almost similar to the one from Recipe 2-9. The only difference is the absence of the @InitBinder-annotated method. Spring MVC detects a jakarta.validation.Validator if that is in the classpath. We added hibernate-validator to the classpath, and that is an implementation.

Next, you can find the controller's HTTP POST handler method used to handle the submission of user data. Since the handler method is expecting an instance of the Reservation object, which you decorated with JSR-303 annotations, you can validate its data.

The remainder of the submitForm method is exactly the same as from Recipe 2-9.

2-11. Creating Excel and PDF Views

Problem

Although HTML is the most common method of displaying web contents, sometimes your users may wish to export contents from your web application in Excel or PDF format. In Java, there are several libraries that can help generate Excel and PDF files. However, to use these libraries directly in a web application, you have to generate the files behind the scenes and return them to users as binary attachments. You have to deal with HTTP response headers and output streams for this purpose.

Solution

Spring integrates the generation of Excel and PDF files into its MVC framework. You can consider Excel and PDF files as special kinds of views, so you can consistently handle a web request in a controller and add data to a model for passing to Excel and PDF views. In this way, you have no need to deal with HTTP response headers and output streams. Spring MVC supports generating Excel files using the Apache POI library. The corresponding view classes are AbstractXlsView, AbstractXlsxView, and AbstractXlsxStreamingView. PDF files are generated by the iText API, and the corresponding view class is AbstractPdfView.

How It Works

Suppose your users wish to generate a report of the reservation summary for a particular day. They want this report to be generated in either Excel, PDF, or the basic HTML format. For this report generation function, you need to declare a method in the service layer that returns all the reservations of a specified day:

```
package com.apress.spring6recipes.court.service;

import com.apress.spring6recipes.court.domain.Reservation;
import java.time.LocalDate;
import java.util.List;

public interface ReservationService {

  List<Reservation> findByDate(LocalDate summaryDate);
}
```

Then you provide a simple implementation for this method by iterating over all the made reservations:

```
package com.apress.spring6recipes.court.service;

import com.apress.spring6recipes.court.domain.Reservation;
import java.time.LocalDate;
import java.util.Objects;
import java.util.stream.Collectors;

@Service
class InMemoryReservationService implements ReservationService {

  @Override
  public List<Reservation> findByDate(LocalDate summaryDate) {
    return reservations.stream()
            .filter( (r) -> Objects.equals(r.getDate(), summaryDate))
}
```

Now you can write a simple controller to get the date parameter from the URL. The date parameter is formatted into a date object and passed to the service layer for querying reservations. The controller relies on the content negotiation resolver described in Recipe 2-7; therefore, the controller returns a single logic view and lets the resolver determine if a report should be generated in Excel, PDF, or a default HTML web page:

```
package com.apress.spring6recipes.court.web;

import com.apress.spring6recipes.court.service.ReservationService;
import org.springframework.format.annotation.DateTimeFormat;
import org.springframework.stereotype.Controller;
import org.springframework.ui.Model;
import org.springframework.web.bind.ServletRequestBindingException;
import org.springframework.web.bind.annotation.ExceptionHandler;
import org.springframework.web.bind.annotation.RequestMapping;
import org.springframework.web.bind.annotation.RequestMethod;
import org.springframework.web.bind.annotation.RequestParam;

import java.text.ParseException;
import java.time.LocalDate;
```

```
@Controller
@RequestMapping("/reservationSummary*")
public class ReservationSummaryController {

  private final ReservationService reservationService;

  public ReservationSummaryController(ReservationService reservationService) {
    this.reservationService = reservationService;
  }

  @RequestMapping(method = RequestMethod.GET)
  public String generateSummary(
          @RequestParam(value = "date") @DateTimeFormat(pattern = "yyyy-MM-dd")
          LocalDate selectedDate,
          Model model) {
    var reservations = reservationService.findByDate(selectedDate);
    model.addAttribute("reservations", reservations);
    return "reservationSummary";
  }

  @ExceptionHandler
  public void handle(ServletRequestBindingException ex) {
    if (ex.getRootCause() instanceof ParseException) {
      throw new ReservationWebException("Invalid date format for reservation summary", ex);
    }
  }
}
```

This controller only contains a default HTTP GET handler method. The method invokes the findByDate method on the ReservationService to get a list of Reservation objects for that date. You can also see an @ExceptionHandler to handle errors in the date parameter. If parsing of the LocalDate fails, a custom exception named ReservationWebException is thrown.

If no errors are raised, the Reservation list is placed into the controller's Model object. Once this is done, the method returns control to the reservationSummary view.

Note that the controller returns a single view, even though it supports PDF, XLS, and HTML views. This is possible due to the ContentNegotiatingViewResolver that determines on the basis of this single view name which of these multiple views to use. See Recipe 2-7 for more information on this resolver.

Creating Excel Views

An Excel view can be created by extending the AbstractXlsView or AbstractXlsxView class. Here, AbstractXlsxView is used as an example. In the buildExcelDocument() method, you can access the model passed from the controller and also a precreated Excel workbook. Your task is to populate the workbook with the data in the model.

ℹ️   To generate Excel files with Apache POI in a web application, you must have the Apache POI dependencies in your CLASSPATH.

Gradle dependencies for Apache POI

implementation group: 'org.apache.poi', name: 'poi-ooxml', version: '5.2.3'

Maven dependencies for Apache POI

```
<dependency>
  <groupId>org.apache.poi</groupId>
  <artifactId>poi-ooxml</artifactId>
  <version>5.2.3</version>
</dependency>
```

```
package com.apress.spring6recipes.court.web.view;

import com.apress.spring6recipes.court.domain.Reservation;
import jakarta.servlet.http.HttpServletRequest;
import jakarta.servlet.http.HttpServletResponse;
import org.apache.poi.ss.usermodel.Sheet;
import org.apache.poi.ss.usermodel.Workbook;
import org.springframework.web.servlet.view.document.AbstractXlsxView;

import java.time.format.DateTimeFormatter;
import java.util.List;
import java.util.Map;

public class ExcelReservationSummary extends AbstractXlsxView {

  private static final DateTimeFormatter DATE_FORMAT = DateTimeFormatter.
  ofPattern("yyyy-MM-dd");

  @Override
  protected void buildExcelDocument(Map<String, Object> model, Workbook workbook,
                                    HttpServletRequest request,
                                    HttpServletResponse response) {
    @SuppressWarnings({ "unchecked" })
    var reservations = (List<Reservation>) model.get("reservations");
    var sheet = workbook.createSheet();

    addHeaderRow(sheet);

    reservations.forEach(reservation -> createRow(sheet, reservation));
  }
```

```java
    private void addHeaderRow(Sheet sheet) {
      var header = sheet.createRow(0);
      header.createCell(0).setCellValue("Court Name");
      header.createCell(1).setCellValue("Date");
      header.createCell(2).setCellValue("Hour");
      header.createCell(3).setCellValue("Player Name");
      header.createCell(4).setCellValue("Player Phone");
    }

    private void createRow(Sheet sheet, Reservation reservation) {
      var row = sheet.createRow(sheet.getLastRowNum() + 1);
      row.createCell(0).setCellValue(reservation.getCourtName());
      row.createCell(1).setCellValue(DATE_FORMAT.format(reservation.getDate()));
      row.createCell(2).setCellValue(reservation.getHour());
      row.createCell(3).setCellValue(reservation.getPlayer().getName());
      row.createCell(4).setCellValue(reservation.getPlayer().getPhone());
    }
}
```

In the preceding Excel view, you first create a sheet in the workbook. In this sheet, you show the headers of this report in the first row. Then you iterate over the reservation list to create a row for each reservation.

As you have @RequestMapping("/reservationSummary*") configured in your controller and the handler method requires the date as a request parameter, you can access this Excel view through the following URL:

```
http://localhost:8080/court/reservationSummary.xlsx?date=2022-01-14
```

Creating PDF Views

A PDF view is created by extending the AbstractPdfView class. In the buildPdfDocument() method, you can access the model passed from the controller and also a precreated PDF document. Your task is to populate the document with the data in the model.

ℹ️   To generate PDF files with iText in a web application, you must have the iText or LibrePDF library in your CLASSPATH.

Gradle dependencies for OpenPDF

```
implementation group: 'com.github.librepdf', name: 'openpdf', version: '1.3.30'
```

Maven dependencies for OpenPDF

```xml
<dependency>
  <groupId>com.github.librepdf</groupId>
  <artifactId>openpdf</artifactId>
  <version>1.3.30</version>
</dependency>
```

```java
package com.apress.spring6recipes.court.web.view;

import com.apress.spring6recipes.court.domain.Reservation;
import com.lowagie.text.BadElementException;
import com.lowagie.text.Document;
import com.lowagie.text.Table;
import com.lowagie.text.pdf.PdfWriter;
import org.springframework.web.servlet.view.document.AbstractPdfView;

import jakarta.servlet.http.HttpServletRequest;
import jakarta.servlet.http.HttpServletResponse;
import java.time.format.DateTimeFormatter;
import java.util.List;
import java.util.Map;

public class PdfReservationSummary extends AbstractPdfView {

  private static final DateTimeFormatter DATE_FORMAT = DateTimeFormatter.ISO_LOCAL_DATE;

  @Override
  protected void buildPdfDocument(Map<String, Object> model, Document document,
                                  PdfWriter writer, HttpServletRequest request,
                                  HttpServletResponse response) {
    @SuppressWarnings("unchecked")
    var reservations = (List<Reservation>) model.get("reservations");
    var table = new Table(5);
    addTableHeader(table);
    reservations.forEach(reservation -> addContent(table, reservation));
    document.add(table);
  }

  private void addContent(Table tab, Reservation res) throws BadElementException {
    tab.addCell(res.getCourtName());
    tab.addCell(DATE_FORMAT.format(res.getDate()));
    tab.addCell(Integer.toString(res.getHour()));
    tab.addCell(res.getPlayer().getName());
    tab.addCell(res.getPlayer().getPhone());
  }

  private void addTableHeader(Table table) throws BadElementException {
    table.addCell("Court Name");
    table.addCell("Date");
    table.addCell("Hour");
    table.addCell("Player Name");
    table.addCell("Player Phone");
  }
}
```

As you have @RequestMapping("/reservationSummary*") configured in your controller and the handler method requires the date as a request parameter, you can access this PDF view through the following URL:

```
http://localhost:8080/court/reservationSummary.pdf?date=2022-10-14
```

Creating Resolvers for Excel and PDF Views

In Recipe 2-6, you learned different strategies for resolving logical view names to specific view implementations. One of these strategies was resolving views through a bean name. The ContentNegotiatingViewResolver has a little trick up its sleeve to resolve multiple views with the same name for different content types. It tries to resolve the view by name with the added prefix. So in our case, it will try to resolve either reservationSummary.xls or reservationSummary.pdf. We need to make sure that we have a BeanNameViewResolver in place and that we register both views with the proper name in the ApplicationContext.

This results in the configuration as seen in the next listing:

```java
package com.apress.spring6recipes.court.config;

import com.apress.spring6recipes.court.web.view.ExcelReservationSummary;
import com.apress.spring6recipes.court.web.view.PdfReservationSummary;
import org.springframework.context.annotation.Bean;
import org.springframework.context.annotation.Configuration;
import org.springframework.http.MediaType;
import org.springframework.web.servlet.config.annotation.ContentNegotiationConfigurer;
import org.springframework.web.servlet.config.annotation.ViewResolverRegistry;
import org.springframework.web.servlet.config.annotation.WebMvcConfigurer;
import org.springframework.web.servlet.view.BeanNameViewResolver;

@Configuration
public class ViewResolverConfiguration implements WebMvcConfigurer {

  public static final MediaType APPLICATION_EXCEL = MediaType.valueOf("application/vnd.
  ms-excel");

  @Override
  public void configureContentNegotiation(ContentNegotiationConfigurer configurer) {
    configurer.mediaType("html", MediaType.TEXT_HTML);
    configurer.mediaType("pdf", MediaType.APPLICATION_PDF);
    configurer.mediaType("xls", APPLICATION_EXCEL);
    configurer.favorPathExtension(true);
  }

  @Override
  public void configureViewResolvers(ViewResolverRegistry registry) {
    registry.enableContentNegotiation();
    registry.jsp("/WEB-INF/jsp/", ".jsp");
    registry.viewResolver(new BeanNameViewResolver());
  }
```

```
@Bean(name = "reservationSummary.pdf")
public PdfReservationSummary pdfReservationSummaryView() {
  return new PdfReservationSummary();
}

@Bean(name = "reservationSummary.xls")
public ExcelReservationSummary excelReservationSummaryView() {
  return new ExcelReservationSummary();
}
}
```

To request a PDF or XLS file, you have to pass the proper Accept header (application/pdf or application/vnd.ms-excel). However, with a browser without resorting to JavaScript, this is pretty hard to accomplish. With a tool like cURL or HTTPie, it is pretty easy. It is also an option to enable content negotiation based on the URL path, but it isn't recommended. To enable set the favorPathExtension property on the ContentNegotiationConfigurer to true:

```
$ http http://localhost:8080/court/reservationSummary.pdf date==2022-10-18
Accept:application/pdf
```

Now when requesting a PDF or XLS file, it will resolve to the proper view and render either the PDF or Excel document.

Creating Date-Based PDF and XLS Filenames

The browser should prompt the user with a question like "Save as reservationSummary.pdf?" or "Save as reservationSummary.xls?" This convention is based on the type of file a user is requesting a resource from. However, given that a user is also providing a date in the URL, a nice feature can be an automatic prompt in the form "Save as ReservationSummary_2022_10_24.xlsx?" or "Save as ReservationSummary_2022_10_14.pdf?" This can be done by applying an interceptor to rewrite the returning URL. The following listing illustrates this interceptor:

```
package com.apress.spring6recipes.court.web;

import jakarta.servlet.http.HttpServletRequest;
import jakarta.servlet.http.HttpServletResponse;

import org.springframework.web.servlet.HandlerInterceptor;
import org.springframework.web.servlet.ModelAndView;

public class ExtensionInterceptor implements HandlerInterceptor {

  public void postHandle(HttpServletRequest request, HttpServletResponse response,
                         Object handler, ModelAndView modelAndView) throws Exception {
    String reportName = null;
    var reportDate = request.getParameter("date").replace("-", "_");
    var path = request.getServletPath();
    if (path.endsWith(".pdf")) {
      reportName = "ReservationSummary_" + reportDate + ".pdf";
    } else if (path.endsWith(".xlsx")) {
      reportName = "ReservationSummary_" + reportDate + ".xlsx";
```

```
    }
    if (reportName != null) {
        response.setHeader("Content-Disposition", "attachment; filename=" + reportName);
    }
  }
}
```

The interceptor extracts the entire URL if it contains a .pdf or .xlsx extension. If it detects such an extension, it creates a value for the return filename in the form ReservationSummary_<report_date>.<.pdf|.xlsx>. To ensure a user receives a download prompt in this form, the HTTP header Content-Disposition is set with this filename format.

In order to deploy this interceptor and that it only is applied to the URL corresponding to the controller charged with generating PDF and XLS files, we advise you to look over Recipe 2-3, which contains this particular configuration and more details about interceptor classes.

CONTENT NEGOTIATION AND SETTING HTTP HEADERS IN AN INTERCEPTOR

Though this application uses the ContentNegotiatingViewResolver to select an appropriate view, the process of modifying a return URL is outside the scope of view resolvers. Therefore, it's necessary to use an interceptor to manually inspect a request extension, as well as set the necessary HTTP headers to modify the outgoing URL.

2-12. Asynchronous Request Handling with Controllers

Problem

To reduce the load on the servlet container, you want to asynchronously handle the request.

Solution

When a request comes in, it is handled synchronously, which blocks the HTTP request handling thread. You can use an async return type like Callable or DeferredResult to unblock that thread. The response stays open and is available to be written to. This is useful when a call, for instance, takes some time to finish, and instead of blocking threads, you can have this processed in the background and return a value to the user when finished.

How It Works

Writing an Asynchronous Controller

Writing a controller and having it handle the request asynchronously is as simple as changing the return type of the controller's handler method. Let's imagine that the call to ReserverationService.make takes quite some time, but we don't want to lock up the server for that:

```
package com.apress.spring6recipes.court.web;

import com.apress.spring6recipes.court.domain.Player;
import com.apress.spring6recipes.court.domain.Reservation;
import com.apress.spring6recipes.court.domain.SportType;
import com.apress.spring6recipes.court.service.ReservationService;
import com.apress.spring6recipes.utils.Utils;
import jakarta.validation.Valid;
import org.springframework.stereotype.Controller;
import org.springframework.ui.Model;
import org.springframework.validation.BindingResult;
import org.springframework.web.bind.annotation.GetMapping;
import org.springframework.web.bind.annotation.ModelAttribute;
import org.springframework.web.bind.annotation.PostMapping;
import org.springframework.web.bind.annotation.RequestMapping;
import org.springframework.web.bind.annotation.RequestParam;
import org.springframework.web.bind.annotation.SessionAttributes;
import org.springframework.web.bind.support.SessionStatus;

import java.time.Duration;
import java.util.List;
import java.util.concurrent.Callable;
import java.util.concurrent.ThreadLocalRandom;

@Controller
@RequestMapping("/reservationForm")
@SessionAttributes("reservation")
public class ReservationFormController {

    @PostMapping
    public Callable<String> submitForm(@ModelAttribute("reservation") @Valid
                                       Reservation reservation,
                                       BindingResult result, SessionStatus status) {
        return () -> {
            if (result.hasErrors()) {
                return "reservationForm";
            } else {
                // Simulate a slow service call
                Utils.sleep(Duration.ofMillis(ThreadLocalRandom.current().nextInt(1000)));
                reservationService.make(reservation);
                status.setComplete();
                return "redirect:reservationSuccess";
            }
        };
    }
}
```

If you look at the submitForm method, it now returns a Callable<String> instead of returning a String directly. Inside the newly constructed Callable<String>, there is a Thread.sleep() to simulate a delay before calling the make method.

Spring MVC supports various return types that will be handled in an asynchronous fashion:

- `java.util.concurrent.Callable`

- `org.springframework.web.context.request.async.DeferredResult;`

- `java.util.concurrent.CompletionStage` / `java.util.concurrent.CompletableFuture`

- `org.springframework.web.context.request.async.WebAsyncTask`

- Reactive types from Project Reactor, RxJava 3, SmallRye Mutiny, and Kotlin co-routines

Configuring Async Processing

To use the async processing features of Spring MVC, you first have to enable them. To do this you can call the `setAsyncSupported()` method when registering a filter or servlet.

When writing a `WebApplicationInitializer`, you have to do the following:

```
public class CourtWebApplicationInitializer implements WebApplicationInitializer {

  public void onStartup(ServletContext ctx) {
    var servlet = new DispatcherServlet();
    var registration = ctx.addServlet("dispatcher", servlet);
    registration.setAsyncSupported(true);
  }
}
```

ℹ️ When doing async processing, all the servlet filters and servlets in your app should have this property switched to `true`; else, it won't work!

Luckily, Spring helps us with this, and when using the `AbstractAnnotationConfigDispatcherServletInitializer` as a superclass, this property is switched to `true` by default for the registered `DispatcherServlet` and filters. To change it override the `isAsyncSupported()` and implement the logic to determine if it should be on or off.

Next, you also need to configure an `AsyncTaskExecutor` and wire that in the MVC configuration:

```
package com.apress.spring6recipes.court.config;

import org.springframework.context.annotation.Bean;
import org.springframework.context.annotation.Configuration;
import org.springframework.core.task.AsyncTaskExecutor;
import org.springframework.scheduling.concurrent.ThreadPoolTaskExecutor;
import org.springframework.web.servlet.config.annotation.AsyncSupportConfigurer;
import org.springframework.web.servlet.config.annotation.WebMvcConfigurer;

import java.time.Duration;
```

```
@Configuration
public class AsyncConfiguration implements WebMvcConfigurer {

  @Override
  public void configureAsyncSupport(AsyncSupportConfigurer configurer) {
    configurer.setDefaultTimeout(Duration.ofSeconds(5).toMillis());
    configurer.setTaskExecutor(mvcTaskExecutor());
  }

  @Bean
  public AsyncTaskExecutor mvcTaskExecutor() {
    var taskExecutor = new ThreadPoolTaskExecutor();
    taskExecutor.setThreadGroupName("mvcTaskExecutor");
    return taskExecutor;
  }
}
```

To configure async processing, you need to override the configureAsyncSupport method of the WebMvcConfigurationSupport. Overriding this method gives you access to the AsyncSupportConfigurer and allows you to set the defaultTimeout and the AsyncTaskExecutor to use. The timeout is set to 5 seconds, and as an executor you will use a ThreadPoolTaskExecutor (see also Recipe 1-23).

Now when making a reservation, you will see something similar in the logs:

```
2022-10-31 19:15:03.077 [http-nio-8080-exec-3] [DEBUG] WebAsyncManager - Started
async request
2022-10-31 19:15:03.079 [http-nio-8080-exec-3] [DEBUG] DispatcherServlet - Exiting but
response remains open for further handling
2022-10-31 19:15:03.970 [mvcTaskExecutor-1] [DEBUG] WebAsyncManager - Async result set,
dispatch to /court/reservationForm
2022-10-31 19:15:03.972 [http-nio-8080-exec-4] [DEBUG] DispatcherServlet - "ASYNC" dispatch
for POST "/court/reservationForm", parameters={masked}
2022-10-31 19:15:03.974 [http-nio-8080-exec-4] [DEBUG] RequestMappingHandlerAdapter - Resume
with async result ["redirect:reservationSuccess"]
```

You notice that a request is handled on a certain thread, and when that is released, then another thread is doing the processing and returning the result.

2-13. Summary

In this chapter, you have learned how to develop a Java web application using the Spring MVC framework. The central component of Spring MVC is DispatcherServlet, which acts as a front controller that dispatches requests to appropriate handlers for them to handle requests. In Spring MVC, controllers are standard Java classes that are decorated with the @Controller annotation. Throughout the various recipes, you learned how to leverage other annotations used in Spring MVC controllers, which included @RequestMapping to indicate access URLs, @Autowired to automatically inject bean references, and @SessionAttributes to maintain objects in a user's session, among many others. You also learned how to incorporate interceptors into an application, which allow you to alter request and response objects in a controller. In addition, you explored how Spring MVC supports form processing, including data validation using both Spring validators and the Jakarta Bean Validation API. You also explored how Spring MVC incorporates SpEL to facilitate certain configuration tasks and how Spring MVC supports different types of views for different presentation technologies. Finally, you learned how to utilize the Servlet Async API to handle requests.

CHAPTER 3

■ ■ ■

Spring MVC: REST Services

In this chapter, you will learn how Spring addresses Representational State Transfer, usually referred to by its acronym REST. REST has had an important impact on web applications since the term was coined by Roy Fielding in the year 2000.

Based on the foundations of the Web's protocol, Hypertext Transfer Protocol (HTTP), the architecture set forth by REST has become increasingly popular in the implementation of web services. Web services in and of themselves have become the cornerstone for much machine-to-machine communication taking place on the Web. It's the fragmented technology choices (e.g., Java, Python, Ruby, .NET) made by many organizations that have necessitated a solution capable of bridging the gaps between these disparate environments. How is information in an application backed by Java accessed by one written in Python? How can a Java application obtain information from an application written in .NET? Web services fill this void.

There are various approaches to implementing web services, but RESTful web services have become the most common choice in web applications. They are used by some of the largest Internet portals (e.g., Google and Yahoo) to provide access to their information, used to back access to Ajax calls made by browsers, in addition to providing the foundations for the distribution of information like news feeds (e.g., RSS).

In this chapter, you will learn how Spring applications can use REST, so you can both access and provide information using this popular approach.

3-1. Publishing XML with REST Services

Problem

You want to publish an XML-based REST service with Spring.

Solution

There are two possibilities when designing REST services in Spring. One involves publishing an application's data as a REST service; the other one involves accessing data from third-party REST services to be used in an application. This recipe describes how to publish an application's data as a REST service. Recipe 3-4 describes how to access data from third-party REST services. Publishing an application's data as a REST service revolves around the use of the Spring MVC annotations @RequestMapping and @PathVariable. By using these annotations to decorate a Spring MVC handler method, a Spring application is capable of publishing its data as a REST service.

In addition, Spring supports a series of mechanisms to generate a REST service's payload. This recipe will explore the simplest mechanism, which involves the use of Spring's MarshallingView class. As the recipes in this chapter progress, you will learn about more advanced mechanisms supported by Spring to generate REST service payloads.

© Marten Deinum, Daniel Rubio, Josh Long 2023
M. Deinum et al., *Spring 6 Recipes*, https://doi.org/10.1007/978-1-4842-8649-4_3

How It Works

Publishing a web application's data as a REST service, or as it's more technically known in web services parlance "creating an endpoint," is strongly tied to Spring MVC, which you explored in Chapter 4. Since Spring MVC relies on the annotation @RequestMapping to decorate handler methods and define access points (i.e., URLs), it's the preferred way in which to define a REST service's endpoint.

Using a MarshallingView to Produce XML

The following listing illustrates a Spring MVC controller class with a handler method that defines a REST service endpoint:

```
package com.apress.spring6recipes.court.web;

import com.apress.spring6recipes.court.domain.Members;
import com.apress.spring6recipes.court.service.MemberService;
import org.springframework.stereotype.Controller;
import org.springframework.ui.Model;
import org.springframework.web.bind.annotation.GetMapping;

@Controller
public class RestMemberController {

  private final MemberService memberService;

  public RestMemberController(MemberService memberService) {
    this.memberService = memberService;
  }

  @GetMapping("/members")
  public String getRestMembers(Model model) {
    var members = new Members();
    members.addMembers(memberService.findAll());
    model.addAttribute("members", members);
    return "membertemplate";
  }
}
```

By using @GetMapping("/members") to decorate a controller's handler method, a REST service endpoint is made accessible at http://[host_name]/[app-name]/members. You can observe that control is relinquished to a logical view named membertemplate. The following listing illustrates the declaration used to define the logical view named membertemplate:

```
package com.apress.spring6recipes.court.web.config;

import com.apress.spring6recipes.court.domain.Member;
import com.apress.spring6recipes.court.domain.Members;
import org.springframework.context.annotation.Bean;
import org.springframework.context.annotation.ComponentScan;
import org.springframework.context.annotation.Configuration;
import org.springframework.oxm.Marshaller;
```

```
import org.springframework.oxm.jaxb.Jaxb2Marshaller;
import org.springframework.web.servlet.config.annotation.EnableWebMvc;
import org.springframework.web.servlet.view.BeanNameViewResolver;
import org.springframework.web.servlet.view.xml.MarshallingView;

import java.util.Map;

import static jakarta.xml.bind.Marshaller.JAXB_FORMATTED_OUTPUT;

@Configuration
@EnableWebMvc
@ComponentScan(basePackages = "com.apress.spring6recipes.court")
public class CourtRestConfiguration {

  @Bean
  public MarshallingView membertemplate(Marshaller marshaller) {
    return new MarshallingView(marshaller);
  }

  @Bean
  public Jaxb2Marshaller jaxb2Marshaller() {
    var marshaller = new Jaxb2Marshaller();
    marshaller.setClassesToBeBound(Member.class, Members.class);
    marshaller.setMarshallerProperties(Map.of(JAXB_FORMATTED_OUTPUT, Boolean.TRUE));
    return marshaller;
  }

  @Bean
  public BeanNameViewResolver viewResolver() {
    return new BeanNameViewResolver();
  }
}
```

The membertemplate view is defined as a MarshallingView type, which is a general-purpose class that allows a response to be rendered using a marshaller. Marshalling is the process of transforming an in-memory representation of an object into a data format. Therefore, for this particular case, a marshaller is charged with transforming Members and Member objects into an XML data format. The marshaller used by MarshallingView belongs to one of a series of XML marshallers provided by Spring.

Marshallers themselves also require configuration. We opted to use the Jaxb2Marshaller due to its simplicity and Java Architecture for XML Binding (JAXB) foundations. However, if you're more comfortable using the XStream framework, you might find it easier to use the XStreamMarshaller.

The Jaxb2Marshaller requires to be configured with either a property named classesToBeBound or contextPath. In the case of classesToBeBound, the classes assigned to this property indicate the class (i.e., object) structure that is to be transformed into XML. The following listing illustrates the Member and Members classes assigned to the Jaxb2Marshaller:

```
package com.apress.spring6recipes.court.domain;

import jakarta.xml.bind.annotation.XmlRootElement;

@XmlRootElement
```

```java
public class Member {

  private String name;
  private String email;
  private String phone;

  public Member() {}

  public Member(String name, String phone, String email) {
    this.name=name;
    this.phone=phone;
    this.email=email;
  }

  public String getEmail() {
    return email;
  }

  public String getName() {
    return name;
  }

  public String getPhone() {
    return phone;
  }

  public void setEmail(String email) {
    this.email = email;
  }

  public void setName(String name) {
    this.name = name;
  }

  public void setPhone(String phone) {
    this.phone = phone;
  }
}
```

The Members class

```java
package com.apress.spring6recipes.court.domain;

import jakarta.xml.bind.annotation.XmlAccessType;
import jakarta.xml.bind.annotation.XmlAccessorType;
import jakarta.xml.bind.annotation.XmlElement;
import jakarta.xml.bind.annotation.XmlRootElement;

import java.util.ArrayList;
import java.util.List;
```

```
@XmlRootElement
@XmlAccessorType(XmlAccessType.FIELD)
public class Members {

  @XmlElement(name = "member")
  private List<Member> members = new ArrayList<>();

  public List<Member> getMembers() {
    return members;
  }

  public void setMembers(List<Member> members) {
    this.members = members;
  }

  public void addMembers(Iterable<Member> members) {
    members.forEach(member -> this.members.add(member));
  }
}
```

Note the Members class is a POJO decorated with the @XmlRootElement annotation. This annotation allows the Jaxb2Marshaller to detect a class's (i.e., object's) fields and transform them into XML data (e.g., name=John into <name>john</name>, email=john@doe.com into <email>john@doe.com</email>).

To recap what's been described, this means that when a request is made to a URL in the form http://[host_name]//app-name]/members, the corresponding handler is charged with creating a Members object, which is then passed to a logical view named membertemplate. Based on this last view's definition, a marshaller is used to convert a Members object into an XML payload that is returned to the REST service's requesting party. The XML payload returned by the REST service is illustrated in the following listing.

```
<?xml version="1.0" encoding="UTF-8" standalone="yes"?>
<members>
    <member>
        <email>marten@deinum.biz</email>
        <name>Marten Deinum</name>
        <phone>00-31-1234567890</phone>
    </member>
    <member>
        <email>john@doe.com</email>
        <name>John Doe</name>
        <phone>1-800-800-800</phone>
    </member>
    <member>
        <email>jane@doe.com</email>
        <name>Jane Doe</name>
        <phone>1-801-802-803</phone>
    </member>
</members>
```

This last XML payload represents a very simple approach to generating a REST service's response. As the recipes in this chapter progress, you will learn more sophisticated approaches, such as the ability to create widely used REST service payloads like RSS, Atom, and JSON.

Since REST service requests typically have HTTP headers in the form `Accept: application/xml`, Spring MVC configured to use content negotiation can determine to serve XML (REST) payloads to such requests even if requests are made extensionless. This also allows extensionless requests to be made in formats like HTML, PDF, and XLS, all simply based on HTTP headers.

Using @ResponseBody to Produce XML

Using a `MarshallingView` to produce XML is one way of producing results. However, when you want to have multiple representations (JSON, for instance) of the same data (a list of `Member` objects), adding another view can be a cumbersome task. Instead, we can rely on the Spring MVC `HttpMessageConverter` implementations to convert an object to the representation requested by the user. The following listing shows the changes made to the `RestMemberController`:

```
package com.apress.spring6recipes.court.web;

import com.apress.spring6recipes.court.domain.Members;
import com.apress.spring6recipes.court.service.MemberService;
import org.springframework.stereotype.Controller;
import org.springframework.web.bind.annotation.GetMapping;
import org.springframework.web.bind.annotation.ResponseBody;

@Controller
public class RestMemberController {

  private final MemberService memberService;

  public RestMemberController(MemberService memberService) {
    this.memberService = memberService;
  }

  @GetMapping("/members")
  @ResponseBody
  public Members getRestMembers() {
    var members = new Members();
    members.addMembers(memberService.findAll());
    return members;
  }
}
```

The first change is that we have now, additionally, annotated our controller method with @ResponseBody. This annotation tells Spring MVC that the result of the method should be used as the body of the response. As we want XML, this marshalling is done by the `Jaxb2RootElementHttpMessageConverter` provided by Spring. The second change is that, due to the @ResponseBody annotation, we don't need the view name anymore but can simply return the `Members` object.

Instead of annotating the method with @ResponseBody, you can also annotate your controller with @RestController instead of @Controller, which would give the same result. This is especially convenient if you have a single controller with multiple methods.

These changes also allow us to clean up our configuration, as we don't need the `MarshallingView` and `Jaxb2Marshaller` anymore:

```
package com.apress.spring6recipes.court.web.config;

import org.springframework.context.annotation.ComponentScan;
import org.springframework.context.annotation.Configuration;
import org.springframework.web.servlet.config.annotation.EnableWebMvc;

@Configuration
@EnableWebMvc
@ComponentScan(basePackages = "com.apress.spring6recipes.court")
public class CourtRestConfiguration { }
```

When the application is deployed and you do request the members from `http://localhost:8080/court/members`, it will yield the same results as before:

```
<?xml version="1.0" encoding="UTF-8" standalone="yes"?>
<members>
    <member>
        <email>marten@deinum.biz</email>
        <name>Marten Deinum</name>
        <phone>00-31-1234567890</phone>
    </member>
    <member>
        <email>john@doe.com</email>
        <name>John Doe</name>
        <phone>1-800-800-800</phone>
    </member>
    <member>
        <email>jane@doe.com</email>
        <name>Jane Doe</name>
        <phone>1-801-802-803</phone>
    </member>
</members>
```

Using @PathVariable to Limit the Results

It's common for REST service requests to have parameters. This is done to limit or filter a service's payload. For example, a request in the form `http://[host_name]/[app-name]/members/353/` can be used to retrieve information exclusively on member 353. Another variation can be a request like `http://[host_name]/[app-name]/reservations/07-07-2010/` to retrieve reservations made on the date 07-07-2010.

In order to use parameters for constructing a REST service in Spring, you use the `@PathVariable` annotation. The `@PathVariable` annotation is added as an input parameter to the handler method, per Spring's MVC conventions, in order for it to be used inside the handler method body. The following snippet illustrates a handler method for a REST service using the `@PathVariable` annotation:

```
@GetMapping("/members/{memberid}")
public Member getMember(@PathVariable("memberid") long memberID) {
  return memberService.findById(memberID).orElse(null);
}
```

Notice the @RequestMapping value contains {memberid}. Values surrounded by { } are used to indicate URL parameters are variables. Further, note the handler method is defined with the input parameter @PathVariable("memberid") long memberID. This last declaration associates whatever memberid value forms part of the URL and assigns it to a variable named memberID that can be accessible inside the handler method. Therefore, REST endpoints in the form /members/353/ and /members/777/ will be processed by this last handler method, with the memberID variable being assigned values of 353 and 777, respectively. Inside the handler method, the appropriate queries can be made for members 353 and 777—via the memberID variable—and returned as the REST service's payload.

A request to http://localhost:8080/court/members/2 will result in an XML representation of the member with ID 2:

```xml
<?xml version="1.0" encoding="UTF-8" standalone="yes"?>
<member>
  <email>john@doe.com</email>
  <name>John Doe</name>
  <phone>1-800-800-800</phone>
</member>
```

Using the ResponseEntity to Inform the Client

The endpoint for retrieval of a single Member instance either returns a valid member or nothing at all. Both lead to a request that will send an HTTP response code 200, which means OK, back to the client. However, this is probably not what our users will expect. When working with resources, we should inform them of the fact that a resource cannot be found. Ideally, we would want to return an HTTP response code 404, which indicates not found. The following code snippets show the modified getMember method:

```java
@GetMapping("/members/{memberid}")
public ResponseEntity<Member> getMember(@PathVariable("memberid") long memberID) {
  return memberService.findById(memberID)
          .map(ResponseEntity::ok)
          .orElseGet(() -> ResponseEntity.notFound().build());
}
```

The return value of the method has been changed to ResponseEntity<Member>. The ResponseEntity is a class in Spring MVC that acts as a wrapper for an object to be used as the body of the result together with an HTTP status code. When we find a Member, it is returned together with an HttpStatus.OK; the latter corresponds to an HTTP status code of 200. When there is no result, we return the HttpStatus.NOT_FOUND, corresponding to the HTTP status code 404, not found.

As this is a very common pattern to follow, there is an easier way to achieve this by using the ResponseEntity.of, which takes an Optional method, which already incorporates this pattern. This makes the code a little smaller and more readable:

```java
@GetMapping("/members/{memberid}")
public ResponseEntity<Member> getMember(@PathVariable("memberid") long memberID) {
  return ResponseEntity.of(memberService.findById(memberID));
}
```

3-2. Publishing JSON with REST Services

Problem

You want to publish a JSON (JavaScript Object Notation)–based REST service with Spring.

Solution

JSON has blossomed into a favorite payload format for REST services. However, unlike most REST service payloads, which rely on XML markup, JSON is different in the sense that its content is a special notation based on the JavaScript language. For this recipe, in addition to relying on Spring's REST support, we will also use the MappingJackson2JsonView class that forms part of Spring to facilitate the publication of JSON content.

ⓘ The MappingJackson2JsonView class depends on the presence of the Jackson JSON processor library, version 2.

Gradle dependencies for Jackson 2

```
implementation group:'com.fasterxml.jackson.core', name: 'jackson-databind', version:
'2.14.1'
```

Maven dependencies for Jackson 2

```
<dependency>
  <groupId>com.fasterxml.jackson.core</groupId>
  <artifactId>jackson-databind</artifactId>
  <version>2.14.1</version>
</dependency>
```

Example 1. Why Publish JSON?

It's very likely that you'll find yourself designing REST services that publish JSON as their payload. This is mainly due to the limited processing capabilities in browsers. Although browsers can process and extract information from REST services that publish XML payloads, it's not very efficient. By instead delivering payloads in JSON, which is based on a language for which browsers have a native interpreter—JavaScript—the processing and extraction of data become more efficient. Unlike RSS and Atom feeds, which are standards, JSON has no specific structure it needs to follow—except its syntax, which you'll explore shortly. Therefore, a JSON element's payload structure is likely to be determined in coordination with the team members charged with an application's design.

How It Works

The first thing you need to do is determine the information you wish to publish as a JSON payload. This information can be located in a RDBMS or text file, accessed through JDBC or object/relational mapping (ORM), inclusively being part of a Spring bean or some other type of construct. Describing how to obtain this information would go beyond the scope of this recipe, so we will assume you'll use whatever means you deem appropriate to access it. In case you're unfamiliar with JSON, the following snippet illustrates a fragment of this format:

```
{
  "members" : {
    "members" : [ {
      "name" : "Marten Deinum",
      "phone" : "00-31-1234567890",
      "email" : "marten@deinum.biz"
    }, {
      "name" : "John Doe",
      "phone" : "1-800-800-800",
      "email" : "john@doe.com"
    }, {
      "name" : "Jane Doe",
      "phone" : "1-801-802-803",
      "email" : "jane@doe.com"
    } ]
  }
}
```

As you can observe, a JSON payload consists of text and separators like {, }, [,], :, and ". We won't go into details about using one separator over another, but it suffices to say this type of syntax makes it easier for a JavaScript engine to access and manipulate data than if it was to process it in an XML-type format.

Using a MappingJackson2JsonView to Produce JSON

Since you've already explored how to publish data using a REST service in Recipe 3-1, we'll cut to the chase and show you the actual handler method needed in a Spring MVC controller to achieve this process:

```
@GetMapping("/members")
public String getRestMembersJson(Model model) {
  var members = new Members();
  members.addMembers(memberService.findAll());
  model.addAttribute("members", members);
  return "jsonmembertemplate";
}
```

You probably notice that it is quite similar to the controller method mentioned in Recipe 3-1. The only difference is that we return a different name for the view. The name of the view we are returning, jsonmembertemplate, is different and maps to a MappingJackson2JsonView. This view we need to configure in our configuration class:

```java
package com.apress.spring6recipes.court.web.config;

import org.springframework.context.annotation.Bean;
import org.springframework.context.annotation.ComponentScan;
import org.springframework.context.annotation.Configuration;
import org.springframework.web.servlet.config.annotation.EnableWebMvc;
import org.springframework.web.servlet.view.BeanNameViewResolver;
import org.springframework.web.servlet.view.json.MappingJackson2JsonView;

@Configuration
@EnableWebMvc
@ComponentScan(basePackages = "com.apress.spring6recipes.court")
public class CourtRestConfiguration {

  @Bean
  public MappingJackson2JsonView jsonmembertemplate() {
    var view = new MappingJackson2JsonView();
    view.setPrettyPrint(true);
    return view;
  }

  @Bean
  public BeanNameViewResolver viewResolver() {
    return new BeanNameViewResolver();
  }
}
```

The MappingJackson2JsonView uses the Jackson2 library to convert objects to and from JSON. It uses a Jackson ObjectMapper instance for the conversion. When a request is made to http://localhost:8080/court/members, the controller method will be invoked, and a JSON representation will be returned:

```json
{
  "members" : {
    "members" : [ {
      "name" : "Marten Deinum",
      "phone" : "00-31-1234567890",
      "email" : "marten@deinum.biz"
    }, {
      "name" : "John Doe",
      "phone" : "1-800-800-800",
      "email" : "john@doe.com"
    }, {
      "name" : "Jane Doe",
      "phone" : "1-801-802-803",
      "email" : "jane@doe.com"
    } ]
  }
}
```

Let's add the method and view from Recipe 3-1 to our controller:

```
package com.apress.spring6recipes.court.web;

import com.apress.spring6recipes.court.domain.Members;
import com.apress.spring6recipes.court.service.MemberService;
import org.springframework.http.MediaType;
import org.springframework.stereotype.Controller;
import org.springframework.ui.Model;
import org.springframework.web.bind.annotation.GetMapping;

@Controller
public class RestMemberController {

  private final MemberService memberService;

  public RestMemberController(MemberService memberService) {
    this.memberService = memberService;
  }

  @GetMapping(value = "/members", produces = MediaType.APPLICATION_XML_VALUE)
  public String getRestMembersXml(Model model) {
    prepareModel(model);
    return "xmlmembertemplate";
  }

  @GetMapping(value = "/members", produces = MediaType.APPLICATION_JSON_VALUE)
  public String getRestMembersJson(Model model) {
    prepareModel(model);
    return "jsonmembertemplate";
  }

  private void prepareModel(Model model) {
    var members = new Members();
    members.addMembers(memberService.findAll());
    model.addAttribute("members", members);
  }
}
```

We have now a getRestMembersXml and getRestMembersJson method; both are basically the same with the distinction that they return a different view name. Notice the produces attribute on the @GetMapping annotation; this is used to determine which method to call. /members with an accept header for XML will now produce XML, whereas /members with an accept header for JSON will produce JSON. However, this approach works duplicating all the methods for the different supported view types and isn't a feasible solution for enterprise applications.

Using @ResponseBody to Produce JSON

Using a MappingJackson2JsonView to produce JSON is one way of producing results. However, as mentioned in the previous section, this can be troublesome, especially with multiple supported view types. Instead, we can rely on the Spring MVC HttpMessageConverter implementations to convert an object to the representation requested by the user. The following listing shows the changes made to the RestMemberController:

```
@Controller
public class RestMemberController {

  @GetMapping("/members")
  @ResponseBody
  public Members getRestMembers() {
    var members = new Members();
    members.addMembers(memberService.findAll());
    return members;
  }
}
```

The first change is that we have now, additionally, annotated our controller method with @ResponseBody. This annotation tells Spring MVC that the result of the method should be used as the body of the response. As we want JSON, this marshalling is done by the MappingJackson2HttpMessageConverter provided by Spring. The second change is that, due to the @ResponseBody annotation, we don't need the view name anymore but can simply return the Members object.

💡 Instead of annotating the method with @ResponseBody, you can also annotate your controller with @RestController instead of @Controller, which would give the same result. This is especially convenient if you have a single controller with multiple methods.

These changes also allow us to clean up our configuration, as we don't need the MappingJackson2JsonView anymore:

```
package com.apress.spring6recipes.court.web.config;

import org.springframework.context.annotation.ComponentScan;
import org.springframework.context.annotation.Configuration;
import org.springframework.web.servlet.config.annotation.EnableWebMvc;


@Configuration
@EnableWebMvc
@ComponentScan(basePackages = "com.apress.spring6recipes.court")
public class CourtRestConfiguration { }
```

When the application is deployed and you do request the members from http://localhost:8080/court/members with the Accept header for JSON (application/json), it will give the same results as before:

```
{
  "members" : {
    "members" : [ {
      "name" : "Marten Deinum",
      "phone" : "00-31-1234567890",
      "email" : "marten@deinum.biz"
```

```
  }, {
    "name" : "John Doe",
    "phone" : "1-800-800-800",
    "email" : "john@doe.com"
  }, {
    "name" : "Jane Doe",
    "phone" : "1-801-802-803",
    "email" : "jane@doe.com"
  } ]
  }
}
```

You probably noticed that the RestMemberController and CourtRestConfiguration are now exactly the same as those in Recipe 3-1. When calling http://localhost:8080/court/members and the Accept header is for XML (application/xml), you will get XML.

How is this possible without any additional configuration? Spring MVC will detect what is in the classpath; it automatically detects JAXB2, Jackson/GSON, and Rome (see Recipe 3-4). It will register the appropriate HttpMessageConverter for the available technologies.

Using GSON to Produce JSON

Up until now you have been using Jackson to produce JSON from our objects. Another popular library is GSON, and Spring has out-of-the-box support for it. To use GSON you will need to add it to your classpath (instead of Jackson), and then it will be used to produce the JSON.

Add the following dependency.

Gradle dependency for GSON

```
implementation  group: 'com.google.code.gson', name: 'gson', version: '2.10'
```

Maven dependency for GSON

```
<dependency>
    <groupId>com.google.code.gson</groupId>
    <artifactId>gson</artifactId>
    <version>2.10</version>
</dependency>
```

This, just like using Jackson, is all you need to have JSON serialization with GSON. If you start the application and call http://localhost:8080/court/members, you will still receive JSON but now instead through GSON.

3-3. Receiving Payloads with a REST Controller

Problem

You want to receive JSON, XML, or another type of supported payload in your controller to add new records to your system.

Solution

Receiving an HTTP payload in your controller is accomplished by annotating one of the parameters with @RequestBody. The @RequestBody annotation instructs Spring to deserialize the incoming HTTP payload onto the type that has been annotated. Generally, the argument you annotate is the type you want to store in your system. Next to only receiving the payload, it could also be validated by adding the @Valid annotation next to @ResponseBody. More on validation can be found in Recipe 2-10.

How It Works

Generally, when receiving a payload, this is in a method that can handle a POST request, hence a method annotated with @PostMapping. This method then receives an object, here a Member, to be added to the database. As this is a Member, we can use the same snippets of XML or JSON, when receiving a single Member, to add it.

Receive and Handle the Request with @RequestBody

Example JSON for the POST request

```
{
  "name" : "Nick Fury",
  "phone" : "secret",
  "email" : "nick.fury@shield.org"
}
```

Example XML for the POST request

```
<?xml version="1.0" encoding="UTF-8" standalone="yes"?>
<member>
  <name>Nick Fury</name>
  <phone>secret</phone>
  <email>nick.fury@shield.org</email>
</member>
```

Now that the data structure is known, the controller can be modified to receive it:

```
@PostMapping
public ResponseEntity<Member> newMember(@RequestBody Member newMember) {
  return ResponseEntity.ok(memberService.save(newMember));
}
```

The newMember method has been added to the controller. It is tied to the POST request through the @PostMapping annotation. Notice that the Member parameter is annotated with @RequestBody; this will deserialize the body into the object. Finally, a response is returned with the newly created entity.

Validating the Request Payload

Spring has a validation abstraction that can be used to automatically validate the incoming request. Although you could write your own implementation of a Spring validator, the most common use case is to use the Jakarta Bean Validation API (see also Recipe 2-10). To enable validation support, first, you need to add a Jakarta Bean Validation provider, like hibernate-validator. Next to the @RequestBody annotation, add an additional jakarta.validation.@Valid on the method argument:

```
@PostMapping
public ResponseEntity<Member> newMember(@Valid @RequestBody Member newMember) {
  return ResponseEntity.ok(memberService.save(newMember));
}
```

In this code notice the addition of the @Valid annotation on the method argument. This instructs Spring MVC to apply validation to the Member object. Now let's add some validations to the Member object. The name and email fields are required; for this we can use the @NotBlank annotation. The email field needs to be a valid email address as well, so additionally we add @Email to validate this.

ⓘ To validate content in a text-based field, you can use @NotNull, @NotEmpty, and @NotBlank, but which to use? The @NotNull will only check if the field is not null, the @NotEmpty will check if the field is not null and not an empty string, and the @NotBlank will check not null and not a string containing only spaces/ control characters. Which to use depends on your needs. Here we use @NotBlank as a name with only blank spaces isn't really a name.

Member with validation annotations

```
package com.apress.spring6recipes.court.domain;

import jakarta.validation.constraints.Email;
import jakarta.validation.constraints.NotBlank;
import jakarta.xml.bind.annotation.XmlRootElement;

@XmlRootElement
public class Member {

  @NotBlank
  private String name;
  @NotBlank
  @Email
  private String email;
  private String phone;
}
```

Now when sending a request without a name or email or with an invalid email, the request won't be handled, and instead an HTTP status of 400 (bad request) is returned.

Error Handling with Spring MVC

The default error handlers registered by Spring MVC are the ExceptionHandlerExceptionResolver and the ResponseStatusExceptionResolver. The ExceptionHandlerExceptionResolver will try to find a method annotated with @ExceptionHandler, which can handle the thrown exception, whereas the ResponseStatusExceptionResolver will use the @ResponseStatus annotation (if present) on the thrown Exception to determine the response code.

In our case the ResponseStatusExceptionResolver is resolving the error because there is no @ExceptionHandler method capable of handling the thrown Exception. Let's improve our error handling by adding such a method. Let's return a better response indicating what is wrong with the request.

For this let's add an @ExceptionHandler method to the RestMemberController that is capable of handling the MethodArgumentNotValidException. The MethodArgumentNotValidException is the exception that is being thrown when the validation process has validation errors. The exception itself contains the error messages and a bit more information:

```
@ExceptionHandler
@ResponseStatus(HttpStatus.BAD_REQUEST)
public Map<String, String> handle(MethodArgumentNotValidException ex) {
  return ex.getFieldErrors().stream()
    .collect(
        Collectors.toMap(FieldError::getField,
                         FieldError::getDefaultMessage));
}
```

The method takes the MethodArgumentNotValidException and converts the field errors (which contain the errors from the validation) to a Map consisting of the field and the error message. There is also the @ResponseStatus annotation to indicate which status to return; in this case we stick with the HTTP 400 error code.

When writing an @ExceptionHandler method, it can receive many different types of objects. One is the thrown exception, but one can include much of what is supported for request handling methods as well. See Table 3-1 for the most used attributes that are supported.

Table 3-1. Most Used Method Arguments for @ExceptionHandler Methods

Method Argument	Description
Exception type	The Exception that will be handled
jakarta.servlet.ServletRequest jakarta.servlet.ServletResponse	Get access to the request and/or response
jakarta.servlet.http.HttpSession	The HTTP session if any
java.security.Principal	The current principal, a.k.a. the currently authenticated user
java.util.Map org.springframework.ui.Model org.springframework.ui.ModelMap	The model for the error response, always empty. Can be used to add data to the response

These are the most commonly used method arguments for exception handling methods.

The modified method will now handle the erroneous situation and return a nicer result (see Figure 3-1).

```
HTTP/1.1 400
Connection: close
Content-Type: application/json
Date: Fri, 25 Nov 2022 10:01:09 GMT
Transfer-Encoding: chunked

{
    "email": "must be a well-formed email address",
    "name": "must not be blank"
}
```

Figure 3-1. Error result

Error Handling with Spring MVC Using RFC-7807

As JSON has become the de facto standard of communicating on the Web, there is now also a (at the moment still proposed) standard for returning error responses to the client. This is RFC-7807, which might be better known as the Problem Details API for HTTP. This standard describes a response in which one can tell what is wrong with the incoming request or what happened on the server.

The response consists of a couple of fields that contain the information; all fields are optional. There is also room to extend this response with additional fields and information.

Field	Type	Description
type	String	A URI that represents the error, generally a link describing the status code
title	String	A short readable explanation of what's wrong
status	Numeric	The HTTP status code
detail	String	A readable explanation of the problem
instance	String	A URI reference to the actual instance causing the issue, generally the called URL

Next to these fields, one can have their own extensions to this.

Spring has support for this standard, but it isn't enabled by default. The support comes in the form of a dedicated exception handler that can be extended.

Let's rewrite our exception handling code from the previous section to use this standard approach. For this we can extend the org.springframework.web.servlet.mvc.method.annotation. ResponseEntityExceptionHandler class and override the handleMethodArgumentNotValid method to add our own customizations:

```
package com.apress.spring6recipes.court.web;

import org.springframework.context.i18n.LocaleContextHolder;
import org.springframework.http.HttpHeaders;
import org.springframework.http.HttpStatusCode;
import org.springframework.http.ResponseEntity;
import org.springframework.validation.FieldError;
```

```java
import org.springframework.validation.ObjectError;
import org.springframework.web.bind.MethodArgumentNotValidException;
import org.springframework.web.bind.annotation.ControllerAdvice;
import org.springframework.web.context.request.WebRequest;
import org.springframework.web.servlet.mvc.method.annotation.ResponseEntityExceptionHandler;

import java.util.stream.Collectors;

@ControllerAdvice
public class CourtExceptionHandlers extends ResponseEntityExceptionHandler {

  @Override
  protected ResponseEntity<Object> handleMethodArgumentNotValid(MethodArgumentNotValidExce
  ption ex,

                                                    HttpHeaders headers,
                                                    HttpStatusCode status,
                                                    WebRequest request) {
    var errors = ex.getAllErrors().stream()
            .collect(Collectors.toMap(this::getKey, this::resolveMessage));
    ex.getBody().setProperty("errors", errors);
    return super.handleExceptionInternal(ex, null, headers, status, request);
  }

  private String getKey(ObjectError error) {
    return (error instanceof FieldError fe) ? fe.getCode() : error.getObjectName();
  }

  private String resolveMessage(ObjectError error) {
    return getMessageSource() != null
        ? getMessageSource().getMessage(error, LocaleContextHolder.getLocale())
        : error.getDefaultMessage();
  }
}
```

The CourtExceptionHandlers class is itself annotated with @ControllerAdvice. Classes with @ControllerAdvice contain logic that applies to all controllers and are an ideal place for exception handling code. The class also extends the ResponseEntityExceptionHandler, and we override the handleMethodArgumentNotValid method.

We use the createProblemDetail helper method from the base class to create the initial ProblemDetail object. The map of errors created earlier still gets created and added as a property to the ProblemDetail object. Finally, we use another helper method to create the ResponseEntity with the ProblemDetail object. With this in place, the error handling will now return a RFC-7807-compliant result (see Figure 3-2).

```
HTTP/1.1 400
Connection: close
Content-Type: application/json
Date: Fri, 25 Nov 2022 10:45:45 GMT
Transfer-Encoding: chunked

{
    "detail": "Validation errors",
    "errors": {
        "email": "must be a well-formed email address",
        "name": "must not be blank"
    },
    "instance": "/court/members",
    "status": 400,
    "title": "Bad Request",
    "type": "about:blank"
}
```

Figure 3-2. *Problem Details error response*

3-4. Accessing a REST Service with Spring

Problem

You want to access a REST service from a third party (e.g., Google, Yahoo, another business partner) and use its payload inside a Spring application.

Solution

Accessing a third-party REST service inside a Spring application revolves around the use of the Spring RestTemplate class. The RestTemplate class is designed on the same principles as the many other Spring *Template classes (e.g., JdbcTemplate, JmsTemplate), providing a simplified approach with default behaviors for performing lengthy tasks. This means the processes of invoking a REST service and using its returning payload are streamlined in Spring applications.

How It Works

Before describing the particularities of the RestTemplate class, it's worth exploring the life cycle of a REST service, so you're aware of the actual work the RestTemplate class performs. Exploring the life cycle of a REST service can best be done from a browser, so open your favorite browser on your workstation to get started. The first thing that's needed is a REST service endpoint. We are going to reuse the endpoint we created in Recipe 3-2. This endpoint should be available at http://localhost:8080/court/members.xml (or .json). If you load this last REST service endpoint on your browser, the browser performs a GET request, which is one of the most popular HTTP requests supported by REST services. Upon loading the REST service, the browser displays a responding payload like the following:

```xml
<?xml version="1.0" encoding="UTF-8" standalone="yes"?>
<members>
    <member>
        <email>marten@deinum.biz</email>
        <name>Marten Deinum</name>
        <phone>00-31-1234567890</phone>
    </member>
    <member>
        <email>john@doe.com</email>
        <name>John Doe</name>
        <phone>1-800-800-800</phone>
    </member>
    <member>
        <email>jane@doe.com</email>
        <name>Jane Doe</name>
        <phone>1-801-802-803</phone>
    </member>
</members>
```

This last payload represents a well-formed XML fragment, which is in line with most REST service responses. The actual meaning of the payload is highly dependent on a REST service. In this case, the XML tags (<members>, <member>, etc.) are definitions set forth by ourselves, while the character data enclosed in each XML tag represents information related to a REST service's request.

It's the task of a REST service consumer (i.e., you) to know the payload structure—sometimes referred to as vocabulary—of a REST service to appropriately process its information. Though this last REST service relies on what can be considered a custom vocabulary, a series of REST services often rely on standardized vocabularies (e.g., RSS), which make the processing of REST service payloads uniform. In addition, it's also worth noting that some REST services provide Web Application Description Language (WADL) contracts to facilitate the discovery and consumption of payloads.

Now that you're familiar with a REST service's life cycle using your browser, we can take a look at how to use the Spring RestTemplate class in order to incorporate a REST service's payload into a Spring application. Given that the RestTemplate class is designed to call REST services, it should come as no surprise that its main methods are closely tied to REST's underpinnings, which are the HTTP's methods: HEAD, GET, POST, PUT, DELETE, and OPTIONS. Table 3-2 contains the main methods supported by the RestTemplate class.

Table 3-2. *RestTemplate class methods based on HTTP's request methods*

Method	Description
headForHeaders	Performs an HTTP HEAD operation
getForObject	Performs an HTTP GET operation and returns the result as a type of the given class
getForEntity	Performs an HTTP GET operation and returns a ResponseEntity
patchForObject	Performs an HTTP PATCH operation and returns the result as a type of the given class
postForLocation	Performs an HTTP POST operation and returns the value of the location header
postForObject	Performs an HTTP POST operation and returns the result as a type of the given class
postForEntity	Performs an HTTP POST operation and returns a ResponseEntity
put	Performs an HTTP PUT operation
delete	Performs an HTTP DELETE operation
optionsForAllow	Performs an HTTP OPTIONS operation
execute	Can perform any HTTP operation with the exception of CONNECT

As you can observe in Table 3-2, the RestTemplate class methods are prefixed with a series of HTTP methods that include HEAD, GET, POST, PUT, DELETE, and OPTIONS. In addition, the execute method serves as a general-purpose method that can perform any HTTP operation, including the more esoteric HTTP TRACE method, albeit not the CONNECT method, which is not supported by the underlying HttpMethod enum used by the execute method.

> ℹ By far the most common HTTP method used in REST services is GET, since it represents a safe operation to obtain information (i.e., it doesn't modify any data). On the other hand, HTTP methods such as PUT, POST, and DELETE are designed to modify a provider's information, which makes them less likely to be supported by a REST service provider. For cases in which data modification needs to take place, many providers opt for SOAP, which is an alternative mechanism to using REST services.

Now that you're aware of the RestTemplate class methods, we can move on to invoking the same REST service you did with your browser previously, except this time using Java code from the Spring Framework. The following listing illustrates a class that accesses the REST service and returns its contents to the System.out:

```
package com.apress.spring6recipes.court;

import org.springframework.web.client.RestTemplate;

public class Main {

  public static void main(String[] args) {
    var uri = "http://localhost:8080/court/members";
    var restTemplate = new RestTemplate();
```

```
    var result = restTemplate.getForObject(uri, String.class);
    System.out.println(result);
  }
}
```

🔥 Some REST service providers restrict access to their data feeds depending on the requesting party. Access is generally denied by relying on data present in a request (e.g., HTTP headers or IP address). So depending on the circumstances, a provider can return an access denied response even when a data feed appears to be working in another medium (e.g., you might be able to access a REST service in a browser but get an access denied response when attempting to access the same feed from a Spring application). This depends on the terms of use set forth by a REST provider.

The first line declares the import statement needed to access the RestTemplate class within a class's body. First, we need to create an instance of the RestTemplate. Next, you can find a call made to the getForObject method that belongs to the RestTemplate class, which as described in Table 3-2 is used to perform an HTTP GET operation—just like the one performed by a browser to obtain a REST service's payload. There are two important aspects related to this last method, its response and its parameters.

The response of calling the getForObject method is assigned to a String object. This means the same output you saw on your browser for this REST service (i.e., the XML structure) is assigned to a string. Even if you've never processed XML in Java, you're likely aware that extracting and manipulating data as a Java string is not an easy task. In other words, there are classes better suited for processing XML data, and with it a REST service's payload, than a String object. For the moment just keep this in mind; other recipes in the chapter illustrate how to better extract and manipulate the data obtained from a REST service.

The parameters passed to the getForObject method consist of the actual REST service endpoint. The first parameter corresponds to the URL (i.e., endpoint) declaration. Notice the URL is identical to the one used when you relied on a browser to call it.

When executed the output will be the same as in the browser except that it is now printed in the console.

Retrieving Data from a Parameterized URL

The previous section showed how we can call a URI to retrieve data, but what about a URI that requires parameters? We don't want to hard-code parameters into the URL. With the RestTemplate we can use a URL with placeholders; these placeholders will be replaced with actual values upon execution. Placeholders are defined using { and }, just as with a request mapping (see Recipes 3-1 and 3-2).

The URI http://localhost:8080/court/members/{memberId} is an example of such a parameterized URI. To be able to call this method, we need to pass in a value for the placeholder. We can do this by using a Map and pass that as the third parameter to the getForObject method of the RestTemplate:

```
package com.apress.spring6recipes.court;

import org.springframework.web.client.RestTemplate;

import java.util.Map;
```

```
public class Main {

  public static void main(String[] args) {
    var uri = "http://localhost:8080/court/members/{memberId}";
    var params = Map.of("memberId", "1");
    var restTemplate = new RestTemplate();
    var result = restTemplate.getForObject(uri, String.class, params);
    System.out.println(result);
  }
}
```

This last snippet makes use of the Map class creating an instance with the corresponding REST service parameters, which is later passed to the getForObject method of the RestTemplate class. The results obtained by passing either a series of String parameters or a single Map parameter to the various RestTemplate methods is identical.

Retrieving Data as a Mapped Object

Instead of returning a string to be used in our application, we can also (re)use our Members and Member classes to map the result. Instead of passing in String.class as the second parameter, pass Members.class, and the response will be mapped onto this class:

```
package com.apress.spring6recipes.court;

import com.apress.spring6recipes.court.domain.Members;
import org.springframework.web.client.RestTemplate;

public class Main {

  public static void main(String[] args) {
    var uri = "http://localhost:8080/court/members";
    var restTemplate = new RestTemplate();
    var result = restTemplate.getForObject(uri, Members.class);
    System.out.println(result);
  }
}
```

The RestTemplate makes use of the same HttpMessageConverter infrastructure as a controller with @ResponseBody-marked methods. As JAXB2 (as well as Jackson) is automatically detected, mapping to a JAXB mapped object is quite easy.

3-5. Publishing RSS and Atom Feeds

Problem

You want to publish an RSS or Atom feed in a Spring application.

Solution

RSS and Atom feeds have become a popular means by which to publish information. Access to these types of feeds is provided by means of a REST service, which means building a REST service is a prerequisite to publishing RSS and Atom feeds. In addition to relying on Spring's REST support, it's also convenient to rely on a third-party library especially designed to deal with the particularities of RSS and Atom feeds. This makes it easier for a REST service to publish this type of XML payload. For this last purpose, we will use Project Rome.

Even though RSS and Atom feeds are often categorized as news feeds, they have surpassed this initial usage scenario of providing just news. Nowadays, RSS and Atom feeds are used to publish information related to blogs, weather, travel, and many other things in a cross-platform manner (i.e., using XML). Hence, if you require publishing information of any sort that's to be accessible in a cross-platform manner, doing so as RSS or Atom feeds can be an excellent choice given their wide adoption (e.g., many applications support them, and many developers know their structure).

How It Works

The first thing you need to do is determine the information you wish to publish as an RSS or Atom news feed. This information can be located in a RDBMS or text file, accessed through JDBC or ORM, inclusively being part of a Spring bean or some other type of construct. Describing how to obtain this information would go beyond the scope of this recipe, so we will assume you'll use whatever means you deem appropriate to access it. Once you've pinpointed the information you wish to publish, it's necessary to structure it as either an RSS or Atom feed, which is where Project Rome comes into the picture.

In case you're unfamiliar with an Atom feed's structure, the following snippet illustrates a fragment of this format:

```
<?xml version="1.0" encoding="utf-8"?>
<feed xmlns="http://www.w3.org/2005/Atom">
  <title>Example Feed</title>
  <link href="http://example.org/"/>
  <updated>2010-08-31T18:30:02Z</updated>
  <Author>
    <name>John Doe</name>
  </author>
  <id>urn:uuid:60a76c80-d399-11d9-b93C-0003939e0af6</id>
  <entry>
    <title>Atom-Powered Robots Run Amok</title>
    <link href="http://example.org/2010/08/31/atom03"/>
    <id>urn:uuid:1225c695-cfb8-4ebb-aaaa-80da344efa6a</id>
    <updated>2010-08-31T18:30:02Z</updated>
    <summary>Some text.</summary>
  </entry>
</feed>
```

The following snippet illustrates a fragment of an RSS feed's structure:

```xml
<?xml version="1.0" encoding="utf-8"?>
<rss version="2.0">
  <channel>
    <title>RSS Example</title>
    <description>This is an example of an RSS feed</description>
    <link>http://www.example.org/link.htm</link>
    <lastBuildDate>Mon, 28 Aug 2006 11:12:55 -0400 </lastBuildDate>
    <pubDate>Tue, 31 Aug 2010 09:00:00 -0400</pubDate>
    <item>
      <title>Item Example</title>
      <description>This is an example of an Item</description>
      <link>http://www.example.org/link.htm</link>
      <guid isPermaLink="false"> 1102345</guid>
      <pubDate>Tue, 31 Aug 2010 09:00:00 -0400</pubDate>
    </item>
  </channel>
</rss>
```

As you can observe from these last two snippets, RSS and Atom feeds are just XML payloads that rely on a series of elements to publish information. Though going into the finer details of either an RSS or Atom feed structure would require a book in itself, both formats possess a series of common characteristics; chief among them are these:

- They have a metadata section to describe the contents of a feed (e.g., the `<Author>` and `<title>` elements for the Atom format and the `<description>` and `<pubDate>` elements for the RSS format).

- They have recurring elements to describe information (e.g., the `<entry>` element for the Atom feed format and the `<item>` element for the RSS feed format). In addition, each recurring element also has its own set of elements with which to further describe information.

- They have multiple versions. RSS versions include 0.90, 0.91 Netscape, 0.91 Userland, 0.92, 0.93, 0.94, 1.0, and 2.0. Atom versions include 0.3 and 1.0. Project Rome allows you to create a feed's metadata section, recurring elements, as well as any of the previously mentioned versions, from information available in Java code (e.g., `String`, `Map`, or other such constructs).

To be able to use the Rome classes, you need to add the dependencies to your classpath.

Gradle dependency for Project Rome

```
implementation group: 'com.rometools', name: 'rome', version: '1.18.0'
```

Maven dependency for Project ROme

```xml
<dependency>
  <groupId>com.rometools</groupId>
  <artifactId>rome</artifactId>
  <version>1.18.0</version>
</dependency>
```

Now that you're aware of the structure of an RSS or Atom feed, as well as the role Project Rome plays in this recipe, let's take a look at a Spring MVC controller charged with presenting a feed to an end user:

```
package com.apress.spring6recipes.court.web;

import com.apress.spring6recipes.court.feeds.TournamentContent;
import org.springframework.stereotype.Controller;
import org.springframework.ui.Model;
import org.springframework.web.bind.annotation.GetMapping;

import java.time.LocalDate;
import java.util.List;

@Controller
public class FeedController {

    @GetMapping("/atomfeed")
    public String getAtomFeed(Model model) {
        var date = LocalDate.now();
        var tournaments = List.of(
            TournamentContent.of("ATP", date, "Australian Open", "www.australianopen.com"),
            TournamentContent.of("ATP", date, "Roland Garros", "www.rolandgarros.com"),
            TournamentContent.of("ATP", date, "Wimbledon", "www.wimbledon.org"),
            TournamentContent.of("ATP", date, "US Open", "www.usopen.org"));
        model.addAttribute("feedContent", tournaments);
        return "atomfeedtemplate";
    }

    @GetMapping("/rssfeed")
    public String getRSSFeed(Model model) {
        prepareModel(model);
        return "rssfeedtemplate";
    }

    private void prepareModel(Model model) {
        var date = LocalDate.now();
        var tournaments = List.of(
            TournamentContent.of("FIFA", date, "World Cup", "www.fifa.com/worldcup/"),
            TournamentContent.of("FIFA", date, "U-20 World Cup", "www.fifa.com/u20worldcup/"),
            TournamentContent.of("FIFA", date, "U-17 World Cup", "www.fifa.com/u17worldcup/"),
            TournamentContent.of("FIFA", date, "Confederations Cup", "www.fifa.com/
            confederationscup/"));
        model.addAttribute("feedContent", tournaments);
    }
}
```

This last Spring MVC controller has two handler methods: one called getAtomFeed(), which is mapped to a URL in the form http://[host_name]/[app-name]/atomfeed, and another called getRSSFeed(), which is mapped to a URL in the form http://[host_name]/[app-name]/rssfeed.

Each handler method defines a List of TournamentContent objects, where the backing class for a TournamentContent object is a POJO. This List is then assigned to the handler method's model object in order for it to become accessible to the returning view. The returning logical views for each handler method are atomfeedtemplate and rssfeedtemplate, respectively. These logical views are defined in the following manner inside a Spring configuration class:

```
package com.apress.spring6recipes.court.web.config;

import com.apress.spring6recipes.court.feeds.AtomFeedView;
import com.apress.spring6recipes.court.feeds.RSSFeedView;
import org.springframework.context.annotation.Bean;
import org.springframework.context.annotation.ComponentScan;
import org.springframework.context.annotation.Configuration;
import org.springframework.web.servlet.config.annotation.EnableWebMvc;
import org.springframework.web.servlet.view.BeanNameViewResolver;

@Configuration
@EnableWebMvc
@ComponentScan(basePackages = "com.apress.spring6recipes.court")
public class CourtRestConfiguration {

  @Bean
  public AtomFeedView atomfeedtemplate() {
    return new AtomFeedView();
  }

  @Bean
  public RSSFeedView rssfeedtemplate() {
    return new RSSFeedView();
  }
}
```

As you can observe, each logical view is mapped to a class. Each of these classes is charged with implementing the necessary logic to build either an Atom or RSS view. If you recall from Chapter 2, you used an identical approach (i.e., using classes) for implementing PDF and Excel views.

In the case of Atom and RSS views, Spring comes equipped with two classes specially equipped and built on the foundations of Project Rome. These classes are AbstractAtomFeedView and AbstractRssFeedView. Such classes provide the foundations to build an Atom or RSS feed, without dealing with the finer details of each of these formats.

The following listing illustrates the AtomFeedView class, which implements the AbstractAtomFeedView class and is used to back the atomfeedtemplate logical view:

```
package com.apress.spring6recipes.court.feeds;

import com.rometools.rome.feed.atom.Content;
import com.rometools.rome.feed.atom.Entry;
import com.rometools.rome.feed.atom.Feed;
import jakarta.servlet.http.HttpServletRequest;
import jakarta.servlet.http.HttpServletResponse;
import org.springframework.web.servlet.view.feed.AbstractAtomFeedView;
```

```java
import java.time.LocalDate;
import java.time.ZoneId;
import java.time.format.DateTimeFormatter;
import java.util.Date;
import java.util.List;
import java.util.Map;
import java.util.stream.Collectors;

public class AtomFeedView extends AbstractAtomFeedView {

  @Override
  protected void buildFeedMetadata(Map<String, Object> model, Feed feed,
                                   HttpServletRequest request) {
    feed.setId("tag:tennis.org");
    feed.setTitle("Grand Slam Tournaments");

    @SuppressWarnings({ "unchecked" })
    var tournaments = (List<TournamentContent>) model.get("feedContent");

    var updated = tournaments.stream()
            .map(TournamentContent::publicationDate).sorted().findFirst()
            .map(this::toDate).orElse(null);
    feed.setUpdated(updated);
  }

  @Override
  protected List<Entry> buildFeedEntries(Map<String, Object> model,
                                         HttpServletRequest request,
                                         HttpServletResponse response) {
    @SuppressWarnings({ "unchecked" })
    var tournaments = (List<TournamentContent>) model.get("feedContent");
    return tournaments.stream().map(this::toEntry).collect(Collectors.toList());
  }

  private Entry toEntry(TournamentContent tc) {
    var summary = new Content();
    summary.setValue(String.format("%s - %s", tc.name(), tc.link()));

    var entry = new Entry();
    var date = DateTimeFormatter.ISO_DATE.format(tc.publicationDate());
    entry.setId(String.format("tag:tennis.org,%s:%d", date, tc.id()));
    entry.setTitle(String.format("%s - Posted by %s", tc.name(), tc.author()));
    entry.setUpdated(toDate(tc.publicationDate()));
    entry.setSummary(summary);
    return entry;
  }

  private Date toDate(LocalDate in) {
    return Date.from(in.atStartOfDay(ZoneId.systemDefault()).toInstant());
  }
}
```

The first thing to notice about this class is that it imports several Project Rome classes from the com.sun. syndication.feed.atom package, in addition to implementing the AbstractAtomFeedView class provided by the Spring Framework. In doing so, the only thing that's needed next is to provide a feed's implementation details for two methods inherited from the AbstractAtomFeedView class: buildFeedMetadata and buildFeedEntries.

The buildFeedMetadata has three input parameters: a Map object, which represents the data used to build the feed (i.e., data assigned inside the handler method, in this case a List of TournamentContent objects), a Feed object based on a Project Rome class that is used to manipulate the feed itself, and an HttpServletRequest object in case it's necessary to manipulate the HTTP request.

Inside the buildFeedMetadata method, you can observe several calls are made to the Feed object's setter methods (e.g., setId, setTitle, setUpdated). Two of these calls are made using hard-coded strings, while another is made with a value determined after looping over a feed's data (i.e., the Map object). All these calls represent the assignment of an Atom feed's metadata information.

ℹ️   Consult Project Rome's API if you want to assign more values to an Atom feed's metadata section, as well as specify a particular Atom version. The default version is Atom 1.0.

The buildFeedEntries method also has three input parameters: a Map object that represents the data used to build the feed (i.e., data assigned inside the handler method, in this case a List of TournamentContent objects), an HttpServletRequest object in case it's necessary to manipulate the HTTP request, and an HttpServletResponse object in case it's necessary to manipulate the HTTP response. It's also important to note the buildFeedEntries method returns a List of objects, which in this case corresponds to a List of Entry objects based on a Project Rome class and containing an Atom feed's recurring elements.

Inside the buildFeedEntries method, you can observe that the Map object is accessed to obtain the feedContent object assigned inside the handler method. Once this is done, an empty List of Entry objects is created. Next, a loop is performed on the feedContent object, which contains a List of TournamentContent objects, and for each element, an Entry object is created that is assigned to the top-level List of Entry objects. Once the loop is finished, the method returns a filled List of Entry objects.

ℹ️   Consult Project Rome's API if you want to assign more values to an Atom feed's recurring elements section.

Upon deploying this last class, in addition to the previously cited Spring MVC controller, accessing a URL in the form http://[host_name]/[app-name]/atomfeed.atom would result in the following response:

```
<feed xmlns="http://www.w3.org/2005/Atom">
  <title>Grand Slam Tournaments</title>
  <id>tag:tennis.org</id>
  <updated>2022-12-23T00:00:00Z</updated>
  <entry>
    <title>Australian Open - Posted by ATP</title>
    <id>tag:tennis.org,2022-12-23:9</id>
    <updated>2022-12-23T00:00:00Z</updated>
    <summary>Australian Open - www.australianopen.com</summary>
  </entry>
```

```
  <entry>
    <title>Roland Garros - Posted by ATP</title>
    <id>tag:tennis.org,2022-12-23:10</id>
    <updated>2022-12-23T00:00:00Z</updated>
    <summary>Roland Garros - www.rolandgarros.com</summary>
  </entry>
  <entry>
    <title>Wimbledon - Posted by ATP</title>
    <id>tag:tennis.org,2022-12-23:11</id>
    <updated>2022-12-23T00:00:00Z</updated>
    <summary>Wimbledon - www.wimbledon.org</summary>
  </entry>
  <entry>
    <title>US Open - Posted by ATP</title>
    <id>tag:tennis.org,2022-12-23:12</id>
    <updated>2022-12-23T00:00:00Z</updated>
    <summary>US Open - www.usopen.org</summary>
  </entry>
</feed>
<?xml version="1.0" encoding="UTF-8"?>
<feed xmlns="http://www.w3.org/2005/Atom">
  <title>Grand Slam Tournaments</title>
  <id>tag:tennis.org</id>
  <updated>2017-05-19T01:32:52Z</updated>
  <entry>
    <title>Australian Open - Posted by ATP</title>
    <id>tag:tennis.org,2017-05-19:5</id>
    <updated>2017-05-19T01:32:52Z</updated>
    <summary>Australian Open - www.australianopen.com</summary>
  </entry>
  <entry>
    <title>Roland Garros - Posted by ATP</title>
    <id>tag:tennis.org,2017-05-19:6</id>
    <updated>2017-05-19T01:32:52Z</updated>
    <summary>Roland Garros - www.rolandgarros.com</summary>
  </entry>
  <entry>
    <title>Wimbledon - Posted by ATP</title>
    <id>tag:tennis.org,2017-05-19:7</id>
    <updated>2017-05-19T01:32:52Z</updated>
    <summary>Wimbledon - www.wimbledon.org</summary>
  </entry>
  <entry>
    <title>US Open - Posted by ATP</title>
    <id>tag:tennis.org,2017-05-19:8</id>
    <updated>2017-05-19T01:32:52Z</updated>
    <summary>US Open - www.usopen.org</summary>
  </entry>
</feed>
```

Turning your attention to the remaining handler method—getRSSFeed—from the previous Spring MVC controller charged with building an RSS feed, you'll see that the process is similar to the one just described for building Atom feeds. The handler method also creates a List of TournamentContent objects, which is then assigned to the handler method's model object for it to become accessible to the returning view. The returning logical view in this case, though, now corresponds to one named rssfeedtemplate. As described earlier, this logical view is mapped to a class named RssFeedView.

The following listing illustrates the RssFeedView class, which implements the AbstractRssFeedView class:

```
package com.apress.spring6recipes.court.feeds;

import com.rometools.rome.feed.rss.Channel;
import com.rometools.rome.feed.rss.Item;
import jakarta.servlet.http.HttpServletRequest;
import jakarta.servlet.http.HttpServletResponse;
import org.springframework.web.servlet.view.feed.AbstractRssFeedView;

import java.time.LocalDate;
import java.time.ZoneId;
import java.util.Date;
import java.util.List;
import java.util.Map;
import java.util.stream.Collectors;

public class RSSFeedView extends AbstractRssFeedView {

  @Override
  protected void buildFeedMetadata(Map<String, Object> model, Channel feed,
                                   HttpServletRequest request) {
    feed.setTitle("World Soccer Tournaments");
    feed.setDescription("FIFA World Soccer Tournament Calendar");
    feed.setLink("fifa.com");

    @SuppressWarnings({ "unchecked" })
    var tournaments = (List<TournamentContent>) model.get("feedContent");
    var lastBuildDate = tournaments.stream()
           .map(TournamentContent::publicationDate).sorted().findFirst()
           .map(this::toDate).orElse(null);
    feed.setLastBuildDate(lastBuildDate);
  }

  @Override
  protected List<Item> buildFeedItems(Map<String, Object> model,
                                      HttpServletRequest request,
                                      HttpServletResponse response) {
    @SuppressWarnings({ "unchecked" })
    var tournamentList = (List<TournamentContent>) model.get("feedContent");
    return tournamentList.stream().map(this::toItem).collect(Collectors.toList());
  }
```

```java
private Item toItem(TournamentContent tc) {
    var item = new Item();
    item.setAuthor(tc.author());
    item.setTitle(String.format("%s - Posted by %s", tc.name(), tc.author()));
    item.setPubDate(toDate(tc.publicationDate()));
    item.setLink(tc.link());
    return item;
}

private Date toDate(LocalDate in) {
    return Date.from(in.atStartOfDay(ZoneId.systemDefault()).toInstant());
}
}
```

The first thing to notice about this class is that it imports several Project Rome classes from the com.sun.syndication.feed.rss package, in addition to implementing the AbstractRssFeedView class provided by the Spring Framework. Once it does so, the only thing that's needed next is to provide a feed's implementation details for two methods inherited from the AbstractRssFeedView class: buildFeedMetadata and buildFeedItems. The buildFeedMetadata method is similar in nature to the one by the same name used in building an Atom feed. Notice the buildFeedMetadata method manipulates a Channel object based on a Project Rome class, which is used to build RSS feeds, instead of a Feed object, which is used to build Atom feeds. The setter method calls made on the Channel object (e.g., setTitle, setDescription, setLink) represent the assignment of an RSS feed's metadata information. The buildFeedItems method, which differs in name from its Atom counterpart buildFeedEntries, is so named because an Atom feed's recurring elements are called entries and an RSS feed's recurring elements are items. Naming conventions aside, their logic is similar.

Inside the buildFeedItems method, you can observe that the Map object is accessed to obtain the feedContent object assigned inside the handler method. Once this is done, an empty List of Item objects is created. Next, a loop is performed on the feedContent object, which contains a List of TournamentContent objects, and for each element, an Item object is created, which is assigned to the top-level List of Item objects. Once the loop is finished, the method returns a filled List of Item objects.

ℹ️ Consult Project Rome's API if you want to assign more values to an RSS feed's metadata and recurring elements sections, as well as specify a particular RSS version. The default version is RSS 2.0.

When you deploy this last class, in addition to the previously cited Spring MVC controller, accessing a URL in the form http://[host_name]/rssfeed.rss (or http://[host_name]/rssfeed.xml) results in the following response:

```xml
<?xml version="1.0" encoding="UTF-8"?>
<rss version="2.0">
  <channel>
    <title>World Soccer Tournaments</title>
    <link>fifa.com</link>
    <description>FIFA World Soccer Tournament Calendar</description>
    <lastBuildDate>Fri, 23 Dec 2022 00:00:00 GMT</lastBuildDate>
    <item>
      <title>World Cup - Posted by FIFA</title>
      <link>www.fifa.com/worldcup/</link>
```

```
        <pubDate>Fri, 23 Dec 2022 00:00:00 GMT</pubDate>
        <Author>FIFA</author>
    </item>
    <item>
        <title>U-20 World Cup - Posted by FIFA</title>
        <link>www.fifa.com/u20worldcup/</link>
        <pubDate>Fri, 23 Dec 2022 00:00:00 GMT</pubDate>
        <Author>FIFA</author>
    </item>
    <item>
        <title>U-17 World Cup - Posted by FIFA</title>
        <link>www.fifa.com/u17worldcup/</link>
        <pubDate>Fri, 23 Dec 2022 00:00:00 GMT</pubDate>
        <Author>FIFA</author>
    </item>
    <item>
        <title>Confederations Cup - Posted by FIFA</title>
        <link>www.fifa.com/confederationscup/</link>
        <pubDate>Fri, 23 Dec 2022 00:00:00 GMT</pubDate>
        <Author>FIFA</author>
    </item>
  </channel>
</rss>
```

3-6. Response Writers

Problem

You have a service, or multiple calls, and want to send the response in chunks to the client.

Solution

Use a ResponseBodyEmitter (or its sibling SseEmitter) to send the response in chunks.

How It Works

Send Multiple Results in a Response

Spring MVC has a class named ResponseBodyEmitter that is particularly useful if instead of a single result (like a view name or ModelAndView), you want to return multiple objects to the client. When sending an object, it is converted to a result using an HttpMessageConverter. To use the ResponseBodyEmitter, you have to return it from the request handling method in an asynchronous fashion (see Recipe 2-12 for more information on async controllers).

Modify the getRestMembers method of the RestMemberController to return a ResponseBodyEmitter and send the results one by one to the client:

```java
package com.apress.spring6recipes.court.web;

import com.apress.spring6recipes.court.domain.Member;
import com.apress.spring6recipes.court.service.MemberService;
import com.apress.spring6recipes.utils.Utils;
import org.springframework.core.task.TaskExecutor;
import org.springframework.web.bind.annotation.GetMapping;
import org.springframework.web.bind.annotation.RequestMapping;
import org.springframework.web.bind.annotation.RestController;
import org.springframework.web.servlet.mvc.method.annotation.ResponseBodyEmitter;

import java.io.IOException;
import java.time.Duration;

@RestController
@RequestMapping("/members")
public class RestMemberController {

  private final MemberService memberService;
  private final TaskExecutor taskExecutor;

  public RestMemberController(MemberService memberService, TaskExecutor taskExecutor) {
    this.memberService = memberService;
    this.taskExecutor = taskExecutor;
  }

  @GetMapping
  public ResponseBodyEmitter getRestMembers() {
    var emitter = new ResponseBodyEmitter();
    taskExecutor.execute(() -> {
      var members = memberService.findAll();
      try {
        for (var member : members) {
          emitter.send(member);
          Utils.sleep(Duration.ofMillis(25));
        }
        emitter.complete();
      } catch (IOException ex) {
        emitter.completeWithError(ex);
      }
    });
    return emitter;
  }
}
```

First, a `ResponseBodyEmitter` is created and in the end returned from this method. Next, a task is executed, which will find all the members using the `MemberService.findAll` method. All the results from that call are returned one by one using the `send` method of the `ResponseBodyEmitter` (and we added a small delay between the elements). When all the objects have been sent, the `complete()` method needs to be called, so that the thread responsible for sending the response can complete the request and be freed up for the next response to handle. When an exception occurs and you want to inform the user of this, you call the `completeWithError`; the exception will pass through the normal exception handling of Spring MVC (see also Recipe 2-8), and after that the response is completed.

When using a tool like HTTPie or cURL, calling the URL `http://localhost:8080/court/members` will yield something like the following result. The result will be chunked and has a status of 200 (OK) (Figure 3-3).

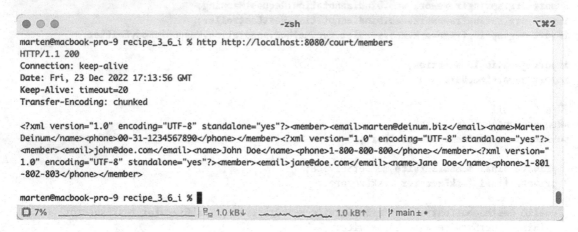

Figure 3-3. *Chunked result*

If you want to change the status code or add custom headers, you could also wrap the `ResponseBodyEmitter` in a `ResponseEntity,` which would allow for customization of the return code, headers, etc.:

```
@GetMapping
public ResponseEntity<ResponseBodyEmitter> getRestMembers() {
  var emitter = new ResponseBodyEmitter();
  ....
  return ResponseEntity.status(HttpStatus.I_AM_A_TEAPOT)
          .header("Custom-Header", "Custom-Value")
          .body(emitter);
}
```

Now the status code will be changed to 418, and it will contain a custom header (see Figure 3-4).

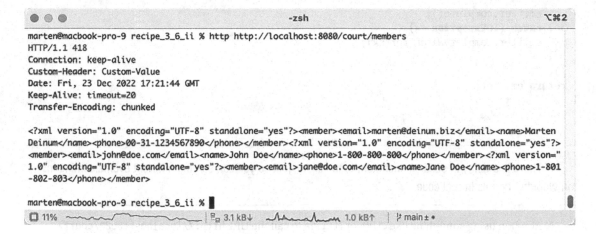

```
marten@macbook-pro-9 recipe_3_6_ii % http http://localhost:8080/court/members
HTTP/1.1 418
Connection: keep-alive
Custom-Header: Custom-Value
Date: Fri, 23 Dec 2022 17:21:44 GMT
Keep-Alive: timeout=20
Transfer-Encoding: chunked

<?xml version="1.0" encoding="UTF-8" standalone="yes"?><member><email>marten@deinum.biz</email><name>Marten
Deinum</name><phone>00-31-1234567890</phone></member><?xml version="1.0" encoding="UTF-8" standalone="yes"?>
<member><email>john@doe.com</email><name>John Doe</name><phone>1-800-800-800</phone></member><?xml version="
1.0" encoding="UTF-8" standalone="yes"?><member><email>jane@doe.com</email><name>Jane Doe</name><phone>1-801
-802-803</phone></member>

marten@macbook-pro-9 recipe_3_6_ii %
```

Figure 3-4. Modified chunked result

Sending Multiple Results as Events

A sibling of the ResponseBodyEmitter is the SseEmitter that can deliver events from the server to the client.
For this Server-Sent Events are utilized. Server-Sent Events are messages from the server side to the client,
and they have a content type header of text/event-stream. They are quite lightweight and allow for four
fields to be defined (see Table 3-3).

Table 3-3. Allowed Fields for Server-Sent Events

Field	Description
id	The ID of the event
event	The type of event
data	The event data
retry	Reconnection time for the event stream

To send events from a request handling method, you need to create an instance of SseEmitter and
return it from the request handling method. Then use the send method to send individual elements to
the client:

```java
@GetMapping
public ResponseBodyEmitter getRestMembers() {
  var emitter = new SseEmitter();
  taskExecutor.execute(() -> {
    var members = memberService.findAll();
    try {
      for (var member : members) {
        emitter.send(member);
        Utils.sleep(Duration.ofMillis(50));
      }
```

```
        emitter.complete();
    } catch (IOException ex) {
        emitter.completeWithError(ex);
    }
  });
  return emitter;
}
```

ℹ️ There is a delay in sending each item to the client, just so you can see the different events coming in. You wouldn't do this in real code.

Now when using something like cURL or HTTPie to call the URL http://localhost:8080/court/members, you will see events coming in one by one (Figure 3-5).

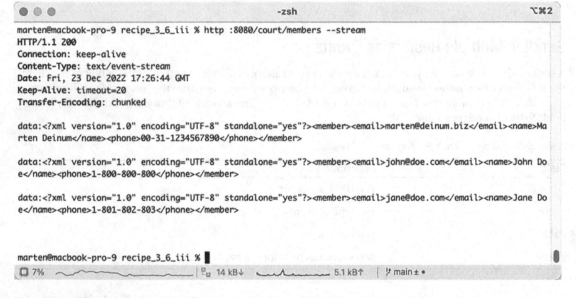

Figure 3-5. *Server-Sent Events result*

Note the Content-Type header; it has a value of text/event-stream to indicate that we get a stream of events. We could keep the stream open and keep receiving event notifications. You will also notice that each object written is converted to JSON; this is done with an HttpMessageConverter just as with a plain ResponseBodyEmitter. Each object is written in the data tag as the event data.

If you want to add more info to the event (fill one of the other fields as mentioned in Table 3-3), you can use the SseEventBuilder; to get an instance of that, you can call the event() factory method on the SseEmitter. Let's use it to fill the id field with the hashcode of the Member:

```
@GetMapping
public ResponseBodyEmitter getRestMembers() {
  var emitter = new SseEmitter();
  taskExecutor.execute(() -> {
```

```java
  var members = memberService.findAll();
  try {
    for (var member : members) {
      var data = SseEmitter.event()
               .id(String.valueOf(member.hashCode()))
               .data(member);
      emitter.send(data);
      Utils.sleep(Duration.ofMillis(50));
    }
    emitter.complete();
  } catch (IOException ex) {
    emitter.completeWithError(ex);
  }
});
  return emitter;
}
```

Now when using something like cURL to call the URL http://localhost:8080/court/members, you will see events coming in one by one, and now they contain both an id and data field (see Figure 3-6).

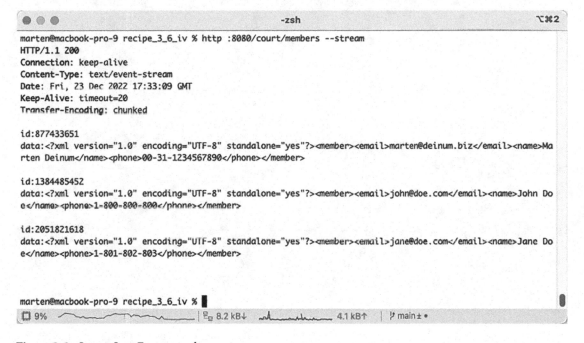

Figure 3-6. *Server-Sent Events result*

3-7. Summary

In this chapter, you have learned how to develop and access REST services using Spring. REST services are closely tied to Spring MVC, whereby a controller acts to dispatch requests made to REST services, as well as access third-party REST services to use this information for application content.

You learned how REST services leverage annotations used in Spring MVC controllers, which included @RequestMapping to indicate service endpoints, as well as @PathVariable to specify access parameters for filtering a service's payload. In addition, you learned about Spring's XML marshallers, such as Jaxb2Marshaller, which allow application objects to be transformed into XML and be output as a REST service's payload. You also learned about Spring's RestTemplate class and how it supports the series of HTTP methods that include HEAD, GET, POST, PUT, and DELETE—all of which allow you to access and perform operations on third-party REST services directly from the context of a Spring application.

Next, you explored how to publish Atom and RSS feeds in a Spring application by leveraging the Project Rome API.

Finally, you had a quick look at the ResponseBodyEmitter and SseEmitter for asynchronous sending of content to the client.

CHAPTER 4

■ ■ ■

Spring WebFlux

When the Servlet API was initially released, the majority of the implementing containers used a thread per request, which meant a thread was blocked until the request processing had finished and the response was sent to the client. However, in those early days, there weren't as many devices connected to the Internet as nowadays. Due to the increased number of devices, the number of HTTP requests handled has grown significantly. Due to this increase, for a lot of web applications, keeping a thread blocked isn't feasible anymore. In the last couple of years, there has been an uprising in reactive programming, and with Spring it is possible to write reactive web applications. To be reactive Spring utilizes Project Reactor as an implementation of the Reactive Streams API. It goes beyond the scope of this book to do a full dive into reactive programming, but in short it is a way of doing non-blocking functional programming.

Traditionally, when working with web applications, there would be a request, HTML would be rendered on the server, and that got sent back to the client. In the last couple of years, rendering of HTML moved to the client, and communication was done not through HTML but by returning JSON, XML, or another representation to the client. This was traditionally still a request and response cycle although driven through an async call by the client through the XmlHttpRequest. However, there are also other ways of communicating between the client and server. One could utilize Server-Sent Events to have one-way communication from the server to the client, and for full-duplex communication, one could use websockets.

4-1. Developing a Reactive Application with Spring WebFlux

Problem

You want to develop a simple reactive web application with Spring WebFlux to learn the basic concepts and configurations of this framework.

Solution

The lowest component of Spring WebFlux is the `org.springframework.http.server.reactive.HttpHandler`; this is an interface with a single `handle` method:

```
package org.springframework.http.server.reactive;

import reactor.core.publisher.Mono;

public interface HttpHandler {

  Mono<Void> handle(ServerHttpRequest request, ServerHttpResponse response);

}
```

The `handle` method returns a `reactor.core.publisher.Mono<Void>`, which is the reactive way of saying it returns void. It takes both a `ServerHttpRequest` and `ServerHttpResponse` both from the `org.springframework.http.server.reactive` package. These are again interfaces, and depending on the container used for running, an instance of the interface is created. For this several adapters or bridges for containers exist. When running on a servlet container (supporting non-blocking IO), the `ServletHttpHandlerAdapter` (or one of its subclasses) is used to adapt from the plain servlet world to the reactive world. When running on a native reactive engine like Netty, the `ReactorHttpHandlerAdapter` is used.

When a web request is sent to a Spring WebFlux application, the `HandlerAdapter` first receives the request. Then it organizes the different components configured in Spring's application context all needed to handle the request.

To define a controller class in Spring WebFlux, a class has to be marked with the `@Controller` or `@RestController` annotation (just as with Spring MVC–see Chapters 3 and 4), or you can write them in a functional way using a `RouterFunction`.

When a `@Controller`-annotated class (i.e., a controller class) receives a request, it looks for an appropriate handler method to handle the request. This requires that a controller class map each request to a handler method by one or more handler mappings. In order to do so, a controller class's methods are decorated with the `@RequestMapping` annotation, making them handler methods.

The signature for these handler methods—as you can expect from any standard class—is open ended. You can specify an arbitrary name for a handler method and define a variety of method arguments. Equally, a handler method can return any of a series of values (e.g., string or void), depending on the application logic it fulfills. The following is only a partial list of valid argument types, just to give you an idea:

- `ServerHttpRequest` or `ServerHttpResponse`

- Request parameters from the URL of arbitrary type, annotated with `@RequestParam`

- Model attributes of arbitrary type, annotated with `@ModelAttribute`

- Cookie values included in an incoming request, annotated with `@CookieValue`

- Request header values of arbitrary type, annotated with `@RequestHeader`

- Request attributes of arbitrary type, annotated with `@RequestAttribute`

- `Map` or `ModelMap`, for the handler method to add attributes to the model

- `WebSession`, for the session

Once the controller class has picked an appropriate handler method, it invokes the handler method's logic with the request. Usually, a controller's logic invokes back-end services to handle the request. In addition, a handler method's logic is likely to add or remove information to or from the numerous input arguments (e.g., `ServerHttpRequest`, `Map`, or `Errors`) that will form part of the ongoing flow.

After a handler method has finished processing the request, it returns a value to the client. Often, this is serialized to JSON or XML (see Recipe 4-2) to be consumed by the client. But it could also be the name of a view to be rendered (see Recipe 4-4).

How It Works

Let's create a simple controller that accepts, optionally, a name and returns a message to the client.

First, we need the configuration for Spring WebFlux, followed by the code to bootstrap Netty and pass it our configuration. Finally, we will write our controller to reactively return the message to the client.

Setting Up a Spring WebFlux Application

Before you are able to use and work with Spring WebFlux, you will need to add some dependencies to your classpath, the most obvious being `spring-webflux`. To fully utilize the reactive nature of the application, you will also need a reactive runtime. Here we choose to use Project Reactor Netty.

Gradle dependencies for WebFlux and Netty

```
implementation group: 'org.springframework', name: 'spring-webflux', version: '6.0.3'
implementation group: 'io.projectreactor.netty', name: 'reactor-netty-http', version: '1.1.0'
```

Maven dependencies for WebFlux and Netty

```xml
<dependency>
  <groupId>org.springframework</groupId>
  <artifactId>spring-webflux</artifactId>
  <version>6.0.3</version>
</dependency>

<dependency>
  <groupId>io.projectreactor.netty</groupId>
  <artifactId>reactor-netty-http</artifactId>
  <version>1.1.0</version>
</dependency>
```

To be able to handle a request in a reactive way, you need to enable WebFlux. This is done by adding @ EnableWebFlux to a @Configuration class:

```java
package com.apress.spring6recipes.reactive.court;

import org.springframework.context.annotation.ComponentScan;
import org.springframework.context.annotation.Configuration;
import org.springframework.web.reactive.config.EnableWebFlux;
import org.springframework.web.reactive.config.WebFluxConfigurer;


@Configuration
@EnableWebFlux
@ComponentScan
public class WebFluxConfiguration implements WebFluxConfigurer { }
```

The @EnableWebFlux annotation is what is turning on reactive processing. For further configuration of WebFlux, you can implement the WebFluxConfigurer and add additional converters, view resolvers, codecs, etc.

Bootstrapping the Application

How to bootstrap the application depends a little on the runtime you choose to run on. For all supported containers (see Table 4-1), there are different handler adapters, so the runtime can work with the HttpHandler abstraction from Spring WebFlux. All the adapter classes reside in the org.springframework. http.server.reactive package.

Table 4-1. *Supported Runtimes and HandlerAdapters*

Runtime	Adapter
Any servlet container	ServletHttpHandlerAdapter
Tomcat	TomcatHttpHandlerAdapter
Jetty	ServletHttpHandlerAdapter
Reactor Netty	ReactorHttpHandlerAdapter
Reactor Netty 5	ReactorNetty2HttpHandlerAdapter
Undertow	UndertowHttpHandlerAdapter

> ℹ️ For both Tomcat and Jetty, it is possible to use the regular ServletHttpHandlerAdapter; however, it is recommended to use the specific one for the container for better integration.

Before adapting to the runtime, you would need to bootstrap the application using an AnnotationConfigApplicationContext and use that to configure an HttpHandler. To make it easier to configure the HttpHandler, use the HttpWebHandlerAdapter to configure it for the given ApplicationContext:

```
var context = new AnnotationConfigApplicationContext(WebFluxConfiguration.class);
var handler = WebHttpHandlerBuilder.applicationContext(context).build();
```

Next, you would adapt the HttpHandler to the runtime.
For Reactor Netty it would be something like this:

```
var adapter = new ReactorHttpHandlerAdapter(handler);
HttpServer.create().host("0.0.0.0").port(8080).handle(adapter).bind().block();
System.in.read();
```

First, you create a ReactorHttpHandlerAdapter, the component that knows how to adapt from the Reactor Netty handling to the internal HttpHandler. Next, you register this adapter as a handler to the newly created Reactor Netty server.

When deploying an application to a servlet container, you can create a class implementing the WebApplicationInitializer and do the setup manually:

```
package com.apress.spring6recipes.reactive.court;

import jakarta.servlet.ServletContext;
import org.springframework.context.annotation.AnnotationConfigApplicationContext;
import org.springframework.http.server.reactive.ServletHttpHandlerAdapter;
import org.springframework.web.WebApplicationInitializer;
import org.springframework.web.server.adapter.WebHttpHandlerBuilder;

public class WebFluxInitializer implements WebApplicationInitializer {
```

```java
@Override
public void onStartup(ServletContext servletContext) {
    var context = new AnnotationConfigApplicationContext(WebFluxConfiguration.class);
    var httpHandler = WebHttpHandlerBuilder.applicationContext(context).build();
    var adapter = new ServletHttpHandlerAdapter(httpHandler);

    var registration = servletContext.addServlet("dispatcher-handler", adapter);
    registration.setLoadOnStartup(1);
    registration.addMapping("/");
    registration.setAsyncSupported(true);
}
}
```

First, you create an AnnotationConfigApplicationContext as you want to use annotations for configuration and pass that your WebFluxConfiguration class. Next, you need an HttpHandler to handle and dispatch the request; for this you use the WebHttpHandlerBuilder class. This HttpHandler needs to be registered to the servlet container you are using as a Servlet; for this you wrap it in a ServletHttpHandlerAdapter. To be able to do reactive processing, asyncSupported needs to be true.

To make this configuration easier, Spring WebFlux provides a convenience implementation for you to extend the AbstractReactiveWebInitializer. The configuration now looks like:

```java
package com.apress.spring6recipes.reactive.court;

import org.springframework.web.server.adapter.AbstractReactiveWebInitializer;

public class WebFluxInitializer extends AbstractReactiveWebInitializer {

    @Override
    protected Class<?>[] getConfigClasses() {
        return new Class<?>[] { WebFluxConfiguration.class };
    }
}
```

The only thing required is the getConfigClasses method. All the moving parts are now handled by the base configuration provided by Spring WebFlux.

Now you are ready to run your application on a regular servlet container.

ℹ️ When running on a regular servlet container, you won't be fully reactive. It will only utilize the async features of the Servlet API and the non-blocking I/O; it won't give you things like backpressure and elasticity (as it is still using the underlying thread pool/blocking nature of Tomcat).

Creating Spring WebFlux Controllers

An annotation-based controller class can be an arbitrary class that doesn't implement a particular interface or extend a particular base class. You can annotate it with the @Controller or @RestController annotation. There can be one or more handler methods defined in a controller to handle single or multiple actions. The signature of the handler methods is flexible enough to accept a range of arguments. (See also Recipe 2-2 for more information on request mapping.)

The @RequestMapping annotation can be applied to the class level or the method level. The first mapping strategy is to map a particular URL pattern to a controller class and then a particular HTTP method to each handler method:

```java
package com.apress.spring6recipes.reactive.court.web;

import org.springframework.web.bind.annotation.GetMapping;
import org.springframework.web.bind.annotation.RequestMapping;
import org.springframework.web.bind.annotation.RequestParam;
import org.springframework.web.bind.annotation.RestController;
import reactor.core.publisher.Mono;

@RestController
@RequestMapping("/welcome")
public class WelcomeController {

  @GetMapping
  public Mono<String> welcome(@RequestParam(defaultValue = "World") String name) {
    return Mono.just("Hello " + name+" from Spring WebFlux!");
  }
}
```

This controller receives an optional name parameter (if not present, it will default to World) and returns a simple message to the client. Note the Mono<String> as a return type. This is the reactive type from Project Reactor indicating a single return value (or none). Instead of Project reactor, you could also use the return types from RxJava 3 or Mutiny.

Since you've already activated annotation scanning on the com.apress.spring6recipes.reactive. court package using @ComponentScan, the annotations for the controller class are detected upon deployment.

The @RestController annotation defines the class as a controller. The @RequestMapping annotation is more interesting since it contains properties and can be declared at the class or handler method level. The first value used in this class—("/welcome")—is used to specify the URL on which the controller is actionable, meaning any request received on the /welcome URL is attended by the WelcomeController class.

Once a request is attended by the controller class, it delegates the call to the default HTTP GET handler method declared in the controller. The reason for this behavior is that every initial request made on a URL is of the HTTP GET kind. So when the controller attends a request on the /welcome URL, it subsequently delegates to the default HTTP GET handler method for processing.

The annotation @GetMapping is used to decorate the welcome method as the controller's default HTTP GET handler method. It's worth mentioning that if no default HTTP GET handler method is declared, a ResponseStatusException is thrown, hence the importance of a Spring WebFlux controller having at a minimum a URL route and default HTTP GET handler method.

Another variation to this approach can be declaring both values—URL route and default HTTP GET handler method—in the @GetMapping annotation used at the method level. This declaration is illustrated next:

```
@RestController
public class WelcomeController {

  @GetMapping("/welcome")
  public String welcome(Model model) { ... }

}
```

This last controller illustrates the basic principles of Spring WebFlux.

Running the Web Application

Depending on the runtime, you can either just run the application by executing the main method or build a web archive (WAR) and deploy it to a servlet container. Here we are going to use the reactive runtime and launch the main method. After launching you can use the browser or something like cURL or HTTPie to issue a request to http://localhost:8080/welcome and get a greeting (see Figure 4-1).

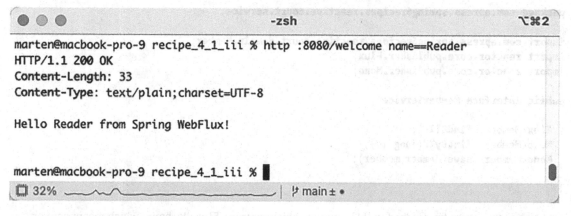

Figure 4-1. *Welcome controller calling and output*

💡 The project can also create a Docker container with the app: run `gradle docker` to get a container with Tomcat and the application. You can then start a Docker container to test the application (`gradle dockerRun`).

4-2. Publishing and Consuming JSON with Reactive REST Services

Problem

You want to develop a simple reactive REST-based application with Spring WebFlux.

Solution

Using the @RestController annotation and the Jackson library, Spring WebFlux can send and receive JSON. To receive data into an object, use the @RequestBody annotation, and it will deserialize the JSON to a Java object.

How It Works

First, you write the following domain class, which is a regular class, nothing reactive so far. The class used here is the same as the regular servlet version in Recipe 4-1:

```java
package com.apress.spring6recipes.reactive.court.domain;

public record Member(String name, String email, String phone) { }
```

Then you define the following service interface to provide member services to the presentation layer:

```java
package com.apress.spring6recipes.reactive.court.service;

import com.apress.spring6recipes.reactive.court.domain.Member;
import reactor.core.publisher.Flux;
import reactor.core.publisher.Mono;

public interface MemberService {

  Flux<Member> findAll();
  Mono<Member> findById(long id);
  Mono<Member> save(Member member);

}
```

Notice the return type of the findAll method, which returns a Flux<Member>, which means zero or more members.

In a production application, you should implement this interface with datastore persistence and preferably one that supports reactive programming. But for simplicity's sake, you can store the members in a map and hard-code several members for testing purposes:

```java
package com.apress.spring6recipes.reactive.court.service;

import com.apress.spring6recipes.reactive.court.domain.Member;
import jakarta.annotation.PostConstruct;
import org.springframework.stereotype.Service;
import reactor.core.publisher.Flux;
import reactor.core.publisher.Mono;

import java.util.Map;
import java.util.concurrent.ConcurrentHashMap;
import java.util.concurrent.atomic.AtomicLong;
```

```java
@Service
class InMemoryMemberService implements MemberService {

  private final AtomicLong sequence = new AtomicLong(1);
  private final Map<Long, Member> members = new ConcurrentHashMap<>();

  @PostConstruct
  public void init() {
    Flux.just(
        new Member("Marten Deinum", "00-31-1234567890", "marten@deinum.biz"),
        new Member("John Doe", "1-800-800-800", "john@doe.com"),
        new Member("Jane Doe", "1-801-802-803", "jane@doe.com"))
          .flatMap(this::save)
          .subscribe();
  }

  @Override
  public Flux<Member> findAll() {
    return Flux.fromIterable(members.values());
  }

  @Override
  public Mono<Member> findById(long id) {
    return Mono.justOrEmpty(members.get(id));
  }

  @Override
  public Mono<Member> save(Member member) {
    var id = sequence.getAndIncrement();
    this.members.put(id, member);
    return Mono.just(member);
  }
}
```

The findById method returns a Mono containing the Member or an empty Mono when the Member isn't found.

Publishing JSON

By annotating the request handling method with @ResponseBody, the output will be returned as JSON, XML, or any representation depending on the request return type and available libraries in the classpath. Instead of annotating the method with @ResponseBody, you could also use the @RestController annotation on the class level, which automatically implies @ResponseBody for all request handling methods.

Let's write a REST controller that returns all members in the system. You do this by annotating a class with @RestController and giving it a @GetMapping-annotated method, which returns a Flux<Member>:

```java
package com.apress.spring6recipes.reactive.court.web;

import com.apress.spring6recipes.reactive.court.domain.Member;
import com.apress.spring6recipes.reactive.court.service.MemberService;
import org.springframework.web.bind.annotation.GetMapping;
```

```
import org.springframework.web.bind.annotation.RequestMapping;
import org.springframework.web.bind.annotation.RestController;
import reactor.core.publisher.Flux;
import reactor.core.publisher.Mono;

@RestController
@RequestMapping("/members")
public class MemberController {

  private final MemberService memberService;

  public MemberController(MemberService memberService) {
    this.memberService = memberService;
  }

  @GetMapping
  public Flux<Member> list() {
    return memberService.findAll();
  }
}
```

To be able to generate JSON, the Jackson JSON library has to be in the classpath. Spring WebFlux will detect its presence and will configure the appropriate message Encoder/Decoder for this. This Encoder/Decoder implementation in turn is then used by an HttpMessageWriter/HttpMessageReader to either write or read an HTTP message (the body of a request or response).

When returning a reactive type like this, it will either be streamed to the client as streaming JSON/XML or as Server-Sent Events (see Recipe 3-6). The result depends on the Accept header from the client. Using HTTPie and executing http http://localhost:8080/members will get you JSON. When adding --stream the result will be published as Server-Sent Events.

Consuming JSON

Next to producing JSON, you can also consume it. For this add a method argument and annotate it with @RequestBody. The incoming request body will be mapped onto the object. For a reactive controller, you can wrap it in a Mono or Flux for, respectively, a single result or multiple results:

```
@PostMapping
public Mono<Member> create(@RequestBody Member member) {
  return memberService.save(member);
}
```

The new method has been annotated with @PostMapping so that it binds to the POST HTTP method. It can receive a Member object, and finally it will save it using the service. The newly created Member will be returned to the user.

Now when a request with a JSON body comes in, this will be deserialized into the Member object. For this Spring WebFlux uses, just as Spring MVC, a converter. The conversion is delegated to an instance of the HttpMessageReader in this case, the DecoderHttpMessageReader; this class will decode the reactive stream into the object. This again is delegated to a Decoder. As we want to use JSON (and have the Jackson 2 JSON library in the classpath), it will use the Jackson2JsonDecoder for this. The HttpMessageReader and Decoder implementations are the reactive counterpart of the HttpMessageConverter used by regular Spring MVC.

Using HTTPie and issuing the following request `http POST http://localhost:8080/members/`
`name="Josh Long" email="josh@example.com"` will add a new member. Now when retrieving all the
members, it will be part of the result.

Validating the Incoming Payload

When receiving a payload, one wants to know whether it is valid or not. When using Spring WebFlux this
can be achieved by using the Jakarta Bean Validation API. This allows one to annotate the different fields
to prevent invalid values. For our member, we want the `name` and `email` to be required (not empty), and
`email` has to be in a valid email format as well. For this we can use, respectively, the `@NotBlank` and `@Email`
annotations:

```
package com.apress.spring6recipes.reactive.court.domain;

import jakarta.validation.constraints.Email;
import jakarta.validation.constraints.NotBlank;

public record Member(@NotBlank String name,
                     @NotBlank @Email String email,
                     String phone) { }
```

For the Jakarta Bean Validation API to work, we also need to have an implementation in our classpath.
Spring supports the Hibernate Validator project. This needs to be added as a dependency to our application.
The Hibernate Validator, by default, needs an EL (expression language) implementation as well.

Gradle dependency

```
implementation group: 'jakarta.validation', name: 'jakarta.validation-api', version: '3.0.2'
runtimeOnly group: 'org.hibernate.validator', name: 'hibernate-validator', version: '8.0.0.Final'
runtimeOnly group: 'org.glassfish', name: 'jakarta.el', version: '4.0.2'
```

Maven dependency

```
<dependency>
  <groupId>jakarta.validation</groupId>
  <artifactId>jakarta.validation-api</artifactId>
  <version>3.0.2</version>
</dependency>
<dependency>
  <groupId>org.hibernate.validator</groupId>
  <artifactId>hibernate-validator</artifactId>
  <version>8.0.0.Final</version>
  <scope>runtime</scope>
</dependency>
<dependency>
  <groupId>org.glassfish</groupId>
  <artifactId>jakarta.el</artifactId>
  <version>4.0.2</version>
  <scope>runtime</scope>
</dependency>
```

Finally, we need to instruct our controller to validate the incoming payload. For this add @Valid next to the @RequestBody annotation:

```
@PostMapping
public Mono<Member> create(@Valid @RequestBody Member member) {
  return memberService.save(member);
}
```

When we now send an invalid request, we will get a response with HTTP status 400, bad request. The response however isn't telling much about what was wrong (which field or what was wrong with a field). For this we could use a more elaborate exception handling (see Recipe 4-3).

4-3. Exception Handling with Reactive Controllers

Problem

A web application has to deal with exceptions, like from validation errors or some technical errors with the database. You want to expose a nice error to the user and explain what is wrong.

Solution

In Spring WebFlux you can use an exception handler to convert exceptions into meaningful error responses. You can use an annotated method in the controller or a more global approach with a controller advice such that it applies to all (or a subset) of your controllers.

How It Works

Recipe 4-2 explained how to receive a request body and do validation of it. To convert the validation exception into a meaningful response for the client, you implement a method and annotate it with @ExceptionHandler. The @ExceptionHandler-annotated method, like the @RequestMapping-annotated methods, can use different types of objects to help writing a meaningful error. One of them is the Exception being handled. Table 4-2 lists another (limit) set of possibilities.

Table 4-2. *Most Used Method Arguments for @ExceptionHandler Methods*

Method Argument	Description
Exception type	The `Exception` that will be handled
`ServerHttpRequest` `ServerHttpResponse`	Get access to the request and/or response
`ServerWebExchange`	The full, current `ServerWebExchange`. Container for all HTTP-related information (method, request, response, session, etc.)
`java.security.Principal`	The current principal, a.k.a. the currently authenticated user

`java.util.Map`
`org.springframework.ui.Model`
`org.springframework.ui.ModelMap`
	The model for the error response, always empty. Can be used to add data to the response

`Errors` `BindingResult`	Access the errors from validation and binding results for the command object

Create an Exception Handler for Validation Errors

The `@ExceptionHandler` annotation can be applied to methods that are either in the `@Controller/`
`@RestController`-annotated class or in a `@ControllerAdvice`-annotated class. In the first case, it will only
apply exception handling to errors from that specific controller; in the second case, it can be a global error
handler for all or a subset of the controllers.

In this recipe you will be creating a global exception handler so as to handle all validation/binding
errors. For this create a class and annotate the class with `@ControllerAdvice`. Next, add a method.

 Next to `@ControllerAdvice` there is also `@RestControllerAdvice`. For this recipe you can
use either one. The main difference is that `@ControllerAdvice` applies to all controllers, whereas
`@RestControllerAdvice` is limited to only `@RestController`-annotated controllers.

```
package com.apress.spring6recipes.reactive.court.web;

import org.springframework.validation.FieldError;
import org.springframework.web.bind.annotation.ControllerAdvice;
import org.springframework.web.bind.annotation.ExceptionHandler;
import org.springframework.web.bind.annotation.ResponseBody;
import org.springframework.web.bind.support.WebExchangeBindException;
import reactor.core.publisher.Flux;
```

```
@ControllerAdvice
public class GlobalErrorHandler {

  @ExceptionHandler(WebExchangeBindException.class)
  @ResponseBody
  public Flux<ErrorMessage> handleValidationErrors(WebExchangeBindException ex) {
    return Flux.fromIterable(ex.getFieldErrors())
            .map(this::toErrorMessage);
  }

  private ErrorMessage toErrorMessage(FieldError fe) {
    return new ErrorMessage(fe.getField(), fe.getDefaultMessage());
  }

  record ErrorMessage(String field, String message) { }

}
```

The @ExceptionHandler-annotated method will handle all WebExchangeBindExceptions that occur within the application. It takes the exception, retrieves the field errors, and converts them into a small object identifying which field has an error and which error it was. The method also has the @ResponseBody annotation to denote that we want to write a response with that content. Various return types are supported; see Table 4-3.

Table 4-3. *Partial List of Supported Return Types*

Response Type	Description
Supported reactive type	Types like Flux/Mono are supported as well as those from other supported reactive libraries
String	Interpreted as the name of a view to render
java.util.Map org.springframework. ui.Model	The model for the error response–a view will be rendered based on the URL
View	The actual View to render
ErrorResponse ProblemDetail	To render a RFC-7807 response with details in the body

Now when posting an empty member to http://localhost:8080/members, we will get a status 400 indicating the response is invalid (see Figure 4-2).

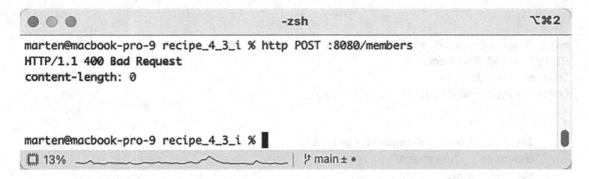

marten@macbook-pro-9 recipe_4_3_i % http POST :8080/members
HTTP/1.1 400 Bad Request
content-length: 0

marten@macbook-pro-9 recipe_4_3_i % ▌

□ 13% 〰〰〰〰〰〰〰 ⑂ main ± •

Figure 4-2. *Exception output*

While the HTTP status code of 400 is correct, it doesn't give much more detail on what is wrong. This is where the Problem Details API (RFC-7807) can help by providing more information in a standardized way.

Use Problem Details (RFC-7808) with Spring WebFlux

Spring WebFlux also supports, just as Spring Web, Problem Details for HTTP APIs (RFC-7807). To use this there are two options: you can return a ProblemDetail/ErrorResponse from an @ExceptionHandler method, or you can extend the provided ResponseEntityExceptionHandler to make things easier.

The easiest starting point is to extend the ResponseEntityExceptionHandler. Let's modify the GlobalErrorHandler in such a way that it extends the ResponseEntityExceptionHandler:

```
package com.apress.spring6recipes.reactive.court.web;

import org.springframework.web.bind.annotation.ControllerAdvice;
import org.springframework.web.reactive.result.method.annotation.
ResponseEntityExceptionHandler;

@ControllerAdvice
public class GlobalErrorHandler extends ResponseEntityExceptionHandler { }
```

The class is now merely a class with an extends and the @ControllerAdvice annotation. This is enough to make Spring WebFlux return a response with Problem Details information (see Figure 4-3).

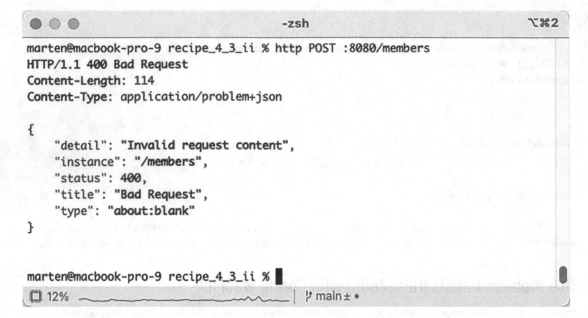

```
● ● ●                                  -zsh                              ⌥⌘2

marten@macbook-pro-9 recipe_4_3_ii % http POST :8080/members
HTTP/1.1 400 Bad Request
Content-Length: 114
Content-Type: application/problem+json

{
    "detail": "Invalid request content",
    "instance": "/members",
    "status": 400,
    "title": "Bad Request",
    "type": "about:blank"
}


marten@macbook-pro-9 recipe_4_3_ii % █

🔲 12% ───────────────~~──────────────  | ⑂ main ± •
```

Figure 4-3. *Default Problem Details exception output*

However, for a WebExchangeBindException, the information is still very sparse. It would be nice if it included the information on which fields are invalid. As the Problem Details RFC allows for extension of the default building blocks, this is very easy to achieve.

As we already extend the ResponseEntityExceptionHandler, we can override the handleWebExchangeBindException and enrich the response with the needed information:

```
package com.apress.spring6recipes.reactive.court.web;

import java.util.Map;

import org.springframework.http.HttpHeaders;
import org.springframework.http.HttpStatusCode;
import org.springframework.http.ResponseEntity;
import org.springframework.web.bind.annotation.ControllerAdvice;
import org.springframework.web.bind.support.WebExchangeBindException;
import org.springframework.web.reactive.result.method.annotation.
ResponseEntityExceptionHandler;
import org.springframework.web.server.MissingRequestValueException;
import org.springframework.web.server.ServerWebExchange;
import org.springframework.web.server.ServerWebInputException;

import reactor.core.publisher.Mono;

@ControllerAdvice
public class GlobalErrorHandler extends ResponseEntityExceptionHandler {
```

```
@Override
protected Mono<ResponseEntity<Object>> handleWebExchangeBindException(
        WebExchangeBindException ex, HttpHeaders headers,
        HttpStatusCode status, ServerWebExchange exchange) {
    var locale = exchange.getLocaleContext().getLocale();
    var errors = ex.resolveErrorMessages(getMessageSource(), locale);
    ex.getBody().setProperty("errors", errors.values());
    return super.handleExceptionInternal(ex, null, headers, status, exchange);
}
}
```

First, we resolve the error messages that might be there. For this we can obtain the MessageSource from our parent class and the Locale from the ServerWebExchange. We add the resolved messages as a new property, named errors, to the Problem Details response. We can do this because the WebExchangeBindException is an implementation of the ErrorResponse interface, which allows that. All exceptions thrown by the web processing parts of Spring implement that interface for convenience.

When we now make an error in our request, we get a nice list of errors explaining what was wrong with our request (see Figure 4-4).

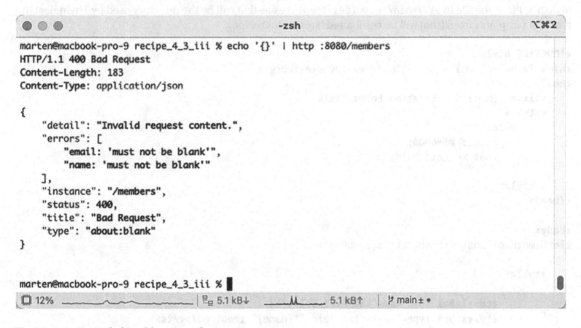

Figure 4-4. Extended Problem Details exception output

4-4. Handling Forms with Reactive Controllers

Problem

In a web application, you often have to deal with forms. A form controller has to show a form to a user and also handle the form submission. Form handling can be a complex and variable task.

Solution

When a user interacts with a form, it requires support for two operations from a controller. First, when a form is initially requested, it asks the controller to show a form by an HTTP GET request that renders the form view to the user. Then when the form is submitted, an HTTP POST request is made to handle things like validation and business processing for the data present in the form. If the form is handled successfully, it renders the success view to the user. Otherwise, it renders the form view again with errors.

How It Works

Suppose you want to allow a user to register as a member by filling out a form. To give you a better idea of the data handled by a controller, we will introduce the controller's view (i.e., the form) first.

Creating a Form's views

Let's create the form view member.html. The form relies on the Thymeleaf library, as this simplifies a form's data binding, the display of error messages, and the redisplay of original values entered by the user in case of errors. Place the file in src/main/resources/templates as that will be the directory used by Thymeleaf to read the templates from (that will be configured later in this recipe):

```
<!DOCTYPE html>
<html lang="en" xmlns:th="http://www.thymeleaf.org">
<head>
    <title>Member Registration Form</title>
    <style>
        .error {
            color: #ff0000;
            font-weight: bold;
        }
    </style>
</head>

<body>
<form method="post" th:object="${member}">

    <table>
        <tr>
            <td><label for="name">Name</label></td>
            <td><input type="text" th:field="*{name}" required/></td>
            <td><span class="error" th:if="${#fields.hasErrors('name')}"
                th:errors="*{name}"></span></td>
        </tr>
        <tr>
            <td><label for="email">Email</label></td>
            <td><input type="email" th:field="*{email}" required/></td>
            <td><span class="error" th:if="${#fields.hasErrors('email')}"
                th:errors="*{email}"></span></td>
        </tr>
        <tr>
            <td><label for="phone">Phone</label></td>
```

```
        <td><input type="text" th:field="*{phone}"/></td>
        <td><span class="error" th:if="${#fields.hasErrors('phone')}"
        th:errors="*{phone}"></span></td>
    </tr>
    <tr>
        <td colspan="3"><input type="submit"/></td>
    </tr>
    </table>
</form>
</body>
</html>
```

This form uses Thymeleaf to bind all form fields to a model attribute named member due to the
th:object=${member} on the form tag. Each field will bind and display the value of the actual field on
the Member object; this is what the th:field tag is used for. When there are errors on the field, those are
displayed through the usage of the th:errors tag.

Finally, you can find the standard HTML tag <input type="submit" /> that generates a "Submit"
button and triggers the sending of data to the server.

In case the form and its data are processed correctly, you need to create a success view to notify the user
of a successful registration. The member-success.html illustrated next serves this purpose:

```
<!DOCTYPE html>
<html lang="en">
<head>
    <meta charset="UTF-8">
    <title>Member registered successfully</title>
</head>
<body>
Your registration has been received successfully.
</body>
</html>
```

It's also possible for errors to occur due to invalid values being submitted in a form. For example, if
the email is not in a valid format or a required field is missing, the controller is designed to reject such field
values. The controller will then generate a list of selective error codes for each error to be returned to the
form view, values that are placed through the th:errors tag.

For example, for an invalid value input in the email field, the following error codes are generated by the
data binding:

```
typeMismatch.command.email
typeMismatch.email
typeMismatch.java.time.LocalDate
typeMismatch
```

If you have a ResourceBundleMessageSource defined, you can include the following error messages in
your resource bundle for the appropriate locale (e.g., messages.properties for the default locale) (see also
Recipe 2-5 on how to externalize localization concerns):

```
typeMismatch.date=Invalid date format
typeMismatch.hour=Invalid hour format
```

The corresponding error codes and their values are what is returned to a user if a failure occurs processing form data.

Now that you know the structure of the views involved with a form, as well as the data handled by it, let's take a look at the logic that handles the submitted data (i.e., the member) in a form.

Creating a Form's Service Processing

We can reuse the `MemberService` from the previous recipes, for which we define an interface and an in-memory implementation:

```
package com.apress.spring6recipes.reactive.court.service;

import com.apress.spring6recipes.reactive.court.domain.Member;
import reactor.core.publisher.Flux;
import reactor.core.publisher.Mono;

public interface MemberService {

  Flux<Member> findAll();
  Mono<Member> findById(long id);
  Mono<Member> save(Member member);

}
```

```
package com.apress.spring6recipes.reactive.court.service;

import com.apress.spring6recipes.reactive.court.domain.Member;
import jakarta.annotation.PostConstruct;
import org.springframework.stereotype.Service;
import reactor.core.publisher.Flux;
import reactor.core.publisher.Mono;

import java.util.Map;
import java.util.concurrent.ConcurrentHashMap;
import java.util.concurrent.atomic.AtomicLong;

@Service
class InMemoryMemberService implements MemberService {

  private final AtomicLong sequence = new AtomicLong(1);
  private final Map<Long, Member> members = new ConcurrentHashMap<>();

  @PostConstruct
  public void init() {
    Flux.just(
        new Member("Marten Deinum", "00-31-1234567890", "marten@deinum.biz"),
        new Member("John Doe", "1-800-800-800", "john@doe.com"),
        new Member("Jane Doe", "1-801-802-803", "jane@doe.com"))
        .flatMap(this::save)
        .subscribe();
  }
```

```java
@Override
public Flux<Member> findAll() {
  return Flux.fromIterable(members.values());
}

@Override
public Mono<Member> findById(long id) {
  return Mono.justOrEmpty(members.get(id));
}

@Override
public Mono<Member> save(Member member) {
  var id = sequence.getAndIncrement();
  this.members.put(id, member);
  return Mono.just(member);
}
}
```

Now that you have a better understanding of the two elements that interact with a controller—a form's views and the member service class—let's create a controller to handle the member registration form.

Creating a Form's Controller

A controller used to handle forms makes use of practically the same annotations you've already used in the previous recipes. So let's get right to the code:

```java
package com.apress.spring6recipes.reactive.court.web;

import com.apress.spring6recipes.reactive.court.domain.Member;
import com.apress.spring6recipes.reactive.court.service.MemberService;
import org.springframework.stereotype.Controller;
import org.springframework.ui.Model;
import org.springframework.validation.BindingResult;
import org.springframework.web.bind.annotation.GetMapping;
import org.springframework.web.bind.annotation.ModelAttribute;
import org.springframework.web.bind.annotation.PostMapping;
import org.springframework.web.bind.annotation.RequestMapping;
import reactor.core.publisher.Mono;

@Controller
@RequestMapping("/members")
public class MemberController {

  private final MemberService memberService;

  public MemberController(MemberService memberService) {
    this.memberService = memberService;
  }
```

```java
@GetMapping
public Mono<String> add(Model model) {
  model.addAttribute("member", new Member(null, null, null));
  return Mono.just("member");
}

@PostMapping
public Mono<String> create(@ModelAttribute("member") Member member,
                           BindingResult bindingResult) {
  return Mono.just(member)
          .map(memberService::save)
          .then(Mono.just("redirect:member-success"));
}
}
```

The controller starts by using the standard @Controller annotation, as well as the @RequestMapping annotation that allows access to the controller through the following URL:

`http://localhost:8080/members`

When you enter this URL in your browser, it will send an HTTP GET request to your web application. This in turn triggers the execution of the add method, which is designated to attend to this type of request based on its @GetMapping annotation.

The add method defines a Model object as an input parameter, which serves to send model data to the view (i.e., the form). Inside the handler method, an empty Member object is created that is added as an attribute to the controller's Model object. Then the controller returns the execution flow to the member view, which in this case is resolved to member.html (i.e., the form).

The most important aspect of this last method is the addition of an empty Member object. If you analyze the form in member.html, you will notice the form tag declares an attribute th:object="${member}". This means that upon rendering the view, the form expects an object named member to be available, which is achieved by placing it inside the handler method's Model. In fact, further inspection reveals that the th:field=*{expression} values for each input tag correspond to the field names belonging to the Member object. Since the form is being loaded for the first time, it should be evident that an empty Member object is expected.

Now let's turn our attention to submitting the form for the first time. After you have filled in the form fields, submitting the form triggers an HTTP POST request that in turn invokes the create method—on account of this method's @PostMapping value.

The input fields declared for the create method are the @ModelAttribute("member") Member member used to reference the member object and the BindingResult object that contains newly submitted data by the user.

At this juncture, the handler method doesn't incorporate validation, which is the purpose of the BindingResult object.

The only operation performed by the handler method is memberService.save(member);. This operation invokes the member service using the current state of the member object.

Generally, controller objects are first validated prior to performing this type of operation on them.

Finally, note the handler method returns a view named redirect:member-success. The actual name of the view in this case is member-success, which is resolved to the member-success.html page you created earlier.

The redirect: prefix in the view name is used to avoid a problem known as duplicate form submission.

When you refresh the web page in the form success view, the form you just submitted is resubmitted again. To avoid this problem, you can apply the post/redirect/get design pattern, which recommends redirecting to another URL after a form submission is handled successfully, instead of returning an HTML page directly. This is the purpose of prefixing a view name with `redirect:`.

Initializing a Model Attribute Object and Pre-populating a Form with Values

The form is designed to register new members. However, if we pre-populate the member variable with an existing member, we could also use the form for editing member information.

Let's add a method to the controller that would reuse the same view but would pre-populate the model with an existing Member object:

```
@GetMapping("/{id}")
public Mono<String> add(@PathVariable("id") long id, Model model) {
  return memberService.findById(id)
          .defaultIfEmpty(new Member(null, null, null))
          .doOnNext( (member) -> model.addAttribute("member", member))
          .then(Mono.just("member"));
}
```

The method receives an id variable in the path and uses this to retrieve an existing member. If nothing is found, it will initialize an empty Member instance so the form can still be rendered. The member.html doesn't need to be changed.

Now when calling http://localhost:8080/members/1, it will open with a form with the form fields pre-filled. This is due to the usage of the th:object and th:field tags in the HTML. Those tags are processed by Thymeleaf, and the values are obtained from the model (which is filled in the controller method).

Providing Form Reference Data

When a form controller is requested to render the form view, it may have some types of reference data to provide to the form (e.g., the items to display in an HTML selection). Now suppose you want to allow a member to select the sport type they generally register:

```
package com.apress.spring6recipes.reactive.court.domain;

public record SportType(int id, String name) { }
```

We need to modify the Member so we can pass it a SportType:

```
package com.apress.spring6recipes.reactive.court.domain;

public record Member(String name, String email,
                     String phone, SportType preferredType) {

  public Member(String name, String email, String phone) {
    this(name, email, phone, null);
  }
}
```

Notice the additional constructor. This is needed to let our InMemoryMemberService still function correctly; else, it would complain about not finding the correct constructor.

Now in the member.html add a drop-down to be able to select a SportType from the list. The list of SportTypes will be added to the model in the controller:

```
<!DOCTYPE html>
<html lang="en" xmlns:th="http://www.thymeleaf.org">
<body>
<form method="post" th:object="${member}">
    <tr>
        <td><label for="preferredType">Preferred Sport</label></td>
        <td>
            <select th:field="*{preferredType}">
                <option th:each="sportType : ${sportTypes}" th:value="${sportType.id}"
                    th:text="${sportType.name}"/>
            </select>
        </td>
        <td><span class="error" th:if="${#fields.hasErrors('preferredType')}"
            th:errors="*{preferredType}"></span></td>
    </tr>
    <tr>
        <td colspan="3"><input type="submit"/></td>
    </tr>
    </table>
</form>
</body>
</html>
```

The <select> tag provides a way to generate a drop-down list of values passed to the view by the controller. Thus, the form represents the preferredType field as a set of HTML <select> elements, instead of the previous open-ended fields—<input>—that require a user to introduce text values.

Next, let's take a look at how the controller assigns the sportType field as a model attribute. The process is a little different than the previous fields.

For simplicity's sake lets add a simple SportTypeRepository, which holds an internal list of sport types and exposes a method to list them all and to find a specific one:

```
package com.apress.spring6recipes.reactive.court.web;

import com.apress.spring6recipes.reactive.court.domain.SportType;
import org.springframework.stereotype.Repository;
import reactor.core.publisher.Flux;

import java.util.List;
import java.util.Optional;

@Repository
public class SportTypeRepository {

    private final List<SportType> sportTypes = List.of(
            new SportType(1, "Tennis"),
            new SportType(2, "Soccer"),
            new SportType(3, "Swimming"));
```

```
    public Flux<SportType> findAll() {
        return Flux.fromIterable(this.sportTypes);
    }

    public Optional<SportType> findById(int id) {
        return sportTypes.stream().filter( (type) -> type.id() == id).findFirst();
    }
}
```

Now that you have an implementation that returns a hard-coded list of SportType objects, let's take a look at how the controller associates this list for it to be returned to the form view:

```
package com.apress.spring6recipes.reactive.court.web;

import com.apress.spring6recipes.reactive.court.service.MemberService;
import org.springframework.stereotype.Controller;
import org.springframework.web.bind.annotation.GetMapping;
import org.springframework.web.bind.annotation.ModelAttribute;
import org.springframework.web.bind.annotation.PathVariable;
import org.springframework.web.bind.annotation.RequestMapping;
import reactor.core.publisher.Flux;
import reactor.core.publisher.Mono;

@Controller
@RequestMapping("/members")
public class MemberController {

    private final MemberService memberService;
    private final SportTypeRepository sportTypeRepository;

    public MemberController(MemberService memberService,
                            SportTypeRepository sportTypeRepository) {
        this.memberService = memberService;
        this.sportTypeRepository = sportTypeRepository;
    }

    @ModelAttribute("sportTypes")
    public Flux<SportType> sportTypes() {
        return sportTypeRepository.findAll();
    }

    @GetMapping("/{id}")
    public Mono<String> add(@PathVariable("id") long id, Model model) {
        return memberService.findById(id)
                .defaultIfEmpty(new Member(null, null, null, null))
                .doOnNext( (member) -> model.addAttribute("member", member))
                .then(Mono.just("member"));
    }
}
```

Notice that the add handler method charged with returning the Member object to the form view remains unchanged.

The new addition and what is responsible for passing a SportType list as a model attribute to the form view is the method decorated with the @ModelAttribute("sportTypes") annotation. The @ModelAttribute annotation is used to define global model attributes, available to any returning view used in handler methods, in the same way a handler method declares a Model object as an input parameter and assigns attributes that can be accessed in the returning view. This last model attribute is used in the form view to populate a drop-down list (i.e., <select> tag). The resulting page should look like the one in Figure 4-5.

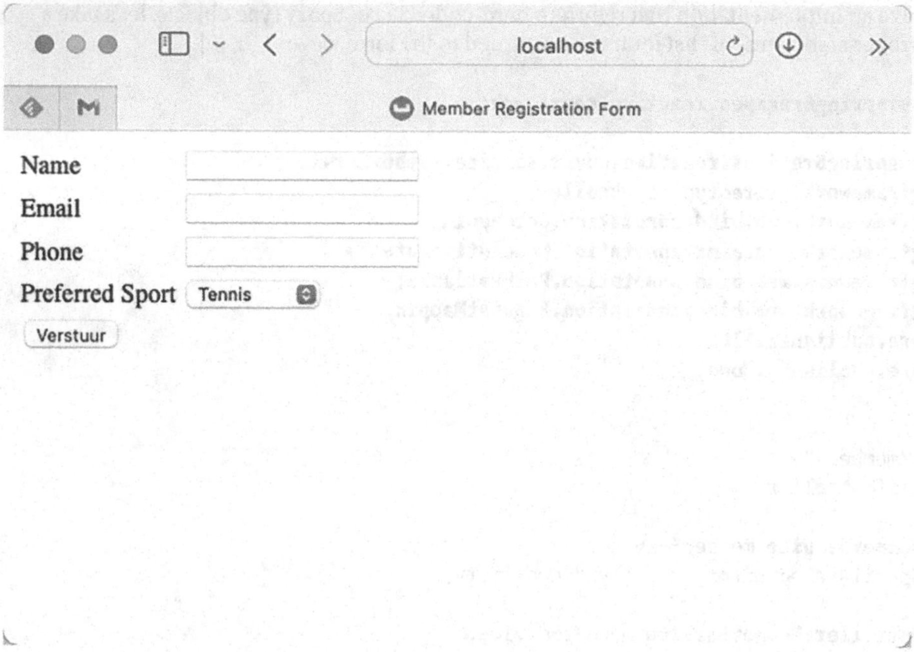

Figure 4-5. *Complete member form*

Binding Properties of Custom Types

When a form is submitted, a controller binds the form field values to a model object's properties of the same name, in this case a Member object. However, for properties of custom types, a controller is not able to convert them unless you specify the corresponding property editors for them.

For example, the sport type selection field only submits the selected sport type ID—as this is the way HTML <select> fields operate. Therefore, you have to convert this ID into a SportType object with a property editor. First, we need to make sure we have a findById method (or another method that returns the request object based on the input):

```
public Optional<SportType> findById(int id) {
  return sportTypes.stream().filter( (type) -> type.id() == id).findFirst();
}
```

Then you create the SportTypeConverter class to convert a sport type ID into a SportType object. This converter requires SportTypeRepository to perform the lookup:

```
package com.apress.spring6recipes.reactive.court.web;

import com.apress.spring6recipes.reactive.court.domain.SportType;
import org.springframework.core.convert.converter.Converter;
import org.springframework.stereotype.Component;

@Component
public class SportTypeConverter implements Converter<String, SportType> {

  private final SportTypeRepository repository;

  public SportTypeConverter(SportTypeRepository repository) {
    this.repository = repository;
  }

  @Override
  public SportType convert(String source) {
    var sportTypeId = Integer.parseInt(source);
    return repository.findById(sportTypeId).orElse(null);
  }
}
```

Now that you have the supporting SportTypeConverter class required to bind form properties to a custom class like SportType, you need to associate it with the controller. For this purpose, we can use the addFormatters method from the WebFluxConfigurer.

By overriding this method in your configuration class, custom types can be associated with a controller, like a SportType through the SportTypeConverter class:

```
package com.apress.spring6recipes.reactive.court;

import com.apress.spring6recipes.reactive.court.web.SportTypeConverter;
import org.springframework.context.annotation.Bean;
import org.springframework.context.annotation.ComponentScan;
import org.springframework.context.annotation.Configuration;
import org.springframework.format.FormatterRegistry;
import org.springframework.web.reactive.config.EnableWebFlux;
@Configuration
@EnableWebFlux
@ComponentScan
public class WebFluxConfiguration implements WebFluxConfigurer {

  private final SportTypeConverter sportTypeConverter;

  public WebFluxConfiguration(SportTypeConverter sportTypeConverter) {
    this.sportTypeConverter = sportTypeConverter;
  }
```

```
@Override
public void addFormatters(FormatterRegistry registry) {
    registry.addConverter(this.sportTypeConverter);
}
}
```

The only field for this last class corresponds to sportTypeConverter, used to access the application's SportTypeConverter bean. This converter is added to the registry in the addFormatters method by calling registry.addConverter. By using this approach, every annotation-based controller (i.e., classes using the @Controller annotation) can have access to the same custom converters and formatters in their handler methods.

Validating Form Data

When a form is submitted, it's standard practice to validate the data provided by a user before a submission is successful. Spring WebFlux, like Spring MVC, supports validation by means of a validator object that implements the Validator interface. You can write your own implementation, but the most commonly used approach is to use the Jakarta Bean Validation API. With this you can add annotations to your model object, and Spring WebFlux will automatically validate them for you.

For this let's add some validation constraints to our Member object:

```
package com.apress.spring6recipes.reactive.court.domain;

import jakarta.validation.constraints.Email;
import jakarta.validation.constraints.NotBlank;
import jakarta.validation.constraints.NotNull;

public record Member(@NotBlank String name,
                     @NotBlank @Email String email,
                     String phone,
                     @NotNull SportType preferredType) {
}
```

The Member class now defines some validation constraints. The name field is required (it doesn't allow blank values like all spaces or null); the email field needs to be a proper email address and is required. Finally, we need a preferredType as well.

The next modification takes place in the HTTP POST handler method, which is always called when a user submits a form. Next to the @ModelAttribute annotation, there is now a @Valid annotation; this annotation triggers validation of the object. After the validation, the result parameter BindingResult object contains the results for the validation process. So next, a conditional based on the value of result.hasErrors() is made. If the validation class detects errors, this value is true.

In case errors are detected in the validation process, the handler method returns the view member, which corresponds to the same form so that a user can resubmit information. In case no errors are detected in the validation process, the flow proceeds as before:

```
@PostMapping
public Mono<String> create(@Valid @ModelAttribute("member") Member member,
                           BindingResult bindingResult) {
    if (bindingResult.hasErrors()) {
        return Mono.just("member");
    }
```

```
return Mono.just(member)
        .map(memberService::save)
        .then(Mono.just("redirect:member-success"));
}
```

4-5. Asynchronous Web Client

Problem

You want to access a REST service from a third party (e.g., Google, Yahoo, another business partner) and use its payload inside a Spring application.

Solution

Accessing a third-party REST service inside a Spring application revolves around the use of the Spring `WebClient` abstraction. The `WebClient` is designed on the same principles as the many other Spring `*Template` classes (e.g., `JdbcTemplate`, `JmsTemplate`), providing a simplified approach with default behaviors for performing lengthy tasks.

This means the processes of invoking a REST service and using its returning payload are streamlined in Spring applications.

How It Works

Before describing the particularities of the `WebClient`, it's worth exploring the life cycle of a REST service, so you're aware of the actual work the `WebClient` class performs (see Recipe 3-4). Exploring the life cycle of a REST service can best be done from a browser, so open your favorite browser on your workstation to get started.

The first thing that's needed is a REST service endpoint. We are going to reuse the endpoint we created in Recipe 4-2. This endpoint should be available at `http://localhost:8080/members`. If you load this last REST service endpoint on your browser, the browser performs a GET request, which is one of the most popular HTTP requests supported by REST services. Upon loading the REST service, the browser displays a responding payload like that in Figure 4-6.

```
[
    {
      "name": "Marten Deinum",
      "email": "00-31-1234567890",
      "phone": "marten@deinum.biz"
    },
    {
      "name": "John Doe",
      "email": "1-800-800-800",
      "phone": "john@doe.com"
    },
    {
      "name": "Jane Doe",
      "email": "1-801-802-803",
      "phone": "jane@doe.com"
    }
]
```

Figure 4-6. *Result JSON*

It's the task of a REST service consumer (i.e., you) to know the payload structure—sometimes referred to as vocabulary—of a REST service to appropriately process its information. Though this last REST service relies on what can be considered a custom vocabulary, a series of REST services often rely on standardized vocabularies (e.g., RSS), which make the processing of REST service payloads uniform. In addition, it's also worth noting that some REST services provide Web Application Description Language (WADL) contracts to facilitate the discovery and consumption of payloads.

Now that you're familiar with a REST service's life cycle using your browser, we can take a look at how to use the Spring WebClient class in order to incorporate a REST service's payload into a Spring application. Given that the WebClient is designed to call REST services, it should come as no surprise that its main methods are closely tied to REST's underpinnings, which are the HTTP's methods: HEAD, GET, POST, PUT, DELETE, and OPTIONS. Table 4-4 contains the main methods supported by the WebClient class.

Table 4-4. *WebClient Class Methods Based on HTTP's Request Methods*

Method	Description
create	Creates a WebClient (optionally, you can give a default URL)
head()	Prepares an HTTP HEAD operation
get()	Prepares an HTTP GET operation
post()	Prepares an HTTP POST operation
put()	Prepares an HTTP PUT operation
options()	Prepares an HTTP OPTIONS operation
patch()	Prepares an HTTP PATCH operation
delete()	Prepares an HTTP DELETE operation

As you can observe in Table 4-4, the WebClient builder methods are modeled after HTTP methods that include HEAD, GET, POST, PUT, DELETE, and OPTIONS.

ℹ By far the most common HTTP method used in REST services is GET, since it represents a safe operation to obtain information (i.e., it doesn't modify any data). On the other hand, HTTP methods such as PUT, POST, and DELETE are designed to modify a provider's information, which makes them less likely to be supported by a REST service provider. For cases in which data modification needs to take place, many providers opt for SOAP, which is an alternative mechanism to using REST services.

Now that you're aware of the WebClient basic builder methods, we can move on to invoking the same REST service you did with your browser previously, except this time using Java code from the Spring Framework. The following listing illustrates a class that accesses the REST service and returns its contents to the System.out:

```java
package com.apress.spring6recipes.reactive.court;

import org.springframework.http.MediaType;
import org.springframework.web.reactive.function.client.WebClient;

import java.io.IOException;

public class Main {

  public static void main(String[] args) throws IOException {
    var url = "http://localhost:8080/";

    WebClient.create(url).get().uri("/members")
            .accept(MediaType.APPLICATION_JSON)
            .exchangeToFlux( (cr) -> cr.bodyToFlux(String.class))
            .subscribe(System.out::println);
```

```
    System.in.read();
  }
}
```

Some REST service providers restrict access to their data feeds depending on the requesting party. Access is generally denied by relying on data present in a request (e.g., HTTP headers or IP address). So depending on the circumstances, a provider can return an access denied response even when a data feed appears to be working in another medium (e.g., you might be able to access a REST service in a browser but get an access denied response when attempting to access the same feed from a Spring application). This depends on the terms of use set forth by a REST provider.

The first lines declare the import statements needed to access the WebClient within a class's body. First, we need to create an instance of the WebClient using WebClient.create. Next, you can find a call made to the get() method that belongs to the WebClient, which as described in Table 4-4 is used to prepare an HTTP GET operation—just like the one performed by a browser to obtain a REST service's payload. Next, we extend the base URL to call as we want to call http://localhost:8080/members and we want to have JSON, hence the accept(MediaType.APPLICATION_JSON).

Next, the call to exchangeToFlux() will switch the configuration from setting up the request to define the response handling. As we probably get zero or more elements, we need to convert the ClientResponse body to a Flux, hence the exchangeToFlux. If you need a Mono, use the exchangeToMono to convert to a single-element result. Each element we want to write to System.out, so we subscribe to that.

When executed the output will be the same as in the browser except that it is now printed in the console.

Retrieving Data from a Parameterized URL

The previous section showed how we can call a URI to retrieve data, but what about a URI that requires parameters? We don't want to hard-code parameters into the URL. With the WebClient we can use a URL with placeholders; these placeholders will be replaced with actual values upon execution. Placeholders are defined using { and }, just as with a request mapping and path variables.

The URI http://localhost:8080/members/{id} is an example of such a parameterized URI. To be able to call this method, we need to pass in a value for the placeholder. We can do this by passing the parameters as arguments to the uri method of the WebClient:

```
public class Main {

    public static void main(String[] args) throws Exception {
      WebClient.create(url)
                  .get()
                  .uri("/members/{id}", "1")
                  .accept(MediaType.APPLICATION__JSON)
                  .exchangeToFlux( (cr) -> cr.bodyToFlux(String.class))
                  .subscribe(System.out::println);

      System.in.read();    }
}
```

Retrieving Data as a Mapped Object

Instead of returning a String to be used in our application, we can also (re)use our Member class to map the result. Instead of passing in String.class as a parameter to the bodyToFlux method, pass Member.class, and the response will be mapped onto this class:

```
package com.apress.spring6recipes.reactive.court;

import com.apress.spring6recipes.reactive.court.domain.Member;
import org.springframework.http.MediaType;
import org.springframework.web.reactive.function.client.WebClient;

import java.io.IOException;

public class ClientWithMapping {

  public static void main(String[] args) throws IOException {
    var url = "http://localhost:8080/";

    WebClient.create(url).get().uri("/members")
            .accept(MediaType.APPLICATION_JSON)
            .exchangeToFlux( (cr) -> cr.bodyToFlux(Member.class))
            .subscribe(System.out::println);

    System.in.read();
  }
}
```

The WebClient makes use of the same HttpMessageReader infrastructure as a controller with @ResponseBody-marked methods. As JAXB2 (as well as Jackson) is automatically detected, mapping to an object is quite easy.

4-6. Writing Reactive Handler Functions

Problem

You want to write functions that react to incoming requests.

Solution

You can write a method that takes a ServerRequest and returns a Mono<ServerResponse> and map it as a router function.

How It Works

Instead of mapping requests to methods using @RequestMapping, you can also write functions that are essentially honoring the HandlerFunction interface:

```
package org.springframework.web.reactive.function.server;

import reactor.core.publisher.Mono;

@FunctionalInterface
public interface HandlerFunction<T extends ServerResponse> {

  Mono<T> handle(ServerRequest request);

}
```

A HandlerFunction, as shown in the preceding code, is basically a method that takes a ServerRequest as an argument and returns a Mono<ServerResponse>. Both the ServerRequest and ServerResponse provide full reactive access to the underlying request and response, by exposing various parts of it as either Mono or Flux streams.

After a function has been written, it can be mapped to incoming requests using the RouterFunctions class. The mapping can be done on URLs, headers, methods, or custom written RequestPredicates implementing classes. The default available request predicates are accessible through the RequestPredicates class.

Writing Handler Functions

Let's rewrite the MemberController to simple request handling functions instead of a controller.

To do so remove all request mapping annotations and add a simple @Component to the class. Although @Controller would work as well, it isn't really a controller anymore. Next, rewrite the methods to adhere to the signature as outlined by the HandlerFunction interface:

```
package com.apress.spring6recipes.reactive.court.web;

import com.apress.spring6recipes.reactive.court.domain.Member;
import com.apress.spring6recipes.reactive.court.service.MemberService;
import org.springframework.stereotype.Component;
import org.springframework.web.reactive.function.server.ServerRequest;
import org.springframework.web.reactive.function.server.ServerResponse;
import reactor.core.publisher.Mono;

@Component
public class MemberController {

  private final MemberService memberService;

  public MemberController(MemberService memberService) {
    this.memberService = memberService;
  }

  public Mono<ServerResponse> list(ServerRequest request) {
    return ServerResponse
            .ok()
            .body(memberService.findAll(), Member.class);
  }
}
```

```
public Mono<ServerResponse> create(ServerRequest request) {
    var member = request.bodyToMono(Member.class)
                        .flatMap(memberService::save);
    return ServerResponse.ok().body(member, Member.class);
  }
}
```

The class still needs the MemberService as a dependency. Notice the change in the list and create methods. They now both return a Mono<ServerResponse> and accept a ServerRequest as input. As we want to return an HTTP status of OK (200), we can use ServerResponse.ok() to build that response. We need to add a body, the Flux<Member> in this case, and we need to specify the type of elements, Member.class. The latter is needed due to the reactive and generic nature, type information cannot be read when composing the function.

In the create method, something similar happens, but first we map the body of the incoming request to a Member using bodyToMono. This result is then used to eventually call the save method on the MemberService.

When accessing the application, the result should be the same as in Recipe 4-4 (see Figure 4-5).

Routing Requests to Handler Functions

As we now have simple functions instead of annotation-based request handling methods, routing needs to be done differently. You can use the RouterFunctions to do the mapping instead:

```
@Bean
public RouterFunction<ServerResponse> membersRouter(MemberController handler) {
  return RouterFunctions.route()
          .GET("/members", handler::list)
          .POST("/members", handler::create)
        .build();
}
```

When an HTTP GET request comes in for /members, the list method will be invoked and for an HTTP POST the create method.

The RequestPredicates.GET is the same as writing RequestPredicates.method(HttpMethod.GET).and(RequestPredicates.path("/members")). You can combine as many RequestPredicate statements as you want. The following are exposed through the RequestPredicates class (see Table 4-5).

Table 4-5. *Default Available RequestPredicates*

Method	Description
method	RequestPredicate for the HTTP METHOD
path	RequestPredicate for the URL or a part of the URL
accept	RequestPredicate for the Accept header to match requested media types
queryParam	RequestPredicate to check the existence of query parameters
headers	RequestPredicate to check the existence of request headers

The RequestPredicates helper also provides shorthand methods for GET, POST, PUT, DELETE, HEAD, PATCH, and OPTIONS. This saves you from combining two expressions.

4-7. Summary

In this chapter you learned how to write reactive controllers, which wasn't all that different from what was learned in the previous chapters and recipes. This also shows the power of the abstractions Spring has. You can use almost the same programming model for a totally different technology. After writing reactive controllers, you looked at writing reactive handler functions, which can do much of the same stuff that the reactive controllers can do in a more functional programming kind of way.

In between you also looked at the WebClient to do asynchronous consumption of a REST API.

CHAPTER 5

∎∎∎

Spring Security

In this chapter, you will learn how to secure applications using the Spring Security framework. Spring Security was initially known as Acegi Security, but its name has been changed since joining with the Spring Portfolio projects. Spring Security can be used to secure any Java application, but it's mostly used for web-based applications. Web applications, especially those that can be accessed through the Internet, are vulnerable to hacker attacks if they are not secured properly.

If you've never handled security in an application, there are several terms and concepts that you must understand first. Authentication is the process of verifying a principal's identity against what it claims to be. A principal can be a user, a device, or a system, but most typically, it's a user. A principal has to provide evidence of identity to be authenticated. This evidence is called a credential, which is usually a password when the target principal is a user.

Authorization is the process of granting authority to an authenticated user so that this user is allowed to access particular resources of the target application. The authorization process must be performed after the authentication process. Typically, authorities are granted in terms of roles.

Access control means controlling access to an application's resources. It entails making a decision on whether a user is allowed to access a resource. This decision is called an access control decision, and it's made by comparing the resource's access attributes with the user's granted authorities or other characteristics.

After finishing this chapter, you will understand basic security concepts and know how to secure your web applications at the URL access level, the method invocation level, the view rendering level, and the domain object level.

ℹ️   Before starting this chapter, take a look at the application for `recipe_5_1_i` (check also `recipe_5_shared` for the shared code). This is the initial unsecured application you will use in this chapter. It is a basic todo app in which you can list, create, and mark todos completed. When you deploy the application, you will be greeted with the content as shown in Figure 5-1.

© Marten Deinum, Daniel Rubio, Josh Long 2023
M. Deinum et al., *Spring 6 Recipes*, https://doi.org/10.1007/978-1-4842-8649-4_5

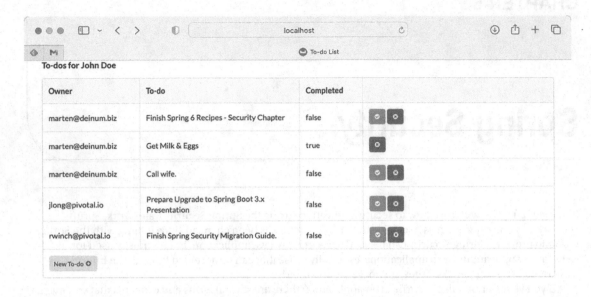

Figure 5-1. *Initial todo application*

5-1. Securing URL Access

Problem

Many web applications have some particular URLs that are critically important and private. You must secure these URLs by preventing unauthorized access to them.

Solution

Spring Security enables you to secure a web application's URL access in a declarative way through simple configuration. It handles security by applying servlet filters to HTTP requests. To register this filter and detect the configuration, Spring Security provides a convenience base class to extend, the AbstractSecurityWebApplicationInitializer.

Spring Security allows you to configure web application security through using the HttpSecurity class and WebSecurity class in @Bean methods, which will (re)configure parts of Spring Security. If your web application's security requirements are straightforward and typical, you can leave the configuration as is and use the default enabled security settings including the following:

- Form-based login service: This provides a default page that contains a login form for users to log into this application.

- HTTP basic authentication: This can process the basic authentication credentials presented in HTTP request headers. It can also be used for authenticating requests made with remoting protocols and web services.

- Logout service: This provides a handler mapped with a URL for users to log out of this application.

- Anonymous login: This assigns a principal and grants authorities to an anonymous user so that you can handle an anonymous user like a normal user.

- Servlet API integration: This allows you to access security information in your web application via standard Servlet APIs, such as HttpServletRequest.isUserInRole() and HttpServletRequest.getUserPrincipal().

- CSRF: Cross-Site Request Forgery protection. It will create a token and put it in the HttpSession.

- Security headers: Like disabled caching for secured packages, XSS protection, transport security, and X-Frame security.

With these security services registered, you can specify the URL patterns that require particular authorities to access. Spring Security will perform security checks according to your configurations. A user must log into an application before accessing the secure URLs, unless these URLs are opened for anonymous access. Spring Security provides a set of authentication providers for you to choose from. An authentication provider authenticates a user and returns the authorities granted to this user.

How It Works

First, you need to enable security by applying the @EnableWebSecurity annotation on a @Configuration class. As our application is set up with component scanning, this @Configuration class is automatically picked up, and security will be applied to our application.

Listing 5 1. Simple security configuration

```
package com.apress.spring6recipes.board.security;

import org.springframework.context.annotation.Configuration;
import org.springframework.security.config.annotation.web.configuration.EnableWebSecurity;

@Configuration
@EnableWebSecurity
public class TodoSecurityConfig { }
```

ℹ️ Although you can configure Spring Security in the same configuration class as the web and service layers, it's better to separate the security configurations in an isolated class (e.g., TodoSecurityConfig).

As Spring Security for HTTP works using a servlet filter, we need to register this as well. This is easily done by extending the AbstractSecurityWebApplicationInitializer (see the following listing).

Listing 5-2. Security initializer

```
package com.apress.spring6recipes.board.security;

import org.springframework.security.web.context.AbstractSecurityWebApplicationInitializer;

public class TodoSecurityInitializer extends AbstractSecurityWebApplicationInitializer { }
```

The AbstractSecurityWebApplicationInitializer will automatically detect the ApplicationContext containing the security configuration and use that to set up the filter. If using Spring Security without Spring (like in a JAX-RS application), you could pass in the configuration to the AbstractSecurityWebApplicationInitializer using the constructor (there is a constructor taking configuration classes).

When building and deploying the application and trying to access http://localhost:8080/todos/todos, you will now be greeted by the default Spring Security login page (see Figure 5-2).

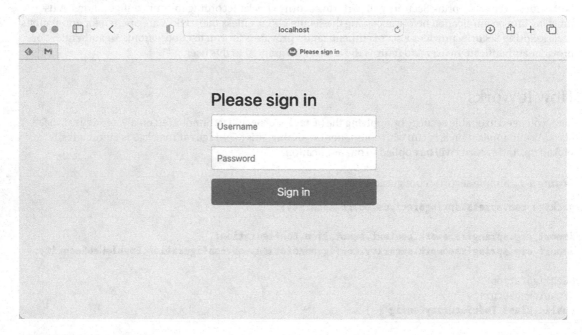

Figure 5-2. *Default Spring Security login page*

Securing URL Access

The default configuration is part of the org.springframework.security.config.annotation.web.configuration.HttpSecurityConfiguration class. This configuration provides a bean of type HttpSecurity with the default configuration. Contributing to this default configuration is the org.springframework.security.config.annotation.web.configuration.WebSecurityConfiguration, which takes care of the web part (setting up a filter chain to apply security). If you look at the latter class, it will create a bean named springSecurityFilterChain. Here you will see that it includes the anyRequest().authenticated() call. This tells Spring Security that for every request that comes in, you have to be authenticated with the system. You will also see that by default HTTP basic authentication and form-based login are enabled. Form-based login also includes a default login page creator, which will be used if you don't explicitly specify a login page.

Listing 5-3. Configuration method from the WebSecurityConfiguration class

```
@Bean(name = AbstractSecurityWebApplicationInitializer.DEFAULT_FILTER_NAME)
public Filter springSecurityFilterChain() throws Exception {
    boolean hasFilterChain = !this.securityFilterChains.isEmpty();
    if (!hasFilterChain) {
        this.webSecurity.addSecurityFilterChainBuilder(() -> {
            this.httpSecurity.authorizeHttpRequests(
            (authorize) -> authorize.anyRequest().authenticated());
            this.httpSecurity.formLogin(Customizer.withDefaults());
            this.httpSecurity.httpBasic(Customizer.withDefaults());
            return this.httpSecurity.build();
        });
    }
    for (SecurityFilterChain securityFilterChain : this.securityFilterChains) {
        this.webSecurity.addSecurityFilterChainBuilder(() -> securityFilterChain);
    }
    for (WebSecurityCustomizer customizer : this.webSecurityCustomizers) {
        customizer.customize(this.webSecurity);
    }
    return this.webSecurity.build();
}
```

Let's write a couple of security rules ourselves. Instead of only needing to be logged in, you can write some powerful access rules for the URLs. To do this you need to create a method that accepts the HttpSecurity bean provided by the HttpSecurityConfiguration and returns a SecurityFilterChain. When providing a SecurityFilterChain yourself, the default configuration in the WebSecurityConfiguration won't apply anymore, and you would need to specify the authentication mechanisms as well.

Listing 5-4. Todo security configuration

```
package com.apress.spring6recipes.board.security;

import org.springframework.context.annotation.Bean;
import org.springframework.context.annotation.Configuration;
import org.springframework.http.HttpMethod;
import org.springframework.security.config.Customizer;
import org.springframework.security.config.annotation.web.builders.HttpSecurity;
import org.springframework.security.config.annotation.web.configuration.EnableWebSecurity;
import org.springframework.security.core.userdetails.User;
import org.springframework.security.provisioning.InMemoryUserDetailsManager;
import org.springframework.security.provisioning.UserDetailsManager;
import org.springframework.security.web.SecurityFilterChain;

@Configuration
@EnableWebSecurity
public class TodoSecurityConfig {
```

```
@Bean
public UserDetailsManager userDetailsService() {
  var user = User.withDefaultPasswordEncoder()
            .username("user").password("user").authorities("USER").build();
  var admin = User.withDefaultPasswordEncoder()
            .username("admin").password("admin").authorities("USER", "ADMIN").build();
  return new InMemoryUserDetailsManager(user, admin);
}

@Bean
public SecurityFilterChain securityFilterChain(HttpSecurity http) throws Exception {

  http.csrf().disable();
  http.formLogin(Customizer.withDefaults());
  http.authorizeHttpRequests( auth ->
            auth
                .requestMatchers(HttpMethod.DELETE, "/todos/*").hasAuthority("ADMIN")
                .requestMatchers("/todos", "/todos/*").hasAuthority("USER"));
  return http.build();
  }
}
```

With authorizeHttpRequests() you start securing your URLs. You can then use one of the matchers–here you use the requestMatchers–to define the matching rules and which authorities a user needs to have. You have secured all access to /todos to users that have the authority USER. To be able to call /todos with a DELETE request, you need to be a user with the role ADMIN.

Most authentication mechanisms will use a UserDetailsService to look up the users. This is an interface with a single method loadByUsername to load user details. In this recipe we will use an InMemoryUserDetailsManager that will store the users internally in a java.util.Map. We use the User.UserBuilder to create some users for testing purposes. Generally, you don't want to use this approach for your live application but rather use something like a database, LDAP, or even tokens to store the user information.

ⓘ   There is a call to disable CSRF protection, for now, as that would disable the working of the forms. See the later part of this recipe on how to enable it.

You can configure authentication services as regular beans. Spring Security supports several ways of authenticating users, including authenticating against a database or an LDAP repository. It also supports defining user details directly for simple security requirements. You can specify a username, a password, and a set of authorities for each user.

Now, you can redeploy this application to test its security configurations. You must log into this application with a correct username and password to see the todos. Finally, to delete a todo, you must log in as an administrator.

Working with CSRF Protection

It is generally a good idea to leave the default for CSRF enabled, as this will reduce the risk you have with the Cross-Site Request Forgery attack. It is enabled by default in Spring Security, and the line `csrf().disable()` can be removed from the configuration. When CSRF protection is enabled, Spring Security adds the `CsrfFilter` to the list of filters it uses for protection. This filter in turn uses an implementation of the `CsrfTokenRepository` to generate and store tokens. By default this is the `HttpSessionCsrfTokenRepository` that, as the name implies, stores the generated token in the `HttpSession`. There is also a `CookieCsrfTokenRepository` that stores the token information in a cookie. If you want to switch the `CsrfTokenRepository`, you can use the `csrfTokenRepository()` configuration method to change it. You could also use this to configure an explicitly configured `HttpSessionCsrfTokenRepository`, `CookieCsrfTokenRepository`, or your own implementation of the `CsrfTokenRepository` interface. For now we will use the `CookieCsrfTokenRepository`.

Listing 5-5. Todo security configuration

```
@Bean
public SecurityFilterChain securityFilterChain(HttpSecurity http)
        throws Exception {
    http.csrf().csrfTokenRepository(csrfTokenRepository());
}

private CookieCsrfTokenRepository csrfTokenRepository() {
    return new CookieCsrfTokenRepository();
}
```

When CSRF is enabled, then after login, trying to complete or delete a todo item will fail in the absence of a CSRF token. To fix this you need to pass the CSRF token back to the server on requests that modify content. You can easily do this with a `hidden` input in your form. The `CookieCsrfTokenRepository` exposes the token as an HTTP cookie with the name `XSRF-TOKEN` (by default, unless you configured it explicitly), and for a form you can use the `parameterName` and `token` properties.

Add the following to the forms that need the CSRF token as part of the submit.

Listing 5-6. CSRF token hidden form fields

```
<input type="hidden" name="${_csrf.parameterName}" value="${_csrf.token}"/>
```

Now when submitting the form, the token will be part of the request, and you will again be able to complete or delete a todo item.

ℹ As the application uses Thymeleaf to render our pages and forms, it will automatically add the hidden input field to all the forms it processes.

There is also a form in the `todo-create.html`; however, as this is using the Spring MVC form tags, you don't need to modify this. When using the Spring MVC form tags, the CSRF token is added to the form automatically. To make this possible, Spring Security registers an `org.springframework.security.web.servlet.support.csrf.CsrfRequestDataValueProcessor`, which takes care of adding the token to the form.

5-2. Logging Into Web Applications

Problem

A secure application requires its users to log in before they can access certain secure functions. This is especially important for web applications running on the open Internet, because hackers can easily reach them. Most web applications have to provide a way for users to input their credentials to log in.

Solution

Spring Security supports multiple ways for users to log into a web application:

- Form-based login

- HTTP basic authentication

- HTTP digest authentication

- OAuth2 authentication

- Certificate-based authentication (X.509)

- J2EE authentication (delegate to the underlying Jakarta container)

Some parts of your application may allow for anonymous access (e.g., access to the welcome page). Spring Security provides an anonymous login service that can assign a principal and grant authorities to an anonymous user so that you can handle an anonymous user like a normal user when defining security policies.

Spring Security also supports remember-me login, which is able to remember a user's identity across multiple browser sessions so that a user needn't log in again after logging in for the first time.

How It Works

To help you better understand the various login mechanisms in isolation, let's first investigate the default Spring Security configuration.

Listing 5-7. HttpSecurity Bean method in HttpSecurityConfiguration

```
@Bean(HTTPSECURITY_BEAN_NAME)
@Scope("prototype")
HttpSecurity httpSecurity() throws Exception {
  // Setup for http element removed
  http
      .csrf(withDefaults())
      .addFilter(webAsyncManagerIntegrationFilter)
      .exceptionHandling(withDefaults())
      .headers(withDefaults())
      .sessionManagement(withDefaults())
      .securityContext(withDefaults())
      .requestCache(withDefaults())
      .anonymous(withDefaults())
      .servletApi(withDefaults())
      .apply(new DefaultLoginPageConfigurer<>());
  http.logout(withDefaults());
```

```
    applyDefaultConfigurers(http);
    return http;
}
```

The aforementioned listing (Listing 5-7) comes from the HttpSecurityConfiguration class and is the default configuration supplied to an HttpSecurity bean. Each method that requires an HttpSecurity instance will receive its own instance due to it being scoped prototype (see Chapter 1 for more information on scopes).

Important in the working of Spring Security are the securityContext and exceptionHandling. Without these basics Spring Security wouldn't store the user after doing a login, and it wouldn't do proper exception translation for security-related exceptions (they would simply bubble up, which might expose some of your internals to the outside world).

As this is the HttpSecurity and thus relies on the Servlet API, the integration with that is automatically enabled through the servletApi() method.

Spring Security will also add specific headers to the responses to disable certain features in the browser, like the X-Frame header to disallow frames, the X-Content-Type-Options to disable content sniffing, and more.

Out of the box, Spring Security assumes that information can be stored in the HTTP session, and thus it will set up basic session management to prevent session hijacking or at least make it harder. As mentioned in Recipe 5-1, the csrf protection is also enabled by default, and with the HttpSessionCsrfTokenRepository to store the information in the HTTP session, this is in the csrf method. The requestCache is for storing an HTTP servlet request in a cache so that after login the original request can be issued again. Again by default this is stored in the HTTP session.

HTTP Basic Authentication

The HTTP basic authentication support can be configured via the httpBasic() method. When HTTP basic authentication is required, a browser will typically display a login dialog or a specific login page for users to log in.

Listing 5-8. Todo security configuration–HTTP basic

```
package com.apress.spring6recipes.board.security;

import org.springframework.context.annotation.Bean;
import org.springframework.context.annotation.Configuration;
import org.springframework.http.HttpMethod;
import org.springframework.security.config.Customizer;
import org.springframework.security.config.annotation.web.builders.HttpSecurity;
import org.springframework.security.config.annotation.web.configuration.EnableWebSecurity;
import org.springframework.security.web.SecurityFilterChain;

@Configuration
@EnableWebSecurity
public class TodoSecurityConfig {

  @Bean
  public SecurityFilterChain securityFilterChain(HttpSecurity http) throws Exception {

    http.formLogin().disable();
    http.httpBasic(Customizer.withDefaults());
```

```
  http.authorizeHttpRequests(
    auth -> auth
      .requestMatchers(HttpMethod.DELETE, "/todos/*").hasAuthority("ADMIN")
      .requestMatchers("/todos", "/todos/*").hasAuthority("USER"));
  return http.build();
  }
}
```

ℹ️   When HTTP basic authentication and form-based login are enabled at the same time, instead of an HTTP basic pop-up, you will get the form login.

Form-Based Login

The form-based login service will render a web page that contains a login form for users to input their login details and process the login form submission. It's configured via the formLogin method.

Listing 5-9. Todo security configuration–form login

```
package com.apress.spring6recipes.board.security;

import org.springframework.context.annotation.Bean;
import org.springframework.context.annotation.Configuration;
import org.springframework.http.HttpMethod;
import org.springframework.security.config.Customizer;
import org.springframework.security.config.annotation.web.builders.HttpSecurity;
import org.springframework.security.config.annotation.web.configuration.EnableWebSecurity;
import org.springframework.security.web.SecurityFilterChain;

@Configuration
@EnableWebSecurity
public class TodoSecurityConfig {

  @Bean
  public SecurityFilterChain securityFilterChain(HttpSecurity http)
          throws Exception {
    http.formLogin(Customizer.withDefaults());
    http.httpBasic().disable();
    http.authorizeHttpRequests(
      auth -> auth
        .requestMatchers(HttpMethod.DELETE, "/todos/*").hasAuthority("ADMIN")
        .requestMatchers("/todos", "/todos/*").hasAuthority("USER"));
    return http.build();
  }
```

By default, Spring Security automatically creates a login page and maps it to the URL /login. So you can add a link to your application (e.g., in todos.html) referring to this URL for login.

Listing 5-10. Login URL link

```
<a th:href="@{/login}">Login</a>
```

If you don't prefer the default login page, you can provide a custom login page of your own. For example, you can create the following login.html file in the templates directory.

Listing 5-11. Custom login page

```html
<!DOCTYPE html>
<html xmlns:th="http://www.thymeleaf.org">
<head>
    <title>Login</title>
    <link type="text/css" rel="stylesheet"
        href="https://cdnjs.cloudflare.com/ajax/libs/semantic-ui/2.2.10/semantic.min.css">
    <style type="text/css">
        body {
            background-color: #DADADA;
        }

        body > .grid {
            height: 100%;
        }

        .column {
            max-width: 450px;
        }
    </style>
</head>

<body>
<div class="ui middle aligned center aligned grid">
    <div class="column">
        <h2 class="ui header">Log-in to your account</h2>
        <form method="POST" th:action="@{/login}" class="ui large form">
            <div class="ui stacked segment">
                <div class="field">
                    <div class="ui left icon input">
                        <i class="user icon"></i>
                        <input type="text" name="username" placeholder="E-mail address">
                    </div>
                </div>
                <div class="field">
                    <div class="ui left icon input">
                        <i class="lock icon"></i>
                        <input type="password" name="password" placeholder="Password">
```

251

```
                    </div>
                </div>
                <button class="ui fluid large submit green button">Login</button>
            </div>
        </form>
    </div>
</div>
</div>
</body>
</html>
```

For this login page to be used, we need to write a controller or rather use a
UrlFilenameViewController, which maps a URL to a name of the view (see Chapter 2 for more on
controllers and views). This is easily done by implementing the WebMvcConfigurer interface and the
addViewControllers method.

Listing 5-12. Todo security configuration–form login

```
package com.apress.spring6recipes.board.security;

@Configuration
@EnableWebSecurity
public class TodoSecurityConfig implements WebMvcConfigurer {

    @Override
    public void addViewControllers(ViewControllerRegistry registry) {
        registry.addViewController("/login").setViewName("login");
    }
}
```

If you stick with the default naming of Spring Security, that is enough to render your own custom login
page. Next, you need to instruct Spring Security to display your custom login page when a login is requested;
you have to specify its URL in the loginPage configuration method.

Listing 5-13. Todo security configuration–form login

```
@Configuration
@EnableWebSecurity
public class TodoSecurityConfig implements WebMvcConfigurer {
    @Bean
    public SecurityFilterChain securityFilterChain(HttpSecurity http) throws Exception {

        http.formLogin().loginPage("/login").permitAll();
    }
}
```

Notice the permitAll after the loginPage element. Without this the login page would be inaccessible by
anonymous users as it would fall under the protection of Spring Security.

If the login page is displayed by Spring Security when a user requests a secure URL, the user will be
redirected to the target URL once the login succeeds. However, if the user requests the login page directly via
its URL, by default the user will be redirected to the context path's root (i.e., http://localhost:8080/) after a
successful login. If you have not defined a welcome page in your web deployment descriptor, you may wish
to redirect the user to a default target URL when the login succeeds.

Listing 5-14. Todo security configuration–form login with defaultSuccessUrl

```
@Configuration
@EnableWebSecurity
public class TodoSecurityConfig implements WebMvcConfigurer {

    @Bean
    public SecurityFilterChain securityFilterChain(HttpSecurity http)
            throws Exception {
        http
            .formLogin().loginPage("/login").defaultSuccessUrl("/todos");
        return http.build();
    }
}
```

If you use the default login page created by Spring Security, then when a login fails, Spring Security will render the login page again with the error message. However, if you specify a custom login page, you will have to configure the authentication failure URL to specify which URL to redirect to on login error. For example, you can redirect to the custom login page again with the error request parameter.

Listing 5-15. Todo security configuration–form login with failureUrl

```
@Configuration
@EnableWebSecurity
public class TodoSecurityConfig implements WebMvcConfigurer {

    @Bean
    public SecurityFilterChain securityFilterChain(HttpSecurity http)
            throws Exception {
        http
            ...
            .formLogin()
              .loginPage("/login")
              .defaultSuccessUrl("/todos")
              .failureUrl("/login?error=true");
        return http.build();
    }
}
```

Then your login page should test whether the error request parameter is present. If an error has occurred, you will have to display the error message by accessing the session scope attribute SPRING_SECURITY_LAST_EXCEPTION, which stores the last exception for the current user.

Listing 5-16. Login page with error display

```
<form method="POST" th:action="@{/login}" class="ui large form">
    <div th:if="${param.error !=null}" class="ui error message" style="display: block;">
        Authentication Failed<br/>
        Reason: <span th:text="${session.SPRING_SECURITY_LAST_EXCEPTION.message}">Reason of
        login error</span>
        </font>
    </div>
</form>
```

The Logout Service

The logout service provides a handler to handle logout requests. It can be configured via the logout() configuration method.

Listing 5-17. Todo security configuration–logout service

```
@Configuration
@EnableWebSecurity
public class TodoSecurityConfig implements WebMvcConfigurer {

  @Bean
  public SecurityFilterChain securityFilterChain(HttpSecurity http)
        throws Exception {
    http.logout();
    return http.build();
  }
}
```

By default, it's mapped to the URL /logout and will react to POST requests only. You can add a small HTML form to your page to log out.

Listing 5-18. Logout form

```
<form th:action="@{/logout}" method="post"><button>Logout</button><form>
```

ℹ️   When using CSRF protection, don't forget to add the CSRF token to the form (see Recipe 5-1); else, logout will fail.

By default, a user will be redirected to the context path's root when the logout succeeds, but sometimes, you may wish to direct the user to another URL, which you can do by using the logoutSuccessUrl configuration method.

Listing 5-19. Todo security configuration–logout service with logoutSuccessUrl

```
@Configuration
@EnableWebSecurity
public class TodoSecurityConfig implements WebMvcConfigurer {

  @Bean
  public SecurityFilterChain securityFilterChain(HttpSecurity http)
        throws Exception {
    http.logout().logoutSuccessUrl("/logout-success");
    return http.build();
  }
}
```

After logout you might notice that when using the browser back button, you will still be able to see the previous pages, even if your logout was successful. This has to do with the fact that the browser caches the pages. By enabling the security headers, with the headers() configuration method, the browser will be instructed to not cache the page.

Listing 5-20. Todo security configuration–header security

```java
@Configuration
@EnableWebSecurity
public class TodoSecurityConfig implements WebMvcConfigurer {

  @Bean
  public SecurityFilterChain securityFilterChain(HttpSecurity http)
      throws Exception {
    http.headers();
    return http.build();
  }
}
```

Next to the no-cache headers, this will also disable content sniffing and enable X-Frame protection (see Recipe 5-1 for more information). With this enabled and using the browser back button, you will be redirected to the login page again.

Anonymous Login

The anonymous login service can be configured via the anonymous() method in Java Config, where you can customize the username and authorities of an anonymous user, whose default values are anonymousUser and ROLE_ANONYMOUS:

Listing 5-21. Todo security configuration–anonymous login

```java
@Configuration
@EnableWebSecurity
public class TodoSecurityConfig implements WebMvcConfigurer {

  @Bean
  public SecurityFilterChain securityFilterChain(HttpSecurity http)
      throws Exception {
    http.anonymous().principal("guest").authorities("ROLE_GUEST");
    return http.build();
  }
}
```

Remember-Me Support

Remember-me support can be configured via the rememberMe() method in Java Config. By default, it encodes the username, password, remember-me expiration time, and a private key as a token, stored as a cookie in the user's browser. The next time the user accesses the same web application, this token will be detected so that the user can log in automatically.

Listing 5-22. Todo Security configuration–Remember Me

```
@Configuration
@EnableWebSecurity
public class TodoSecurityConfig implements WebMvcConfigurer {

    @Bean
    public SecurityFilterChain securityFilterChain(HttpSecurity http)
            throws Exception {
        http.rememberMe();
        return http.build();
    }
}
```

However, static remember-me tokens can cause security issues, because they may be captured by hackers. Spring Security supports rolling tokens for more advanced security needs, but this requires a database to persist the tokens. For details about rolling remember-me token deployment, please refer to the Spring Security reference documentation.

5-3. Authenticating Users

Problem

When a user attempts to log into your application to access its secure resources, you have to authenticate the user's principal and grant authorities to this user.

Solution

In Spring Security, authentication is performed by one or more AuthenticationProviders, connected as a chain. If any of these providers authenticates a user successfully, that user will be able to log into the application. If any provider reports that the user is disabled or locked or that the credential is incorrect or if no provider can authenticate the user, then the user will be unable to log into this application.

Spring Security supports multiple ways of authenticating users and includes built-in provider implementations for them. You can easily configure these providers with the built-in XML elements. Most common authentication providers authenticate users against a user repository storing user details (e.g., in an application's memory, a relational database, or an LDAP repository).

When storing user details in a repository, you should avoid storing user passwords in clear text, because that makes them vulnerable to hackers. Instead, you should always store encrypted passwords in your repository. A typical way of encrypting passwords is to use a one-way hash function to encode the passwords. When a user enters a password to log in, you apply the same hash function to this password and compare the result with the one stored in the repository. Spring Security supports several algorithms for encoding passwords (including MD5 and SHA) and provides built-in password encoders for these algorithms.

If you retrieve a user's details from a user repository every time a user attempts to log in, your application may incur a performance impact. This is because a user repository is usually stored remotely, and it has to perform some kinds of queries in response to a request. For this reason, Spring Security supports caching user details in local memory and storage to save you the overhead of performing remote queries.

How It Works

Authenticating Users with In-Memory Definitions

If you have only a few users in your application and you seldom modify their details, you can consider defining the user details in Spring Security's configuration file so that they will be loaded into your application's memory.

Listing 5-23. InMemoryUserDetailsManager with users

```
@Configuration
@EnableWebSecurity
public class TodoSecurityConfig implements WebMvcConfigurer {

  @Bean
  public UserDetailsManager userDetailsService() {
    var user1 = User.withDefaultPasswordEncoder()
            .username("marten@deinum.biz").password("user").authorities("USER").build();
    var user2 = User.withDefaultPasswordEncoder()
            .username("jdoe@does.net").password("unknown").disabled(true).
            authorities("USER").build();
    var admin = User.withDefaultPasswordEncoder()
            .username("admin@ya2do.io").password("admin").authorities("USER", "ADMIN").
            build();
    return new InMemoryUserDetailsManager(user1, user2, admin);
  }
}
```

You can define user details with the User class and the different with* methods. Here we use the withDefaultPasswordEncoder as we want to be able to supply plaintext passwords but still have them encoded. For each user, you can specify a username, a password, a disabled status, and a set of granted authorities. A disabled user cannot log into an application.

Authenticating Users Against a Database

More typically, user details should be stored in a database for easy maintenance. Spring Security has built-in support for querying user details from a database. By default, it queries user details, including authorities, with the following SQL statements.

Listing 5-24. Spring Security default SQL select statements

```
SELECT username, password, enabled
FROM   users
WHERE  username = ?

SELECT username, authority
FROM   authorities
WHERE  username = ?
```

In order for Spring Security to query user details with these SQL statements, you have to create the corresponding tables in your database. For example, you can create them in the todo schema with the following SQL statements.

Listing 5-25. Spring Security USERS and AUTHORITIES tables

```
-- Spring Security User / Authorities setup
-- See also users.ddl from Spring Security
CREATE TABLE USERS
(
    USERNAME VARCHAR(50) NOT NULL,
    PASSWORD VARCHAR(60) NOT NULL,
    ENABLED  SMALLINT    NOT NULL DEFAULT 0,
    PRIMARY KEY (USERNAME)
);

CREATE TABLE AUTHORITIES
(
    USERNAME  VARCHAR(50) NOT NULL,
    AUTHORITY VARCHAR(50) NOT NULL,
    FOREIGN KEY (USERNAME) REFERENCES USERS
);
```

Next, you can input some user details into these tables for testing purposes. The data for these two tables is shown in Tables 5-1 and 5-2.

Table 5-1. Testing User Data for the USERS Table

USERNAME	PASSWORD	ENABLED
admin@ya2do.io	secret	1
marten@deinum.biz	user	1
jdoe@does.net	unknown	0

Table 5-2. Testing User Data for the AUTHORITIES Table

USERNAME	AUTHORITY
admin@ya2do.io	ADMIN
admin@ya2do.io	USER
marten@deinum.biz	USER
jdoe@does.net	USER

In order for Spring Security to access these tables, you have to declare a data source to be able to create connections to this database. In this case the DataSource was already defined in the TodoWebConfig, and we can just inject it into our userDetailsService method through an argument. In the userDetailsService we now construct an instance of the JdbcUserDetailsManager, which allows us to not only find users but also create them. If you don't need to create them, you can do with the org.springframework.security.core. userdetails.jdbc.JdbcDaoImpl, which only provides the lookup.

Listing 5-26. Todo security configuration with JDBC

```
@Configuration
@EnableWebSecurity
public class TodoSecurityConfig implements WebMvcConfigurer {

  @Bean
  public UserDetailsManager userDetailsService(DataSource dataSource) {
    var userDetailsManager = new JdbcUserDetailsManager(dataSource);
    initializeUsers(userDetailsManager);
    return userDetailsManager;
  }

  private void initializeUsers(JdbcUserDetailsManager users) {
    var user1 = User.withDefaultPasswordEncoder()
      .username("marten@deinum.biz").password("user").authorities("USER").build();
    var user2 = User.withDefaultPasswordEncoder()
      .username("jdoe@does.net").password("unknown").disabled(true).authorities("USER").
build();
    var admin = User.withDefaultPasswordEncoder()
      .username("admin@ya2do.io").password("admin").authorities("USER", "ADMIN").build();

    users.createUser(user1);
    users.createUser(user2);
    users.createUser(admin);
  }
}
```

However, in some cases, you may already have your own user repository defined in a legacy database. For example, suppose that the tables are created with the following SQL statements and that all users in the MEMBER table have the enabled status.

Listing 5-27. Legacy table structure (sample)

```
CREATE TABLE MEMBER (
    ID          BIGINT          NOT NULL,
    USERNAME    VARCHAR(50)     NOT NULL,
    PASSWORD    VARCHAR(32)     NOT NULL,
    PRIMARY KEY (ID)
);

CREATE TABLE MEMBER_ROLE (
    MEMBER_ID   BIGINT          NOT NULL,
    ROLE        VARCHAR(10)     NOT NULL,
    FOREIGN KEY (MEMBER_ID) REFERENCES MEMBER
);
```

Suppose you have the legacy user data stored in these tables as shown in Tables 5-3 and 5-4.

Table 5-3. *Legacy User Data in the MEMBER Table*

ID	USERNAME	PASSWORD
1	admin@ya2do.io	secret
2	marten@deinum.biz	user

Table 5-4. *Legacy User Data in the MEMBER_ROLE Table*

MEMBER_ID	ROLE
1	ROLE_ADMIN
1	ROLE_USER
2	ROLE_USER

Fortunately, Spring Security also supports using custom SQL statements to query a legacy database for user details. You can specify the statements for querying a user's information and authorities using the usersByUsernameQuery and authoritiesByUsernameQuery properties of the JdbcDaoImpl/JdbcUserDetailsManager.

Listing 5-28. Todo security with custom JDBC queries

```
@Configuration
@EnableWebSecurity
public class TodoSecurityConfig implements WebMvcConfigurer {

  private static final String USERS_BY_USERNAME =
      "SELECT username, password, 'true' as enabled FROM member WHERE username = ?";
  private static final String AUTHORITIES_BY_USERNAME = """
      SELECT member.username, member_role.role as authorities
      FROM member, member_role
      WHERE  member.username = ? AND member.id = member_role.member_id
      """;

@Bean
  public UserDetailsManager userDetailsService(DataSource dataSource) {
    var userDetailsManager = new JdbcUserDetailsManager(dataSource);
    userDetailsManager.setUsersByUsernameQuery(USERS_BY_USERNAME);
    userDetailsManager.setAuthoritiesByUsernameQuery(AUTHORITIES_BY_USERNAME);
    initializeUsers(userDetailsManager);
    return userDetailsManager;
  }
}
```

Encrypting Passwords

Until now, you have been storing user details with the default configured password encoder, which is the BCryptPasswordEncoder. Or rather it uses the DelegatingPasswordEncoder, which detects the type of encoding from the password and when none found uses the default. Passwords are stored in the format {id} encodedPassword, where id refers to a configured encoder. Out of the box, Spring Security comes configured with the following encoders.

Table 5-5. *Default configured password encoders*

id	Password Encoder	Encoding	Deprecated
bcrypt	BCryptPasswordEncoder	BCrypt	No
ldap	LdapShaPasswordEncoder	SHA and SSHA	Yes
MD4	Md4PasswordEncoder	MD4	Yes
MD5	MessageDigestPasswordEncoder	MD5	Yes
noop	NoOpPasswordEncoder	Plaintext	Yes
pbkdf2	Pbkdf2PasswordEncoder	PBKDF2	No
scrypt	SCryptPasswordEncoder	SCrypt	No
SHA-1	MessageDigestPasswordEncoder	SHA-1	Yes
SHA-256	MessageDigestPasswordEncoder	SHA-256	Yes
sha-256	StandardPasswordEncoder	SHA-256	Yes
argon2	Argon2PasswordEncoder	Argon2	No

Some of the provided PasswordEncoders are deprecated and are mainly there for backward compatibility. If you are still using one of those in your application, it might be time to upgrade to one that is still supported. This would however need a password reset for the users, unless the passwords are stored in plaintext.

Instead of relying on the delegating password encoder, you can also specify a specific one in your configuration. If there is only a single PasswordEncoder in your configuration, it will be automatically picked up and used by Spring Security.

Listing 5-29. Todo security with an explicit PasswordEncoder

```
@Configuration
@EnableWebSecurity
public class TodoSecurityConfig implements WebMvcConfigurer {

  @Bean
  public BCryptPasswordEncoder passwordEncoder() {
    return new BCryptPasswordEncoder();
  }
}
```

To store BCrypt hashes in the password field, the length of the field has to be at least 60 chars long (that is the length of the BCrypt hash), and if you are using a SQL script, like data.sql to insert data into the database, the passwords need to be inserted encoded. Table 5-6 contains the BCrypt encoded passwords for the test users.

Table 5-6. *Testing User Data with Encrypted Passwords for the USERS Table*

Username	Password	Enabled
admin@ya2do.io	$2a$10$E3mPTZb50e7sSW15fDx8Ne7hDZpfDjrmMPTTUp8wVjLTu.G5oPYCO	1
marten@deinum.biz	$2a$10$5VWqjwoMYnFRTTmbWCRZT.iY3WW8ny27kQuUL9yPK1/WJcPcBLFWO	1
jdoe@does.net	$2a$10$cFKh0.XCUOA9L.in5smIiO2QIOT8.6ufQSwIIC.AVz26WctxhSWC6	0

Authenticating Users Against an LDAP Repository

Spring Security also supports accessing an LDAP repository for authenticating users. First, you have to prepare some user data for populating the LDAP repository. Let's prepare the user data in the LDAP Data Interchange Format (LDIF), a standard plaintext data format for importing and exporting LDAP directory data. For example, create the users.ldif file containing the following contents.

Listing 5-30. LDIF file for LDAP setup

```
dn: dc=spring6recipes,dc=com
objectClass: top
objectClass: domain
dc: spring6recipes

dn: ou=groups,dc=spring6recipes,dc=com
objectclass: top
objectclass: organizationalUnit
ou: groups

dn: ou=people,dc=spring6recipes,dc=com
objectclass: top
objectclass: organizationalUnit
ou: people

dn: uid=admin,ou=people,dc=spring6recipes,dc=com
objectclass: top
objectclass: uidObject
objectclass: person
uid: admin
cn: admin
sn: admin
userPassword: secret

dn: uid=user1,ou=people,dc=spring6recipes,dc=com
objectclass: top
objectclass: uidObject
objectclass: person
uid: user1
cn: user1
sn: user1
```

```
userPassword: 1111

dn: cn=admin,ou=groups,dc=spring6recipes,dc=com
objectclass: top
objectclass: groupOfNames
cn: admin
member: uid=admin,ou=people,dc=spring6recipes,dc=com

dn: cn=user,ou=groups,dc=spring6recipes,dc=com
objectclass: top
objectclass: groupOfNames
cn: user
member: uid=admin,ou=people,dc=spring6recipes,dc=com
member: uid=user1,ou=people,dc=spring6recipes,dc=com
```

Don't worry if you don't understand this LDIF file very well. You probably won't need to use this file format to define LDAP data often, because most LDAP servers support GUI-based configuration. This users.ldif file includes the following contents:

- The default LDAP domain, dc=spring6recipes,dc=com

- The groups and people organization units for storing groups and users

- The admin and user1 users with the passwords secret and 1111

- The admin group (including the admin user) and the user group (including the admin and user1 users)

For testing purposes, you can install an LDAP server on your local machine to host this user repository. For the sake of easy installation and configuration, we recommend installing OpenDS, a Java-based open source directory service engine that supports LDAP.

💡 In the bin directory, there is a ldap.sh script that will start a Dockerized version of OpenDS and that will import earlier mentioned users.ldif. Note that the root user and password for this LDAP server are cn=Directory Manager and ldap, respectively. Later, you will have to use this user to connect to this server.

After the LDAP server has started up, you can configure Spring Security to authenticate users against its repository.

There are two options for using LDAP: One is to use bind authentication, which entails that the user is authenticated against the LDAP server with the given username/password. The other option is to use password authentication in which the user information will be retrieved from LDAP but Spring Security will do the password validation. The drawback of the latter approach is that you need to have some read-only user that has access to the LDAP to be able to retrieve the user information. The most common way to use LDAP is with bind authentication. To enable this you need to configure a BindAuthenticator. To help do the setup, there is the LdapBindAuthenticationManagerFactory.

Before we can configure the BindAuthenticator, we need to have a connection to LDAP; for this we use a ContextSource. Spring Security provides one to make it a little easier, the DefaultSpringSecurityContextSource. It takes a single argument in the constructor for the LDAP server URL; based on that it will connect to our LDAP server.

The `ContextSource` is passed into the `authenticationManager` method and used to configure the `BindAuthenticator` and a `DefaultLdapAuthoritiesPopulator`. The latter is needed to retrieve the groups a user is a member of and translate them into authorities to be used with Spring Security. By default a `NullLdapAuthoritiesPopulator` is being used, which allows for authenticating the user, but it won't set up any authorities.

To be able to find the proper users in LDAP, we need to set up either one or more `userDnPatterns` or a `userSearchFilter`. For our application it is enough to specify a pattern of `uid={0},ou=people`, as all of our users are in the people unit. The `{0}` will be replaced with the username as passed in from the login form. For the `DefaultLdapAuthoritiesPopulator` we need to have a `groupSearchBase`, so we specify `ou=groups` as that is the unit containing the groups. With this the populator will obtain the groups the user is part of and convert them into authorities.

Listing 5-31. Todo security configuration for LDAP

```
@Configuration
@EnableWebSecurity
public class TodoSecurityConfig implements WebMvcConfigurer {

  @Bean
  public DefaultSpringSecurityContextSource contextSource() {
    var url = "ldap://ldap-server:389/dc=spring6recipes,dc=com";
    return new DefaultSpringSecurityContextSource(url);
  }

  @Bean
  public AuthenticationManager authenticationManager(
          DefaultSpringSecurityContextSource contextSource) {
    var populator = new DefaultLdapAuthoritiesPopulator(contextSource, "ou=groups");
    populator.setRolePrefix("");

    var factory = new LdapBindAuthenticationManagerFactory(contextSource);
    factory.setUserDnPatterns("uid={0},ou=people");
    factory.setLdapAuthoritiesPopulator(populator);
    return factory.createAuthenticationManager();
  }
}
```

5-4. Making Access Control Decisions

Problem

In the authentication process, an application will grant a successfully authenticated user a set of authorities. When this user attempts to access a resource in the application, the application has to decide whether the resource is accessible with the granted authorities or other characteristics.

Solution

The decision on whether a user is allowed to access a resource in an application is called an authorization decision. It is made based on the user's authentication status and the resource's nature and access attributes. In Spring Security, authorization decisions are made by authorization managers, which have to implement the `AuthorizationManager` interface. You are free to create your own authorization managers by implementing this interface, but Spring Security comes with several implementations already. Most of them are configurable through the `http.authorizeHttpRequest` or by using method security (see recipe 5-5).

How It Works

Without knowing we have already been using these `AuthorizationManager` instances. In the expression `.requestMatchers("/todos", "/todos/*").hasAuthority("USER")`, the hasAuthority part is actually using a `AuthorizationManager`, the `AuthorityAuthorizationManager` to be precise. However, this is just a single instance. We could apply more or a specific one using the `access` method. For example, we could create an `AuthorizationManager` that would only allow access from localhost instead of for every URL.

Listing 5-32. Custom AuthorizationManager implementation

```
package com.apress.spring6recipes.board.security;

import org.springframework.security.authorization.AuthorizationDecision;
import org.springframework.security.authorization.AuthorizationManager;
import org.springframework.security.core.Authentication;
import org.springframework.security.web.authentication.WebAuthenticationDetails;

import java.util.function.Supplier;

public class LocalhostAuthorizationManager<T> implements AuthorizationManager<T> {

  @Override
  public AuthorizationDecision check(Supplier<Authentication> authentication, T object) {
    var auth = authentication.get();
    var granted = false;
    if (auth.getDetails() instanceof WebAuthenticationDetails details) {
      String address = details.getRemoteAddress();
      granted = address.equals("127.0.0.1") || address.equals("0:0:0:0:0:0:0:1");
    }
    return new AuthorizationDecision(granted);
  }
}
```

If the user is a web client whose IP address is equal to 127.0.0.1 or 0:0:0:0:0:0:0:1, their voter will decide to allow access; else, access will be denied. If the currently authenticated user (expressed through the `Authentication` object) is not a web client, access is denied as well.

Next, you have to define a custom access rule to include this authorization manager.

Listing 5-33. Todo security configuration–with a custom authorization manager

```
.requestMatchers(HttpMethod.DELETE, "/todos/*").access(
    AuthorizationManagers.allOf(
        AuthorityAuthorizationManager.hasAuthority("ADMIN"),
        new LocalhostAuthorizationManager<>()))
```

There is a helper class, the AuthorizationManagers, to make it easier to combine multiple authorization managers in either an all-of or any-of fashion. Here we want both to apply, so we use the allOf helper method to combine the two. The AuthorityAuthorizationManager is now also explicitly configured as we want both the authority and the IP address to be checked.

Using Expressions to Make Access Control Decisions

Although the authorization managers allow for a certain degree of flexibility, sometimes one wants more complex access control rules or to be more flexible. With Spring Security it is also possible to use Spring Expression Language (SpEL) to create powerful access control rules. Spring Security supports a couple of expressions out of the box (see Table 5-7 for a list). Using constructs like and, or, and not, one can create very powerful and flexible expressions.

Table 5-7. *Spring Security Built-In Expressions*

Expression	Description
hasRole('role') or hasAuthority('authority')	Returns true if the current user has the given role/authority
hasAnyRole('role1','role2') / hasAnyAuthority('auth1','auth2')	Returns true if the current user has at least one of the given roles
hasIpAddress('ip-address')	Returns true if the current user has the given IP address
principal	The current user
authentication	Access to the Spring Security authentication object
permitAll	Always evaluates to true
denyAll	Always evaluates to false
isAnonymous()	Returns true if the current user is anonymous
isRememberMe()	Returns true if the current user logged in by means of the remember-me functionality
isAuthenticated()	Returns true if this is not an anonymous user
isFullyAuthenticated()	Returns true if the user is not an anonymous nor a remember-me user

Although role and authority are almost the same, there is a slight, but important, difference in how they are processed. When using hasRole the passed-in value for the role will be checked if it starts with ROLE_ (the default role prefix); if not, this will be added before checking the authority. So hasRole('ADMIN') will actually check if the current user has the authority ROLE_ADMIN. When using hasAuthority it will check the value as is.

Listing 5-34. Todo security configuration–with an expression

```
auth
  .requestMatchers(HttpMethod.DELETE, "/todos/*").access(
    new WebExpressionAuthorizationManager("hasRole('ROLE_ADMIN') and
(hasIpAddress('127.0.0.1') or hasIpAddress('0:0:0:0:0:0:0:1'))"))
```

The preceding expression would give access to deletion of a post if someone had the ADMIN role and was logged in on the local machine. In the previous section, we needed to create our own custom AuthorizationManager. Now you only have to write an expression.

Using Expressions to Make Access Control Decisions Using Spring Beans

Although Spring Security has already several built-in functions that can be used when creating expressions, it is also possible to use your own functions. Using the @ syntax in the expression, you can reference any bean in the application context. So you could write an expression like @accessChecker. hasLocalAccess(authentication) and provide a bean named accessChecker that has a hasLocalAccess method that takes an Authentication object.

Listing 5-35. AccessChecker class

```
package com.apress.spring6recipes.board.security;

import org.springframework.security.core.Authentication;
import org.springframework.security.web.authentication.WebAuthenticationDetails;
import org.springframework.stereotype.Component;

@Component
public class AccessChecker {

  public boolean hasLocalAccess(Authentication authentication) {
    var access = false;
    if (authentication.getDetails() instanceof WebAuthenticationDetails details) {
      var address = details.getRemoteAddress();
      access = address.equals("127.0.0.1") || address.equals("0:0:0:0:0:0:0:1");
    }
    return access;
  }
}
```

The AccessChecker still does the same checks as the earlier LocalhostAuthorizationManager but doesn't need to extend the Spring Security classes.

Listing 5-36. Todo security configuration–with an expression using a bean

```
auth
  .requestMatchers(HttpMethod.DELETE, "/todos/*").access(
    new WebExpressionAuthorizationManager(
      "hasRole('ROLE_ADMIN') and @accessChecker.hasLocalAccess(authentication)"))
```

5-5. Securing Method Invocations

Problem

As an alternative or a complement to securing URL access in the web layer, sometimes you may need to secure method invocations in the service layer. For example, in the case that a single controller has to invoke multiple methods in the service layer, you may wish to enforce fine-grained security controls on these methods.

Solution

Spring Security enables you to secure method invocations in a declarative way. You annotate methods declared in a bean interface or an implementation class with the @Secured, @PreAuthorize/ @PostAuthorize, or @PreFilter/@PostFilter annotation and then enable security for them using the @EnableGlobalMethodSecurity annotation.

How It Works

Securing Methods with Annotations

The approach to securing methods is by annotating them with @Secured. For example, you can annotate each of the methods in TodoServiceImpl with the @Secured annotation and specify the access attribute as its value, whose type is String[] and which takes one or more authorities that will have access to the method.

Listing 5-37. TodoService implementation–using @Secured

```
package com.apress.spring6recipes.board;

import org.springframework.security.access.annotation.Secured;
import org.springframework.stereotype.Service;
import org.springframework.transaction.annotation.Transactional;

import java.util.List;
import java.util.Optional;

@Service
@Transactional
class TodoServiceImpl implements TodoService {

  private final TodoRepository todoRepository;

  TodoServiceImpl(TodoRepository todoRepository) {
    this.todoRepository = todoRepository;
  }

  @Override
  @Secured("USER")
  public List<Todo> listTodos() {
    return todoRepository.findAll();
  }
```

```
@Override
@Secured("USER")
public void save(Todo todo) {
  this.todoRepository.save(todo);
}

@Override
@Secured("USER")
public void complete(long id) {
  findById(id)
          .ifPresent((todo) -> {
            todo.setCompleted(true);
            todoRepository.save(todo);
          });
}

@Override
@Secured({ "USER", "ADMIN" })
public void remove(long id) {
  todoRepository.remove(id);
}

@Override
@Secured("USER")
public Optional<Todo> findById(long id) {
  return todoRepository.findOne(id);
}
}
```

Finally, you need to enable the method security. To do so you have to add the @EnableMethodSecurity annotation to your configuration class. As you want to use @Secured, you have to set the securedEnabled attribute to true.

Listing 5-38. Todo security configuration–method security enabled

```
package com.apress.spring6recipes.board.security;

@Configuration
@EnableWebSecurity
@EnableMethodSecurity(securedEnabled = true)
public class TodoSecurityConfig implements WebMvcConfigurer {
}
```

ℹ️ It is important that you add the @EnableMethodSecurity annotation to the application context configuration that contains the beans you want to secure!

269

Securing Methods with Annotations and Expressions

If you need more elaborate security rules, you can, just like with URL protection, use security expressions based on SpEL to secure your application. For this you can use the @PreAuthorize and @PostAuthorize annotations. With those you can write security-based expressions just as with the URL-based security. To enable processing of those annotations, you have to set the prePostEnabled attribute on the @EnableMethodSecurity to true (which is also the default).

Listing 5-39. Todo security configuration–method security enabled

```
package com.apress.spring6recipes.board.security;

@Configuration
@EnableWebSecurity
@EnableMethodSecurity(prePostEnabled = true)
public class TodoSecurityConfig implements WebMvcConfigurer {
}
```

Now you can use the @PreAuthorize and @PostAuthorize annotations to secure your application.

Listing 5-40. TodoService implementation–using @PreAuthorize/@PostAuthorize

```
package com.apress.spring6recipes.board;

import org.springframework.security.access.prepost.PostAuthorize;
import org.springframework.security.access.prepost.PreAuthorize;
import org.springframework.stereotype.Service;
import org.springframework.transaction.annotation.Transactional;

import java.util.List;
import java.util.Optional;

@Service
@Transactional
class TodoServiceImpl implements TodoService {

  private final TodoRepository todoRepository;

  TodoServiceImpl(TodoRepository todoRepository) {
    this.todoRepository = todoRepository;
  }

  @Override
  @PreAuthorize("hasAuthority('USER')")
  public List<Todo> listTodos() {
    return todoRepository.findAll();
  }
```

```java
@Override
@PreAuthorize("hasAuthority('USER')")
public void save(Todo todo) {
  this.todoRepository.save(todo);
}

@Override
@PreAuthorize("hasAuthority('USER')")
public void complete(long id) {
  findById(id)
          .ifPresent((todo) -> {
            todo.setCompleted(true);
            todoRepository.save(todo);
          });
}

@Override
@PreAuthorize("hasAnyAuthority('USER', 'ADMIN')")
public void remove(long id) {
  todoRepository.remove(id);
}

@Override
@PreAuthorize("hasAuthority('USER')")
@PostAuthorize("returnObject.owner == authentication.name")
public Optional<Todo> findById(long id) {
  return todoRepository.findOne(id);
}
}
```

The @PreAuthorize will be triggered before the actual method call and the @PostAuthorize after the method call. You can also write a security expression and use the result of the method invocation using the returnObject expression. See the expression on the findById method. Now if someone else aside from the owner would try to access the Todo, a security exception would be thrown.

Filtering with Annotations and Expressions

Next to the @PreAuthorize and @PostAuthorize, there are also the @PreFilter and @PostFilter annotations. The main difference between the two sets of annotations is the @*Authorize will throw an exception if the security rules don't apply, whereas the @*Filter will simply filter the input and output variables of elements you don't have access to.

Currently, when calling the listTodos, everything is returned from the database. You want to restrict the retrieval of all elements to a user with the authority ADMIN, and others can only see their own list of todos. This can be simply implemented with a @PostFilter annotation; adding @PostFilter ("hasAuthority('ADMIN') or filterObject.owner == authentication.name") will implement this rule.

Listing 5-41. TodoService (snippet) implementation–using @PostFilter

```java
@PostFilter("hasAnyAuthority('ADMIN') or filterObject.owner == authentication.name")
```

When you redeploy the application and log in as a user, you will now only see your own todos, and when using a user with the ADMIN authority, you will still see all the available todos. See also Recipe 5-7 for a more elaborate use of the @*Filter annotations.

Although the @PostFilter and @PreFilter are a very simple way of filtering the input/output of a method, use it with caution. When using this with large results, it can severely impact the performance of your application.

5-6. Handling Security in Views

Problem

Sometimes, you may wish to display a user's authentication information, such as the principal name and the granted authorities, in the views of your web application. In addition, you would like to render the view contents conditionally according to the user's authorities.

Solution

Although you can write some expressions in your Thymeleaf template files to retrieve the needed authentication and/or authorization information, it is not an ideal nor efficient solution. Thymeleaf and Spring Security provide a Thymeleaf dialect so you can use tags and additional expressions in your view templates. With these expressions you can either disable rendering for a part of the view or display additional user information (like login name and so on).

How It Works

Displaying Authentication Information

Suppose you would like to display a user's principal name and granted authorities in the header of the todos listing page (i.e., todos.html). First, you have to add the security dialect for Thymeleaf (for JSP you can import the Spring Security tag library) and make Thymeleaf aware of this dialect.

Listing 5-42. Gradle dependency for Thymeleaf and Spring Security

```
implementation group: 'org.thymeleaf.extras', name: 'thymeleaf-extras-springsecurity6',
version: '3.1.1.RELEASE'
```

Listing 5-43. Maven dependency for Thymeleaf and Spring Security

```
<dependency>
  <groupId>org.thymeleaf.extras</groupId>
  <artifactId>thymeleaf-extras-springsecurity6</artifactId>
  <version>3.1.1.RELEASE</version>
</dependency>
```

Listing 5-44. Todo web configuration with an additional dialect

```
@Bean
public SpringTemplateEngine templateEngine(ITemplateResolver templateResolver) {
  var templateEngine = new SpringTemplateEngine();
  templateEngine.setTemplateResolver(templateResolver);
  templateEngine.addDialect(new SpringSecurityDialect());
  return templateEngine;
}
```

With this dialect you will get new expression objects to use `authentication` and `authorization`, which you can use to write expressions for both Thymeleaf and Spring Security expression rules. The `authentication` object exposes the current user's `Authentication` object for you to render its properties or use in an expression. For example, you can render a user's principal name through the `name` property. The `authorization` object can be used to add Spring Security expressions to (part of) the page you are trying to render.

Listing 5-45. Use of an authentication expression

```
<h4>To-dos for <span th:text="${#authentication?.name}">John Doe</span></h4>
```

Rendering View Contents Conditionally

If you would like to render view contents conditionally according to a user's authorities, you can use the `<sec:authorize>` tag. For example, you can decide whether to render the message authors according to the user's authorities.

Listing 5-46. Use of authorization with a security expression

```
<td>
  <span th:if="{#authorization.expression('hasAuthority(''ADMIN'')')}">...</span>
</td>
```

If you want the enclosing content to be rendered only when the user has been granted certain authorities at the same time, you have to specify them in the `ifAllGranted` attribute. Otherwise, if the enclosing content can be rendered with any of the authorities, you have to specify them in the `ifAnyGranted` attribute.

Listing 5-47. Use of authorization with a security expression

```
<td>
  <span th:if="{#authorization.expression('hasAnyAuthority(''ADMIN'',''US
ER'')')}">...</span>
</td>
```

5-7. Handling Domain Object Security

Problem

Sometimes, you may have complicated security requirements that require handling security at the domain object level. That means you have to allow each domain object to have different access attributes for different principals.

Solution

Spring Security provides a module named ACL that allows each domain object to have its own access control list (ACL). An ACL contains a domain object's object identity to associate with the object and also holds multiple access control entries (ACEs), each of which contains the following two core parts:

- Permissions: An ACE's permissions are represented by a particular bit mask, with each bit value for a particular type of permission. The BasePermission class predefines five basic permissions as constant values for you to use: READ (bit 0 or integer 1), WRITE (bit 1 or integer 2), CREATE (bit 2 or integer 4), DELETE (bit 3 or integer 8), and ADMINISTRATION (bit 4 or integer 16). You can also define your own using other unused bits.

- Security identity (SID): Each ACE contains permissions for a particular SID. An SID can be a principal (`PrincipalSid`) or an authority (`GrantedAuthoritySid`) to associate with permissions. In addition to defining the ACL object model, Spring Security defines APIs for reading and maintaining the model and provides high-performance JDBC implementations for these APIs. To simplify ACL's usages, Spring Security also provides facilities, such as access decision voters and expressions, for you to use ACL consistently with other security facilities in your application.

How It Works

Setting Up an ACL Service

Spring Security provides built-in support for storing ACL data in a relational database and accessing it with JDBC. First, you have to create the following tables in your database for storing ACL data.

Listing 5-48. ACL table structure

```
CREATE TABLE ACL_SID(
    ID          BIGINT      NOT NULL GENERATED BY DEFAULT AS IDENTITY,
    PRINCIPAL   SMALLINT    NOT NULL,
    SID         VARCHAR(100) NOT NULL,
    PRIMARY KEY (ID),
    UNIQUE (SID, PRINCIPAL)
);

CREATE TABLE ACL_CLASS(
    ID          BIGINT      NOT NULL GENERATED BY DEFAULT AS IDENTITY,
    CLASS       VARCHAR(100) NOT NULL,
    CLASS_ID_TYPE VARCHAR(100),
```

```
    PRIMARY KEY (ID),
    UNIQUE (CLASS)
);

CREATE TABLE ACL_OBJECT_IDENTITY(
    ID                    BIGINT    NOT NULL GENERATED BY DEFAULT AS IDENTITY,
    OBJECT_ID_CLASS       BIGINT    NOT NULL,
    OBJECT_ID_IDENTITY    BIGINT    NOT NULL,
    PARENT_OBJECT         BIGINT,
    OWNER_SID             BIGINT,
    ENTRIES_INHERITING    SMALLINT  NOT NULL,
    PRIMARY KEY (ID),
    UNIQUE (OBJECT_ID_CLASS, OBJECT_ID_IDENTITY),
    FOREIGN KEY (PARENT_OBJECT)    REFERENCES ACL_OBJECT_IDENTITY,
    FOREIGN KEY (OBJECT_ID_CLASS) REFERENCES ACL_CLASS,
    FOREIGN KEY (OWNER_SID)        REFERENCES ACL_SID
);

CREATE TABLE ACL_ENTRY(
    ID                    BIGINT    NOT NULL GENERATED BY DEFAULT AS IDENTITY,
    ACL_OBJECT_IDENTITY   BIGINT    NOT NULL,
    ACE_ORDER             INT       NOT NULL,
    SID                   BIGINT    NOT NULL,
    MASK                  INTEGER   NOT NULL,
    GRANTING              SMALLINT  NOT NULL,
    AUDIT_SUCCESS         SMALLINT  NOT NULL,
    AUDIT_FAILURE         SMALLINT  NOT NULL,
    PRIMARY KEY (ID),
    UNIQUE (ACL_OBJECT_IDENTITY, ACE_ORDER),
    FOREIGN KEY (ACL_OBJECT_IDENTITY) REFERENCES ACL_OBJECT_IDENTITY,
    FOREIGN KEY (SID)                 REFERENCES ACL_SID
);
```

Spring Security defines APIs and provides JDBC implementations for you to access ACL data stored in these tables, so you'll seldom have a need to access ACL data from the database directly. As each domain object can have its own ACL, there may be a large number of ACLs in your application. Fortunately, Spring Security supports caching ACL objects and uses the Spring Cache abstraction for this. For the sample we will use Caffeine as a cache implementation (see Chapter 14 for more information on Spring and caching).

Listing 5-49. ACL cache configuration

```
@Bean
public Caffeine<Object, Object> caffeine() {
    return Caffeine.newBuilder().expireAfterWrite(Duration.ofMinutes(15));
}

@Bean
public CacheManager cacheManager(Caffeine<Object, Object> caffeine) {
    var cacheManager = new CaffeineCacheManager();
    cacheManager.setCaffeine(caffeine);
    return cacheManager;
}
```

Next, you have to set up an ACL service for your application. You have to configure this module with a group of normal Spring beans. For this reason, let's create a separate bean configuration class named TodoAclConfig, which will store ACL-specific configurations.

In an ACL configuration file, the core bean is an ACL service. In Spring Security, there are two interfaces that define operations of an ACL service: AclService and MutableAclService. AclService defines operations for you to read ACLs. MutableAclService is a sub-interface of AclService that defines operations for you to create, update, and delete ACLs. If your application only needs to read ACLs, you can simply choose an AclService implementation, such as JdbcAclService. Otherwise, you should choose a MutableAclService implementation, such as JdbcMutableAclService.

Listing 5-50. Todo ACL security configuration

```
package com.apress.spring6recipes.board.security;

import com.github.benmanes.caffeine.cache.Caffeine;
import org.springframework.cache.CacheManager;
import org.springframework.cache.caffeine.CaffeineCacheManager;
import org.springframework.context.annotation.Bean;
import org.springframework.context.annotation.Configuration;
import org.springframework.security.acls.AclEntryVoter;
import org.springframework.security.acls.AclPermissionEvaluator;
import org.springframework.security.acls.domain.AclAuthorizationStrategy;
import org.springframework.security.acls.domain.AclAuthorizationStrategyImpl;
import org.springframework.security.acls.domain.AuditLogger;
import org.springframework.security.acls.domain.BasePermission;
import org.springframework.security.acls.domain.ConsoleAuditLogger;
import org.springframework.security.acls.domain.DefaultPermissionGrantingStrategy;
import org.springframework.security.acls.domain.SpringCacheBasedAclCache;
import org.springframework.security.acls.jdbc.BasicLookupStrategy;
import org.springframework.security.acls.jdbc.JdbcMutableAclService;
import org.springframework.security.acls.jdbc.LookupStrategy;
import org.springframework.security.acls.model.AclCache;
import org.springframework.security.acls.model.AclService;
import org.springframework.security.acls.model.Permission;
import org.springframework.security.acls.model.PermissionGrantingStrategy;
import org.springframework.security.core.authority.SimpleGrantedAuthority;

import javax.sql.DataSource;
import java.time.Duration;

@Configuration
public class TodoAclConfig {

  private final DataSource dataSource;

  public TodoAclConfig(DataSource dataSource) {
    this.dataSource = dataSource;
  }
```

```java
@Bean
public AclEntryVoter aclEntryVoter(AclService aclService) {
    return new AclEntryVoter(aclService, "ACL_MESSAGE_DELETE",
        new Permission[] { BasePermission.ADMINISTRATION, BasePermission.DELETE });
}


@Bean
public Caffeine<Object, Object> caffeine() {
    return Caffeine.newBuilder().expireAfterWrite(Duration.ofMinutes(15));
}


@Bean
public CacheManager cacheManager(Caffeine<Object, Object> caffeine) {
    var cacheManager = new CaffeineCacheManager();
    cacheManager.setCaffeine(caffeine);
    return cacheManager;
}


@Bean
public AuditLogger auditLogger() {
    return new ConsoleAuditLogger();
}


@Bean
public PermissionGrantingStrategy permissionGrantingStrategy(AuditLogger auditLogger) {
    return new DefaultPermissionGrantingStrategy(auditLogger);
}


@Bean
public AclAuthorizationStrategy aclAuthorizationStrategy() {
    return new AclAuthorizationStrategyImpl(new SimpleGrantedAuthority("ADMIN"));
}


@Bean
public AclCache aclCache(CacheManager cacheManager,
                         PermissionGrantingStrategy permissionGrantingStrategy,
                         AclAuthorizationStrategy aclAuthorizationStrategy) {
    var aclCache = cacheManager.getCache("aclCache");
    return new SpringCacheBasedAclCache(aclCache, permissionGrantingStrategy,
        aclAuthorizationStrategy);
}


@Bean
public LookupStrategy lookupStrategy(AclCache aclCache,
                                     PermissionGrantingStrategy
                                     permissionGrantingStrategy,
                                     AclAuthorizationStrategy aclAuthorizationStrategy) {
    return new BasicLookupStrategy(this.dataSource, aclCache, aclAuthorizationStrategy,
    permissionGrantingStrategy);
}
```

```
@Bean
public AclService aclService(LookupStrategy lookupStrategy, AclCache aclCache) {
  return new JdbcMutableAclService(this.dataSource, lookupStrategy, aclCache);
}

@Bean
public AclPermissionEvaluator permissionEvaluator(AclService aclService) {
  return new AclPermissionEvaluator(aclService);
}
}
```

The core bean definition in this ACL configuration file is the ACL service, which is an instance of JdbcMutableAclService that allows you to maintain ACLs. This class requires three constructor arguments. The first is a data source for creating connections to a database that stores ACL data. You should have a data source defined beforehand so that you can simply refer to it here (assuming that you have created the ACL tables in the same database). The third constructor argument is a cache instance to use with an ACL, which you can configure using a Spring Cache implementation as the back-end cache implementation.

The only implementation that comes with Spring Security is BasicLookupStrategy, which performs basic lookup using standard and compatible SQL statements. If you want to make use of advanced database features to increase lookup performance, you can create your own lookup strategy by implementing the LookupStrategy interface. A BasicLookupStrategy instance also requires a data source and a cache instance. Besides, it requires a constructor argument whose type is AclAuthorizationStrategy. This object determines whether a principal is authorized to change certain properties of an ACL, usually by specifying a required authority for each category of properties. For the preceding configurations, only a user who has the ADMIN authority can change an ACL's ownership, an ACE's auditing details, or other ACL and ACE details, respectively. Finally, it needs a constructor argument whose type is PermissionGrantingStrategy. This object's responsibility is to check if the ACL grants access to the given Sid with the permissions it has.

Finally, JdbcMutableAclService embeds standard SQL statements for maintaining ACL data in a relational database. However, those SQL statements may not be compatible with all database products. For example, you have to customize the identity query statement for Apache Derby.

Maintaining ACLs for Domain Objects

In your back-end services and DAOs, you can maintain ACLs for domain objects with the previously defined ACL service via dependency injection. For your todo service, you have to create an ACL for a todo when it is posted and delete the ACL when this todo is deleted.

Listing 5-51. TodoService implementation with ACL

```
package com.apress.spring6recipes.board;

import org.springframework.security.access.prepost.PreAuthorize;
import org.springframework.security.acls.domain.GrantedAuthoritySid;
import org.springframework.security.acls.domain.ObjectIdentityImpl;
import org.springframework.security.acls.domain.PrincipalSid;
import org.springframework.security.acls.model.MutableAclService;
import org.springframework.stereotype.Service;
import org.springframework.transaction.annotation.Transactional;
```

```
import static org.springframework.security.acls.domain.BasePermission.DELETE;
import static org.springframework.security.acls.domain.BasePermission.READ;
import static org.springframework.security.acls.domain.BasePermission.WRITE;

@Service
@Transactional
class TodoServiceImpl implements TodoService {

  private final TodoRepository todoRepository;
  private final MutableAclService mutableAclService;

  TodoServiceImpl(TodoRepository todoRepository, MutableAclService mutableAclService) {
    this.todoRepository = todoRepository;
    this.mutableAclService = mutableAclService;
  }
  @PreAuthorize("hasAuthority('USER')")
  public void save(Todo todo) {

    this.todoRepository.save(todo);

    var oid = new ObjectIdentityImpl(Todo.class, todo.getId());
    var acl = mutableAclService.createAcl(oid);
    var principalSid = new PrincipalSid(todo.getOwner());
    var authoritySid = new GrantedAuthoritySid("ADMIN");

    acl.insertAce(0, READ, principalSid, true);
    acl.insertAce(1, WRITE, principalSid, true);
    acl.insertAce(2, DELETE, principalSid, true);

    acl.insertAce(3, READ, authoritySid, true);
    acl.insertAce(4, WRITE, authoritySid, true);
    acl.insertAce(5, DELETE, authoritySid, true);
  }
  @PreAuthorize("hasPermission(#id, 'com.apress.springrecipes.board.Todo', 'delete')")
  public void remove(long id) {
    todoRepository.remove(id);

    var oid = new ObjectIdentityImpl(Todo.class, id);
    mutableAclService.deleteAcl(oid, false);
  }
}
```

When a user creates a todo, you create a new ACL for this message at the same time, using the ID as the ACL's object identity. When a user deletes a todo, you delete the corresponding ACL as well. For a new todo, you insert the following ACEs into its ACL:

- The owner of the todo can READ, WRITE, and DELETE the todo.

- A user who has the ADMIN authority can also READ, WRITE, and DELETE the todos.

JdbcMutableAclService requires that the calling methods have transactions enabled so that its SQL statements can run within transactions. See the recipes in Chapter 7 on information on how to enable them.

Making Access Control Decisions Using Expressions

With an ACL for each domain object, you can use an object's ACL to make access control decisions on methods that involve this object. For example, when a user attempts to delete a todo, you can consult this message's ACL about whether the user is permitted to delete this todo.

Configuring ACL can be a daunting task. Luckily, you can use annotations and expressions to make your life easier. We can use the @PreAuthorize and @PreFilter annotations to check if someone is allowed to execute the method or use certain method arguments. The @PostAuthorize and @PostFilter can be used to check if a user is allowed to access the result or to filter results based on the ACL. To enable the processing of these annotations, you need to set the prePostEnabled attribute of the @EnableMethodSecurity annotation to true (which is also the default).

In addition, you need to configure infrastructure components to be able to make decisions. You need to set up an AclPermissionEvaluator, which is needed to evaluate the permission for an object. As you want to use ACL to secure the methods using an expression, it needs the custom permission evaluator. The AclPermissionEvaluator requires an AclService to obtain the ACL for the objects it needs to check. When doing Java-based configuration, this is enough as the PermissionEvaluator will be automatically detected and wired to the DefaultMethodSecurityExpressionHandler.

Now everything is in place to use the annotations together with expressions to control our access.

Listing 5-52. TodoService ACL expressions

```
package com.apress.spring6recipes.board;

@Service
@Transactional
class TodoServiceImpl implements TodoService {

  @Override
  @PreAuthorize("hasAuthority('USER')")
  @PostFilter("hasAnyAuthority('ADMIN') or hasPermission(filterObject, 'read')")
  public List<Todo> listTodos() {
  }

  @Override
  @PreAuthorize("hasAuthority('USER')")
  public void save(Todo todo) {
  }

  @Override
  @PreAuthorize("hasPermission(#id, 'com.apress.springrecipes.board.Todo', 'write')")
  public void complete(long id) {
  }

  @Override
  @PreAuthorize("hasPermission(#id, 'com.apress.springrecipes.board.Todo', 'delete')")
  public void remove(long id) {
  }
```

```
@Override
@PostFilter("hasPermission(filterObject, 'read')")
public Optional<Todo> findById(long id) {
}
}
```

You probably noticed the different annotations and the expressions inside these annotations. The @PreAuthorize annotation can be used to check if someone has the correct permissions to execute the method. The expression uses #message; this refers to the method argument with the name message. The hasPermission expression is a built-in expression from Spring Security (see Table 5-7).

The @PostFilter annotation allows you to filter the collection and remove the elements someone isn't allowed to read. In the expression the keyword filterObject refers to an element in the collection. To remain in the collection, the logged-in user needs to have read permission.

@PostAuthorize can be used to check if a single return value can be used (i.e., if the user has the right permissions). To use the return value in an expression, use the keyword returnObject.

5-8. Adding Security to a WebFlux Application

Problem

You have an application built with Spring WebFlux (see Chapter 4), and you want to add security.

Solution

Enable security by adding @EnableWebFluxSecurity to your configuration and create a SecurityWebFilterChain containing the security configuration.

How It Works

A Spring WebFlux application is very different in nature from a regular Spring MVC application. Nonetheless, Spring Security strives to make the configuration as easy (and equal) as possible, and it tries to be as similar to regular web configuration as possible.

Securing URL Access

First, let's create a SecurityConfiguration class and put @EnableWebFluxSecurity on that class.

Listing 5-53. Basic security configuration for Spring WebFlux

```
@Configuration
@EnableWebFluxSecurity
public class SecurityConfiguration { }
```

The @EnableWebFluxSecurity configuration registers a WebFluxConfigurer (see Recipe 5-5) to add the AuthenticationPrincipalArgumentResolver, which allows you to inject the Authentication into a Spring WebFlux handler method. It also registers the WebFluxSecurityConfiguration class from Spring Security, which detects instances of SecurityWebFilterChain (containing the security configuration), which is wrapped as a WebFilter (comparable to a regular servlet filter), which in turn is used by Spring WebFlux to add behavior to an incoming request (just as a normal servlet filter).

Without any further configuration, Spring Security will run with some defaults, which are that certain HTTP headers are being written and logout on /logout is enabled. Next, it will enable both HTTP basic authentication and a form login. For security it will now require an authenticated user for all URLs that are being accessed.

The org.springframework.security.config.web.server.ServerHttpSecurity should look familiar (see Recipe 5-1) and is used to add security rules and do further configuration (like adding/removing headers and configuring the login method). With the authorizeExchange it is possible to write rules. Here we secure URLs: the /welcome is permitted for everyone, and the /reservation URLs are only available for the role USER. For other requests you have to be authenticated. Finally, you need to call build() to actually build the SecurityWebFilterChain.

Next to the authorizeExchange, it is also possible to use the headers() configuration method to add security headers to requests (see also Recipe 5-2), like Cross-Site scripting protection, cache headers, etc.

Authenticating Users

Authenticating users in a Spring WebFlux–based application is done through a ReactiveAuthenticationManager; this is an interface with a single authenticate method. You can either provide your own implementation or use one of the provided implementations. The first is the UserDetailsRepositoryReactiveAuthenticationManager, which wraps an instance of the ReactiveUserDetailsService. The other implementation, the ReactiveAuthenticationManagerAdapter, is a wrapper for a regular AuthenticationManager (see Recipe 5-3). It will wrap a regular instance, and this allows you to use the blocking implementations in a reactive way. This doesn't make them reactive; they still block, but they are reusable in this way. With this you could use JDBC, LDAP, etc. also for your reactive application.

When configuring Spring Security in a Spring WebFlux application, you can either add an instance of a ReactiveAuthenticationManager to your Java configuration class or a ReactiveUserDetailsService. When the latter is detected, it will automatically be wrapped in a UserDetailsRepositoryReactiveAuthenticationManager.

Listing 5-54. Reactive todo security configuration

```
package com.apress.spring6recipes.todo;

import org.springframework.context.annotation.Bean;
import org.springframework.context.annotation.Configuration;
import org.springframework.security.config.annotation.web.reactive.EnableWebFluxSecurity;
import org.springframework.security.core.userdetails.MapReactiveUserDetailsService;
import org.springframework.security.core.userdetails.User;

@Configuration
@EnableWebFluxSecurity
public class SecurityConfiguration {

    @Bean
    public MapReactiveUserDetailsService userDetailsRepository() {
        var marten = User.withDefaultPasswordEncoder()
                .username("marten").password("secret").authorities("USER").build();
```

```
var admin = User.withDefaultPasswordEncoder()
        .username("admin").password("admin").authorities("USER", "ADMIN").build();
    return new MapReactiveUserDetailsService(marten, admin);
  }
}
```

When you would now deploy the application (or run the ReactorNettyBootstrap class) and access http://localhost:8080/todos, you would be greeted by the default login from Spring Security. It will render the login page because we request a URL that would render a web page; if we would request a URL that would return JSON (or require JSON), it would need HTTP basic authentication.

HTTP Basic Authentication

The HTTP basic authentication support can be configured via the httpBasic() method. When HTTP basic authentication is required, a browser will typically display a login dialog or a specific login page for users to log in.

Listing 5-55. Reactive todo security configuration–HTTP basic authentication

```
@Bean
public SecurityWebFilterChain springWebFilterChain(ServerHttpSecurity http) {
  return http.httpBasic().and().build();
}
```

Form-Based Login

The form-based login service will render a web page that contains a login form for users to input their login details and process the login form submission. It's configured via the formLogin() method.

Listing 5-56. Reactive todo security configuration–form login

```
@Bean
public SecurityWebFilterChain springWebFilterChain(ServerHttpSecurity http) {
  return http.formLogin().and().build();
}
```

By default, Spring Security automatically creates a login page and maps it to the URL /login. So you can add a link to your application (e.g., in todos.html) referring to this URL for login.

Listing 5-57. Login link sample

```
<a th:href="@{/login}">">Login</a>
```

If you don't prefer the default login page, you can provide a custom login page of your own. For example, you can create the following login.html file in the templates directory.

Listing 5-58. Custom login page

```html
<!DOCTYPE html>
<html xmlns:th="http://www.thymeleaf.org">
<head>
    <title>Login</title>
    <link type="text/css" rel="stylesheet"
          href="https://cdnjs.cloudflare.com/ajax/libs/semantic-ui/2.2.10/semantic.min.css">
    <style type="text/css">
        body {
            background-color: #DADADA;
        }

        body > .grid {
            height: 100%;
        }

        .column {
            max-width: 450px;
        }
    </style>
</head>

<body>
<div class="ui middle aligned center aligned grid">
    <div class="column">
        <h2 class="ui header">Log-in to your account</h2>
        <form method="POST" th:action="@{/login}" class="ui large form">
            <div class="ui stacked segment">
                <div class="field">
                    <div class="ui left icon input">
                        <i class="user icon"></i>
                        <input type="text" name="username" placeholder="E-mail address">
                    </div>
                </div>
                <div class="field">
                    <div class="ui left icon input">
                        <i class="lock icon"></i>
                        <input type="password" name="password" placeholder="Password">
                    </div>
                </div>
                <button class="ui fluid large submit green button">Login</button>
            </div>
            <div th:if="${param.error != null}" class="ui error message" style="display:
            block;">
                Authentication Failed<br/>
            </div>
        </form>
    </div>
</div>
</body>
</html>
```

For this login page to be used, we need to write a handler. It is quite easy to use the `RouterFunction` for this. We need to map the `GET` request for `/login` to a view named `login`. To do this we can add a bean of type `RouterFunction` to our configuration and use the `RouterFunctions` helper class to add a handler method.

Listing 5-59. Login page WebFlux configuration

```
@Bean
public RouterFunction<ServerResponse> securityPages() {
  return RouterFunctions
          .route().GET("/login", (req) -> ServerResponse.ok().render("login")).build();
}
```

If you stick with the default naming of Spring Security, that is enough to render your own custom login page. Next, you need to instruct Spring Security to display your custom login page when a login is requested. You have to specify its URL in the `loginPage` configuration method.

Listing 5-60. Reactive todo security configuration–form login

```
@Bean
public SecurityWebFilterChain springWebFilterChain(ServerHttpSecurity http) {
  return http
          .formLogin( (formLogin) -> formLogin.loginPage("/login"))
          .csrf(ServerHttpSecurity.CsrfSpec::disable)
          .authorizeExchange( (auth) -> auth.pathMatchers("/login").permitAll())
          .build();
}
```

Notice the `permitAll` for the `/login` URL. Without this the login page would be inaccessible by anonymous users as it would fall under the protection of Spring Security. For now we also disable CSRF protection; else, we wouldn't be able to log in due to a CSRF token being required. See the next section on how to enable it. If the login page is displayed by Spring Security when a user requests a secure URL, the user will be redirected to the target URL once the login succeeds.

Working with CSRF Protection

It is generally a good idea to leave the default for CSRF enabled, as this will reduce the risk you have with the Cross-Site Request Forgery attack. It is enabled by default in Spring Security, and the line `csrf().disable()` can be removed from the configuration. When CSRF protection is enabled, Spring Security adds the `CsrfWebFilter` to the list of filters it uses for protection. This filter in turn uses an implementation of the `ServerCsrfTokenRepository` to generate and store tokens. By default this is the `WebSessionServerCsrfTokenRepository`, which, as the name implies, stores the generated token in the `Websession`. There is also a `CookieServerCsrfTokenRepository`, which stores the token information in a cookie. If you want to switch the `ServerCsrfTokenRepository`, you can use the `csrfTokenRepository()` configuration method to change it. You could also use this to configure an explicitly configured `WebSessionServerCsrfTokenRepository`, `CookieServerCsrfTokenRepository`, or your own implementation of the `ServerCsrfTokenRepository` interface. For now we will use the default `WebSessionServerCsrfTokenRepository`.

When CSRF is enabled, then after login, trying to complete or delete a todo item will fail in the absence of a CSRF token. To fix this you need to pass the CSRF token back to the server on requests that modify content. When using a supported view technology, like Thymeleaf, this can be done, mostly, automatically by virtue of the CsrfRequestDataValueProcessor, which exposes the token in a well-known location. However, for this to work, we need to copy the CSRF token to a specific attribute. We can use a HandlerFilterFunction and a @ControllerAdvice to expose the CsrfToken under the proper name.

Listing 5-61. Reactive todo security configuration–CSRF configuration

```
@Bean
public RouterFunction<ServerResponse> securityPages() {
  return RouterFunctions
          .route().filter(csrfToken())
          .GET("/login", (req) -> ServerResponse.ok().render("login")).build();
}

public HandlerFilterFunction<ServerResponse, ServerResponse> csrfToken() {
  var name = CsrfToken.class.getName();
  return (req, next) -> req.exchange()
          .getAttributeOrDefault(name, Mono.empty().ofType(CsrfToken.class))
          .flatMap(token -> {
            req.exchange()
                .getAttributes()
                .put(CsrfRequestDataValueProcessor.DEFAULT_CSRF_ATTR_NAME, token);
            return next.handle(req);
          });
}
```

Now the preceding filter will work for the RouterFunction; it will not work for the @(Rest)Controller-annotated classes. For that add a @ControllerAdvice, which will have a @ModelAttribute method. This will then be invoked before each method invocation of a @(Rest)Controller.

Listing 5-62. ControllerAdvice to copy a CSRF token

```
package com.apress.spring6recipes.todo.web;

import org.springframework.security.web.reactive.result.view.CsrfRequestDataValueProcessor;
import org.springframework.security.web.server.csrf.CsrfToken;
import org.springframework.web.bind.annotation.ControllerAdvice;
import org.springframework.web.bind.annotation.ModelAttribute;
import org.springframework.web.server.ServerWebExchange;
import reactor.core.publisher.Mono;

@ControllerAdvice
public class SecurityControllerAdvice {

  @ModelAttribute
  public Mono<CsrfToken> csrfToken(ServerWebExchange exchange) {
    Mono<CsrfToken> csrfToken = exchange.getAttribute(CsrfToken.class.getName());
    return csrfToken.doOnSuccess( (token) -> exchange.getAttributes()
            .put(CsrfRequestDataValueProcessor.DEFAULT_CSRF_ATTR_NAME, token));
  }
}
```

Now that all this is in place, you can expose the CSRF token in a hidden field. You can easily do this with a `hidden` input in your form. The `WebSessionServerCsrfTokenRepository` exposes the token in the session, and for a form you can use the `parameterName` and `token` properties.

Add the following to the two forms that complete and delete a todo item.

Listing 5-63. CSRF token hidden field for forms

```
<input type="hidden" name="${_csrf.parameterName}" value="${_csrf.token}"/>
```

Now when submitting the form, the token will be part of the request, and you will again be able to complete or delete a todo item.

ℹ️   As the application uses Thymeleaf to render our pages and forms, it will automatically add the hidden input field to all the forms it processes.

There is also a form in the `todo-create.html`; however, as this is using the Spring MVC form tags, you don't need to modify this. When using the Spring MVC form tags, the CSRF token is added to the form automatically. To make this possible Spring Security registers a `org.springframework.security.web.reactive.result.view.CsrfRequestDataValueProcessor`, which takes care of adding the token to the form.

Making Access Control Decisions

The decision on whether a user is allowed to access a resource in an application is called an authorization decision. It is made based on the user's authentication status and the resource's nature and access attributes. In Spring Security, authorization decisions are made by authorization managers, which have to implement the `ReactiveAuthorizationManager` interface. You are free to create your own authorization managers by implementing this interface, but Spring Security comes with several implementations already. Most of them are configurable through the `http.authorizeExchange` or by using method security (see Recipe 5-5).

Without knowing we have already been using these authorization managers. In the expression `.pathMatchers("/login").permitAll()`, the `permitAll` part is actually using a `ReactiveAuthorizationManager`, a simple one that always returns true for allowing access. However, this is just a single instance. We could apply more of those through the convenience methods (see Table 5-8) or by using the `access` method use a more complex function to determine if access is allowed.

Table 5-8. *Spring Security WebFlux Built-In Expressions*

Expression	Description
hasRole('role') or hasAuthority('authority')	Returns true if the current user has the given role
hasAnyRole('role') or hasAnyAuthority('authority')	Returns true if the current user has one of given roles
permitAll()	Always evaluates to true
denyAll()	Always evaluates to false
authenticated()	Returns true if the user is authenticated
hasIpAddress()	Returns true if the user has the selected IP address (or range)
access()	Uses a function to determine if access is granted

Although role and authority are almost the same, there is a slight, but important, difference in how they are processed. When using hasRole the passed-in value for the role will be checked if it starts with ROLE_ (the default role prefix); if not, this will be added before checking the authority. So hasRole('ADMIN') will actually check if the current user has the authority ROLE_ADMIN. When using hasAuthority it will check the value as is.

Listing 5-64. Reactive todo security configuration

```
@Bean
public SecurityWebFilterChain springWebFilterChain(ServerHttpSecurity http) {
  return http
    .formLogin( (formLogin) -> formLogin.loginPage("/login"))
    .csrf( (csrf) -> csrf.csrfTokenRepository(new CookieServerCsrfTokenRepository()))
    .authorizeExchange( (auth) -> {
        auth.pathMatchers("/login").permitAll();
        auth.pathMatchers("/todos").hasAuthority("USER");
        auth.pathMatchers(HttpMethod.DELETE, "/todos").access(this::todoRemoveAllowed);
      }
    )
    .build();
}

private Mono<AuthorizationDecision> todoRemoveAllowed(Mono<Authentication> authentication,
AuthorizationContext context) {
  return authentication
        .map ( (auth) -> auth.getAuthorities().contains(
        new SimpleGrantedAuthority("ADMIN")) || isOwner(auth, context))
        .map(AuthorizationDecision::new);
}
```

```
private boolean isOwner(Authentication auth, AuthorizationContext context) {
  var id = Long.valueOf(context.getVariables().getOrDefault("id", "-1").toString());
  return todoService.findById(id)
          .map( (todo) -> Objects.equals(todo.getOwner(), auth.getName())).
          defaultIfEmpty(false).block();
}
```

The access() expression can be used to write a very powerful expression. The preceding snippet uses a path parameter in the URL {user}, and access is allowed if the current user is the actual user or if someone has the ADMIN authority. The AuthorizationContext contains the parsed variables, which you could use to compare the name from the URI. The Authentication contains the collection of GrantedAuthorities, which you can check for the ROLE_ADMIN. Of course you can write as many complex expressions as you like. You could check for the IP address, request headers, etc.

5-9. Summary

In this chapter, you learned how to secure applications using Spring Security. It can be used to secure any Java application, but it's mostly used for web applications. The concepts of authentication, authorization, and access control are essential in the security area, so you should have a clear understanding of them.

You often have to secure critical URLs by preventing unauthorized access to them. Spring Security can help you achieve this in a declarative way. It handles security by applying servlet filters, which can be configured with simple Java-based configuration. Spring Security will automatically configure the basic security services for you and try to be as secure as possible by default.

Spring Security supports multiple ways for users to log into a web application, such as form-based login and HTTP basic authentication. It also provides an anonymous login service that allows you to handle an anonymous user just like a normal user. Remember-me support allows an application to remember a user's identity across multiple browser sessions.

Spring Security supports multiple ways of authenticating users and has built-in provider implementations for them. For example, it supports authenticating users against in-memory definitions, a relational database, and an LDAP repository. You should always store encrypted passwords in your user repository, because clear-text passwords are vulnerable to hacker attacks. Spring Security also supports caching user details locally to save you the overhead of performing remote queries.

Decisions on whether a user is allowed to access a given resource are made by access decision managers. Spring Security comes with three access decision managers that are based on the voting approach. All of them require a group of voters to be configured for voting on access control decisions.

Spring Security enables you to secure method invocations in a declarative way, either by embedding a security interceptor in a bean definition or matching multiple methods with AspectJ pointcut expressions or annotations. Spring Security also allows you to display a user's authentication information in JSP views and render view contents conditionally according to a user's authorities.

Spring Security provides an ACL module that allows each domain object to have an ACL for controlling access. You can read and maintain an ACL for each domain object with Spring Security's high-performance APIs, which are implemented with JDBC. Spring Security also provides facilities such as access decision voters and JSP tags for you to use ACLs consistently with other security facilities.

Spring Security also has support for securing Spring WebFlux–based applications. In the last recipe, you explored how you could add security to such an application.

CHAPTER 6

■ ■ ■

Data Access

In this chapter, you will learn how Spring can simplify your database access tasks (Spring can also simplify your NoSQL and BigData tasks, which is covered in Chapter 9). Data access is a common requirement for most enterprise applications, which usually require accessing data stored in relational databases. As an essential part of Java SE, Java Database Connectivity (JDBC) defines a set of standard APIs for you to access relational databases in a vendor-independent fashion.

The purpose of JDBC is to provide APIs through which you can execute SQL statements against a database. However, when using JDBC, you have to manage database-related resources by yourself and handle database exceptions explicitly. To make JDBC easier to use, Spring provides an abstraction framework for interfacing with JDBC. As the heart of the Spring JDBC framework, JDBC templates are designed to provide template methods for different types of JDBC operations. Each template method is responsible for controlling the overall process and allows you to override particular tasks of the process.

If raw JDBC doesn't satisfy your requirement or you feel your application would benefit from something slightly higher level, then Spring's support for ORM solutions will interest you. In this chapter, you will also learn how to integrate object/relational mapping (ORM) frameworks into your Spring applications. Spring supports most of the popular ORM (or data mapper) frameworks, including Hibernate and the Java Persistence API (JPA). The focus of this chapter will be on Hibernate and JPA. However, Spring's support for ORM frameworks is consistent, so you can easily apply the techniques in this chapter to other ORM frameworks as well.

ORM is a technology for persisting objects into a relational database. An ORM framework persists your objects according to the mapping metadata you provide (XML- or annotation-based), such as the mappings between classes and tables, properties and columns, and so on. It generates SQL statements for object persistence at runtime, so you don't need to write database-specific SQL statements unless you want to take advantage of database-specific features or provide optimized SQL statements of your own. Compared with the direct use of JDBC, an ORM framework can significantly reduce the data access effort of your applications.

Hibernate is a popular open source and high-performance ORM framework in the Java community. Hibernate supports most JDBC-compliant databases and can use specific dialects to access particular databases. Beyond the basic ORM features, Hibernate supports more advanced features such as caching, cascading, and lazy loading. It also defines a querying language called Hibernate Query Language (HQL) for you to write simple but powerful object queries.

JPA defines a set of standard annotations and APIs for object persistence in both the Java SE and Java EE platforms. JPA is defined as the Jakarta Persistence specification. JPA is just a set of standard APIs that require a JPA-compliant engine to provide persistence services. You can compare JPA with the JDBC API and a JPA engine with a JDBC driver. Hibernate can be configured as a JPA-compliant engine through an extension module called Hibernate EntityManager. This chapter will mainly demonstrate JPA with Hibernate as the underlying engine.

© Marten Deinum, Daniel Rubio, Josh Long 2023
M. Deinum et al., *Spring 6 Recipes*, https://doi.org/10.1007/978-1-4842-8649-4_6

6-1. Problems with Direct JDBC

Suppose you are going to develop an application for vehicle registration, whose major functions are the basic create, read, update, and delete (CRUD) operations on vehicle records. These records will be stored in a relational database and accessed with JDBC. First, you design the following Vehicle class, which represents a vehicle in Java.

Listing 6-1. Vehicle class

```
package com.apress.spring6recipes.vehicle;

public class Vehicle {

    private String vehicleNo;
    private String color;
    private int wheel;
    private int seat;

    // Constructors, Getters and Setters
    ...
}
```

6-2. Setting Up the Application Database

The database you are going to work with is PostgreSQL.

ℹ   The sample code for this chapter provides scripts in the bin directory to start and connect to a Docker-based PostgreSQL instance. To start the instance and create the database, follow these steps:

1. Execute bin\postgres.sh; this will download and start the Postgres Docker container.

2. Execute bin\psql.sh; this will connect to the running Postgres container.

3. Execute CREATE DATABASE vehicle; to create the database to use for the samples.

4. Next, you have to create the VEHICLE table for storing vehicle records with the following SQL statement. By default, this table will be created in the APP database's APP database schema:

   ```
   CREATE TABLE VEHICLE (
       VEHICLE_NO    VARCHAR(10)    NOT NULL,
       COLOR         VARCHAR(10),
       WHEEL         INT,
       SEAT          INT,
       PRIMARY KEY (VEHICLE_NO)
   );
   ```

Table 6-1. *JDBC Properties for Connecting to the Application Database*

Property	Value
Driver class	org.postgresql.Driver
URL	jdbc:postgresql://localhost:5432/vehicle
Username	postgres
Password	password

Understanding the Data Access Object Design Pattern

A typical design mistake is to mix different types of logic (e.g., presentation logic, business logic, and data access logic) in a single large module. This reduces the module's reusability and maintainability because of the tight coupling it introduces. The general purpose of the Data Access Object (DAO) pattern is to avoid these problems by separating data access logic from business logic and presentation logic. This pattern recommends that data access logic be encapsulated in independent modules called Data Access Objects.

For your vehicle registration application, you can abstract the data access operations to insert, update, delete, and query a vehicle. These operations should be declared in a DAO interface to allow for different DAO implementation technologies.

Listing 6-2. VehicleDao interface

```
package com.apress.spring6recipes.vehicle;

import java.util.Collection;
import java.util.List;

public interface VehicleDao {

  void insert(Vehicle vehicle);
  void update(Vehicle vehicle);
  void delete(Vehicle vehicle);
  Vehicle findByVehicleNo(String vehicleNo);
  List<Vehicle> findAll();

  default void insert(Collection<Vehicle> vehicles) {
    vehicles.forEach(this::insert);
  }

}
```

Most parts of the JDBC APIs declare throwing java.sql.SQLException. But because this interface aims to abstract the data access operations only, it should not depend on the implementation technology. So it's unwise for this general interface to declare throwing the JDBC-specific SQLException. A common practice when implementing a DAO interface is to wrap this kind of exception with a runtime exception (either your own business Exception subclass or a generic one).

Implementing the DAO with JDBC

To access the database with JDBC, you create an implementation for this DAO interface (e.g., JdbcVehicleDao). Because your DAO implementation has to connect to the database to execute SQL statements, you may establish database connections by specifying the driver class name, database URL, username, and password. However, you can obtain database connections from a preconfigured javax.sql. DataSource object without knowing about the connection details.

Listing 6-3. Plain JDBC VehicleDao implementation

```java
package com.apress.spring6recipes.vehicle;

import javax.sql.DataSource;
import java.sql.PreparedStatement;
import java.sql.ResultSet;
import java.sql.SQLException;
import java.util.ArrayList;
import java.util.List;

public class PlainJdbcVehicleDao implements VehicleDao {

  private static final String INSERT_SQL = "INSERT INTO VEHICLE (COLOR, WHEEL, SEAT,
  VEHICLE_NO) VALUES (?, ?, ?, ?)";
  private static final String UPDATE_SQL = "UPDATE VEHICLE SET COLOR=?,WHEEL=?,SEAT=? WHERE
  VEHICLE_NO=?";
  private static final String SELECT_ALL_SQL = "SELECT * FROM VEHICLE";
  private static final String SELECT_ONE_SQL = "SELECT * FROM VEHICLE WHERE VEHICLE_NO = ?";
  private static final String DELETE_SQL = "DELETE FROM VEHICLE WHERE VEHICLE_NO=?";

  private final DataSource dataSource;

  public PlainJdbcVehicleDao(DataSource dataSource) {
    this.dataSource = dataSource;
  }

  @Override
  public void insert(Vehicle vehicle) {
    try (var conn = dataSource.getConnection();
        var ps = conn.prepareStatement(INSERT_SQL)) {
      prepareStatement(ps, vehicle);
      ps.executeUpdate();
    } catch (SQLException e) {
      throw new RuntimeException(e);
    }
  }

  @Override
  public Vehicle findByVehicleNo(String vehicleNo) {
    try (var conn = dataSource.getConnection();
        var ps = conn.prepareStatement(SELECT_ONE_SQL)) {
      ps.setString(1, vehicleNo);
```

```
    Vehicle vehicle = null;
    try (var rs = ps.executeQuery()) {
      if (rs.next()) {
        vehicle = toVehicle(rs);
      }
    }
    return vehicle;
    } catch (SQLException e) {
      throw new RuntimeException(e);
    }
  }

  @Override
  public void update(Vehicle vehicle) {
    try (var conn = dataSource.getConnection();
        var ps = conn.prepareStatement(UPDATE_SQL)) {
      prepareStatement(ps, vehicle);
      ps.executeUpdate();
    } catch (SQLException e) {
      throw new RuntimeException(e);
    }
  }

  @Override
  public void delete(Vehicle vehicle) {
    try (var conn = dataSource.getConnection();
        var ps = conn.prepareStatement(DELETE_SQL)) {
      ps.setString(1, vehicle.getVehicleNo());
      ps.executeUpdate();
    } catch (SQLException e) {
      throw new RuntimeException(e);
    }
  }

  private Vehicle toVehicle(ResultSet rs) throws SQLException {
    return new Vehicle(rs.getString("VEHICLE_NO"), rs.getString("COLOR"),
    rs.getInt("WHEEL"), rs.getInt("SEAT"));
  }

  private void prepareStatement(PreparedStatement ps, Vehicle vehicle) throws SQLException {
    ps.setString(1, vehicle.getColor());
    ps.setInt(2, vehicle.getWheel());
    ps.setInt(3, vehicle.getSeat());
    ps.setString(4, vehicle.getVehicleNo());
  }
}
```

The vehicle insert operation is a typical JDBC update scenario. Each time this method is called, you obtain a connection from the data source and execute the SQL statement on this connection. Your DAO interface doesn't declare throwing any checked exceptions, so if a SQLException occurs, you have to wrap it with an unchecked RuntimeException. (There is a detailed discussion on handling exceptions in your DAOs later in this chapter.) The code shown here uses a so-called try-with-resources mechanism, which

295

will automatically close the used resources (i.e. the Connection, PreparedStatement, and ResultSet). If you don't use a try-with-resources block, you have to remember to correctly close the used resources. Failing to do so will lead to connection leaks.

Here, the update and delete operations will be skipped, because they are much the same as the insert operation from a technical point of view. For the query operation, you have to extract the data from the returned result set to build a vehicle object in addition to executing the SQL statement. The toVehicle method is a simple helper method to be able to reuse the mapping logic, and the prepareStatement method helps set the parameters for the insert and update methods.

Configuring a DataSource in Spring

The javax.sql.DataSource interface is a standard interface defined by the JDBC specification that factories Connection instances. There are many data source implementations provided by different vendors and projects: HikariCP and Apache Commons DBCP are popular open source options, and most application servers will provide their own implementation. It is very easy to switch between different data source implementations, because they implement the common DataSource interface. As a Java application framework, Spring also provides several convenient but less powerful data source implementations. The simplest one is DriverManagerDataSource, which opens a new connection every time one is requested.

Listing 6-4. Vehicle JDBC configuration

```
package com.apress.spring6recipes.vehicle.config;

import javax.sql.DataSource;

import org.postgresql.Driver;
import org.springframework.context.annotation.Bean;
import org.springframework.context.annotation.Configuration;
import org.springframework.jdbc.datasource.SimpleDriverDataSource;

import com.apress.spring6recipes.vehicle.PlainJdbcVehicleDao;
import com.apress.spring6recipes.vehicle.VehicleDao;

@Configuration
public class VehicleConfiguration {

  @Bean
  public VehicleDao vehicleDao(DataSource dataSource) {
    return new PlainJdbcVehicleDao(dataSource);
  }

  @Bean
  public DataSource dataSource() {
    var dataSource = new SimpleDriverDataSource();
    dataSource.setDriverClass(Driver.class);
    dataSource.setUrl("jdbc:postgresql://localhost:5432/vehicle");
    dataSource.setUsername("postgres");
    dataSource.setPassword("password");
    return dataSource;
  }
}
```

SimpleDriverDataSource (and its cousin DriverManagerDataSource) is not an efficient data source implementation because it opens a new connection for the client every time it's requested. Another data source implementation provided by Spring is SingleConnectionDataSource (a DriverManagerDataSource subclass). As its name indicates, this maintains only a single connection that's reused all the time and never closed. Obviously, it is not suitable in a multithreaded environment.

Spring's own data source implementations are mainly used for testing purposes. However, many production data source implementations support connection pooling. For example, HikariCP provides the HikariDataSource, which accepts the same connection properties as DriverManagerDataSource and allows you to specify, among others, the minimum pool size and maximum active connections for the connection pool.

Listing 6-5. Vehicle JDBC configuration with a connection pool

```
@Bean
public DataSource dataSource() {
  var dataSource = new HikariDataSource();
  dataSource.setDataSourceClassName("org.postgresql.ds.PGSimpleDataSource");
  dataSource.setJdbcUrl("jdbc:postgresql://localhost:5432/vehicle");
  dataSource.setUsername("postgres");
  dataSource.setPassword("password");
  dataSource.setMinimumIdle(2);
  dataSource.setMaximumPoolSize(5);
  return dataSource;
}
```

ℹ️ To use the data source implementations provided by HikariCP, you have to add them to your CLASSPATH.

Gradle dependency

```
implementation 'com.zaxxer:HikariCP:5.0.1'
```

Maven dependency

```
<dependency>
  <groupId>com.zaxxer</groupId>
  <artifactId>HikariCP</artifactId>
  <version>5.0.1</version>
</dependency>
```

Many Jakarta EE application servers have built-in data source implementations that you can configure from the server console or in configuration files. If you have a data source configured in an application server and exposed for JNDI lookup, you can use JndiDataSourceLookup to look it up.

Listing 6-6. JNDI lookup

```
@Bean
public DataSource dataSource() {
  return new JndiDataSourceLookup().getDataSource("jdbc/VehicleDS");
}
```

Running the DAO

The following Main class tests your DAO by using it to insert a new vehicle to the database. If it succeeds, you can query the vehicle from the database immediately.

Listing 6-7. Main class

```
package com.apress.spring6recipes.vehicle;

import org.springframework.context.annotation.AnnotationConfigApplicationContext;

import com.apress.spring6recipes.vehicle.config.VehicleConfiguration;

public class Main {

  public static void main(String[] args) throws Exception {
    var cfg = VehicleConfiguration.class;
    try (var ctx = new AnnotationConfigApplicationContext(cfg)) {
      var vehicleDao = ctx.getBean(VehicleDao.class);
      var vehicle = new Vehicle("TEM0001", "Red", 4, 4);
      vehicleDao.insert(vehicle);

      vehicle = vehicleDao.findByVehicleNo("TEM0001");
      System.out.println(vehicle);
    }
  }
}
```

Now you can implement a DAO using JDBC directly. However, as you can see from the preceding DAO implementation, most of the JDBC code is similar and needs to be repeated for each database operation. Such redundant code will make your DAO methods much longer and less readable.

Taking It a Step Further

An alternative approach is to use an ORM (an object/relational mapping) tool, which lets you code the logic specifically for mapping an entity in your domain model to a database table. The ORM will, in turn, figure out how to write the logic to usefully persist your class's data to the database. This can be very liberating: you are suddenly beholden only to your business and domain model, not to whims of your database's SQL parser. The flip side, of course, is that you are also divesting yourself from the complete control over the communication between your client and the database—you have to trust that the ORM layer will do the right thing.

6-3. Using a JDBC Template to Work with a Database

Problem

Using JDBC is tedious and fraught with redundant API calls, many of which could be managed for you. To implement a JDBC update operation, you have to perform the following tasks, most of which are redundant:

1. Obtain a database connection from the data source.

2. Create a PreparedStatement object from the connection.

3. Bind the parameters to the PreparedStatement object.

4. Execute the PreparedStatement object.

5. Handle SQLException.

JDBC is a low-level API, but with the JDBC template, the surface area of the API that you need to work with becomes more expressive (you spend less time in the weeds and more time working on your application logic) and is simpler to work with safely.

Solution

The `org.springframework.jdbc.core.JdbcTemplate` class declares a number of overloaded `update()` template methods to control the overall update process. Different versions of the `update()` method allow you to override different task subsets of the default process. The Spring JDBC framework predefines several callback interfaces to encapsulate different task subsets. You can implement one of these callback interfaces and pass its instance to the corresponding `update()` method to complete the process.

How It Works

Updating a Database with a Statement Creator

The first callback interface to introduce is `PreparedStatementCreator`. You implement this interface to override the statement creation task (task 2) and the parameter binding task (task 3) of the overall update process. To insert a vehicle into the database, you implement the `PreparedStatementCreator` interface as follows.

Listing 6-8. Spring JdbcTemplate-based VehicleDao implementation

```
package com.apress.spring6recipes.vehicle;

import java.sql.Connection;
import java.sql.PreparedStatement;
import java.sql.ResultSet;
import java.sql.SQLException;
import java.util.ArrayList;
import java.util.List;

import javax.sql.DataSource;

import org.springframework.jdbc.core.JdbcTemplate;
import org.springframework.jdbc.core.PreparedStatementCreator;
```

```java
public class JdbcVehicleDao implements VehicleDao {

  private void prepareStatement(PreparedStatement ps, Vehicle vehicle)
          throws SQLException {
    ps.setString(1, vehicle.getColor());
    ps.setInt(2, vehicle.getWheel());
    ps.setInt(3, vehicle.getSeat());
    ps.setString(4, vehicle.getVehicleNo());
  }

  private class InsertVehicleStatementCreator implements PreparedStatementCreator {

    private final Vehicle vehicle;

    InsertVehicleStatementCreator(Vehicle vehicle) {
      this.vehicle = vehicle;
    }

    @Override
    public PreparedStatement createPreparedStatement(Connection conn)
            throws SQLException {
      var ps = conn.prepareStatement(INSERT_SQL);
      prepareStatement(ps, this.vehicle);
      return ps;
    }
  }
}
```

When implementing the PreparedStatementCreator interface, you will get the database connection as the createPreparedStatement() method's argument. All you have to do in this method is to create a PreparedStatement object on this connection and bind your parameters to this object. Finally, you have to return the PreparedStatement object as the method's return value. Notice that the method signature declares throwing SQLException, which means that you don't need to handle this kind of exception yourself. As you are creating this class as an inner class for the DAO, you can call the prepareStatement helper method from your implementation.

Now, you can use this statement creator to simplify the vehicle insert operation. First of all, you have to create an instance of the JdbcTemplate class and pass in the data source for this template to obtain a connection from it. Then, you just make a call to the update() method and pass in your statement creator for the template to complete the update process.

Listing 6-9. Spring JdbcTemplate-based VehicleDao implementation - using PreparedStatementCreator

```java
package com.apress.spring6recipes.vehicle;

import java.sql.Connection;
import java.sql.PreparedStatement;
import java.sql.ResultSet;
import java.sql.SQLException;
import java.util.ArrayList;
import java.util.List;
```

```
import javax.sql.DataSource;

import org.springframework.jdbc.core.JdbcTemplate;
import org.springframework.jdbc.core.PreparedStatementCreator;

public class JdbcVehicleDao implements VehicleDao {
  @Override
  public void insert(Vehicle vehicle) {
    var jdbcTemplate = new JdbcTemplate(this.dataSource);
    jdbcTemplate.update(new InsertVehicleStatementCreator(vehicle));
  }
}
```

Typically, it is better to implement the PreparedStatementCreator interface and other callback interfaces as anonymous inner classes if they are used within one method only. This is because you can get access to the local variables and method arguments directly from the inner class, instead of passing them as constructor arguments. When using local variables, those have to be marked as final.

Listing 6-10. Spring JdbcTemplate-based VehicleDao implementation - using anonymous inner class

```
package com.apress.spring6recipes.vehicle;

import java.sql.Connection;
import java.sql.PreparedStatement;
import java.sql.ResultSet;
import java.sql.SQLException;
import java.util.ArrayList;
import java.util.List;

import javax.sql.DataSource;

import org.springframework.jdbc.core.JdbcTemplate;

public class JdbcVehicleDao implements VehicleDao {

  @Override
  public void insert(Vehicle vehicle) {
    var jdbcTemplate = new JdbcTemplate(this.dataSource);
    jdbcTemplate.update( (conn) -> {
      var ps = conn.prepareStatement(INSERT_SQL);
      prepareStatement(ps, vehicle);
      return ps;
    });
  }

  private void prepareStatement(PreparedStatement ps, Vehicle vehicle) throws SQLException {
    ps.setString(1, vehicle.getColor());
    ps.setInt(2, vehicle.getWheel());
    ps.setInt(3, vehicle.getSeat());
    ps.setString(4, vehicle.getVehicleNo());
  }
}
```

301

Now, you can delete the preceding InsertVehicleStatementCreator inner class, because it will not be used anymore.

Updating a Database with a Statement Setter

The second callback interface, PreparedStatementSetter, as its name indicates, performs only the parameter binding task (task 3) of the overall update process.

Another version of the update() template method accepts a SQL statement and a PreparedStatementSetter object as arguments. This method will create a PreparedStatement object for you from your SQL statement. All you have to do with this interface is to bind your parameters to the PreparedStatement object (and for this you can delegate to the prepareStatement method again).

Listing 6-11. Spring JdbcTemplate-based VehicleDao implementation - using PreparedStatementSetter

```
package com.apress.spring6recipes.vehicle;
...
import org.springframework.jdbc.core.JdbcTemplate;
import org.springframework.jdbc.core.PreparedStatementSetter;

public class JdbcVehicleDao implements VehicleDao {
  ...
  public void insert(final Vehicle vehicle) {
    JdbcTemplate jdbcTemplate = new JdbcTemplate(dataSource);

    jdbcTemplate.update(INSERT_SQL, new PreparedStatementSetter() {

        public void setValues(PreparedStatement ps)
            throws SQLException {
              prepareStatement(ps, vehicle);
        }
      });
  }
}
```

Or even more compact, it can be as a Java lambda expression.

Listing 6-12. Spring JdbcTemplate-based VehicleDao implementation - using lambda expression

```
@Override
public void insert(Vehicle vehicle) {
  var jdbcTemplate = new JdbcTemplate(this.dataSource);
  jdbcTemplate.update(INSERT_SQL, ps -> prepareStatement(ps, vehicle));
}
```

Updating a Database with a SQL Statement and Parameter Values

Finally, the simplest version of the update() method accepts a SQL statement and an object array as statement parameters. It will create a PreparedStatement object from your SQL statement and bind the parameters for you. Therefore, you don't have to override any of the tasks in the update process.

Listing 6-13. Spring JdbcTemplate-based VehicleDao implementation - simple update with parameters

```
}

@Override
public void insert(Vehicle vehicle) {
  var jdbcTemplate = new JdbcTemplate(this.dataSource);
  jdbcTemplate.update(INSERT_SQL, vehicle.getColor(), vehicle.getWheel(), vehicle.getSeat(),
                      vehicle.getVehicleNo());
```

Of the three different versions of the update() method introduced, the last is the simplest because you don't have to implement any callback interfaces. Additionally, we've managed to remove all set–style methods for parameterizing the query. In contrast, the first is the most flexible because you can do any preprocessing of the PreparedStatement object before its execution. In practice, you should always choose the simplest version that meets all your needs.

There are also other overloaded update() methods provided by the JdbcTemplate class. Please refer to Javadoc for details.

Batch Updating a Database

Suppose you want to insert a batch of vehicles into the database. If you call the update() method multiple times, the update will be very slow as the SQL statement will be compiled and executed repeatedly. So it would be better to implement it using batch updates to insert a batch of vehicles.

The JdbcTemplate class also offers a few batchUpdate() template methods for batch update operations. The one you are going to use takes a SQL statement, a collection of items, a batch size, and a ParameterizedPreparedStatementSetter.

Listing 6-14. Spring JdbcTemplate-based VehicleDao implementation - batch insert using PreparedStatementSetter

```
package com.apress.spring6recipes.vehicle;
...
import org.springframework.jdbc.core.BatchPreparedStatementSetter;
import org.springframework.jdbc.core.JdbcTemplate;

public class JdbcVehicleDao implements VehicleDao {
  ...
  @Override
  public void insert(Collection<Vehicle> vehicles) {
    var jdbcTemplate = new JdbcTemplate(this.dataSource);
  var ppss = new ParameterizedPreparedStatementSetter<Vehicle>() {
      @Override
      public void setValues(PreparedStatement ps, Vehicle argument)
      throws SQLException {
        prepareStatement(ps, argument);
      }
    });
    jdbcTemplate.batchUpdate(INSERT_SQL, vehicles, vehicles.size(), ppss);
  }
}
```

Or it can be as a Java lambda expression.

Listing 6-15. Spring JdbcTemplate-based VehicleDao implementation - batch insert with lambda expression

```
@Override
public void insert(Collection<Vehicle> vehicles) {
  var jdbcTemplate = new JdbcTemplate(this.dataSource);
  jdbcTemplate.batchUpdate(INSERT_SQL, vehicles, vehicles.size(), this::prepareStatement);
}
```

You can test your batch insert operation with the following code snippet in the Main class.

Listing 6-16. Main class

```
package com.apress.spring6recipes.vehicle;

import java.util.Arrays;
import java.util.List;

import org.springframework.context.ApplicationContext;
import org.springframework.context.annotation.AnnotationConfigApplicationContext;

import com.apress.spring6recipes.vehicle.config.VehicleConfiguration;

public class Main {

  public static void main(String[] args) throws Exception {

    var cfg = VehicleConfiguration.class;
    try (var context = new AnnotationConfigApplicationContext(cfg)) {

      var vehicleDao = context.getBean(VehicleDao.class);
      var vehicle1 = new Vehicle("TEM0022", "Blue", 4, 4);
      var vehicle2 = new Vehicle("TEM0023", "Black", 4, 6);
      var vehicle3 = new Vehicle("TEM0024", "Green", 4, 5);
      vehicleDao.insert(List.of(vehicle1, vehicle2, vehicle3));

      vehicleDao.findAll().forEach(System.out::println);
    }
  }
}
```

6-4. Using a JDBC Template to Query a Database

Problem

To implement a JDBC query operation, you have to perform the following tasks, two of which (tasks 5 and 6) are additional as compared with an update operation:

1. Obtain a database connection from the data source.

2. Create a PreparedStatement object from the connection.

3. Bind the parameters to the PreparedStatement object.

4. Execute the PreparedStatement object.

5. Iterate the returned result set.

6. Extract data from the result set.

7. Handle SQLException.

The only steps relevant to your business logic, however, are the definition of the query and the extraction of the results from the result set! The rest is better handled by the JDBC template.

Solution

The JdbcTemplate class declares a number of overloaded query() template methods to control the overall query process. You can override the statement creation (task 2) and the parameter binding (task 3) by implementing the PreparedStatementCreator and PreparedStatementSetter interfaces, just as you did for the update operations. Moreover, the Spring JDBC framework supports multiple ways for you to override the data extraction (task 6).

How It Works

Extracting Data with a Row Callback Handler

RowCallbackHandler is the primary interface that allows you to process the current row of the result set. One of the query() methods iterates the result set for you and calls your RowCallbackHandler for each row. So the processRow() method will be called once for each row of the returned result set.

Listing 6-17. Spring JdbcTemplate-based VehicleDao implementation - plain JDBC

```
package com.apress.spring6recipes.vehicle;

@Override
public Vehicle findByVehicleNo(String vehicleNo) {
  try (var conn = dataSource.getConnection();
       var ps = conn.prepareStatement(SELECT_ONE_SQL)) {
    ps.setString(1, vehicleNo);

    Vehicle vehicle = null;
    try (ResultSet rs = ps.executeQuery()) {
      if (rs.next()) {
        vehicle = toVehicle(rs);
      }
    }
    ps.setString(1, vehicle.getVehicleNo());
```

It would be a bit more compact when using a Java lambda.

Listing 6-18. Method using JdbcTemplate with a lambda callback

```
@Override
public Vehicle findByVehicleNo(String vehicleNo) {
  var jdbcTemplate = new JdbcTemplate(dataSource);

  var vehicle = new Vehicle();
  jdbcTemplate.query(SELECT_ONE_SQL,
      rs -> {
        vehicle.setVehicleNo(rs.getString("VEHICLE_NO"));
        vehicle.setColor(rs.getString("COLOR"));
        vehicle.setWheel(rs.getInt("WHEEL"));
        vehicle.setSeat(rs.getInt("SEAT"));
      }, vehicleNo);
  return vehicle;
}
```

As there will be one row returned for the SQL query at maximum, you can create a vehicle object as a local variable and set its properties by extracting data from the result set. For a result set with more than one row, you should collect the objects as a list.

💡 The best use for the RowCallbackHandler is not for returning a result from a query method, as done here, but to process records row by row, for example, to export them to a CSV or Excel document.

Extracting Data with a Row Mapper

The RowMapper interface is more general than RowCallbackHandler. Its purpose is to map a single row of the result set to a customized object, so it can be applied to a single-row result set as well as a multiple-row result set.

From the viewpoint of reuse, it's better to implement the RowMapper interface as a normal class than as an inner class. In the mapRow() method of this interface, you have to construct the object that represents a row and return it as the method's return value.

Listing 6-19. Spring JdbcTemplate-based VehicleDao implementation - using RowMapper

```
package com.apress.spring6recipes.vehicle;

import java.sql.ResultSet;
import java.sql.SQLException;

import org.springframework.jdbc.core.RowMapper;

public class JdbcVehicleDao implements VehicleDao {

  private Vehicle toVehicle(ResultSet rs) throws SQLException {
    return new Vehicle(rs.getString("VEHICLE_NO"), rs.getString("COLOR"),
      rs.getInt("WHEEL"), rs.getInt("SEAT"));
  }
```

```
private class VehicleRowMapper implements RowMapper<Vehicle> {

  @Override
  public Vehicle mapRow(ResultSet rs, int rowNum) throws SQLException {
    return toVehicle(rs);
  }
}
}
```

As mentioned, RowMapper can be used for either a single-row or multiple-row result set. When querying for a unique object like in findByVehicleNo(), you have to make a call to the queryForObject() method of JdbcTemplate.

Listing 6-20. Spring JdbcTemplate-based VehicleDao implementation

```
package com.apress.spring6recipes.vehicle;

import org.springframework.jdbc.core.JdbcTemplate;

public class JdbcVehicleDao implements VehicleDao {

  @Override
  public Vehicle findByVehicleNo(String vehicleNo) {
    var jdbcTemplate = new JdbcTemplate(dataSource);
    return jdbcTemplate.queryForObject(SELECT_ONE_SQL, new VehicleRowMapper(), vehicleNo);
  }
}
```

Spring comes with a convenient RowMapper implementation, BeanPropertyRowMapper, which can automatically map a row to a new instance of the specified class. Note that the specified class must be a top-level class and must have a default or no-argument constructor. It first instantiates this class and then maps each column value to a property by matching their names. It supports matching a property name (e.g., vehicleNo) to the same column name or the column name with underscores (e.g., VEHICLE_NO).

Listing 6-21. Spring JdbcTemplate-based VehicleDao implementation - using BeanPropertyRowMapper

```
package com.apress.spring6recipes.vehicle;

import org.springframework.jdbc.core.BeanPropertyRowMapper;
import org.springframework.jdbc.core.JdbcTemplate;

public class JdbcVehicleDao implements VehicleDao {

  @Override
  public Vehicle findByVehicleNo(String vehicleNo) {
    var jdbcTemplate = new JdbcTemplate(dataSource);
    var mapper = BeanPropertyRowMapper.newInstance(Vehicle.class);
    return jdbcTemplate.queryForObject(SELECT_ONE_SQL, mapper , vehicleNo);
  }
}
```

Querying for Multiple Rows

Now, let's look at how to query for a result set with multiple rows. For example, suppose that you need a findAll() method in the DAO interface to get all vehicles.

Listing 6-22. VehicleDao interface–findAll declaration

```
package com.apress.spring6recipes.vehicle;
...
public interface VehicleDao {
  ...
  List<Vehicle> findAll();
}
```

Without the help of RowMapper, you can still call the queryForList() method and pass in a SQL statement. The returned result will be a list of maps. Each map stores a row of the result set with the column names as the keys.

Listing 6-23. Spring JdbcTemplate-based VehicleDao implementation - result as list of maps

```
package com.apress.spring6recipes.vehicle;

import java.util.List;

import org.springframework.jdbc.core.JdbcTemplate;

public class JdbcVehicleDao implements VehicleDao {

  @Override
  public List<Vehicle> findAll() {
    var jdbcTemplate = new JdbcTemplate(dataSource);
    var rows = jdbcTemplate.queryForList(SELECT_ALL_SQL);
    return rows.stream().map(row -> {
      var vehicle = new Vehicle();
      vehicle.setVehicleNo((String) row.get("VEHICLE_NO"));
      vehicle.setColor((String) row.get("COLOR"));
      vehicle.setWheel((Integer) row.get("WHEEL"));
      vehicle.setSeat((Integer) row.get("SEAT"));
      return vehicle;
    }).collect(Collectors.toList());
  }
}
```

You can test your findAll() method with the following code snippet in the Main class.

Listing 6-24. Main class

```
package com.apress.spring6recipes.vehicle;

import org.springframework.context.annotation.AnnotationConfigApplicationContext;

import com.apress.spring6recipes.vehicle.config.VehicleConfiguration;
```

```
public class Main {

  public static void main(String[] args) throws Exception {
    var cfg = VehicleConfiguration.class;
    try (var context = new AnnotationConfigApplicationContext(cfg)) {

      var vehicleDao = context.getBean(VehicleDao.class);
      var vehicles = vehicleDao.findAll();
      for (var vehicle : vehicles) {
        System.out.println("Vehicle No: " + vehicle.getVehicleNo());
        System.out.println("Color: " + vehicle.getColor());
        System.out.println("Wheel: " + vehicle.getWheel());
        System.out.println("Seat: " + vehicle.getSeat());
      }
    }
  }
}
```

If you use a RowMapper object to map the rows in a result set, you will get a list of mapped objects from the query() method.

Listing 6-25. JdbcTemplate with a RowMapper sample

```
package com.apress.spring6recipes.vehicle;
...
import org.springframework.jdbc.core.BeanPropertyRowMapper;
import org.springframework.jdbc.core.JdbcTemplate;

public class JdbcVehicleDao implements VehicleDao {
  ...
  public List<Vehicle> findAll() {
    var jdbcTemplate = new JdbcTemplate(dataSource);
    var mapper = BeanPropertyRowMapper.newInstance(Vehicle.class);
    return jdbcTemplate.query (SELECT_ALL_SQL, mapper);
  }
}
```

Querying for a Single Value

Finally, let's consider querying for a single-row and single-column result set. As an example, add the following operations to the DAO interface.

Listing 6-26. VehicleDao single find with RowMapper

```
package com.apress.spring6recipes.vehicle;

public interface VehicleDao {

  default String getColor(String vehicleNo) {
    throw new IllegalStateException("Method is not implemented!");
  }
```

```
default int countAll() {
  throw new IllegalStateException("Method is not implemented!");
}
}
```

ℹ️   They are added as default methods so as not to break existing implementations of the VehicleDao interface.

To query for a single string value, you can call the overloaded queryForObject() method, which requires an argument of java.lang.Class type. This method will help you map the result value to the type you specified.

Listing 6-27. Spring JdbcTemplate-based VehicleDao implementation - count with queryForObject

```
package com.apress.spring6recipes.vehicle;

public class JdbcVehicleDao implements VehicleDao {

  private static final String COUNT_ALL_SQL = "SELECT COUNT(*) FROM VEHICLE";
  private static final String SELECT_COLOR_SQL = "SELECT COLOR FROM VEHICLE WHERE
VEHICLE_NO=?";

  @Override
  public String getColor(String vehicleNo) {
    var jdbcTemplate = new JdbcTemplate(dataSource);
    return jdbcTemplate.queryForObject(SELECT_COLOR_SQL, String.class, vehicleNo);
  }

  @Override
  public int countAll() {
    var jdbcTemplate = new JdbcTemplate(dataSource);
    return jdbcTemplate.queryForObject(COUNT_ALL_SQL, Integer.class);
  }
}
```

You can test these two methods with the following code snippet in the Main class.

Listing 6-28. Main class

```
package com.apress.spring6recipes.vehicle;

import org.springframework.context.annotation.AnnotationConfigApplicationContext;

import com.apress.spring6recipes.vehicle.config.VehicleConfiguration;

public class Main {

  public static void main(String[] args) throws Exception {
    var cfg = VehicleConfiguration.class;
```

```
try (var ctx = new AnnotationConfigApplicationContext(cfg)) {

    var vehicleDao = ctx.getBean(VehicleDao.class);
    var count = vehicleDao.countAll();
    System.out.println("Vehicle Count: " + count);
    var color = vehicleDao.getColor("TEM0001");
    System.out.println("Color for [TEM0001]: " + color);
  }
 }
}
```

6-5. Simplifying JDBC Template Creation

Problem

It's not efficient to create a new instance of JdbcTemplate every time you need it, because you have to repeat the creation statement and incur the cost of creating a new object.

Solution

The JdbcTemplate class is designed to be thread-safe, so you can declare a single instance of it in the IoC container and inject this instance into all your DAO instances. Furthermore, the Spring JDBC framework offers a convenient class, org.springframework.jdbc.core.support.JdbcDaoSupport, to simplify your DAO implementation. This class declares a jdbcTemplate property, which can be injected from the IoC container or created automatically from a data source, for example, JdbcTemplate jdbcTemplate = new JdbcTemplate(dataSource). Your DAO can extend this class to have this property inherited.

How It Works

Injecting a JDBC Template

Until now, you have created a new instance of JdbcTemplate in each DAO method. Actually, you can have it injected at the class level and use this injected instance in all DAO methods. For simplicity's sake, the following code shows only the change to the insert() method.

Listing 6-29. Injecting JdbcTemplate at the class level

```
package com.apress.spring6recipes.vehicle;

import org.springframework.jdbc.core.JdbcTemplate;

public class JdbcVehicleDao implements VehicleDao {

  private final JdbcTemplate jdbcTemplate;

  public JdbcVehicleDao(JdbcTemplate jdbcTemplate) {
    this.jdbcTemplate = jdbcTemplate;
  }
```

```
  @Override
  public void insert(Vehicle vehicle) {
    jdbcTemplate.update(INSERT_SQL, vehicle.getColor(), vehicle.getWheel(),
                                    vehicle.getSeat(), vehicle.getVehicleNo());
  }
}
```

A JDBC template requires a data source to be set. You can inject this property by either a setter method or a constructor argument. Then, you can inject this JDBC template into your DAO.

Listing 6-30. VehicleDao configuration

```
package com.apress.spring6recipes.vehicle.config;

import javax.sql.DataSource;

import org.springframework.context.annotation.Bean;
import org.springframework.context.annotation.Configuration;
import org.springframework.jdbc.core.JdbcTemplate;

import com.apress.spring6recipes.vehicle.JdbcVehicleDao;
import com.apress.spring6recipes.vehicle.VehicleDao;
import com.zaxxer.hikari.HikariDataSource;

@Configuration
public class VehicleConfiguration {

  @Bean
  public VehicleDao vehicleDao(JdbcTemplate jdbcTemplate) {
    return new JdbcVehicleDao(jdbcTemplate);
  }

  @Bean
  public JdbcTemplate jdbcTemplate(DataSource dataSource) {
    return new JdbcTemplate(dataSource);
  }

  @Bean
  public DataSource dataSource() {
    var dataSource = new HikariDataSource();
    dataSource.setDataSourceClassName("org.postgresql.ds.PGSimpleDataSource");
    dataSource.setJdbcUrl("jdbc:postgresql://localhost:5432/vehicle");
    dataSource.setUsername("postgres");
    dataSource.setPassword("password");
    dataSource.setMinimumIdle(2);
    dataSource.setMaximumPoolSize(5);
    return dataSource;
  }

}
```

Extending the JdbcDaoSupport Class

The org.springframework.jdbc.core.support.JdbcDaoSupport class has a setDataSource() method and a setJdbcTemplate() method. Your DAO class can extend this class to have these methods inherited. Then, you can either inject a JDBC template directly or inject a data source for it to create a JDBC template.

In your DAO methods, you can simply call the getJdbcTemplate() method to retrieve the JDBC template. You also have to delete the dataSource and jdbcTemplate properties, as well as their setter methods, from your DAO class, because they have already been inherited. Again, for simplicity's sake, only the change to the insert() method is shown.

Listing 6-31. Spring JdbcDaoSupport-based VehicleDao implementation

```
package com.apress.spring6recipes.vehicle;

public class JdbcVehicleDao implements VehicleDao {

  private static final String INSERT_SQL = "INSERT INTO VEHICLE (COLOR, WHEEL, SEAT,
  VEHICLE_NO) VALUES (?, ?, ?, ?)";

  public JdbcVehicleDao(JdbcTemplate jdbcTemplate) {
    this.jdbcTemplate = jdbcTemplate;
  }

  @Override
  public void insert(Vehicle vehicle) {
    jdbcTemplate.update(INSERT_SQL, vehicle.getColor(), vehicle.getWheel(),
                            vehicle.getSeat(), vehicle.getVehicleNo());
  }
}
```

By extending JdbcDaoSupport, your DAO class inherits the setDataSource() method. You can inject a data source into your DAO instance for it to create a JDBC template.

Listing 6-32. VehicleDao configuration

```
@Configuration
public class VehicleConfiguration {
...
  @Bean
  public VehicleDao vehicleDao(DataSource dataSource) {
    var vehicleDao = new JdbcVehicleDao();
    vehicleDao.setDataSource(dataSource);
    return vehicleDao;
  }
}
```

6-6. Using Named Parameters in a JDBC Template

Problem

In classic JDBC usage, SQL parameters are represented by the placeholder ? and are bound by position. The trouble with positional parameters is that whenever the parameter order is changed, you have to change the parameter bindings as well. For a SQL statement with many parameters, it is very cumbersome to match the parameters by position.

Solution

Another option when binding SQL parameters in the Spring JDBC framework is to use named parameters. As the term implies, named SQL parameters are specified by name (starting with a colon) rather than by position. Named parameters are easier to maintain and also improve readability. At runtime, the framework classes replace named parameters with placeholders. Named parameters are supported by the NamedParameterJdbcTemplate.

How It Works

When using named parameters in your SQL statement, you can provide the parameter values in a map with the parameter names as the keys.

Listing 6-33. Spring NamedParameterJdbcDaoSupport-based VehicleDao implementation - using a Map

```
package com.apress.spring6recipes.vehicle;
...
import org.springframework.jdbc.core.namedparam.NamedParameterJdbcDaoSupport;

public class JdbcVehicleDao extends NamedParameterJdbcDaoSupport
                implements VehicleDao {

  private static final String INSERT_SQL = "INSERT INTO VEHICLE (COLOR, WHEEL, SEAT,
VEHICLE_NO) VALUES (:color, :wheel, :seat, :vehicleNo)";

  public void insert(Vehicle vehicle) {
    getNamedParameterJdbcTemplate().update(INSERT_SQL, toParameterMap(vehicle));
  }

  private Map<String, Object> toParameterMap(Vehicle vehicle) {
    var parameters = new HashMap<String, Object>();
    parameters.put("vehicleNo", vehicle.getVehicleNo());
    parameters.put("color", vehicle.getColor());
    parameters.put("wheel", vehicle.getWheel());
    parameters.put("seat", vehicle.getSeat());
    return parameters;
  }
  ...
}
```

You can also provide a SQL parameter source, whose responsibility is to offer SQL parameter values for named SQL parameters. There are three implementations of the SqlParameterSource interface. The basic one is MapSqlParameterSource, which wraps a map as its parameter source. In this example, this is a net loss compared with the previous example, as we've introduced one extra object—the SqlParameterSource.

Listing 6-34. Spring NamedParameterJdbcDaoSupport-based VehicleDao implementation - using a MapSqlParameterSource

```
package com.apress.spring6recipes.vehicle;
...
import org.springframework.jdbc.core.namedparam.MapSqlParameterSource;
import org.springframework.jdbc.core.namedparam.SqlParameterSource;
import org.springframework.jdbc.core.namedparam.NamedParameterJdbcDaoSupport;

public class JdbcVehicleDao extends NamedParameterJdbcDaoSupport
                implements VehicleDao {

  public void insert(Vehicle vehicle) {
    var parameterSource = new MapSqlParameterSource(toParameterMap(vehicle));
    getNamedParameterJdbcTemplate().update(INSERT_SQL, parameterSource);
  }
  ...
}
```

The power comes when we need an extra level of indirection between the parameters passed into the update method and the source of their values. For example, what if we want to get properties from a JavaBean? Here is where the SqlParameterSource intermediary starts to benefit us! SqlParameterSource is BeanPropertySqlParameterSource, which wraps a normal Java object as a SQL parameter source. For each of the named parameters, the property with the same name will be used as the parameter value.

Listing 6-35. Spring NamedParameterJdbcDaoSupport-based VehicleDao implementation - using a BeanPropertySqlParameterSource

```
package com.apress.spring6recipes.vehicle;

import org.springframework.jdbc.core.namedparam.BeanPropertySqlParameterSource;
import org.springframework.jdbc.core.namedparam.SqlParameterSource;
import org.springframework.jdbc.core.namedparam.NamedParameterJdbcDaoSupport;

public class JdbcVehicleDao extends NamedParameterJdbcDaoSupport
                implements VehicleDao {

  public void insert(Vehicle vehicle) {
    var parameterSource = new BeanPropertySqlParameterSource(vehicle);
    getNamedParameterJdbcTemplate ().update(INSERT_SQL, parameterSource);
  }
}
```

Named parameters can also be used in batch update. You can provide either a Map, an array, or a SqlParameterSource array for the parameter values.

Listing 6-36. Spring NamedParameterJdbcDaoSupport-based VehicleDao implementation - batch update

```
package com.apress.spring6recipes.vehicle;
...
import org.springframework.jdbc.core.namedparam.BeanPropertySqlParameterSource;
import org.springframework.jdbc.core.namedparam.SqlParameterSource;
import org.springframework.jdbc.core.namedparam.NamedParameterJdbcDaoSupport;

public class JdbcVehicleDao extends NamedParameterJdbcDaoSupport implements VehicleDao {
  ...
  @Override
  public void insert(Collection<Vehicle> vehicles) {
    var sources = vehicles.stream()
        .map(BeanPropertySqlParameterSource::new)
        .toArray(SqlParameterSource[]::new);
    getNamedParameterJdbcTemplate().batchUpdate(INSERT_SQL, sources);
  }
}
```

6-7. Handling Exceptions in the Spring JDBC Framework

Problem

Many of the JDBC APIs declare throwing java.sql.SQLException, a checked exception that must be caught. It's very troublesome to handle this kind of exception every time you perform a database operation. You often have to define your own policy to handle this kind of exception. Failure to do so may lead to inconsistent exception handling.

Solution

The Spring Framework offers a consistent data access exception handling mechanism for its data access module, including the JDBC framework. In general, all exceptions thrown by the Spring JDBC framework are subclasses of org.springframework.dao.DataAccessException, a type of RuntimeException that you are not forced to catch. It's the root exception class for all exceptions in Spring's data access module.

Figure 6-1 shows only part of the DataAccessException hierarchy in Spring's data access module. In total, there are more than 30 exception classes defined for different categories of data access exceptions.

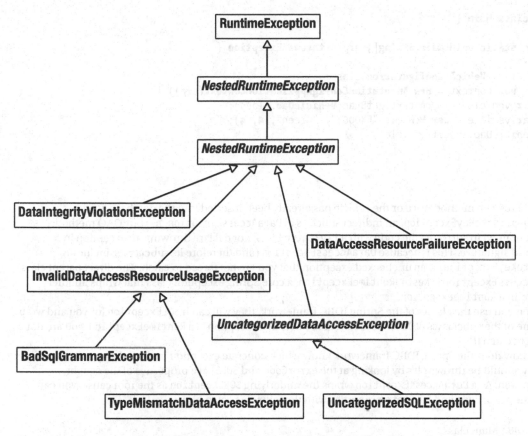

Figure 6-1. *Common exception classes in the DataAccessException hierarchy*

How It Works

Understanding Exception Handling in the Spring JDBC Framework

Until now, you haven't handled JDBC exceptions explicitly when using a JDBC template or JDBC operation objects. To help you understand the Spring JDBC framework's exception handling mechanism, let's consider the following code fragment in the Main class, which inserts a vehicle. What happens if you insert a vehicle with a duplicate vehicle number?

Listing 6-37. Main class

```
package com.apress.spring6recipes.vehicle;

import org.springframework.context.annotation.AnnotationConfigApplicationContext;

import com.apress.spring6recipes.vehicle.config.VehicleConfiguration;
```

```java
public class Main {

  public static void main(String[] args) throws Exception {

    var cfg = VehicleConfiguration.class;
    try (var context = new AnnotationConfigApplicationContext(cfg)) {
      var vehicleDao = context.getBean(VehicleDao.class);
      var vehicle = new Vehicle("EX0001", "Green", 4, 4);
      vehicleDao.insert(vehicle);
    }
  }
}
```

If you run the method twice or the vehicle has already been inserted into the database, it will throw a DuplicateKeyException, an indirect subclass of DataAccessException. In your DAO methods, you neither need to surround the code with a try/catch block nor declare throwing an exception in the method signature. This is because DataAccessException (and therefore its subclasses, including DuplicateKeyException) is an unchecked exception that you are not forced to catch. The direct parent class of DataAccessException is NestedRuntimeException, a core Spring exception class that wraps another exception in a RuntimeException.

When you use the classes of the Spring JDBC framework, they will catch SQLException for you and wrap it with one of the subclasses of DataAccessException. As this exception is a RuntimeException, you are not required to catch it.

But how does the Spring JDBC framework know which concrete exception in the DataAccessException hierarchy should be thrown? It's by looking at the errorCode and SQLState properties of the caught SQLException. As a DataAccessException wraps the underlying SQLException as the root cause, you can inspect the errorCode and SQLState properties with the following catch block.

Listing 6-38. Main class

```java
package com.apress.spring6recipes.vehicle;
...
import java.sql.SQLException;

import org.springframework.dao.DataAccessException;

public class Main {

  public static void main(String[] args) {
    ...
    var vehicleDao = context.getBean(VehicleDao.class);
    var vehicle = new Vehicle("EX0001", "Green", 4, 4);
    try {
      vehicleDao.insert(vehicle);
    } catch (DataAccessException e) {
      var sqle = (SQLExcption) e.getCause();
      System.out.println("Error code: " + sqle.getErrorCode());
      System.out.println("SQL state: " + sqle.getSQLState());
    }
  }
}
```

When you insert the duplicate vehicle again, notice that PostgreSQL returns the following error code and SQL state:

```
Error code : 0
SQL state : 23505
```

If you refer to the PostgreSQL reference manual, you will find the error code description shown in Table 6-2.

Table 6-2. *PostgreSQL Error Code Description*

SQL State	Message Text
23505	unique_violation

How does the Spring JDBC framework know that state 23505 should be mapped to DuplicateKeyException? The error code and SQL state are database specific, which means different database products may return different codes for the same kind of error. Moreover, some database products will specify the error in the errorCode property, while others (like PostgreSQL) will do so in the SQLState property.

As an open Java application framework, Spring understands the error codes of most popular database products. Because of the large number of error codes, however, it can only maintain mappings for the most frequently encountered errors. The mapping is defined in the sql-error-codes.xml file, located in the org. springframework.jdbc.support package. The following snippet for PostgreSQL is taken from this file.

Listing 6-39. Snippet from the sql-error-codes.xml file

```xml
<?xml version="1.0" encoding="UTF-8"?>
<!DOCTYPE beans PUBLIC "-//SPRING//DTD BEAN 3.0//EN"
  "http://www.springframework.org/dtd/spring-beans-3.0.dtd">

<beans>
  ...

  <bean id="PostgreSQL" class="org.springframework.jdbc.support.SQLErrorCodes">
    <property name="useSqlStateForTranslation">
      <value>true</value>
    </property>
    <property name="badSqlGrammarCodes">
      <value>03000,42000,42601,42602,42622,42804,42P01</value>
    </property>
    <property name="duplicateKeyCodes">
      <value>23505</value>
    </property>
    <property name="dataIntegrityViolationCodes">
      <value>23000,23502,23503,23514</value>
    </property>
    <property name="dataAccessResourceFailureCodes">
      <value>53000,53100,53200,53300</value>
    </property>
```

```
      <property name="cannotAcquireLockCodes">
        <value>55P03</value>
      </property>
      <property name="cannotSerializeTransactionCodes">
        <value>40001</value>
      </property>
      <property name="deadlockLoserCodes">
        <value>40P01</value>
      </property>
    </bean>
  ...
</beans>
```

The useSqlStateForTranslation property means that the SQLState property, rather than the errorCode property, should be used to match the error code. Finally, the SQLErrorCodes class defines several categories for you to map database error codes. The code 23505 lies in the dataIntegrityViolationCodes category.

Customizing Data Access Exception Handling

The Spring JDBC framework only maps well-known error codes. Sometimes, you may wish to customize the mapping yourself. For example, you might decide to add more codes to an existing category or define a custom exception for particular error codes.

In Table 6-2, the error code 23505 indicates a duplicate key error in PostgreSQL. It is mapped by default to DataIntegrityViolationException. Suppose that you want to create a custom exception type, MyDuplicateKeyException, for this kind of error. It should extend DataIntegrityViolationException because it is also a kind of data integrity violation error. Remember that for an exception to be thrown by the Spring JDBC framework, it must be compatible with the root exception class DataAccessException.

Listing 6-40. Custom exception class

```java
package com.apress.spring6recipes.vehicle;

import org.springframework.dao.DataIntegrityViolationException;

public class MyDuplicateKeyException extends DataIntegrityViolationException {

  public MyDuplicateKeyException(String msg) {
    super(msg);
  }

  public MyDuplicateKeyException(String msg, Throwable cause) {
    super(msg, cause);
  }
}
```

By default, Spring will look up an exception from the sql-error-codes.xml file located in the org.springframework.jdbc.support package. However, you can override some of the mappings by providing a file with the same name in the root of the classpath. If Spring can find your custom file, it will look up an exception from your mapping first. However, if it does not find a suitable exception there, Spring will look up the default mapping.

For example, suppose that you want to map your custom DuplicateKeyException type to error code 23505. You have to add the binding via a CustomSQLErrorCodesTranslation bean and then add this bean to the customTranslations category.

Listing 6-41. Custom sql-error-codes.xml file

```xml
<?xml version="1.0" encoding="UTF-8"?>
<!DOCTYPE beans PUBLIC "-//SPRING//DTD BEAN 2.0//EN"
  "http://www.springframework.org/dtd/spring-beans-2.0.dtd">

<beans>
  <bean id="PostgreSQL"
      class="org.springframework.jdbc.support.SQLErrorCodes">
    <property name="useSqlStateForTranslation">
      <value>true</value>
    </property>
    <property name="customTranslations">
      <list>
        <ref bean="myDuplicateKeyTranslation" />
      </list>
    </property>
  </bean>

  <bean id="myDuplicateKeyTranslation"
    class="org.springframework.jdbc.support.CustomSQLErrorCodesTranslation">
    <property name="errorCodes">
      <value>23505</value>
    </property>
    <property name="exceptionClass">
      <value>
        com.apress.spring6recipes.vehicle.MyDuplicateKeyException
      </value>
    </property>
  </bean>
</beans>
```

Now, if you remove the try/catch block surrounding the vehicle insert operation and insert a duplicate vehicle, the Spring JDBC framework will throw a MyDuplicateKeyException instead.

However, if you are not satisfied with the basic code-to-exception mapping strategy used by the SQLErrorCodes class, you may further implement the SQLExceptionTranslator interface and inject its instance into a JDBC template via the setExceptionTranslator() method.

6-8. Problems with Using ORM Frameworks Directly

Problem

You've decided to go to the next level—you have a sufficiently complex domain model, and manually writing all the code for each entity is getting tedious, so you begin to investigate a few alternatives, like Hibernate. You're stunned to find that while they're powerful, they can be anything but simple!

Solution

Let Spring lend a hand; it has facilities for dealing with ORM layers that rival those available for plain ol' JDBC access.

How It Works

Suppose you are developing a course management system for a training center. The first class you create for this system is Course. This class is called an entity class or a persistent class because it represents a real-world entity and its instances will be persisted to a database. Remember that for each entity class to be persisted by an ORM framework, a default constructor with no argument is required.

Listing 6-42. Course class

```
package com.apress.spring6recipes.course;

public class Course {

  private Long id;
  private String title;
  private LocalDate beginDate;
  private LocalDate endDate;
  private int fee;
}
```

For each entity class, you must define an identifier property to uniquely identify an entity. It's a best practice to define an auto-generated identifier because this has no business meaning and thus won't be changed under any circumstances. Moreover, this identifier will be used by the ORM framework to determine an entity's state. If the identifier value is null, this entity will be treated as a new and unsaved entity. When this entity is persisted, an insert SQL statement will be issued; otherwise, an update statement will. To allow the identifier to be null, choose a primitive wrapper type like java.lang.Integer and java.lang.Long for the identifier.

In your course management system, you need a DAO interface to encapsulate the data access logic. Let's define the following operations in the CourseDao interface.

Listing 6-43. CourseDao interface

```
package com.apress.spring6recipes.course;

import java.util.List;

public interface CourseDao {

  Course store(Course course);
  void delete(Long courseId);
  Course findById(Long courseId);
  List<Course> findAll();
}
```

Usually, when using ORM for persisting objects, the insert and update operations are combined into a single operation (e.g., store). This is to let the ORM framework (not you) decide whether an object should be inserted or updated. In order for an ORM framework to persist your objects to a database, it must know the mapping metadata for the entity classes. You have to provide mapping metadata to it in its supported format. Historically, Hibernate used XML to provide the mapping metadata. However, because each ORM framework may have its own format for defining mapping metadata, JPA defines a set of persistent annotations for you to define mapping metadata in a standard format that is more likely to be reusable in other ORM frameworks.

Hibernate also supports the use of JPA annotations to define mapping metadata, so there are essentially three different strategies for mapping and persisting your objects with Hibernate and JPA:

- Using the Hibernate API to persist objects with Hibernate XML mappings

- Using the Hibernate API to persist objects with JPA annotations

- Using JPA to persist objects with JPA annotations

The core programming elements of Hibernate, JPA, and other ORM frameworks resemble those of JDBC. They are summarized in Table 6-3.

Table 6-3. *Core Programming Elements for Different Data Access Strategies*

Concept	JDBC	Hibernate	JPA
Resource	Connection	Session	EntityManager
Resource factory	DataSource	SessionFactory	EntityManagerFactory
Exception	SQLException	HibernateException	PersistenceException

In Hibernate, the core interface for object persistence is Session, whose instances can be obtained from a SessionFactory instance. In JPA, the corresponding interface is EntityManager, whose instances can be obtained from an EntityManagerFactory instance. The exceptions thrown by Hibernate are of type HibernateException, while those thrown by JPA may be of type PersistenceException or other Java SE exceptions like IllegalArgumentException and IllegalStateException. Note that all these exceptions are subclasses of RuntimeException, which you are not forced to catch and handle.

Persisting Objects Using the Hibernate API with JPA Annotations

JPA annotations are standardized by the Jakarta Persistence specification, so they're supported by all JPA-compliant ORM frameworks, including Hibernate. Moreover, the use of annotations will be more convenient for you to edit mapping metadata in the same source file.

The following Course class illustrates the use of JPA annotations to define mapping metadata.

Listing 6-44. Course class with JPA annotations

```
package com.apress.spring6recipes.course;

import jakarta.persistence.Column;
import jakarta.persistence.Entity;
import jakarta.persistence.GeneratedValue;
import jakarta.persistence.GenerationType;
import jakarta.persistence.Id;
import jakarta.persistence.Table;
```

```java
import java.time.LocalDate;
import java.util.Objects;

@Entity
@Table(name = "COURSE")
public class Course {

  @Id
  @GeneratedValue(strategy = GenerationType.IDENTITY)
  @Column(name = "ID")
  private Long id;

  @Column(name = "TITLE", length = 100, nullable = false)
  private String title;

  @Column(name = "BEGIN_DATE")
  private LocalDate beginDate;

  @Column(name = "END_DATE")
  private LocalDate endDate;

  @Column(name = "FEE")
  private int fee;
}
```

Each entity class must be annotated with the @Entity annotation. You can assign a table name for an entity class in this annotation. For each property, you can specify a column name and column details using the @Column annotation.

Each entity class must have an identifier defined by the @Id annotation. You can choose a strategy for identifier generation using the @GeneratedValue annotation. Here, the identifier will be generated by a table identity column.

Now, let's implement the DAO interface in the hibernate subpackage using the plain Hibernate API. Before you call the Hibernate API for object persistence, you have to initialize a Hibernate session factory (e.g., in the constructor).

Listing 6-45. Hibernate-based CourseDao implementation

```java
package com.apress.spring6recipes.course.hibernate;

import java.util.List;

import org.hibernate.SessionFactory;
import org.hibernate.cfg.AvailableSettings;
import org.hibernate.cfg.Configuration;

import com.apress.spring6recipes.course.Course;
import com.apress.spring6recipes.course.CourseDao;

public class HibernateCourseDao implements CourseDao {

  private final SessionFactory sessionFactory;
```

```java
public HibernateCourseDao() {
  var url = "jdbc:postgresql://localhost:5432/course";
  var configuration = new Configuration()
      .setProperty(AvailableSettings.URL, url)
      .setProperty(AvailableSettings.USER, "postgres")
      .setProperty(AvailableSettings.PASS, "password")
      .setProperty(AvailableSettings.SHOW_SQL, String.valueOf(true))
      .setProperty(AvailableSettings.HBM2DDL_AUTO, "update")
      .addClass(Course.class);

  this.sessionFactory = configuration.buildSessionFactory();
}

@Override
public Course store(Course course) {
  var session = sessionFactory.openSession();
  try (session) {
    session.getTransaction().begin();
    if (course.getId() == null) {
      session.persist(course);
    } else {
      session.merge(course);
    }
    session.getTransaction().commit();
    return course;
  } catch (RuntimeException e) {
    session.getTransaction().rollback();
    throw e;
  }
}

@Override
public void delete(Long courseId) {
  var session = sessionFactory.openSession();
  try (session) {
    session.getTransaction().begin();
    Course course = session.get(Course.class, courseId);
    session.remove(course);
    session.getTransaction().commit();
  } catch (RuntimeException e) {
    session.getTransaction().rollback();
    throw e;
  }
}

@Override
public Course findById(Long courseId) {
  try (var session = sessionFactory.openSession()) {
    return session.find(Course.class, courseId);
  }
}
```

325

```java
@Override
public List<Course> findAll() {
  try (var session = sessionFactory.openSession()) {
    return session.createQuery("SELECT c FROM Course c", Course.class).getResultList();
  }
}
}
```

The first step in using Hibernate is to create a Configuration object and to configure properties such as the database settings (either JDBC connection properties or a data source's JNDI name), the database dialect, the mapping metadata's locations, and so on. When using XML mapping files to define mapping metadata, you use the addClass method to tell Hibernate what classes it has to manage. Then, you build a Hibernate session factory from this Configuration object. The purpose of a session factory is to produce sessions for you to persist your objects. Before you can persist your objects, you have to create tables in a database schema to store the object data. When using an ORM framework like Hibernate, you usually needn't design the tables by yourself. If you set the hibernate.hbm2ddl.auto property to update, Hibernate can help you update the database schema and create the tables when necessary.

 Naturally, you shouldn't enable this in production, but it can be a great speed boost for development.

In the preceding DAO methods, you first open a session from the session factory. For any operation that involves database update, such as persist() and remove(), you must start a Hibernate transaction on that session. If the operation completes successfully, you commit the transaction. Otherwise, you roll it back if any RuntimeException happens. For read-only operations such as get() and HQL queries, there's no need to start a transaction. Finally, you must remember to close a session to release the resources held by this session.

You can create the following Main class to test run all the DAO methods. It also demonstrates an entity's typical life cycle.

Listing 6-46. Main class

```java
package com.apress.spring6recipes.course;

import java.time.LocalDate;

import com.apress.spring6recipes.course.hibernate.HibernateCourseDao;

public class Main {

  public static void main(String[] args) {

    var courseDao = new HibernateCourseDao();

    var course = new Course();
    course.setTitle("Core Spring Framework 6");
    course.setBeginDate(LocalDate.of(2022, 8, 1));
    course.setEndDate(LocalDate.of(2022, 9, 1));
    course.setFee(1000);
```

```java
System.out.println("\nCourse before persisting");
System.out.println(course);

courseDao.store(course);

System.out.println("\nCourse after persisting");
System.out.println(course);

var courseId = course.getId();
var courseFromDb = courseDao.findById(courseId);

System.out.println("\nCourse fresh from database");
System.out.println(courseFromDb);

courseDao.delete(courseId);

System.exit(0);
  }

}
```

Persisting Objects Using JPA with Hibernate as the Engine

In addition to persistent annotations, JPA defines a set of programming interfaces for object persistence. However, JPA is not a persistence implementation; you have to pick up a JPA-compliant engine to provide persistence services. Hibernate can be JPA-compliant through the Hibernate EntityManager. With this Hibernate can work as an underlying JPA engine to persist objects. This lets you retain both the valuable investment in Hibernate (perhaps it's faster or handles certain operations more to your satisfaction) and write code that is JPA-compliant and portable among other JPA engines. This can also be a useful way to transition a code base to JPA. New code is written strictly against the JPA APIs, and older code is transitioned to the JPA interfaces.

In a Jakarta EE environment, you can configure the JPA engine in a Java EE container. But in a Java SE application, you have to set up the engine locally. The configuration of JPA is through the central XML file persistence.xml, located in the META-INF directory of the classpath root. In this file, you can set any vendor-specific properties for the underlying engine configuration. When using Spring to configure the EntityManagerFactory, this isn't needed, and the configuration can be done through Spring.

Now, let's create the JPA configuration file persistence.xml in the META-INF directory of the classpath root. Each JPA configuration file contains one or more <persistence-unit> elements. A persistence unit defines a set of persistent classes and how they should be persisted. Each persistence unit requires a name for identification. Here, you assign the name course to this persistence unit.

Listing 6-47. JPA persistence.xml file

```xml
<?xml version="1.0" encoding="UTF-8" standalone="yes"?>
<persistence xmlns="https://jakarta.ee/xml/ns/persistence"
             xmlns:xsi="http://www.w3.org/2001/XMLSchema-instance"
             xsi:schemaLocation="https://jakarta.ee/xml/ns/persistence
             https://jakarta.ee/xml/ns/persistence/persistence_3_1.xsd"
             version="3.1">
```

```
<persistence-unit name="course" transaction-type="RESOURCE_LOCAL">
  <provider>org.hibernate.jpa.HibernatePersistenceProvider</provider>
  <class>com.apress.spring6recipes.course.Course</class>

  <properties>
    <property name="jakarta.persistence.jdbc.url"
              value="jdbc:postgresql://localhost:5432/course"/>
    <property name="jakarta.persistence.jdbc.user" value="postgres"/>
    <property name="jakarta.persistence.jdbc.password" value="password"/>

    <property name="hibernate.dialect"
              value="org.hibernate.dialect.PostgreSQL95Dialect"/>
    <property name="hibernate.hbm2ddl.auto" value="update"/>
    <property name="hibernate.show_sql" value="true"/>
  </properties>
</persistence-unit>
</persistence>
```

In this JPA configuration file, you configure Hibernate as your underlying JPA engine. Notice that there are a few generic javax.persistence properties to configure the location of the database and username/password combination to use. Next, there are some Hibernate-specific properties to configure the dialect and again the hibernate.hbm2ddl.auto property. Finally, there is a <class> element to specify which classes to use for mapping.

In a Jakarta EE environment, a Jakarta EE container is able to manage the entity manager for you and inject it into your components directly. But when you use JPA outside of a Jakarta EE container (e.g., in a Java SE application), you have to create and maintain the entity manager by yourself.

Now, let's implement the CourseDao interface using JPA in a Java SE application. Before you call JPA for object persistence, you have to initialize an entity manager factory. The purpose of an entity manager factory is to produce entity managers for you to persist your objects.

Listing 6-48. JPA-based CourseDao implementation

```java
package com.apress.spring6recipes.course.jpa;

import java.util.List;

import jakarta.persistence.EntityManagerFactory;
import jakarta.persistence.Persistence;

import com.apress.spring6recipes.course.Course;
import com.apress.spring6recipes.course.CourseDao;

public class JpaCourseDao implements CourseDao {

  private final EntityManagerFactory entityManagerFactory
          = Persistence.createEntityManagerFactory("course");

  @Override
  public Course store(Course course) {
    var manager = entityManagerFactory.createEntityManager();
    var tx = manager.getTransaction();
    try {
```

```
      tx.begin();
      var persisted = manager.merge(course);
      tx.commit();
      return persisted;
    } catch (RuntimeException e) {
      tx.rollback();
      throw e;
    } finally {
      manager.close();
    }
  }

  @Override
  public void delete(Long courseId) {
    var manager = entityManagerFactory.createEntityManager();
    var tx = manager.getTransaction();
    try {
      tx.begin();
      Course course = manager.find(Course.class, courseId);
      manager.remove(course);
      tx.commit();
    } catch (RuntimeException e) {
      tx.rollback();
      throw e;
    } finally {
      manager.close();
    }
  }

  @Override
  public Course findById(Long courseId) {
    var manager = entityManagerFactory.createEntityManager();
    try {
      return manager.find(Course.class, courseId);
    } finally {
      manager.close();
    }
  }

  @Override
  public List<Course> findAll() {
    var manager = entityManagerFactory.createEntityManager();
    try {
      return manager.createQuery("select course from Course course", Course.class).
      getResultList();
    } finally {
      manager.close();
    }
  }
}
```

329

The entity manager factory is built by the static method createEntityManagerFactory() of the jakarta.persistence.Persistence class. You have to pass in a persistence unit name defined in persistence.xml for an entity manager factory.

In the preceding DAO methods, you first create an entity manager from the entity manager factory. For any operation that involves database update, such as merge() and remove(), you must start a JPA transaction on the entity manager. For read-only operations such as find() and JPA queries, there's no need to start a transaction. Finally, you must close an entity manager to release the resources.

You can test this DAO with the similar Main class, but this time, you instantiate the JPA DAO implementation instead.

Listing 6-49. Main class

```
package com.apress.spring6recipes.course;
public class Main {

  public static void main(String[] args) {

    var courseDao = new JpaCourseDao();
}
```

In the preceding DAO implementations for both Hibernate and JPA, there are only one or two lines that are different for each DAO method. The rest of the lines are boilerplate routine tasks that you have to repeat. Moreover, each ORM framework has its own API for local transaction management.

6-9. Configuring ORM Resource Factories in Spring

Problem

When using an ORM framework on its own, you have to configure its resource factory with its API. For Hibernate and JPA, you have to build a session factory and an entity manager factory from the native Hibernate API and JPA. You have no choice but to manage these objects manually, without Spring's support.

Solution

Spring provides several factory beans for you to create a Hibernate session factory or a JPA entity manager factory as a singleton bean in the IoC container. These factories can be shared between multiple beans via dependency injection. Moreover, this allows the session factory and the entity manager factory to integrate with other Spring data access facilities, such as data sources and transaction managers.

How It Works

Configuring a Hibernate Session Factory in Spring

First of all, let's modify HibernateCourseDao to accept a session factory via dependency injection, instead of creating it directly with the native Hibernate API in the constructor.

Listing 6-50. Hibernate-based CourseDao implementation

```
package com.apress.spring6recipes.course.hibernate;
...
import org.hibernate.SessionFactory;

public class HibernateCourseDao implements CourseDao {

  private final SessionFactory sessionFactory;

  public HibernateCourseDao(SessionFactory sessionFactory) {
    this.sessionFactory = sessionFactory;
  }

  ...
}
```

Then, you create a configuration class for using Hibernate as the ORM framework. You can also declare a HibernateCourseDao instance under Spring's management.

Listing 6-51. Course configuration - SessionFactory only

```
package com.apress.spring6recipes.course.config;

import java.util.Properties;

import org.hibernate.SessionFactory;
import org.hibernate.cfg.AvailableSettings;
import org.springframework.context.annotation.Bean;
import org.springframework.context.annotation.Configuration;
import org.springframework.orm.hibernate5.LocalSessionFactoryBuilder;

import com.apress.spring6recipes.course.Course;
import com.apress.spring6recipes.course.CourseDao;
import com.apress.spring6recipes.course.hibernate.HibernateCourseDao;

@Configuration
public class CourseConfiguration {

  @Bean
  public CourseDao courseDao(SessionFactory sessionFactory) {
    return new HibernateCourseDao(sessionFactory);
  }

  @Bean
  public SessionFactory sessionFactory() {
    return new LocalSessionFactoryBuilder(null)
            .addAnnotatedClasses(Course.class)
            .addProperties(hibernateProperties())
            .buildSessionFactory();
  }
```

```
  private Properties hibernateProperties() {
    var url = "jdbc:postgresql://localhost:5432/course";
    var properties = new Properties();
    properties.setProperty(AvailableSettings.URL, url);
    properties.setProperty(AvailableSettings.USER, "postgres");
    properties.setProperty(AvailableSettings.PASS, "password");
    properties.setProperty(AvailableSettings.SHOW_SQL, String.valueOf(true));
    properties.setProperty(AvailableSettings.HBM2DDL_AUTO, "update");
    return properties;
  }
}
```

All the properties that were set earlier on the Hibernate configuration are now translated to a
Properties object and added to the LocalSessionFactoryBuilder. The annotated class is passed in
through the addAnnotatedClasses method so that eventually Hibernate knowns about the annotated class.
The constructed SessionFactory is passed to the HibernateCourseDao through its constructor.

If you are in a project that still uses Hibernate mapping files, you can use the addDirectory and addFile
methods to specify the mapping directories or files.

Now, you can modify the Main class to retrieve the HibernateCourseDao instance from the Spring IoC
container.

Listing 6-52. Main class

```
package com.apress.spring6recipes.course;

import org.springframework.context.annotation.AnnotationConfigApplicationContext;

import com.apress.spring6recipes.course.config.CourseConfiguration;

public class Main {

  public static void main(String[] args) {

    var cfg = CourseConfiguration.class;
    try (var context = new AnnotationConfigApplicationContext(cfg)) {
      var courseDao = context.getBean(CourseDao.class);
    }
  }
}
```

The preceding builder creates a session factory by loading the Hibernate configuration file, which
includes the database settings (either JDBC connection properties or a data source's JNDI name). Now,
suppose you have a data source defined in the Spring IoC container. If you want to use this data source
for your session factory, you can inject it into the constructor of the LocalSessionFactoryBuilder. The
data source specified in this property will override the database settings of the Hibernate configuration.
If this is set, the Hibernate settings should not define a connection provider to avoid meaningless double
configuration.

Listing 6-53. Course configuration - SessionFactory with DataSource

```java
package com.apress.spring6recipes.course.config;

import java.util.Properties;

import javax.sql.DataSource;

import org.hibernate.SessionFactory;
import org.hibernate.cfg.AvailableSettings;
import org.springframework.context.annotation.Bean;
import org.springframework.context.annotation.Configuration;
import org.springframework.orm.hibernate5.LocalSessionFactoryBuilder;

import com.apress.spring6recipes.course.Course;
import com.apress.spring6recipes.course.CourseDao;
import com.apress.spring6recipes.course.hibernate.HibernateCourseDao;
import com.zaxxer.hikari.HikariDataSource;

@Configuration
public class CourseConfiguration {

  @Bean
  public CourseDao courseDao(SessionFactory sessionFactory) {
    return new HibernateCourseDao(sessionFactory);
  }

  @Bean
  public DataSource dataSource() {
    var dataSource = new HikariDataSource();
    dataSource.setUsername("postgres");
    dataSource.setPassword("password");
    dataSource.setJdbcUrl("jdbc:postgresql://localhost:5432/course");
    dataSource.setMinimumIdle(2);
    dataSource.setMaximumPoolSize(5);
    return dataSource;
  }

  @Bean
  public SessionFactory sessionFactory(DataSource dataSource) {
    return new LocalSessionFactoryBuilder(dataSource)
            .addAnnotatedClasses(Course.class)
            .addProperties(hibernateProperties())
            .buildSessionFactory();
  }

  private Properties hibernateProperties() {
    var properties = new Properties();
    properties.setProperty(AvailableSettings.SHOW_SQL, String.valueOf(true));
    properties.setProperty(AvailableSettings.HBM2DDL_AUTO, "update");
    return properties;
  }
}
```

333

Configuring a JPA Entity Manager Factory in Spring

First of all, let's modify JpaCourseDao to accept an entity manager factory via dependency injection, instead of creating it directly in the class.

Listing 6-54. JPA-based CourseDao implementation

```
package com.apress.spring6recipes.course;
...
import javax.persistence.EntityManagerFactory;
import javax.persistence.Persistence;

public class JpaCourseDao implements CourseDao {

  private final EntityManagerFactory entityManagerFactory;

  public JpaCourseDao (EntityManagerFactory entityManagerFactory) {
    this.entityManagerFactory = entityManagerFactory;
  }
  ...
}
```

Let's create a bean configuration file for using JPA. Spring provides a factory bean, LocalEntityManagerFactoryBean, for you to create an entity manager factory in the IoC container. You must specify the persistence unit name defined in the JPA configuration file. You can also declare a JpaCourseDao instance under Spring's management.

Listing 6-55. Course configuration - using existing persistence.xml

```
package com.apress.spring6recipes.course.config;

import jakarta.persistence.EntityManagerFactory;

import org.springframework.context.annotation.Bean;
import org.springframework.context.annotation.Configuration;
import org.springframework.orm.jpa.LocalEntityManagerFactoryBean;

import com.apress.spring6recipes.course.CourseDao;
import com.apress.spring6recipes.course.jpa.JpaCourseDao;

@Configuration
public class CourseConfiguration {

  @Bean
  public CourseDao courseDao(EntityManagerFactory entityManagerFactory) {
    return new JpaCourseDao(entityManagerFactory);
  }

  @Bean
  public LocalEntityManagerFactoryBean entityManagerFactory() {
    var emf = new LocalEntityManagerFactoryBean();
```

```
    emf.setPersistenceUnitName("course");
    return emf;
  }
}
```

Now, you can test this JpaCourseDao instance with the Main class by retrieving it from the Spring IoC container.

Listing 6-56. Main class

```
package com.apress.spring6recipes.course;

import org.springframework.context.annotation.AnnotationConfigApplicationContext;

import com.apress.spring6recipes.course.config.CourseConfiguration;

public class Main {

  public static void main(String[] args) {

    try (var context = new AnnotationConfigApplicationContext(CourseConfiguration.class)) {
      var courseDao = context.getBean(CourseDao.class);
    }
  }
}
```

In a Jakarta EE environment, you can look up an entity manager factory from a Java EE container with JNDI. In Spring, you can perform a JNDI lookup by using the JndiLocatorDelegate object (which is simpler than constructing a JndiObjectFactoryBean, which would also work).

Listing 6-57. JNDI lookup for EntityManagerFactory

```
@Bean
public EntityManagerFactory entityManagerFactory() throws NamingException {
  return JndiLocatorDelegate.createDefaultResourceRefLocator()
      .lookup("jpa/coursePU", EntityManagerFactory.class);
}
```

LocalEntityManagerFactoryBean creates an entity manager factory by loading the JPA configuration file (i.e., persistence.xml). Spring supports a more flexible way to create an entity manager factory by another factory bean, LocalContainerEntityManagerFactoryBean. It allows you to override some of the configurations in the JPA configuration file, such as the data source and database dialect. So you can take advantage of Spring's data access facilities to configure the entity manager factory.

Listing 6-58. Course configuration - Spring configuration

```
@Configuration
public class CourseConfiguration {

  @Bean
  public CourseDao courseDao(EntityManagerFactory entityManagerFactory) {
    return new JpaCourseDao(entityManagerFactory);
  }
```

```java
@Bean
public LocalContainerEntityManagerFactoryBean entityManagerFactory(DataSource ds) {
    var emf = new LocalContainerEntityManagerFactoryBean();
    emf.setPersistenceUnitName("course");
    emf.setDataSource(ds);
    emf.setJpaVendorAdapter(jpaVendorAdapter());
    return emf;
}

private JpaVendorAdapter jpaVendorAdapter() {
    var jpaVendorAdapter = new HibernateJpaVendorAdapter();
    jpaVendorAdapter.setShowSql(true);
    jpaVendorAdapter.setGenerateDdl(true);
    return jpaVendorAdapter;
}

@Bean
public DataSource dataSource() {
    var dataSource = new HikariDataSource();
    dataSource.setUsername("postgres");
    dataSource.setPassword("password");
    dataSource.setJdbcUrl("jdbc:postgresql://localhost:5432/course");
    dataSource.setMinimumIdle(2);
    dataSource.setMaximumPoolSize(5);
    return dataSource;
}
}
```

In the preceding bean configurations, you inject a data source into this entity manager factory. It will override the database settings in the JPA configuration file. You can set a JPA vendor adapter to LocalContainerEntityManagerFactoryBean to specify JPA engine–specific properties. With Hibernate as the underlying JPA engine, you should choose HibernateJpaVendorAdapter. Other properties that are not supported by this adapter can be specified in the jpaProperties property.

Now your JPA configuration file (i.e., persistence.xml) can be simplified as follows because its configurations have been ported to Spring.

Listing 6-59. Simplified JPA persistence.xml file

```xml
<persistence xmlns="https://jakarta.ee/xml/ns/persistence"
             xmlns:xsi="http://www.w3.org/2001/XMLSchema-instance"
             xsi:schemaLocation="https://jakarta.ee/xml/ns/persistence
                         https://jakarta.ee/xml/ns/persistence/persistence_3_1.xsd"
             version="3.1">

  <persistence-unit name="course" transaction-type="RESOURCE_LOCAL">
    <class>com.apress.spring6recipes.course.Course</class>
  </persistence-unit>

</persistence>
```

Spring also makes it possible to configure the JPA EntityManagerFactory **without** a persistence.xml; if we want, we can fully configure it in a Spring configuration file. Instead of a persistenceUnitName, we need to specify the packagesToScan property. After this you can remove the persistence.xml completely.

Listing 6-60. Course configuration - Spring only configuration

```
@Bean
public LocalContainerEntityManagerFactoryBean entityManagerFactory(DataSource dataSource) {
  var emf = new LocalContainerEntityManagerFactoryBean();
  emf.setDataSource(dataSource);
  emf.setJpaVendorAdapter(jpaVendorAdapter());
  emf.setPackagesToScan("com.apress.spring6recipes.course");
  return emf;
}
```

6-10. Persisting Objects with Hibernate's Contextual Sessions

Problem

You want to write a DAO based on the plain Hibernate API but still rely on Spring-managed transactions.

Solution

As of Hibernate 3, a session factory can manage contextual sessions for you and allows you to retrieve them by the getCurrentSession() method on org.hibernate.SessionFactory. Within a single transaction, you will get the same session for each getCurrentSession() method call. This ensures that there will be only one Hibernate session per transaction, so it works nicely with Spring's transaction management support.

How It Works

To use the contextual session approach, your DAO methods require access to the session factory, which can be injected via a setter method or a constructor argument. Then, in each DAO method, you get the contextual session from the session factory and use it for object persistence.

Listing 6-61. Hibernate-based CourseDao implementation

```
package com.apress.spring6recipes.course.hibernate;

import java.util.List;

import org.hibernate.SessionFactory;
import org.springframework.stereotype.Repository;
import org.springframework.transaction.annotation.Transactional;

import com.apress.spring6recipes.course.Course;
import com.apress.spring6recipes.course.CourseDao;
```

```java
@Repository
public class HibernateCourseDao implements CourseDao {

  private final SessionFactory sessionFactory;

  public HibernateCourseDao(SessionFactory sessionFactory) {
    this.sessionFactory = sessionFactory;
  }

  @Override
  @Transactional
  public Course store(Course course) {
    var session = sessionFactory.getCurrentSession();
    if (course.getId() == null) {
      session.persist(course);
    } else {
      course = session.merge(course);
    }
    return course;
  }

  @Override
  @Transactional
  public void delete(Long courseId) {
    var session = sessionFactory.getCurrentSession();
    var course = session.getReference(Course.class, courseId);
    session.remove(course);
  }

  @Override
  @Transactional(readOnly = true)
  public Course findById(Long courseId) {
    var session = sessionFactory.getCurrentSession();
    return session.get(Course.class, courseId);
  }

  @Override
  @Transactional(readOnly = true)
  public List<Course> findAll() {
    var session = sessionFactory.getCurrentSession();
    return session.createQuery("from Course", Course.class).list();
  }
}
```

Note that all your DAO methods must be made transactional. This is required because Spring integrates with Hibernate through Hibernate's contextual session support. Spring has its own implementation of the CurrentSessionContext interface from Hibernate. It will attempt to find a transaction and then fail, complaining that no Hibernate session's been bound to the thread. You can achieve this by annotating each method or the entire class with @Transactional. This ensures that the persistence operations within a DAO method will be executed in the same transaction and hence by the same session. Moreover, if a service layer component's method calls multiple DAO methods and it propagates its own transaction to these methods, then all these DAO methods will run within the same session as well.

🔥 When configuring Hibernate with Spring, make sure **not** to set the **hibernate.current_session_context_ class** property, as that will interfere with Spring's ability to properly manage the transactions. You should only set this property when you are in need of JTA transactions.

In the bean configuration file, you have to declare a HibernateTransactionManager instance for this application and enable declarative transaction management via @EnableTransactionManagement.

Listing 6-62. Course configuration - Hibernate Transaction Management

```
@Configuration
@EnableTransactionManagement
public class CourseConfiguration {

    return new HibernateTransactionManager(sf);
  }
}
```

When calling the native methods on a Hibernate session, the exceptions thrown will be of native type HibernateException. If you want the Hibernate exceptions to be translated into Spring's DataAccessException for consistent exception handling, you have to apply the @Repository annotation to your DAO class that requires exception translation.

Listing 6-63. Hibernate-based CourseDao implementation

```
package com.apress.spring6recipes.course.hibernate;

import org.springframework.stereotype.Repository;

@Repository
public class HibernateCourseDao implements CourseDao {

  public List<Course> findAll() {
```

A PersistenceExceptionTranslationPostProcessor takes care of translating the native Hibernate exceptions into data access exceptions in Spring's DataAccessException hierarchy. This bean post-processor will only translate exceptions for beans annotated with @Repository. When using Java-based configuration, this bean is automatically registered in the AnnotationConfigApplicationContext. Hence, there is no need to explicitly declare a bean for it.

In Spring, @Repository is a stereotype annotation. By annotating it, a component class can be auto-detected through component scanning. You can assign a component name in this annotation and have the session factory autowired by the Spring IoC container.

Listing 6-64. Hibernate-based CourseDao implementation with @Repository

```
package com.apress.spring6recipes.course.hibernate;
...
import org.hibernate.SessionFactory;
import org.springframework.beans.factory.annotation.Autowired;
import org.springframework.stereotype.Repository;

@Repository("courseDao")
public class HibernateCourseDao implements CourseDao {

  private final SessionFactory sessionFactory;

  public HibernateCourseDao (SessionFactory sessionFactory) {
    this.sessionFactory = sessionFactory;
  }
  ...
}
```

Then, you can simply add the @ComponentScan annotation and delete the original HibernateCourseDao bean declaration.

Listing 6-65. Course configuration with component scanning

```
@Configuration
@EnableTransactionManagement
@ComponentScan("com.apress.spring6recipes.course")
public class CourseConfiguration { ... }
```

6-11. Persisting Objects with JPA's Context Injection

Problem

In a Jakarta EE environment, a Jakarta EE container can manage entity managers for you and inject them into your EJB components directly. An EJB component can simply perform persistence operations on an injected entity manager without caring much about the entity manager creation and transaction management.

Solution

Originally, the @PersistenceContext annotation is used for entity manager injection in EJB components. Spring can also interpret this annotation by means of a bean post-processor. It will inject an entity manager into a property with this annotation. Spring ensures that all your persistence operations within a single transaction will be handled by the same entity manager.

How It Works

To use the context injection approach, you can declare an entity manager field in your DAO and annotate it with the @PersistenceContext annotation. Spring will inject an entity manager into this field for you to persist your objects.

Listing 6-66. JPA-based CourseDao implementation

```java
package com.apress.spring6recipes.course.jpa;

import java.util.List;

import jakarta.persistence.EntityManager;
import jakarta.persistence.PersistenceContext;
import jakarta.persistence.TypedQuery;

import org.springframework.transaction.annotation.Transactional;

import com.apress.spring6recipes.course.Course;
import com.apress.spring6recipes.course.CourseDao;

public class JpaCourseDao implements CourseDao {

  @PersistenceContext
  private EntityManager entityManager;

  @Override
  @Transactional
  public Course store(Course course) {
    return entityManager.merge(course);
  }

  @Override
  @Transactional
  public void delete(Long courseId) {
    Course course = entityManager.find(Course.class, courseId);
    entityManager.remove(course);
  }

  @Override
  @Transactional(readOnly = true)
  public Course findById(Long courseId) {
    return entityManager.find(Course.class, courseId);
  }

  @Override
  @Transactional(readOnly = true)
  public List<Course> findAll() {
    TypedQuery<Course> query = entityManager.createQuery("SELECT c FROM Course c",
    Course.class);
    return query.getResultList();
  }
}
```

You can annotate each DAO method or the entire DAO class with @Transactional to make all these methods transactional. It ensures that the persistence operations within a single method will be executed in the same transaction and hence by the same entity manager.

In the bean configuration file, you have to declare a JpaTransactionManager instance and enable declarative transaction management via @EnableTransactionManagement. A PersistenceAnnotationBeanPostProcessor instance is registered automatically when using Java-based configuration, to inject entity managers into properties annotated with @PersistenceContext.

Listing 6-67. Course configuration - JPA Transaction Management

```java
package com.apress.spring6recipes.course.config;

import jakarta.persistence.EntityManagerFactory;

import javax.sql.DataSource;

import org.hibernate.dialect.PostgreSQL95Dialect;
import org.springframework.context.annotation.Bean;
import org.springframework.context.annotation.Configuration;
import org.springframework.orm.jpa.JpaTransactionManager;
import org.springframework.orm.jpa.JpaVendorAdapter;
import org.springframework.orm.jpa.LocalContainerEntityManagerFactoryBean;
import org.springframework.orm.jpa.vendor.HibernateJpaVendorAdapter;
import org.springframework.transaction.annotation.EnableTransactionManagement;

import com.apress.spring6recipes.course.CourseDao;
import com.apress.spring6recipes.course.jpa.JpaCourseDao;
import com.zaxxer.hikari.HikariDataSource;

@Configuration
@EnableTransactionManagement
public class CourseConfiguration {

  @Bean
  public CourseDao courseDao() {
    return new JpaCourseDao();
  }

  @Bean
  public LocalContainerEntityManagerFactoryBean entityManagerFactory(DataSource ds) {
    var emf = new LocalContainerEntityManagerFactoryBean();
    emf.setPackagesToScan("com.apress.springrecipes.course");
    emf.setDataSource(ds);
    emf.setJpaVendorAdapter(jpaVendorAdapter());
    return emf;
  }

  private JpaVendorAdapter jpaVendorAdapter() {
    var jpaVendorAdapter = new HibernateJpaVendorAdapter();
    jpaVendorAdapter.setShowSql(true);
```

```
    jpaVendorAdapter.setGenerateDdl(true);
    return jpaVendorAdapter;
}

@Bean
public DataSource dataSource() {
    var dataSource = new HikariDataSource();
    dataSource.setUsername("postgres");
    dataSource.setPassword("password");
    dataSource.setJdbcUrl("jdbc:postgresql://localhost:5432/course");
    dataSource.setMinimumIdle(2);
    dataSource.setMaximumPoolSize(5);
    return dataSource;
}

@Bean
public JpaTransactionManager transactionManager(EntityManagerFactory emf) {
    return new JpaTransactionManager(emf);
}

}
```

The PersistenceAnnotationBeanPostProcessor can also inject the entity manager factory into a property with the @PersistenceUnit annotation. This allows you to create entity managers and manage transactions by yourself. It's no different from injecting the entity manager factory via a setter method.

Listing 6-68. JPA-based CourseDao implementation showing JPA annotations

```
package com.apress.spring6recipes.course;
...
import javax.persistence.EntityManagerFactory;
import javax.persistence.PersistenceUnit;

public class JpaCourseDao implements CourseDao {
    @PersistenceContext
    private EntityManager entityManager;

    @PersistenceUnit
    private EntityManagerFactory entityManagerFactory;
    ...
}
```

When calling native methods on a JPA entity manager, the exceptions thrown will be of native type PersistenceException or other Java SE exceptions like IllegalArgumentException and IllegalStateException. If you want JPA exceptions to be translated into Spring's DataAccessException, you have to apply the @Repository annotation to your DAO class.

Listing 6-69. JPA-based CourseDao implementation with @Repository

```java
package com.apress.spring6recipes.course.jpa;

import java.util.List;

import org.springframework.stereotype.Repository;
import org.springframework.transaction.annotation.Transactional;

import com.apress.spring6recipes.course.Course;
import com.apress.spring6recipes.course.CourseDao;

import jakarta.persistence.EntityManager;
import jakarta.persistence.PersistenceContext;

@Repository("courseDao")
public class JpaCourseDao implements CourseDao {

  @PersistenceContext
  private EntityManager entityManager;

  @Transactional
  public Course store(Course course) {
    return entityManager.merge(course);
  }

  @Transactional
  public void delete(Long courseId) {
    var course = entityManager.getReference(Course.class, courseId);
    entityManager.remove(course);
  }

  @Transactional(readOnly = true)
  public Course findById(Long courseId) {
    return entityManager.find(Course.class, courseId);
  }

  @Transactional(readOnly = true)
  public List<Course> findAll() {
    return entityManager.createQuery("select c from Course c", Course.class).
    getResultList();
  }
}
```

A PersistenceExceptionTranslationPostProcessor instance will translate the native JPA exceptions into exceptions in Spring's DataAccessException hierarchy. When using Java-based configuration, this bean is automatically registered in the AnnotationConfigApplicationContext. Hence, there is no need to explicitly declare a bean for it.

6-12. Simplify JPA with Spring Data JPA

Problem

Writing data access code, even with JPA, can be a tedious and repetitive task. You often need access to the `EntityManager` or `EntityManagerFactory` and have to create queries–not to mention the fact that when one has a lot of DAOs, there's a repetitive declaration of `findById` and `findAll` methods for all different entities.

Solution

Spring Data JPA allows you, just as Spring itself, to focus on the parts that are important and not on the boilerplate needed to accomplish this. It also provides default implementations for the most commonly used data access methods (i.e., `findAll`, `delete`, `save`, etc.).

How It Works

To use Spring Data JPA, you have to extend one of its interfaces. These interfaces are detected, and a default implementation of such repository is generated at runtime. In most cases it is enough to extend the `CrudRepository` interface.

Listing 6-70. Spring Data JPA–based CourseRepository

```
package com.apress.spring6recipes.course;

import com.apress.spring6recipes.course.Course;
import org.springframework.data.repository.CrudRepository;

public interface CourseRepository extends CrudRepository<Course, Long>{}
```

This is enough to be able to do all necessary CRUD actions for the `Course` entity. When extending the Spring Data interfaces, we have to specify the type, `Course`, and the type of the primary key, `Long`. This information is needed to generate the repository at runtime.

ℹ️   You could also extend `JpaRepository`, which adds some JPA-specific methods (`flush`, `saveAndFlush`) and provides query methods with paging/sorting capabilities.

To enable detection of the Spring Data–enabled repositories, add the `@EnableJpaRepositories` annotation provided by Spring Data JPA.

Listing 6-71. Spring Data JPA Course configuration

```
@Configuration
@EnableTransactionManagement
@EnableJpaRepositories("com.apress.spring6recipes.course")
public class CourseConfiguration { ... }
```

This will bootstrap Spring Data JPA and will construct a usable repository. By default all repository methods are marked with @Transactional, so no additional annotations are needed.

Now, you can test this CourseRepository instance with the Main class by retrieving it from the Spring IoC container.

Listing 6-72. Main class

```
package com.apress.spring6recipes.course.datajpa;
...
import org.springframework.context.ApplicationContext;
import org.springframework.context.support.ClassPathXmlApplicationContext;

public class Main {

  public static void main(String[] args) {
    var context = new AnnotationConfigApplicationContext(CourseConfiguration.class);

    var repository = context.getBean(CourseRepository.class);
    ...
  }
}
```

All other things like exception translation, transaction management, and easy configuration of your EntityManagerFactory still apply to Spring Data JPA–based repositories. It just makes your life a lot easier and lets you focus on what is important.

6-13. Reactive Database Access with R2DBC

Most Java developers will know, or at least have heard of, the JDBC API (see the beginning of this chapter). JDBC however is blocking by nature and will not venture well in an environment with reactive programming. For reactive programming and SQL databases, there is R2DBC. This is a low-level reactive API (or rather SPI) developed by the community. Several databases already have a driver implementation based on this SPI, like (but not limited to) PostgreSQL, Oracle, MySQL, and H2.

Problem with Plain R2DBC

While R2DBC provides, sort of, an API, it is more or less meant as being a set of interfaces for drivers to implement. It is quite a low-level API and can be cumbersome to work with. Let's take a look at a plain R2DBC implementation of a repository, and let's use the Vehicle sample from JDBC.

First, we need a Vehicle class.

Listing 6-73. Vehicle class

```
package com.apress.spring6recipes.vehicle;

import java.util.Objects;

public class Vehicle {

  private String vehicleNo;
```

```java
private String color;
private int wheel;
private int seat;

public Vehicle() {}

public Vehicle(String vehicleNo, String color, int wheel, int seat) {
    this.vehicleNo = vehicleNo;
    this.color = color;
    this.wheel = wheel;
    this.seat = seat;
}

public String getColor() {
    return color;
}

public void setColor(String color) {
    this.color = color;
}

public int getSeat() {
    return seat;
}

public void setSeat(int seat) {
    this.seat = seat;
}

public String getVehicleNo() {
    return vehicleNo;
}

public void setVehicleNo(String vehicleNo) {
    this.vehicleNo = vehicleNo;
}

public int getWheel() {
    return wheel;
}

public void setWheel(int wheel) {
    this.wheel = wheel;
}

@Override
public boolean equals(Object o) {
    if (this == o)
        return true;
```

```java
  if (vehicleNo != null && o instanceof Vehicle vehicle) {
    return Objects.equals(this.vehicleNo, vehicle.vehicleNo);
  }
  return false;
}

@Override
public int hashCode() {
  return Objects.hash(vehicleNo);
}

@Override
public String toString() {
  var fmt = "Vehicle [vehicleNo='%s', color='%s', wheel=%d, seat=%d]";
  return String.format(fmt, vehicleNo, color, wheel, seat);
}

}
```

Next, we need a reactive version of the VehicleDao interface. The return types of the methods are either a Mono (zero or one value) or a Flux (zero or more values). We could also have used one of the other supported reactive types like RxJava 3 or Mutiny Rye. But here we use Project Reactor.

Listing 6-74. Reactive VehicleDao interface

```java
package com.apress.spring6recipes.vehicle;

import reactor.core.publisher.Flux;
import reactor.core.publisher.Mono;

public interface VehicleDao {

  Mono<Vehicle> save(Vehicle vehicle);
  Mono<Vehicle> findByVehicleNo(String vehicleNo);
  Flux<Vehicle> findAll();
  Mono<Void> delete(Vehicle vehicle);
}
```

Listing 6-75. Project Reactor R2DBC-based VehicleDao implementation

```java
package com.apress.spring6recipes.vehicle;

import io.r2dbc.spi.ConnectionFactory;
import io.r2dbc.spi.Result;
import io.r2dbc.spi.Row;
import io.r2dbc.spi.Statement;
import reactor.core.publisher.Flux;
import reactor.core.publisher.Mono;
```

```java
public class R2dbcVehicleDao implements VehicleDao {

  private static final String INSERT_SQL = "INSERT INTO VEHICLE (COLOR, WHEEL, SEAT,
  VEHICLE_NO) VALUES ($1, $2, $3, $4)";
  private static final String SELECT_ALL_SQL = "SELECT * FROM VEHICLE";
  private static final String SELECT_ONE_SQL = "SELECT * FROM VEHICLE WHERE VEHICLE_
  NO = $1";
  private static final String DELETE_SQL = "DELETE FROM VEHICLE WHERE VEHICLE_NO=$1";

  private final ConnectionFactory connectionFactory;

  public R2dbcVehicleDao(ConnectionFactory connectionFactory) {
    this.connectionFactory = connectionFactory;
  }

  @Override
  public Mono<Vehicle> save(Vehicle vehicle) {
    return Mono.usingWhen(
            connectionFactory.create(),
            c -> Mono.from(prepareStatement(c.createStatement(INSERT_SQL), vehicle).
            execute())
                    .flatMap(res -> Mono.from(res.getRowsUpdated()))
                    .doOnNext( (cnt) -> System.out.printf("Rows inserted: %d%n", cnt)),
            c -> c.close())
            .then(this.findByVehicleNo(vehicle.getVehicleNo()));
  }

  @Override
  public Mono<Vehicle> findByVehicleNo(String vehicleNo) {
    return Mono.usingWhen(
            connectionFactory.create(),
            con -> Mono.from(con.createStatement(SELECT_ONE_SQL).bind("$1", vehicleNo).
            execute())
                    .flatMap((rs) -> Mono.from(rs.map((row, meta) -> toVehicle(row)))),
            c -> c.close());
  }

  @Override
  public Flux<Vehicle> findAll() {
    return Flux.usingWhen(
            connectionFactory.create(),
            con -> Flux.from(con.createStatement(SELECT_ALL_SQL).execute())
                    .flatMap((rs) -> Flux.from(rs.map((row, meta) -> toVehicle(row)))),
            con -> con.close());
  }

  @Override
  public Mono<Void> delete(Vehicle vehicle) {
    return Mono.usingWhen(
            connectionFactory.create(),
```

```
                con -> Mono.from(con.createStatement(DELETE_SQL).bind("$1", vehicle.
        getVehicleNo()).execute())
                    .flatMap(res -> Mono.from(res.getRowsUpdated()))
                    .doOnNext( (cnt) -> System.out.printf("Rows deleted: %d%n", cnt)),
            c -> c.close()).then();
    }

    private Statement prepareStatement(Statement st, Vehicle vehicle) {
      return st.bind("$1", vehicle.getColor())
            .bind("$2", vehicle.getWheel())
            .bind("$3", vehicle.getSeat())
            .bind("$4", vehicle.getVehicleNo());
    }

    private Vehicle toVehicle(Row row) {
      return new Vehicle(row.get("VEHICLE_NO", String.class),
            row.get("COLOR", String.class),
            row.get("WHEEL", Integer.class),
            row.get("SEAT", Integer.class));
    }
}
```

The R2dbcVehicleDao needs a bit of explaining. To connect to our database, we need a
ConnectionFactory, which is the reactive equivalent of the Datasource from JDBC. We need this so we can
obtain a Connection that we can use to create one or more Statements, which we can use to execute queries.
As R2DBC doesn't really care which reactive runtime we use, it all returns the top-level Publisher from the
reactive API, so we need to do some wrapping with Mono or Flux in our code. When we execute a Statement,
we get a Result, which we can use to obtain the number of rows that got changed or to get the Row and map
that to a result we want (here a Vehicle).

Finally, when all the code is executed, we need to make sure we are closing the connection to prevent
a connection leak. Using a Mono.usingWhen/Flux.usingWhen, we can simplify the code a bit. The first
statement is the creation of a resource (the Connection), which is used in the second statement. The last
statement is called when the reactive pipeline finishes (successfully or not) and will close the connection.

We will also need some configuration for the ConnectionFactory and the VehicleDao.

Listing 6-76. Reactive vehicle configuration

```
package com.apress.spring6recipes.vehicle.config;

import static io.r2dbc.spi.ConnectionFactoryOptions.DATABASE;
import static io.r2dbc.spi.ConnectionFactoryOptions.DRIVER;
import static io.r2dbc.spi.ConnectionFactoryOptions.HOST;
import static io.r2dbc.spi.ConnectionFactoryOptions.PASSWORD;
import static io.r2dbc.spi.ConnectionFactoryOptions.PORT;
import static io.r2dbc.spi.ConnectionFactoryOptions.USER;

import org.springframework.context.annotation.Bean;
import org.springframework.context.annotation.Configuration;
import org.springframework.core.io.ClassPathResource;
import org.springframework.r2dbc.connection.init.ConnectionFactoryInitializer;
import org.springframework.r2dbc.connection.init.ResourceDatabasePopulator;
```

```
import com.apress.spring6recipes.vehicle.R2dbcVehicleDao;

import io.r2dbc.spi.ConnectionFactories;
import io.r2dbc.spi.ConnectionFactory;
import io.r2dbc.spi.ConnectionFactoryOptions;

@Configuration
public class VehicleConfiguration {

  @Bean
  public R2dbcVehicleDao vehicleDao(ConnectionFactory cf) {
    return new R2dbcVehicleDao(cf);
  }

  @Bean
  public ConnectionFactory connectionFactory() {
    var options = ConnectionFactoryOptions.builder()
            .option(DRIVER, "postgresql")
            .option(HOST, "localhost").option(PORT, 5432)
            .option(DATABASE, "vehicle")
            .option(USER, "postgres").option(PASSWORD, "password")
            .build();
    return ConnectionFactories.get(options);
  }

  @Bean
  public ConnectionFactoryInitializer initializer(ConnectionFactory cf) {
    var initializer = new ConnectionFactoryInitializer();
    initializer.setConnectionFactory(cf);
    initializer.setDatabasePopulator(new ResourceDatabasePopulator(
            new ClassPathResource("/sql/vehicle.sql")));
    return initializer;
  }
}
```

The ConnectionFactory needs the information to connect to the database. Here we use the ConnectionFactoryOptions through a builder pattern to provide the information. There is also a ConnectionFactories.get method that takes a URL in the form of a string, much like the JDBC URL used for JDBC. The ConnectionFactory is then injected into the R2dbcVehicleDao and used by a ConnectionFactoryInitializer. The ConnectionFactoryInitializer will create the vehicle table so we can use it in our code.

Finally, we will need a class to run all this.

Listing 6-77. Main class

```
package com.apress.spring6recipes.vehicle;

import java.util.concurrent.CountDownLatch;

import org.springframework.context.annotation.AnnotationConfigApplicationContext;

import com.apress.spring6recipes.vehicle.config.VehicleConfiguration;
```

```
import reactor.core.publisher.Flux;

public class Main {

    public static void main(String[] args) throws Exception {
        var cfg = VehicleConfiguration.class;
        try (var ctx = new AnnotationConfigApplicationContext(cfg)) {
            var vehicleDao = ctx.getBean(VehicleDao.class);
            var vehicle1 = new Vehicle("TEMO442", "Blue", 4, 4);
            var vehicle2 = new Vehicle("TEMO443", "Black", 4, 6);

            var latch = new CountDownLatch(1);
            var vehicles = Flux.just(vehicle1, vehicle2);

            vehicles.flatMap(vehicleDao::save)
                    .thenMany(vehicleDao.findAll().doOnNext(System.out::println).
                    flatMap(vehicleDao::delete))
                    .doOnTerminate(latch::countDown).subscribe();

            latch.await();
        }
    }
}
```

The main class will store two vehicles, retrieve them, print the information to the console, and finally delete them again.

Problem

You want to use reactive programming and want to utilize a regular SQL database for persistence.

Solution

Use R2DBC as a driver and let Spring and Spring Data R2DBC help you in working with the reactive resource.

How It Works

As R2DBC itself is quite a low-level API, it is recommended to use a client API. Luckily, the Spring Framework itself provides such a client, the DatabaseClient; this is part of the spring-r2dbc module of the Spring Framework. Spring Data R2DBC builds further on Spring R2DBC and allows for a repository-style approach (just as with JPA).

ℹ️ Before using Spring R2DBC or Spring Data R2DBC, the relevant jars need to be added to the classpath. When using Maven add the following dependency:

```
<dependency>
  <groupId>org.postgresql</groupId>
  <artifactId>r2dbc-postgresql</artifactId>
  <version>1.0.0.RELEASE</version>
</dependency>
<dependency>
  <groupId>org.springframework</groupId>
  <artifactId>spring-r2dbc</artifactId>
  <version>6.0.3</version>
</dependency>
<dependency>
  <groupId>org.springframework.data</groupId>
  <artifactId>spring-data-r2dbc</artifactId>
  <version>3.0.0</version>
</dependency>
```

Or add the following when using Gradle:

```
implementation group: 'org.postgresql', name: 'r2dbc-postgresql', version: '1.0.0.RELEASE'

implementation group: 'org.springframework', name: 'spring-r2dbc', version: '6.0.3'

implementation group: 'org.springframework.data', name: 'spring-data-r2dbc', version: '3.0.0'
```

Spring R2DBC DatabaseClient

Spring R2DBC provides a DatabaseClient much akin to the JdbcTemplate for JDBC. It makes working with R2DBC easier. It still requires the ConnectionFactory for managing the connections and operating with R2DBC, but much of this is abstracted away.

First, we need to modify the R2dbcVehicleDao to use the DatabaseClient instead of the ConnectionFactory.

Listing 6-78. DatabaseClient-based VehicleDao implementation

```java
package com.apress.spring6recipes.vehicle;

import org.springframework.r2dbc.core.DatabaseClient;

import io.r2dbc.spi.Row;
import reactor.core.publisher.Flux;
import reactor.core.publisher.Mono;

public class R2dbcVehicleDao implements VehicleDao {

  private static final String INSERT_SQL = "INSERT INTO VEHICLE (COLOR, WHEEL, SEAT,
VEHICLE_NO) VALUES ($1, $2, $3, $4)";
  private static final String UPDATE_SQL = "UPDATE VEHICLE SET COLOR=$1,WHEEL=$2,SEAT=$3
WHERE VEHICLE_NO=$4";
  private static final String SELECT_ALL_SQL = "SELECT * FROM VEHICLE";
```

```java
private static final String SELECT_ONE_SQL = "SELECT * FROM VEHICLE WHERE VEHICLE_
NO = $1";
private static final String DELETE_SQL = "DELETE FROM VEHICLE WHERE VEHICLE_NO=$1";

private final DatabaseClient client;

public R2dbcVehicleDao(DatabaseClient client) {
  this.client = client;
}

@Override
public Mono<Vehicle> save(Vehicle vehicle) {
  return prepareStatement(client.sql(INSERT_SQL), vehicle)
          .fetch()
          .rowsUpdated().doOnNext((cnt) -> System.out.printf("Rows inserted: %d%n", cnt))
          .then(this.findByVehicleNo(vehicle.getVehicleNo())));
}

@Override
public Mono<Vehicle> findByVehicleNo(String vehicleNo) {
  return client.sql(SELECT_ONE_SQL)
          .bind("$1", vehicleNo)
          .map( (r, rmd) -> toVehicle(r))
          .one();
}

@Override
public Flux<Vehicle> findAll() {
  return client.sql(SELECT_ALL_SQL)
          .map( (r, rmd) -> toVehicle(r))
          .all();
}

@Override
public Mono<Void> delete(Vehicle vehicle) {
  return client.sql(DELETE_SQL)
          .bind("$1", vehicle.getVehicleNo())
          .fetch().rowsUpdated()
          .doOnNext( (cnt) -> System.out.printf("Rows deleted: %d%n", cnt))
          .then();
}

private DatabaseClient.GenericExecuteSpec prepareStatement(DatabaseClient.
GenericExecuteSpec st, Vehicle vehicle) {
  return st.bind("$1", vehicle.getColor())
          .bind("$2", vehicle.getWheel())
          .bind("$3", vehicle.getSeat())
          .bind("$4", vehicle.getVehicleNo());
}
```

```
  private Vehicle toVehicle(Row row) {
    return new Vehicle(row.get("VEHICLE_NO", String.class),
            row.get("COLOR", String.class),
            row.get("WHEEL", Integer.class),
            row.get("SEAT", Integer.class));
  }
}
```

The DatabaseClient makes it easier to work with R2DBC. We now don't need to manage the connection anymore; all of that is done for us. Executing a query is done by calling the fetch method, even for modifying queries. When doing a select query, we can map the result, and depending on what we need, we can return a Flux by calling all or a Mono by calling one. The code looks cleaner now and more focused on what we want to do.

Next, the configuration needs to be slightly modified. We need a DatabaseClient next to the ConnectionFactory.

Listing 6-79. Reactive vehicle configuration - using DatabaseClient

```
package com.apress.spring6recipes.vehicle.config;

import static io.r2dbc.spi.ConnectionFactoryOptions.DATABASE;
import static io.r2dbc.spi.ConnectionFactoryOptions.DRIVER;
import static io.r2dbc.spi.ConnectionFactoryOptions.HOST;
import static io.r2dbc.spi.ConnectionFactoryOptions.PASSWORD;
import static io.r2dbc.spi.ConnectionFactoryOptions.PORT;
import static io.r2dbc.spi.ConnectionFactoryOptions.USER;

import org.springframework.context.annotation.Bean;
import org.springframework.context.annotation.Configuration;
import org.springframework.core.io.ClassPathResource;
import org.springframework.r2dbc.connection.init.ConnectionFactoryInitializer;
import org.springframework.r2dbc.connection.init.ResourceDatabasePopulator;
import org.springframework.r2dbc.core.DatabaseClient;

import com.apress.spring6recipes.vehicle.R2dbcVehicleDao;

import io.r2dbc.spi.ConnectionFactories;
import io.r2dbc.spi.ConnectionFactory;
import io.r2dbc.spi.ConnectionFactoryOptions;

@Configuration
public class VehicleConfiguration {

  @Bean
  public ConnectionFactory connectionFactory() {
    var options = ConnectionFactoryOptions.builder()
            .option(DRIVER, "postgresql")
            .option(HOST, "localhost").option(PORT, 5432)
            .option(DATABASE, "vehicle")
            .option(USER, "postgres").option(PASSWORD, "password")
            .build();
```

```
    return ConnectionFactories.get(options);
  }

  @Bean
  public DatabaseClient databaseClient(ConnectionFactory cf) {
    return DatabaseClient.create(cf);
  }

  @Bean
  public R2dbcVehicleDao vehicleDao(DatabaseClient dc) {
    return new R2dbcVehicleDao(dc);
  }

  @Bean
  public ConnectionFactoryInitializer initializer(ConnectionFactory cf) {
    var initializer = new ConnectionFactoryInitializer();
    initializer.setConnectionFactory(cf);
    initializer.setDatabasePopulator(new ResourceDatabasePopulator(
            new ClassPathResource("/sql/vehicle.sql")));
    return initializer;
  }
}
```

The main class can remain unchanged, and when running the code, the output will still be the same.

Spring Data R2DBC Template

The code can be even more slick by using the R2dbcEntityTemplate provided by Spring Data R2DBC. This uses the Vehicle class itself to determine what the queries need by using Spring Data annotations like @Id, @Column, and @Table. The @Id is necessary as to mark the primary key field(s) of an entity. The @Column and @Table are optional, and by default the table used is the same as the name of the class, and the fields will map to column names. If they aren't the same, you can specify that by adding the @Column and/or @Table annotation.

For our Vehicle we only need to add the @Id annotation to our vehicleNo field. The rest of the class can remain untouched.

Listing 6-80. Vehicle class with the @Id annotation

```
package com.apress.spring6recipes.vehicle;

import java.util.Objects;

import org.springframework.data.annotation.Id;

public class Vehicle {

  @Id
  private String vehicleNo;

}
```

Next, we need to modify the R2dbcVehicleDao to make use of the R2dbcEntityTemplate instead of the DatabaseClient.

Listing 6-81. R2dbcEntityTemplate-based VehicleDao implementation

```java
package com.apress.spring6recipes.vehicle;

import static org.springframework.data.relational.core.query.Criteria.where;
import static org.springframework.data.relational.core.query.Query.query;

import org.springframework.data.r2dbc.core.R2dbcEntityTemplate;
import org.springframework.r2dbc.core.DatabaseClient;

import io.r2dbc.spi.Row;
import reactor.core.publisher.Flux;
import reactor.core.publisher.Mono;

public class R2dbcVehicleDao implements VehicleDao {

  private final R2dbcEntityTemplate template;

  public R2dbcVehicleDao(R2dbcEntityTemplate template) {
    this.template = template;
  }

  @Override
  public Mono<Vehicle> save(Vehicle vehicle) {
    return template.insert(vehicle);
  }

  @Override
  public Mono<Vehicle> findByVehicleNo(String vehicleNo) {
    var query = query(where("vehicleNo").is(vehicleNo));
    return template.selectOne(query, Vehicle.class);
  }

  @Override
  public Flux<Vehicle> findAll() {
    return template.select(Vehicle.class).all();
  }

  @Override
  public Mono<Void> delete(Vehicle vehicle) {
    return template.delete(vehicle).then();
  }
}
```

The implementation now uses the R2dbcEntityTemplate, and we don't need to specify SQL queries anymore (you still could if needed/wanted), and inserting and selecting is a lot easier now. We simply pass the Vehicle instance to persist to the insert method on the template, and that will take care of the rest. For the select we can define a Query, which is basically the where clause of the SQL to be generated, and use that to select one row or multiple rows (a Mono or a Flux). All in all the code is now a lot cleaner and easier to understand.

Finally, Spring Data R2DBC also helps in simplifying the configuration as it provides a base class that provides all needed components. The only thing we need to provide is the ConnectionFactory. The base class is the AbstractR2dbcConfiguration and requires one method to be implemented, the connectionFactory.

Listing 6-82. Vehicle configuration with the Spring Data R2DBC base class (snippet)

```
@Configuration
@EnableR2dbcRepositories("com.apress.spring6recipes.vehicle")
public class VehicleConfiguration extends AbstractR2dbcConfiguration {

  @Override
  @Bean
  public ConnectionFactory connectionFactory() {
    var options = ConnectionFactoryOptions.builder()
            .option(DRIVER, "postgresql")
            .option(HOST, "localhost").option(PORT, 5432)
            .option(DATABASE, "vehicle")
            .option(USER, "postgres").option(PASSWORD, "password")
            .build();
    return ConnectionFactories.get(options);
  }

  @Bean
  public R2dbcVehicleDao vehicleDao(R2dbcEntityTemplate template) {
    return new R2dbcVehicleDao(template);
  }
}
```

The AbstractR2dbcConfiguration will take care of configuring a DatabaseClient and a R2dbcEntityTemplate for us to use.

Spring Data R2DBC Repository

Finally, we could even remove the whole implementation of the R2dbcVehicleDao by extending the ReactiveCrudRepository from Spring Data and enable R2DBC repository support in our configuration.

The VehicleDao interface can now extend the ReactiveCrudRepository and have all the methods, except findByVehicleNo, removed (although as that is also the primary key, we could use findById as well!):

```
package com.apress.spring6recipes.vehicle;

import org.springframework.data.r2dbc.repository.Query;
import org.springframework.data.r2dbc.repository.R2dbcRepository;
import org.springframework.data.repository.reactive.ReactiveCrudRepository;
```

```
import reactor.core.publisher.Flux;
import reactor.core.publisher.Mono;

public interface VehicleDao extends ReactiveCrudRepository<Vehicle, String> {

  Mono<Vehicle> findByVehicleNo(String vehicleNo);
}
```

Next in the configuration, the @EnableR2dbcRepositories annotation needs to be added, and the configuration of the R2dbcVehicleDao can be removed:

```
package com.apress.spring6recipes.vehicle.config;

import static io.r2dbc.spi.ConnectionFactoryOptions.DATABASE;
import static io.r2dbc.spi.ConnectionFactoryOptions.DRIVER;
import static io.r2dbc.spi.ConnectionFactoryOptions.HOST;
import static io.r2dbc.spi.ConnectionFactoryOptions.PASSWORD;
import static io.r2dbc.spi.ConnectionFactoryOptions.PORT;
import static io.r2dbc.spi.ConnectionFactoryOptions.USER;

import org.springframework.context.annotation.Bean;
import org.springframework.context.annotation.Configuration;
import org.springframework.core.io.ClassPathResource;
import org.springframework.data.r2dbc.config.AbstractR2dbcConfiguration;
import org.springframework.data.r2dbc.repository.config.EnableR2dbcRepositories;
import org.springframework.r2dbc.connection.init.ConnectionFactoryInitializer;
import org.springframework.r2dbc.connection.init.ResourceDatabasePopulator;

import io.r2dbc.spi.ConnectionFactories;
import io.r2dbc.spi.ConnectionFactory;
import io.r2dbc.spi.ConnectionFactoryOptions;

@Configuration
@EnableR2dbcRepositories("com.apress.spring6recipes.vehicle")
public class VehicleConfiguration extends AbstractR2dbcConfiguration {

  @Bean
  public ConnectionFactory connectionFactory() {
    var options = ConnectionFactoryOptions.builder()
            .option(DRIVER, "postgresql")
            .option(HOST, "localhost").option(PORT, 5432)
            .option(DATABASE, "vehicle")
            .option(USER, "postgres").option(PASSWORD, "password")
            .build();
    return ConnectionFactories.get(options);
  }

  @Bean
  public ConnectionFactoryInitializer initializer(ConnectionFactory cf) {
    var initializer = new ConnectionFactoryInitializer();
    initializer.setConnectionFactory(cf);
```

```
        initializer.setDatabasePopulator(new ResourceDatabasePopulator(
                new ClassPathResource("/sql/vehicle.sql")));
        return initializer;
    }
}
```

With @EnableR2dbcRepositories we instruct Spring to register the support classes to create dynamic repositories based on the interfaces it detects in the specified package(s). It will need some infrastructure, but most of that is provided by the AbstractR2dbcConfiguration, and we need only to provide the ConnectionFactory.

The original main class will still work and save the vehicles, retrieve them, and eventually delete them again. However, the code we have written is far less and less complex than it initially was.

6-14. Summary

This chapter discussed how to use Spring's support for JDBC, Hibernate + JPA, and R2DBC. You learned how to configure a DataSource to connect to a database and how to use Spring's JdbcTemplate and NamedParameterJdbcTemplate to rid your code of tedious boilerplate handling. You saw how to use the utility base classes to build DAO classes with JDBC and Hibernate, as well as how to use Spring's support for stereotype annotations and component scanning to easily build new DAOs and services.

Next was a trip around Hibernate and JPA and how Spring and Spring Data help you in reducing the code you need to write as well as the complexity in programming in such an environment.

The final technology, R2DBC, is a relatively new one in the database area. It allows for reactive access to your database. The usage of plain R2DBC is pretty cumbersome, but through the use of Spring R2DBC and Spring Data R2DBC, this can be made far easier and less complex.

CHAPTER 7

■ ■ ■

Spring Transaction Management

In this chapter, you will learn about the basic concept of transactions and Spring's capabilities in the area of transaction management. Transaction management is an essential technique in enterprise applications to ensure data integrity and consistency. Spring, as an enterprise application framework, provides an abstract layer on top of different transaction management APIs. As an application developer, you can use Spring's transaction management facilities without having to know much about the underlying transaction management APIs.

Like the bean-managed transaction (BMT) and container-managed transaction (CMT) approaches in EJB, Spring supports both programmatic and declarative transaction management. The aim of Spring's transaction support is to provide an alternative to EJB transactions by adding transaction capabilities to POJOs.

Programmatic transaction management is achieved by embedding transaction management code in your business methods to control the commit and rollback of transactions. You usually commit a transaction if a method completes normally and roll back a transaction if a method throws certain types of exceptions. With programmatic transaction management, you can define your own rules to commit and roll back transactions.

However, when managing transactions programmatically, you have to include transaction management code in each transactional operation. As a result, the boilerplate transaction code is repeated in each of these operations. Moreover, it's hard for you to enable and disable transaction management for different applications. If you have a solid understanding of AOP, you may already have noticed that transaction management is a kind of crosscutting concern.

Declarative transaction management is preferable to programmatic transaction management in most cases. It's achieved by separating transaction management code from your business methods via declarations. Transaction management, as a kind of crosscutting concern, can be modularized with the AOP approach. Spring supports declarative transaction management through the Spring AOP framework. This can help you enable transactions for your applications more easily and define a consistent transaction policy. Declarative transaction management is less flexible than programmatic transaction management.

Programmatic transaction management allows you to control transactions through your code—explicitly starting, committing, and joining them as you see fit. You can specify a set of transaction attributes to define your transactions at a fine level of granularity. The transaction attributes supported by Spring include the propagation behavior, isolation level, rollback rules, transaction timeout, and whether or not the transaction is read-only. These attributes allow you to further customize the behavior of your transactions.

Upon finishing this chapter, you will be able to apply different transaction management strategies in your application. Moreover, you will be familiar with different transaction attributes to finely define your transactions.

© Marten Deinum, Daniel Rubio, Josh Long 2023
M. Deinum et al., *Spring 6 Recipes*, https://doi.org/10.1007/978-1-4842-8649-4_7

Programmatic transaction management is a good idea in certain cases where you don't feel the addition of Spring proxies is worth the trouble or negligible performance loss. Here, you might access the native transaction yourself and control the transaction manually. A more convenient option that avoids the overhead of Spring proxies is the `TransactionTemplate` class, which provides a template method around which a transactional boundary is started and then committed.

7-1. Problems with Transaction Management

Transaction management is an essential technique in enterprise application development to ensure data integrity and consistency. Without transaction management, your data and resources may be corrupted and left in an inconsistent state. Transaction management is particularly important for recovering from unexpected errors in a concurrent and distributed environment.

In simple words, a transaction is a series of actions that are treated as a single unit of work. These actions should either complete entirely or take no effect at all. If all the actions go well, the transaction should be committed permanently. In contrast, if any of them goes wrong, the transaction should be rolled back to the initial state as if nothing had happened.

The concept of transactions can be described with four key properties–atomicity, consistency, isolation, and durability (ACID):

- Atomicity: A transaction is an atomic operation that consists of a series of actions. The atomicity of a transaction ensures that the actions either complete entirely or take no effect at all.

- Consistency: Once all actions of a transaction have completed, the transaction is committed. Then your data and resources will be in a consistent state that conforms to business rules.

- Isolation: Because there may be many transactions processing with the same dataset at the same time, each transaction should be isolated from others to prevent data corruption.

- Durability: Once a transaction has completed, its result should be durable to survive any system failure (imagine if the power to your machine was cut right in the middle of a transaction's commit). Usually, the result of a transaction is written to persistent storage.

To understand the importance of transaction management, let's begin with an example about purchasing books from an online bookshop. First, you have to create a new schema for this application in your database. We have chosen to use PostgreSQL as the database to use for these samples. The source code for this chapter contains a `bin` directory with two scripts, one (`postgres.sh`) to download a Docker container and start a default Postgres instance and another (`psql.sh`) to connect to the running Postgres instance. The properties for connecting to the database can be found in Table 7-1.

ⓘ The sample code for this chapter provides scripts in the `bin` directory to start and connect to a Docker-based PostgreSQL instance. To start the instance and create the database, follow these steps:

1. Execute `bin\postgres.sh`; this will download and start the Postgres Docker container.

2. Execute `bin\psql.sh`; this will connect to the running Postgres container.

3. Execute `CREATE DATABASE bookstore` to create the database to use for the samples.

Table 7-1. *JDBC Properties for Connecting to the Application Database*

Property	Value
Driver class	org.postgresql.Driver
URL	jdbc:postgresql://localhost:5432/bookstore
Username	postgres
Password	password

For your bookshop application, you need a place to store the data. You'll create a simple database to manage books and accounts.

The entity relational (ER) diagram for the tables looks like Figure 7-1.

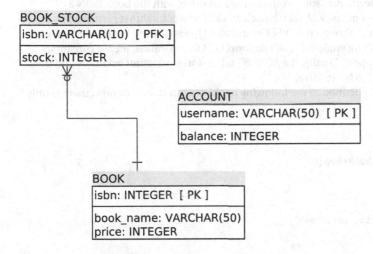

Figure 7-1. *BOOK_STOCK describes how many given BOOKs exist*

Now, let's create the SQL for the preceding model. Execute the `bin\psql.sh` command to connect to the running container and open the `psql` tool.

Paste the following SQL into the shell and verify its success.

Listing 7-1. Bookstore tables

```
CREATE TABLE BOOK (
    ISBN          VARCHAR(50)     NOT NULL,
    BOOK_NAME     VARCHAR(100)    NOT NULL,
    PRICE         INT,
    PRIMARY KEY (ISBN)
);

CREATE TABLE BOOK_STOCK (
    ISBN      VARCHAR(50)     NOT NULL,
    STOCK     INT             NOT NULL,
    PRIMARY KEY (ISBN),
    CONSTRAINT positive_stock CHECK (STOCK >= 0)
);
```

```
CREATE TABLE ACCOUNT (
    USERNAME    VARCHAR(50)     NOT NULL,
    BALANCE     INT             NOT NULL,
    PRIMARY KEY (USERNAME),
    CONSTRAINT positive_balance CHECK (BALANCE >= 0)
);
```

ℹ️   A real-world application of this type would probably feature a price field with a decimal type, but using an int makes the programming simpler to follow, so leave it as an int.

The BOOK table stores basic book information such as the name and price, with the book ISBN as the primary key. The BOOK_STOCK table keeps track of each book's stock. The stock value is restricted by a CHECK constraint to be a positive number. Although the CHECK constraint type is defined in SQL-99, not all database engines support it. If your database engine doesn't support CHECK constraints, please consult its documentation for similar constraint support. Finally, the ACCOUNT table stores customer accounts and their balances. Again, the balance is restricted to be positive.

The operations of your bookshop are defined in the following BookShop interface. For now, there is only one operation: purchase.

Listing 7-2. Bookstore interface

```
package com.apress.spring6recipes.bookshop;

public interface BookShop {

    void purchase(String isbn, String username);
}
```

Because you will implement this interface with JDBC, you create the following JdbcBookShop class. To better understand the nature of transactions, let's implement this class without the help of Spring's JDBC support.

Listing 7-3. Bookstore JDBC implementation

```
package com.apress.spring6recipes.bookshop;

import java.sql.SQLException;

import javax.sql.DataSource;

public class JdbcBookShop implements BookShop {

    private final DataSource dataSource;

    public JdbcBookShop(DataSource dataSource) {
        this.dataSource = dataSource;
    }
```

```java
public void purchase(String isbn, String username) {
  try (var conn = dataSource.getConnection()) {
    int price;
    var PRICE_SQL = "SELECT PRICE FROM BOOK WHERE ISBN = ?";
    try (var stmt1 = conn.prepareStatement(PRICE_SQL)) {
      stmt1.setString(1, isbn);
      try (var rs = stmt1.executeQuery()) {
        rs.next();
        price = rs.getInt("PRICE");
      }
    }
    var STOCK_SQL = "UPDATE BOOK_STOCK SET STOCK = STOCK - 1 WHERE ISBN = ?";
    try (var stmt2 = conn.prepareStatement(STOCK_SQL)) {
      stmt2.setString(1, isbn);
      stmt2.executeUpdate();

      var BALANCE_SQL = "UPDATE ACCOUNT SET BALANCE = BALANCE - ? WHERE USERNAME = ?";
      try (var stmt3 = conn.prepareStatement(BALANCE_SQL)) {
        stmt3.setInt(1, price);
        stmt3.setString(2, username);
        stmt3.executeUpdate();
      }
    }
  } catch (SQLException e) {
    throw new RuntimeException(e);
  }
}
}
```

For the purchase() operation, you have to execute three SQL statements in total. The first is to query the book price. The second and third update the book stock and account balance accordingly. Then, you can declare a bookshop instance in the Spring IoC container to provide purchasing services. For simplicity's sake, you can use DriverManagerDataSource, which opens a new connection to the database for every request.

 To access a PostgreSQL database, you have to add the Postgres client library to your CLASSPATH.

Listing 7-4. Bookstore configuration

```java
package com.apress.spring6recipes.bookshop.config;

import javax.sql.DataSource;

import org.springframework.context.annotation.Bean;
import org.springframework.context.annotation.Configuration;
import org.springframework.jdbc.datasource.DriverManagerDataSource;
```

```
import com.apress.spring6recipes.bookshop.JdbcBookShop;

@Configuration
public class BookstoreConfiguration {

    @Bean
    public DriverManagerDataSource dataSource() {
        var dataSource = new DriverManagerDataSource();
        dataSource.setDriverClassName(org.postgresql.Driver.class.getName());
        dataSource.setUrl("jdbc:postgresql://localhost:5432/bookstore");
        dataSource.setUsername("postgres");
        dataSource.setPassword("password");
        return dataSource;
    }

    @Bean
    public JdbcBookShop bookShop(DataSource dataSource) {
        return new JdbcBookShop(dataSource);
    }
}
```

To demonstrate the problems that can arise without transaction management, suppose you have the data shown in Tables 7-2, 7-3, and 7-4 entered in your bookshop database.

Table 7-2. Sample Data in the BOOK Table for Testing Transactions

ISBN	BOOK_NAME	PRICE
0001	The First Book	30

Table 7-3. Sample Data in the BOOK_STOCK Table for Testing Transactions

ISBN	STOCK
0001	10

Table 7-4. Sample Data in the ACCOUNT Table for Testing Transactions

USERNAME	BALANCE
user1	20

Then, write the following Main class for purchasing the book with ISBN 0001 by the user user1. Because that user's account has only $20, the funds are not sufficient to purchase the book.

Listing 7-5. Main class to test the bookstore app

```
package com.apress.spring6recipes.bookshop;

import com.apress.spring6recipes.bookshop.config.BookstoreConfiguration;
import org.springframework.context.annotation.AnnotationConfigApplicationContext;
```

```
public class Main {

  public static void main(String[] args) {
    var cfg = BookstoreConfiguration.class;
    try(var context = new AnnotationConfigApplicationContext(cfg)) {
      var bookShop = context.getBean(BookShop.class);
      bookShop.purchase("0001", "user1");
    }
  }
}
```

When you run this application, you will encounter a SQLException, because the CHECK constraint of the ACCOUNT table has been violated. This is an expected result because you were trying to debit more than the account balance.

However, if you check the stock for this book in the BOOK_STOCK table, you will find that it was accidentally deducted by this unsuccessful operation! The reason is that you executed the second SQL statement to deduct the stock before you got an exception in the third statement.

As you can see, the lack of transaction management causes your data to be left in an inconsistent state. To avoid this inconsistency, your three SQL statements for the purchase operation should be executed within a single transaction. Once any of the actions in a transaction fail, the entire transaction should be rolled back to undo all changes made by the executed actions.

Managing Transactions with JDBC Commit and Rollback

When using JDBC to update a database, by default, each SQL statement will be committed immediately after its execution. This behavior is known as auto-commit. However, it does not allow you to manage transactions for your operations. JDBC supports the primitive transaction management strategy of explicitly calling the commit() and rollback() methods on a connection. But before you can do that, you must turn off auto-commit, which is turned on by default.

Listing 7-6. Bookstore JDBC implementation with transactions

```
package com.apress.spring6recipes.bookshop;

public class JdbcBookShop implements BookShop {

  public void purchase(String isbn, String username) {
    try (var conn = dataSource.getConnection()) {
      try {
      conn.setAutoCommit(false);
        int price;
        var BOOK_SQL = "SELECT PRICE FROM BOOK WHERE ISBN = ?";
        try (var stmt1 = conn.prepareStatement(BOOK_SQL)) {
          stmt1.setString(1, isbn);
          try (var rs = stmt1.executeQuery()) {
            rs.next();
            price = rs.getInt("PRICE");
          }
        }
```

```
      var STOCK_SQL = "UPDATE BOOK_STOCK SET STOCK = STOCK - 1 WHERE ISBN = ?";
      try (var stmt2 = conn
              .prepareStatement(STOCK_SQL)) {
        stmt2.setString(1, isbn);
        stmt2.executeUpdate();
      }

      var ACCOUNT_SQL = "UPDATE ACCOUNT SET BALANCE = BALANCE - ? WHERE USERNAME = ?";
      try (var stmt3 = conn
              .prepareStatement(ACCOUNT_SQL)) {
        stmt3.setInt(1, price);
        stmt3.setString(2, username);
        stmt3.executeUpdate();
      }
      conn.commit();
    } catch (SQLException ex) {
      conn.rollback();
      throw ex;
    }
  } catch (SQLException ex) {
    throw new RuntimeException(ex);
  }
 }
}
```

The auto-commit behavior of a database connection can be altered by calling the setAutoCommit() method. By default, auto-commit is turned on to commit each SQL statement immediately after its execution. To enable transaction management, you must turn off this default behavior and commit the connection only when all the SQL statements have been executed successfully. If any of the statements go wrong, you must roll back all changes made by this connection.

Now, if you run your application again, the book stock will not be deducted when the user's balance is insufficient to purchase the book.

Although you can manage transactions by explicitly committing and rolling back JDBC connections, the code required for this purpose is boilerplate code that you have to repeat for different methods. Moreover, this code is JDBC specific, so once you have chosen another data access technology, it needs to be changed also. Spring's transaction support offers a set of technology-independent facilities, including transaction managers (e.g., org.springframework.transaction.PlatformTransactionManager), a transaction template (e.g., org.springframework.transaction.support.TransactionTemplate), and transaction declaration support to simplify your transaction management tasks.

7-2. Choosing a Transaction Manager Implementation

Problem

Typically, if your application involves only a single data source, you can simply manage transactions by calling the commit() and rollback() methods on a database connection. However, if your transactions extend across multiple data sources or you prefer to make use of the transaction management capabilities provided by your Java EE application server, you may choose the Jakarta Transaction API (JTA). Besides, you may have to call different proprietary transaction APIs for different object/relational mapping frameworks such as Hibernate and JPA.

As a result, you have to deal with different transaction APIs for different technologies. It would be hard for you to switch from one set of APIs to another.

Solution

Spring abstracts a general set of transaction facilities from different transaction management APIs. As an application developer, you can simply utilize Spring's transaction facilities without having to know much about the underlying transaction APIs. With these facilities, your transaction management code will be independent of any specific transaction technology.

Spring's core transaction management abstraction is based on the interface `PlatformTransactionManager`. It encapsulates a set of technology-independent methods for transaction management. Remember that a transaction manager is needed no matter which transaction management strategy (programmatic or declarative) you choose in Spring. The `PlatformTransactionManager` interface provides three methods for working with transactions:

- `TransactionStatus getTransaction(TransactionDefinition definition) throws TransactionException`

- `void commit(TransactionStatus status) throws TransactionException;`

- `void rollback(TransactionStatus status) throws TransactionException;`

Spring's reactive transaction management abstraction is based on the interface `ReactiveTransactionManager`, which very closely mimics the regular `PlatformTransactionManager` but then in a reactive fashion. The `ReactiveTransactionManager` interface provides three methods for working with transactions:

- `Mono<ReactiveTransaction> getReactiveTransaction(TransactionDefinition definition) throws TransactionException;`

- `Mono<Void> commit(ReactiveTransaction transaction) throws TransactionException;`

- `Mono<Void> rollback(ReactiveTransaction transaction) throws TransactionException;`

How It Works

`PlatformTransactionManager` and `ReactiveTransactionManager` are general interfaces for all Spring transaction managers. Spring has several built-in implementations of these interfaces for use with different transaction management APIs:

- If you have to deal with only a single data source in your application and access it with JDBC, `DataSourceTransactionManager` should meet your needs.

- If you are using JTA for transaction management on a Jakarta EE application server, you should use `JtaTransactionManager` to look up a transaction from the application server. Additionally, `JtaTransactionManager` is appropriate for distributed transactions (transactions that span multiple resources). Note that while it's common to use a JTA transaction manager to integrate the application server's transaction manager, there's nothing stopping you from using a stand-alone JTA transaction manager such as Atomikos.

- If you are using an object/relational mapping framework to access a database, you should choose a corresponding transaction manager for this framework, such as HibernateTransactionManager or JpaTransactionManager.

- When working with R2DBC, you need the R2dbcTransactionManager.

Figure 7-2 shows the common implementations available in Spring.

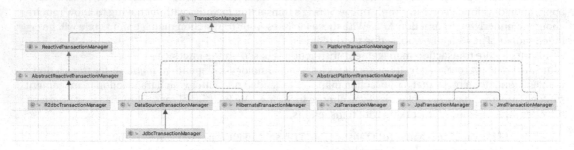

Figure 7-2. *Common transaction manager implementations in Spring*

A transaction manager is declared in the Spring IoC container as a normal bean. For example, the following bean configuration declares a DataSourceTransactionManager instance. It requires a DataSource so that it can manage transactions for connections made by this data source.

Listing 7-7. Bean for DataSourceTransactionManager

```
@Bean
public DataSourceTransactionManager transactionManager(DataSource dataSource) {
    return new DataSourceTransactionManager(dataSource)
}
```

7-3. Managing Transactions Programmatically with the Transaction Manager API

Problem

You need to precisely control when to commit and roll back transactions in your business methods, but you don't want to deal with the underlying transaction API directly.

Solution

Spring's transaction manager provides a technology-independent API that allows you to start a new transaction (or obtain the currently active transaction) by calling the getTransaction() method and manage it by calling the commit() and rollback() methods. Because PlatformTransactionManager is an abstract unit for transaction management, the methods you call for transaction management are guaranteed to be technology independent.

How It Works

While both the PlatformTransactionManager and ReactiveTransactionManager are similar in nature, the programming model is different. However, for both you need to declare a bean in the application context and inject it into the class where you want to use it. First, we will show how to do it with the PlatformTransactionManager followed by the ReactiveTransactionManager.

Use and Configure the PlatformTransactionManager

To demonstrate how to use the transaction manager API, let's create a new class, TransactionalJdbcBookShop, which will make use of the Spring JDBC template. Because it has to deal with a transaction manager, you add a field of type PlatformTransactionManager and allow it to be injected via the constructor.

Listing 7-8. Bookstore JDBC implementation with PlatformTransactionManager

```java
package com.apress.spring6recipes.bookshop;

import org.springframework.dao.DataAccessException;
import org.springframework.jdbc.core.support.JdbcDaoSupport;
import org.springframework.transaction.PlatformTransactionManager;
import org.springframework.transaction.TransactionDefinition;
import org.springframework.transaction.TransactionStatus;
import org.springframework.transaction.support.DefaultTransactionDefinition;

import javax.sql.DataSource;

public class TransactionalJdbcBookShop extends JdbcDaoSupport implements BookShop {

    private final PlatformTransactionManager transactionManager;

    public TransactionalJdbcBookShop(PlatformTransactionManager transactionManager,
                                     DataSource dataSource) {
        this.transactionManager = transactionManager;
        setDataSource(dataSource);
    }

    public void purchase(String isbn, String username) {
        var def = new DefaultTransactionDefinition();
        var status = transactionManager.getTransaction(def);

        try {
            var BOOK_SQL = "SELECT PRICE FROM BOOK WHERE ISBN = ?";
            var price = getJdbcTemplate().queryForObject(BOOK_SQL, Integer.class, isbn);

            var STOCK_SQL = "UPDATE BOOK_STOCK SET STOCK = STOCK - 1 WHERE ISBN = ?";
            getJdbcTemplate().update(STOCK_SQL, isbn);
```

```
    var BALANCE_SQL = "UPDATE ACCOUNT SET BALANCE = BALANCE - ? WHERE USERNAME = ?";
    getJdbcTemplate().update(BALANCE_SQL, price, username);

    transactionManager.commit(status);
  }
  catch (DataAccessException e) {
    transactionManager.rollback(status);
    throw e;
  }
  }
}
```

Before you start a new transaction, you have to specify the transaction attributes in a transaction definition object of type TransactionDefinition. For this example, you can simply create an instance of DefaultTransactionDefinition to use the default transaction attributes.

Once you have a transaction definition, you can ask the transaction manager to start a new transaction with that definition by calling the getTransaction() method. Then, it will return a TransactionStatus object to keep track of the transaction status. If all the statements execute successfully, you ask the transaction manager to commit this transaction by passing in the transaction status. Because all exceptions thrown by the Spring JDBC template are subclasses of DataAccessException, you ask the transaction manager to roll back the transaction when this kind of exception is caught.

In this class, you have declared the transaction manager property of the general type PlatformTransactionManager. Now, you have to inject an appropriate transaction manager implementation. Because you are dealing with only a single data source and accessing it with JDBC, you should choose DataSourceTransactionManager. Here, you also wire a DataSource because the class is a subclass of Spring's JdbcDaoSupport, which requires it.

Listing 7-9. Bookstore configuration

```
@Configuration
public class BookstoreConfiguration {

  @Bean
  public DataSourceTransactionManager transactionManager(DataSource dataSource) {
    return new DataSourceTransactionManager(dataSource);
  }

  @Bean
  public TransactionalJdbcBookShop bookShop(DataSource dataSource,
PlatformTransactionManager transactionManager) {
    return new TransactionalJdbcBookShop(transactionManager, dataSource);
  }
}
```

Use and Configure the ReactiveTransactionManager

To demonstrate how to use the reactive transaction manager API, let's create a new class, TransactionalR2dbcBookShop, which will make use of the Spring R2DBC DatabaseClient. Because it has to deal with a transaction manager, you add a field of type ReactiveTransactionManager and allow it to be injected via the constructor.

Listing 7-10. Reactive bookstore implementation with ReactiveTransactionManager

```
package com.apress.spring6recipes.bookshop.reactive;

import org.springframework.r2dbc.core.DatabaseClient;
import org.springframework.transaction.ReactiveTransactionManager;
import org.springframework.transaction.support.DefaultTransactionDefinition;

import io.r2dbc.spi.ConnectionFactory;
import reactor.core.publisher.Mono;

public class TransactionalR2dbcBookShop implements BookShop {

    private final ReactiveTransactionManager txManager;
    private final DatabaseClient client;

    public TransactionalR2dbcBookShop(ReactiveTransactionManager txManager,
                                 ConnectionFactory cf) {
        this.txManager = txManager;
        this.client = DatabaseClient.create(cf);
    }

    public Mono<Void> purchase(String isbn, String username) {
        var def = new DefaultTransactionDefinition();
        var tx = txManager.getReactiveTransaction(def);

        var BOOK_SQL = "SELECT PRICE FROM BOOK WHERE ISBN = $1";
        var STOCK_SQL = "UPDATE BOOK_STOCK SET STOCK = STOCK - 1 WHERE ISBN = $1";
        var BALANCE_SQL = "UPDATE ACCOUNT SET BALANCE = BALANCE - $1 WHERE USERNAME = $2";
        return tx.flatMap((status) -> {
            var price = client.sql(BOOK_SQL).bind("$1", isbn)
                    .map((row, meta) -> row.get("PRICE", Integer.class))
                    .one();
            var stock = price.doOnNext((p) -> client.sql(STOCK_SQL)
                    .bind("$1", price).fetch());
            var balance = stock.doOnNext((p) -> client.sql(BALANCE_SQL)
                    .bind("$1", price)
                    .bind("$2", username).fetch());
            return balance.then(txManager.commit(status))
                    .onErrorResume((ex) -> txManager.rollback(status).then(Mono.error(ex)));
        });
    }
}
```

Before you start a new transaction, you have to specify the transaction attributes in a transaction definition object of type TransactionDefinition. For this example, you can simply create an instance of DefaultTransactionDefinition to use the default transaction attributes.

Once you have a transaction definition, you can ask the transaction manager to start a new transaction with that definition by calling the getReactiveTransaction() method. Then, it will return a Mono<ReactiveTransaction> object to keep track of the transaction status. If all the statements execute successfully, you ask the transaction manager to commit this transaction by passing in the transaction status. In case of an error, you do a rollback.

In this class, you have declared the transaction manager property of the general type ReactiveTransactionManager. Now, you have to inject an appropriate transaction manager implementation. Because you are dealing with only a single data source and accessing it with R2DBC, you should choose R2dbcTransactionManager. Here, you also wire a ConnectionFactory as to be able to create a DatabaseClient to do data access.

Listing 7-11. Reactive bookstore configuration

```
@Configuration
public class ReactiveBookstoreConfiguration {

  @Bean
  public R2dbcTransactionManager transactionManager(ConnectionFactory cf) {
    return new R2dbcTransactionManager(cf);
  }

  @Bean
  public TransactionalR2dbcBookShop bookShop(ReactiveTransactionManager txManager,
                                             ConnectionFactory cf) {
    return new TransactionalR2dbcBookShop(txManager, cf);
  }
}
```

7-4. Managing Transactions Programmatically with a Transaction Template

Problem

Suppose that you have a code block, but not the entire body, of a business method that has the following transaction requirements:

- Start a new transaction at the beginning of the block.

- Commit the transaction after the block completes successfully.

- Roll back the transaction if an exception is thrown in the block.

If you call Spring's transaction manager API directly, the transaction management code can be generalized in a technology-independent manner. However, you may not want to repeat the boilerplate code for each similar code block.

Solution

Spring provides for both regular data access and reactive data access a template approach to manage transactions. For regular data access, you can use the TransactionTemplate; for reactive data access, there is the TransactionalOperator. Both classes make it easier to do programmatic transaction management. They make it easier in a way that you don't need to explicitly start, commit or roll back a transaction. The code that is part of the TransactionCallback passed to either of the execute methods is the transactional unit. A transaction will be started at the moment of execution and committed (or rolled back) at the end.

The template objects that Spring provides are lightweight and usually can be discarded or recreated with no performance impact. A JDBC template can be recreated on the fly with a DataSource reference, for example, and so too can a TransactionTemplate be recreated by providing a reference to a transaction manager. You can, of course, simply create one in your Spring application context too.

How It Works

Use the TransactionTemplate

As with the JDBC template, Spring also provides a TransactionTemplate to help you control the overall transaction management process and transaction exception handling. You just have to encapsulate your code block in a callback class that implements the TransactionCallback interface and pass it to the TransactionTemplate execute method for execution. In this way, you don't need to repeat the boilerplate transaction management code for this block.

A TransactionTemplate is created on a transaction manager just as a JDBC template is created on a data source. A transaction template executes a transaction callback object that encapsulates a transactional code block. You can implement the callback interface either as a separate class or as an inner class. If it's implemented as an inner class, you have to make the method arguments final for it to access.

Listing 7-12. Bookstore JDBC implementation with TransactionTemplate - injecting PlatformTransactionManager

```
package com.apress.spring6recipes.bookshop;

import org.springframework.jdbc.core.support.JdbcDaoSupport;
import org.springframework.transaction.PlatformTransactionManager;
import org.springframework.transaction.TransactionStatus;
import org.springframework.transaction.support.TransactionCallbackWithoutResult;
import org.springframework.transaction.support.TransactionTemplate;

import javax.sql.DataSource;

public class TransactionalJdbcBookShop extends JdbcDaoSupport implements BookShop {

  private final PlatformTransactionManager transactionManager;

  public TransactionalJdbcBookShop(PlatformTransactionManager txManager, DataSource ds) {
    this.transactionManager = txManager;
    setDataSource(ds);
  }

  public void purchase(final String isbn, final String username) {
    var txTemplate = new TransactionTemplate(transactionManager);

    txTemplate.execute(new TransactionCallbackWithoutResult() {

      protected void doInTransactionWithoutResult(TransactionStatus ts) {

        var BOOK_SQL = "SELECT PRICE FROM BOOK WHERE ISBN = ?";
        int price = getJdbcTemplate().queryForObject(BOOK_SQL, Integer.class, isbn);

        var STOCK_SQL = "UPDATE BOOK_STOCK SET STOCK = STOCK - 1 WHERE ISBN = ?";
```

```
        getJdbcTemplate().update(STOCK_SQL, isbn);

        var BALANCE_SQL = "UPDATE ACCOUNT SET BALANCE = BALANCE - ? WHERE USERNAME = ?";
        getJdbcTemplate().update(BALANCE_SQL, price, username);
      }
    });
  }
}
```

A TransactionTemplate can accept a transaction callback object that implements either the TransactionCallback or an instance of the one implementer of that interface provided by the framework, the TransactionCallbackWithoutResult class. For the code block in the purchase() method for deducting the book stock and account balance, there's no result to be returned, so TransactionCallbackWithoutResult is fine. For any code blocks with return values, you should use the TransactionCallback<T> interface instead. The return value of the callback object will finally be returned by the template's T execute() method. The main benefit is that the responsibility of starting, rolling back, or committing the transaction has been removed.

During the execution of the callback object, if it throws an unchecked exception (e.g., RuntimeException and DataAccessException fall into this category) or if you explicitly called setRollbackOnly() on the TransactionStatus argument in the doInTransactionWithoutResult method, the transaction will be rolled back. Otherwise, it will be committed after the callback object completes.

In the bean configuration file, the bookshop bean still requires a transaction manager to create a TransactionTemplate.

Listing 7-13. Bookstore configuration

```
@Configuration
public class BookstoreConfiguration {

  @Bean
  public DataSourceTransactionManager transactionManager(DataSource ds) {
    return new DataSourceTransactionManager(ds);
  }

  @Bean
  public TransactionalJdbcBookShop bookShop(PlatformTransactionManager ptm,
                                            DataSource dataSource) {
    return new TransactionalJdbcBookShop(ptm, dataSource);
  }
}
```

You can also have the IoC container inject a transaction template instead of creating it directly. Because a transaction template handles all transactions, there's no need for your class to refer to the transaction manager anymore.

Listing 7-14. Bookstore JDBC implementation with injected TransactionTemplate

```
package com.apress.spring6recipes.bookshop;

import org.springframework.jdbc.core.support.JdbcDaoSupport;
import org.springframework.transaction.TransactionStatus;
import org.springframework.transaction.support.TransactionCallbackWithoutResult;
```

```java
import org.springframework.transaction.support.TransactionTemplate;

import javax.sql.DataSource;

public class TransactionalJdbcBookShop extends JdbcDaoSupport implements BookShop {

    private final TransactionTemplate transactionTemplate;

    public TransactionalJdbcBookShop(TransactionTemplate txTemplate, DataSource ds) {
        this.transactionTemplate = txTemplate;
        setDataSource(ds);
    }

    public void purchase(final String isbn, final String username) {

        transactionTemplate.execute(new TransactionCallbackWithoutResult() {

            protected void doInTransactionWithoutResult(TransactionStatus ts) {

                var BOOK_SQL = "SELECT PRICE FROM BOOK WHERE ISBN = ?";
                int price = getJdbcTemplate().queryForObject(BOOK_SQL, Integer.class, isbn);

                var STOCK_SQL = "UPDATE BOOK_STOCK SET STOCK = STOCK - 1 WHERE ISBN = ?";
                getJdbcTemplate().update(STOCK_SQL, isbn);

                var BALANCE_SQL = "UPDATE ACCOUNT SET BALANCE = BALANCE - ? WHERE USERNAME = ?";
                getJdbcTemplate().update(BALANCE_SQL, price, username);
            }
        });
    }
}
```

Then you define a transaction template in the bean configuration file and inject it, instead of the transaction manager, into your bookshop bean. Notice that the transaction template instance can be used for more than one transactional bean because it is a thread-safe object. Finally, don't forget to set the transaction manager property for your transaction template.

Listing 7-15. Bookstore configuration

```java
@Configuration
public class BookstoreConfiguration {
    @Bean
    public DataSourceTransactionManager transactionManager(DataSource dataSource) {
        return new DataSourceTransactionManager(dataSource);
    }

    @Bean
    public TransactionTemplate transactionTemplate(PlatformTransactionManager ptm) {
        return new TransactionTemplate(ptm);
    }
```

```
@Bean
public TransactionalJdbcBookShop bookShop(DataSource ds, TransactionTemplate tt) {
    return new TransactionalJdbcBookShop(tt, ds);
  }
}
```

Use the TransactionalOperator

A TransactionalOperator is created on a transaction manager. A TransactionalOperator executes a transaction callback object that encapsulates a transactional code block. You can implement the callback interface either as a separate class or as an inner class. If it's implemented as an inner class, you have to make the method arguments final for it to access.

Listing 7-16. Reactive bookstore implementation with injected TransactionalOperator

```
package com.apress.spring6recipes.bookshop.reactive;

import org.springframework.r2dbc.core.DatabaseClient;
import org.springframework.transaction.ReactiveTransactionManager;
import org.springframework.transaction.reactive.TransactionalOperator;

import io.r2dbc.spi.ConnectionFactory;
import reactor.core.publisher.Mono;

public class TransactionalR2dbcBookShop implements BookShop {

    private final ReactiveTransactionManager txManager;
    private final DatabaseClient client;

    public TransactionalR2dbcBookShop(ReactiveTransactionManager txManager,
                                      ConnectionFactory cf) {
        this.txManager = txManager;
        this.client = DatabaseClient.create(cf);
    }

    public Mono<Void> purchase(String isbn, String username) {
        var tx = TransactionalOperator.create(txManager);

        var BOOK_SQL = "SELECT PRICE FROM BOOK WHERE ISBN = $1";
        var STOCK_SQL = "UPDATE BOOK_STOCK SET STOCK = STOCK - 1 WHERE ISBN = $1";
        var BALANCE_SQL = "UPDATE ACCOUNT SET BALANCE = BALANCE - $1 WHERE USERNAME = $2";

        var price = client.sql(BOOK_SQL).bind("$1", isbn)
                .map((row, meta) -> row.get("PRICE", Integer.class))
                .one();
        var stock = price.doOnNext((p) -> client.sql(STOCK_SQL)
                .bind("$1", price).fetch());
        var balance = stock.doOnNext((p) -> client.sql(BALANCE_SQL)
                .bind("$1", price)
```

```
            .bind("$2", username).fetch());
    return balance.as(tx::transactional).then();
    }
}
```

A `TransactionalOperator` can accept a transaction callback object that implements the `TransactionCallback` interface. The return value of the callback object will finally be returned by the template's `T execute()` method. The main benefit is that the responsibility of starting, rolling back, or committing the transaction has been removed.

During the execution of the callback object, if it throws an unchecked exception (e.g., `RuntimeException` and `DataAccessException` fall into this category) or if you explicitly called `setRollbackOnly()` on the `ReactiveTransaction` argument in the execute method, the transaction will be rolled back. Otherwise, it will be committed after the callback object completes.

In the bean configuration file, the bookshop bean still requires a transaction manager to create a `TransactionalOperator`.

Listing 7-17. Reactive bookstore configuration

```
@Configuration
public class ReactiveBookstoreConfiguration {

  @Bean
  public R2dbcTransactionManager transactionManager(ConnectionFactory cf) {
    return new R2dbcTransactionManager(cf);
  }

  @Bean
  public TransactionalR2dbcBookShop bookShop(ReactiveTransactionManager rtm,
                                             ConnectionFactory cf) {
    return new TransactionalR2dbcBookShop(rtm, cf);
  }
}
```

You can also have the IoC container inject a TransactionalOperator instead of creating it directly. Because a `TransactionalOperator` handles all transactions, there's no need for your class to refer to the transaction manager anymore.

Listing 7-18. Reactive bookstore implementation with injected TransactionalOperator

```
package com.apress.spring6recipes.bookshop.reactive;

import org.springframework.r2dbc.core.DatabaseClient;
import org.springframework.transaction.reactive.TransactionalOperator;

import io.r2dbc.spi.ConnectionFactory;
import reactor.core.publisher.Mono;

public class TransactionalR2dbcBookShop implements BookShop {

  private final TransactionalOperator txOperator;
  private final DatabaseClient client;
```

```java
public TransactionalR2dbcBookShop(TransactionalOperator txOperator,
                                  ConnectionFactory cf) {
    this.txOperator = txOperator;
    this.client = DatabaseClient.create(cf);
}

public Mono<Void> purchase(String isbn, String username) {
    var BOOK_SQL = "SELECT PRICE FROM BOOK WHERE ISBN = $1";
    var STOCK_SQL = "UPDATE BOOK_STOCK SET STOCK = STOCK - 1 WHERE ISBN = $1";
    var BALANCE_SQL = "UPDATE ACCOUNT SET BALANCE = BALANCE - $1 WHERE USERNAME = $2";

    var price = client.sql(BOOK_SQL).bind("$1", isbn)
            .map((row, meta) -> row.get("PRICE", Integer.class))
            .one();
    var stock = price.doOnNext((p) -> client.sql(STOCK_SQL)
            .bind("$1", price).fetch());
    var balance = stock.doOnNext((p) -> client.sql(BALANCE_SQL)
            .bind("$1", price)
            .bind("$2", username).fetch());
    return balance.as(txOperator::transactional).then();
}
}
```

Then you define a TransactionalOperator in the bean configuration file and inject it, instead of the transaction manager, into your bookshop bean. Notice that the TransactionalOperator instance can be used for more than one transactional bean because it is a thread-safe object.

Listing 7-19. Reactive bookstore configuration

```java
@Configuration
public class ReactiveBookstoreConfiguration {

    @Bean
    public R2dbcTransactionManager transactionManager(ConnectionFactory cf) {
        return new R2dbcTransactionManager(cf);
    }
}
```

7-5. Managing Transactions Declaratively with the @Transactional Annotation

Problem

Declaring transactions in the bean configuration file requires knowledge of AOP concepts such as pointcuts, advices, and advisors. Developers who lack this knowledge might find it hard to enable declarative transaction management.

Solution

Spring allows you to declare transactions simply by annotating your transactional methods with @Transactional and adding the @EnableTransactionManagement annotation to your configuration class.

How It Works

To define a method as transactional, you can simply annotate it with @Transactional. Note that you should only annotate public methods due to the proxy-based limitations of Spring AOP.

Listing 7-20. JDBC bookstore implementation with @Transactional

```
package com.apress.spring6recipes.bookshop;

import org.springframework.jdbc.core.support.JdbcDaoSupport;
import org.springframework.transaction.annotation.Transactional;

import javax.sql.DataSource;

public class JdbcBookShop extends JdbcDaoSupport implements BookShop {

  public JdbcBookShop(DataSource dataSource) {
    setDataSource(dataSource);
  }

  @Transactional
  public void purchase(String isbn, String username) {
    var BOOK_SQL = "SELECT PRICE FROM BOOK WHERE ISBN = ?";
    int price = getJdbcTemplate().queryForObject(BOOK_SQL, Integer.class, isbn);

    var STOCK_SQL = "UPDATE BOOK_STOCK SET STOCK = STOCK - 1 WHERE ISBN = ?";
    getJdbcTemplate().update(STOCK_SQL, isbn);

    var BALANCE_SQL = "UPDATE ACCOUNT SET BALANCE = BALANCE - ? WHERE USERNAME = ?";
    getJdbcTemplate().update(BALANCE_SQL, price, username);
  }
}
```

Note that, as we are extending JdbcDaoSupport, we no longer need the mutators for the DataSource; remove it from your DAO class.

Listing 7-21. Reactive bookstore implementation with @Transactional

```
package com.apress.spring6recipes.bookshop.reactive;

import org.springframework.r2dbc.core.DatabaseClient;
import org.springframework.transaction.annotation.Transactional;

import io.r2dbc.spi.ConnectionFactory;
import reactor.core.publisher.Mono;
```

```
public class TransactionalR2dbcBookShop implements BookShop {

  private final DatabaseClient client;

  public TransactionalR2dbcBookShop(ConnectionFactory cf) {
    this.client = DatabaseClient.create(cf);
  }

  @Transactional
  public Mono<Void> purchase(String isbn, String username) {
    var BOOK_SQL = "SELECT PRICE FROM BOOK WHERE ISBN = $1";
    var STOCK_SQL = "UPDATE BOOK_STOCK SET STOCK = STOCK - 1 WHERE ISBN = $1";
    var BALANCE_SQL = "UPDATE ACCOUNT SET BALANCE = BALANCE - $1 WHERE USERNAME = $2";

    var price = client.sql(BOOK_SQL).bind("$1", isbn)
                      .map((row, meta) -> row.get("PRICE", Integer.class))
                      .one();
    var stock = price.doOnNext((p) -> client.sql(STOCK_SQL).bind("$1", price).fetch());
    var balance = stock.doOnNext((p) -> client.sql(BALANCE_SQL)
                                       .bind("$1", price)
                                       .bind("$2", username).fetch());
    return balance.then();
  }
}
```

You may apply the @Transactional annotation at the method level or the class level. When applying this annotation to a class, all of the public methods within this class will be defined as transactional. Although you can apply @Transactional to interfaces or method declarations in an interface, it's not recommended because it may not work properly with class-based proxies (i.e., CGLIB proxies).

In the Java configuration class, you have to add the @EnableTransactionManagement annotation. That's all you need to make it work. Spring will advise methods with @Transactional, or methods in a class with @Transactional, from beans declared in the IoC container. As a result, Spring can manage transactions for these methods.

Listing 7-22. Configuration for @EnableTransactionManagement

```
@Configuration
@EnableTransactionManagement
public class BookstoreConfiguration { ... }
```

7-6. Setting the Propagation Transaction Attribute

Problem

When a transactional method is called by another method, it is necessary to specify how the transaction should be propagated. For example, the method may continue to run within the existing transaction, or it may start a new transaction and run within its own transaction.

Solution

A transaction's propagation behavior can be specified by the propagation transaction attribute. Spring defines seven propagation behaviors, as shown in Table 7-5. These behaviors are defined in the org. springframework.transaction.TransactionDefinition interface. Note that not all types of transaction managers support all of these propagation behaviors. Their behavior is contingent on the underlying resource. Databases, for example, may support varying isolation levels, which constrains what propagation behaviors the transaction manager can support.

Table 7-5. *Propagation Behaviors Supported by Spring*

Propagation	Description
REQUIRED	If there's an existing transaction in progress, the current method should run within this transaction. Otherwise, it should start a new transaction and run within its own transaction.
REQUIRES_NEW	The current method must start a new transaction and run within its own transaction. If there's an existing transaction in progress, it should be suspended.
SUPPORTS	If there's an existing transaction in progress, the current method can run within this transaction. Otherwise, it is not necessary to run within a transaction.
NOT_SUPPORTED	The current method should not run within a transaction. If there's an existing transaction in progress, it should be suspended.
MANDATORY	The current method must run within a transaction. If there's no existing transaction in progress, an exception will be thrown.
NEVER	The current method should not run within a transaction. If there's an existing transaction in progress, an exception will be thrown.
NESTED	If there's an existing transaction in progress, the current method should run within the nested transaction of this transaction. Otherwise, it should start a new transaction and run within its own transaction. This feature is unique to Spring (whereas the previous propagation behaviors have analogs in Jakarta EE transaction propagation). The behavior is useful for situations such as batch processing, in which you've got a long running process (imagine processing 1 million records) and you want to chunk the commits on the batch. So you commit every 10,000 records. If something goes wrong, you roll back the nested transaction, and you've lost only 10,000 records' worth of work (as opposed to the entire 1 million).

How It Works

Transaction propagation happens when a transactional method is called by another method. For example, suppose a customer would like to check out all books to purchase at the bookshop cashier. To support this operation, you define the Cashier interface as follows.

Listing 7-23. Cashier interface

```
package com.apress.spring6recipes.bookshop;

import java.util.List;

public interface Cashier {

  void checkout(List<String> isbns, String username);

}
```

You can implement this interface by delegating the purchases to a bookshop bean by calling its purchase() method multiple times. Note that the checkout() method is made transactional by applying the @Transactional annotation.

Listing 7-24. Cashier implementation

```
package com.apress.spring6recipes.bookshop;

import java.util.List;

import org.springframework.transaction.annotation.Transactional;

public class BookShopCashier implements Cashier {

  private final BookShop bookShop;

  public BookShopCashier(BookShop bookShop) {
    this.bookShop = bookShop;
  }

  @Transactional
  public void checkout(List<String> isbns, String username) {
    isbns.forEach(isbn -> bookShop.purchase(isbn, username));
  }
}
```

Then define a cashier bean in your bean configuration file and refer to the bookshop bean for purchasing books.

Listing 7-25. Bookstore configuration for Cashier

```
@Configuration
@EnableTransactionManagement()
public class BookstoreConfiguration {
...

    @Bean
    public Cashier cashier(BookShop bookShop) {
        return new BookShopCashier(bookShop);
    }
}
```

To illustrate the propagation behavior of a transaction, enter the data shown in Tables 7-6, 7-7, and 7-8 in your bookshop database.

Table 7-6. *Sample Data in the BOOK Table for Testing Propagation Behaviors*

ISBN	BOOK_NAME	PRICE
0001	The First Book	30
0002	The Second Book	50

Table 7-7. *Sample Data in the BOOK_STOCK Table for Testing Propagation Behaviors*

ISBN	STOCK
0001	10
0002	10

Table 7-8. *Sample Data in the ACCOUNT Table for Testing Propagation Behaviors*

USERNAME	BALANCE
user1	40

The REQUIRED Propagation Behavior

When the user user1 checks out the two books from the cashier, the balance is sufficient to purchase the first book but not the second.

Listing 7-26. Main class for testing Cashier

```
package com.apress.spring6recipes.bookshop;

import java.util.List;

import com.apress.spring6recipes.bookshop.config.BookstoreConfiguration;

import org.springframework.context.annotation.AnnotationConfigApplicationContext;

public class Main {

  public static void main(String[] args) {
    var cfg = BookstoreConfiguration.class;
    try (var context = new AnnotationConfigApplicationContext(cfg)) {
      var isbnList = List.of("0001", "0002");
      var cashier = context.getBean(Cashier.class);
      cashier.checkout(isbnList, "user1");
    }
  }
}
```

When the bookshop's purchase() method is called by another transactional method, such as checkout(), it will run within the existing transaction by default. This default propagation behavior is called REQUIRED. That means there will be only one transaction whose boundary is the beginning and ending of the checkout() method. This transaction will be committed only at the end of the checkout() method. As a result, the user can purchase none of the books.

Figure 7-3 illustrates the REQUIRED propagation behavior.

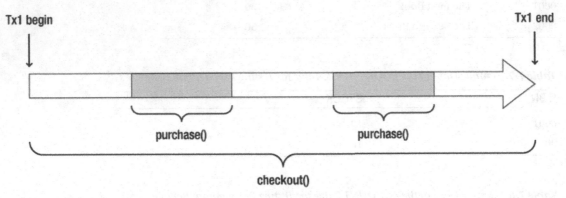

Figure 7-3. *The REQUIRED transaction propagation behavior*

However, if the purchase() method is called by a non-transactional method and there's no existing transaction in progress, it will start a new transaction and run within its own transaction. The propagation transaction attribute can be defined in the @Transactional annotation. For example, you can set the REQUIRED behavior for this attribute as follows. In fact, this is unnecessary, because it's the default behavior.

Listing 7-27. Bookshop using @Transactional with propagation REQUIRED

```
package com.apress.spring6recipes.bookshop.spring;
...
import org.springframework.transaction.annotation.Propagation;
import org.springframework.transaction.annotation.Transactional;

public class JdbcBookShop extends JdbcDaoSupport implements BookShop {
    @Transactional(propagation = Propagation.REQUIRED)
    public void purchase(String isbn, String username) {
        ...
    }
}
```

Listing 7-28. Cashier using @Transactional with propagation REQUIRED

```
package com.apress.spring6recipes.bookshop.spring;
...
import org.springframework.transaction.annotation.Propagation;
import org.springframework.transaction.annotation.Transactional;

public class BookShopCashier implements Cashier {
    ...
```

```
@Transactional(propagation = Propagation.REQUIRED)
public void checkout(List<String> isbns, String username) {
    ...
}
}
```

The REQUIRES_NEW Propagation Behavior

Another common propagation behavior is REQUIRES_NEW. It indicates that the method must start a new transaction and run within its new transaction. If there's an existing transaction in progress, it should be suspended first (as, e.g., with the checkout method on BookShopCashier, with a propagation of REQUIRED).

Listing 7-29. Bookshop using @Transactional with propagation REQUIRES_NEW

```
package com.apress.spring6recipes.bookshop.spring;
...
import org.springframework.transaction.annotation.Propagation;
import org.springframework.transaction.annotation.Transactional;

public class JdbcBookShop extends JdbcDaoSupport implements BookShop {

    @Transactional(propagation = Propagation.REQUIRES_NEW)
    public void purchase(String isbn, String username) {
        ...
    }
}
```

In this case, there will be three transactions started in total. The first transaction is started by the checkout() method, but when the first purchase() method is called, the first transaction will be suspended and a new transaction will be started. At the end of the first purchase() method, the new transaction completes and commits. When the second purchase() method is called, another new transaction will be started. However, this transaction will fail and roll back. As a result, the first book will be purchased successfully, while the second will not. Figure 7-4 illustrates the REQUIRES_NEW propagation behavior.

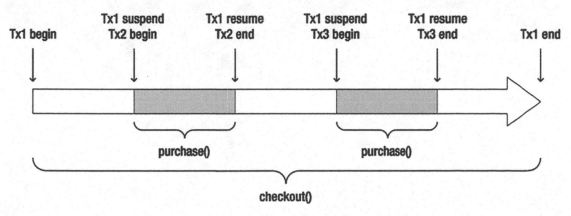

Figure 7-4. The REQUIRES_NEW transaction propagation behavior

7-7. Setting the Isolation Transaction Attribute

Problem

When multiple transactions of the same application or different applications are operating concurrently on the same dataset, many unexpected problems may arise. You must specify how you expect your transactions to be isolated from one another.

Solution

The problems caused by concurrent transactions can be categorized into four types:

- Dirty read: For two transactions T1 and T2, T1 reads a field that has been updated by T2 but not yet committed. Later, if T2 rolls back, the field read by T1 will be temporary and invalid.

- Nonrepeatable read: For two transactions T1 and T2, T1 reads a field, and then T2 updates the field. Later, if T1 reads the same field again, the value will be different.

- Phantom read: For two transactions T1 and T2, T1 reads some rows from a table, and then T2 inserts new rows into the table. Later, if T1 reads the same table again, there will be additional rows.

- Lost updates: For two transactions T1 and T2, they both select a row for update and, based on the state of that row, make an update to it. Thus, one overwrites the other when the second transaction to commit should have waited until the first one committed before performing its selection.

In theory, transactions should be completely isolated from each other (i.e., serializable) to avoid all the mentioned problems. However, this isolation level will have great impact on performance, because transactions have to run in serial order. In practice, transactions can run in lower isolation levels in order to improve performance.

A transaction's isolation level can be specified by the isolation transaction attribute. Spring supports five isolation levels, as shown in Table 7-9. These levels are defined in the org.springframework.transaction. TransactionDefinition interface.

Table 7-9. *Isolation Levels Supported by Spring*

Isolation	Description
DEFAULT	Uses the default isolation level of the underlying database. For most databases, the default isolation level is READ_COMMITTED.
READ_UNCOMMITTED	Allows a transaction to read uncommitted changes by other transactions. The dirty read, nonrepeatable read, and phantom read problems may occur.
READ_COMMITTED	Allows a transaction to read only those changes that have been committed by other transactions. The dirty read problem can be avoided, but the nonrepeatable read and phantom read problems may still occur.
REPEATABLE_READ	Ensures that a transaction can read identical values from a field multiple times. For the duration of this transaction, updates made by other transactions to this field are prohibited. The dirty read and nonrepeatable read problems can be avoided, but the phantom read problem may still occur.
SERIALIZABLE	Ensures that a transaction can read identical rows from a table multiple times. For the duration of this transaction, inserts, updates, and deletes made by other transactions to this table are prohibited. All the concurrency problems can be avoided, but the performance will be low.

ℹ️ Transaction isolation is supported by the underlying database engine but not an application or a framework. However, not all database engines support all these isolation levels. You can change the isolation level of a JDBC connection by calling the `setTransactionIsolation()` method on the `java.sql.Connection` interface.

How It Works

To illustrate the problems caused by concurrent transactions, let's add two new operations to your bookshop for increasing and checking the book stock.

Listing 7-30. Modified BookShop interface

```java
package com.apress.spring6recipes.bookshop;

public interface BookShop {

    void purchase(String isbn, String username);
    void increaseStock(String isbn, int stock);
    int checkStock(String isbn);
}
```

Then, you implement these operations as follows. Note that these two operations must be declared as transactional.

Listing 7-31. Modified BookShop implementation

```
package com.apress.spring6recipes.bookshop;

import com.apress.spring6recipes.utils.Utils;
import org.springframework.jdbc.core.support.JdbcDaoSupport;
import org.springframework.transaction.annotation.Isolation;
import org.springframework.transaction.annotation.Transactional;

import javax.sql.DataSource;

public class JdbcBookShop extends JdbcDaoSupport implements BookShop {

  public JdbcBookShop(DataSource dataSource) {
    setDataSource(dataSource);
  }

  @Transactional
  public void purchase(String isbn, String username) {
    var BOOK_SQL = "SELECT PRICE FROM BOOK WHERE ISBN = ?";
    int price = getJdbcTemplate().queryForObject(BOOK_SQL, Integer.class, isbn);

    var STOCK_SQL = "UPDATE BOOK_STOCK SET STOCK = STOCK - 1 WHERE ISBN = ?";
    getJdbcTemplate().update(STOCK_SQL, isbn);

    var BALANCE_SQL = "UPDATE ACCOUNT SET BALANCE = BALANCE - ? WHERE USERNAME = ?";
    getJdbcTemplate().update(BALANCE_SQL, price, username);

  }

  @Transactional
  public void increaseStock(String isbn, int stock) {
    String threadName = Thread.currentThread().getName();
    System.out.println(threadName + " - Prepare to increase book stock");

    var STOCK_SQL = "UPDATE BOOK_STOCK SET STOCK = STOCK + ? WHERE ISBN = ?";
    getJdbcTemplate().update(STOCK_SQL, stock, isbn);

    System.out.println(threadName + " - Book stock increased by " + stock);
    sleep(threadName);

    System.out.println(threadName + " - Book stock rolled back");
    throw new RuntimeException("Increased by mistake");
  }

  @Transactional(isolation = Isolation.READ_UNCOMMITTED)
  public int checkStock(String isbn) {
    String threadName = Thread.currentThread().getName();
    System.out.println(threadName + " - Prepare to check book stock");
```

```
var STOCK_SQL = "SELECT STOCK FROM BOOK_STOCK WHERE ISBN = ?";
int stock = getJdbcTemplate().queryForObject(STOCK_SQL, Integer.class, isbn);

System.out.println(threadName + " - Book stock is " + stock);
sleep(threadName);

return stock;
}

private void sleep(String threadName) {
    System.out.println(threadName + " - Sleeping");
    Utils.sleep(10000);
    System.out.println(threadName + " - Wake up");
}

}
```

To simulate concurrency, your operations need to be executed by multiple threads. You can track the current status of the operations through the println statements. For each operation, you print a couple of messages to the console around the SQL statement's execution. The messages should include the thread name for you to know which thread is currently executing the operation.

After each operation executes the SQL statement, you ask the thread to sleep for 10 seconds. As you know, the transaction will be committed or rolled back immediately once the operation completes. Inserting a sleep statement can help postpone the commit or rollback. For the increase() operation, you eventually throw a RuntimeException to cause the transaction to roll back. Let's look at a simple client that runs these examples.

Before you start with the isolation level examples, enter the data from Tables 7-10 and 7-11 into your bookshop database. (Note that the ACCOUNT table isn't needed in this example.)

Table 7-10. *Sample Data in the BOOK Table for Testing Isolation Levels*

ISBN	BOOK_NAME	PRICE
0001	The First Book	30

Table 7-11. *Sample Data in the BOOK_STOCK Table for Testing Isolation Levels*

ISBN	STOCK
0001	10

The READ_UNCOMMITTED and READ_COMMITTED Isolation Levels

READ_UNCOMMITTED is the lowest isolation level that allows a transaction to read uncommitted changes made by other transactions. You can set this isolation level in the @Transaction annotation of your checkStock() method.

Listing 7-32. BookShop with isolation level READ_UNCOMMITTED

```
package com.apress.spring6recipes.bookshop.spring;
...
import org.springframework.transaction.annotation.Isolation;
import org.springframework.transaction.annotation.Transactional;

public class JdbcBookShop extends JdbcDaoSupport implements BookShop {
    ...
    @Transactional(isolation = Isolation.READ_UNCOMMITTED)
    public int checkStock(String isbn) {
        ...
    }
}
```

You can create some threads to experiment on this transaction isolation level. In the following Main
class, there are two threads you are going to create. Thread 1 increases the book stock, while thread 2 checks
the book stock. Thread 1 starts 5 seconds before thread 2.

Listing 7-33. Main class

```
package com.apress.spring6recipes.bookshop;

import com.apress.spring6recipes.bookshop.config.BookstoreConfiguration;
import com.apress.spring6recipes.utils.Utils;
import org.springframework.context.annotation.AnnotationConfigApplicationContext;

public class Main {

  public static void main(String[] args) {
    var cfg = BookstoreConfiguration.class;
    try (var context = new AnnotationConfigApplicationContext(cfg)) {

      var bookShop = context.getBean(BookShop.class);

      var thread1 = new Thread(() -> {
        try {
          bookShop.increaseStock("0001", 5);
        } catch (RuntimeException e) {
        }

      }, "Thread 1");

      var thread2 = new Thread(() -> bookShop.checkStock("0001"), "Thread 2");

      thread1.start();
      Utils.sleep(5000);
      thread2.start();

    }
  }

}
```

If you run the application, you will get the following result.

Listing 7-34. Console output

```
Thread 1 - Prepare to increase book stock
Thread 1 - Book stock increased by 5
Thread 1 - Sleeping
Thread 2 - Prepare to check book stock
Thread 2 - Book stock is 15
Thread 2 - Sleeping
Thread 1 - Wake up
Thread 1 - Book stock rolled back
Thread 2 - Wake up
```

First, thread 1 increased the book stock and then went to sleep. At that time, thread 1's transaction had not yet been rolled back. While thread 1 was sleeping, thread 2 started and attempted to read the book stock. With the READ_UNCOMMITTED isolation level, thread 2 would be able to read the stock value that had been updated by an uncommitted transaction.

However, when thread 1 woke up, its transaction was rolled back due to a RuntimeException, so the value read by thread 2 was temporary and invalid. This problem is known as dirty read, because a transaction may read values that are "dirty."

To avoid the dirty read problem, you should raise the isolation level of checkStock() to READ_COMMITTED.

Listing 7-35. BookShop with isolation level READ_COMMITTED

```
package com.apress.spring6recipes.bookshop.spring;
...
import org.springframework.transaction.annotation.Isolation;
import org.springframework.transaction.annotation.Transactional;

public class JdbcBookShop extends JdbcDaoSupport implements BookShop {
    ...
    @Transactional(isolation = Isolation.READ_COMMITTED)
    public int checkStock(String isbn) {
        ...
    }
}
```

If you run the application again, thread 2 won't be able to read the book stock until thread 1 has rolled back the transaction. In this way, the dirty read problem can be avoided by preventing a transaction from reading a field that has been updated by another uncommitted transaction.

Listing 7-36. Console output

```
Thread 1 - Prepare to increase book stock
Thread 1 - Book stock increased by 5
Thread 1 - Sleeping
Thread 2 - Prepare to check book stock
Thread 1 - Wake up
Thread 1 - Book stock rolled back
```

```
Thread 2 - Book stock is 10
Thread 2 - Sleeping
Thread 2 - Wake up
```

In order for the underlying database to support the READ_COMMITTED isolation level, it may acquire an update lock on a row that was updated but not yet committed. Then, other transactions must wait to read that row until the update lock is released, which happens when the locking transaction commits or rolls back.

The REPEATABLE_READ Isolation Level

Now, let's restructure the threads to demonstrate another concurrency problem. Swap the tasks of the two threads so that thread 1 checks the book stock before thread 2 increases the book stock.

Listing 7-37. Main class

```java
package com.apress.spring6recipes.bookshop;

import com.apress.spring6recipes.bookshop.config.BookstoreConfiguration;
import com.apress.spring6recipes.utils.Utils;
import org.springframework.context.annotation.AnnotationConfigApplicationContext;

public class Main {

  public static void main(String[] args) {
    try (var context = new AnnotationConfigApplicationContext(BookstoreConfiguration.
    class)) {

      var bookShop = context.getBean(BookShop.class);

      var thread1 = new Thread(() -> bookShop.checkStock("0001"), "Thread 1");

      var thread2 = new Thread(() -> {
        try {
          bookShop.increaseStock("0001", 5);
        } catch (RuntimeException e) {
        }
      }, "Thread 2");

      thread1.start();
      Utils.sleep(5000);
      thread2.start();

    }
  }
}
```

If you run the application, you will get the following result.

Listing 7-38. Console output

```
Thread 1 - Prepare to check book stock
Thread 1 - Book stock is 10
Thread 1 - Sleeping
Thread 2 - Prepare to increase book stock
Thread 2 - Book stock increased by 5
Thread 2 - Sleeping
Thread 1 - Wake up
Thread 2 - Wake up
Thread 2 - Book stock rolled back
```

First, thread 1 read the book stock and then went to sleep. At that time, thread 1's transaction had not yet been committed. While thread 1 was sleeping, thread 2 started and attempted to increase the book stock. With the READ_COMMITTED isolation level, thread 2 would be able to update the stock value that was read by an uncommitted transaction.

However, if thread 1 read the book stock again, the value would be different from its first read. This problem is known as nonrepeatable read because a transaction may read different values for the same field.

To avoid the nonrepeatable read problem, you should raise the isolation level of checkStock() to REPEATABLE_READ.

Listing 7-39. BookShop with isolation level REPEATABLE_READ

```
package com.apress.spring6recipes.bookshop.spring;
...
import org.springframework.transaction.annotation.Isolation;
import org.springframework.transaction.annotation.Transactional;

public class JdbcBookShop extends JdbcDaoSupport implements BookShop {
    ...
    @Transactional(isolation = Isolation.REPEATABLE_READ)
    public int checkStock(String isbn) {
        ...
    }
}
```

If you run the application again, thread 2 won't be able to update the book stock until thread 1 has committed the transaction. In this way, the nonrepeatable read problem can be avoided by preventing a transaction from updating a value that has been read by another uncommitted transaction.

Listing 7-40. Console output

```
Thread 1 - Prepare to check book stock
Thread 1 - Book stock is 10
Thread 1 - Sleeping
Thread 2 - Prepare to increase book stock
Thread 1 - Wake up
Thread 2 - Book stock increased by 5
Thread 2 - Sleeping
Thread 2 - Wake up
Thread 2 - Book stock rolled back
```

In order for the underlying database to support the REPEATABLE_READ isolation level, it may acquire a read lock on a row that was read but not yet committed. Then, other transactions must wait to update the row until the read lock is released, which happens when the locking transaction commits or rolls back.

The SERIALIZABLE Isolation Level

After a transaction has read several rows from a table, another transaction inserts new rows into the same table. If the first transaction reads the same table again, it will find additional rows that are different from the first read. This problem is known as phantom read. Actually, phantom read is very similar to nonrepeatable read but involves multiple rows.

To avoid the phantom read problem, you should raise the isolation level to the highest: SERIALIZABLE. Notice that this isolation level is the slowest because it may acquire a read lock on the full table. In practice, you should always choose the lowest isolation level that can satisfy your requirements.

7-8. Setting the Rollback Transaction Attribute

Problem

By default, only unchecked exceptions (i.e., of type RuntimeException and Error) will cause a transaction to roll back, while checked exceptions will not. Sometimes, you may wish to break this rule and set your own exceptions for rolling back.

Solution

The exceptions that cause a transaction to roll back or not can be specified by the rollback transaction attribute. Any exceptions not explicitly specified in this attribute will be handled by the default rollback rule (i.e., rolling back for unchecked exceptions and not rolling back for checked exceptions).

How It Works

A transaction's rollback rule can be defined in the @Transactional annotation via the rollbackFor and noRollbackFor attributes. These two attributes are declared as Class[], so you can specify more than one exception for each attribute.

Listing 7-41. BookShop with @Transactional attributes

```
package com.apress.spring6recipes.bookshop.spring;
...
import org.springframework.transaction.annotation.Propagation;
import org.springframework.transaction.annotation.Transactional;
import java.io.IOException;

public class JdbcBookShop extends JdbcDaoSupport implements BookShop {
    ...
    @Transactional(
            propagation = Propagation.REQUIRES_NEW,
            rollbackFor = IOException.class,
            noRollbackFor = ArithmeticException.class)
```

```
    public void purchase(String isbn, String username) throws Exception{
        throw new ArithmeticException();
    }
}
```

7-9. Setting the Timeout and Read-Only Transaction Attributes

Problem

Because a transaction may acquire locks on rows and tables, a long transaction will tie up resources and have an impact on overall performance. Besides, if a transaction only reads but does not update data, the database engine could optimize this transaction. You can specify these attributes to increase the performance of your application.

Solution

The timeout transaction attribute (an integer that describes seconds) indicates how long your transaction can survive before it is forced to roll back. This can prevent a long transaction from tying up resources. The read-only attribute indicates that this transaction will only read but not update data. The read-only flag is just a hint to enable a resource to optimize the transaction, and a resource might not necessarily cause a failure if a write is attempted.

How It Works

The timeout and read-only transaction attributes can be defined in the @Transactional annotation. Note that timeout is measured in seconds.

Listing 7-42. BookShop with @Transactional attributes timeout/read-only

```
package com.apress.spring6recipes.bookshop.spring;
...
import org.springframework.transaction.annotation.Isolation;
import org.springframework.transaction.annotation.Transactional;

public class JdbcBookShop extends JdbcDaoSupport implements BookShop {
    ...
    @Transactional(
            isolation = Isolation.REPEATABLE_READ,
            timeout = 30,
            readOnly = true)
    public int checkStock(String isbn) {
        ...
    }
}
```

7-10. Managing Transactions with Load-Time Weaving

Problem

By default, Spring's declarative transaction management is enabled via its AOP framework. However, as Spring AOP can only advise public methods of beans declared in the IoC container, you are restricted to managing transactions within this scope using Spring AOP. Sometimes, you may wish to manage transactions for nonpublic methods or methods of objects created outside the Spring IoC container (e.g., domain objects).

Solution

Spring provides an AspectJ aspect named AnnotationTransactionAspect that can manage transactions for any methods of any objects, even if the methods are nonpublic or the objects are created outside the Spring IoC container. This aspect will manage transactions for any methods with the @Transactional annotation. You can choose either AspectJ's compile-time weaving or load-time weaving to enable this aspect.

How It Works

To weave this aspect into your domain classes at load time, you have to put the @EnableLoadTimeWeaving annotation on your configuration class. To enable Spring's AnnotationTransactionAspect for transaction management, you just define the @EnableTransactionManagement annotation and set its mode attribute to ASPECTJ. The @EnableTransactionManagement annotation takes two values for the mode attribute: ASPECTJ and PROXY. ASPECTJ stipulates that the container should use load-time or compile-time weaving to enable the transaction advice. This requires the spring-instrument jar to be in the classpath, as well as the appropriate configuration at load time or compile time.

Alternatively, PROXY stipulates that the container should use the Spring AOP mechanisms. It's important to note that the ASPECTJ mode doesn't support configuration of the @Transactional annotation on interfaces. Then the transaction aspect will automatically get enabled. You also have to provide a transaction manager for this aspect. By default, it will look for a transaction manager whose name is transactionManager.

Listing 7-43. Bookstore configuration for load-time weaving

```
package com.apress.spring6recipes.bookshop;

@Configuration
@EnableTransactionManagement(mode = AdviceMode.ASPECTJ)
@EnableLoadTimeWeaving
public class BookstoreConfiguration { ... }
```

ℹ️ To use the Spring aspect library for AspectJ, you have to include the spring-aspects module in your CLASSPATH. To enable load-time weaving, we also have to include a java agent; this is available in the spring-instrument module.

For a simple Java application, you can weave this aspect into your classes at load time with the Spring agent specified as a VM argument.

Listing 7-44. Shell command to execute

```
java -javaagent:lib/spring-instrument-6.0.3.RELEASE.jar -jar recipe_7_10_i.jar
```

7-11. Summary

This chapter discussed transactions and why you should use them. You explored the approach taken for transaction management historically in Jakarta EE and then learned how the approach the Spring Framework offers differs. You explored explicit use of transactions in your code as well as implicit use with annotation-driven aspects. You set up a database and used transactions to enforce valid state in the database.

In the next chapter, you will explore Spring Batch. Spring Batch provides infrastructure and components that can be used as the foundation for batch processing jobs.

CHAPTER 8

■ ■ ■

Spring Batch

Batch processing has been around for decades. The earliest widespread applications of technology for managing information (information technology) were applications of batch processing. These environments didn't have interactive sessions and usually didn't have the capability to load multiple applications in memory. Computers were expensive and bore no resemblance to today's servers. Typically, machines were multiuser and in use during the day (time-shared). During the evening, however, the machines would sit idle, which was a tremendous waste. Businesses invested in ways to utilize the offline time to do work aggregated through the course of the day. Out of this practice emerged batch processing.

Batch processing solutions typically run offline, indifferent to events in the system. In the past, batch processes ran offline out of necessity. Today, however, most batch processes are run offline because having work done at a predictable time and having chunks of work done is a requirement for a lot of architectures. A batch processing solution doesn't usually respond to requests, although there's no reason it couldn't be started as a consequence of a message or request. Batch processing solutions tend to be used on large datasets where the duration of the processing is a critical factor in its architecture and implementation. A process might run for minutes, hours, or days! Jobs may have unbounded durations (i.e., run until all work is finished, even if this means running for a few days), or they may be strictly bounded (jobs must proceed in constant time, with each row taking the same amount of time regardless of bound, which lets you, say, predict that a given job will finish in a certain time window).

Batch processing has had a long history that informs even modern batch processing solutions.

Mainframe applications used batch processing, and one of the largest modern-day environments for batch processing, CICS on z/OS, is still fundamentally a mainframe operating system. Customer Information Control System (CICS) is very well suited to a particular type of task: take input, process it, and write it to output. CICS is a transaction server used most in financial institutions and government that runs programs in a number of languages (COBOL, C, PLI, etc.). It can easily support thousands of transactions per second. CICS was one of the first containers, a concept familiar to Spring and Jakarta EE users, even though CICS itself debuted in 1969! A CICS installation is very expensive, and although IBM still sells and installs CICS, many other solutions have come along since then. These solutions are usually specific to a particular environment: COBOL/CICS on mainframes, C on Unix, and, today, Java on any number of environments. The problem is that there's very little standardized infrastructure for dealing with these types of batch processing solutions. Very few people are even aware of what they're missing because there's very little native support on the Java platform for batch processing. Businesses that need a solution typically end up writing it in-house, resulting in fragile, domain-specific code.

The pieces are there, however: transaction support, fast I/O, schedulers such as Quartz, and solid threading support, as well as a very powerful concept of an application container in Jakarta EE and Spring. It was only natural that Dave Syer and his team would come along and build Spring Batch, a batch processing solution for the Spring platform.

© Marten Deinum, Daniel Rubio, Josh Long 2023
M. Deinum et al., *Spring 6 Recipes*, https://doi.org/10.1007/978-1-4842-8649-4_8

It's important to think about the kinds of problems this framework solves before diving into the details. A technology is defined by its solution space. A typical Spring Batch application typically reads in a lot of data and then writes it back out in a modified form. Decisions about transactional barriers, input size, concurrency, and order of steps in processing are all dimensions of a typical integration.

A common requirement is loading data from a comma-separated value (CSV) file, perhaps as a business-to-business (B2B) transaction, perhaps as an integration technique with an older legacy application. Another common application is nontrivial processing on records in a database. Perhaps the output is an update of the database record itself. An example might be resizing of images on the file system whose metadata is stored in a database or needing to trigger another process based on some condition.

ⓘ Fixed-width data is a format of rows and cells, quite like a CSV file. CSV file cells are separated by commas or tabs however, and fixed-width data works by presuming certain lengths for each value. The first value might be the first nine characters, the second value the next four characters after that, and so on.

Fixed-width data, which is often used with legacy or embedded systems, is a fine candidate for batch processing. Processing that deals with a resource that's fundamentally non-transactional (e.g., a web service or a file) begs for batch processing, because batch processing provides retry/skip/fail functionality that most web services will not.

It's also important to understand what Spring Batch doesn't do. Spring Batch is a flexible but not all-encompassing solution. Just as Spring doesn't reinvent the wheel when it can be avoided, Spring Batch leaves a few important pieces to the discretion of the implementor. Case in point: Spring Batch provides a generic mechanism by which to launch a job, be it by the command line, a Unix cron, an operating system service, or Quartz (discussed in Chapter 10) or in response to an event on an enterprise service bus (ESB) (e.g., the Mule ESB or Spring's own ESB-like solution, Spring Integration, which is discussed in Chapter 12). Another example is the way Spring Batch manages the state of batch processes. Spring Batch requires a durable store. The only useful implementation of a JobRepository (an interface provided by Spring Batch for storing runtime data) requires a database, because a database is transactional and there's no need to reinvent it. To which database you should deploy, however, is largely unspecified, although there are useful defaults provided for you, of course.

8-1. Runtime Metadata Model

Spring Batch works with a JobRepository, which is the keeper of all the knowledge and metadata for each job (including component parts such as JobInstances, JobExecution, and StepExecution). Each Job is composed of one or more Steps, one after another. With Spring Batch, a Step can conditionally follow another Step, allowing for primitive workflows.

These steps can also be concurrent: two steps can run at the same time.

When a job is run, it's often coupled with JobParameters to parameterize the behavior of the Job itself. For example, a job might take a date parameter to determine which records to process. This coupling is called a JobInstance. A JobInstance is unique because of the JobParameters associated with it. Each time the same JobInstance (i.e., the same Job and JobParameters) is run, it's called a JobExecution. This is a runtime context for a version of the Job. Ideally, for every JobInstance there'd be only one JobExecution: the JobExecution that was created the first time the JobInstance ran. However, if there were any errors, the JobInstance should be restarted; the subsequent run would create another JobExecution. For every step in the original job, there is a StepExecution in the JobExecution.

Thus, you can see that Spring Batch has a mirrored object graph, one reflecting the design/build time view of a job and another reflecting the runtime view of a job. This split between the prototype and the instance is very similar to the way many workflow engines—including jBPM—work.

For example, suppose that a daily report is generated at 2 AM. The parameter to the job would be the date (most likely the previous day's date). The job, in this case, would model a loading step, a summary step, and an output step. Each day the job is run, a new JobInstance and JobExecution would be created. If there are any retries of the same JobInstance, conceivably many JobExecutions would be created.

8-2. Setting Up Spring Batch's Infrastructure

Problem

Spring Batch provides a lot of flexibility and guarantees to your application, but it cannot work in a vacuum. To do its work, the JobRepository requires a database. Additionally, there are several collaborators required for Spring Batch to do its work. This configuration is mostly boilerplate.

Solution

In this recipe, you'll set up the Spring Batch database and also create a Spring application configuration that can be imported by subsequent solutions. This configuration is repetitive and largely uninteresting. It will also tell Spring Batch what database to use for the metadata it stores.

How It Works

The JobRepository interface is the first thing that you'll have to deal with when setting up a Spring Batch process. You usually don't deal with it in code, but in Spring configuration it is key to getting everything else working. There's only one really useful implementation of the JobRepository interface called SimpleJobRepository, which stores information about the state of the batch processes in a database. Creation is done through a JobRepositoryFactoryBean. Another standard factory, MapJobRepositoryFactoryBean, is useful mainly for testing because its state is not durable–it's an in-memory implementation. Both factories create an instance of SimpleJobRepository.

Because this JobRepository instance works on your database, you need to set up the schema for Spring Batch to work with. The schemas for different databases are in the Spring Batch distribution. The simplest way to initialize your database is to use a DataSourceInitializer in Java Config. The files can be found in the org/springframework/batch/core directory. There are several .sql files, each containing the data definition language (DDL, the subset of SQL used for defining and examining the structure of a database) for the required schema for the database of your choice. In these examples, we will use H2, so we will use the DDL for H2: schema-h2.sql. Make sure you configure it and tell Spring Batch about it as in the following configuration.

Listing 8-1. Batch configuration with explicit defaults

```
@ComponentScan("com.apress.spring6recipes.springbatch")
@PropertySource("classpath:batch.properties")
public class BatchConfiguration {

    @Bean
    public DataSource dataSource(Environment env) {
        var dataSource = new DriverManagerDataSource();
        dataSource.setUrl(env.getRequiredProperty("datasource.url"));
```

```java
    dataSource.setUsername(env.getRequiredProperty("datasource.username"));
    dataSource.setPassword(env.getRequiredProperty("datasource.password"));
    return dataSource;
}

@Bean
public DataSourceInitializer dataSourceInitializer(
        DataSource dataSource,
        DatabasePopulator databasePopulator) {
    var initializer = new DataSourceInitializer();
    initializer.setDataSource(dataSource);
    initializer.setDatabasePopulator(databasePopulator);
    return initializer;
}

@Bean
public DatabasePopulator databasePopulator() {
    var databasePopulator = new ResourceDatabasePopulator();
    databasePopulator.setContinueOnError(true);
    databasePopulator.addScript(
            new ClassPathResource("org/springframework/batch/core/schema-h2.sql"));
    databasePopulator.addScript(
            new ClassPathResource("sql/reset_user_registration.sql"));
    return databasePopulator;
}

@Bean
public DataSourceTransactionManager transactionManager(DataSource dataSource) {
    return new DataSourceTransactionManager(dataSource);
}

@Bean
public JobRepositoryFactoryBean jobRepository(
        DataSource dataSource,
        PlatformTransactionManager transactionManager) {
    var jobRepositoryFactoryBean = new JobRepositoryFactoryBean();
    jobRepositoryFactoryBean.setDataSource(dataSource);
    jobRepositoryFactoryBean.setTransactionManager(transactionManager);
    return jobRepositoryFactoryBean;
}

@Bean
public TaskExecutorJobLauncher jobLauncher(JobRepository jobRepository) {
    var jobLauncher = new TaskExecutorJobLauncher();
    jobLauncher.setJobRepository(jobRepository);
    return jobLauncher;
}
```

```
@Bean
public JobRegistryBeanPostProcessor jobRegistryBeanPostProcessor(
        JobRegistry jobRegistry) {
  var jobRegistryBeanPostProcessor = new JobRegistryBeanPostProcessor();
  jobRegistryBeanPostProcessor.setJobRegistry(jobRegistry);
  return jobRegistryBeanPostProcessor;
}
```

The first few beans are related strictly to configuration—nothing particularly novel or peculiar to Spring Batch: a data source, a transaction manager, and a data source initializer.

Eventually, we get to the declaration of a MapJobRegistry instance. This is critical—it is the central store for information regarding a given job, and it controls the "big picture" about all jobs in the system. Everything else works with this instance.

Next, we have a TaskExecutorJobLauncher, whose sole purpose is to give you a mechanism to launch batch jobs, where a "job" in this case is our batch solution. The jobLauncher is used to specify the name of the batch solution to run as well as any parameters required. We'll follow up more on that in the next recipe.

Next, you define a JobRegistryBeanPostProcessor. This bean scans your Spring context file and associates any configured jobs with the MapJobRegistry.

Finally, we get to the SimpleJobRepository (that is, in turn, created by the JobRepositoryFactoryBean). The JobRepository is an implementation of "repository" (in the patterns of enterprise application architecture sense of the word): it handles persistence and retrieval for the domain models surrounding steps, jobs, and so on.

The @PropertySource annotation will instruct Spring to load our batch.properties file. The properties we need we are going to retrieve using the Environment class. The batch.properties contains the following.

💡 We could have also used a @Value annotation to inject all individual properties, but when needing multiple properties in a configuration class, it is easier to use the Environment object.

Listing 8-2. Database properties

```
datasource.password=sa
datasource.username=
datasource.url=jdbc:h2:~/batch
```

Although this works, Spring Batch also has support to configure these defaults out of the box using the @EnableBatchProcessing annotation. This makes things a little easier.

Listing 8-3. Batch configuration with implicit defaults

```
@Configuration
@EnableBatchProcessing
@ComponentScan("com.apress.spring6recipes.springbatch")
@PropertySource("classpath:/batch.properties")
public class BatchConfiguration {

  @Bean
  public DataSource dataSource(Environment env) {
    var dataSource = new DriverManagerDataSource();
```

```
    dataSource.setUrl(env.getRequiredProperty("datasource.url"));
    dataSource.setUsername(env.getProperty("datasource.username"));
    dataSource.setPassword(env.getProperty("datasource.password"));
    return dataSource;
}

@Bean
public DataSourceTransactionManager transactionManager(DataSource dataSource) {
    return new DataSourceTransactionManager(dataSource);
}

@Bean
public DataSourceInitializer databasePopulator(DataSource dataSource) {
    var populator = new ResourceDatabasePopulator();
    populator.addScript(
            new ClassPathResource("org/springframework/batch/core/schema-h2.sql"));
    populator.addScript(
            new ClassPathResource("sql/reset_user_registration.sql"));
    populator.setContinueOnError(true);
    populator.setIgnoreFailedDrops(true);
```

This class only contains three bean definitions: one for the data source, one for the transaction manager, and one for initializing the database. Everything else is taken care of due to the @EnableBatchProcessing annotation. The preceding configuration class will bootstrap Spring Batch with some sensible defaults.

The default configuration will configure a JobRepository, JobRegistry, and JobLauncher.

If there are multiple data sources in your application, you need to add an explicit BatchConfigurer to select the data source to use for the batch part of your application.

The following Main class will use the Java-based configuration for running the batch application.

Listing 8-4. Main class

```
package com.apress.spring6recipes.springbatch;

import com.apress.spring6recipes.springbatch.config.BatchConfiguration;
import org.springframework.batch.core.configuration.JobRegistry;
import org.springframework.batch.core.launch.JobLauncher;
import org.springframework.batch.core.repository.JobRepository;
import org.springframework.context.annotation.AnnotationConfigApplicationContext;

public class Main {
  public static void main(String[] args) {

    var cfg = BatchConfiguration.class;
    try (var context = new AnnotationConfigApplicationContext(cfg)) {

      var jobRegistry = context.getBean("jobRegistry", JobRegistry.class);
      var jobLauncher = context.getBean("jobLauncher", JobLauncher.class);
      var jobRepository = context.getBean("jobRepository", JobRepository.class);
```

```
        System.out.println("JobRegistry: " + jobRegistry);
        System.out.println("JobLauncher: " + jobLauncher);
        System.out.println("JobRepository: " + jobRepository);
    }
  }
}
```

8-3. Reading and Writing

Problem

You want to insert data from a file into a database. This solution will be one of the simplest solutions and will give you a chance to explore the moving pieces of a typical solution.

Solution

You'll build a solution that does a minimal amount of work while being a viable application of the technology. The solution will read in a file of arbitrary length and write out the data into a database. The end result will be almost 100 percent code-free. You will rely on an existing model class and write one class (a class containing the public static void main(String [] args() method) to round out the example. There's no reason the model class couldn't be a Hibernate class or something from your DAO layer, though in this case it's a brainless POJO. This solution will use the components we configured in Recipe 8-1.

How It Works

This example demonstrates the simplest possible use of Spring Batch: to provide scalability. This program will do nothing but read data from a CSV file, with fields delimited by commas and rows delimited by new lines. It then inserts the records into a table. You are exploiting the intelligent infrastructure that Spring Batch provides to avoid worrying about scaling. This application could easily be done manually. You will not exploit any of the smart transactional functionality made available to you, nor will you worry about retries for the time being.

This solution is as simple as Spring Batch solutions get. Spring Batch models solutions using XML schema. The abstractions and terms are in the spirit of classical batch processing solutions so will be portable from previous technologies and perhaps to subsequent technologies. Spring Batch provides useful default classes that you can override or selectively adjust. In the following example, you'll use a lot of the utility implementations provided by Spring Batch. Fundamentally, most solutions look about the same and feature a combination of the same set of interfaces. It's usually just a matter of picking and choosing the right ones.

When I ran this program, it worked on files with 20,000 rows, and it worked on files with 1 million rows. I experienced no increase in memory, which indicates there were no memory leaks. Naturally, it took a lot longer! (The application ran for several hours with the 1-million-row insert.)

Of course, it would be catastrophic if you worked with a million rows and it failed on the penultimate record, because you'd lose all your work when the transaction rolled back! Read on for examples on chunking. Additionally, you might want to read through Chapter 7 to brush up on transactions.

Listing 8-5. User registration SQL

```
create table USER_REGISTRATION
(
  ID BIGINT NOT NULL PRIMARY KEY GENERATED ALWAYS AS IDENTITY (START WITH 1,
INCREMENT BY 1),
  FIRST_NAME VARCHAR(255) not null,
  LAST_NAME VARCHAR(255) not null,
  COMPANY VARCHAR(255) not null,
  ADDRESS VARCHAR(255) not null,
  CITY VARCHAR(255) not null,
  STATE VARCHAR(255) not null,
  ZIP VARCHAR(255) not null,
  COUNTY VARCHAR(255) not null,
  URL VARCHAR(255) not null,
  PHONE_NUMBER VARCHAR(255) not null,
  FAX VARCHAR(255) not null
) ;
```

DATA LOADS AND DATA WAREHOUSES

I didn't tune the table at all. For example, there are no indexes on any of the columns besides the primary key. This is to avoid complicating the example. Great care should be taken with a table like this one in a nontrivial, production-bound application.

Spring Batch applications are workhorse applications and have the potential to reveal bottlenecks in your application you didn't know you had. Imagine suddenly being able to achieve 1 million new database insertions every 10 minutes. Would your database grind to a halt? Insert speed can be a critical factor in the speed of your application. Software developers will (hopefully) think about their database schema in terms of how well it enforces the constraints of the business logic and how well it serves the overall business model. However, it's important to wear another hat, that of a DBA, when writing applications such as this one. A common solution is to create a denormalized table whose contents can be coerced into valid data once inside the database, perhaps by a trigger on inserts. This is typical in data warehousing. Later, you'll explore using Spring Batch to do processing on a record before insertion. This lets the developer verify or override the input into the database. This processing, in tandem with a conservative application of constraints that are best expressed in the database, can make for applications that are very robust and quick.

The Job Configuration

The configuration for the job is as follows.

Listing 8-6. User job definition

```
package com.apress.spring6recipes.springbatch.config;

import com.apress.spring6recipes.springbatch.UserRegistration;
import org.springframework.batch.core.Job;
import org.springframework.batch.core.Step;
import org.springframework.batch.core.job.builder.JobBuilder;
import org.springframework.batch.core.repository.JobRepository;
import org.springframework.batch.core.step.builder.StepBuilder;
import org.springframework.batch.item.ItemReader;
import org.springframework.batch.item.ItemWriter;
import org.springframework.batch.item.database.BeanPropertyItemSqlParameterSourceProvider;
import org.springframework.batch.item.database.JdbcBatchItemWriter;
import org.springframework.batch.item.file.FlatFileItemReader;
import org.springframework.batch.item.file.LineMapper;
import org.springframework.batch.item.file.mapping.BeanWrapperFieldSetMapper;
import org.springframework.batch.item.file.mapping.DefaultLineMapper;
import org.springframework.batch.item.file.mapping.FieldSetMapper;
import org.springframework.batch.item.file.transform.DelimitedLineTokenizer;
import org.springframework.batch.item.file.transform.LineTokenizer;
import org.springframework.beans.factory.annotation.Value;
import org.springframework.context.annotation.Bean;
import org.springframework.context.annotation.Configuration;
import org.springframework.core.io.Resource;
import org.springframework.transaction.PlatformTransactionManager;

import javax.sql.DataSource;

@Configuration
public class UserJob {

  private static final String INSERT_REGISTRATION_QUERY = """
          insert into USER_REGISTRATION (FIRST_NAME, LAST_NAME, COMPANY, ADDRESS,CITY,STATE,
          ZIP,COUNTY,URL,PHONE_NUMBER,FAX)
          values
          (:firstName,:lastName,:company,:address,:city,:state,:zip,:county,:url,
          :phoneNumber,:fax)""";

  private final JobRepository jobRepository;

  @Value("file:${user.home}/batches/registrations.csv")
  private Resource input;

  public UserJob(JobRepository jobRepository) {
    this.jobRepository = jobRepository;
  }
```

```
@Bean
public Job insertIntoDbFromCsvJob(Step step1) {
  var name = "User Registration Import Job";
  var builder = new JobBuilder(name, jobRepository);
  return builder.start(step1).build();
}


@Bean
public Step step1(ItemReader<UserRegistration> reader,
                  ItemWriter<UserRegistration> writer,
                  PlatformTransactionManager txManager) {
  var name = "User Registration CSV To DB Step";
  var builder = new StepBuilder(name, jobRepository);
  return builder
          .<UserRegistration, UserRegistration>chunk(5, txManager)
          .reader(reader)
          .writer(writer)
          .build();
}


@Bean
public FlatFileItemReader<UserRegistration> csvFileReader(
        LineMapper<UserRegistration> lineMapper) {
  var itemReader = new FlatFileItemReader<UserRegistration>();
  itemReader.setLineMapper(lineMapper);
  itemReader.setResource(input);
  return itemReader;
}


@Bean
public DefaultLineMapper<UserRegistration> lineMapper(LineTokenizer tokenizer,
                                                     FieldSetMapper<UserRegistration>
                                                     mapper) {
  var lineMapper = new DefaultLineMapper<UserRegistration>();
  lineMapper.setLineTokenizer(tokenizer);
  lineMapper.setFieldSetMapper(mapper);
  return lineMapper;
}


@Bean
public BeanWrapperFieldSetMapper<UserRegistration> fieldSetMapper() {
  var fieldSetMapper = new BeanWrapperFieldSetMapper<UserRegistration>();
  fieldSetMapper.setTargetType(UserRegistration.class);
  return fieldSetMapper;
}


@Bean
public DelimitedLineTokenizer tokenizer() {
  var tokenizer = new DelimitedLineTokenizer();
  tokenizer.setDelimiter(",");
```

```
    tokenizer.setNames("firstName", "lastName", "company", "address", "city",
                    "state", "zip", "county", "url", "phoneNumber", "fax");
    return tokenizer;
  }

  @Bean
  public JdbcBatchItemWriter<UserRegistration> jdbcItemWriter(DataSource dataSource) {
    var provider = new BeanPropertyItemSqlParameterSourceProvider<UserRegistration>();
    var itemWriter = new JdbcBatchItemWriter<UserRegistration>();
    itemWriter.setDataSource(dataSource);
    itemWriter.setSql(INSERT_REGISTRATION_QUERY);
    itemWriter.setItemSqlParameterSourceProvider(provider);
    return itemWriter;
  }
}
```

As described earlier, a job consists of steps, which are the real workhorse of a given job. The steps can be as complex or as simple as you like. Indeed, a step could be considered the smallest unit of work for a job. Input (what's read) is passed to the Step and potentially processed; then output (what's written) is created from the step. This processing is spelled out using a Tasklet. You can provide your own Tasklet implementation or simply use some of the preconfigured configurations for different processing scenarios. These implementations are made available in terms of subelements of the Tasklet element. One of the most important aspects of batch processing is chunk-oriented processing, which is employed here using the chunk configuration method.

In chunk-oriented processing, input is read from a reader, optionally processed, and then aggregated. Finally, at a configurable interval—as specified by the commit interval attribute to configure how many items will be processed before the transaction is committed—all the input is sent to the writer. If there is a transaction manager in play, the transaction is also committed. Right before a commit, the metadata in the database is updated to mark the progress of the job.

There are some nuances surrounding the aggregation of the input (read) values when a transaction-aware writer (or processor) rolls back. Spring Batch caches the values it reads and writes them to the writer. If the writer component is transactional, like a database, and the reader is not, there's nothing inherently wrong with caching the read values and perhaps retrying or taking some alternative approach. If the reader itself is also transactional, then the values read from the resource will be rolled back and could conceivably change, rendering the in-memory cached values stale. If this happens, you can configure the chunk to not cache the values using reader-transactional-queue="true" on the chunk element.

Input

The first responsibility is reading a file from the file system. You use a provided implementation for the example. Reading CSV files is a very common scenario, and Spring Batch's support does not disappoint. The org.springframework.batch.item.file.FlatFileItemReader<T> class delegates the task of delimiting fields and records within a file to a LineMapper<T>, which in turn delegates the task of identifying the fields within that record to LineTokenizer. You use a org.springframework.batch.item.file.transform. DelimitedLineTokenizer, which is configured to delineate fields separated by a "," character.

The DefaultLineMapper also declares a fieldSetMapper attribute that requires an implementation of FieldSetMapper. This bean is responsible for taking the input name/value pairs and producing a type that will be given to the writer component.

In this case, you use a BeanWrapperFieldSetMapper that will create a JavaBean POJO of type UserRegistration. You name the fields so that you can reference them later in the configuration. These names don't have to be the values of some header row in the input file; they just have to correspond to the order in which the fields are found in the input file. These names are also used by the FieldSetMapper to match properties on a POJO. As each record is read, the values are applied to an instance of a POJO, and that POJO is returned.

Listing 8-7. User job definition–CSV item reader

```
@Bean
public FlatFileItemReader<UserRegistration> csvFileReader(
        LineMapper<UserRegistration> lineMapper) {
  var itemReader = new FlatFileItemReader<UserRegistration>();
  itemReader.setLineMapper(lineMapper);
  itemReader.setResource(input);
  return itemReader;
}


@Bean
public DefaultLineMapper<UserRegistration> lineMapper(LineTokenizer tokenizer,
                                          FieldSetMapper<UserRegistration>
                                          mapper) {
  var lineMapper = new DefaultLineMapper<UserRegistration>();
  lineMapper.setLineTokenizer(tokenizer);
  lineMapper.setFieldSetMapper(mapper);
  return lineMapper;
}


@Bean
public BeanWrapperFieldSetMapper<UserRegistration> fieldSetMapper() {
  var fieldSetMapper = new BeanWrapperFieldSetMapper<UserRegistration>();
  fieldSetMapper.setTargetType(UserRegistration.class);
  return fieldSetMapper;
}

@Bean
public DelimitedLineTokenizer tokenizer() {
  var tokenizer = new DelimitedLineTokenizer();
  tokenizer.setDelimiter(",");
  tokenizer.setNames("firstName", "lastName", "company", "address", "city",
                      "state", "zip", "county", "url", "phoneNumber", "fax");
  return tokenizer;
}
```

The class returned from the reader, UserRegistration, is a rather plain Java record.

Listing 8-8. UserRegistration class

```
package com.apress.spring6recipes.springbatch;

public record UserRegistration(

        String firstName,
        String lastName,
        String company,
```

```
        String address,
        String city,
        String stat,
        String zip,
        String county,
        String url,
        String phoneNumber,
        String fax) {
}
```

Output

The next component to do work is the writer, which is responsible for taking the aggregated collection of items read from the reader. In this case, you might imagine that a new collection (`java.util.List<UserRegistration>`) is created, then written, and then reset each time the collection exceeds the commit interval attribute on the chunk element. Because you're trying to write to a database, you use Spring Batch's `org.springframework.batch.item.database.JdbcBatchItemWriter`. This class contains support for taking input and writing it to a database. It is up to the developer to provide the input and to specify what SQL should be run for the input. It will run the SQL specified by the sql property, in essence reading from the database, as many times as specified by the chunk element's commit interval, and then commit the whole transaction. Here, you're doing a simple insert. The names and values for the named parameters are being created by the bean configured for the `itemSqlParameterSourceProvider` property, an instance of `BeanPropertyItemSqlParameterSourceProvider`, whose sole job it is to take JavaBean properties and make them available as named parameters corresponding to the property name on the JavaBean.

Listing 8-9. User job definition–JDBC item writer

```
@Bean
public JdbcBatchItemWriter<UserRegistration> jdbcItemWriter(DataSource dataSource) {
  var provider = new BeanPropertyItemSqlParameterSourceProvider<UserRegistration>();
  var itemWriter = new JdbcBatchItemWriter<UserRegistration>();
  itemWriter.setDataSource(dataSource);
  itemWriter.setSql(INSERT_REGISTRATION_QUERY);
  itemWriter.setItemSqlParameterSourceProvider(provider);
  return itemWriter;
}
```

And that's it! A working solution. With little configuration and no custom code, you've built a solution for taking large CSV files and reading them into a database. This solution is bare-bones and leaves a lot of edge cases uncared for. You might want to do processing on the item as it's read (before it's inserted), for example.

This exemplifies a simple job. It's important to remember that there are similar classes for doing the exact opposite transformation: reading from a database and writing to a CSV file.

Listing 8-10. User job definition–Job and Step

```
@Bean
public Job insertIntoDbFromCsvJob(Step step1) {
  var name = "User Registration Import Job";
  var builder = new JobBuilder(name, jobRepository);
  return builder.start(step1).build();
}


@Bean
public Step step1(ItemReader<UserRegistration> reader,
                  ItemWriter<UserRegistration> writer,
                  PlatformTransactionManager txManager) {
  var name = "User Registration CSV To DB Step";
  var builder = new StepBuilder(name, jobRepository);
  return builder
        .<UserRegistration, UserRegistration>chunk(5, txManager)
        .reader(reader)
        .writer(writer)
        .build();
}
```

To configure the step, we give it the name User Registration CSV To DB Step. We are using chunk-based processing, and we need to tell it that we want a chunk size of 5. Next, we supply it with a reader and writer, and finally we tell the builder to build the step. The configured step is finally wired as a starting point to our job, named User Registration Import Job, which consists only of this step.

Simplifying the ItemReader and ItemWriter Configurations

Configuring the ItemReader and ItemWriter can be a daunting task. You need to know quite a lot of the internals of Spring Batch (which classes to use and so on). As of Spring Batch 4, configuring the readers and writers has become easier as there are now specific builders for the different readers and writers.

To configure the FlatFileItemReader, one could use the FlatFileItemReaderBuilder, and instead of configuring four individual beans, it is now six lines of code (mainly due to the formatting in the sample).

Listing 8-11. User job definition–CSV item reader

```
@Bean
public FlatFileItemReader<UserRegistration> csvFileReader() {
  var names = new String[] {
          "firstName", "lastName", "company", "address", "city",
          "state", "zip", "county", "url", "phoneNumber", "fax"
  };
  return new FlatFileItemReaderBuilder<UserRegistration>()
          .name(ClassUtils.getShortName(FlatFileItemReader.class))
          .resource(input)
          .targetType(UserRegistration.class)
          .delimited()
          .names(names)
          .build();
}
```

This builder will automatically create the DefaultLineMapper, BeanWrapperFieldSetMapper, and DelimitedLineTokenizer, and you don't have to know that they are used internally. You can now basically describe your configuration rather than explicitly configure all the different items.

The same can be applied to the JdbcBatchItemWriter using the JdbcBatchItemWriterBuilder.

Listing 8-12. User job definition–JDBC item writer

```
@Bean
public JdbcBatchItemWriter<UserRegistration> jdbcItemWriter(DataSource dataSource) {
    return new JdbcBatchItemWriterBuilder<UserRegistration>()
            .dataSource(dataSource)
            .sql(INSERT_REGISTRATION_QUERY)
            .beanMapped()
            .build();
}
```

8-4. Writing a Custom ItemWriter and ItemReader

Problem

You want to talk to a resource (you might imagine an RSS feed or any other custom data format) that Spring Batch doesn't know how to connect to.

Solution

You can easily write your own ItemWriter or ItemReader. The interfaces are drop-dead simple, and there's not a lot of responsibility placed on the implementations.

How It Works

As easy and trivial as this process is to do, it's still not better than just reusing any of the numerous provided options. If you look, you'll likely find something. There's support for writing JMS (JmsItemWriter), JPA (JpaItemWriter), JDBC (JdbcBatchItemWriter), files (FlatFileItemWriter), Hibernate (HibernateItemWriter), and more. There's even support for writing by invoking a method on a bean (PropertyExtractingDelegatingItemWriter) and passing to it as arguments the properties on the item to be written! One of the more useful writers lets you write to a set of files that are numbered. This implementation—MultiResourceItemWriter<T>—delegates to other proper ItemWriter<T> implementations for the work, but lets you write to multiple files, not just one very large one. There's a slightly smaller but impressive set of implementations for ItemReader. If it doesn't exist, look again. If you still can't find one, consider writing your own. In this recipe, we will do just that.

Writing a Custom ItemReader

The ItemReader example is trivial. Here, an ItemReader is created that knows how to retrieve UserRegistration objects from a remote procedure call (RPC) endpoint.

Listing 8-13. UserRegistrationItemReader source

```java
package com.apress.spring6recipes.springbatch;

import org.springframework.batch.item.ItemReader;

import java.time.LocalDate;

public class UserRegistrationItemReader implements ItemReader<UserRegistration> {

  private final UserRegistrationService usr;

  public UserRegistrationItemReader(UserRegistrationService usr) {
    this.usr = usr;
  }

  public UserRegistration read() throws Exception {
    var today = LocalDate.now();
    var registrations = usr.getOutstandingUserRegistrationBatchForDate(1, today);
    var iter = registrations.iterator();
    return iter.hasNext() ? iter.next() : null;
  }
}
```

As you can see, the interface is trivial. In this case, you defer most work to a remote service to provide you with the input. The interface requires that you return one record. The interface is parameterized to the type of object (the "item") to be returned. All the read items will be aggregated and then passed to the ItemWriter.

Writing a Custom ItemWriter

The ItemWriter example is also trivial. Imagine wanting to write by invoking a remote service using any of the numerous options for remoting that Spring provides. The ItemWriter interface is parameterized by the type of item you're expecting to write. Here, you expect a UserRegistration object from the ItemReader. The interface consists of one method, which expects a Chunk of the class's parameterized type. These are the objects read from ItemReader and aggregated. If your commit interval were ten, you might expect ten or fewer items in the Chunk.

Listing 8-14. UserRegistrationServiceItemWriter source

```java
package com.apress.spring6recipes.springbatch;

import org.slf4j.Logger;
import org.slf4j.LoggerFactory;
import org.springframework.batch.item.Chunk;
import org.springframework.batch.item.ItemWriter;

import java.util.List;

public class UserRegistrationServiceItemWriter implements ItemWriter<UserRegistration> {

  private final Logger logger = LoggerFactory.getLogger(getClass());
```

```
private final UserRegistrationService urs;

public UserRegistrationServiceItemWriter(UserRegistrationService urs) {
  this.urs = urs;
}

@Override
public void write(Chunk<? extends UserRegistration> items) throws Exception {
  items.forEach(this::write);
}

private void write(UserRegistration ur) {
  var registration = urs.registerUser(ur);
  logger.debug("Registered: {}", registration);
}
}
```

Here, you've wired in the service's client interface. You simply loop through the UserRegistration objects and invoke the service, which in turn hands you back an identical instance of UserRegistration. If you remove the gratuitous spacing, curly brackets, and logging output, it becomes two lines of code to satisfy the requirement.

The interface for UserRegistrationService follows.

Listing 8-15. UserRegistrationService interface

```
package com.apress.spring6recipes.springbatch;

import java.time.LocalDate;

public interface UserRegistrationService {

  Iterable<UserRegistration> getOutstandingUserRegistrationBatchForDate(int quantity,
  LocalDate date);

  UserRegistration registerUser(UserRegistration userRegistrationRegistration);
}
```

In our example, we have no particular implementation for the interface, as it is irrelevant: it could be any interface that Spring Batch doesn't know about already.

8-5. Processing Input Before Writing

Problem

While transferring data directly from a spreadsheet or CSV dump might be useful, one can imagine having to do some sort of processing on the data before it's written. Data in a CSV file, and more generally from any source, is not usually exactly the way you expect it to be or immediately suitable for writing. Just because Spring Batch can coerce it into a POJO on your behalf doesn't mean the state of the data is correct. There may be additional data that you need to infer or fill in from other services before the data is suitable for writing.

Solution

Spring Batch will let you do processing on reader output. This processing can do virtually anything to the output before it gets passed to the writer, including changing the type of the data.

How It Works

Spring Batch gives the implementor a chance to perform any custom logic on the data read from the reader. The processor attribute on the chunk configuration expects a reference to a bean of the interface org. springframework.batch.item.ItemProcessor. Thus, the revised definition for the job from the previous recipe looks like this.

Listing 8-16. UserRegistrationValidationItemProcessor modified step configuration

```
@Bean
public Step step1(ItemReader<UserRegistration> reader,
    ItemProcessor<UserRegistration, UserRegistration> processor,
    ItemWriter<UserRegistration> writer,
    PlatformTransactionManager txManager) {
  var name = "User Registration CSV To DB Step";
  var builder = new StepBuilder(name, jobRepository);
  return builder
          .<UserRegistration, UserRegistration>chunk(5, txManager)
          .reader(reader)
          .processor(processor)
          .writer(writer)
          .build();
}
```

The goal is to do certain validations on the data before you authorize it to be written to the database. If you determine the record is invalid, you can stop further processing by returning null from the ItemProcessor. This is crucial and provides a necessary safeguard. One thing that you want to do is ensure that the data is the right format (e.g., the schema may require a valid two-letter state name instead of the longer full state name). Telephone numbers are expected to follow a certain format, and you can use this processor to strip the telephone number of any extraneous characters, leaving only a valid (in the United States) ten-digit phone number. The same applies for US zip codes, which consist of five characters and optionally a hyphen followed by a four-digit code. Finally, while a constraint guarding against duplicates is best implemented in the database, there may very well be some other eligibility criteria for a record that can be met only by querying the system before insertion.

Here's the configuration for the ItemProcessor.

Listing 8-17. UserRegistrationValidationItemProcessor bean configuration

```
@Bean
public UserRegistrationValidationItemProcessor validatingItemProcessor() {
  return new UserRegistrationValidationItemProcessor();
}
```

In the interest of keeping this class short, I won't reprint it in its entirety, but the salient bits should be obvious.

Listing 8-18. UserRegistrationValidationItemProcessor source

```
package com.apress.spring6recipes.springbatch;

import org.springframework.batch.item.ItemProcessor;
import org.springframework.util.StringUtils;

import java.util.Arrays;
import java.util.Collection;

public class UserRegistrationValidationItemProcessor
        implements ItemProcessor<UserRegistration, UserRegistration> {

  private String stripNonNumbers(String input) {
  }

  private boolean isTelephoneValid(String telephone) {
  }

  private boolean isZipCodeValid(String zip) {
  }

  private boolean isValidState(String state) {
  }

  public UserRegistration process(UserRegistration input) {
    var zipCode = stripNonNumbers(input.zip());
    var telephone = stripNonNumbers(input.phoneNumber());
    var state = input.state();

    if (isTelephoneValid(telephone) && isZipCodeValid(zipCode) && isValidState(state)) {
      return new UserRegistration(
              input.firstName(), input.lastName(), input.company(), input.address(),
              input.city(), input.state(), zipCode, input.county(), input.url(),
              telephone, input.fax());
    }
    return null;
  }
}
```

The class is a parameterized type. The type information is the type of the input, as well as the type of the output. The input is what's given to the method for processing, and the output is the returned data from the method. Because you're not transforming anything in this example, the two parameterized types are the same. Once this process has completed, there's a lot of useful information to be had in the Spring Batch metadata tables. Issue the following query on your database.

Listing 8-19. UserRegistrationValidationItemProcessor sample query

```
select * from BATCH_STEP_EXECUTION;
```

Among other things, you'll get back the exit status of the job, how many commits occurred, how many items were read, and how many items were filtered. So if the preceding job was run on a batch with 100 rows, each item was read and passed through the processor, and it found 10 items invalid (it returned null 10 times), the value for the filter_count column would be 10. You could see that a 100 items were read from the read_count. The write_count column would reflect that 10 items didn't make it and would show 90.

Chaining Processors Together

Sometimes you might want to add extra processing that isn't congruous with the goals of the processor you've already set up. Spring Batch provides a convenience class, CompositeItemProcessor<I,O>, which forwards the output of the filter to the input of the successive filter. In this way, you can write many, singly focused ItemProcessor<I,O>s and then reuse them and chain them as necessary.

Listing 8-20. CompositeItemProcessor sample configuration

```
@Bean
public CompositeItemProcessor<Customer, Customer> compositeBankCustomerProcessor() {
    return new CompositeItemProcessor<>(
        creditScoreValidationProcessor(),
        salaryValidationProcessor(),
        customerEligibilityProcessor());
}
```

The example created a very simple workflow. The first ItemProcessor will take an input of whatever's coming from the ItemReader configured for this job, presumably a Customer object. It will check the credit score of the Customer and, if approved, forward the Customer to the salary and income validation processor. If everything checks out there, the Customer will be forwarded to the eligibility processor, where the system is checked for duplicates or any other invalid data. It will finally be forwarded to the writer to be added to the output. If at any point in the three processors the customer fails a check, the executing ItemProcessor can simply return null and arrest processing.

8-6. Better Living Through Transactions

Problem

You want your reads and writes to be robust. Ideally, they'll use transactions where appropriate and correctly react to exceptions.

Solution

Transaction capabilities are built on top of the first-class support already provided by the core Spring Framework. Where relevant, Spring Batch surfaces the configuration so that you can control it. Within the context of chunk-oriented processing, it also exposes a lot of control over the frequency of commits, rollback semantics, and so on.

How It Works

Transactions

Spring's core framework provides first-class support for transactions. You simply wire up a PlatformTransactionManager and give Spring Batch a reference, just as you would in any regular JdbcTemplate or HibernateTemplate solution. As you build your Spring Batch solutions, you'll be given opportunities to control how steps behave in a transaction. You've already seen some of the support for transactions baked right in.

The configuration used in all these examples established a DriverManagerDataSource and a DataSourceTransactionManager bean. The PlatformTransactionManager and DataSource were then wired to the JobRepositoryFactoryBean, which was in turn wired to the JobLauncher, which you used to launch all jobs thus far. This enabled all the metadata your jobs created to be written to the database in a transactional way.

If you looked at the preceding samples, you already noticed the call to the chunk method contained both a number and a transaction manager. There is also a chunk method that accepts only a number, but that has been deprecated and will be removed in future Spring Batch releases. If you used the chunk method without a transaction manager for a step, Spring Batch would, by default, try to pluck the PlatformTransactionManager named transactionManager from the context and use it. If you want to explicitly configure this, you can specify the transactionManager property. A simple transaction manager for JDBC work might look like the following.

Listing 8-21. Step configuration with PlatformTransactionManager

```
@Bean
protected Step step1(PlatformTransactionManager txManager) {
    var name = "step1";
    var builder = new StepBuilder(name, jobRepository);
    return builder
            .<UserRegistration,UserRegistration>chunk(5)
            .reader(csvFileReader())
            .processor(userRegistrationValidationItemProcessor())
            .writer(jdbcItemWriter())
            .transactionManager(txManager)
            .build();
}
```

However, as the chunk(5) has been deprecated, you want to favor chunk(5, transactionManager) over setting it again through the transactionManager property.

Items read from an ItemReader are normally aggregated. If a commit on the ItemWriter fails, the aggregated items are kept and then resubmitted. This process is efficient and works most of the time. One place where it breaks semantics is when reading from a transactional resource (like a JMS queue or database). Reads from a message queue can and should be rolled back if the transaction they participate in (in this case, the transaction for the writer) fails.

Listing 8-22. Step configuration with a transactional queue

```
@Bean
protected Step step1(PlatformTransactionManager txManager) {
    var name = "step1";
    var builder = new StepBuilder(name, jobRepository);
    return builder
```

```
        .<UserRegistration,UserRegistration>chunk(5, txManager)
        .reader(csvFileReader()).readerIsTransactionalQueue()
        .processor(userRegistrationValidationItemProcessor())
        .writer(jdbcItemWriter())
        .build();
}
```

Rollbacks

Handling the simple case ("read X items, and commit a database transaction every Y items") is easy. Spring Batch excels in the robustness it surfaces as simple configuration options for the edge and failure cases.

If a write fails on an `ItemWriter` or some other exception occurs in processing, Spring Batch will roll back the transaction. This is valid handling for a majority of the cases. There may be some scenarios when you want to control which exceptional cases cause the transaction to roll back.

When using Java-based configuration to enable rollbacks, first, the step needs to be a fault-tolerant step, which in turn can be used to specify the no-rollback exceptions. First, use `faultTolerant()` to obtain a fault-tolerant step. Next, the `skipLimit()` method can be used to specify the number of ignored rollbacks before actually stopping the job execution. Finally, the `noRollback()` method can be used to specify the exceptions that don't trigger a rollback. To specify multiple exceptions, you can simply chain calls to the `noRollback()` method.

Listing 8-23. Sample configuration with rollback rules

```
@Bean
protected Step step1(PlatformTransactionManager txManager) {
    var name = "step1";
    var builder = new StepBuilder(name, jobRepository);
    return builder
            .<UserRegistration,UserRegistration>chunk(10, txManager)
                .faultTolerant()
                    .noRollback(com.yourdomain.exceptions.YourBusinessException.class)
            .reader(csvFileReader())
            .processor(userRegistrationValidationItemProcessor())
            .writer(jdbcItemWriter())
            .build();
}
```

8-7. Retrying

Problem

You are dealing with a requirement for functionality that may fail but is not transactional. Perhaps it is transactional but unreliable. You want to work with a resource that may fail when you try to read from or write to it. It may fail because of networking connectivity because an endpoint is down or for any other number of reasons. You know that it will likely be back up soon, though, and that it should be retried.

Solution

Use Spring Batch's retry capabilities to systematically retry the read or write.

How It Works

As you saw in the last recipe, it's easy to handle transactional resources with Spring Batch. When it comes to transient or unreliable resources, a different tack is required. Such resources tend to be distributed or manifest problems that eventually resolve themselves. Some (such as web services) cannot inherently participate in a transaction because of their distributed nature. There are products that can start a transaction on one server and propagate the transactional context to a distributed server and complete it there, although this tends to be very rare and inefficient. Alternatively, there's good support for distributed ("global" or XA) transactions if you can use it. Sometimes, however, you may be dealing with a resource that isn't either of those. A common example might be a call made to a remote service, such as an RMI service or a REST endpoint. Some invocations will fail but may be retried with some likelihood of success in a transactional scenario. For example, an update to the database resulting in `org.springframework.dao.DeadlockLoserDataAccessException` might be usefully retried.

Configuring a Step

The simplest example is in the configuration of a step. Here, you can specify exception classes on which to retry the operation. As with the rollback exceptions, you can delimit this list of exceptions with newlines or commas.

When using Java-based configuration to enable retrying, first, the step needs to be a fault-tolerant step, which in turn can be used to specify the retry limit and retriable exceptions. First, use `faultTolerant()` to obtain a fault-tolerant step. Next, the `retryLimit()` method can be used to specify the number of retry attempts. Finally, the `retry` method can be used to specify the exceptions that trigger a retry. To specify multiple exceptions, you can simply chain calls to the `retry` method.

Listing 8-24. Step configuration for retry

```
@Bean
public Step step1(ItemReader<UserRegistration> reader,
        ItemWriter<UserRegistration> writer,
        PlatformTransactionManager txManager) {
  var name = "User Registration CSV To DB Step";
  var builder = new StepBuilder(name, jobRepository);
  return builder
          .<UserRegistration, UserRegistration>chunk(5, txManager)
          .faultTolerant()
            .retryLimit(3).retry(DeadlockLoserDataAccessException.class)
          .reader(reader)
          .writer(writer)
          .build();
}
```

Retry Template

Alternatively, you can leverage Spring Retry support for retries and recovery in your own code. For example, you can have a custom ItemWriter in which retry functionality is desired or even an entire service interface for which retry support is desired.

Spring Batch supports these scenarios through the RetryTemplate that (much like its various other template cousins) isolates your logic from the nuances of retries and instead enables you to write the code as though you were only going to attempt it once. Let Spring Batch handle everything else through declarative configuration.

The RetryTemplate supports many use cases, with convenient APIs to wrap otherwise tedious retry/ fail/recover cycles in concise, single-method invocations.

Let's take a look at the modified version of a simple ItemWriter from Recipe 8-3 on how to write a custom ItemWriter. The solution was simple enough and would ideally work all the time. It fails to handle the error cases for the service, however. When dealing with RPC, always proceed as if it's almost impossible for things to go right; the service itself may surface a semantic or system violation. An example might be a duplicate database key, invalid credit card number, and so on. This is true whether the service is distributed or in-VM, of course.

Next, the RPC layer below the system may also fault. Here's the rewritten code, this time allowing for retries.

Listing 8-25. RetryableUserRegistrationServiceItemWriter implementation

```
package com.apress.spring6recipes.springbatch;

import org.springframework.batch.item.Chunk;
import org.springframework.batch.item.ItemWriter;
import org.springframework.retry.RetryCallback;
import org.springframework.retry.support.RetryTemplate;

public class RetryableUserRegistrationServiceItemWriter
        implements ItemWriter<UserRegistration> {

  private final UserRegistrationService userRegistrationService;

  private final RetryTemplate retryTemplate;

  public RetryableUserRegistrationServiceItemWriter(UserRegistrationService usr,
                                            RetryTemplate retryTemplate) {
    this.userRegistrationService = usr;
    this.retryTemplate = retryTemplate;
  }

  public void write(Chunk<? extends UserRegistration> items)
          throws Exception {
    for (var userRegistration : items) {
      retryTemplate.execute(context ->
              userRegistrationService.registerUser(userRegistration));
    }
  }
}
```

As you can see, the code hasn't changed much, and the result is much more robust. The `RetryTemplate` itself is configured in the Spring context, although it's trivial to create in code. I declare it in the Spring context only because there is some surface area for configuration when creating the object, and I try to let Spring handle the configuration.

One of the more useful settings for the `RetryTemplate` is the `BackOffPolicy` in use. The `BackOffPolicy` dictates how long the `RetryTemplate` should back off between retries. Indeed, there's even support for growing the delay between retries after each failed attempt to avoid lock stepping with other clients attempting the same invocation. This is great for situations in which there are potentially many concurrent attempts on the same resource and a race condition may ensue. There are other BackOffPolicies, including one that delays retries by a fixed amount called `FixedBackOffPolicy`.

Listing 8-26. RetryTemplate configuration

```
@Bean
public RetryTemplate retryTemplate(BackOffPolicy backOffPolicy) {
  var retryTemplate = new RetryTemplate();
  retryTemplate.setBackOffPolicy(backOffPolicy);
  return retryTemplate;
}


@Bean
public ExponentialBackOffPolicy backOffPolicy() {
  var backOffPolicy = new ExponentialBackOffPolicy();
  backOffPolicy.setInitialInterval(1000);
  backOffPolicy.setMaxInterval(10000);
  backOffPolicy.setMultiplier(2);
  return backOffPolicy;
}
```

You have configured a `RetryTemplate`'s `BackOffPolicy` so that the `BackOffPolicy` will wait 1 second (1,000 milliseconds) before the initial retry. Subsequent attempts will double that value (the growth is influenced by the multiplier). It'll continue until the `maxInterval` is met, at which point all subsequent retry intervals will level off, retrying at a consistent interval.

AOP-Based Retries

An alternative is an AOP advisor provided by Spring Batch that will wrap invocations of methods whose success is not guaranteed in retries, as you did with the `RetryTemplate`. In the previous example, you rewrote an `ItemWriter<T>` to make use of the template. Another approach might be to merely advise the entire `userRegistrationService` proxy with this retry logic. In this case, the code could go back to the way it was in the original example, with no `RetryTemplate`!

To do so you would annotate the method(s) to be retriable with the `@Retryable` annotation. To achieve the same as in the code with an explicit `RetryTemplate`, you would need to add the following.

Listing 8-27. Annotation-based retry on UserRegistrationService

```
@Retryable(backoff = @Backoff(delay = 1000, maxDelay = 10000, multiplier = 2))
public UserRegistration registerUser(UserRegistration registration) { ... }
```

Only adding this annotation isn't enough. You would also need to enable annotation processing for this with the `@EnableRetry` annotation on your configuration.

Listing 8-28. Configuration for annotation-based retry

```
@Configuration
@EnableBatchProcessing
@EnableRetry
@ComponentScan("com.apress.spring6recipes.springbatch")
@PropertySource("classpath:/batch.properties")
public class BatchConfiguration {
}
```

8-8. Controlling Step Execution

Problem

You want to control how steps are executed, perhaps to eliminate a needless waste of time by introducing concurrency or by executing steps only if a condition is true.

Solution

There are different ways to change the runtime profile of your jobs, mainly by exerting control over the way steps are executed: concurrent steps, decisions, and sequential steps.

How It Works

Thus far, you have explored running one step in a job. Typical jobs of almost any complexity will have multiple steps, however. A step provides a boundary (transactional or not) to the beans and logic it encloses. A step can have its own reader, writer, and processor. Each step helps decide what the next step will be. A step is isolated and provides focused functionality that can be assembled using the updated schema and configuration options in Spring Batch in very sophisticated workflows. In fact, some of the concepts and patterns you're about to see will be very familiar if you have an interest in business process management (BPM) systems and workflows. BPM provides many constructs for process or job control that are similar to what you're seeing here. A step often corresponds to a bullet point when you outline the definition of a job on paper. For example, a batch job to load the daily sales and produce a report might be proposed as follows.

Daily Sales Report Job

1. Load customers from the CSV file into the database.

2. Calculate daily statistics, and write to a report file.

3. Send messages to the message queue to notify an external system of the successful registration for each of the newly loaded customers.

Sequential Steps

In the previous example, there's an implied sequence between the first two steps: the audit file can't be written until all the registrations have completed. This sort of relationship is the default relationship between two steps. One occurs after the other. Each step executes with its own execution context and shares only a parent job execution context and an order.

Listing 8-29. Job with multiple steps

```
@Bean
public Job nightlyRegistrationsJob () {
    var name = "nightlyRegistrationsJob";
    var builder = new JobBuilder(name, jobRegistry);
    return builder
            .start(loadRegistrations())
            .next(reportStatistics())
            .next(...)
            .build();
    }
}
```

Concurrency

The first version of Spring Batch was oriented toward batch processing inside the same thread and, with some alteration, perhaps inside the virtual machine. There were workarounds, of course, but the situation was less than ideal.

In the outline for this example job, the first step has to come before the second two because the second two are dependent on the first. The second two, however, do not share any such dependencies. There's no reason the audit log couldn't be written at the same time as the JMS messages are being delivered. Spring Batch provides the capability to fork processing to enable just this sort of arrangement.

Listing 8-30. Job with multiple steps, with a fork

```
@Bean
public Job insertIntoDbFromCsvJob() {
    var name = "insertIntoDbFromCsvJob";
    var builder = new JobBuilder(name, jobRegistry);
    return builder
            .start(loadRegistrations())
            .split(taskExecutor())
                .add(
                    builder.flow(reportStatistics()),
                    builder.flow(sendJmsNotifications()))
            .build();
}
```

You can use the split() method on the job builder. To make a step into a flow, the flow() method of the job builder can be used. Then to add more steps to the flow, these can be added with the next() method. The split() method requires a TaskExecutor to be set. See Recipe 1-23 for more information on scheduling and concurrency.

In this example, there's nothing to prevent you from having many steps within the flow elements, nor is there anything preventing you from having more steps after the split element. The split element, like the step elements, takes a next attribute as well.

Spring Batch provides a mechanism to offload processing to another process. This distribution requires some sort of durable, reliable connection. This is a perfect use of JMS because it's rock-solid and transactional, fast, and reliable. Spring Batch support is modeled at a slightly higher level, on top of the Spring Integration abstractions for Spring Integration channels. This support is not in the main Spring Batch code; it can be found in the spring-batch-integration project. Remote chunking lets individual steps read and aggregate items as usual in the main thread. This step is called the master. Items read are sent to the ItemProcessor/ItemWriter running in another process (this is called the slave). If the slave is an aggressive consumer, you have a simple, generic mechanism to scale: work is instantly farmed out over as many JMS clients as you can throw at it. The aggressive consumer pattern refers to the arrangement of multiple JMS clients all consuming the same queue's messages. If one client consumes a message and is busy processing, other idle queues will get the message instead. As long as there's a client that's idle, the message will be processed instantly.

Additionally, Spring Batch supports implicitly scaling out using a feature called partitioning. This feature is interesting because it's built in and generally very flexible. You replace your instance of a step with a subclass, PartitionStep, which knows how to coordinate distributed executors and maintains the metadata for the execution of the step, thus eliminating the need for a durable medium of communication as in the "remote chunking" technology.

The functionality here is also very generic. It could, conceivably, be used with any sort of grid fabric technology such as GridGain or Hadoop. Spring Batch ships with only a TaskExecutorPartitionHandler, which executes steps in multiple threads using a TaskExecutor strategy. This simple improvement might be enough of a justification for this feature! If you're really hurting, however, you can extend it.

Conditional Steps with Statuses

Using the ExitStatus of a given job or step to determine the next step is the simplest example of a conditional flow. Spring Batch facilitates this through the use of the stop, next, fail, and end elements. By default, assuming no intervention, a step will have an ExitStatus that matches its BatchStatus, which is a property whose values are defined as an enum (the BatchStatus mentioned before) and may be any of the following: COMPLETED, STARTING, STARTED, STOPPING, STOPPED, FAILED, ABANDONED, or UNKNOWN.

Let's look at an example that executes one of two steps based on the success of a preceding step.

Listing 8-31. Job with conditional steps

```
@Bean
public Job insertIntoDbFromCsvJob() {
    var name = "User Registration Import Job";
    var builder = new JobBuilder(name, jobRegistry);
    return builder
            .start(step1())
                .on("COMPLETED").to(step2())
                .on("FAILED").to(failureStep())
            .build();
}
```

It's also possible to provide a wildcard. This is useful if you want to ensure a certain behavior for any number of BatchStatuses, perhaps in tandem with a more specific next element that matches only one BatchStatus.

Listing 8-32. Job with conditional steps, with a catch-all

```
@Bean
public Job insertIntoDbFromCsvJob() {
    var name = "User Registration Import Job";
    var builder = new JobBuilder(name, jobRegistry);
    return builder
            .start(step1())
                .on("COMPLETED").to(step2())
                .on("*").to(failureStep())
            .build();
}
```

In this example, you are instructing Spring Batch to perform some step based on any unaccounted-for ExitStatus. Another option is to just stop processing altogether with a BatchStatus of FAILED. You can do this using the fail element. A less aggressive rewrite of the preceding example might be the following.

Listing 8-33. Job with a conditional step or failure

```
@Bean
public Job insertIntoDbFromCsvJob() {
    var name = "User Registration Import Job";
    var builder = new JobBuilder(name, jobRegistry);
    return builder
            .start(step1())
                .on("COMPLETED").to(step2())
                .on("FAILED").fail()
            .build();
}
```

In all these examples, you're reacting to the standard BatchStatuses that the Spring Batch framework provides. But it's also possible to raise your own ExitStatus. If, for example, you wanted the whole job to fail with a custom ExitStatus of "MAN DOWN", you might do something like this.

Listing 8-34. Job with a conditional step or end step

```
@Bean
public Job insertIntoDbFromCsvJob() {
    var name = "User Registration Import Job";
    var builder = new JobBuilder(name, jobRegistry);
    return builder
            .start(step1())
                .on("COMPLETED").to(step2())
                .on("FAILED").end("MAN DOWN")
            .build();
}
```

Finally, if all you want to do is end processing with a BatchStatus of COMPLETED, you can use the end() method. This is an explicit way of ending a flow as if it had run out of steps and incurred no errors.

Listing 8-35. Job with conditional steps

```
@Bean
public Job insertIntoDbFromCsvJob() {
    var name = "User Registration Import Job";
    var builder = new JobBuilder(name, jobRegistry);
    return builder
            .start(step1())
                .on("COMPLETED").end()
                .on("FAILED").to(errorStep())
            .build();
}
```

Conditional Steps with Decisions

If you want to vary the execution flow based on some logic more complex than a job's ExitStatuses, you may give Spring Batch a helping hand by using a decision element and providing it with an implementation of a JobExecutionDecider.

Listing 8-36. HoroscopeDecider class

```
package com.apress.spring6recipes.springbatch;

import org.springframework.batch.core.JobExecution;
import org.springframework.batch.core.StepExecution;
import org.springframework.batch.core.job.flow.FlowExecutionStatus;
import org.springframework.batch.core.job.flow.JobExecutionDecider;

import java.util.concurrent.ThreadLocalRandom;

public class HoroscopeDecider implements JobExecutionDecider {

  private boolean isMercuryIsInRetrograde() {
    return ThreadLocalRandom.current().nextDouble() > .9;
  }

  public FlowExecutionStatus decide(JobExecution jobExecution, StepExecution
  stepExecution) {
    if (isMercuryIsInRetrograde()) {
      return FlowExecutionStatus.FAILED;
    }
    return FlowExecutionStatus.COMPLETED;
  }
}
```

All that remains is the configuration.

Listing 8-37. Job with conditional steps based on JobExecutionDecider

```
@Bean
public Job insertIntoDbFromCsvJob(JobExecutionDecider decider) {
    var name = "User Registration Import Job";
    var builder = new JobBuilder(name, jobRegistry);
    return builder
            .start(step1())
            .next(decider)
                .on("MERCURY_IN_RETROGRADE").to(step2())
                .on("COMPLETED").to(step3())
            .build();
}
```

8-9. Launching a Job

Problem

What deployment scenarios does Spring Batch support? How does Spring Batch launch? How does Spring Batch work with a system scheduler such as cron or autosys or from a web application?

Solution

Spring Batch works well in all environments that Spring runs: your `public static void main`, a web application, anywhere! Some use cases are uniquely challenging, though: it is rarely practical to run Spring Batch in the same thread as an HTTP response because it might end up stalling execution, for example. Spring Batch supports asynchronous execution for just this scenario. Spring Batch also provides a convenience class that can be readily used with cron or autosys to support launching jobs. Additionally, Spring's excellent scheduler namespace provides a great mechanism to schedule jobs.

How It Works

Before you get into creating a solution, it's important to know what options are available for deploying and running these solutions. All solutions require, at minimum, a job and a `JobLauncher`. You already configured these components in the previous recipe. The job is configured in your Spring application context, as you'll see later. The simplest example of launching a Spring Batch solution from Java code is about five lines of Java code, three if you've already got a handle to the `ApplicationContext`!

Listing 8-38. Main class launching a job

```
package com.apress.spring6recipes.springbatch;

public class Main {
    public static void main(String[] args) throws Throwable {
        var context = new AnnotationConfigApplicationContext(BatchConfiguration.class)
        var jobLauncher = ctx.getBean("jobLauncher", JobLauncher.class);
```

```
        var job = ctx.getBean("myJobName". Job.class);
        var jobExecution = jobLauncher.run(job, new JobParameters());
    }
}
```

As you can see, the JobLauncher reference you configured previously is obtained and used to then launch an instance of a Job with the given JobParameters. The result is a JobExecution. You can interrogate the JobExecution for information on the state of the Job, including its exit status and runtime status.

Listing 8-39. Code checking the status of job execution

```
var jobExecution = jobLauncher.run(job, jobParameters);
var batchStatus = jobExecution.getStatus();
while(batchStatus.isRunning()) {
        System.out.println( "Still running..." );
        Utils.sleep( 5, SECONDS );
}
```

You can also get the ExitStatus.

Listing 8-40. Code reading the exit status

```
System.out.printf( "Exit code: %s%n", jobExecution.getExitStatus().getExitCode());
```

The JobExecution also provides a lot of other very useful information like the create time of the Job, the start time, the last updated date, and the end time—all as java.time.LocalDateTime instances. If you want to correlate the job back to the database, you'll need the jobInstance and the ID.

Listing 8-41. Code reading the jobInstance ID

```
var jobInstance = jobExecution.getJobInstance();
System.out.printf( "job instance Id: %d%n", jobInstance.getId());
```

In our simple example, we use an empty JobParameters instance. In practice, this will only work once. Spring Batch builds a unique key based on the parameters and uses this to uniquely identify one run of a given Job from another. You'll learn about parameterizing a Job in detail in the next recipe.

Launching from a Web Application

Launching a job from a web application requires a slightly different approach, because the client thread (presumably an HTTP request) can't usually wait for a batch job to finish. The ideal solution is to have the job execute asynchronously when launched from a controller or action in the web tier, unattended by the client thread. Spring Batch supports this scenario through the use of a Spring TaskExecutor. This requires a simple change to the configuration for the JobLauncher, although the Java code can stay the same. Here, we will use a SimpleAsyncTaskExecutor that will spawn a thread of execution and manage that thread without blocking.

Listing 8-42. Batch configuration with TaskExecutor

```
package com.apress.spring6recipes.springbatch.config;

@Configuration
@EnableBatchProcessing
@ComponentScan("com.apress.springrecipes.springbatch")
@PropertySource("classpath:/batch.properties")
public class BatchConfiguration {

    @Bean
    public SimpleAsyncTaskExecutor taskExecutor() {
        return new SimpleAsyncTaskExecutor();
    }
}
```

Spring Batch will, by default, look for a TaskExecutor named taskExecutor and if a bean with that name is found will use it as the TaskExecutor of its choice. If for some reason you cannot use the TaskExecutor named taskExecutor, you can pass the name of the TaskExecutor to use to the @ EnableBatchProcessing annotation through the taskExecutorRef attribute.

Listing 8-43. Batch configuration with custom named TaskExecutor

```
@Configuration
@EnableBatchProcessing(taskExecutorRef = "customTaskExecutor")
@ComponentScan("com.apress.spring6recipes.springbatch")
@PropertySource("classpath:/batch.properties")
public class BatchConfiguration {

    @Bean
    public SimpleAsyncTaskExecutor customTaskExecutor() {
      return new SimpleAsyncTaskExecutor();
    }
}
```

Running from the Command Line

Another common use case is deployment of a batch process from a system scheduler such as cron or autosys or even Window's event scheduler. Spring Batch provides a convenience class that takes as its parameters the name of the application context (that contains everything required to run a job) as well as the name of the job bean itself. Additional parameters may be provided and used to parameterize the job. These parameters must be in the form name=value. An example invocation of this class on the command line (on a Linux/Unix system), assuming that you set up the classpath, might look like the following.

Listing 8-44. Shell command to launch

```
java -cp "userjob.jar:libs/*" org.springframework.batch.core.launch.support.
CommandLineJobRunner \
 com.apress.spring6recipes.springbatch.confug.UserJob \
 insertIntoDbFromCsvJob date=`date +%m/%d/%Y` time=`date +%H`
```

The `org.springframework.batch.core.launch.support.CommandLineJobRunner` will even return system error codes (0 for success, 1 for failure, and 2 for an issue with loading the batch job) so that a shell (such as used by most system schedulers) can react or do something about the failure. More complicated return codes can be returned by creating and declaring a top-level bean that implements the interface `ExitCodeMapper`, in which you can specify a more useful translation of exit status messages to integer-based error codes that the shell will see on process exit.

Running on a Schedule

Spring has support for a scheduling framework (see also Recipes 10-5 and 10-6). This framework lends itself perfectly to running Spring Batch. First, let's modify our existing application context configuration to enable scheduling with the `@EnableScheduling` annotation and by adding a `ThreadPoolTaskScheduler`.

Listing 8-45. BatchConfiguration with TaskScheduler

```
package com.apress.springrecipes.springbatch.config;

@Configuration
@EnableBatchProcessing
@ComponentScan("com.apress.springrecipes.springbatch")
@PropertySource("classpath:/batch.properties")
@EnableScheduling
@EnableAsync
public class BatchConfiguration {

    @Bean
    public ThreadPoolTaskScheduler taskScheduler() {
        var taskScheduler = new ThreadPoolTaskScheduler();
        taskScheduler.setThreadGroupName("batch-scheduler");
        taskScheduler.setPoolSize(10);
        return taskScheduler;
    }

}
```

These imports enable the simplest possible support for scheduling. The preceding annotations ensure that any bean under the package `com.apress.spring6recipes.springbatch` will be configured and scheduled as required. Our scheduler bean is as follows.

Listing 8-46. JobScheduler class

```
package com.apress.spring6recipes.springbatch.scheduler;

import org.springframework.batch.core.Job;
import org.springframework.batch.core.JobParametersBuilder;
import org.springframework.batch.core.launch.JobLauncher;
import org.springframework.scheduling.annotation.Scheduled;
import org.springframework.stereotype.Component;
```

```java
import java.time.LocalDate;
import java.time.LocalDateTime;
import java.time.ZoneId;
import java.util.Date;

@Component
public class JobScheduler {

  private final JobLauncher jobLauncher;
  private final Job job;

  public JobScheduler(JobLauncher jobLauncher, Job job) {
    this.jobLauncher = jobLauncher;
    this.job = job;
  }

  public void runRegistrationsJob(LocalDateTime date) throws Exception{
    System.out.println("Starting job at " + date.toString());

    var jobParametersBuilder = new JobParametersBuilder();
    jobParametersBuilder.addLocalDateTime("date", date);
    jobParametersBuilder.addString("input.file", "registrations");

    var jobParameters = jobParametersBuilder.toJobParameters();
    var jobExecution = jobLauncher.run(job, jobParameters);
    var exitcode = jobExecution.getExitStatus().getExitCode();
    System.out.printf("jobExecution finished, exit code: %s%n", exitcode);
  }

  @Scheduled(fixedDelay = 10_0000)
  public void runRegistrationsJobOnASchedule() throws Exception {
    runRegistrationsJob(LocalDateTime.now());
  }
}
```

There is nothing particularly novel; it's a good study of how the different components of the Spring Framework work well together. The bean is recognized and becomes part of the application context because of the @Component annotation, which we enabled with the @ComponentScan annotation in our configuration class. There's only one Job in the UserJob class and only one JobLauncher, so we simply have those autowired into our bean. Finally, the logic for kicking off a batch run is inside the runRegistrationsJob(java.time.LocalDateTime date) method. This method could be called from anywhere. Our only client for this functionality is the scheduled method runRegistrationsJobOnASchedule. The framework will invoke this method for us, according to the timeline dictated by the @Scheduled annotation.

There are other options for this sort of thing; traditionally in the Java and Spring world, this sort of problem would be a good fit for Quartz. It might still be, as the Spring scheduling support isn't designed to be as extensible as Quartz. If you are in an environment requiring more traditional, ops-friendly scheduling tools, there are of course old standbys like cron, autosys, and BMC too.

8-10. Parameterizing a Job

Problem

The previous examples work well enough, but they leave something to be desired in terms of flexibility. To apply the batch code to some other file, you'd have to edit the configuration and hard-code the name in there. The ability to parameterize the batch solution would be very helpful.

Solution

Use JobParameters to parameterize a job, which is then available to your steps through Spring Batch's expression language or via API calls.

How It Works

Launching a Job with Parameters

A job is a prototype of a JobInstance. JobParameters are used to provide a way of identifying a unique run of a job (a JobInstance). These JobParameters allow you to give input to your batch process, just as you would with a method definition in Java. You've seen the JobParameters in previous examples but not in detail. The JobParameters object is created as you launch the job using the JobLauncher. To launch a job called dailySalesFigures, with the date for the job to work with, you would write something like the following.

Listing 8-47. Main class

```java
package com.apress.spring6recipes.springbatch;

import java.time.LocalDateTime;

import org.springframework.batch.core.Job;
import org.springframework.batch.core.JobParametersBuilder;
import org.springframework.batch.core.launch.JobLauncher;
import org.springframework.context.annotation.AnnotationConfigApplicationContext;

import com.apress.spring6recipes.springbatch.config.BatchConfiguration;

public class Main {
  public static void main(String[] args) throws Throwable {
    var cfg = BatchConfiguration.class;
    try (var ctx = new AnnotationConfigApplicationContext(cfg)) {
      var jobLauncher = ctx.getBean(JobLauncher.class);
      var job = ctx.getBean("dailySalesFigures", Job.class);
      var builder = new JobParametersBuilder();
      var parameters = builder.addLocalDateTime("date", LocalDateTime.now())
              .toJobParameters();
      jobLauncher.run(job, parameters);
  }}
}
```

Accessing JobParameters

Technically, you can get at JobParameters via any of the ExecutionContexts (step and job). Once you have it, you can access the parameters in a type-safe way by calling getLong(), getString(), and so on. A simple way to do this is to bind to the @BeforeStep event, save the StepExecution, and iterate over the parameters this way. From here, you can inspect the parameters and do anything you want with them. Let's look at that in terms of the ItemProcessor you wrote earlier.

Listing 8-48. Access the JobParameters through the StepExecution

```
// ...
private StepExecution stepExecution;

@BeforeStep
public void saveStepExecution(StepExecution stepExecution) {
  this.stepExecution = stepExecution;
}

public UserRegistration process(UserRegistration input) throws Exception {

    var params = stepExecution.getJobParameters().getParameters();

  // iterate over all of the parameters
  for (var key : params.keySet()) {
    var value = params.get(key).getValue().toString();
    System.out.printf("%s=%s%n", key, value);
  ));
  }

  // access specific parameters in a type safe way
  var date = stepExecution.getJobParameters().getDate("date");
  // etc ...
}
```

This turns out to be of limited value. The 80 percent case is that you'll need to bind parameters from the job's launch to the Spring beans in the application context. These parameters are available only at runtime, whereas the steps in the application context are configured at design time. This happens in many places. Previous examples demonstrated ItemWriter and ItemReader instances with hard-coded paths. That works fine unless you want to parameterize the filename. This is hardly acceptable unless you plan on using a job just once!

The core Spring Framework features an enhanced expression language that Spring Batch uses to defer binding of the parameter until the correct time—or, in this case, until the bean is in the correct scope. Spring Batch has the "step" scope for just this purpose. Let's take a look at how you'd rework the previous example to use a parameterized filename for the ItemReader's resource:

```
@Bean
@StepScope
public ItemReader<UserRegistration> csvFileReader(
    @Value("file:${user.home}/batches/#{jobParameters['input.fileName']}.csv")
    Resource input) { ... }
```

All you did is scope the bean (the FlatFileItemReader) to the life cycle of a step (at which point those JobParameters will resolve correctly) and then use the EL syntax to parameterize the path to work off.

8-11. Summary

This chapter introduced you to the concepts of batch processing, some of its history, and why it fits in a modern-day architecture. You learned about Spring Batch, the batch processing from Spring, and how to do reading and writing with ItemReader and ItemWriter implementations in your batch jobs. You wrote your own ItemReader and ItemWriter implementations as needed and saw how to control the execution of steps inside a job.

■ ■ ■

CHAPTER 9

Spring Data Access with NoSQL

Most applications use a relational database like Oracle, MySQL, or PostgreSQL; however, there is more to data storage than just SQL databases. There are

1. Relational databases (Oracle, MySQL, PostgreSQL, etc.)

2. Document stores (MongoDB, Couchbase)

3. Key-value stores (Redis, Voldemort)

4. Column stores (Cassandra)

5. Graph stores (Neo4j, Apache Giraph)

Although each of these different technologies (and even the different implementations) has its own use, it can also be hard to use or configure. Additionally, sometimes it might feel that one writes a lot of duplicated plumbing code for handling transactions and error translation.

The Spring Data project can help make life easier; it can help configure the different technologies with the plumbing code. Each of the integration modules will have support for exception translation to Spring's consistent DataAccessException hierarchy and the use of Spring's templating approach. Spring Data also provides a cross-storage solution for some technologies, which means part of your model can be stored in a relational database with JPA and the other part can be stored in a graph or document store.

💡 Although each section describes how to download and install the needed persistence store, the bin directory contains scripts that set up Docker containers for each persistence store.

9-1. Using MongoDB

Problem

You want to use MongoDB to store and retrieve documents.

Solution

Download and configure MongoDB.

© Marten Deinum, Daniel Rubio, Josh Long 2023
M. Deinum et al., *Spring 6 Recipes*, https://doi.org/10.1007/978-1-4842-8649-4_9

How It Works

Downloading and Starting MongoDB

First, download MongoDB from www.mongodb.org. Select the one that is applicable for the system in use and follow the installation instructions in the manual (https://docs.mongodb.org/manual/installation/). When the installation is complete, MongoDB can be started. To start MongoDB execute the mongodb command on the command line (see Figure 9-1). This will start a MongoDB server on port 27017. If a different port is required, this can be done by specifying the --port option on the command line when starting the server.

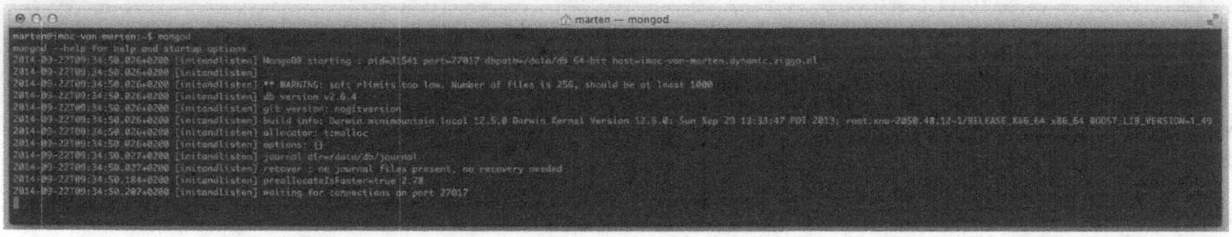

Figure 9-1. *Output after initial start of MongoDB*

The default location for storing data is \data\db (for Windows users this is from the root of the disk where MongoDB was installed!). To change the path, use the --dbpath option on the command line. Make sure that the directory exists and is writeable for MongoDB.

Connecting to MongoDB

For a connection to MongoDB, an instance of Mongo is needed. This instance can be used to get the database to use and the actual underlying collection(s). Let's create a small system that uses MongoDB. First, create an object to use for storage.

Listing 9-1. The Vehicle record

```
package com.apress.spring6recipes.nosql;

public record Vehicle(String vehicleNo, String color, int wheel, int seat) { }
```

To work with this object, create a repository interface.

Listing 9-2. VehicleRepository interface

```
package com.apress.spring6recipes.nosql;

import java.util.List;

public interface VehicleRepository {

  long count();
  void save(Vehicle vehicle);
  void delete(Vehicle vehicle);
  List<Vehicle> findAll();
  Vehicle findByVehicleNo(String vehicleNo);
}
```

For MongoDB create the `MongoVehicleRepository` implementation of the `VehicleRepository`.

Listing 9-3. MongoDB implementation of VehicleRepository

```java
package com.apress.spring6recipes.nosql;

import com.mongodb.client.MongoClient;
import com.mongodb.client.MongoCollection;
import org.bson.Document;

import java.util.List;
import java.util.stream.Collectors;
import java.util.stream.StreamSupport;

import static com.mongodb.client.model.Filters.eq;

public class MongoVehicleRepository implements VehicleRepository {

  private final MongoClient mongo;
  private final String collectionName;
  private final String databaseName;

  public MongoVehicleRepository(MongoClient mongo, String databaseName,
                                String collectionName) {
    this.mongo = mongo;
    this.databaseName = databaseName;
    this.collectionName = collectionName;
  }

  @Override
  public long count() {
    return getCollection().countDocuments();
  }

  @Override
  public void save(Vehicle vehicle) {
    var dbVehicle = transform(vehicle);
    getCollection().insertOne(dbVehicle);
  }

  @Override
  public void delete(Vehicle vehicle) {
    getCollection().deleteOne(eq("vehicleNo", vehicle.vehicleNo()));
  }

  @Override
  public List<Vehicle> findAll() {
    return StreamSupport.stream(getCollection().find().spliterator(), false)
            .map(this::transform)
            .collect(Collectors.toList());
  }
}
```

```java
@Override
public Vehicle findByVehicleNo(String vehicleNo) {
    return transform(getCollection().find(eq("vehicleNo", vehicleNo)).first());
}

private MongoCollection<Document> getCollection() {
    return mongo.getDatabase(databaseName).getCollection(collectionName);
}

private Vehicle transform(Document dbVehicle) {
    if (dbVehicle == null) {
        return null;
    }
    return new Vehicle(
            dbVehicle.getString("vehicleNo"),
            dbVehicle.getString("color"),
            dbVehicle.getInteger("wheel"),
            dbVehicle.getInteger("seat"));
}

private Document transform(Vehicle vehicle) {
    return new Document("vehicleNo", vehicle.vehicleNo())
            .append("color", vehicle.color())
            .append("wheel", vehicle.wheel())
            .append("seat", vehicle.seat());
}
}
```

First, notice the constructor; it takes three arguments. The first is the actual MongoDB client, the second is the name of the database that is going to be used, and the last is the name of the collection in which the objects are stored. Documents in MongoDB are stored in collections, and a collection belongs to a database.

For easy access to the MongoCollection used, there is the getCollection method, which gets a connection to the DB and returns the configured MongoCollection. This MongoCollection can then be used to execute operations like storing, deleting, or updating documents.

The save method will first try to update an existing document. If this fails a new document for the given Vehicle will be created. To store objects, start by transforming the domain object Vehicle into a Document. The Document takes key/value pairs of the different properties of our Vehicle object. When querying for a document, the same Document is used. The key/value pairs that are present on the given object are used to look up documents. An example can be found in the findByVehicleNo method in the repository. Conversion from and to vehicle objects is done through the two transform methods.

To use this class, create the following Main class.

Listing 9-4. Main class to run the code

```java
package com.apress.spring6recipes.nosql;

import com.mongodb.client.MongoClients;

public class Main {

    private static final String DB_NAME = "vehicledb";
    private static final String COUNT = "Number of Vehicles: %d%n";
```

```
public static void main(String[] args) {
    try (var mongo = MongoClients.create()) {

        var repository = new MongoVehicleRepository(mongo, DB_NAME, "vehicles");

        System.out.printf(COUNT, repository.count());

        repository.save(new Vehicle("TEM0001", "RED", 4, 4));
        repository.save(new Vehicle("TEM0002", "RED", 4, 4));

        System.out.printf(COUNT, repository.count());

        var v = repository.findByVehicleNo("TEM0001");

        System.out.println(v);

        var vehicleList = repository.findAll();

        System.out.printf(COUNT, vehicleList.size());
        vehicleList.forEach(System.out::println);
        System.out.printf(COUNT, repository.count());

        mongo.getDatabase(DB_NAME).drop();
    }
  }
}
```

The main class constructs an instance of the MongoClient (through the use of the MongoClients helper), which will try to connect to port 27017 on localhost for a MongoDB instance. If another port or host is needed, there is also a create method, which takes a connection string or MongoClientSettings for more specific configuration as parameters. Next, an instance of the MongoVehicleRepository is constructed. The earlier created MongoClient is passed as well as the name of the database, vehicledb, and name of the collection, vehicles.

The next lines of code will insert two vehicles into the database, try to find them, and finally delete them. The last lines in the main class will drop the database. The latter is something you don't want to do when using a production database. Finally, the try-with-resources block will close the MongoClient used to communicate with MongoDB.

The output for all the recipes should be the same as listed here:

```
Number of Vehicles: 0
Number of Vehicles: 2
Vehicle[vehicleNo=TEM0001, color=RED, wheel=4, seat=4]
Number of Vehicles: 2
Vehicle[vehicleNo=TEM0001, color=RED, wheel=4, seat=4]
Vehicle[vehicleNo=TEM0002, color=RED, wheel=4, seat=4]
Number of Vehicles: 2
```

Using Spring for Configuration

The setup and configuration of the MongoClient and MongoVehicleRepository can easily be moved to Spring configuration.

Listing 9-5. Spring @Configuration to use MongoDB

```java
package com.apress.spring6recipes.nosql.config;

import com.apress.spring6recipes.nosql.MongoVehicleRepository;
import com.apress.spring6recipes.nosql.VehicleRepository;
import com.mongodb.client.MongoClient;
import com.mongodb.client.MongoClients;
import org.springframework.context.annotation.Bean;
import org.springframework.context.annotation.Configuration;

@Configuration
public class MongoConfiguration {

  private static final String DB_NAME = "vehicledb";
  private static final String COLLECTION_NAME = "vehicles";

  @Bean
  public MongoClient mongo() {
    return MongoClients.create();
  }

  @Bean
  public MongoVehicleRepository vehicleRepository(MongoClient mongo) {
    return new MongoVehicleRepository(mongo, DB_NAME, COLLECTION_NAME);
  }
}
```

The following @PreDestroy-annotated method has been added to the MongoVehicleRepository to take care of the cleanup of the database.

Listing 9-6. MongoVehicleRepository for Spring with a PreDestroy method

```java
  @PreDestroy
  public void cleanUp() {
    mongo.getDatabase(databaseName).drop();
  }
}
```

Finally, the Main program needs to be updated to reflect the changes.

Listing 9-7. Main class to run the code

```java
package com.apress.spring6recipes.nosql;

import com.apress.spring6recipes.nosql.config.MongoConfiguration;
import org.springframework.context.annotation.AnnotationConfigApplicationContext;
```

```java
import java.util.List;

public class Main {

  private static final String COUNT = "Number of Vehicles: %d%n";

  public static void main(String[] args) {
    var cfg = MongoConfiguration.class;
    try (var ctx = new AnnotationConfigApplicationContext(cfg)) {
      var repository = ctx.getBean(VehicleRepository.class);

      System.out.printf(COUNT, repository.count());

      repository.save(new Vehicle("TEM0001", "RED", 4, 4));
      repository.save(new Vehicle("TEM0002", "RED", 4, 4));

      System.out.printf(COUNT, repository.count());

      var v = repository.findByVehicleNo("TEM0001");

      System.out.println(v);

      var vehicleList = repository.findAll();

      System.out.printf(COUNT, vehicleList.size());

      vehicleList.forEach(System.out::println);

      System.out.printf(COUNT, repository.count());
    }
  }
}
```

The configuration is loaded by an AnnotationConfigApplicationContext. From this context the VehicleRepository bean is retrieved and used to execute the operations. When the code that has run the context is closed, it triggers the cleanUp method in the MongoVehicleRepository.

Using a MongoTemplate to Simplify MongoDB Code

At the moment the MongoVehicleRepository uses the plain MongoDB API. Although not very complex, it still requires knowledge about the API. Next to that there are some repetitive tasks like mapping from and to a Vehicle object. Using a MongoTemplate can simplify the repository considerably.

ⓘ   Before using Spring Data MongoDB, the relevant jars need to be added to the classpath. When using Maven add the following dependency:

```
<dependency>
  <groupId>org.springframework.data</groupId>
  <artifactId>spring-data-mongodb</artifactId>
  <version>4.0.0</version>
</dependency>
```

Or add the following when using Gradle:

```
compile 'org.springframework.data:spring-data-mongodb:4.0.0'
```

Listing 9-8. MongoVehicleRepository using MongoTemplate

```java
package com.apress.spring6recipes.nosql;

import jakarta.annotation.PreDestroy;
import org.springframework.data.mongodb.core.MongoTemplate;
import org.springframework.data.mongodb.core.query.Query;

import java.util.List;

import static org.springframework.data.mongodb.core.query.Criteria.where;

public class MongoVehicleRepository implements VehicleRepository {

  private final MongoTemplate mongo;
  private final String collectionName;

  public MongoVehicleRepository(MongoTemplate mongo, String collectionName) {
    this.mongo = mongo;
    this.collectionName = collectionName;
  }

  @Override
  public long count() {
    return mongo.count(new Query(), collectionName);
  }

  @Override
  public void save(Vehicle vehicle) {
    mongo.save(vehicle, collectionName);
  }

  @Override
  public void delete(Vehicle vehicle) {
    mongo.remove(vehicle, collectionName);
  }
```

```
@Override
public List<Vehicle> findAll() {
  return mongo.findAll(Vehicle.class, collectionName);
}

@Override
public Vehicle findByVehicleNo(String vehicleNo) {
  var query = new Query(where("vehicleNo").is(vehicleNo));
  return mongo.findOne(query, Vehicle.class, collectionName);
}

@PreDestroy
public void cleanUp() {
  mongo.execute(db -> {
    db.drop();
    return null;
  });
}
}
```

The code looks a lot cleaner when using a MongoTemplate. It has convenience methods for almost every operation: save, update, and delete. Additionally, it has a very nice query builder approach (see the findByVehicleNo method). There are no more mappings to and from the Mongo classes, so there is no need to create a Document anymore. That burden is now handled by the MongoTemplate. To convert the Vehicle object to the MongoDB classes, a MongoConverter is used. By default a MappingMongoConverter is used. This mapper maps properties to attribute names and vice versa and while doing so also tries to convert from and to the correct datatype. If a specific mapping is needed, it is possible to write your own implementation of a MongoConverter and register it with the MongoTemplate.

Due to the use of the MongoTemplate, the configuration needs to be modified.

Listing 9-9. MongoConfiguration class modified for MongoTemplate

```
package com.apress.spring6recipes.nosql.config;

import com.apress.spring6recipes.nosql.MongoVehicleRepository;
import com.mongodb.client.MongoClient;
import org.springframework.context.annotation.Bean;
import org.springframework.context.annotation.Configuration;
import org.springframework.data.mongodb.core.MongoClientFactoryBean;
import org.springframework.data.mongodb.core.MongoTemplate;

@Configuration
public class MongoConfiguration {

  private static final String DB_NAME = "vehicledb";
  private static final String COLLECTION_NAME = "vehicles";

  @Bean
  public MongoTemplate mongo(MongoClient mongo) throws Exception {
    return new MongoTemplate(mongo, DB_NAME);
  }
```

```
@Bean
public MongoClientFactoryBean mongoFactoryBean() {
  return new MongoClientFactoryBean();
}

@Bean
public MongoVehicleRepository vehicleRepository(MongoTemplate mongo) {
  return new MongoVehicleRepository(mongo, COLLECTION_NAME);
}
}
```

Notice the use of the `MongoClientFactoryBean`. It allows for easy setup of the `MongoClient`. It isn't a requirement for using the `MongoTemplate`, but it makes it easier to configure the client.

The `MongoTemplate` has various constructors. The one used here takes a `MongoClient` instance and the name of the database to use. To resolve the database, an instance of a `MongoDatabaseFactory` is used, by default the `SimpleMongoClientDatabaseFactory`. In most cases this is sufficient, but if some special case arises, like encrypted connections, it is quite easy to extend the default implementation. Finally, the `MongoTemplate` is injected, together with the name of the collection, into the `MongoVehicleRepository`.

A final addition needs to be made to the `Vehicle` object. It is required that a field is available for storing the generated ID. This can be either a field with the name `id` or a field with the Spring Data `@Id` annotation.

Listing 9-10. Vehicle record with an id field

```
package com.apress.spring6recipes.nosql;

public record Vehicle(String id, String vehicleNo, String color, int wheel, int seat) { }
```

Using Annotations to Specify Mapping Information

Currently, the `MongoVehicleRepository` needs to know the name of the collection we want to access. It would be easier and more flexible if this could be specified on the object we want to store, here the `Vehicle`. With Spring Data Mongo, this is possible using the `@Document` annotation, just as with a JPA `@Table` annotation.

Listing 9-11. Vehicle record with @Document

```
package com.apress.spring6recipes.nosql;

import org.springframework.data.mongodb.core.mapping.Document;

@Document(collection = "vehicles")
public record Vehicle(String id, String vehicleNo, String color, int wheel, int seat) { }
```

The `@Document` annotation can take three attributes: `collection`, `language`, and `collation`. The `collection` property is for specifying the name of the collection to use; the `language` property is for specifying the language for this object. The `collation` property can be used to specify language-specific rules for string comparison, such as rules for letter case and accent marks. Now that the mapping information is on the `Vehicle` class, the collection name can be removed from the `MongoVehicleRepository`.

Listing 9-12. Modified MongoVehicleRepository without the collection name

```
package com.apress.spring6recipes.nosql;

import jakarta.annotation.PreDestroy;
import org.springframework.data.mongodb.core.MongoTemplate;
import org.springframework.data.mongodb.core.query.Query;

import java.util.List;

import static org.springframework.data.mongodb.core.query.Criteria.where;

public class MongoVehicleRepository implements VehicleRepository {

  private final MongoTemplate mongo;

  public MongoVehicleRepository(MongoTemplate mongo) {
    this.mongo = mongo;
  }

  @Override
  public long count() {
    return mongo.count(new Query(), Vehicle.class);
  }

  @Override
  public void save(Vehicle vehicle) {
    mongo.save(vehicle);
  }

  @Override
  public void delete(Vehicle vehicle) {
    mongo.remove(vehicle);
  }

  @Override
  public List<Vehicle> findAll() {
    return mongo.findAll(Vehicle.class);
  }

  @Override
  public Vehicle findByVehicleNo(String vehicleNo) {
    var query = new Query(where("vehicleNo").is(vehicleNo));
    return mongo.findOne(query, Vehicle.class);
  }

  @PreDestroy
  public void cleanUp() {
    mongo.execute(db -> {
      db.drop();
```

```
      return null;
  });
  }
}
```

Of course the collection name can be removed from the configuration of the MongoVehicleRepository as well. The remainder of the configuration (the MongoTemplate and so on) can stay the same.

Listing 9-13. Modified MongoVehicleRepository configuration

```
package com.apress.spring6recipes.nosql.config;

import org.springframework.context.annotation.Bean;
import org.springframework.context.annotation.Configuration;

@Configuration
public class MongoConfiguration {

  @Bean
  public MongoVehicleRepository vehicleRepository(MongoTemplate mongo) {
    return new MongoVehicleRepository(mongo);
  }
}
```

When running the Main class, the result should still be the same as it was before.

Create a Spring Data MongoDB Repository

Although the code has been reduced a lot in that there is no more mapping from and to MongoDB classes and no more collection names passing around, it can still be reduced even further. Leveraging another feature of Spring Data Mongo, the complete implementation of the MongoVehicleRepository could be removed.

First, the configuration needs to be modified.

Listing 9-14. MongoDB configuration

```
package com.apress.spring6recipes.nosql.config;

import com.mongodb.client.MongoClient;
import org.springframework.context.annotation.Bean;
import org.springframework.context.annotation.Configuration;
import org.springframework.data.mongodb.core.MongoClientFactoryBean;
import org.springframework.data.mongodb.core.MongoTemplate;
import org.springframework.data.mongodb.repository.config.EnableMongoRepositories;

@Configuration
@EnableMongoRepositories(basePackages = "com.apress.spring6recipes.nosql")
public class MongoConfiguration {

  public static final String DB_NAME = "vehicledb";
```

```
@Bean
public MongoTemplate mongoTemplate(MongoClient mongo) {
  return new MongoTemplate(mongo, DB_NAME);
}

@Bean
public MongoClientFactoryBean mongoFactoryBean() {
  return new MongoClientFactoryBean();
}
}
```

First, notice the removal of the @Bean method that constructed the MongoVehicleRepository. Second, notice the addition of the @EnableMongoRepositories annotation. This enables detection of interfaces that extend the Spring Data Repository interface (or one of its sub-interfaces) and are used for domain objects annotated with @Document.

To have our VehicleRepository detected by Spring Data, we need to let it extend CrudRepository or one of its sub-interfaces like MongoRepository.

Listing 9-15. Spring Data–based VehicleRepository interface

```
package com.apress.spring6recipes.nosql;

import org.springframework.data.mongodb.repository.MongoRepository;

public interface VehicleRepository extends MongoRepository<Vehicle, String> {

  Vehicle findByVehicleNo(String vehicleNo);

}
```

You might wonder where all the methods have gone. They are already defined in the super-interfaces and as such can be removed from this interface. The findByVehicleNo method is still there. This method will still be used to look up a Vehicle by its vehicleNo property. All the findBy methods are converted into a MongoDB query. The part after the findBy is interpreted as a property name. It is also possible to write more complex queries using different operators like and, or, and between.

Now running the Main class again should still result in the same output; however, the actual code written to work with MongoDB has been minimized.

Create a Reactive Spring Data MongoDB Repository

Instead of creating a traditional MongoDB repository, it is also possible to create a reactive repository. This is done by extending the ReactiveMongoRepository (or one of the other reactive repository interfaces). This will change the return types for methods that return a single value and zero or more elements into Mono and Flux, respectively.

ℹ️ If you want to use RxJava instead of Project Reactor, extend one of the RxJava3*Repository interfaces and use a Single or Observable instead of Mono or Flux.

To be able to use reactive repository implementation, you first have to use a reactive implementation of the MongoDB driver and configure Spring Data to use that driver. To make it easier, you can extend the AbstractReactiveMongoConfiguration and implement the two required methods getDatabaseName and reactiveMongoClient.

Listing 9-16. Reactive MongoDB configuration

```
package com.apress.spring6recipes.nosql.config;

import com.mongodb.reactivestreams.client.MongoClient;
import com.mongodb.reactivestreams.client.MongoClients;
import org.springframework.context.annotation.Bean;
import org.springframework.context.annotation.Configuration;
import org.springframework.data.mongodb.config.AbstractReactiveMongoConfiguration;
import org.springframework.data.mongodb.repository.config.EnableReactiveMongoRepositories;

@Configuration
@EnableReactiveMongoRepositories(basePackages = "com.apress.spring6recipes.nosql")
public class MongoConfiguration extends AbstractReactiveMongoConfiguration {

  private static final String DB_NAME = "vehicledb";

  @Bean
  @Override
  public MongoClient reactiveMongoClient() {
    return MongoClients.create();
  }

  @Override
  protected String getDatabaseName() {
    return DB_NAME;
  }
}
```

Another thing that has changed is the use of @EnableReactiveMongoRepositories instead of @EnableMongoRepositories. The database name is still needed, and we need to connect with a reactive driver to the MongoDB instance. For this you can use one of the MongoClients.create methods; here you can simply use the default.

Next, change the VehicleRepository to extend ReactiveMongoRepository so it will become reactive. You also need to change the return type of the findByVehicleNo method to Mono<Vehicle> instead of a plain Vehicle.

Listing 9-17. Reactive Spring Data–based VehicleRepository interface

```
package com.apress.spring6recipes.nosql;

import org.springframework.data.mongodb.repository.ReactiveMongoRepository;
import reactor.core.publisher.Mono;
```

```
public interface VehicleRepository extends ReactiveMongoRepository<Vehicle, String> {

    Mono<Vehicle> findByVehicleNo(String vehicleNo);

}
```

The final piece that would need to change is the Main class to test all this. Instead of blocking calls, you want to use a stream of methods to be called.

Listing 9-18. Main class to run the code

```
package com.apress.spring6recipes.nosql;

import com.apress.spring6recipes.nosql.config.MongoConfiguration;
import org.springframework.context.annotation.AnnotationConfigApplicationContext;
import reactor.core.publisher.Flux;

import java.util.concurrent.CountDownLatch;

public class Main {

    private static final String COUNT = "Number of Vehicles: %d%n";

    public static void main(String[] args) throws Exception {
        var cfg = MongoConfiguration.class;
        try (var ctx = new AnnotationConfigApplicationContext(cfg)) {
            var repository = ctx.getBean(VehicleRepository.class);
            var countDownLatch = new CountDownLatch(1);

            repository.count().doOnSuccess(cnt -> System.out.printf(COUNT, cnt))
                .thenMany(repository.saveAll(
                    Flux.just(
                        new Vehicle(null, "TEM0001", "RED", 4, 4),
                        new Vehicle(null, "TEM0002", "RED", 4, 4))))
                    .last()
                    .then(repository.count()).doOnSuccess(cnt -> System.out.printf(COUNT, cnt))
                    .then(repository.findByVehicleNo("TEM0001")).doOnSuccess(System.out::println)
                    .then(repository.deleteAll())
                    .doOnTerminate(countDownLatch::countDown)
                    .then(repository.count()).subscribe(cnt -> System.out.printf(COUNT, cnt));

            countDownLatch.await();
        }
    }
}
```

The flow starts with a count, and when that succeeds the Vehicle instances are put into MongoDB. When the last() vehicle has been added, a count is done again, followed by a query that in turn is followed by a deleteAll. All these methods are called in a reactive fashion one after the other, triggered by an event. Because we don't want to block using the block() method, we wait for the code to execute using a CountDownLatch; the counter is decremented after the deletion of all records, after which the program will continue execution. Granted this is still blocking, when using this in a full reactive stack, you would probably return the Mono from the last then and do further composition or give the output a Spring WebFlux controller (see Chapter 4).

9-2. Using Redis

Problem

You want to utilize Redis to store data.

Solution

Download and install Redis and use Spring and Spring Data to access the Redis instance.

How It Works

Redis is an in-memory data structure store that can be used as a database, cache (see Chapter 14), message broker, or streaming engine. Here we will look at the data store capabilities. For this Redis provides lists, (ordered) sets, hashes, strings, bitmaps, geospatial indexes, and streams. To be very performant, Redis uses an in-memory dataset. Depending on your situation, you can store this to disk periodically or have a commit log continuously added.

Downloading and Starting Redis

Redis can be downloaded from https://redis.io/download. At the moment of writing, version 7.0 was the recently released stable version. For installation instructions you can consult https://redis.io/docs/getting-started/installation/, which contains the instructions for most operating systems.

After downloading and installing Redis, start it using the redis-server command from the command line. When started, the output should be similar to that in Figure 9-2. It will output the process ID (PID) and the port number (default 6379) it listens on.

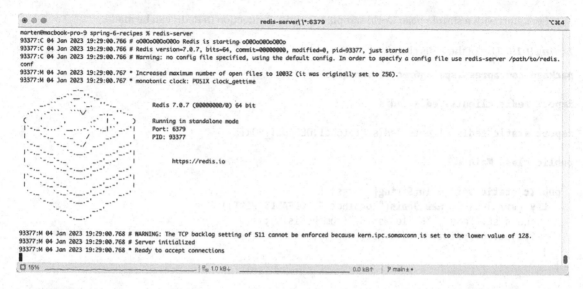

Figure 9-2. *Output after starting Redis*

Connecting to Redis

To be able to connect to Redis, a client is needed, much like a JDBC driver to connect to a database. There are several clients available. A full list can be found on the Redis website (`https://redis.io/clients`). For this recipe the Jedis client will be used as that is quite active and recommended by the Redis team.

ⓘ   The relevant dependencies for Jedis need to be added to the classpath. When using Maven add the following dependency:

```
<dependency>
  <groupId>redis.clients</groupId>
  <artifactId>jedis</artifactId>
  <version>4.3.1</version>
</dependency>
```

Or add the following when using Gradle:

```
compile 'redis.clients:jedis:4.3.1'
```

Let's start with a simple hello world sample to see if a connection to Redis can be made.

Listing 9-19. Use of the Jedis client

```
package com.apress.spring6recipes.nosql;

import redis.clients.jedis.Jedis;

import static redis.clients.jedis.Protocol.DEFAULT_PORT;

public class Main {

  public static void main(String[] args) {
    try (var jedis = new Jedis("localhost", DEFAULT_PORT)) {
      jedis.set("msg", "Hello World, from Redis!");
      System.out.println(jedis.get("msg"));
    }
  }
}
```

A Jedis client is created and passed the name of the host and the port to connect to, in this case simply localhost and the default port (6379). The set method on the Jedis client will put a message in the store, and with get the message is retrieved again. Instead of a simple object, you could also have Redis mimic a List or a Map.

Listing 9-20. Main class to run the code

```
package com.apress.spring6recipes.nosql;

import redis.clients.jedis.Jedis;

import static redis.clients.jedis.Protocol.DEFAULT_PORT;

public class Main {

  public static void main(String[] args) {
    try (var jedis = new Jedis("localhost", DEFAULT_PORT)) {
      jedis.rpush("authors", "Marten Deinum", "Josh Long", "Daniel Rubio", "Gary Mak");
      System.out.println("Authors: " + jedis.lrange("authors", 0, -1));

      jedis.hset("sr_5", "authors", "Josh Long, Marten Deinum");
      jedis.hset("sr_5", "published", "2019");

      jedis.hset("sr_6", "authors", "Josh Long, Marten Deinum");
      jedis.hset("sr_6", "published", "2023");

      System.out.println("Spring 5 Recipes " + jedis.hgetAll("sr_5"));
      System.out.println("Spring 6 Recipes " + jedis.hgetAll("sr_6"));
    }

  }
}
```

With rpush and lpush, one can add elements to a list. rpush adds the elements to the end of the list, and lpush adds them to the start of the list. To retrieve them the lrange and rrange methods can be used. The lrange starts from the left and takes a start and end index. The sample uses -1 that indicates everything.

To add elements to a map, use hset; this takes a key and a field and value. Another option is to use hmset (multi-set), which takes a Map<String, String> or Map<byte[], byte[]> as an argument.

Storing Objects with Redis

Redis is a key/value store and can only handle String or byte[]. The same goes for the keys. So storing an object in Redis isn't as straightforward as with other technologies. The object needs to be serialized to a String or a byte[] before storing.

Let's reuse the Vehicle record from Recipe 9-1 and store and retrieve that using a Jedis client.

Listing 9-21. Vehicle record

```java
package com.apress.spring6recipes.nosql;

import java.io.Serializable;

public record Vehicle (String vehicleNo, String color, int wheel, int seat)
        implements Serializable {

}
```

Let's also declare a VehicleRepository interface (the same as in Recipe 9-1 for MongoDB).

Listing 9-22. VehicleRepository interface

```java
package com.apress.spring6recipes.nosql;

import java.util.List;

public interface VehicleRepository {

  long count();
  void save(Vehicle vehicle);
  void delete(Vehicle vehicle);
  List<Vehicle> findAll();
  Vehicle findByVehicleNo(String vehicleNo);
}
```

Finally, the implementation of the VehicleRepository for Redis.

Listing 9-23. Redis VehicleRepository implementation

```java
package com.apress.spring6recipes.nosql;

import java.util.List;

import org.springframework.util.SerializationUtils;
```

```java
import jakarta.annotation.PreDestroy;
import redis.clients.jedis.Jedis;

public class RedisVehicleRepository implements VehicleRepository {

  private static final String DB_NAME = "vehicles";

  private final Jedis jedis;

  public RedisVehicleRepository(Jedis jedis) {
    this.jedis = jedis;
  }

  @Override
  public long count() {
    return jedis.hkeys(DB_NAME.getBytes()).size();
  }

  @Override
  public void save(Vehicle vehicle) {
    var key = vehicle.vehicleNo();
    var vehicleArray = SerializationUtils.serialize(vehicle);
    jedis.hset(DB_NAME.getBytes(), key.getBytes(), vehicleArray);
  }

  @Override
  public void delete(Vehicle vehicle) {
    jedis.hdel(DB_NAME.getBytes(), vehicle.vehicleNo().getBytes());
  }

  @Override
  public List<Vehicle> findAll() {
    return jedis.hkeys(DB_NAME).stream()
            .map(this::findByVehicleNo).toList();
  }

  @Override
  public Vehicle findByVehicleNo(String vehicleNo) {
    var vehicleArray = jedis.hget(DB_NAME.getBytes(), vehicleNo.getBytes());
    return (Vehicle) SerializationUtils.deserialize(vehicleArray);
  }

  @PreDestroy
  public void cleanUp() {
    findAll().forEach(this::delete);
  }
}
```

The repository will need the Jedis client we used earlier to store the objects we want. As we don't really have a table in Redis, we can use the hash type, which is kind of a distributed map. We will use vehicles as the key for the hash, and this will give us the ability to add vehicles to the resulting hash. The hash key is converted to a byte[ ], and as our Vehicle is Serializable, we can convert that to a byte[ ] as well.

ⓘ   When using Java serialization, one would need to implement the `java.io.Serializable` interface. This is needed to make the object serializable for Java. Before storing the object, it needs to be converted into a `byte[]`. In Java the `ObjectOutputStream` can write objects, and the `ByteArrayOutputStream` can write to a `byte[]`. To transform a `byte[]` into an object again, the `ObjectInputStream` and `ByteArrayInputStream` are of help. Spring has a helper class for this, the `org.springframework.util.SerializationUtils`, which provides the `serialize` and `deserialize` helper methods.

⚠   The implementation is not the most optimized implementation for a Redis-based repository; it is only there to serve this recipe as a sample.

Now in the main class, let's create some Vehicle instances and store and retrieve them using our repository.

Listing 9-24. Main class

```
package com.apress.spring6recipes.nosql;

import org.springframework.context.annotation.AnnotationConfigApplicationContext;

import com.apress.spring6recipes.nosql.config.RedisConfig;

public class Main {

  private static final String COUNT = "Number of Vehicles: %d%n";

  public static void main(String[] args) {
    var cfg = RedisConfig.class;
    try (var ctx = new AnnotationConfigApplicationContext(cfg)) {
      var repository = ctx.getBean(VehicleRepository.class);

      System.out.printf(COUNT, repository.count());

      repository.save(new Vehicle("TEM0001", "RED", 4, 4));
      repository.save(new Vehicle("TEM0002", "RED", 4, 4));

      System.out.printf(COUNT, repository.count());

      var v = repository.findByVehicleNo("TEM0001");

      System.out.println(v);

      var vehicleList = repository.findAll();

      System.out.printf(COUNT, vehicleList.size());
```

```
    vehicleList.forEach(System.out::println);
    System.out.printf(COUNT, repository.count());

  }
 }
}
```

Another option is to use a String representation of the object. Convert the Vehicle into XML or JSON, which would be more flexible than a byte[]. Let's take a look at converting the object into JSON using the excellent Jackson JSON library.

Listing 9-25. Redis Vehicle implementation–storing JSON

```
package com.apress.spring6recipes.nosql;

import java.util.List;

import org.springframework.util.SerializationUtils;

import com.fasterxml.jackson.core.JsonProcessingException;
import com.fasterxml.jackson.databind.ObjectMapper;

import jakarta.annotation.PreDestroy;
import redis.clients.jedis.Jedis;

public class RedisVehicleRepository implements VehicleRepository{

  private static final String DB_NAME = "vehicles";

  private final Jedis jedis;
  private final ObjectMapper mapper;

  public RedisVehicleRepository(Jedis jedis, ObjectMapper mapper) {
    this.jedis = jedis;
    this.mapper = mapper;
  }

  @Override
  public long count() {
    return jedis.hkeys(DB_NAME).size();
  }

  @Override
  public void save(Vehicle vehicle) {
    try {
      var vehicleJson = mapper.writeValueAsString(vehicle);
      jedis.hset(DB_NAME, vehicle.vehicleNo(), vehicleJson);
    } catch (JsonProcessingException e) {
      throw new RuntimeException(e);
    }
  }
```

```
@Override
public void delete(Vehicle vehicle) {
  jedis.hdel(DB_NAME, vehicle.vehicleNo());
}

@Override
public List<Vehicle> findAll() {
  return jedis.hkeys(DB_NAME).stream()
        .map(this::findByVehicleNo).toList();
}

@Override
public Vehicle findByVehicleNo(String vehicleNo) {
  var vehicleJson = jedis.hget(DB_NAME, vehicleNo);
  try {
    return mapper.readValue(vehicleJson, Vehicle.class);
  } catch (JsonProcessingException ex) {
    throw new RuntimeException(ex);
  }
}

@PreDestroy
public void cleanUp() {
  findAll().forEach(this::delete);
}
}
```

First, an instance of the Jackson ObjectMapper is needed. This object is used to convert from and to JSON. When writing the writeValueAsString method is used as it will transform the object into a JSON string. This String is then stored in Redis. Next, the string is read again and passed to the readValue method of the ObjectMapper. Based on the type argument, Vehicle.class here, an object is constructed, and the JSON is mapped to an instance of the given class.

Storing objects when using Redis isn't straightforward, and some argue that this isn't how Redis was intended to be used (storing complex object structures).

Configuring and Using the RedisTemplate

Depending on the client library used to connect to Redis, it might be harder to use the Redis API. To unify this there is the RedisTemplate. It can work with most Redis Java clients out there. Next to providing a unified approach, it also takes care of translating any exceptions into Spring's DataAccessException hierarchy. This lets it to integrate nicely with any already existing data access and allows it to use Spring's transaction support.

ℹ   Before using Spring Data Redis, the relevant jars need to be added to the classpath. When using Maven add the following dependency:

```
<dependency>
  <groupId>org.springframework.data</groupId>
  <artifactId>spring-data-redis</artifactId>
```

```
    <version>3.0.0</version>
</dependency>
```

Or add the following when using Gradle:

```
compile 'org.springframework.data:spring-data-redis:3.0.0'
```

The RedisTemplate requires a RedisConnectionFactory to be able to get a connection. The RedisConnectionFactory is an interface, and several implementations are available. In this case the JedisConnectionFactory is needed.

Listing 9-26. RedisTemplate configuration

```java
package com.apress.spring6recipes.nosql.config;

import com.apress.spring6recipes.nosql.RedisVehicleRepository;
import com.apress.spring6recipes.nosql.Vehicle;
import org.springframework.context.annotation.Bean;
import org.springframework.context.annotation.Configuration;
import org.springframework.data.redis.connection.RedisConnectionFactory;
import org.springframework.data.redis.connection.jedis.JedisConnectionFactory;
import org.springframework.data.redis.core.RedisTemplate;

@Configuration
public class RedisConfig {

  @Bean
  public RedisTemplate<String, Vehicle> redisTemplate(
          RedisConnectionFactory connectionFactory) {
    var template = new RedisTemplate<String, Vehicle>();
    template.setConnectionFactory(connectionFactory);
    return template;
  }

  @Bean
  public RedisConnectionFactory redisConnectionFactory() {
    return new JedisConnectionFactory();
  }

  @Bean
  public RedisVehicleRepository vehicleRepository(RedisTemplate<String, Vehicle> redis) {
    return new RedisVehicleRepository(redis);
  }
}
```

Notice the return type of the redisTemplate bean method. The RedisTemplate is a generic class and requires a key and value type to be specified. In this case string is the type of key, and Vehicle is the type of value. When storing and retrieving objects, the RedisTemplate will take care of the conversion. Conversion is done using a RedisSerializer, which is an interface for which several implementations exist (see Table 9-1). The default RedisSerializer, the JdkSerializationRedisSerializer, uses standard Java serialization to convert objects to a byte[] and back.

Table 9-1. *Default RedisSerializer Implementations*

Name	Description
ByteArrayRedisSerializer	Stores a byte[] as is and returns the same.
GenericToStringSerializer	String to byte[] serializer, uses the Spring ConversionService to convert objects to String before converting to a byte[].
GenericJackson2ToStringSerializer	Read and write JSON using a Jackson 2 ObjectMapper using dynamic typing.
Jackson2JsonRedisRedisSerializer	Read and write JSON using a Jackson 2 ObjectMapper using static typing (one serializer per object type is needed).
JdkSerializationRedisSerializer	Uses default Java serialization and deserialization and is the default implementation used.
OxmSerializer	Read and write XML using Spring's Marshaller and Unmarshaller.
StringRedisSerializer	Simple String to byte[] converter.

To be able to use the RedisTemplate, the RedisVehicleRepository class needs to be modified. The Main class we had can remain unchanged.

Listing 9-27. RedisTemplate VehicleRepository implementation

```
package com.apress.spring6recipes.nosql;

import java.util.List;
import java.util.Map;

import org.springframework.dao.DataAccessException;
import org.springframework.data.redis.connection.DataType;
import org.springframework.data.redis.connection.RedisConnection;
import org.springframework.data.redis.core.RedisCallback;
import org.springframework.data.redis.core.RedisTemplate;
import org.springframework.data.redis.core.ScanOptions;

import com.fasterxml.jackson.core.JsonProcessingException;

import jakarta.annotation.PreDestroy;

public class RedisVehicleRepository implements VehicleRepository{

  private static final String DB_NAME = "vehicles";

  private final RedisTemplate<String, Vehicle> redis;

  public RedisVehicleRepository(RedisTemplate<String, Vehicle> redis) {
    this.redis = redis;
  }
```

```java
@Override
public long count() {
  return redis.opsForHash().size(DB_NAME);
}

@Override
public void save(Vehicle vehicle) {
  redis.opsForHash().put(DB_NAME, vehicle.vehicleNo(), vehicle);
}

@Override
public void delete(Vehicle vehicle) {
  redis.opsForHash().delete(DB_NAME, vehicle.vehicleNo());
}

@Override
public List<Vehicle> findAll() {
  try (var cursor = redis.opsForHash().scan(DB_NAME, ScanOptions.NONE)) {
    return cursor.stream()
            .map(Map.Entry::getValue)
            .map(Vehicle.class::cast).toList();
  }
}

@Override
public Vehicle findByVehicleNo(String vehicleNo) {
  return (Vehicle) redis.opsForHash().get(DB_NAME, vehicleNo);
}

@PreDestroy
public void cleanUp() {
  findAll().forEach(this::delete);
}
}
```

The biggest advantage here is that one can use objects and the template handles the hard work of converting from and to objects. Notice how the set method takes a String and Vehicle as arguments instead of only String or byte[]. This makes code more readable and easier to maintain. By default JDK serialization is used. To use Jackson a different RedisSerializer needs to be configured.

Listing 9-28. VehicleRepository configuration

```java
package com.apress.spring6recipes.nosql.config;

@Configuration
public class RedisConfig {

  @Bean
  public RedisTemplate<String, Vehicle> redisTemplate(
          RedisConnectionFactory connectionFactory) {
    var template = new RedisTemplate<String, Vehicle>();
    template.setConnectionFactory(connectionFactory);
```

```
template.setDefaultSerializer(new GenericJackson2JsonRedisSerializer());
template.setEnableTransactionSupport(true);
return template;
return new JedisConnectionFactory();
```

The RedisTemplate will now use a Jackson ObjectMapper to perform the serialization and deserialization. The remainder of the code can remain the same. When running the main program again, it still works, and the object will be stored using JSON. When Redis is used inside a transaction, it can also participate in that same transaction. For this set the enableTransactionSupport property on the RedisTemplate to true. This will take care of executing the Redis operation inside the transaction, when the transaction commits.

Create a Spring Data Redis Repository

The repository using the RedisTemplate made working with Redis easier. However, it can be made even easier for a lot of use cases. As with JPA, Spring Data Redis also provides the option to write a repository using one of the Spring Data base classes and then use the out-of-the-box methods. For this one needs to extend the Repository interface (or one of the sub-interfaces) of Spring Data.

Underneath it will use the RedisTemplate, but the code is much cleaner. In fact the whole RedisVehicleRepository can be removed, and the VehicleRepository can extend the CrudRepository interface.

First, the configuration can be changed.

Listing 9-29. Spring Data Redis configuration

```
package com.apress.spring6recipes.nosql.config;

import com.apress.spring6recipes.nosql.Vehicle;
import org.springframework.context.annotation.Bean;
import org.springframework.context.annotation.Configuration;
import org.springframework.data.redis.connection.RedisConnectionFactory;
import org.springframework.data.redis.connection.jedis.JedisConnectionFactory;
import org.springframework.data.redis.core.RedisTemplate;
import org.springframework.data.redis.repository.configuration.EnableRedisRepositories;
import org.springframework.data.redis.serializer.GenericJackson2JsonRedisSerializer;

@Configuration
@EnableRedisRepositories(basePackages = "com.apress.spring6recipes.nosql")
public class RedisConfig {

    @Bean
    public RedisTemplate<String, Vehicle> redisTemplate(
            RedisConnectionFactory connectionFactory) {
        var template = new RedisTemplate<String, Vehicle>();
        template.setConnectionFactory(connectionFactory);
        template.setDefaultSerializer(new GenericJackson2JsonRedisSerializer());
        template.setEnableTransactionSupport(true);
        return template;
    }
}
```

```
@Bean
public RedisConnectionFactory redisConnectionFactory() {
  return new JedisConnectionFactory();
}
}
```

First, notice the removal of the @Bean method that constructed the RedisVehicleRepository. Second, notice the addition of the @EnableRedisRepositories annotation. This enables detection of interfaces that extend the Spring Data Repository interface (or one of its sub-interfaces) and are used for domain objects.

Spring Data needs to know which field of the Vehicle to use as the key. By default it will look for a field named id or a field annotated with org.springframework.data.annotation.Id. For the Vehicle let's add an additional field named id. To define the keyspace (the hash used earlier), you can add a @RedisHash annotation on the class. By default it will use the name of the class Vehicle as the keyspace. We want to use vehicles; hence, we need to explicitly add it. Finally, the vehicleNo field needs an @Indexed; without this the field would not be usable in a query. This will generate a secondary index for this field so it can be used in queries.

Listing 9-30. Modified Vehicle class

```
package com.apress.spring6recipes.nosql;

import java.util.UUID;

import org.springframework.data.annotation.Id;
import org.springframework.data.redis.core.RedisHash;
import org.springframework.data.redis.core.index.Indexed;

@RedisHash("vehicles")
public record Vehicle (String id, @Indexed String vehicleNo, String color, int wheel,
int seat) {

  public Vehicle(String vehicleNo, String color, int wheel, int seat) {
    this(UUID.randomUUID().toString(), vehicleNo, color, wheel, seat);
  }
}
```

Finally, the VehicleRepository interface to be used.

Listing 9-31. Spring Data VehicleRepository

```
package com.apress.spring6recipes.nosql;

import org.springframework.data.repository.ListCrudRepository;

public interface VehicleRepository extends ListCrudRepository<Vehicle, String> {

  Vehicle findByVehicleNo(String vehicleNo);
}
```

You might wonder where all the methods have gone. They are already defined in the super-interfaces and as such can be removed from this interface. The findByVehicleNo method is still there. This method will still be used to look up a Vehicle by its vehicleNo property. All the findBy methods are converted into Redis queries. The part after the findBy is interpreted as a property name. It is also possible to write more complex queries using different operators like and, or, and between.

ℹ️   We extend ListCrudRepository for convenience. The findAll now returns a List instead of an Iterable.

Now running the Main class again should still result in the same output. However, the actual code written to work with Redis has been minimized.

Listing 9-32. Main class

```java
package com.apress.spring6recipes.nosql;

import org.springframework.context.annotation.AnnotationConfigApplicationContext;

import com.apress.spring6recipes.nosql.config.RedisConfig;

public class Main {

  private static final String COUNT = "Number of Vehicles: %d%n";

  public static void main(String[] args) {
    var cfg = RedisConfig.class;
    try (var ctx = new AnnotationConfigApplicationContext(cfg)) {
      var repository = ctx.getBean(VehicleRepository.class);

      System.out.printf(COUNT, repository.count());

      repository.save(new Vehicle("TEM0001", "RED", 4, 4));
      repository.save(new Vehicle("TEM0002", "RED", 4, 4));

      System.out.printf(COUNT, repository.count());

      var v = repository.findByVehicleNo("TEM0001");

      System.out.println(v);

      var vehicleList = repository.findAll();

      System.out.printf(COUNT, vehicleList.size());
      vehicleList.forEach(System.out::println);
      System.out.printf(COUNT, repository.count());
      repository.deleteAll();
    }
  }
}
```

Create a Reactive Spring Data Redis Repository

Instead of creating a traditional Redis repository, it is also possible to create a reactive repository. However, as Spring Data Redis, at the moment of writing, doesn't have a reactive counterpart for the repository style but only a `ReactiveRedisTemplate`, this entails implementing the repository ourselves. To use the `ReactiveRedisTemplate`, we also have to use a reactive driver implementation and modify the configuration accordingly.

Listing 9-33. Reactive Redis configuration

```
package com.apress.spring6recipes.nosql.config;

import org.springframework.context.annotation.Bean;
import org.springframework.context.annotation.Configuration;
import org.springframework.data.redis.connection.ReactiveRedisConnectionFactory;
import org.springframework.data.redis.connection.RedisConnectionFactory;
import org.springframework.data.redis.connection.jedis.JedisConnectionFactory;
import org.springframework.data.redis.connection.lettuce.LettuceConnectionFactory;
import org.springframework.data.redis.core.ReactiveRedisTemplate;
import org.springframework.data.redis.core.RedisTemplate;
import org.springframework.data.redis.serializer.GenericJackson2JsonRedisSerializer;
import org.springframework.data.redis.serializer.Jackson2JsonRedisSerializer;
import org.springframework.data.redis.serializer.RedisSerializationContext;
import org.springframework.data.redis.serializer.RedisSerializer;
import org.springframework.data.redis.serializer.StringRedisSerializer;

import com.apress.spring6recipes.nosql.RedisVehicleRepository;
import com.apress.spring6recipes.nosql.Vehicle;

@Configuration
public class RedisConfig {

  @Bean
  public ReactiveRedisTemplate<String, Vehicle> redisTemplate(
          ReactiveRedisConnectionFactory connectionFactory) {

    RedisSerializationContext.RedisSerializationContextBuilder<String, Vehicle> builder =
          RedisSerializationContext.newSerializationContext(new StringRedisSerializer());
    var serializer = new Jackson2JsonRedisSerializer<>(Vehicle.class);
    RedisSerializationContext<String, Vehicle> context = builder.hashValue(serializer).
    build();

    return new ReactiveRedisTemplate<>(connectionFactory, context);
  }

  @Bean
  public ReactiveRedisConnectionFactory redisConnectionFactory() {
    return new LettuceConnectionFactory("localhost", 6379);
  }
}
```

```
@Bean
public RedisVehicleRepository vehicleRepository(ReactiveRedisTemplate<String, Vehicle>
redis) {
  return new RedisVehicleRepository(redis);
}

}
```

To be able to use reactive repository implementation, you first have to use a reactive implementation of the Redis driver. As the Jedis driver isn't reactive, we need to switch to the Lettuce driver. The driver is used by the LettuceConnectionFactory (it can be used in the regular way, and it is both a blocking and non-blocking driver). The ReactiveRedisConnectionFactory is needed to create a ReactiveRedisTemplate. Next to a RedisSerializationContext, this holds the information on how to serialize the keys and values (both regular and for the hash). As we want to use a regular String, we use the StringRedisSerializer as the default, and for the hashValue we want to use the Jackson JSON library and hence the Jackson2JsonRedisSerializer. With this we construct the ReactiveRedisTemplate and inject it into our RedisVehicleRepository.

Next, change the VehicleRepository to use the ReactiveRedisTemplate so it will become reactive. You also need to change the return types of the methods to either a Mono (zero or one value) or a Flux (zero or more values). We could also have used one of the other supported reactive types like RxJava3 or Mutiny Rye. But here we use Project Reactor.

Listing 9-34. Reactive Spring Data–based VehicleRepository interface

```
package com.apress.spring6recipes.nosql;

import java.util.Map;

import org.springframework.data.redis.core.ReactiveRedisTemplate;
import org.springframework.data.redis.core.ScanOptions;

import jakarta.annotation.PreDestroy;
import reactor.core.publisher.Flux;
import reactor.core.publisher.Mono;

public class RedisVehicleRepository implements VehicleRepository{

  private static final String DB_NAME = "vehicles";

  private final ReactiveRedisTemplate<String, Vehicle> redis;

  public RedisVehicleRepository(ReactiveRedisTemplate<String, Vehicle> redis) {
    this.redis = redis;
  }

  @Override
  public Mono<Long> count() {
    return redis.opsForHash().size(DB_NAME);
  }
```

```java
@Override
public Mono<Void> save(Vehicle vehicle) {
  return redis.opsForHash().put(DB_NAME, vehicle.vehicleNo(), vehicle).then();
}

@Override
public Mono<Void> delete(Vehicle vehicle) {
  return redis.opsForHash().remove(DB_NAME, vehicle.vehicleNo()).then();
}

@Override
public Flux<Vehicle> findAll() {
  return redis.opsForHash().scan(DB_NAME, ScanOptions.NONE)
          .map(Map.Entry::getValue)
          .cast(Vehicle.class);
}

@Override
public Mono<Vehicle> findByVehicleNo(String vehicleNo) {
  return redis.opsForHash().get(DB_NAME, vehicleNo).cast(Vehicle.class);
}

@PreDestroy
public void cleanUp() {
  findAll().map(this::delete).subscribe();
}
}
```

The final piece that would need to change is the Main class to test all this. Instead of blocking calls, you want to use a stream of methods to be called.

Listing 9-35. Main class to run the code

```java
package com.apress.spring6recipes.nosql;

import java.util.concurrent.CountDownLatch;

import org.springframework.context.annotation.AnnotationConfigApplicationContext;

import com.apress.spring6recipes.nosql.config.RedisConfig;

import reactor.core.publisher.Flux;

public class Main {

  private static final String COUNT = "Number of Vehicles: %d%n";

  public static void main(String[] args) throws Exception {
    var cfg = RedisConfig.class;
    try (var ctx = new AnnotationConfigApplicationContext(cfg)) {
      var repository = ctx.getBean(VehicleRepository.class);
      var countDownLatch = new CountDownLatch(1);
```

```
var vehicles = Flux.just(
        new Vehicle("TEM0001", "RED", 4, 4),
        new Vehicle("TEM0002", "RED", 4, 4));

  repository.count().doOnSuccess(cnt -> System.out.printf(COUNT, cnt))
    .thenMany(vehicles.flatMap(repository::save))
        .then(repository.count()).doOnSuccess(cnt -> System.out.printf(COUNT, cnt))
        .then(repository.findByVehicleNo("TEM0001")).doOnSuccess(System.out::println)
        .doOnTerminate(countDownLatch::countDown)
        .then(repository.count()).subscribe(cnt -> System.out.printf(COUNT, cnt));

  countDownLatch.await();
  }
 }
}
```

The flow starts with a count, and when that succeeds the Vehicle instances are put into Redis. When the vehicles have been added, a count is done again, followed by a query. All these methods are called in a reactive fashion one after the other, triggered by an event. Because we don't want to block using the block() method, we wait for the code to execute using a CountDownLatch; the counter is decremented after the deletion of all records, after which the program will continue execution. Granted this is still blocking, when using this in a full reactive stack, you would probably return the Mono from the last then and do further composition or give the output a Spring WebFlux controller (see Chapter 4).

9-3. Using Neo4j

Problem

You want to use Neo4j in your application.

Solution

Use the Spring Data Neo4j library to access Neo4j.

How It Works

Downloading and Running Neo4j

Neo4j can be downloaded from the Neo4j website (https://neo4j.com/download/). For this recipe it is enough to download the community edition; however, it should also work with the commercial version of Neo4j. Windows users can run the installer to install. Mac and Linux users can extract the archive and, from inside the directory created, start with bin/neo4j. Mac users can also use Homebrew (https://brew.sh) to install Neo4j with brew install neo4j; starting can then be done with neo4j start on the command line.

After starting on the command line, the output should be similar to that as shown in Listing 9-36.

Listing 9-36. Neo4j startup output

```
2023-01-05 19:48:37.589+0000 INFO  Starting...
2023-01-05 19:48:38.495+0000 INFO  This instance is ServerId{5511a206} (5511a206-9cc1-4cd0-
af11-4c4b10c0a779)
```

```
2023-01-05 19:48:40.121+0000 INFO  ======== Neo4j 4.4.16 ========
2023-01-05 19:48:42.298+0000 INFO  Initializing system graph model for component 'security-
users' with version -1 and status UNINITIALIZED
2023-01-05 19:48:42.312+0000 INFO  Setting up initial user from defaults: neo4j
2023-01-05 19:48:42.313+0000 INFO  Creating new user 'neo4j' (passwordChangeRequired=true,
suspended=false)
2023-01-05 19:48:42.333+0000 INFO  Setting version for 'security-users' to 3
2023-01-05 19:48:42.337+0000 INFO  After initialization of system graph model component
'security-users' have version 3 and status CURRENT
2023-01-05 19:48:42.345+0000 INFO  Performing postInitialization step for component
'security-users' with version 3 and status CURRENT
2023-01-05 19:48:42.992+0000 INFO  Bolt enabled on 0.0.0.0:7687.
2023-01-05 19:48:44.269+0000 INFO  Remote interface available at
2023-01-05 19:48:44.275+0000 INFO  id:
402C3B3CDF4CFDC5FF07BC34F4FD765ADD00594BCF495D316D110FFFC9A38C10
2023-01-05 19:48:44.275+0000 INFO  name: system
2023-01-05 19:48:44.275+0000 INFO  creationDate: 2023-01-05T19:48:40.843Z
2023-01-05 19:48:44.275+0000 INFO  Started.
```

Starting Neo4j

Let's start by creating a simple hello world for Neo4j. Create a Main class that connects to the server, adds some data to Neo4j, and retrieves it again.

Listing 9-37. Main class

```java
package com.apress.spring6recipes.nosql;

import org.neo4j.driver.GraphDatabase;

import java.util.stream.Collectors;

import static org.neo4j.driver.Values.parameters;

public class Main {

    private static final String URL = "bolt://localhost:7687";
    private static final String CREATE_QUERY = "CREATE (:Greetings {msg: $msg})";
    private static final String MATCH_QUERY = "MATCH (g) RETURN g.msg";
    private static final String DELETE_ALL_QUERY = "MATCH (n) DETACH DELETE n";

    public static void main(String[] args) {

        try (var driver = GraphDatabase.driver(URL)) {
            try (var session = driver.session()) {
                session.writeTransaction(tx -> {
                    tx.run(CREATE_QUERY, parameters("msg", "Hello"));
                    tx.run(CREATE_QUERY, parameters("msg", "World"));
                    return null;
                });
```

```
        var readResult = session.readTransaction(tx -> {
          var res = tx.run(MATCH_QUERY);
          return res.stream().map(it -> it.get(0).asString()).collect(Collectors.
          joining(" "));
        });

        System.out.println("After Read: \n\t" + readResult);

        session.run(DELETE_ALL_QUERY);
      }
    }
  }
}
```

This main will connect to the Neo4j server using the Bolt protocol. Next, it will start a transaction and create two nodes. Next, all nodes are retrieved, and the value of the msg property is printed to the console. Neo4j is good at traversing relations between nodes. It is especially optimized for that (just like other graph data stores).

ℹ️ The relevant dependencies for Neo4j need to be added to the classpath. When using Maven add the following dependency:

```xml
<dependency>
  <groupId>org.neo4j</groupId>
  <artifactId>neo4j</artifactId>
  <version>5.3.0</version>
</dependency>
<dependency>
  <groupId>org.neo4j.driver</groupId>
  <artifactId>neo4j-java-driver</artifactId>
  <version>5.3.1</version>
</dependency>
```

Or add the following when using Gradle:

```
implementation group: 'org.neo4j', name: 'neo4j', version: '5.3.0'
implementation group: 'org.neo4j.driver', name: 'neo4j-java-driver', version: '5.3.1'
```

Let's create some nodes that have a relationship between them.

Listing 9-38. Main class

```java
package com.apress.spring6recipes.nosql;

import org.neo4j.driver.GraphDatabase;

import java.util.Map;

public class Main {
```

```java
private static final String URL = "bolt://localhost:7687";
private static final String CREATE_CHARACTER_QUERY = "CREATE (:Character {name: $name})";
private static final String CREATE_PLANET_QUERY = "CREATE (:Planet {name: $name})";
private static final String CREATE_PLANET_REL_QUERY = "MATCH (a:Character), (b:Planet)
WHERE a.name=$cname AND b.name=$pname CREATE (a)-[r:LOCATION]->(b)";
private static final String CREATE_FRIENDS_REL_QUERY = "MATCH (a:Character), (b:Character)
WHERE a.name=$aname AND b.name=$bname CREATE (a)-[r:FRIENDS_WITH]->(b)";
private static final String CREATE_MASTER_REL_QUERY = "MATCH (a:Character), (b:Character)
WHERE a.name=$aname AND b.name=$bname CREATE (a)-[r:MASTER_OF]->(b)";
private static final String DELETE_ALL_QUERY = "MATCH (n) DETACH DELETE n";
public static void main(String[] args) {

    try (var driver = GraphDatabase.driver(URL)) {
        try (var session = driver.session()) {

            // Characters
            session.run(CREATE_CHARACTER_QUERY, Map.of("name", "Yoda"));
            session.run(CREATE_CHARACTER_QUERY, Map.of("name", "Luke Skywalker"));
            session.run(CREATE_CHARACTER_QUERY, Map.of("name", "Leia Organa"));
            session.run(CREATE_CHARACTER_QUERY, Map.of("name", "Han Solo"));
            // Planets
            session.run(CREATE_PLANET_QUERY, Map.of("name", "Dagobah"));
            session.run(CREATE_PLANET_QUERY, Map.of("name", "Tatooine"));
            session.run(CREATE_PLANET_QUERY, Map.of("name", "Alderaan"));

            // Relations
            session.run(CREATE_PLANET_REL_QUERY, Map.of("cname", "Yoda", "pname", "Dagobah"));
            session.run(CREATE_PLANET_REL_QUERY, Map.of("cname", "Leia Organa", "pname",
            "Alderaan"));
            session.run(CREATE_PLANET_REL_QUERY, Map.of("cname", "Luke Skywalker", "pname",
            "Tatooine"));

            session.run(CREATE_FRIENDS_REL_QUERY, Map.of("aname", "Luke Skywalker", "bname",
            "Han Solo"));
            session.run(CREATE_FRIENDS_REL_QUERY, Map.of("aname", "Leia Organa", "bname", "Han
            Solo"));
            session.run(CREATE_FRIENDS_REL_QUERY, Map.of("aname", "Leia Organa", "bname", "Luke
            Skywalker"));

            session.run(CREATE_MASTER_REL_QUERY, Map.of("aname", "Yoda", "bname", "Luke
            Skywalker"));
        }

        try (var session = driver.session()) {
            var result = session.run("MATCH (n) RETURN n.name as name");
            result.stream()
                    .flatMap(m -> m.fields().stream())
                    .map(row -> row.key() + " : " + row.value().asString())
                    .forEach(System.out::println);
```

```
        session.run(DELETE_ALL_QUERY);
      }
    }
  }
}
```

The code reflects a tiny part of the Star Wars universe. It has characters and their locations, which are actually planets. There are also relations between people (see Figure 9-3 for the relationship diagram).

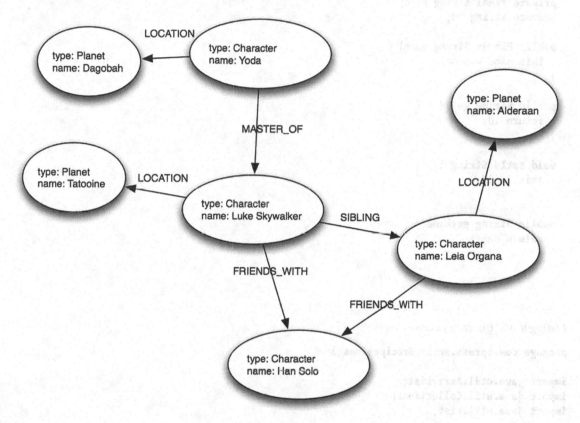

Figure 9-3. *Relationships in sample*

The relationships are created by matching the character to another character or a planet (depending on the type of relationship). After inserting all the data, it will execute the Cypher query MATCH (n) RETURN n.name as name. This selects all nodes and returns the name property of all the nodes.

Mapping Objects with Neo4j

The code until now is quite low level and bound to plain Neo4j and Cypher queries. Creating and manipulating nodes is cumbersome. Ideally, one would use Planet and Character classes and have those stored/retrieved from Neo4j.

First, create the Planet and Character classes.

Listing 9-39. Planet class

```
package com.apress.spring6recipes.nosql;

public class Planet {

  private final String name;
  private String id;

  public Planet(String name) {
    this.name = name;
  }

  public String getId() {
    return id;
  }

  void setId(String id) {
    this.id=id;
  }

  public String getName() {
    return name;
  }

}
```

Listing 9-40. Character class

```
package com.apress.spring6recipes.nosql;

import java.util.ArrayList;
import java.util.Collections;
import java.util.List;

public class Character {

  private final String name;
  private final List<Character> friends = new ArrayList<>();

  private String id;
  private Planet location;
  private Character apprentice;

  public Character(String name) {
    this.name=name;
  }
```

```java
public String getId() {
    return id;
}

void setId(String id) {
    this.id=id;
}

public String getName() {
    return name;
}

public Planet getLocation() {
    return location;
}

public void setLocation(Planet location) {
    this.location = location;
}

public Character getApprentice() {
    return apprentice;
}

public void setApprentice(Character apprentice) {
    this.apprentice = apprentice;
}

public List<Character> getFriends() {
    return Collections.unmodifiableList(friends);
}

public void addFriend(Character friend) {
    friends.add(friend);
}
}
```

The Planet class is quite straightforward. It has an id and name property. The Character class is a bit more complicated. It also has the id and name properties along with some additional properties for the relationships. There is the location for the LOCATION relationship, a collection of Characters for the FRIENDS_WITH relationship, and also an apprentice for the MASTER_OF relationship.

To be able to store these classes, let's create a StarwarsRepository interface to hold the save operations.

Listing 9-41. StarwarsRepository interface

```java
package com.apress.spring6recipes.nosql;

public interface StarwarsRepository {

    Planet save(Planet planet);
    Character save(Character charachter);

}
```

And here's the implementation for Neo4j.

Listing 9-42. Neo4j StarwarsRepository implementation class

```java
package com.apress.spring6recipes.nosql;

import org.neo4j.driver.Driver;

import java.util.Map;

class Neo4jStarwarsRepository implements StarwarsRepository {

  private static final String CREATE_PLANET_QUERY = "CREATE (a:Planet {id: randomUUID(),
name: $name}) RETURN a.id";
  private static final String CREATE_CHARACTER_QUERY = "CREATE (a:Character {id:
randomUUID(), name: $name}) RETURN a.id";

  private static final String CREATE_PLANET_REL_QUERY = "MATCH (a:Character), (b:Planet)
WHERE a.id=$aid AND b.id=$bid CREATE (a)-[r:LOCATION]->(b)";
  private static final String CREATE_FRIENDS_REL_QUERY = "MATCH (a:Character), (b:Character)
WHERE a.id=$aid AND b.id=$bid CREATE (a)-[r:FRIENDS_WITH]->(b)";
  private static final String CREATE_MASTER_REL_QUERY = "MATCH (a:Character), (b:Character)
WHERE a.id=$aid AND b.id=$bid CREATE (a)-[r:MASTER_OF]->(b)";

  private final Driver db;
  Neo4jStarwarsRepository(Driver db) {
    this.db = db;
  }

  @Override
  public Planet save(Planet planet) {
    if (planet.getId() != null) {
      return planet;
    }

    try (var session = db.session()) {
      var res = session.run(CREATE_PLANET_QUERY, Map.of("name", planet.getName()));
      planet.setId(res.single().get(0).asString());
      return planet;
    }
  }

  @Override
  public Character save(Character charr) {
    if (charr.getId() != null) {
      return charr;
    }

    try (var session = db.session()) {
      session.executeWrite(tx -> {
        var res = tx.run(CREATE_CHARACTER_QUERY, Map.of( "name", charr.getName()));
        charr.setId(res.single().get(0).asString());
```

```
      if (charr.getLocation() != null) {
        var location = save(charr.getLocation());
        tx.run(CREATE_PLANET_REL_QUERY, Map.of("aid", charr.getId(),
                                          "bid", location.getId()));
      }
      for (var friend : charr.getFriends()) {
        friend = save(friend);
        tx.run(CREATE_FRIENDS_REL_QUERY, Map.of("aid", charr.getId(),
                                          "bid", friend.getId()));
      }

      if (charr.getApprentice() != null) {
        var apprentice = save(charr.getApprentice());
        tx.run(CREATE_MASTER_REL_QUERY, Map.of("aid", charr.getId(),
                                          "bid", apprentice.getId()));
      }
      return null;
    });
  }
  return charr;
}
}
```

There is a whole lot going on here to store the objects in Neo4j. For the Planet it is pretty easy. First, check if it has already been persisted (the id is not null in that case); if not start a transaction, create a node, set the name property, and transfer the id to the Planet object. However, for the Character class, it is a bit more complicated as all the relationships need to be taken into account.

It isn't recommended to use the technical ID generated by Neo4j, hence the generation of the id in Neo4j. You could also create your own generator for the IDs (or use client-generated UUIDs) and store them directly. Here we chose to let Neo4j handle it and copy it back to the object.

The Main class needs to be modified to reflect the changes to the classes.

Listing 9-43. Main class

```java
package com.apress.spring6recipes.nosql;

import org.neo4j.driver.GraphDatabase;

import java.util.stream.Stream;

public class Main {

  private static final String URL = "bolt://localhost:7687";
  private static final String DELETE_ALL_QUERY = "MATCH (n) DETACH DELETE n";
```

```java
public static void main(String[] args) {

    try (var driver = GraphDatabase.driver(URL)) {
        var repository = new Neo4jStarwarsRepository(driver);

        // Planets
        var dagobah = new Planet("Dagobah");
        var alderaan = new Planet("Alderaan");
        var tatooine = new Planet("Tatooine");

        Stream.of(dagobah, alderaan, tatooine).forEach(repository::save);

        // Characters
        var han = new Character("Han Solo");
        var leia = new Character("Leia Organa");
        leia.setLocation(alderaan);
        leia.addFriend(han);

        var luke = new Character("Luke Skywalker");
        luke.setLocation(tatooine);
        luke.addFriend(han);
        luke.addFriend(leia);

        var yoda = new Character("Yoda");
        yoda.setLocation(dagobah);
        yoda.setApprentice(luke);

        Stream.of(han, luke, leia, yoda).forEach(repository::save);

        try(var session = driver.session()) {
            var result = session.run("MATCH (n) RETURN n.name as name");
            result.stream()
                    .flatMap(m -> m.fields().stream())
                    .map(row -> row.key() + " : " + row.value() + ";")
                    .forEach(System.out::println);

            session.run(DELETE_ALL_QUERY);

        }
    }
  }
}
```

When executing the result should still be the same as before. However, the main difference is now the code is using domain objects instead of working directly with nodes.

Use Spring to Configure Neo4j

Currently there is no Spring involved. Let's move the Driver and Neo4JstarwarsRepository to a Spring configuration class. For this create a StarwarsConfig class.

Listing 9-44. StarwarsConfig

```
package com.apress.spring6recipes.nosql;

import org.neo4j.driver.Driver;
import org.neo4j.driver.GraphDatabase;
import org.springframework.beans.factory.annotation.Value;
import org.springframework.context.annotation.Bean;
import org.springframework.context.annotation.Configuration;
import org.springframework.context.annotation.PropertySource;
import org.springframework.context.support.PropertySourcesPlaceholderConfigurer;

@Configuration
@PropertySource("classpath:/application.properties")
public class StarwarsConfig {

  @Bean
  public Driver driver(@Value("${neo4j.url}") String url) {
    return GraphDatabase.driver(url);
  }

  @Bean
  public Neo4jStarwarsRepository starwarsRepository(Driver driver) {
    return new Neo4jStarwarsRepository(driver);
  }

  @Bean
  public static PropertySourcesPlaceholderConfigurer pspc() {
    return new PropertySourcesPlaceholderConfigurer();
  }
}
```

The creation of the Driver and the Neo4JStarwarsRepository has been moved to the configuration class. The configuration of the url has been moved to a properties file, application. properties, which is loaded through the added @PropertySource and converted through the PropertySourcesPlaceholderConfigurer. This way it is easier to configure different URLs for different environments.

Listing 9-45. Application properties

```
neo4j.url=bolt://localhost:7687
```

Now that the configuration has been created, some minor modifications to our Main class are needed as well. We need to start the Spring context and get the beans needed from there.

Listing 9-46. Main class

```
package com.apress.spring6recipes.nosql;

import org.neo4j.driver.Driver;
import org.springframework.context.annotation.AnnotationConfigApplicationContext;

import java.util.stream.Stream;
```

```
public class Main {

  public static void main(String[] args) {
    var cfg = StarwarsConfig.class;
    try (var ctx = new AnnotationConfigApplicationContext(cfg)) {
      var repository = ctx.getBean(StarwarsRepository.class);
      var driver = ctx.getBean(Driver.class);
      try(var session = driver.session()) {
        var result = session.run("MATCH (n) RETURN n.name as name");
        result.stream()
                .flatMap(m -> m.fields().stream())
                .map(row -> row.key() + " : " + row.value() + ";")
                .forEach(System.out::println);

      }
    }
  }
}
```

Using the Spring Data Neo4j Neo4jTemplate

To make working with Neo4j easier, the Spring Data Neo4j project exists. Apart from providing helpers like the Neo4jTemplate and Neo4jTransactionManager, it is also an object mapping framework. It allows to annotate classes with @Node so that they can be used as domain objects for Neo4j, much like the @Entity annotation from JPA. If one wants to use the Spring Data Neo4j-provided classes and helpers, we need to start by annotating our domain objects.

ℹ️   The relevant dependencies for Spring Data Neo4j need to be added to the classpath. When using Maven add the following dependency:

```
<dependency>
  <groupId>org.springframework.data</groupId>
  <artifactId>spring-data-neo4j</artifactId>
  <version>7.0.0</version>
</dependency>
```

Or add the following when using Gradle:

```
implementation group: 'org.springframework.data', name: 'spring-data-neo4j',
version: '7.0.0'
```

The Character and Planet classes need a @Node annotation. This marks them as a node for Neo4j. Next, we need to specify the field(s) we want to use as identifier with the @Id annotation. Finally, as we want to generate a UUID, we use the @GeneratedValue annotation. We also specify the UUIDStringGenerator as the class to use to generate our IDs. Listing 9-47 shows the modifications to the Planet class. The remainder can be the same as in Listing 9-39.

Listing 9-47. Planet class with mapping annotations

```
package com.apress.spring6recipes.nosql;

import org.springframework.data.neo4j.core.schema.GeneratedValue;
import org.springframework.data.neo4j.core.schema.Id;
import org.springframework.data.neo4j.core.schema.Node;
import org.springframework.data.neo4j.core.support.UUIDStringGenerator;

@Node
public class Planet {

    private final String name;

    @Id
    @GeneratedValue(UUIDStringGenerator.class)
    private String id;

}
```

The Character class deserves some more annotation to map the relationships in there. That is where the @Relationship annotation comes into play. The list of friends is the **FRIENDS_WITH** relation, the apprentice field the **MASTER_OF**, and finally the location field the **LOCATION** relation. An additional @AccessType annotation is needed on the FRIENDS_WITH relationship; as we don't have a setFriends method, we need to instruct Spring Data to use field-based access for this. Finally, a toString method has been added so that we can use that to print information to the console.

Listing 9-48. Character class with mapping annotations

```
package com.apress.spring6recipes.nosql;

import org.springframework.data.annotation.AccessType;
import org.springframework.data.neo4j.core.schema.GeneratedValue;
import org.springframework.data.neo4j.core.schema.Id;
import org.springframework.data.neo4j.core.schema.Node;
import org.springframework.data.neo4j.core.schema.Relationship;
import org.springframework.data.neo4j.core.support.UUIDStringGenerator;

import java.util.ArrayList;
import java.util.Collections;
import java.util.List;

@Node
public class Character {

    private final String name;
    @Relationship(type="FRIENDS_WITH")
    private @AccessType(AccessType.Type.FIELD) List<Character> friends = new ArrayList<>();

    @Id
    @GeneratedValue(UUIDStringGenerator.class)
    private String id;
```

```
@Relationship(type = "LOCATION")
private Planet location;
@Relationship(type = "MASTER_OF")
private Character apprentice;

@Override
public String toString() {
  return String.format("Character[name=%s, planet=%s]",
          this.name, this.location != null ? this.location.getName() : "");
}
```

Let's clean up our Neo4jStarwarsRepository by using Spring-managed transactions and the Neo4jTemplate, also two new methods to find all Planet and Character instances from Neo4j.

Listing 9-49. Spring Data Neo4jStarwarsRepository

```
package com.apress.spring6recipes.nosql;

import jakarta.annotation.PreDestroy;
import org.springframework.data.neo4j.core.Neo4jTemplate;
import org.springframework.stereotype.Repository;
import org.springframework.transaction.annotation.Transactional;

@Repository
@Transactional
class Neo4jStarwarsRepository implements StarwarsRepository {

  private final Neo4jTemplate neo4j;

  Neo4jStarwarsRepository(Neo4jTemplate neo4j) {
    this.neo4j = neo4j;
  }

  @Override
  public Planet save(Planet planet) {
    return neo4j.save(planet);
  }

  @Override
  public Character save(Character character) {
    return neo4j.save(character);
  }

  @Override
  public Iterable<Character> findAllCharacters() {
    return neo4j.find(Character.class).all();
  }

  @Override
  public Iterable<Planet> findAllPlanets() {
    return neo4j.find(Planet.class).all();
  }
```

```
@PreDestroy
public void cleanUp() {
    // Clean up when shutdown
    neo4j.deleteAll(Character.class);
    neo4j.deleteAll(Planet.class);
}
}
```

The class is now annotated with @Transactional, and the constructor takes a Neo4jTemplate. Both the save methods now directly call the save method on the Neo4jTemplate. The findAll is also passed on to the Neo4jTemplate.findAll method. This method takes a type and will return a FluentFindOperation. ExecutableQuery. We could limit the results by using the matching method of this, but as we want all, we just call all().

Finally, we need to modify our StarwarsConfig to include a Neo4jClient (needed to construct a Neo4jTemplate) and a Neo4jTransactionManager to enable Spring-managed transactions.

Listing 9-50. StarwarsConfig with Neo4jTemplate

```
package com.apress.spring6recipes.nosql;

import org.neo4j.driver.Driver;
import org.neo4j.driver.GraphDatabase;
import org.springframework.beans.factory.annotation.Value;
import org.springframework.context.annotation.Bean;
import org.springframework.context.annotation.Configuration;
import org.springframework.context.annotation.PropertySource;
import org.springframework.context.support.PropertySourcesPlaceholderConfigurer;
import org.springframework.data.neo4j.core.Neo4jClient;
import org.springframework.data.neo4j.core.Neo4jTemplate;
import org.springframework.data.neo4j.core.transaction.Neo4jTransactionManager;
import org.springframework.transaction.annotation.EnableTransactionManagement;

@Configuration
@PropertySource("classpath:/application.properties")
@EnableTransactionManagement
public class StarwarsConfig {

    @Bean
    public Driver driver(@Value("${neo4j.url}") String url) {
        return GraphDatabase.driver(url);
    }

    @Bean
    public Neo4jClient neo4jClient(Driver driver) {
        return Neo4jClient.create(driver);
    }

    @Bean
    public Neo4jTemplate neo4jTemplate(Neo4jClient neo4jClient) {
        return new Neo4jTemplate(neo4jClient);
    }
```

```
@Bean
public Neo4jStarwarsRepository starwarsRepository(Neo4jTemplate neo4jTemplate) {
    return new Neo4jStarwarsRepository(neo4jTemplate);
}

@Bean
public Neo4jTransactionManager transactionManager(Driver driver) {
    return Neo4jTransactionManager.with(driver).build();
}

@Bean
public static PropertySourcesPlaceholderConfigurer pspc() {
    return new PropertySourcesPlaceholderConfigurer();
}
}
```

To enable annotation-driven transactions, we added @EnableTransactionManagement, which will need a PlatformTransactionManager, in this case the Neo4jTransactionManager. The Neo4jClient is a wrapper around the Neo4j driver in use and is the basic building block for Spring Data Neo4j. Finally, there is the Neo4jTemplate that uses the Neo4jClient to generate and execute the queries. Finally, the Neo4jTemplate is passed into the Neo4jStarwarsRepository.

To run this the Main class needs some minor modifications as well, mainly concerning the reading of the result (see Listing 9-51 for the modifications).

Listing 9-51. Modifications for the main class

```
public static void main(String[] args) {

    try (var ctx = new AnnotationConfigApplicationContext(StarwarsConfig.class)) {
        var repository = ctx.getBean(StarwarsRepository.class);
        repository.findAllCharacters().forEach(System.out::println);
        repository.findAllPlanets().forEach(System.out::println);
    }
}
```

Using Spring Data Neo4j Repositories

The code has been simplified considerably. The usage of the Neo4jTemplate and Neo4jTransactionManager made it a lot easier to work with entities together with Neo4j. It can be even easier. As with the JPA version of Spring Data, it can generate repositories for you. The only thing you need to do is write an interface. Let's create a PlanetRepository and CharacterRepository to operate on the entities.

Listing 9-52. Spring Data Neo4j-based CharacterRepository

```
package com.apress.spring6recipes.nosql;

import org.springframework.data.repository.CrudRepository;

public interface CharacterRepository extends CrudRepository<Character, String> { }
```

And here's the `PlanetRepository`.

Listing 9-53. Spring Data Neo4j-based PlanetRepository

```
package com.apress.spring6recipes.nosql;

import org.springframework.data.repository.CrudRepository;

public interface PlanetRepository extends CrudRepository<Planet, String> { }
```

The repositories all extend CrudRepository, but it could also have been PagingAndSortingRepository or the special Neo4jRepository interface. For the recipe the CrudRepository is sufficient.

Next, rename the StarwarsRepository, and its implementation, to StarwarsService as it isn't really a repository anymore. The implementation also needs to change to operate on the repositories instead of the Neo4jTemplate. For convenience also add a printAll method.

Listing 9-54. StarwarsService interface

```
package com.apress.spring6recipes.nosql;

/**
 * Created by marten on 10-10-14.
 */
public interface StarwarsService {

  Planet save(Planet planet);

  Character save(Character charachter);

  void printAll();

}
```

Here's the modified Neo4jStarwarsService.

Listing 9-55. StarwarsService implementation

```
package com.apress.spring6recipes.nosql;

import jakarta.annotation.PreDestroy;
import org.springframework.stereotype.Service;
import org.springframework.transaction.annotation.Transactional;

@Service
@Transactional
class Neo4jStarwarsService implements StarwarsService {

  private final PlanetRepository planetRepository;
  private final CharacterRepository characterRepository;

  Neo4jStarwarsService(PlanetRepository planetRepository,
                       CharacterRepository characterRepository) {
```

```
  this.planetRepository = planetRepository;
  this.characterRepository = characterRepository;
}

@Override
public Planet save(Planet planet) {
  return planetRepository.save(planet);
}

@Override
public Character save(Character character) {
  return characterRepository.save(character);
}

@Override
public void printAll() {
  planetRepository.findAll().forEach(System.out::println);
  characterRepository.findAll().forEach(System.out::println);
}

@PreDestroy
public void cleanUp() {
  // Clean up when shutdown
  characterRepository.deleteAll();
  planetRepository.deleteAll();
}
}
```

Now all operations are done on the specific repository interfaces. Those interfaces don't create instances themselves. To enable the creation, the @EnableNeo4jRepositories annotation needs to be added to the configuration class. Also add a @ComponentScan to have the StarwarsService detected and autowired.

Listing 9-56. Spring Data StarwarsConfig

```
@Configuration
@PropertySource("classpath:/application.properties")
@EnableTransactionManagement
@ComponentScan
@EnableNeo4jRepositories
public class StarwarsConfig {
}
```

Notice the @EnableNeo4jRepositories annotation. This annotation will scan the configured base packages for repositories. When one is found, a dynamic implementation is created. This implementation eventually delegates to the Neo4jTemplate.

Finally, modify the Main class to use the refactored StarwarsService.

Listing 9-57. Main class–modifications

```
package com.apress.spring6recipes.nosql;

import org.springframework.context.annotation.AnnotationConfigApplicationContext;

import java.util.stream.Stream;

public class Main {

  public static void main(String[] args) {

    try (var ctx = new AnnotationConfigApplicationContext(StarwarsConfig.class)) {
      var service = ctx.getBean(StarwarsService.class);

      service.printAll();
    }
  }
}
```

Now all the components have been changed to use the dynamically created Spring Data Neo4j repositories.

Simplifying the Spring Neo4j Configuration

Currently, the StarwarsConfig manually configures all the moving parts: the Neo4jClient, Neo4jTemplate, etc. Although you learned that all of this is used underneath the Spring Data Neo4j repositories, it doesn't mean you want to manually configure them. The only thing that changes, generally, from application to application is the configuration of the Driver. Spring Data Neo4j recognizes this and has a base configuration class, AbstractNeo4jConfig, which you can extend. When extending this class, you only need to implement the driver method and annotate it with @Bean, and all other parts are configured automatically.

Listing 9-58. StarwarsConfig with the base class

```
package com.apress.spring6recipes.nosql;

import org.neo4j.driver.Driver;
import org.neo4j.driver.GraphDatabase;
import org.springframework.beans.factory.annotation.Value;
import org.springframework.context.annotation.Bean;
import org.springframework.context.annotation.ComponentScan;
import org.springframework.context.annotation.Configuration;
import org.springframework.context.annotation.PropertySource;
import org.springframework.context.support.PropertySourcesPlaceholderConfigurer;
import org.springframework.data.neo4j.config.AbstractNeo4jConfig;
import org.springframework.data.neo4j.repository.config.EnableNeo4jRepositories;
import org.springframework.transaction.annotation.EnableTransactionManagement;
```

```
@Configuration
@PropertySource("classpath:/application.properties")
@EnableTransactionManagement
@ComponentScan
@EnableNeo4jRepositories
public class StarwarsConfig extends AbstractNeo4jConfig {

  @Value("${neo4j.url}")
  private String url;

  @Override
  @Bean
  public Driver driver() {
    return GraphDatabase.driver(url);
  }

  @Bean
  public static PropertySourcesPlaceholderConfigurer pspc() {
    return new PropertySourcesPlaceholderConfigurer();
  }
}
```

Using Spring Data Neo4j Reactive Repositories

Instead of the blocking repositories, it is also possible to get a reactive repository. It will now return a
Mono for methods returning zero or one element like findById and a Flux for methods returning zero or
more elements like findAll. The default Neo4j Java driver already has reactive support built in. To use
the reactive way of programming, you need either RxJava3 or Project Reactor in the classpath and use
the proper repository RxJava3CrudRepository or ReactiveCrudRepository (or the special Neo4j one,
ReactiveNeo4jRepository). We are going to use the ReactiveCrudRepository to enable reactive access.

First, modify the repositories to extend ReactiveCrudRepository instead of the regular
CrudRepository.

Listing 9-59. Reactive CharacterRepository

```
package com.apress.spring6recipes.nosql;

import org.springframework.data.repository.reactive.ReactiveCrudRepository;

public interface CharacterRepository extends ReactiveCrudRepository<Character, String> { }
```

Listing 9-60. Reactive PlanetRepository

```
package com.apress.spring6recipes.nosql;

import org.springframework.data.repository.reactive.ReactiveCrudRepository;

public interface PlanetRepository extends ReactiveCrudRepository<Planet, String> { }
```

Next, we need to modify the `StarwarsService` (Listing 9-61) and the `Neo4jStarwarsService` (Listing 9-62) implementation to be reactive as well.

Listing 9-61. Reactive StarwarsService

```
package com.apress.spring6recipes.nosql;

import reactor.core.publisher.Mono;

public interface StarwarsService {

  Mono<Planet> save(Planet planet);
  Mono<Character> save(Character charachter);
  Mono<Void> printAll();
  Mono<Void> deleteAll();

}
```

Listing 9-62. Reactive StarwarsService implementation

```
package com.apress.spring6recipes.nosql;

import jakarta.annotation.PreDestroy;
import org.springframework.stereotype.Service;
import org.springframework.transaction.annotation.Transactional;
import reactor.core.publisher.Mono;

@Service
@Transactional
class Neo4jStarwarsService implements StarwarsService {

  private final PlanetRepository planetRepository;
  private final CharacterRepository characterRepository;

  Neo4jStarwarsService(PlanetRepository planetRepository,
                       CharacterRepository characterRepository) {
    this.planetRepository = planetRepository;
    this.characterRepository = characterRepository;
  }

  @Override
  public Mono<Planet> save(Planet planet) {
    return planetRepository.save(planet);
  }

  @Override
  public Mono<Character> save(Character character) {
    return characterRepository.save(character);
  }
```

```
@Override
public Mono<Void> printAll() {
  return planetRepository.findAll().doOnNext(System.out::println)
          .thenMany(characterRepository.findAll().doOnNext(System.out::println)).then();
}

@PreDestroy
public Mono<Void> deleteAll() {
  return characterRepository.deleteAll()
          .then(planetRepository.deleteAll());
}
}
```

As we are now using the reactive parts of Spring Data Neo4j, the configuration needs to follow along as well. We can extend the AbstractReactiveNeo4jConfig class to help set up the parts and only implement the driver method. We also need to replace the @EnableNeo4jRepositories with @ EnableReactiveNeo4jRepositories. See Listing 9-63.

Listing 9-63. Reactive Neo4j configuration

```
package com.apress.spring6recipes.nosql;

import org.neo4j.driver.Driver;
import org.neo4j.driver.GraphDatabase;
import org.springframework.beans.factory.annotation.Value;
import org.springframework.context.annotation.Bean;
import org.springframework.context.annotation.ComponentScan;
import org.springframework.context.annotation.Configuration;
import org.springframework.context.annotation.PropertySource;
import org.springframework.context.support.PropertySourcesPlaceholderConfigurer;
import org.springframework.data.neo4j.config.AbstractReactiveNeo4jConfig;
import org.springframework.data.neo4j.repository.config.EnableReactiveNeo4jRepositories;
import org.springframework.transaction.annotation.EnableTransactionManagement;

@Configuration
@PropertySource("classpath:/application.properties")
@EnableTransactionManagement
@ComponentScan
@EnableReactiveNeo4jRepositories
public class StarwarsConfig extends AbstractReactiveNeo4jConfig {

  @Value("${neo4j.url}")
  private String url;
  @Override
  @Bean
  public Driver driver() {
    return GraphDatabase.driver(url);
  }

  @Bean
  public static PropertySourcesPlaceholderConfigurer pspc() {
    return new PropertySourcesPlaceholderConfigurer();
  }
}
```

Finally, our Main needs to be modified to call the methods in a reactive pipeline.

Listing 9-64. Reactive main class

```java
package com.apress.spring6recipes.nosql;

import org.springframework.context.annotation.AnnotationConfigApplicationContext;
import reactor.core.publisher.Flux;
import reactor.core.publisher.Mono;

import java.util.concurrent.CountDownLatch;

public class Main {

  public static void main(String[] args) throws Exception {

    try (var ctx = new AnnotationConfigApplicationContext(StarwarsConfig.class)) {
      var service = ctx.getBean(StarwarsService.class);
      // Planets
      var dagobah = new Planet("Dagobah");
      var alderaan = new Planet("Alderaan");
      var tatooine = new Planet("Tatooine");

      var planets = Flux.just(dagobah, alderaan, tatooine);

      // Characters
      var han = new Character("Han Solo");
      var leia = new Character("Leia Organa");
      var luke = new Character("Luke Skywalker");
      var yoda = new Character("Yoda");

      leia.setLocation(alderaan);
      leia.addFriend(han);

      luke.setLocation(tatooine);
      luke.addFriend(han);
      luke.addFriend(leia);

      yoda.setLocation(dagobah);
      yoda.setApprentice(luke);

      var characters = Flux.just(han, luke, leia, yoda);
      var countDownLatch = new CountDownLatch(1);
      planets.flatMap(service::save)
              .thenMany(characters.concatMap(service::save))
              .then(service.printAll())
              .then(service.deleteAll())
              .doOnTerminate(countDownLatch::countDown).subscribe();

      countDownLatch.await();
    }
  }
}
```

The main now uses a `Flux` instead of a `Stream` for the planets and characters. When the planets are saved, the characters are saved, and when that is done, we print everything as we did before. Because we don't want to block using the `block()` method, we wait for the code to execute using a `CountDownLatch`; the counter is decremented after the deletion of all records, after which the program will continue execution. Granted this is still blocking, when using this in a full reactive stack, you would probably return the `Mono` from the last `then` and do further composition or give the output a Spring WebFlux controller (see Chapter 4).

9-4. Using Couchbase

Problem

You want to use Couchbase in your application to store documents.

Solution

First, download, install, and set up Couchbase. Then use the Spring Data Couchbase project to store and retrieve documents from the data store.

How It Works

Download and Install Couchbase

Couchbase can be downloaded from `www.Couchbase.com/downloads` for various OSes including Windows. At the moment of writing, version 7.1 was the latest version and is the one used for this recipe.

💡 The `bin` directory also contains a `Couchbase.sh` that starts Couchbase in a Docker container, to save you the installation.

Set Up Couchbase

After downloading and starting Couchbase, open your browser and go to http://localhost:8091, and you should be greeted with a page similar to that of Figure 9-4. You can either start a new one or join an existing cluster. For this recipe you will start a new cluster. Thus, click the **Setup New Cluster** button.

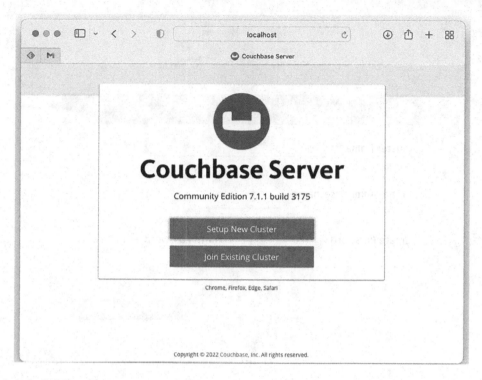

Figure 9-4. *Install Couchbase*

In the next screen (see Figure 9-5), you can configure the cluster and specify the name, user, and password for the user. As the name for the cluster, you can use `vehicle-cluster`. For the user use `s6r-user` and password `s6r-password`, but feel free to choose your own (remember to use those in the code samples as well!). Now click the **Next: Accept Terms** button.

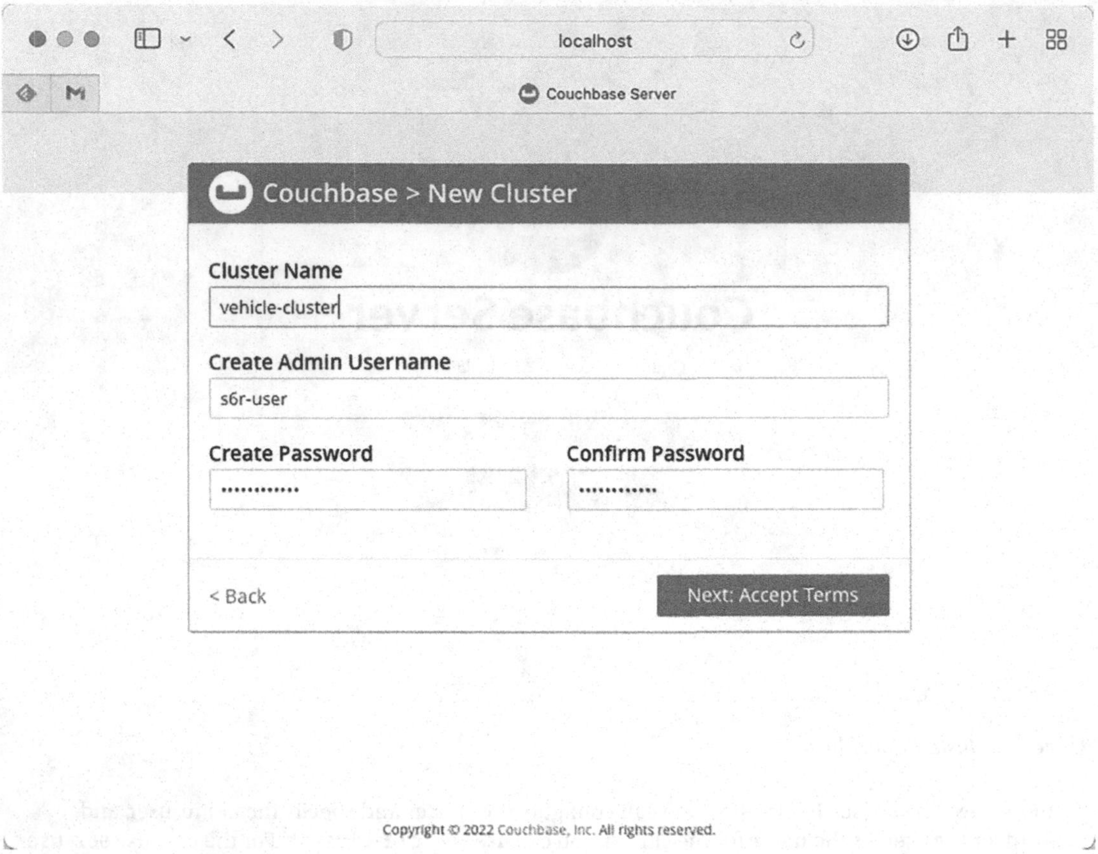

Figure 9-5. *Install Couchbase–new cluster (1/2)*

In the next screen (Figure 9-6), you need to check the box to agree with the **terms and conditions**. Then click **Configure Disk, Memory, Services**.

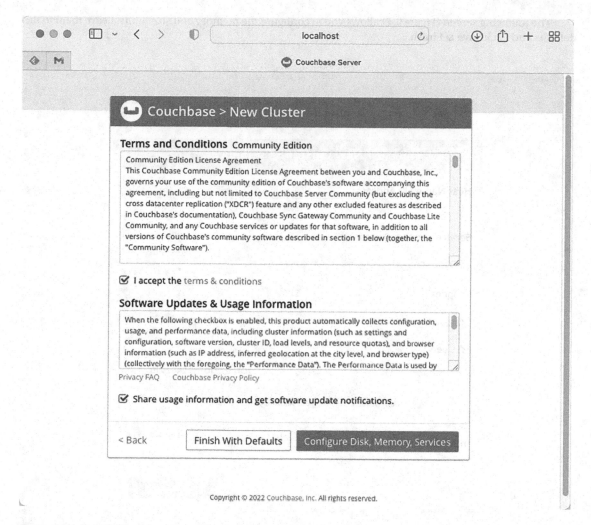

Figure 9-6. *Install Couchbase–new cluster (2/2)*

ℹ️ If you are running the Dockerized Couchbase, you need to reduce the **Data RAM Quota** as that is limited.

The following screen (Figure 9-7) allows you to configure the memory and size limits. Leave them to the defaults and click **Save & Finish**.

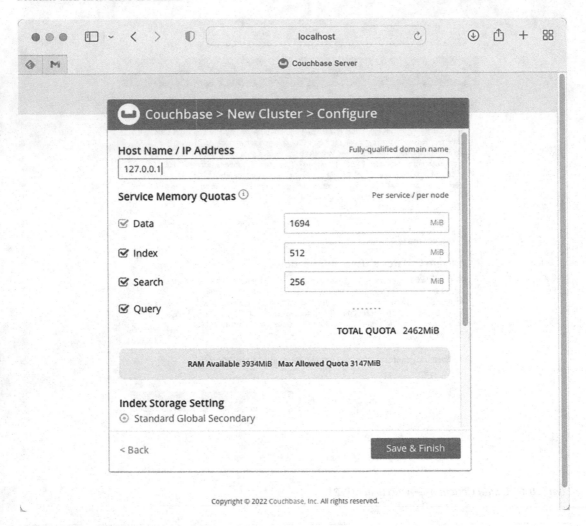

Figure 9-7. *Install Couchbase–configure the cluster*

After a short wait, you are greeted with the administration console/browser of Couchbase and a message stating that you haven't configured any buckets (Figure 9-8).

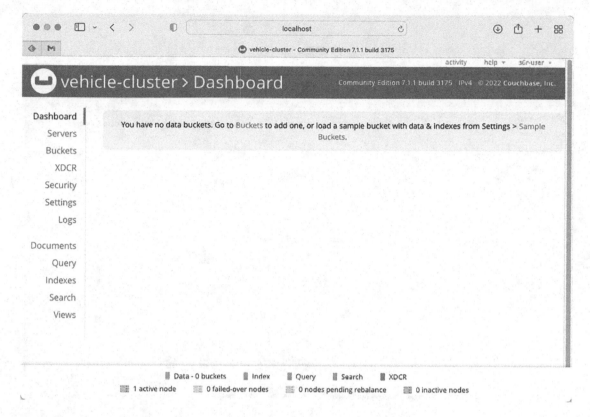

Figure 9-8. *Install Couchbase–create a bucket (1/3)*

To create a bucket, navigate to the Buckets page by clicking **Buckets**. You will then be greeted by the Buckets administration page (Figure 9-9).

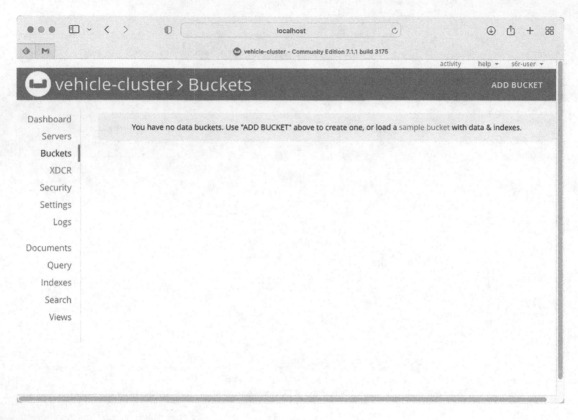

Figure 9-9. *Install Couchbase–create a bucket (2/3)*

Here we have the message again stating there are no buckets configured. Click the **Add Bucket** link in the top right to open the wizard to add a bucket (Figure 9-10).

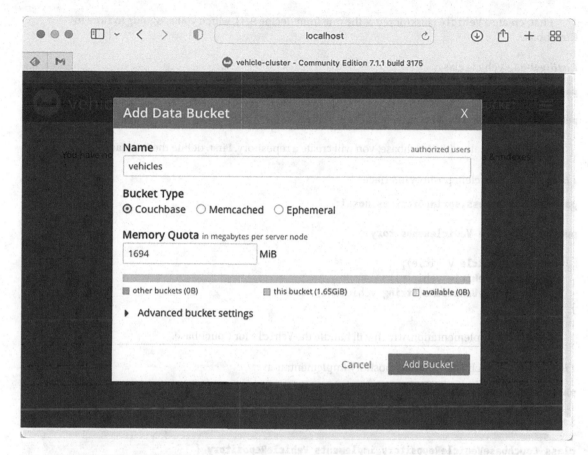

Figure 9-10. Install Couchbase–create a bucket (3/3)

In this screen you can create a bucket and configure the settings of the bucket. We are going to leave the defaults as for this recipe that will suffice. For the name pick vehicles as that is what you are going to store in here. After filling out the required fields and configuring the settings as you like (or leaving the defaults), click the **Add Bucket** button. This will create the bucket with a default scope and collection both aptly named _default.

Storing and Retrieving Documents with Couchbase

To store an object in Couchbase, you need to create a document that can hold various types of content, like Serializable objects, JSON, String date, or binary data in the form of a Netty ByteBuf. However, the primary type of content is JSON. This way you can use it with other technologies as well. When using a binary content, you are restricting yourself to the usage of Java-based solutions. In this recipe we will be using JSON content.

Before storing an object in Couchbase, you need to make a connection to the cluster. To connect to Couchbase, we need a Cluster to be able to access the Bucket you created while doing the setup for Couchbase. You can use the Cluster class to create a connection to the earlier set-up cluster. The resulting Cluster can be used to open a Bucket with the bucket() method. For this recipe we are going to use the default bucket and simplest cluster setup.

First, create a Vehicle class (or reuse the one from Recipe 9-1), which you are going to store in Couchbase.

Listing 9-65. Vehicle class

```
package com.apress.spring6recipes.nosql;

public record Vehicle(String vehicleNo, String color, int wheel, int seat) { }
```

To communicate with Couchbase, you will create a repository. First, define the interface.

Listing 9-66. VehicleRepository interface

```
package com.apress.spring6recipes.nosql;

public interface VehicleRepository {

  void save(Vehicle vehicle);
  void delete(Vehicle vehicle);
  Vehicle findByVehicleNo(String vehicleNo);
}
```

Next is the implementation, which will handle the Vehicle for Couchbase.

Listing 9-67. Couchbase VehicleRepository implementation

```
package com.apress.spring6recipes.nosql;

import com.couchbase.client.java.Bucket;

class CouchbaseVehicleRepository implements VehicleRepository {

  private final Bucket bucket;

  public CouchbaseVehicleRepository(Bucket bucket) {
    this.bucket = bucket;
  }

  @Override
  public void save(Vehicle vehicle) {
    bucket.defaultCollection()
            .upsert(vehicle.vehicleNo(), vehicle);
  }

  @Override
  public void delete(Vehicle vehicle) {
    bucket.defaultCollection().remove(vehicle.vehicleNo());
  }
```

```
@Override
public Vehicle findByVehicleNo(String vehicleNo) {
  return bucket.defaultCollection().get(vehicleNo).contentAs(Vehicle.class);
  }
}
```

The repository needs a Bucket for storing the documents. It is like the table of a database (a Bucket is like the table and the Cluster more like the whole database). When storing the Vehicle, it is converted to JSON, and the vehicleNo is used as the ID. After that the upsert method is called. This will either update or insert the document depending on the fact if it already exists or not. Couchbase comes with its own JSON marshalling framework (a repacked version of Jackson), so when storing a Java object, it will use that to convert it to JSON (and when reading it will use it to convert it back to a Java object).

Let's create a Main class that stores and retrieves the data for a Vehicle in the bucket.

Listing 9-68. Main class

```
package com.apress.spring6recipes.nosql;

import com.couchbase.client.java.Cluster;

public class Main {

  public static void main(String[] args) {

    try (var cluster = Cluster.connect("couchbase://127.0.0.1", "s6r-user",
    "s6r-password")){
      var bucket = cluster.bucket("vehicles");

      var vehicleRepository = new CouchbaseVehicleRepository(bucket);
      vehicleRepository.save(new Vehicle("TEM0001", "GREEN", 3, 1));
      vehicleRepository.save(new Vehicle("TEM0004", "RED", 4, 2));

      var v1 = vehicleRepository.findByVehicleNo("TEM0001");
      var v2 = vehicleRepository.findByVehicleNo("TEM0004");

      System.out.println("Vehicle: " + v1);
      System.out.println("Vehicle: " + v2);

      vehicleRepository.delete(v1);
      vehicleRepository.delete(v2);
    }
  }
}
```

First, a connection is made to the Cluster using the CouchbaseCluster.connect() method. This will connect to the cluster on the given URL, username, and password. When using Couchbase in a production environment, you probably want to use one of the other connect methods and pass in a list of hosts to connect to or to set even more properties using the ClusterOptions and ClusterEnvironment (to set things like queryTimeout, searchTimeout, etc.). For this recipe it is enough to use the default settings. Next, you need to specify the Bucket (the one created in the beginning named vehicles) to use for storing and retrieving documents; using cluster.bucket("vehicles") is enough.

The Bucket is used to create an instance of the CouchbaseVehicleRepository. After that two Vehicles are stored, retrieved, and removed again (as to leave no clutter from this recipe). Finally, the connections are closed.

ℹ️ The relevant dependencies for Spring Data Couchbase need to be added to the classpath. When using Maven add the following dependency:

```
<dependency>
  <groupId>org.springframework.data</groupId>
  <artifactId>spring-data-couchbase</artifactId>
  <version>5.0.0</version>
</dependency>
```

Or add the following when using Gradle:

```
implementation group: 'org.springframework.data', name: 'spring-data-couchbase',
version: '5.0.0'
```

Using Spring

At the moment everything is configured in the Main class. Let's move the configuration parts to a CouchbaseConfiguration class and use it to bootstrap an application.

Listing 9-69. Couchbase configuration class

```
package com.apress.spring6recipes.nosql;

import com.couchbase.client.java.Bucket;
import com.couchbase.client.java.Cluster;
import org.springframework.context.annotation.Bean;
import org.springframework.context.annotation.Configuration;

@Configuration
public class CouchbaseConfiguration {

  @Bean
  public Cluster cluster() {
    return Cluster.connect("couchbase://127.0.0.1", "s6r-user", "s6r-password");
  }

  @Bean
  public Bucket bucket(Cluster cluster) {
    return cluster.bucket("vehicles");
  }
}
```

```
@Bean
public CouchbaseVehicleRepository vehicleRepository(Bucket bucket) {
    return new CouchbaseVehicleRepository(bucket);
  }
}
```

The close method on the Cluster will be called automatically as that is one of the predefined destroyMethods that is automatically detected. The construction of the CouchbaseVehicleRepository is still the same, but you now pass a Spring-managed bean to it.

Modify the Main class to use the CouchbaseConfiguration.

Listing 9-70. Main class

```
package com.apress.spring6recipes.nosql;

import org.springframework.context.annotation.AnnotationConfigApplicationContext;

public class Main {

  public static void main(String[] args) {
    var cfg = CouchbaseConfiguration.class;
    try (var ctx = new AnnotationConfigApplicationContext(cfg)) {
      VehicleRepository vehicleRepository = ctx.getBean(VehicleRepository.class);

      vehicleRepository.save(new Vehicle("TEM0001", "GREEN", 3, 1));
      vehicleRepository.save(new Vehicle("TEM0004", "RED", 4, 2));

      var v1 = vehicleRepository.findByVehicleNo("TEM0001");
      var v2 = vehicleRepository.findByVehicleNo("TEM0004");

      System.out.println("Vehicle: " + v1);
      System.out.println("Vehicle: " + v2);

      vehicleRepository.delete(v1);
      vehicleRepository.delete(v2);
    }
  }
}
```

The VehicleRepository is retrieved from the constructed ApplicationContext, and still there are Vehicle instances stored, retrieved, and removed from the Couchbase cluster.

Using Spring Data CouchbaseTemplate

Although using Couchbase from Java with Jackson for mapping JSON is pretty straightforward, it can become quite cumbersome with larger repositories or when using specific indexes and N1QL queries. Not to mention if you want to integrate this in an application that has also other means of storing data. The Spring Data Couchbase project contains a CouchbaseTemplate that takes away part of the plumbing you are now doing in the repository, like mapping to/from JSON, but also converting exceptions into a DataAccessException, which will make it easier to integrate it with other data access technologies that are utilized with Spring.

First, rewrite the repository to use the CouchbaseTemplate.

Listing 9-71. VehicleRepository with CouchbaseTemplate

```
package com.apress.spring6recipes.nosql;

import org.springframework.data.couchbase.core.CouchbaseTemplate;

public class CouchbaseVehicleRepository implements VehicleRepository {

  private final CouchbaseTemplate couchbase;

  public CouchbaseVehicleRepository(CouchbaseTemplate couchbase) {
    this.couchbase = couchbase;
  }

  @Override
  public void save(Vehicle vehicle) {
    couchbase.upsertById(Vehicle.class).one(vehicle);
  }

  @Override
  public void delete(Vehicle vehicle) {
    couchbase.removeById(Vehicle.class).one(vehicle.getVehicleNo());
  }

  @Override
  public Vehicle findByVehicleNo(String vehicleNo) {
    return couchbase.findById(Vehicle.class).one(vehicleNo);
  }
}
```

Now the repository is reduced to just a couple of lines of code. To be able to store the Vehicle, you need to annotate the Vehicle object as it needs to know which field to use for the ID.

Listing 9-72. Vehicle class with annotations

```
package com.apress.spring6recipes.nosql;

import org.springframework.data.annotation.Id;
import org.springframework.data.couchbase.core.mapping.Field;

public record Vehicle(@Id String vehicleNo,
                      @Field String color,
                      @Field int wheel,
                      @Field int seat) { }
```

The field vehicleNo has been annotated with the @Id annotation and the other fields with @Field. Although the latter isn't required to do, it is recommended to specify it. You can also use the @Field annotation to specify a different name for the name of the JSON property, which can be nice if you need to map existing documents to Java objects.

Finally, you need to configure a CouchbaseTemplate in the configuration class.

Listing 9-73. Couchbase configuration

```
package com.apress.spring6recipes.nosql;

import com.couchbase.client.java.Cluster;
import org.springframework.context.annotation.Bean;
import org.springframework.context.annotation.Configuration;
import org.springframework.data.couchbase.CouchbaseClientFactory;
import org.springframework.data.couchbase.SimpleCouchbaseClientFactory;
import org.springframework.data.couchbase.core.CouchbaseTemplate;
import org.springframework.data.couchbase.core.convert.CouchbaseConverter;
import org.springframework.data.couchbase.core.convert.MappingCouchbaseConverter;

@Configuration
public class CouchbaseConfiguration {

  @Bean
  public Cluster cluster() {
    return Cluster.connect("couchbase://127.0.0.1", "s6r-user", "s6r-password");
  }

  @Bean
  public CouchbaseClientFactory couchbaseClientFactory(Cluster cluster) {
    return new SimpleCouchbaseClientFactory(cluster, "vehicles", null);
  }

  @Bean
  public CouchbaseConverter couchbaseConverter() {
    return new MappingCouchbaseConverter();
  }

  @Bean
  public CouchbaseTemplate couchbaseTemplate(CouchbaseClientFactory ccf,
                                             CouchbaseConverter couchbaseConverter) {
    return new CouchbaseTemplate(ccf, couchbaseConverter);
  }

  @Bean
  public CouchbaseVehicleRepository vehicleRepository(CouchbaseTemplate template) {
    return new CouchbaseVehicleRepository(template);
  }
}
```

A CouchbaseTemplate needs a CouchebaseClientFactory and a CouchebaseConverter. The CouchebaseClientFactory is a Spring Data Couchbase component that handles connecting to the Couchbase cluster (hence, we pass it the Cluster). The MappingCouchebaseConverter is used for mapping objects to/from Couchbase and handles the types not directly supported by Couchbase.

When running the Main class, access is still provided, and storing, retrieving, and removing still works.

To make configuration a little easier, Spring Data Couchbase provides a base configuration class, AbstractCouchbaseConfiguration, which you can extend. With this you don't need to configure the Spring Data Couchbase-specific components anymore.

Listing 9-74. Couchbase configuration using the base class

```
package com.apress.spring6recipes.nosql;

import org.springframework.context.annotation.Bean;
import org.springframework.context.annotation.Configuration;
import org.springframework.data.couchbase.config.AbstractCouchbaseConfiguration;
import org.springframework.data.couchbase.core.CouchbaseTemplate;

@Configuration
public class CouchbaseConfiguration extends AbstractCouchbaseConfiguration {

  @Override
  public String getConnectionString() {
    return "couchbase://127.0.0.1";
  }

  @Override
  public String getUserName() {
    return "s6r-user";
  }

  @Override
  public String getPassword() {
    return "s6r-password";
  }

  @Override
  public String getBucketName() {
    return "vehicles";
  }

  @Bean
  public CouchbaseVehicleRepository vehicleRepository(CouchbaseTemplate template) {
    return new CouchbaseVehicleRepository(template);
  }
}
```

The configuration now extends the `AbstractCouchbaseConfiguration` base class, and you only need the connection URL of the bucket, username, and password. The base configuration class provides the `CouchbaseTemplate` and all the objects it needs.

Using Spring Data Couchbase Repositories

As with other technologies, Spring Data Couchbase also provides the option to specify an interface and have an actual repository implementation available at runtime. This way you only need to create an interface and not the concrete implementation. For this, like with other Spring Data projects, you need to extend `CrudRepository`. Note you could also extend the `CouchbaseRepository` if you need that functionality. For this recipe we are going to use `CrudRepository`.

Listing 9-75. Spring Data Couchbase-based VehicleRepository interface

```
package com.apress.spring6recipes.nosql;

import org.springframework.data.repository.CrudRepository;

public interface VehicleRepository extends CrudRepository<Vehicle, String> { }
```

As you can see the interface has no more methods, as all the CRUD methods are provided already. Next, an @EnableCouchbaseRepositories annotation is needed on the configuration class.

Listing 9-76. Spring Data Couchbase configuration

```
package com.apress.spring6recipes.nosql;

import org.springframework.context.annotation.Configuration;
import org.springframework.data.couchbase.config.AbstractCouchbaseConfiguration;
import org.springframework.data.couchbase.repository.config.EnableCouchbaseRepositories;

@Configuration
@EnableCouchbaseRepositories
public class CouchbaseConfiguration extends AbstractCouchbaseConfiguration {
}
```

Finally, the Main class needs a minor modification as instead of the findByVehicleNo you need to use the findById method.

Listing 9-77. Main class

```
package com.apress.spring6recipes.nosql;

import org.springframework.context.annotation.AnnotationConfigApplicationContext;

public class Main {

  public static void main(String[] args) {

    try (var context = new AnnotationConfigApplicationContext(CouchbaseConfiguration.
    class)) {
      VehicleRepository vehicleRepository = context.getBean(VehicleRepository.class);

      vehicleRepository.save(new Vehicle("TEM0001", "GREEN", 3, 1));
      vehicleRepository.save(new Vehicle("TEM0004", "RED", 4, 2));

      vehicleRepository.findById("TEM0001").ifPresent(System.out::println);
      vehicleRepository.findById("TEM0004").ifPresent(System.out::println);

      vehicleRepository.deleteById("TEM0001");
      vehicleRepository.deleteById("TEM0004");
    }
  }
}
```

The findById method returns a java.util.Optional, and as such you can use the ifPresent method to print it to the console.

Using Spring Data Reactive Couchbase Repositories

Instead of the blocking repositories, it is also possible to utilize the ReactiveCouchbaseRepository to get a reactive repository. It will now return a Mono for methods returning zero or one element like findById and a Flux for methods returning zero or more elements like findAll. The default Couchbase driver already has reactive support built in. To be able to use this, you need to have RxJava and RxJava Reactive Streams in your classpath. To be able to use the reactive types from the ReactiveCouchbaseRepository, you would also need Project Reactor in your classpath.

To configure reactive repositories for Couchbase, modify the CouchbaseConfiguration. Instead of @EnableCouchbaseRepositories use @EnableReactiveCouchbaseRepositories.

Listing 9-78. Reactive Couchbase configuration

```
package com.apress.spring6recipes.nosql;

import org.springframework.context.annotation.Configuration;
import org.springframework.data.couchbase.config.AbstractCouchbaseConfiguration;
import org.springframework.data.couchbase.repository.config.
EnableReactiveCouchbaseRepositories;

@Configuration
@EnableReactiveCouchbaseRepositories
public class CouchbaseConfiguration extends AbstractCouchbaseConfiguration {
```

The remainder of the configuration remains the same as compared to the regular Couchbase configuration. We still need to connect to the same Couchbase server and use the same bucket.

Next, for the VehicleRepository instead of CrudRepository, let it extend ReactiveCrudRepository.

Listing 9-79. Reactive Spring Data VehicleRepository interface

```
package com.apress.spring6recipes.nosql;

import org.springframework.data.couchbase.repository.ReactiveCouchbaseRepository;

public interface VehicleRepository
        extends ReactiveCouchbaseRepository<Vehicle, String> { }
```

This is basically all that is needed to get a reactive repository. To be able to test, you would also need to modify the Main class.

Listing 9-80. Main class

```
package com.apress.spring6recipes.nosql;

import org.springframework.context.annotation.AnnotationConfigApplicationContext;
import reactor.core.publisher.Flux;

import java.util.concurrent.CountDownLatch;
```

```java
public class Main {

  public static void main(String[] args) throws InterruptedException {

    try (var ctx = new AnnotationConfigApplicationContext(CouchbaseConfiguration.class)) {
      var repository = ctx.getBean(VehicleRepository.class);

      var countDownLatch = new CountDownLatch(1);

      repository.saveAll(Flux.just(new Vehicle("TEM0001", "GREEN", 3, 1), //
                  new Vehicle("TEM0004", "RED", 4, 2)))
          .last()
          .then(repository.findById("TEM0001")).doOnSuccess(System.out::println)
          .then(repository.findById("TEM0004")).doOnSuccess(System.out::println)
          .then(repository.deleteById(Flux.just("TEM0001", "TEM00004")))
          .doOnTerminate(countDownLatch::countDown)
          .subscribe();
      countDownLatch.await();
    }
  }
}
```

Creating the `ApplicationContext` and obtaining the `VehicleRepository` isn't any different. However, after that we have a chain of method calls one following the other. First, you add two `Vehicle` instances to the data store. When the `last()` one has been saved, you will query the repository for each instance. When that is done, everything is deleted again. For everything to be able to complete, you could either `block()` or wait yourself. Generally, using `block()` in a reactive system is something you want to avoid, hence the use of the `CountDownLatch`. When the `deleteById` method completes, the `CountDownLatch` is decremented. The `countDownLatch.await()` waits till the counter reaches 0 and then finishes the program.

9-5. Summary

In this recipe you took an introductory journey into different types of data stores, including how to use them and how to make using them easier with different modules of the Spring Data family. You started out by taking a look at document-driven stores in the form of MongoDB and the usage of the Spring Data MongoDB module. Next, the journey took you to key-value stores for which Redis was used as an implementation and the usage of the Spring Data Redis module. This was followed by a small trip to a graph-based data store, in this case Neo4j with Spring Data Neo4j, and you built a repository for storing entities. The last data store you looked at was Couchbase together with Spring Data Couchbase. For all the data stores, you looked at the plain usage and how Spring Data can help you make it easier for both configuration and using the data store. As reactive programming is also very popular, we also dipped into reactive programming with Spring Data and the various data stores using reactive drivers (when needed) and Project Reactor.

■ ■ ■

CHAPTER 10

Spring Java Enterprise Services and Remoting Technologies

In this chapter, you will learn about Spring's support for the most common Java enterprise services: Java Management Extensions (JMX), sending email with Jakarta Mail, and scheduling tasks with and without Quartz. In addition, you'll learn about Spring's support for SOAP web services.

JMX is part of Java SE and is a technology for managing and monitoring system resources such as devices, applications, objects, and service-driven networks. These resources are represented as managed beans (MBeans). Spring supports JMX by exporting any Spring bean as model MBean without programming against the JMX API. In addition, Spring can easily access remote MBeans.

Jakarta Mail is the standard API and implementation for sending email in Java. Spring further provides an abstract layer to send email in an implementation-independent fashion.

There are two main options for scheduling tasks on the Java platform: JDK Timer and Quartz Scheduler. JDK Timer offers simple task scheduling features that are bundled with JDK. Compared with JDK Timer, Quartz offers more powerful job scheduling features. For both options, Spring supplies utility classes to configure scheduling tasks in a bean configuration file, without using either API directly.

You'll learn how to create and consume SOAP web services using Spring Web Services (Spring-WS).

The last recipes will cover how you can use the Java Flight Recorder (JFR) as well as the Micrometer API to get insight into your application's behavior and usage.

10-1. Register Spring POJOs as JMX MBeans
Problem

You want to register an object in your Java application as a JMX MBean, to have the ability to look at services that are running and manipulate their state at runtime. This will allow you to run tasks as follows: rerun batch jobs, invoke methods, and change configuration metadata.

Solution

Spring supports JMX by allowing you to export any beans in its IoC container as model MBeans. This can be done simply by declaring an MBeanExporter instance. With Spring's JMX support, you don't need to deal with the JMX API directly. In addition, Spring enables you to declare JSR-160 (Java Management Extensions Remote API) connectors to expose MBeans for remote access over a specific protocol by using a factory bean. Spring provides factory beans for both servers and clients.

© Marten Deinum, Daniel Rubio, Josh Long 2023
M. Deinum et al., *Spring 6 Recipes*, https://doi.org/10.1007/978-1-4842-8649-4_10

Spring's JMX support comes with other mechanisms by which you can assemble an MBean's management interface. These options include using exporting beans by method names, interfaces, and annotations. Spring can also detect and export MBeans automatically from beans declared in the IoC container and annotated with JMX-specific annotations defined by Spring.

How It Works

Suppose you're developing a utility for replicating files from one directory to another. Let's design the interface for this utility.

Listing 10-1. FileReplicator interface

```
package com.apress.spring6recipes.replicator;

import java.io.IOException;

public interface FileReplicator {

  String getSrcDir();
  void setSrcDir(String srcDir);

  String getDestDir();
  void setDestDir(String destDir);

  void replicate() throws IOException;
}
```

The source and destination directories are designed as properties of a replicator object, not method arguments. That means each file replicator instance replicates files only for a particular source and destination directory. You can create multiple replicator instances in your application.

But before you implement this replicator, let's create another interface that copies a file from one directory to another, given its name.

Listing 10-2. FileCopier interface

```
package com.apress.spring6recipes.replicator;

import java.nio.file.Path;

public interface FileCopier {

  void copyFile(Path srcFile, Path destDir);
}
```

There are many strategies for implementing this file copier. For instance, you can make use of the Java NIO classes.

Listing 10-3. FileCopier implementation

```
package com.apress.spring6recipes.replicator;

import java.io.IOException;
import java.nio.file.Files;
import java.nio.file.Path;

public class NioFileCopier implements FileCopier {

  @Override
  public void copyFile(Path srcFile, Path destDir) {
    var destFile = destDir.resolve(srcFile.getFileName());
    try {
      Files.copy(srcFile, destFile);
    } catch (IOException ex) {
      throw new IllegalStateException("Cannot copy file.", ex);
    }
  }
}
```

With the help of a file copier, you can implement the file replicator, as shown in the following code sample.

Listing 10-4. File replication implementation

```
package com.apress.spring6recipes.replicator;

import java.io.IOException;
import java.nio.file.Files;
import java.nio.file.Path;

public class JMXFileReplicator implements FileReplicator {

  private String srcDir;
  private String destDir;
  private FileCopier fileCopier;

  public String getSrcDir() {
    return srcDir;
  }

  public void setSrcDir(String srcDir) {
    this.srcDir = srcDir;
  }

  public String getDestDir() {
    return destDir;
  }
}
```

```java
public void setDestDir(String destDir) {
  this.destDir = destDir;
}

public FileCopier getFileCopier() {
  return fileCopier;
}

public void setFileCopier(FileCopier fileCopier) {
  this.fileCopier = fileCopier;
}

@Override
public synchronized void replicate() throws IOException {
  var files = Path.of(srcDir);

  try (var fileList = Files.list(files)) {
    fileList.filter(Files::isRegularFile)
            .forEach(it -> fileCopier.copyFile(it, Path.of(destDir)));

  }
 }
}
```

Each time you call the `replicate()` method, all files in the source directory are replicated to the destination directory. To avoid unexpected problems caused by concurrent replication, you declare this method as synchronized.

Now, you can configure one or more file replicator instances in a Java Config class. The documentReplicator instance needs references to two directories: a source directory from which files are read and a target directory to which files are backed up. The code in this example attempts to read from a directory called docs in your operating system user's home directory and then copy to a folder called docs_backup in your operating system user's home directory.

When this bean starts up, it creates the two directories if they don't already exist there.

The "home directory" is different for each operating system, but typically on Unix it's the directory that ~ resolves to. On a Linux box, the folder might be /home/user. On Mac OS X, the folder might be /Users/user, and on Windows it might be similar to C:\Documents and Settings\user.

Listing 10-5. File replicator configuration

```java
package com.apress.spring6recipes.replicator.config;

import com.apress.spring6recipes.replicator.FileCopier;
import com.apress.spring6recipes.replicator.JMXFileReplicator;
import com.apress.spring6recipes.replicator.NioFileCopier;
import jakarta.annotation.PostConstruct;
import org.springframework.beans.factory.annotation.Value;
```

```java
import org.springframework.context.annotation.Bean;
import org.springframework.context.annotation.Configuration;

import java.io.IOException;
import java.nio.file.Files;
import java.nio.file.Path;

@Configuration
public class FileReplicatorConfig {

  @Value("#{systemProperties['user.home']}/docs")
  private String srcDir;
  @Value("#{systemProperties['user.home']}/docs_backup")
  private String destDir;

  @Bean
  public NioFileCopier fileCopier() {
    return new NioFileCopier();
  }

  @Bean
  public JMXFileReplicator documentReplicator(FileCopier fileCopier) {
    var fRep = new JMXFileReplicator();
    fRep.setSrcDir(srcDir);
    fRep.setDestDir(destDir);
    fRep.setFileCopier(fileCopier);
    return fRep;
  }

  @PostConstruct
  public void verifyDirectoriesExist() throws IOException {
    Files.createDirectories(Path.of(srcDir));
    Files.createDirectories(Path.of(destDir));
  }
}
```

Initially, two fields are declared using the @Value annotations to gain access to the user's home directory and define the source and destination directories. Next, two bean instances are created using the @Bean annotation. Notice the @PostConstuct annotation on the verifyDirectoriesExist(), which ensures the source and destination directories exist.

Now that we have the application's core beans, let's take look at how to register and access the beans as an MBean.

Register MBeans Without Spring's Support

First, let's see how to register a model MBean using the JMX API directly. In the following main class, you get the FileReplicator bean from the IoC container and register it as an MBean for management and monitoring. All properties and methods are included in the MBean's management interface.

Listing 10-6. Main class

```
package com.apress.spring6recipes.replicator;

import com.apress.spring6recipes.replicator.config.FileReplicatorConfig;
import org.springframework.context.annotation.AnnotationConfigApplicationContext;

import javax.management.JMException;
import javax.management.ObjectName;
import javax.management.modelmbean.DescriptorSupport;
import javax.management.modelmbean.InvalidTargetObjectTypeException;
import javax.management.modelmbean.ModelMBeanAttributeInfo;
import javax.management.modelmbean.ModelMBeanInfoSupport;
import javax.management.modelmbean.ModelMBeanOperationInfo;
import javax.management.modelmbean.RequiredModelMBean;
import java.io.IOException;
import java.lang.management.ManagementFactory;

public class Main {

  public static void main(String[] args) throws IOException {
    var cfg = FileReplicatorConfig.class;
    try (var ctx = new AnnotationConfigApplicationContext(cfg)) {

      var documentReplicator = ctx.getBean(FileReplicator.class);

      try {
        var mbeanServer = ManagementFactory.getPlatformMBeanServer();
        var objectName = new ObjectName("bean:name=documentReplicator");

        var mbean = new RequiredModelMBean();
        mbean.setManagedResource(documentReplicator, "objectReference");

        var srcDirDescriptor = new DescriptorSupport(
                "name=SrcDir", "descriptorType=attribute",
                "getMethod=getSrcDir", "setMethod=setSrcDir");
        var srcDirInfo = new ModelMBeanAttributeInfo(
                "SrcDir", "java.lang.String", "Source directory",
                true, true, false, srcDirDescriptor);

        var destDirDescriptor = new DescriptorSupport(
                "name=DestDir", "descriptorType=attribute",
                "getMethod=getDestDir", "setMethod=setDestDir");
        var destDirInfo = new ModelMBeanAttributeInfo(
                "DestDir", "java.lang.String", "Destination directory",
                true, true, false, destDirDescriptor);

        var getSrcDirInfo = new ModelMBeanOperationInfo(
                "Get source directory",
                FileReplicator.class.getMethod("getSrcDir"));
```

```
    var setSrcDirInfo = new ModelMBeanOperationInfo(
            "Set source directory",
            FileReplicator.class.getMethod("setSrcDir", String.class));
    var getDestDirInfo = new ModelMBeanOperationInfo(
            "Get destination directory",
            FileReplicator.class.getMethod("getDestDir"));
    var setDestDirInfo = new ModelMBeanOperationInfo(
            "Set destination directory",
            FileReplicator.class.getMethod("setDestDir", String.class));
    var replicateInfo = new ModelMBeanOperationInfo(
            "Replicate files",
            FileReplicator.class.getMethod("replicate"));

    var mbeanInfo = new ModelMBeanInfoSupport(
            "FileReplicator", "File replicator",
            new ModelMBeanAttributeInfo[]{srcDirInfo, destDirInfo},
            null,
            new ModelMBeanOperationInfo[]{getSrcDirInfo, setSrcDirInfo,
                    getDestDirInfo, setDestDirInfo, replicateInfo},
            null
    );
    mbean.setModelMBeanInfo(mbeanInfo);

    mbeanServer.registerMBean(mbean, objectName);
    } catch (JMException | InvalidTargetObjectTypeException |
            NoSuchMethodException ex) {
        System.err.println(ex);
    }
}
System.in.read();
}
}
```

To register an MBean, you need a javax.managment.MBeanServer. You can call the static method ManagementFactory.getPlatformMBeanServer() to locate a platform MBean server. It will create an MBean server if none exists and then register this server instance for future use. Each MBean requires an MBean object name that includes a domain. The preceding MBean is registered under the domain bean with the name documentReplicator.

From the preceding code, you can see that for each MBean attribute and MBean operation, you need to create a ModelMBeanAttributeInfo object and a ModelMBeanOperationInfo object for describing it. After those, you have to create a ModelMBeanInfo object for describing the MBean's management interface by assembling the preceding information. For details about using these types, you can consult their Javadocs. Moreover, you have to handle the JMX-specific exceptions when calling the JMX API. These exceptions are checked exceptions that you must handle. Note that you must prevent your application from terminating before you look inside it with a JMX client tool. Requesting a key from the console using System.in.read() is a good choice.

Finally, you have to add the VM argument -Dcom.sun.management.jmxremote to enable local monitoring of this application. If you're using the book's source code, you can use the following.

Listing 10-7. Shell command for running

```
java -Dcom.sun.management.jmxremote -jar recipe_10_1_i-6.0.0.jar
```

Now, you can use any JMX client tools to monitor your MBeans locally. The simplest one is JConsole, which comes with JDK. To start JConsole, execute the `jconsole` executable file located in the bin directory of the JDK installation.

When JConsole starts, you can see a list of JMX-enabled applications on the Local Process tab of the connection window. Select the process that corresponds to the running Spring app (i.e., `recipe_10_1_i-1.0-6.0.0.jar`). This is illustrated in Figure 10-1.

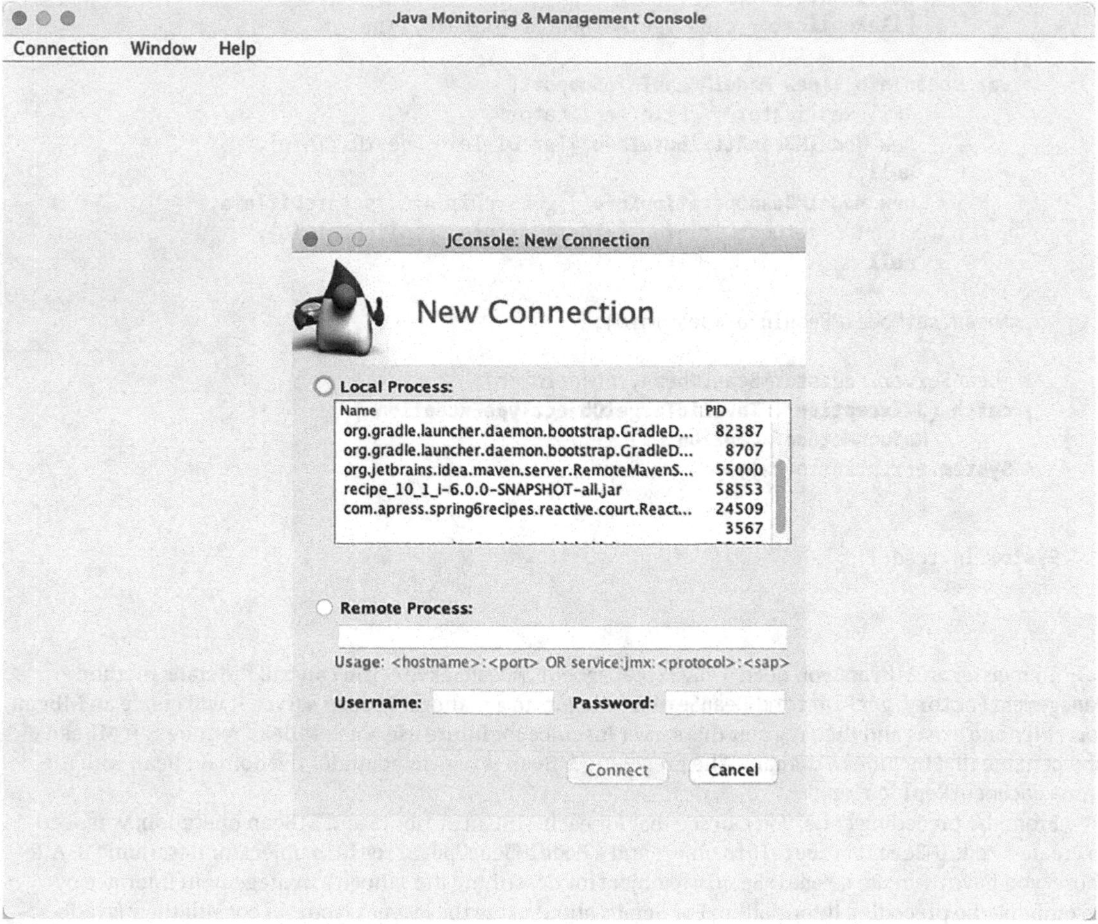

Figure 10-1. *JConsole startup window*

◐ If you're on Windows, you may not see any processes in JConsole. This is a known bug where JConsole isn't able to detect running Java processes. To solve this issue, you'll need to ensure the user has a `hsperfdata` folder in their temp folder. This folder is used by Java and JConsole to keep track of running processes, and it may not exist. For example, if you're running the application as user John.Doe, ensure the following path exists: `C:\Users\John.Doe\AppData\Local\Temp\hsperfdata_John.Doe\`.

After connecting to the replicator application, go to the **MBeans** tab. Next, click the **bean** folder in the left-hand tree and select the documentReplicator, followed by the Operations section. In the main screen, you'll see a series of buttons to invoke the bean's operations. To invoke replicate() simply click the button "replicate." This screen is illustrated in Figure 10-2.

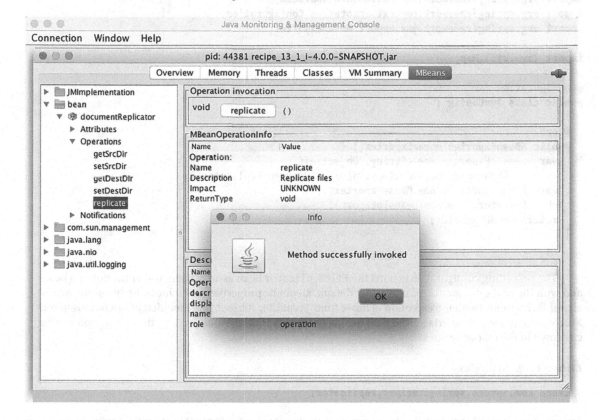

Figure 10-2. JConsole simulating a Spring bean operation

You'll see a "Method successfully invoked" pop-up window. With this action all the files in the source folder are copied/synchronized with those in the destination folder.

Register MBeans with Spring Support

The prior application relied on the use of the JMX API directly. As you saw in the main application class, there's a lot of code that can be difficult to write, manage, and sometimes understand. To export beans configured in the Spring IoC container as MBeans, you simply create an MBeanExporter instance and specify the beans to export, with their MBean object names as the keys. This can be done by adding the following configuration class. Note that the key in the beansToExport map is used as the ObjectName for the bean referenced by the corresponding entry value.

Listing 10-8. JMX configuration

```java
package com.apress.spring6recipes.replicator.config;

import org.springframework.context.annotation.Bean;
import org.springframework.context.annotation.Configuration;
import org.springframework.jmx.export.MBeanExporter;

import java.util.Map;

@Configuration
public class JmxConfig {

    @Bean
    public MBeanExporter mbeanExporter() {
        var beansToExport = Map.<String, Object>of(
                "bean:name=documentReplicator", "documentReplicator");
        var mbeanExporter = new MBeanExporter();
        mbeanExporter.setBeans(beansToExport);
        return mbeanExporter;
    }
}
```

The preceding configuration exports the FileReplicator bean as an MBean, under the domain bean and with the name documentReplicator. By default, all public properties are included as attributes, and all public methods (with the exception of those from java.lang.Object) are included as operations in the MBean's management interface. And with the help of Spring JMX, the main class in the application can be cut down to the following lines.

Listing 10-9. Main class

```java
package com.apress.spring6recipes.replicator;

import org.springframework.context.annotation.AnnotationConfigApplicationContext;

import java.io.IOException;

public class Main {
```

```
public static void main(String[] args) throws IOException {
  var cfg = "com.apress.spring6recipes.replicator.config";
  try (var ctx = new AnnotationConfigApplicationContext(cfg)) {
    System.in.read();
  }
}
}
```

Work with Multiple MBean Server Instances

The Spring MBeanExporter approach can locate an MBean server instance and register MBeans with it implicitly. The JDK creates an MBean server the first time when you locate it, so there's no need to create an MBean server explicitly. The same case applies if an application is running in an environment that provides an MBean server (e.g., a Java application server).

However, if you have multiple MBean servers running, you need to tell the mbeanServer bean to which server it should bind. You do this by specifying the agentId of the server. To figure out the agentId of a given server in JConsole, for example, go to the MBeans tab and in the left-hand tree go to JMImplementation ➤ MBeanServerDelegate ➤ Attributes ➤ MBeanServerId. There, you'll see the string value (see Figure 10-3).

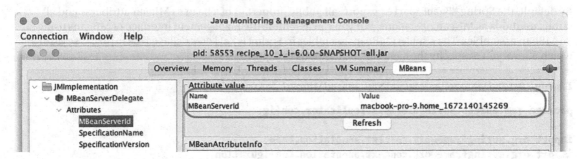

Figure 10-3. *Agent ID attribute*

On our local machine, the value is macbook-pro-9.home_1672140145269. To enable it, configure the agentId property of the MBeanServer.

Listing 10-10. Agent ID configuration

```
@Bean
public MBeanServerFactoryBean mbeanServer() {
    var mbeanServer = new MBeanServerFactoryBean();
    mbeanServer.setLocateExistingServerIfPossible(true);
    mbeanServer.setAgentId("macbook-pro-9.home_1672140145269");
    return mbeanServer;
}
```

If you have multiple MBean server instances in your context, you can explicitly specify a specific MBean server for MBeanExporter to export your MBeans to. In this case, MBeanExporter will not locate an MBean server; it will use the specified MBean server instance. This property is for you to specify a particular MBean server when more than one is available.

Listing 10-11. MBeanExporter with explicit MBeanServer

```
@Bean
public MBeanExporter mbeanExporter(MBeanServer server) {
    var mbeanExporter = new MBeanExporter();
    mbeanExporter.setBeans(beansToExport());
    mbeanExporter.setServer(server);
    return mbeanExporter;
}

@Bean
public MBeanServerFactoryBean mbeanServer() {
    var mbeanServer = new MBeanServerFactoryBean();
    mbeanServer.setLocateExistingServerIfPossible(true);
    return mbeanServer;
}
```

Assemble the Management Interface of MBeans

By default, the Spring MBeanExporter exports all public properties of a bean as MBean attributes and all public methods as MBean operations. But you can assemble the management interface of MBeans using an MBean assembler. The simplest MBean assembler in Spring is MethodNameBasedMBeanInfoAssembler, which allows you to specify the names of the methods to export.

Listing 10-12. JMX config - MethodNameBasedMBeanInfoAssembler

```
package com.apress.spring6recipes.replicator.config;

import org.springframework.context.annotation.Bean;
import org.springframework.context.annotation.Configuration;
import org.springframework.jmx.export.MBeanExporter;
import org.springframework.jmx.export.assembler.MBeanInfoAssembler;
import org.springframework.jmx.export.assembler.MethodNameBasedMBeanInfoAssembler;

import java.util.Map;

@Configuration
public class JmxConfig {

  @Bean
  public MBeanExporter mbeanExporter(MBeanInfoAssembler assembler) {
    var mbeanExporter = new MBeanExporter();
    mbeanExporter.setBeans(Map.of("bean:name=documentReplicator", "documentReplicator"));
    mbeanExporter.setAssembler(assembler);
    return mbeanExporter;
  }

  @Bean
  public MBeanInfoAssembler assembler() {
    var assembler = new MethodNameBasedMBeanInfoAssembler();
```

```
    assembler.setManagedMethods("getSrcDir", "setSrcDir", "getDestDir", "setDestDir",
    "replicate");
    return assembler;
  }
}
```

Another MBean assembler is `InterfaceBasedMBeanInfoAssembler`, which exports all methods defined in the interfaces you specified.

Listing 10-13. JMX config - InterfaceBasedMBeanInfoAssembler

```
@Bean
public MBeanInfoAssembler assembler() {
  var assembler = new InterfaceBasedMBeanInfoAssembler();
  assembler.setManagedInterfaces(FileReplicator.class);
  return assembler;
}
```

Spring also provides `MetadataMBeanInfoAssembler` to assemble an MBean's management interface based on the metadata in the bean class. For a bean class annotated with JDK annotations, you specify an `AnnotationJmxAttributeSource` instance as the attribute source of `MetadataMBeanInfoAssembler`.

Listing 10-14. JMX config - MetadataMBeanInfoAssembler

```
@Bean
public MBeanInfoAssembler assembler() {
  var assembler = new MetadataMBeanInfoAssembler();
  assembler.setAttributeSource(new AnnotationJmxAttributeSource());
  return assembler;
}
```

Then, you annotate your bean class and methods with the annotations `@ManagedResource`, `@ManagedAttribute`, and `@ManagedOperation` for `MetadataMBeanInfoAssembler` to assemble the management interface for this bean. The annotations are easily interpreted. They expose the element that they annotate. If you have a JavaBean-compliant property, JMX will use the term attribute. Classes themselves are referred to as resources. In JMX, methods will be called operations. Knowing that, it's easy to see what the following code does.

Listing 10-15. FileReplicator with JMX annotations

```
package com.apress.spring6recipes.replicator;

import org.springframework.jmx.export.annotation.ManagedAttribute;
import org.springframework.jmx.export.annotation.ManagedOperation;
import org.springframework.jmx.export.annotation.ManagedResource;

import java.io.IOException;
import java.nio.file.Files;
import java.nio.file.Path;
```

```java
@ManagedResource(description = "File replicator")
public class JMXFileReplicator implements FileReplicator {

  private String srcDir;
  private String destDir;
  private FileCopier fileCopier;

  @ManagedAttribute(description = "Get source directory")
  public String getSrcDir() {
    return srcDir;
  }

  @ManagedAttribute(description = "Set source directory")
  public void setSrcDir(String srcDir) {
    this.srcDir = srcDir;
  }

  @ManagedAttribute(description = "Get destination directory")
  public String getDestDir() {
    return destDir;
  }

  @ManagedAttribute(description = "Set destination directory")
  public void setDestDir(String destDir) {
    this.destDir = destDir;
  }

  public FileCopier getFileCopier() {
    return fileCopier;
  }

  public void setFileCopier(FileCopier fileCopier) {
    this.fileCopier = fileCopier;
  }

  @ManagedOperation(description = "Replicate files")
  public synchronized void replicate() throws IOException {
    var files = Path.of(srcDir);

    try (var fileList = Files.list(files)) {
      fileList.filter(Files::isRegularFile)
              .forEach(it -> fileCopier.copyFile(it, Path.of(destDir)));

    }
  }
}
```

Register MBeans with Annotations

In addition to exporting a bean explicitly with MBeanExporter, you can simply configure its subclass AnnotationMBeanExporter to auto-detect MBeans from beans declared in the IoC container. You don't need to configure an MBean assembler for this exporter, because it uses MetadataMBeanInfoAssembler with AnnotationJmxAttributeSource by default. You can delete the previous beans and assembler properties for this registration and simply leave the following.

Listing 10-16. JMX config - AnnotationMBeanExporter

```
package com.apress.spring6recipes.replicator.config;

import org.springframework.context.annotation.Bean;
import org.springframework.context.annotation.Configuration;
import org.springframework.jmx.export.MBeanExporter;
import org.springframework.jmx.export.annotation.AnnotationMBeanExporter;

@Configuration
public class JmxConfig {

  @Bean
  public MBeanExporter mbeanExporter() {
    return new AnnotationMBeanExporter();
  }
}
```

AnnotationMBeanExporter detects any beans configured in the IoC container with the @ManagedResource annotation and exports them as MBeans. By default, this exporter exports a bean to the domain whose name is the same as its package name. Also, it uses the bean's name in the IoC container as its MBean name and the bean's short class name as its type. So the documentReplicator bean will be exported under the following MBean object name: com.apress.spring6recipes.replicator:name=documentReplicator, type=JMXFileReplicator.

If you don't want to use the package name as the domain name, you can set the default domain for the exporter by adding the defaultDomain property.

Listing 10-17. JMX config - AnnotationMBeanExporter with default domain

```
package com.apress.spring6recipes.replicator.config;

import org.springframework.context.annotation.Bean;
import org.springframework.context.annotation.Configuration;
import org.springframework.jmx.export.MBeanExporter;
import org.springframework.jmx.export.annotation.AnnotationMBeanExporter;

@Configuration
public class JmxConfig {

  @Bean
  public MBeanExporter mbeanExporter() {
    var mbeanExporter = new AnnotationMBeanExporter();
```

```
    mbeanExporter.setDefaultDomain("bean");
    return mbeanExporter;
  }
}
```

After setting the default domain to bean, the documentReplicator bean is exported under the following MBean object name:

```
bean:name=documentReplicator,type=JMXFileReplicator
```

In addition, you can specify a bean's MBean object name in the objectName attribute of the @ManagedResource annotation. For example, you can export the file copier as an MBean by annotating it with the following annotations.

Listing 10-18. JMX file replicator with objectName set

```
package com.apress.spring6recipes.replicator;

import org.springframework.jmx.export.annotation.ManagedAttribute;
import org.springframework.jmx.export.annotation.ManagedOperation;
import org.springframework.jmx.export.annotation.ManagedResource;

import java.io.IOException;
import java.nio.file.Files;
import java.nio.file.Path;

@ManagedResource(
        description = "File replicator",
        objectName = "bean:name=fileCopier,type=JMXFileReplicator")
public class JMXFileReplicator implements FileReplicator {
  }
```

However, specifying the object name in this way works only for classes that you're going to create a single instance of in the IoC container (e.g., file copier), not for classes that you may create multiple instances of (e.g., file replicator). This is because you can only specify a single object name for a class. As a result, you shouldn't try to run the same server multiple times without changing the names.

Finally, another possibility is to rely on Spring to export MBeans decorated with @ManagedResource. For this you need to add @EnableMBeanExport to a configuration class. This tells Spring to export any beans that are decorated with the @ManagedResource.

Listing 10-19. Config with @EnableMBeanExport

```
package com.apress.spring6recipes.replicator.config;

import java.io.IOException;
public class FileReplicatorConfig {

  @Value("#{systemProperties['user.home']}/docs")
```

Due to the presence of the @EnableMBeanExport, the bean documentReplicator gets exported as an MBean because it is decorated with the @ManagedResource annotation.

10-2. Publish and Listen to JMX Notifications

Problem

You want to publish JMX notifications from your MBeans and listen to them with JMX notification listeners.

Solution

Spring allows your beans to publish JMX notifications through the NotificationPublisher interface. You can also register standard JMX notification listeners in the IoC container to listen to JMX notifications.

How It Works

Publish JMX Notifications

The Spring IoC container supports the beans that are going to be exported as MBeans to publish JMX notifications. These beans must implement the NotificationPublisherAware interface, to get access to NotificationPublisher, so that they can publish notifications.

Listing 10-20. FileReplicator–publish notifications

```
package com.apress.spring6recipes.replicator;

import org.springframework.jmx.export.notification.NotificationPublisher;
import org.springframework.jmx.export.notification.NotificationPublisherAware;

@ManagedResource(description = "File replicator")
public class JMXFileReplicator implements FileReplicator, NotificationPublisherAware {

    private final AtomicInteger sequenceNumber = new AtomicInteger();
    private NotificationPublisher notificationPublisher;

    @ManagedOperation(description = "Replicate files")
    public synchronized void replicate() throws IOException {
        var files = Path.of(srcDir);

        try (var fileList = Files.list(files)) {
            fileList.filter(Files::isRegularFile)
                    .forEach(it -> fileCopier.copyFile(it, Path.of(destDir)));
        }
        var seqNumber = sequenceNumber.incrementAndGet();
        var notification =new Notification("replication.complete", this, seqNumber);
        notificationPublisher.sendNotification(notification);
    }

    @Override
    public void setNotificationPublisher(NotificationPublisher notificationPublisher) {
        this.notificationPublisher = notificationPublisher;
    }
}
```

In this file replicator, you send a JMX notification whenever a replication starts or completes. The notification is visible both in the standard output in the console and in the JConsole Notifications menu on the MBeans tab, as illustrated in Figure 10-4.

Figure 10-4. *MBean events reported in JConsole*

To see notifications in Jconsole, you must first click the "Subscribe" button that appears toward the bottom, as illustrated in Figure 10-4. Then, when invoking the `replicate()` method using the JConsole button in the MBean "Operations" section, you'll see two new notifications arrive. The first argument in the notification constructor is the notification type, while the second is the notification source. The last one is a sequence number.

Listen to JMX Notifications

Now, let's create a notification listener to listen to JMX notifications. Because a listener will be notified of many different types of notifications, such as `javax.management.AttributeChangeNotification` when an MBean's attribute has changed, you have to filter those notifications that you are interested in handling.

Listing 10-21. NotificationListener implementation

```java
package com.apress.spring6recipes.replicator;

import javax.management.Notification;
import javax.management.NotificationListener;

public class ReplicationNotificationListener implements NotificationListener {

  public void handleNotification(Notification not, Object handback) {
    if (not.getType().startsWith("replication")) {
      System.out.printf("%s %s #%d%n",
            not.getSource(), not.getType(), not.getSequenceNumber());
    }
  }
}
```

Then, you can register this notification listener with your MBean exporter to listen to notifications emitted from certain MBeans.

Listing 10-22. JMX configuration

```
@Bean
public ReplicationNotificationListener replicationNotificationListener() {
  return new ReplicationNotificationListener();
}

@Bean
public AnnotationMBeanExporter mbeanExporter(NotificationListener nl) {
  var mbeanExporter = new AnnotationMBeanExporter();
  mbeanExporter.setDefaultDomain("bean");
  mbeanExporter.setNotificationListenerMappings(
      Map.of("bean:name=documentReplicator,type=JMXFileReplicator", nl));
  return mbeanExporter;
}
```

10-3. Expose and Access Remote JMX MBeans in Spring
Problem

You want to access JMX MBeans running on a remote MBean server exposed by a JMX connector. When accessing remote MBeans directly with the JMX API, you have to write complex JMX-specific code.

Solution

Spring offers two approaches to simplify remote MBean access. First, it provides a factory bean to create an MBean server connection declaratively. With this server connection, you can query and update an MBean's attributes, as well as invoke its operations. Second, Spring provides another factory bean that allows you to create a proxy for a remote MBean. With this proxy, you can operate a remote MBean as if it were a local bean.

How It Works
Expose MBeans Through a JMX Connector Server

If you want your MBeans to be accessed remotely, you need to enable a remoting protocol for JMX. JSR-160 defines a standard for JMX remoting through a JMX connector. Spring allows you to create a JMX connector server through ConnectorServerFactoryBean. By default, ConnectorServerFactoryBean creates and starts a JMX connector server bound to the service URL service:jmx:jmxmp://localhost:9875, which exposes the JMX connector through the JMX Messaging Protocol (JMXMP). However, most JMX implementations don't support JMXMP. Therefore, you should choose a widely supported remoting protocol for your JMX connector, such as RMI. To expose your JMX connector through a specific protocol, you provide the service URL for it.

Listing 10-23. JMX server configuration

```
package com.apress.spring6recipes.replicator.config;

import org.springframework.context.annotation.Bean;
import org.springframework.context.annotation.Configuration;
import org.springframework.context.annotation.Import;
import org.springframework.jmx.support.ConnectorServerFactoryBean;

@Configuration
@Import(FileReplicatorConfig.class)
public class JmxServerConfiguration {

  @Bean
  public ConnectorServerFactoryBean connectorServerFactoryBean() {
    var url ="service:jmx:rmi://localhost/jndi/rmi://localhost:1099/replicator";
    var connectorServer = new ConnectorServerFactoryBean();
    connectorServer.setServiceUrl(url);
    return connectorServer;
  }
}
```

ℹ️   To be able to expose the beans through RMI, you would need an RMI registry. Generally, when using an application server, this is available by default. When running standalone, you want to run the `rmiregistry` provided with Java on the command line. This recipe assumes that that is running.

You specify the preceding URL to bind your JMX connector to an RMI registry listening on port 1099 of localhost. The default port for this registry is 1099, but you can specify another one in its port property.

Now, your MBeans can be accessed remotely via RMI. Note there's no need to start an RMI-enabled app with the JMX -Dcom.sun.management.jmxremote flag, as you did in previous apps. When JConsole starts, you can enter `service:jmx:rmi://localhost/jndi/rmi://localhost:1099/replicator` in the service URL on the "Remote Process" section of the connection window. This is illustrated in Figure 10-5.

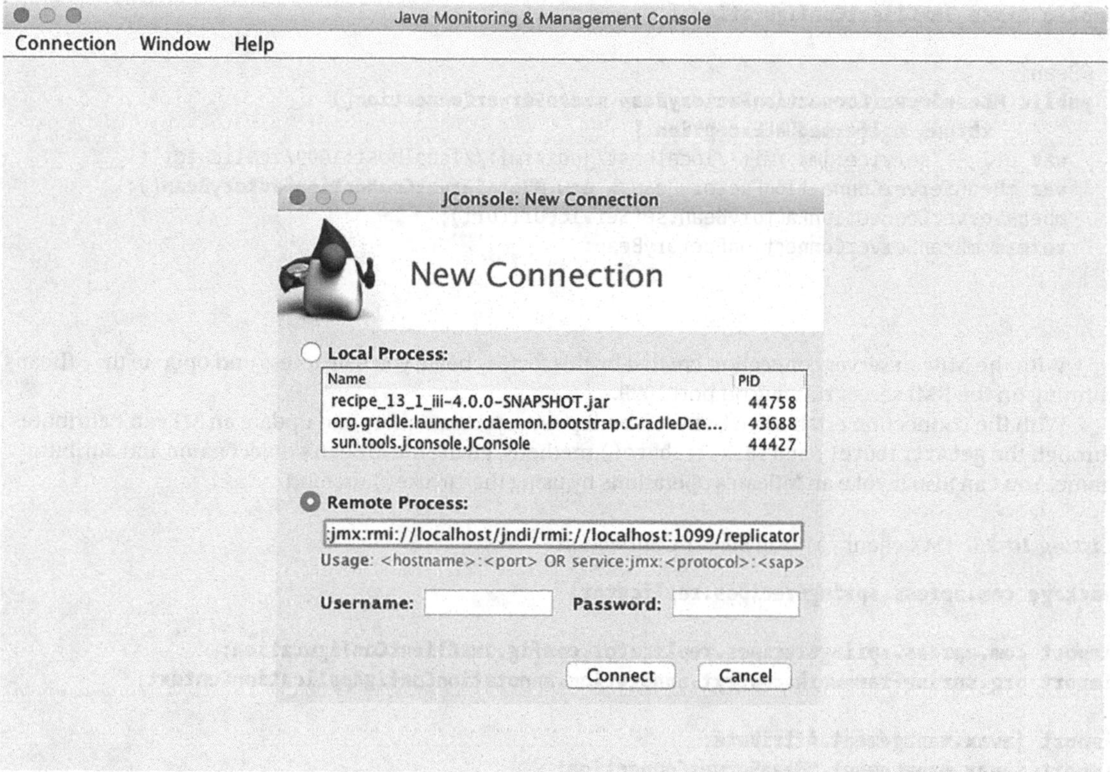

Figure 10-5. *Connecting to service:jmx:rmi://localhost/jndi/rmi://localhost:1099/replicator*

Once the connection is established, you can invoke bean methods just as you did with previous examples.

Access Remote MBeans Through an MBean Server Connection

A JMX client requires an MBean server connection to access MBeans running on a remote MBean server. Spring provides org.springframework.jmx.support.MBeanServerConnectionFactoryBean for you to create a connection to a remote JSR-160–enabled MBean server declaratively. You have to provide the service URL for it to locate the MBean server. Now let's declare this factory bean in your client bean configuration class.

Listing 10-24. JMX client configuration - MBean Server Connection

```
package com.apress.spring6recipes.replicator.config;

import org.springframework.context.annotation.Bean;
import org.springframework.context.annotation.Configuration;
import org.springframework.jmx.support.MBeanServerConnectionFactoryBean;

import java.net.MalformedURLException;

@Configuration
```

```
public class JmxClientConfiguration {

    @Bean
    public MBeanServerConnectionFactoryBean mbeanServerConnection()
            throws MalformedURLException {
        var url = "service:jmx:rmi://localhost/jndi/rmi://localhost:1099/replicator";
        var mBeanServerConnectionFactoryBean = new MBeanServerConnectionFactoryBean();
        mBeanServerConnectionFactoryBean.setServiceUrl(url);
        return mBeanServerConnectionFactoryBean;
    }
}
```

With the MBean server connection created by this factory bean, you can access and operate the MBeans running on the RMI server running on port 1099.

With the connection established between both points, you can query and update an MBean's attributes through the getAttribute() and setAttribute() methods, giving the MBean's object name and attribute name. You can also invoke an MBean's operations by using the invoke() method.

Listing 10-25. JMX client - MBean Server Connection

```
package com.apress.spring6recipes.replicator;

import com.apress.spring6recipes.replicator.config.JmxClientConfiguration;
import org.springframework.context.annotation.AnnotationConfigApplicationContext;

import javax.management.Attribute;
import javax.management.MBeanServerConnection;
import javax.management.ObjectName;

public class Client {

    public static void main(String[] args) throws Exception {
        var cfg = JmxClientConfiguration.class;
        try (var context = new AnnotationConfigApplicationContext(cfg)) {
            var mbeanServerConnection = context.getBean(MBeanServerConnection.class);
            var srcDir = (String) mbeanServerConnection.getAttribute(mbeanName, "SrcDir");
            var destDir = new Attribute("DestDir", srcDir + "_backup");
            mbeanServerConnection.setAttribute(mbeanName, destDir);
            mbeanServerConnection.invoke(mbeanName, "replicate", null, null);
        }
    }
```

In addition, let's create a JMX notification listener, so we can listen in on file replication notifications.

Listing 10-26. Replication notification listener

```
package com.apress.spring6recipes.replicator;

import javax.management.Notification;
import javax.management.NotificationListener;

public class ReplicationNotificationListener implements NotificationListener {
```

```
public void handleNotification(Notification notification, Object handback) {
    if (notification.getType().startsWith("replication")) {
        System.out.println(
                notification.getSource() + " " +
                        notification.getType() + " #" +
                        notification.getSequenceNumber());
    }
  }
}
```

You can register this notification listener to the MBean server connection to listen to notifications emitted from this MBean server.

Listing 10-27. Listener creation and registration

```
var name = "bean:name=documentReplicator,type=JMXFileReplicator";
var mbeanName = new ObjectName(name);
var listener = new ReplicationNotificationListener();
mbeanServerConnection.addNotificationListener(mbeanName, listener, null, null);
```

After you run this application client, check JConsole for the RMI server application—using "Remote Process" at service:jmx:rmi://localhost/jndi/rmi://localhost:1099/replicator. Under the "Notifications" menu of the MBeans tab, you'll see a new notification of type jmx.attribute.change as illustrated in Figure 10-6.

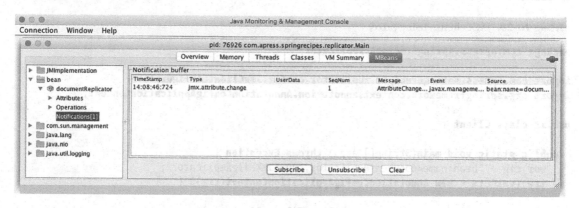

Figure 10-6. *JConsole notification event invoked through RMI*

Access Remote MBeans Through an MBean Proxy

Another approach that Spring offers for remote MBean access is through MBeanProxy, which can be created by MBeanProxyFactoryBean.

Listing 10-28. JMX client configuration - MBean Proxy

```
package com.apress.spring6recipes.replicator.config;

import com.apress.spring6recipes.replicator.FileReplicator;
```

```java
import org.springframework.context.annotation.Bean;
import org.springframework.context.annotation.Configuration;
import org.springframework.jmx.access.MBeanProxyFactoryBean;

@Configuration
public class JmxClientConfiguration {

  @Bean
  public MBeanProxyFactoryBean fileReplicatorProxy() throws Exception {
    var url = "service:jmx:rmi://localhost/jndi/rmi://localhost:1099/replicator";
    var name = "bean:name=documentReplicator,type=JMXFileReplicator";
    var fileReplicatorProxy = new MBeanProxyFactoryBean();
    fileReplicatorProxy.setServiceUrl(url);
    fileReplicatorProxy.setObjectName(name);
    fileReplicatorProxy.setProxyInterface(FileReplicator.class);
    return fileReplicatorProxy;
  }
}
```

You need to specify the object name and the server connection for the MBean you are going to proxy. The most important is the proxy interface, whose local method calls will be translated into remote MBean calls behind the scenes. Now, you can operate the remote MBean through this proxy as if it were a local bean. The preceding MBean operations invoked on the MBean server connection directly can be simplified as follows.

Listing 10-29. JMX client - using proxy

```java
package com.apress.spring6recipes.replicator;

import com.apress.spring6recipes.replicator.config.JmxClientConfiguration;
import org.springframework.context.annotation.AnnotationConfigApplicationContext;

public class Client {

  public static void main(String[] args) throws Exception {
    var cfg = "bean:name=documentReplicator,type=JMXFileReplicator";
    try (var ctx = new AnnotationConfigApplicationContext(cfg)) {

      var fileReplicatorProxy = ctx.getBean(FileReplicator.class);
      var srcDir = fileReplicatorProxy.getSrcDir();
      fileReplicatorProxy.setDestDir(srcDir + "_backup");
      fileReplicatorProxy.replicate();
    }
  }
}
```

10-4. Send Email with Spring's Email Support

Problem

Many applications need to send email. In a Java application, you can send email with the Jakarta Mail API. However, when using Jakarta Mail, you have to handle specific mail sessions and exceptions. As a result, an application becomes Jakarta Mail dependent, and it becomes hard to switch to another email API.

Solution

Spring's email support makes it easier to send email by providing an abstract and implementation-independent API for sending email. The core interface of Spring's email support is MailSender. The Jakarta MailSender interface is a sub-interface of MailSender that includes specialized Jakarta Mail features such as Multipurpose Internet Mail Extensions (MIME) message support. To send an email message with HTML content, inline images, or attachments, you have to send it as a MIME message.

How It Works

Suppose you want the file replicator application from the previous recipes to notify the administrator of any error. First, you create the following ErrorNotifier interface, which includes a method for notifying of a file copy error.

Listing 10-30. ErrorNotifier interface

```
package com.apress.spring6recipes.replicator;

public interface ErrorNotifier {

  void notifyCopyError(String srcDir, String destDir, String filename);
}
```

ℹ️ Invoking this notifier in case of error is left for you to accomplish. As you can consider error handling a crosscutting concern, AOP would be an ideal solution to this problem. You can write an after throwing advice to invoke this notifier.

Next, you can implement this interface to send a notification in a way of your choice. The most common way is to send email. Before you implement the interface in this way, you may need a local email server that supports the Simple Mail Transfer Protocol (SMTP) for testing purposes. We recommend installing GreenMail, which is very easy to install and configure. You can also run the greenmail.sh script to start a Docker container. By default GreenMail uses mail ports with a 3000 offset, so instead of port 25 it is 3025 for SMPT and instead of port 110 it is 3110 for POP3.

Send Email Using the Jakarta Mail API

Now, let's take a look at how to send email using the Jakarta Mail API. Before you can use the Jakarta Mail API, you will need to add the dependencies for the API.

Listing 10-31. Gradle dependency

```
implementation group: 'com.sun.mail', name: 'jakarta.mail', version: '2.0.1'
```

Listing 10-32. Maven dependency

```xml
<dependency>
  <groupId>com.sun.mail</groupId>
  <artifactId>jakarta.mail</artifactId>
  <version>2.0.1</version>
</dependency>
```

You can implement the ErrorNotifier interface to send email notifications in case of errors.

Listing 10-33. EmailErrorNotifier using the Jakarta Mail API

```java
package com.apress.spring6recipes.replicator;

import jakarta.mail.Message;
import jakarta.mail.MessagingException;
import jakarta.mail.Session;
import jakarta.mail.Transport;
import jakarta.mail.internet.InternetAddress;
import jakarta.mail.internet.MimeMessage;

import java.util.Properties;

public class EmailErrorNotifier implements ErrorNotifier {

  private static final String MSG = """
                Dear Administrator,
                An error occurred when copying the following file :
                Source directory: %s
                Destination directory: %s
                Filename : %s
          """;

  @Override
  public void notifyCopyError(String srcDir, String destDir, String filename) {
    var props = new Properties();
    props.put("mail.smtp.host", "localhost");
    props.put("mail.smtp.port", "3025");
    props.put("mail.smtp.username", "system");
    props.put("mail.smtp.password", "12345");
    var session = Session.getDefaultInstance(props, null);
    try {
      var message = new MimeMessage(session);
      message.setFrom(new InternetAddress("system@localhost"));
      message.setRecipients(Message.RecipientType.TO,
              InternetAddress.parse("admin@localhost"));
      message.setSubject("File Copy Error");
```

```
      message.setText(String.format(MSG, srcDir, destDir, filename));
      Transport.send(message);
    } catch (MessagingException e) {
      throw new RuntimeException(e);
    }
  }
}
```

You first open a mail session connecting to an SMTP server by defining the properties. Then, you create a message from this session for constructing your email. After that, you send the email by making a call to Transport.send(). When dealing with the Jakarta Mail API, you have to handle the checked exception MessagingException. Note that all of these classes, interfaces, and exceptions are defined by Jakarta Mail.

Next, declare an instance of EmailErrorNotifier in the Spring IoC container for sending email notifications in case of file replication errors.

Listing 10-34. Mail configuration

```
package com.apress.spring6recipes.replicator.config;

import com.apress.spring6recipes.replicator.EmailErrorNotifier;
import com.apress.spring6recipes.replicator.ErrorNotifier;
import org.springframework.context.annotation.Bean;
import org.springframework.context.annotation.Configuration;

@Configuration
public class MailConfiguration {

  @Bean
  public ErrorNotifier errorNotifier() {
    return new EmailErrorNotifier();
  }
}
```

You can write the following Main class to test EmailErrorNotifier. After running it, you can configure your email application to receive the email from your e-mail server via POP3.

Listing 10-35. Main class

```
package com.apress.spring6recipes.replicator;

import com.apress.spring6recipes.replicator.config.MailConfiguration;
import org.springframework.context.annotation.AnnotationConfigApplicationContext;

public class Main {

  public static void main(String[] args) {
    var cfg = MailConfiguration.class;
    try (var ctx = new AnnotationConfigApplicationContext(cfg)) {
      var errorNotifier = ctx.getBean(ErrorNotifier.class);
      errorNotifier.notifyCopyError("c:/documents", "d:/documents", "spring.doc");
    }
  }
}
```

To verify the email was sent, you can log in to the POP server included with GreenMail. You can telnet, using a console, to port 3110 and run the following commands to view the email for user admin, whose password is the same you set on creation.

Listing 10-36. Console input/output from telnet

```
> telnet localhost 3110
+OK POP3 GreenMail Server v1.6.10 ready
USER admin@localhost
+OK
PASS admin@localhost
+OK
LIST
+ OK 1 698
RETR 1
+OK Message follows
...
```

Send Email with Spring's MailSender

Now, let's look at how to send email with the help of Spring's MailSender interface, which can send SimpleMailMessage in its send() method. With this interface, your code is no longer Jakarta Mail specific, and now it's easier to test.

Listing 10-37. EmailErrorNotifier using Jakarta MailSender

```java
package com.apress.spring6recipes.replicator;

import org.springframework.mail.MailSender;
import org.springframework.mail.SimpleMailMessage;

public class EmailErrorNotifier implements ErrorNotifier {

    private static final String MSG = """
                Dear Administrator,
                An error occurred when copying the following file :
                Source directory: %s
                Destination directory: %s
                Filename : %s
            """;

    private final MailSender mailSender;

    public EmailErrorNotifier(MailSender mailSender) {
        this.mailSender = mailSender;
    }

    @Override
    public void notifyCopyError(String srcDir, String destDir, String filename) {
        var message = new SimpleMailMessage();
```

```
    message.setFrom("system@localhost");
    message.setTo("admin@localhost");
    message.setSubject("File Copy Error");
    message.setText(String.format(MSG, srcDir, destDir, filename));
    mailSender.send(message);
  }
}
```

Next, you have to configure a `MailSender` implementation in the bean configuration file and inject it into `EmailErrorNotifier`. In Spring, the unique implementation of this interface is `JavaMailSenderImpl`, which uses Jakarta Mail to send email.

Listing 10-38. MailConfiguration with Jakarta MailSender

```
package com.apress.spring6recipes.replicator.config;

import com.apress.spring6recipes.replicator.EmailErrorNotifier;
import com.apress.spring6recipes.replicator.ErrorNotifier;
import org.springframework.context.annotation.Bean;
import org.springframework.context.annotation.Configuration;
import org.springframework.mail.javamail.JavaMailSender;
import org.springframework.mail.javamail.JavaMailSenderImpl;

@Configuration
public class MailConfiguration {

  @Bean
  public ErrorNotifier errorNotifier(JavaMailSender mailSender) {
    return new EmailErrorNotifier(mailSender);
  }

  @Bean
  public JavaMailSenderImpl mailSender() {
    var mailSender = new JavaMailSenderImpl();
    mailSender.setHost("localhost");
    mailSender.setPort(3025);
    mailSender.setUsername("system");
    mailSender.setPassword("12345");
    return mailSender;
  }
}
```

The default port used by `JavaMailSenderImpl` is the standard SMTP port 25, so if your email server listens on this port for SMTP, you can simply omit this property. Also, if your SMTP server doesn't require user authentication, you needn't set the `username` and `password`.

If you have a Jakarta Mail session configured in your Java app server, you can first look it up with the help of `JndiLocatorDelegate`.

Listing 10-39. JNDI lookup for a mail session

```
@Bean
public Session mailSession() throws NamingException {
```

```
        return JndiLocatorDelegate
                .createDefaultResourceRefLocator()
                .lookup("mail/Session", Session.class);
}
```

You can inject the Jakarta Mail session into `JavaMailSenderImpl` for its use. In this case, you no longer need to set the host, port, username, or password.

Listing 10-40. MailSender with injected mail session

```
@Bean
public JavaMailSenderImpl mailSender(Session mailSession) {
    var mailSender = new JavaMailSenderImpl();
    mailSender.setSession(mailSession);
    return mailSender;
}
```

Define an Email Template

Constructing an email message from scratch in the method body is not efficient, because you have to hard-code the email properties. Also, you may have difficulty in writing the email text in terms of Java strings. You can consider defining an email message template in the bean configuration file and construct a new email message from it.

Listing 10-41. MailConfiguration using a SimpleMailMessage as template

```
package com.apress.spring6recipes.replicator.config;

import com.apress.spring6recipes.replicator.EmailErrorNotifier;
import com.apress.spring6recipes.replicator.ErrorNotifier;
import org.springframework.context.annotation.Bean;
import org.springframework.context.annotation.Configuration;
import org.springframework.mail.SimpleMailMessage;
import org.springframework.mail.javamail.JavaMailSender;
import org.springframework.mail.javamail.JavaMailSenderImpl;

@Configuration
public class MailConfiguration {

  private static final String MSG = """
                Dear Administrator,
                An error occurred when copying the following file :
                Source directory: %s
                Destination directory: %s
                Filename : %s
        """;
```

```java
@Bean
public ErrorNotifier errorNotifier(JavaMailSender mailSender,
                                   SimpleMailMessage template) {
  return new EmailErrorNotifier(mailSender, template);
}

@Bean
public JavaMailSenderImpl mailSender() {
  var mailSender = new JavaMailSenderImpl();
  mailSender.setHost("localhost");
  mailSender.setPort(3025);
  mailSender.setUsername("system");
  mailSender.setPassword("12345");
  return mailSender;
}

@Bean
public SimpleMailMessage copyErrorMailMessage() {
  var message = new SimpleMailMessage();
  message.setFrom("system@localhost");
  message.setTo("admin@localhost");
  message.setSubject("File Copy Error");
  message.setText(MSG);
  return message;
}
}
```

Note that in the preceding message text, you include the placeholders %s, which will be replaced by message parameters through String.format(). Of course, you can also use a powerful templating language such as Thymeleaf or FreeMarker to generate the message text according to a template. It's also a good practice to separate mail message templates from bean configuration files.

Each time you send email, you can construct a new SimpleMailMessage instance from this injected template. Then you can generate the message text using String.format() to replace the %s placeholders with your message parameters.

Listing 10-42. EmailErrorNotifier with a template message

```java
package com.apress.spring6recipes.replicator;

import org.springframework.mail.MailSender;
import org.springframework.mail.SimpleMailMessage;

public class EmailErrorNotifier implements ErrorNotifier {

  private final MailSender mailSender;
  private final SimpleMailMessage template;

  public EmailErrorNotifier(MailSender mailSender, SimpleMailMessage template) {
    this.mailSender = mailSender;
    this.template = template;
  }
```

```
  @Override
  public void notifyCopyError(String srcDir, String destDir, String filename) {
    var message = new SimpleMailMessage(template);
    message.setText(String.format(
            template.getText(), srcDir, destDir, filename));
    mailSender.send(message);
  }
}
```

Send Email with Attachments (MIME Messages)

So far, the SimpleMailMessage class you used can send only a simple plaintext email message. To send email that contains HTML content, inline images, or attachments, you have to construct and send a MIME message instead. MIME is supported by Jakarta Mail through the jakarta.mail.internet. MimeMessage class.

First of all, you have to use the JavaMailSender interface instead of its parent interface MailSender. The JavaMailSenderImpl instance you injected does implement this interface, so you needn't modify your bean configurations. The following notifier sends Spring's bean configuration file as an email attachment to the administrator.

Listing 10-43. EmailErrorNotifier sending a MIME Message

```
package com.apress.spring6recipes.replicator;

import jakarta.mail.MessagingException;
import jakarta.mail.internet.MimeMessage;
import org.springframework.core.io.ClassPathResource;
import org.springframework.mail.MailParseException;
import org.springframework.mail.SimpleMailMessage;
import org.springframework.mail.javamail.JavaMailSender;
import org.springframework.mail.javamail.MimeMessageHelper;

public class EmailErrorNotifier implements ErrorNotifier {

  private final JavaMailSender mailSender;
  private final SimpleMailMessage template;

  public EmailErrorNotifier(JavaMailSender mailSender,
                            SimpleMailMessage template) {
    this.mailSender = mailSender;
    this.template = template;
  }

  @Override
  public void notifyCopyError(String srcDir, String destDir, String filename) {
    var message = mailSender.createMimeMessage();
    try {
      var helper = new MimeMessageHelper(message, true);
      helper.setFrom(template.getFrom());
      helper.setTo(template.getTo());
```

```
        helper.setSubject(template.getSubject());
        helper.setText(String.format(
                template.getText(), srcDir, destDir, filename));

        helper.addAttachment("beans.xml", new ClassPathResource("beans.xml"));
      } catch (MessagingException e) {
        throw new MailParseException(e);
      }
      mailSender.send(message);
    }
}
```

Unlike SimpleMailMessage, the MimeMessage class is defined by Jakarta Mail, so you can only instantiate it by calling mailSender.createMimeMessage(). Spring provides the helper class MimeMessageHelper to simplify the operations of MimeMessage. It allows you to add an attachment from a Spring resource object. However, the operations of this helper class can still throw Jakarta Mail's MessagingException. You have to convert this exception into Spring's mail runtime exception for consistency. Spring offers another method for you to construct a MIME message, which is through implementing the MimeMessagePreparator interface.

Listing 10-44. EmailErrorNotifier using MimeMessagePreparator

```
package com.apress.spring6recipes.replicator;

import jakarta.mail.internet.MimeMessage;
import org.springframework.core.io.ClassPathResource;
import org.springframework.mail.SimpleMailMessage;
import org.springframework.mail.javamail.JavaMailSender;
import org.springframework.mail.javamail.MimeMessageHelper;
import org.springframework.mail.javamail.MimeMessagePreparator;

public class EmailErrorNotifier implements ErrorNotifier {

  private final JavaMailSender mailSender;
  private final SimpleMailMessage template;

  public EmailErrorNotifier(JavaMailSender mailSender,
                            SimpleMailMessage template) {
    this.mailSender = mailSender;
    this.template = template;
  }

  @Override
  public void notifyCopyError(
          final String srcDir, final String destDir, final String filename) {
    MimeMessagePreparator preparator = (mimeMessage) -> {
      var helper = new MimeMessageHelper(mimeMessage, true);
      helper.setFrom(template.getFrom());
      helper.setTo(template.getTo());
      helper.setSubject(template.getSubject());
      helper.setText(String.format(
              template.getText(), srcDir, destDir, filename));
```

```
    helper.addAttachment("beans.xml", new ClassPathResource("beans.xml"));
  };
  mailSender.send(preparator);
  }
}
```

In the prepare() method, you can prepare the MimeMessage object, which is precreated for Jakarta MailSender. If there's any exception thrown, it will be converted into Spring's mail runtime exception automatically.

 As it is a functional interface, you can write it as a lambda.

10-5. Schedule Tasks with Spring's Quartz Support
Problem

Your application has an advanced scheduling requirement that you want to fulfill using Quartz Scheduler. Such a requirement might be something seemingly complex like the ability to run at arbitrary times or at strange intervals ("every other Thursday, but only after 10 AM and before 2 PM"). Moreover, you want to configure scheduling jobs in a declarative way.

Solution

Spring provides utility classes for Quartz to enable scheduling jobs without programming against the Quartz API.

How It Works
Use Quartz Without Spring's Support

To use Quartz for scheduling, you first need to create a job by implementing the Job interface. For example, the following job executes the replicate() method of the file replicator designed in the previous recipes. It retrieves a job data map—which is a Quartz concept to define jobs—through the JobExecutionContext object.

Listing 10-45. Quartz job for FileReplication

```
package com.apress.spring6recipes.replicator;

import org.quartz.Job;
import org.quartz.JobExecutionContext;
import org.quartz.JobExecutionException;

import java.io.IOException;
```

```
public class FileReplicationJob implements Job {

    @Override
    public void execute(JobExecutionContext context)
            throws JobExecutionException {
        var dataMap = context.getJobDetail().getJobDataMap();
        var fileReplicator = (FileReplicator) dataMap.get("fileReplicator");
        try {
            fileReplicator.replicate();
        } catch (IOException e) {
            throw new JobExecutionException(e);
        }
    }
}
```

After creating the job, you configure and schedule it with the Quartz API. For instance, the following scheduler runs your file replication job every 60 seconds with a 5-second delay for the first time of execution.

Listing 10-46. Main class

```
package com.apress.spring6recipes.replicator;

import com.apress.spring6recipes.replicator.config.FileReplicatorConfig;
import org.quartz.JobBuilder;
import org.quartz.JobDataMap;
import org.quartz.SimpleScheduleBuilder;
import org.quartz.TriggerBuilder;
import org.quartz.impl.StdSchedulerFactory;
import org.springframework.context.annotation.AnnotationConfigApplicationContext;

import java.util.Date;

public class Main {

    public static void main(String[] args) throws Exception {
        var cfg = FileReplicatorConfig.class;
        try (var ctx = new AnnotationConfigApplicationContext(cfg)) {

            var documentReplicator = ctx.getBean(FileReplicator.class);

            var jobDataMap = new JobDataMap();
            jobDataMap.put("fileReplicator", documentReplicator);

            var job = JobBuilder.newJob(FileReplicationJob.class)
                    .withIdentity("documentReplicationJob")
                    .storeDurably()
                    .usingJobData(jobDataMap)
                    .build();

            var trigger = TriggerBuilder.newTrigger()
                    .withIdentity("documentReplicationTrigger")
                    .startAt(new Date(System.currentTimeMillis() + 5000))
```

547

```
                .forJob(job)
                .withSchedule(SimpleScheduleBuilder.simpleSchedule()
                        .withIntervalInSeconds(60)
                        .repeatForever())
                .build();

        var scheduler = new StdSchedulerFactory().getScheduler();
        scheduler.start();
        scheduler.scheduleJob(job, trigger);
    }
  }
}
```

In the Main class, you first create a job map. In this case it's a single job, where the key is a descriptive name and the value is an object reference for the job. Next, you define the job details for the file replication job in a JobDetail object and prepare job data in its jobDataMap property. Next, you create a SimpleTrigger object to configure the scheduling properties. Finally, you create a scheduler to run your job using this trigger.

Quartz supports various types of schedules to run jobs at different intervals. Schedules are defined as part of triggers. In the most recent release, Quartz schedules are SimpleScheduleBuilder, CronScheduleBuilder, CalendarIntervalScheduleBuilder, and DailyTimeIntervalScheduleBuilder. SimpleScheduleBuilder allows you to schedule jobs setting properties such as start time, end time, repeat interval, and repeat count. CronScheduleBuilder accepts a Unix cron expression for you to specify the times to run your job. For example, you can replace the preceding SimpleScheduleBuilder with the following CronScheduleBuilder to run a job at 17:30 every day: .withSchedule(CronScheduleBuilder. cronSchedule(" 0 30 17 * * ?")). A cron expression is made up of seven fields (the last field is optional), separated by spaces. Table 10-1 shows the field descriptions for a cron expression.

Table 10-1. *Field Descriptions for a Cron Expression*

Position	Field Name	Range
1	Second	0–59
2	Minute	0–59
3	Hour	0–23
4	Day of month	1–31
5	Month	1–12 or JAN–DEC
6	Day of week	1–7 or SUN–SAT
7	Year (optional)	1970–2099

Each part of a cron expression can be assigned a specific value (e.g., 3), a range (e.g., 1–5), a list (e.g., 1, 3, 5), a wildcard (* matches all values), or a question mark (? is used in either of the "Day of month" and "Day of week" fields for matching one of these fields but not both). CalendarIntervalScheduleBuilder allows you to schedule jobs based on calendar times (day, week, month, year), whereas DailyTimeIntervalScheduleBuilder provides convenience utilities to set a job's end time (e.g., methods like endingDailyAt() and endingDailyAfterCount()).

Use Quartz with Spring's Support

When using Quartz, you can create a job by implementing the Job interface and retrieve job data from the job data map through JobExecutionContext. To decouple your job class from the Quartz API, Spring provides QuartzJobBean, which you can extend to retrieve job data through setter methods. QuartzJobBean converts the job data map into properties and injects them via the setter methods.

Listing 10-47. Quartz job with the Spring base class

```
package com.apress.spring6recipes.replicator;

import org.quartz.JobExecutionContext;
import org.quartz.JobExecutionException;
import org.springframework.scheduling.quartz.QuartzJobBean;

import java.io.IOException;

public class FileReplicationJob extends QuartzJobBean {

  private FileReplicator fileReplicator;

  public void setFileReplicator(FileReplicator fileReplicator) {
    this.fileReplicator = fileReplicator;
  }

  protected void executeInternal(JobExecutionContext context)
        throws JobExecutionException {
    try {
      fileReplicator.replicate();
    } catch (IOException e) {
      throw new JobExecutionException(e);
    }
  }
}
```

Then, you can configure a Quartz JobDetail object in Spring's bean configuration file through JobDetailBean. By default, Spring uses this bean's name as the job name. You can modify it by setting the name property.

Listing 10-48. Quartz configuration

```
@Bean
public JobDetailFactoryBean documentReplicationJob(FileReplicator fileReplicator) {
  var documentReplicationJob = new JobDetailFactoryBean();
  documentReplicationJob.setJobClass(FileReplicationJob.class);
  documentReplicationJob.setDurability(true);
  documentReplicationJob.setJobDataAsMap(Collections.singletonMap("fileReplicator",
  fileReplicator));
  return documentReplicationJob;
}
```

Spring also offers MethodInvokingJobDetailFactoryBean for you to define a job that executes a single method of a particular object. This saves you the trouble of creating a job class. You can use the following job detail to replace the previous.

Listing 10-49. Example of a MethodInvokingJobDetailFactoryBean bean

```
@Bean
public MethodInvokingJobDetailFactoryBean documentReplicationJob(FileReplicator
fileReplicator) {
    MethodInvokingJobDetailFactoryBean documentReplicationJob =
    new MethodInvokingJobDetailFactoryBean();
    documentReplicationJob.setTargetObject(fileReplicator);
    documentReplicationJob.setTargetMethod("replicatie");
    return documentReplicationJob;
}
```

Once you define a job, you can configure a Quartz trigger. Spring supports the SimpleTriggerFactoryBean and the CronTriggerFactoryBean. The SimpleTriggerFactoryBean requires a reference to a JobDetail object and provides common values for schedule properties, such as start time and repeat count.

Listing 10-50. Quartz configuration for SimpleTriggerFactoryBean

```
@Bean
public SimpleTriggerFactoryBean documentReplicationTrigger(JobDetail
documentReplicationJob) {
  var documentReplicationTrigger = new SimpleTriggerFactoryBean();
  documentReplicationTrigger.setJobDetail(documentReplicationJob);
  documentReplicationTrigger.setStartDelay(5000);
  documentReplicationTrigger.setRepeatInterval(60000);
  return documentReplicationTrigger;
}
```

You can also use the CronTriggerFactoryBean to configure a cron-like schedule.

Listing 10-51. Quartz configuration for CronTriggerFactoryBean

```
@Bean
public SimpleTriggerFactoryBean documentReplicationTrigger(JobDetail
documentReplicationJob) {
  var documentReplicationTrigger = new SimpleTriggerFactoryBean();
  documentReplicationTrigger.setJobDetail(documentReplicationJob);
  documentReplicationTrigger.setStartDelay(5000);
  documentReplicationTrigger.setRepeatInterval(60000);
  return documentReplicationTrigger;
}
```

Finally, once you have the Quartz job and trigger, you can configure a SchedulerFactoryBean instance to create a Scheduler object for running your trigger. You can specify multiple triggers in this factory bean.

Listing 10-52. Quartz configuration for SchedulerFactoryBean

```
@Bean
public SchedulerFactoryBean scheduler(Trigger[] triggers) {
  var scheduler = new SchedulerFactoryBean();
  scheduler.setTriggers(triggers);
  return scheduler;
}
```

Now, you can simply start your scheduler with the following Main class. In this way, you don't require a single line of code for scheduling jobs.

Listing 10-53. Main class

```
package com.apress.spring6recipes.replicator;

import com.apress.spring6recipes.replicator.config.FileReplicatorConfig;
import com.apress.spring6recipes.replicator.config.QuartzConfiguration;
import org.springframework.context.annotation.AnnotationConfigApplicationContext;

public class Main {

  public static void main(String[] args) {
    var cfg = "com.apress.spring6recipes.replicator.config";
    try (var ctx = new AnnotationConfigApplicationContext(cfg)) {}
  }
}
```

10-6. Schedule Tasks with Spring's Scheduling
Problem

You want to schedule a method invocation in a consistent manner, using either a cron expression, an interval, or a rate, and you don't want to have to go through Quartz just to do it.

Solution

Spring has support to configure TaskExecutors and TaskSchedulers. This capability, coupled with the ability to schedule method execution using the @Scheduled annotation, makes Spring scheduling support work with a minimum of fuss: all you need are a method, an annotation, and to have switched on the scanner for annotations.

How It Works

Let's revisit the example in the last recipe: we want to schedule a call to the replication method on the bean using a cron expression. Our configuration class looks like the following.

Listing 10-54. Scheduling configuration

```
package com.apress.spring6recipes.replicator.config;

import org.springframework.context.annotation.Bean;
import org.springframework.context.annotation.Configuration;
import org.springframework.scheduling.TaskScheduler;
import org.springframework.scheduling.annotation.EnableScheduling;
import org.springframework.scheduling.concurrent.ThreadPoolTaskScheduler;


@Configuration
@EnableScheduling
public class SchedulingConfiguration {

  @Bean
  public TaskScheduler taskScheduler() {
    var taskScheduler = new ThreadPoolTaskScheduler();
    taskScheduler.setThreadNamePrefix("s6r-scheduler-");
    taskScheduler.setPoolSize(10);
    return taskScheduler;
  }
}
```

We enable the annotation-driven scheduling support by specifying @EnableScheduling. This will register a bean that scans the beans in the application context for the @Scheduled annotation. We also configure a ThreadPoolTaskScheduler with the name taskScheduler, as we want to set a prefix for the thread names and we want to schedule ten tasks at once. We set the pool size to 10. The scheduling support will automatically detect a single TaskScheduler or detect it by the name taskScheduler.

Listing 10-55. Simple FileReplicator implementation with scheduling

```
package com.apress.spring6recipes.replicator;

import org.springframework.scheduling.annotation.Scheduled;

import java.io.IOException;
import java.nio.file.Files;
import java.nio.file.Path;

public class SimpleFileReplicator implements FileReplicator {

  @Scheduled(fixedDelay = 60_000)
  public synchronized void replicate() throws IOException {
    var files = Path.of(srcDir);
    try (var fileList = Files.list(files)) {
      fileList.filter(Files::isRegularFile)
              .forEach(it -> fileCopier.copyFile(it, Path.of(destDir)));
    }
  }
}
```

Note that we've annotated the `replicate()` method with a `@Scheduled` annotation. Here, we've told the scheduler to execute the method every 60 seconds. Alternatively, we might specify a `fixedRate` value for the `@Scheduled` annotation, which would measure the time between successive starts and then trigger another run.

Listing 10-56. Simple FileReplicator implementation with fixedRate

```
@Scheduled(fixedRate = 60_000)
public synchronized void replicate() throws IOException { ... }
```

Finally, we might want more complex control over the execution of the method. In this case, we can use a cron expression, just as we did in the Quartz example.

Listing 10-57. Simple FileReplicator implementation with a cron expression

```
@Scheduled( cron = "0/60 * * * * ? " )
public synchronized void replicate() throws IOException { ... }
```

There is support for configuring all of this in Java too. This might be useful if you didn't want to, or couldn't, add an annotation to an existing bean method. Here's a look at how we might recreate the preceding annotation-centric examples using the Spring `ScheduledTaskRegistrar`. You can get access to the `ScheduledTaskRegistrar` by letting the configuration class (or another Spring component) implement the `SchedulingConfigurer` interface and implement the `configureTasks` method.

Listing 10-58. Scheduling configuration - manually configuring tasks

```
package com.apress.spring6recipes.replicator.config;

import com.apress.spring6recipes.replicator.FileReplicator;
import org.springframework.context.annotation.Bean;
import org.springframework.context.annotation.Configuration;
import org.springframework.scheduling.TaskScheduler;
import org.springframework.scheduling.annotation.EnableScheduling;
import org.springframework.scheduling.annotation.SchedulingConfigurer;
import org.springframework.scheduling.concurrent.ThreadPoolTaskScheduler;
import org.springframework.scheduling.config.ScheduledTaskRegistrar;

import java.io.IOException;
import java.time.Duration;

@Configuration
@EnableScheduling
public class SchedulingConfiguration implements SchedulingConfigurer {

  private final FileReplicator fileReplicator;

  public SchedulingConfiguration(FileReplicator fileReplicator) {
    this.fileReplicator = fileReplicator;
  }
```

```java
@Override
public void configureTasks(ScheduledTaskRegistrar taskRegistrar) {
  taskRegistrar.addFixedDelayTask(() -> {
    try {
      fileReplicator.replicate();
    } catch (IOException e) {
      e.printStackTrace();
    }
  }, Duration.ofSeconds(60));
}

@Bean
public TaskScheduler taskScheduler() {
  var taskScheduler = new ThreadPoolTaskScheduler();
  taskScheduler.setThreadNamePrefix("s6r-scheduler-");
  taskScheduler.setPoolSize(10);
  return taskScheduler;
}
}
```

10-7. Introduction to Contract-First SOAP Web Services
Problem

You want to develop a contract-first SOAP web service.

Solution

There are two ways to develop SOAP web services. One is called "code-first," which means you start with a Java class and then build out toward a WSDL contract. The other method is called "contract-first," which means you start with an XML data contract—something simpler than WSDL—and build in toward a Java class to implement the service. To create a data contract for a "contract-first" SOAP web service, you'll need an XSD file or XML schema file that describes the operations and data supported by the service. The requirement for an XSD file is because "under the hood" the communication between a SOAP service client and server takes place as XML defined in an XSD file. However, because an XSD file can be difficult to write correctly, it's preferable to start by creating sample XML messages and then generating the XSD file from them. Then with the XSD file, you can leverage something like Spring-WS to build the SOAP web service parting from the XSD file.

How It Works
Create Sample XML Messages

Let's create a weather service using the SOAP "contract-first" approach. So you're asked to write a SOAP service that is able to communicate weather information based on a city and date, returning the minimum, maximum, and average temperatures. Instead of going in head-first and writing code to support the functionality, let's describe the temperature of a particular city and date using a "contract-first" approach with an XML message like the following.

Listing 10-59. Sample XML response

```xml
<TemperatureInfo city="Houston" date="2021-12-01">
  <min>5.0</min>
  <max>10.0</max>
  <average>8.0</average>
</TemperatureInfo>
```

This is the first step toward having a data contract in a SOAP "contract-first" way for the weather service. Now let's define some operations. You want to allow clients to query the temperatures of a particular city for multiple dates. Each request consists of a city element and multiple date elements. We'll also specify the namespace for this request to avoid naming conflicts with other XML documents. Let's create this XML message and save it into a file called request.xml.

Listing 10-60. Sample XML request

```xml
<GetTemperaturesRequest
      xmlns="http://spring6recipes.apress.com/weather/schemas">
  <city>Houston</city>
  <date>2021-12-01</date>
  <date>2021-12-08</date>
  <date>2021-12-15</date>
</GetTemperaturesRequest>
```

The response for a request of the previous type would consist of multiple TemperatureInfo elements, each of which represents the temperature of a particular city and date, in accordance with the requested dates. Let's create this XML message and save it to a file called response.xml.

Listing 10-61. Sample XML response

```xml
<GetTemperaturesResponse
      xmlns="http://spring6recipes.apress.com/weather/schemas">
  <TemperatureInfo city="Houston" date="2021-12-01">
    <min>5.0</min>
    <max>10.0</max>
    <average>8.0</average>
  </TemperatureInfo>
  <TemperatureInfo city="Houston" date="2021-12-08">
    <min>4.0</min>
    <max>13.0</max>
    <average>7.0</average>
  </TemperatureInfo>
  <TemperatureInfo city="Houston" date="2021-12-15">
    <min>10.0</min>
    <max>18.0</max>
    <average>15.0</average>
  </TemperatureInfo>
</GetTemperaturesResponse>
```

Generate an XSD File from Sample XML Messages

Now, you can generate the XSD file from the preceding sample XML messages. Most XML tools and enterprise Java IDEs can generate an XSD file from a couple of XML files. Here, we'll use Apache XMLBeans to generate the XSD file.

ℹ️   You can download Apache XMLBeans (e.g., v5.1.1) from the Apache XMLBeans website and extract it to a directory of your choice to complete the installation.

Apache XMLBeans provides a tool called inst2xsd to generate XSD files from XML files. It supports several design types for generating XSD files. The simplest is called the Russian doll design, which generates local elements and local types for the target XSD file. Because there's no enumeration type used in your XML messages, you can disable the enumeration generation feature. You can execute the following command to generate the XSD file from the previous XML files.

Listing 10-62. Command to generate XSD

```
inst2xsd -design rd -enumerations never request.xml response.xml
```

The generated XSD file will have the default name schema0.xsd, located in the same directory. Let's rename it to temperature.xsd.

Listing 10-63. XSD schema for the weather service

```xml
<?xml version="1.0" encoding="UTF-8"?>
<xs:schema attributeFormDefault="unqualified"
    elementFormDefault="qualified"
    targetNamespace="http://spring6recipes.apress.com/weather/schemas"
    xmlns:xs="http://www.w3.org/2001/XMLSchema">

    <xs:element name="GetTemperaturesRequest">
        <xs:complexType>
            <xs:sequence>
                <xs:element type="xs:string" name="city" />
                <xs:element type="xs:date" name="date"
                    maxOccurs="unbounded" minOccurs="0" />
            </xs:sequence>
        </xs:complexType>
    </xs:element>

    <xs:element name="GetTemperaturesResponse">
        <xs:complexType>
            <xs:sequence>
                <xs:element name="TemperatureInfo"
                    maxOccurs="unbounded" minOccurs="0">
                    <xs:complexType>
                        <xs:sequence>
                            <xs:element type="xs:float" name="min" />
                            <xs:element type="xs:float" name="max" />
                            <xs:element type="xs:float" name="average" />
```

```
            </xs:sequence>
            <xs:attribute type="xs:string" name="city"
                use="optional" />
            <xs:attribute type="xs:date" name="date"
                use="optional" />
        </xs:complexType>
      </xs:element>
    </xs:sequence>
  </xs:complexType>
 </xs:element>
</xs:schema>
```

Optimizing the Generated XSD File

As you can see, the generated XSD file allows clients to query temperatures for unlimited dates. If you want to add a constraint on the maximum and minimum query dates, you can modify the maxOccurs and minOccurs attributes.

Listing 10-64. XSD schema for the weather service with modifications

```
<?xml version="1.0" encoding="UTF-8"?>
<xs:schema xmlns:xs="http://www.w3.org/2001/XMLSchema" attributeFormDefault="unqualified"
          elementFormDefault="qualified"
          targetNamespace="http://springrecipes.apress.com/weather/schemas">
    <xs:element name="GetTemperaturesRequest">
        <xs:complexType>
            <xs:sequence>
                <xs:element type="xs:string" name="city"/>
                <xs:element type="xs:date" name="date" maxOccurs="5" minOccurs="1"/>
            </xs:sequence>
        </xs:complexType>
    </xs:element>
    <xs:element name="GetTemperaturesResponse">
        <xs:complexType>
            <xs:sequence>
                <xs:element name="TemperatureInfo" maxOccurs="5" minOccurs="1">
                    <xs:complexType>
                        <xs:sequence>
                            <xs:element type="xs:float" name="min"/>
                            <xs:element type="xs:float" name="max"/>
                            <xs:element type="xs:float" name="average"/>
                        </xs:sequence>
                        <xs:attribute type="xs:string" name="city" use="optional"/>
                        <xs:attribute type="xs:date" name="date" use="optional"/>
                    </xs:complexType>
                </xs:element>
            </xs:sequence>
        </xs:complexType>
    </xs:element>
</xs:schema>
```

Previewing the Generated WSDL File

As you will learn shortly and in full detail, Spring-WS is equipped to automatically generate a WSDL contract parting from an XSD file. The following snippet illustrates the Spring bean configuration for this purpose—we'll add context on how to use this snippet in the next recipe, which describes how to build SOAP web services with Spring-WS.

Listing 10-65. Sample bean configuration for WSDL

```
@Bean
public XsdSchema temperatureSchema() {
  var xsd = new ClassPathResource("/META-INF/xsd/temperature.xsd");
  return new SimpleXsdSchema(xsd);
}
```

Here, we'll preview the generated WSDL file to better understand the service contract. For simplicity's sake, the less important parts are omitted.

Listing 10-66. Generated WSDL using Spring-WS

```
<?xml version="1.0" encoding="UTF-8" ?>
<wsdl:definitions ...
    targetNamespace="http://spring6recipes.apress.com/weather/schemas">
    <wsdl:types>
        <!-- Copied from the XSD file -->
        ...
    </wsdl:types>
    <wsdl:message name="GetTemperaturesResponse">
        <wsdl:part element="schema:GetTemperaturesResponse"
            name="GetTemperaturesResponse">
        </wsdl:part>
    </wsdl:message>
    <wsdl:message name="GetTemperaturesRequest">
        <wsdl:part element="schema:GetTemperaturesRequest"
            name="GetTemperaturesRequest">
        </wsdl:part>
    </wsdl:message>
    <wsdl:portType name="Weather">
        <wsdl:operation name="GetTemperatures">
            <wsdl:input message="schema:GetTemperaturesRequest"
                name="GetTemperaturesRequest">
            </wsdl:input>
            <wsdl:output message="schema:GetTemperaturesResponse"
                name="GetTemperaturesResponse">
            </wsdl:output>
        </wsdl:operation>
    </wsdl:portType>
    ...
    <wsdl:service name="WeatherService">
        <wsdl:port binding="schema:WeatherBinding" name="WeatherPort">
```

```
    <soap:address
        location="http://localhost:8080/weather/services" />
  </wsdl:port>
 </wsdl:service>
</wsdl:definitions>
```

In the Weather port type, a GetTemperatures operation is defined whose name is derived from the prefix of the input and output messages (i.e., <GetTemperaturesRequest> and <GetTemperaturesResponse>). The definitions of these two elements are included in the <wsdl:types> part, as defined in the data contract.

Now with the WSDL contract in hand, you can generate the necessary Java interfaces and then write the backing code for each of the operations that started out as XML messages. This full technique is explored in the next recipe, which uses Spring-WS for the process.

10-8. Expose and Invoke SOAP Web Services with Spring-WS

Problem

You have an XSD file to develop a "contract-first" SOAP web service and don't know how or what to use to implement the "contract-first" SOAP service.

Spring-WS was designed from the outset to support "contract-first" SOAP web services. However, this does not mean Spring-WS is the only way to create SOAP web services in Java. JAX-WS implementations like CXF also support this technique. Nevertheless, Spring-WS is the more mature and natural approach to do "contract-first" SOAP web services in the context of Spring applications. Describing other "contract-first" SOAP Java techniques would lead us outside the scope of the Spring Framework.

Solution

Spring-WS provides a set of facilities to develop "contract-first" SOAP web services. The essential tasks for building a Spring-WS web service include the following:

- Set up and configure a Spring MVC application for Spring-WS.
- Map web service requests to endpoints.
- Create service endpoints to handle the request messages and return the response messages.
- Publish the WSDL file for the web service.

How It Works

Set Up a Spring-WS Application

To implement a web service using Spring-WS, let's first create a web application initializer class to bootstrap a web application with a SOAP web service. You need to configure the MessageDispatcherServlet, which is part of Spring-WS. This servlet specializes in dispatching web service messages to appropriate endpoints and detecting the framework facilities of Spring-WS.

Listing 10-67. WebApplicationInitializer for Spring-WS

```
package com.apress.spring6recipes.weather.config;

import org.springframework.ws.transport.http.support.
AbstractAnnotationConfigMessageDispatcherServletInitializer;

public class Initializer extends
AbstractAnnotationConfigMessageDispatcherServletInitializer {

  @Override
  protected Class<?>[] getRootConfigClasses() {
    return null;
  }

  @Override
  protected Class<?>[] getServletConfigClasses() {
    return new Class<?>[]{SpringWsConfiguration.class};
  }
}
```

To make configuration easier, there is the
AbstractAnnotationConfigMessageDispatcherServletInitializer base class that you can extend. You
need to supply it with the configuration classes that make up the rootConfig and the servletConfig; the
former can be null, whereas the latter is required.

The preceding configuration will bootstrap a MessageDispatcherServlet using the
SpringWsConfiguration class and register it for the /services/ and .wsdl URLs by default.

Listing 10-68. Spring-WS configuration

```
package com.apress.spring6recipes.weather.config;

import org.springframework.context.annotation.Bean;
import org.springframework.context.annotation.ComponentScan;
import org.springframework.context.annotation.Configuration;
import org.springframework.core.io.ClassPathResource;
import org.springframework.ws.config.annotation.EnableWs;
import org.springframework.ws.wsdl.wsdl11.DefaultWsdl11Definition;
import org.springframework.xml.xsd.SimpleXsdSchema;
import org.springframework.xml.xsd.XsdSchema;

@Configuration
@EnableWs
@ComponentScan("com.apress.spring6recipes.weather")
public class SpringWsConfiguration {
}
```

The SpringWsConfiguration class is annotated with @EnableWs that registers the necessary beans to
make the MessageDispatcherServlet work. There is also the @ComponentScan that scans for @Service and @
Endpoint beans.

Create Service Endpoints

Spring-WS supports annotating an arbitrary class as a service endpoint by the @Endpoint annotation so it becomes accessible as a web service. Besides the @Endpoint annotation, you also need to annotate handler methods with the @PayloadRoot annotation to map service requests. And each handler method also relies on the @ResponsePayload and @RequestPayload annotations to handle the incoming and outgoing service data.

Listing 10-69. Weather service endpoint

```
package com.apress.spring6recipes.weather;

import org.dom4j.DocumentHelper;
import org.dom4j.Element;
import org.dom4j.Node;
import org.dom4j.XPath;
import org.dom4j.xpath.DefaultXPath;
import org.springframework.ws.server.endpoint.annotation.Endpoint;
import org.springframework.ws.server.endpoint.annotation.PayloadRoot;
import org.springframework.ws.server.endpoint.annotation.RequestPayload;
import org.springframework.ws.server.endpoint.annotation.ResponsePayload;

import java.time.LocalDate;
import java.time.format.DateTimeFormatter;
import java.util.Map;

@Endpoint
public class TemperatureEndpoint {

    private static final String namespaceUri = "http://spring6recipes.apress.com/weather/
    schemas";
    private final WeatherService weatherService;
    private final XPath cityPath;
    private final XPath datePath;

    public TemperatureEndpoint(WeatherService weatherService) {
        this.weatherService = weatherService;
        // Create the XPath objects, including the namespace
        var namespaceUris = Map.of("weather", namespaceUri);
        cityPath = new DefaultXPath("/weather:GetTemperaturesRequest/weather:city");
        cityPath.setNamespaceURIs(namespaceUris);
        datePath = new DefaultXPath("/weather:GetTemperaturesRequest/weather:date");
        datePath.setNamespaceURIs(namespaceUris);
    }

    @PayloadRoot(localPart = "GetTemperaturesRequest", namespace = namespaceUri)
    @ResponsePayload
    public Element getTemperature(@RequestPayload Element requestElement) {
        // Extract the service parameters from the request message
        var city = cityPath.valueOf(requestElement);
```

```
var dates = datePath.selectNodes(requestElement).stream()
        .map(Node::getText)
        .map(ds -> LocalDate.parse(ds, DateTimeFormatter.ISO_DATE))
        .toList();

// Invoke the back-end service to handle the request
var temperatures =
        weatherService.getTemperatures(city, dates);

// Build the response message from the result of back-end service
var responseDocument = DocumentHelper.createDocument();
var responseElement = responseDocument.addElement(
        "GetTemperaturesResponse", namespaceUri);
temperatures.forEach(temp -> map(responseElement, temp));
return responseElement;
}

private Element map(Element root, TemperatureInfo temperature) {
    var temperatureElement = root.addElement("TemperatureInfo");
    temperatureElement.addAttribute("city", temperature.city());
    temperatureElement.addAttribute("date", temperature.date().format(DateTimeFormatter.
    ISO_DATE));
    temperatureElement.addElement("min").setText(Double.toString(temperature.min()));
    temperatureElement.addElement("max").setText(Double.toString(temperature.max()));
    temperatureElement.addElement("average").setText(Double.toString(temperature.
    average()));
    return temperatureElement;
}

}
```

In the @PayloadRoot annotation, you specify the local name (getTemperaturesRequest) and namespace (http://spring6recipes.apress.com/weather/schemas) of the payload root element to be handled. Next, the method is decorated with the @ResponsePayload indicating the method's return value is the service response data. In addition, the method's input parameter is decorated with the @RequestPayload annotation to indicate it's the service input value.

Then inside the handler method, you first extract the service parameters from the request message. Here, you use XPath to help locate the elements. The XPath objects are created in the constructor so that they can be reused for subsequent request handling. Note that you must also include the namespace in the XPath expressions, or else they will not be able to locate the elements correctly. After extracting the service parameters, you invoke the back-end service to handle the request. Because this endpoint is configured in the Spring IoC container, it can easily refer to other beans through dependency injection. Finally, you build the response message from the back-end service's result. In this case we used the dom4j library that provides a rich set of APIs for you to build an XML message. But you can use any other XML processing API or Java parser you wish (e.g., DOM).

Because you already defined a @ComponentScan in the SpringWsConfiguration class, Spring automatically picks up all the Spring-WS annotations and deploys the endpoint to the servlet.

Publish the WSDL File

The last step to complete the SOAP web service is to publish the WSDL file. In Spring-WS, it's not necessary for you to write the WSDL file manually. You only need to add a bean to the SpringWsConfiguration class.

Listing 10-70. XSD and WSDL configuration

```
@Bean
public DefaultWsdl11Definition temperature() {
    var temperature = new DefaultWsdl11Definition();
    temperature.setPortTypeName("Weather");
    temperature.setLocationUri("/");
    temperature.setSchema(temperatureSchema());
    return temperature;
}


@Bean
public XsdSchema temperatureSchema() {
    var xsd = new ClassPathResource("/META-INF/xsd/temperature.xsd")
    return new SimpleXsdSchema(xsd);
}
```

The DefaultWsdl11Definition class requires that you specify two properties: a portTypeName for the service and a locationUri on which to deploy the final WSDL. In addition, it also requires that you specify the location of the XSD file from which to create the WSDL—see the previous recipe for details on how to create an XSD file. In this case, the XSD file will be located inside the application's META-INF directory. Because you have defined <GetTemperaturesRequest> and <GetTemperaturesResponse> in your XSD file and you have specified the port type name as Weather, the WSDL builder will generate the following WSDL port type and operation for you. The following snippet is taken from the generated WSDL file.

Listing 10-71. WSDL port type definition

```
<wsdl:portType name="Weather">
    <wsdl:operation name="GetTemperatures">
        <wsdl:input message="schema:GetTemperaturesRequest"
            name="GetTemperaturesRequest" />
        <wsdl:output message="schema:GetTemperaturesResponse"
            name="GetTemperaturesResponse" />
    </wsdl:operation>
</wsdl:portType>
```

Finally, you can access this WSDL file by joining its definition's bean name and the .wsdl suffix. Assuming the web application is packaged in a WAR file named springws, then the service is deployed in http://localhost:8080/springws/—because the Spring-WS servlet in the initializer is deployed on the /services directory—and the WSDL file's URL would be http://localhost:8080/springws/services/weather/temperature.wsdl, given that the bean name of the WSDL definition is temperature.

Invoke SOAP Web Services with Spring-WS

Now, let's create a Spring-WS client to invoke the weather service according to the contract it publishes. You can create a Spring-WS client by parsing the request and response XML messages. As an example, we will use dom4j to implement it. But you are free to choose any other XML parsing APIs for it.

To shield the client from the low-level invocation details, we'll create a local proxy to call the SOAP web service. This proxy also implements the WeatherService interface, and it translates local method calls into remote SOAP web service calls.

Listing 10-72. WeatherServiceProxy interface

```java
package com.apress.spring6recipes.weather;

import org.dom4j.DocumentHelper;
import org.dom4j.Element;
import org.dom4j.io.DocumentResult;
import org.dom4j.io.DocumentSource;
import org.springframework.ws.client.core.WebServiceTemplate;

import java.time.LocalDate;
import java.time.format.DateTimeFormatter;
import java.util.List;

public class WeatherServiceProxy implements WeatherService {

  private static final String uri = "http://spring6recipes.apress.com/weather/schemas";

  private final WebServiceTemplate webServiceTemplate;

  public WeatherServiceProxy(WebServiceTemplate webServiceTemplate) {
    this.webServiceTemplate = webServiceTemplate;
  }

  @Override
  public List<TemperatureInfo> getTemperatures(String city, List<LocalDate> dates) {

    // Build the request document from the method arguments
    var doc = DocumentHelper.createDocument();
    var el = doc.addElement("GetTemperaturesRequest", uri);
    el.addElement("city").setText(city);
    dates.forEach(date -> el.addElement("date")
            .setText(date.format(DateTimeFormatter.ISO_DATE)));

    // Invoke the remote web service
    var source = new DocumentSource(doc);
    var result = new DocumentResult();
    webServiceTemplate.sendSourceAndReceiveToResult(source, result);

    // Extract the result from the response document
    var responseDocument = result.getDocument();
    var responseElement = responseDocument.getRootElement();
    return responseElement.elements("TemperatureInfo")
            .stream().map( (e) -> this.map(city, e))
            .toList();
  }
```

```
private TemperatureInfo map(String city, Element element) {
    var date = LocalDate.parse(element.attributeValue("date"), DateTimeFormatter.ISO_DATE);
    var min = Double.parseDouble(element.elementText("min"));
    var max = Double.parseDouble(element.elementText("max"));
    var average = Double.parseDouble(element.elementText("average"));
    return new TemperatureInfo(city, date, min, max, average);
  }
}
```

In the getTemperatures() method, you first build the request message using the dom4j
API. WebServiceTemplate provides a sendSourceAndReceiveToResult() method that accepts a java.xml.
transform.Source and a java.xml.transform.Result object as arguments. You have to build a dom4j
DocumentSource object to wrap your request document and create a new dom4j DocumentResult object
for the method to write the response document to it. Finally, you get the response message and extract the
results from it.

With the service proxy written, we can declare it in a configuration class and later call it using a
standalone class.

Listing 10-73. Weather service client configuration

```
package com.apress.spring6recipes.weather.config;

import com.apress.spring6recipes.weather.WeatherService;
import com.apress.spring6recipes.weather.WeatherServiceClient;
import com.apress.spring6recipes.weather.WeatherServiceProxy;
import org.springframework.context.annotation.Bean;
import org.springframework.context.annotation.Configuration;
import org.springframework.ws.client.core.WebServiceTemplate;

@Configuration
public class SpringWsClientConfiguration {

  @Bean
  public WeatherServiceClient weatherServiceClient(WeatherService weatherService) {
    return new WeatherServiceClient(weatherService);
  }

  @Bean
  public WeatherServiceProxy weatherServiceProxy(WebServiceTemplate wst) {
    return new WeatherServiceProxy(wst);
  }

  @Bean
  public WebServiceTemplate webServiceTemplate() {
    var webServiceTemplate = new WebServiceTemplate();
    webServiceTemplate.setDefaultUri("http://localhost:8080/springws/services");
    return webServiceTemplate;
  }
}
```

Note the webServiceTemplate has its defaultUri value set to the endpoint defined for the Spring-WS endpoint in the previous sections. Once the configuration is loaded by an application, you can call the SOAP service using the following class.

Listing 10-74. Weather service client

```
package com.apress.spring6recipes.weather;

import com.apress.spring6recipes.weather.config.SpringWsClientConfiguration;
import org.springframework.context.annotation.AnnotationConfigApplicationContext;

public class SpringWSInvokerClient {

  public static void main(String[] args) {
    var cfg = SpringWsClientConfiguration.class;
    try (var context = new AnnotationConfigApplicationContext(cfg)) {

      var client = context.getBean(WeatherServiceClient.class);
      var temperature = client.getTodayTemperature("Houston");
      System.out.println("Min temperature : " + temperature.min());
      System.out.println("Max temperature : " + temperature.max());
      System.out.println("Average temperature : " + temperature.average());
    }
  }
}
```

10-9. Develop SOAP Web Services with Spring-WS and XML Marshalling
Problem

To develop web services with the contract-first approach, you have to process request and response XML messages. If you parse the XML messages with XML parsing APIs directly, you'll have to deal with the XML elements one by one with low-level APIs, which is a cumbersome and inefficient task.

Solution

Spring-WS supports using XML marshalling technology to marshal and unmarshal objects to and from XML documents. In this way, you can deal with object properties instead of XML elements. This technology is also known as object/XML mapping (OXM), because you are actually mapping objects to and from XML documents. To implement endpoints with an XML marshalling technology, you can configure an XML marshaller for it. Table 10-2 lists the marshallers provided by Spring for different XML marshalling APIs.

Table 10-2. *Marshallers for Different XML Marshalling APIs*

API	Marshaller
JAXB	org.springframework.oxm.jaxb.Jaxb2Marshaller
XStream	org.springframework.oxm.xstream.XStreamMarshaller

Spring-WS clients can use this marshalling and unmarshalling technique to simplify XML data processing.

How It Works

Create Service Endpoints with XML Marshalling

Spring-WS supports various XML marshalling APIs, including JAXB and XStream. As an example, you'll create a service endpoint using JAXB as the marshaller. Using other XML marshalling APIs is very similar. The first step in using XML marshalling is creating the object model according to the XML message formats. This model can usually be generated by the marshalling API. For some marshalling APIs, the object model must be generated by them so that they can insert marshalling-specific information. With JAXB you generally start from the XSD and based on that generate the Java classes.

To generate the Java classes from the XSD, you need a tool called `xjc`, which transforms the XSD into a Java object (or generate a schema from a Java object). The XJC for JAXB can be downloaded from the Jakarta EE homepage. When downloaded and unpacked, the `xjc` launch scripts are available in the `bin` directory.

To generate the classes, execute the following command (from the directory where you download the `xjc` program).

Listing 10-75. XJC command line

```
xjc <path-to-project-sources>/spring-6-recipes/code/ch10/recipe_10_9_SpringWS_Server/src/
main/resources/META-INF/xsd/temperature.xsd
```

This will generate four java classes, which you can copy into the sources of your project.

When using a build tool like Gradle or Maven, there are plugins that will generate the code while building the project; this will save you from manually needing to generate the Java code from the XSD.

Listing 10-76. JAXB-generated request and response

```java
package com.apress.spring6recipes.weather.schemas;

@XmlAccessorType(XmlAccessType.FIELD)
@XmlType(name = "", propOrder = {
    "city",
    "date"
})
@XmlRootElement(name = "GetTemperaturesRequest")
public class GetTemperaturesRequest {
    protected List<XMLGregorianCalendar> date;
}

package com.apress.spring6recipes.weather.schemas;

@XmlAccessorType(XmlAccessType.FIELD)
@XmlType(name = "", propOrder = {
```

```
    "temperatureInfo"
})
@XmlRootElement(name = "GetTemperaturesResponse")
public class GetTemperaturesResponse {

    @XmlElement(name = "TemperatureInfo", required = true)
    protected List<TemperatureInfo> temperatureInfo;
}
```

With the object model created, you can easily integrate marshalling on any endpoint. Let's apply this technique to the endpoint presented in the previous recipe.

Listing 10-77. Temperature Endpoint

```
package com.apress.spring6recipes.weather;

import com.apress.spring6recipes.weather.schemas.GetTemperaturesRequest;
import com.apress.spring6recipes.weather.schemas.GetTemperaturesResponse;
import org.springframework.ws.server.endpoint.annotation.Endpoint;
import org.springframework.ws.server.endpoint.annotation.PayloadRoot;
import org.springframework.ws.server.endpoint.annotation.RequestPayload;
import org.springframework.ws.server.endpoint.annotation.ResponsePayload;

import javax.xml.datatype.DatatypeConfigurationException;
import javax.xml.datatype.DatatypeFactory;
import java.time.LocalDate;

@Endpoint
public class TemperatureEndpoint {

  private static final String namespaceUri = "http://spring6recipes.apress.com/weather/
  schemas";
  private final WeatherService weatherService;

  public TemperatureEndpoint(WeatherService weatherService) {
    this.weatherService = weatherService;
  }

  @PayloadRoot(localPart = "GetTemperaturesRequest", namespace = namespaceUri)
  @ResponsePayload
  public GetTemperaturesResponse getTemperature(@RequestPayload GetTemperaturesRequest
  request) {
    // Extract the service parameters from the request message
    var city = request.getCity();
    var dates = request.getDate().stream()
            .map(ds -> LocalDate.of(ds.getYear(), ds.getMonth(), ds.getDay()))
            .toList();

    // Invoke the back-end service to handle the request
    var temperatures =
            weatherService.getTemperatures(city, dates);
```

```java
    // Build the response message from the result of back-end service
    var response = new GetTemperaturesResponse();
    temperatures.forEach(temp -> response.getTemperatureInfo().add(map(temp)));
    return response;
}

private GetTemperaturesResponse.TemperatureInfo map(TemperatureInfo temperature) {
    var temperatureInfo = new GetTemperaturesResponse.TemperatureInfo();
    temperatureInfo.setCity(temperature.city());
    temperatureInfo.setMax(temperature.max());
    temperatureInfo.setMin(temperature.min());
    temperatureInfo.setAverage(temperature.average());
    try {
        temperatureInfo.setDate(DatatypeFactory.newInstance().newXMLGregorianCalendar(temperat
        ure.date().toString()));
    } catch (DatatypeConfigurationException e) {
        throw new IllegalStateException(e);
    }
    return temperatureInfo;
}
}
```

Notice that all you have to do in this new method endpoint is handle the request object and return the response object. Then, it will be marshalled to the response XML message. In addition to this endpoint modification, a marshalling endpoint also requires that both the marshaller and unmarshaller properties be set. Usually, you can specify a single marshaller for both properties. For JAXB, you declare a Jaxb2Marshaller bean as the marshaller and configure it with the packages to scan (the packages with the generated classes in them). Next to the marshaller, we also need to register a MethodArgumentResolver and MethodReturnValueHandler to actually handle the marshalling of the method argument and return type. For this we extend the WsConfigurerAdapter and override the addArgumentResolvers and addReturnValueHandlers methods and add the MarshallingPayloadMethodProcessor to both the lists.

Listing 10-78. Spring-WS with JAXB marshaller configuration

```java
package com.apress.spring6recipes.weather.config;

import org.springframework.context.annotation.Bean;
import org.springframework.context.annotation.ComponentScan;
import org.springframework.context.annotation.Configuration;
import org.springframework.core.io.ClassPathResource;
import org.springframework.oxm.jaxb.Jaxb2Marshaller;
import org.springframework.ws.config.annotation.EnableWs;
import org.springframework.ws.config.annotation.WsConfigurerAdapter;
import org.springframework.ws.server.endpoint.adapter.method.
MarshallingPayloadMethodProcessor;
import org.springframework.ws.server.endpoint.adapter.method.MethodArgumentResolver;
import org.springframework.ws.server.endpoint.adapter.method.MethodReturnValueHandler;
import org.springframework.ws.wsdl.wsdl11.DefaultWsdl11Definition;
import org.springframework.xml.xsd.SimpleXsdSchema;
import org.springframework.xml.xsd.XsdSchema;

import java.util.List;
```

```
@Configuration
@EnableWs
@ComponentScan("com.apress.spring6recipes.weather")
public class SpringWsConfiguration extends WsConfigurerAdapter {

  @Bean
  public DefaultWsdl11Definition temperature() {
    var temperature = new DefaultWsdl11Definition();
    temperature.setPortTypeName("Weather");
    temperature.setLocationUri("/");
    temperature.setSchema(temperatureSchema());
    return temperature;
  }

  @Bean
  public XsdSchema temperatureSchema() {
    var xsd = new ClassPathResource("/META-INF/xsd/temperature.xsd");
    return new SimpleXsdSchema(xsd);
  }

  @Bean
  public Jaxb2Marshaller marshaller() {
    var marshaller = new Jaxb2Marshaller();
    marshaller.setPackagesToScan("com.apress.spring6recipes.weather.schemas");
    return marshaller;
  }

  @Override
  public void addArgumentResolvers(List<MethodArgumentResolver> argumentResolvers) {
    argumentResolvers.add(new MarshallingPayloadMethodProcessor(marshaller()));
  }

  @Override
  public void addReturnValueHandlers(List<MethodReturnValueHandler> returnValueHandlers) {
    returnValueHandlers.add(new MarshallingPayloadMethodProcessor(marshaller()));
  }
}
```

Invoking Web Services with XML Marshalling

A Spring-WS client can also marshal and unmarshal the request and response objects to and from XML messages. As an example, we will create a client using JAXB as the marshaller so that you can reuse the object models GetTemperaturesRequest, GetTemperaturesResponse, and TemperatureInfo, from the service endpoint. Let's implement the service proxy with XML marshalling. WebServiceTemplate provides a marshalSendAndReceive() method that accepts a request object as the method argument, which will be marshalled to the request message. This method has to return a response object that will be unmarshalled from the response message.

Listing 10-79. Weather service proxy with marshalling

```java
package com.apress.spring6recipes.weather;

import com.apress.spring6recipes.weather.schemas.GetTemperaturesRequest;
import com.apress.spring6recipes.weather.schemas.GetTemperaturesResponse;
import org.springframework.ws.client.core.WebServiceTemplate;

import javax.xml.datatype.DatatypeConfigurationException;
import javax.xml.datatype.DatatypeFactory;
import java.time.LocalDate;
import java.util.List;

public class WeatherServiceProxy implements WeatherService {

  private final WebServiceTemplate webServiceTemplate;

  public WeatherServiceProxy(WebServiceTemplate webServiceTemplate) throws Exception {
    this.webServiceTemplate = webServiceTemplate;
  }

  public List<TemperatureInfo> getTemperatures(String city, List<LocalDate> dates) {
    var request = createRequest(city, dates);
    var response = (GetTemperaturesResponse) webServiceTemplate.marshalSendAndReceive
    (request);
    return response.getTemperatureInfo().stream().map( (ti) -> map(city, ti)).toList();
  }

  private TemperatureInfo map(String city, GetTemperaturesResponse.TemperatureInfo info) {
    var date = info.getDate();
    var min = info.getMin();
    var max = info.getMax();
    var average = info.getAverage();
    return new TemperatureInfo(city, LocalDate.of(date.getYear(), date.getMonth(), date.
    getDay()),
            min, max, average);
  }

  private GetTemperaturesRequest createRequest(String city, List<LocalDate> dates) {
    var request = new GetTemperaturesRequest();
    request.setCity(city);
    dates.forEach(ld -> {
      try {
        request.getDate().add(DatatypeFactory.newInstance().newXMLGregorianCalendar(ld.
        toString()));
      } catch (DatatypeConfigurationException e) {
        throw new IllegalStateException(e);
      }
    });
    return request;
  }
}
```

When you are using XML marshalling, WebServiceTemplate requires both the marshaller and unmarshaller properties to be set. Usually, you can specify a single marshaller for both properties. For JAXB, you declare a Jaxb2Marshaller bean as the marshaller.

Listing 10-80. Spring-WS client configuration

```java
package com.apress.spring6recipes.weather.config;

import com.apress.spring6recipes.weather.WeatherService;
import com.apress.spring6recipes.weather.WeatherServiceClient;
import com.apress.spring6recipes.weather.WeatherServiceProxy;
import org.springframework.context.annotation.Bean;
import org.springframework.context.annotation.Configuration;
import org.springframework.oxm.Marshaller;
import org.springframework.oxm.jaxb.Jaxb2Marshaller;
import org.springframework.ws.client.core.WebServiceTemplate;

@Configuration
public class SpringWsClientConfiguration {

  @Bean
  public WeatherServiceClient weatherServiceClient(WeatherService weatherService) {
    return new WeatherServiceClient(weatherService);
  }

  @Bean
  public WeatherServiceProxy weatherServiceProxy(WebServiceTemplate webServiceTemplate)
          throws Exception {
    return new WeatherServiceProxy(webServiceTemplate);
  }

  @Bean
  public Jaxb2Marshaller marshaller() {
    var marshaller = new Jaxb2Marshaller();
    marshaller.setPackagesToScan("com.apress.spring6recipes.weather.schemas");
    return marshaller;
  }

  @Bean
  public WebServiceTemplate webServiceTemplate(Marshaller marshaller) {
    var webServiceTemplate = new WebServiceTemplate(marshaller);
    webServiceTemplate.setDefaultUri("http://localhost:8080/springws/services");
    return webServiceTemplate;
  }
}
```

10-10. Use the Java Flight Recorder to Investigate Application Startup

Problem

You want to investigate the startup of your Spring-based application and determine what can be improved using the Java Flight Recorder (JFR). The Java Flight Recorder is a tool for recording diagnostic and profiling information about a running application on a JVM. It does this with almost no performance overhead, which makes it useful in almost every environment. JFR will collect data about the JVM it runs on as well as the application it runs.

Solution

The core Spring container provides an API to monitor the setup and start of the application context. This API, the ApplicationStartup interface, has one implementation, the FlightRecorderApplicationStartup, which can be used to publish JFR events. However, by default the ApplicationStartup is no-op and doesn't do anything, so you would need to activate it.

After enabling the FlightRecorderApplicationStartup, you would also need to instruct the JDK to record the JFR events. Finally, to investigate the events, you would need a tool like Java Mission Control.

How It Works

First, we would need to set the proper ApplicationStartup implementation we want to use. Next, we would start with the proper command-line properties, and finally we would be able to inspect the events.

Enable JFR Event Processing

To enable JFR event publishing, we need to configure the application context with the FlightRecorderApplicationStartup class, instead of the default no-op one. You can do this by calling the setApplicationStartup method, which is defined in a base class used by most, so not all, application context implementations. After the registration, you call refresh to start loading the application context.

Listing 10-81. Main class with ApplicationStartup configuration

```
package com.apress.spring6recipes.replicator;

import org.springframework.context.annotation.AnnotationConfigApplicationContext;
import org.springframework.core.metrics.jfr.FlightRecorderApplicationStartup;

public class Main {

  public static void main(String[] args) throws Exception {
    var cfg = "com.apress.spring6recipes.replicator.config";
    try (var ctx = new AnnotationConfigApplicationContext()) {
      ctx.setApplicationStartup(new FlightRecorderApplicationStartup());
      ctx.scan(cfg);
      ctx.refresh();
```

```
        System.in.read();
    }
  }
}
```

However, with only this in place, the events won't be recorded. For that you would need to add the StartFlightRecording attribute to the JVM.

Listing 10-82. Java launch command

```
java -XX:StartFlightRecording:filename=recording.jfr,duration=30s -jar recipe_10_10_i.jar
```

This will start the application with flight recording enabled. It will write the events in a file named recording.jfr and will record 30 seconds of data.

Another option is to enable flight recording in-flight, meaning in a running application. You can use the jcmd command for that. Using the process explorer (Windows) of the ps command on Unix-based systems, you need to determine the process ID of the Java process in which you want to enable flight recording. Let's say the process ID is 4321. Then the following would enable flight recording.

Listing 10-83. JCMD launch command

```
jcmd 4321 JFR.start duration=30s filename=recording.jfr
```

When starting flight recording, you will see some output in the console indicating this.

Listing 10-84. Flight recording–enabled output

```
[0.462s][info][jfr,startup] Started recording 1. The result will be written to:
[0.462s][info][jfr,startup]
[0.462s][info][jfr,startup] /Users/marten/Repositories/apress/spring-6-recipes/code/
recording.jfr
[0.481s][info][jfr,startup] Started recording 2. The result will be written to:
[0.481s][info][jfr,startup]
[0.481s][info][jfr,startup] /Users/marten/Repositories/apress/spring-6-recipes/code/
recording.jfr
```

After stopping the application, you can open the recording.jfr file in Java Mission Control to observe the events (see Figure 10-7).

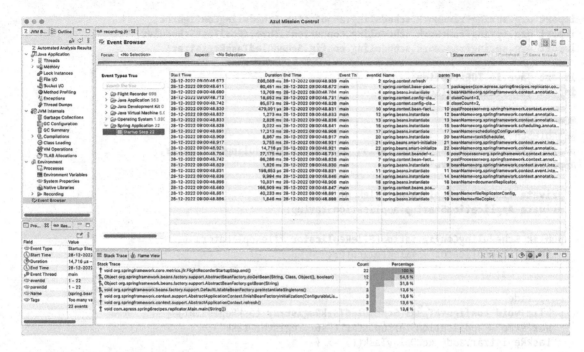

Figure 10-7. *Java Mission Control*

As you can see, there are several `spring.*` named events all corresponding to a part of the life cycle of the application context and/or the beans in it. This makes it a very powerful tool to help identify which parts of the application startup are slowing things down.

Publishing JFR Events

Next to publishing the standard events, it is also possible to publish/write your own events. To accomplish this you would need to obtain the `ApplicationStartup` instance in use and use its `start` method to create a `StartupStep`. When done you can call end on the provided `StartupStep` to record the event. To get a reference to the `ApplicationStartup` used in this context, you can implement the `ApplicationStartupAware` interface to have it injected. Using `@Autowired` might not work as annotation-based processing might not yet have been fully initialized.

Let's publish an event when we register a task through the `ScheduledTaskRegistrar`.

Listing 10-85. Scheduling configuration with an event

```
package com.apress.spring6recipes.replicator.config;

import com.apress.spring6recipes.replicator.FileReplicator;

import org.springframework.context.ApplicationStartupAware;
import org.springframework.context.annotation.Bean;
import org.springframework.context.annotation.Configuration;
import org.springframework.core.metrics.ApplicationStartup;
import org.springframework.scheduling.TaskScheduler;
import org.springframework.scheduling.annotation.EnableScheduling;
```

```java
import org.springframework.scheduling.annotation.SchedulingConfigurer;
import org.springframework.scheduling.concurrent.ThreadPoolTaskScheduler;
import org.springframework.scheduling.config.ScheduledTaskRegistrar;

import java.io.IOException;
import java.time.Duration;

@Configuration
@EnableScheduling
public class SchedulingConfiguration implements SchedulingConfigurer,
ApplicationStartupAware {

  private final FileReplicator fileReplicator;
  private ApplicationStartup applicationStartup;

  public SchedulingConfiguration(FileReplicator fileReplicator) {
    this.fileReplicator = fileReplicator;
  }

  @Override
  public void configureTasks(ScheduledTaskRegistrar taskRegistrar) {
    var step = applicationStartup.start("s6r.register-task");
    taskRegistrar.addFixedDelayTask(() -> {
      try {
        fileReplicator.replicate();
      } catch (IOException e) {
        e.printStackTrace();
      }
    }, Duration.ofSeconds(60));
    step.end();
  }
...
  @Override
  public void setApplicationStartup(ApplicationStartup applicationStartup) {
    this.applicationStartup=applicationStartup;
  }
}
```

Now when running the application with the appropriate settings (see Listing 10-83), you will see this event being registered as well (see Figure 10-8).

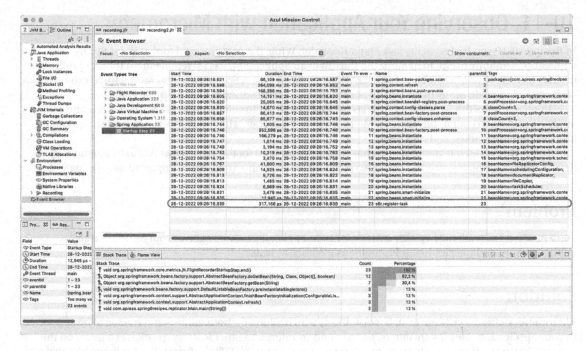

Figure 10-8. *Java Mission Control–registered event*

Registering an event is relatively easy. You can also enrich the events with additional tags (just as the ones in the `spring.*` namespace). For instance, you could add a tag that would include the name of the task/job you register.

Listing 10-86. Scheduling configuration with an event with a tag

```
public void configureTasks(ScheduledTaskRegistrar taskRegistrar) {

  var step = applicationStartup.start("s6r.register-task");
  step.tag("task", "file-replicator");
  taskRegistrar.addFixedDelayTask(() -> {
    try {
      fileReplicator.replicate();
    } catch (IOException e) {
      e.printStackTrace();
    }
  }, Duration.ofSeconds(60));
  step.end();
}
```

The tag, created with `tag` on the `StartupStep,` will now also be written with the event and will show up in Java Mission Control when doing the investigation.

10-11. Observing Your Application with Micrometer

In Recipe 10-10 you looked at the Java Flight Recorder. While that is a powerful tool, it is, for Spring applications, mainly useful to monitor the startup of an application. It is no replacement for Java profilers or metrics libraries like Micrometer. However, when the need arises, Spring also integrates with Micrometer out of the box, and so do many of the Spring portfolio projects like Spring Security, Spring Data, etc.

In recent years the Micrometer API has become the de facto standard for recording metrics and applying tracing to your application(s). Micrometer can integrate with many different monitoring systems, like Prometheus, Influx, and New Relic.

To provide better integration, Spring has embedded support for the Micrometer API in its internals, by default using a no-op registry, but it can be configured to send data to one of the supported monitoring systems.

Problem

You are using Prometheus to gather metrics for your application, and you want your Spring-based application to send metrics to this Prometheus instance as well.

Solution

Micrometer defines a concept of an `Observation,` which allows for both metrics and tracing to be supported in your application. Metrics are timers, gauges, and counters and provide a way to collect statistics on the runtime behavior of your application, for instance, the number of HTTP requests that are being handled and the respective outcome. Metrics help in analyzing performance, application usage patterns, and error rates. Tracing allows a more holistic view of your application landscape and enables you to track requests (HTTP, messages, etc.) through your entire system.

Micrometer Concepts

Here is a quick overview of the concepts of Micrometer Observation:

- `Observation` is the actual recording of something happening in your application. `Observation` is handled by an `ObservationHandler` to provide metrics and/or traces.

- Every observation has an `ObservationContext` implementation, which holds all relevant metadata for the `Observation`. For example, in case of an HTTP request, it will hold the HTTP method, response status, etc.

- Each `Observation` consists of one or more `KeyValues`. In the case of an HTTP request, this will be the HTTP method, response status, processing time, etc. The `KeyValues` are provided to a `ObservationConvention` implementation (for which there are many), which is tied to a specific `ObservationContext` implementation.

- `KeyValues` are called "low cardinality" when there are a low and bound number of possible values for the `KeyValue` (for instance, HTTP method for which there are just a few). Low-cardinality values are contributed to metrics only.

- `KeyValues` are called "high cardinality" when there are an (possible) unbounded number of possibilities (like the URL). High-cardinality values are contributed to traces only.

- Finally, there is an `ObservationDocumentation,` which documents all possible observations in a domain, describing the expected key names and their meaning.

To record metrics we need to configure a `MeterRegistry` so the `Observation` instance can use this to create the counters, timers, etc. Different technologies have different `MeterRegistry` implementations. Here we are going to use the JMX version, the `JmxMeterRegistry`.

How It Works

To publish metrics to JMX, we need the appropriate implementation to be available in the classpath. For this we need to add a dependency.

Listing 10-87. Gradle dependency

```
implementation group: 'io.micrometer', name: 'micrometer-registry-jmx', version: '1.10.2'
```

Listing 10-88. Maven dependency

```
<dependency>
  <groupId>io.micrometer</groupId>
  <artifactId>micrometer-registry-jmx</artifactId>
  <version>1.10.2</version>
</dependency>
```

With the dependency in place, we can configure our application to record and send metrics. Let's reuse the applications from Recipes 3-3 and 3-4 to enable metrics on both the server and the client.

Micrometer Configuration for the Client

Let's start with the client. First, we need a `JmxMeterRegistry` configured. With this `MeterRegistry` we can construct an `ObservationHandler` to be used with the `ObservationRegistry` to create and publish metrics through JMX.

Listing 10-89. Client metrics configuration

```
@Bean
public JmxMeterRegistry meterRegistry() {
  return new JmxMeterRegistry(JmxConfig.DEFAULT, Clock.SYSTEM);
}

@Bean
public ObservationRegistry observationRegistry(MeterRegistry meterRegistry) {
  var registry = ObservationRegistry.create();
  var handler = new DefaultMeterObservationHandler(meterRegistry);
  registry.observationConfig().observationHandler(handler);
  return registry;
}

@Bean
public RestTemplate restTemplate(ObservationRegistry observationRegistry) {
  var restTemplate = new RestTemplate();
  restTemplate.setObservationRegistry(observationRegistry);
  return restTemplate;
}
```

We can then use the `MeterRegistry` to configure the `ObservationRegistry` by supplying it with an `ObservationHandler`. For this we can use the `DefaultMeterObservationHandler`. You can see we use the factory method `create` on the `ObservationRegistry` to create an instance for us instead of using the default no-op implementation. The configuration can be obtained and modified by calling the `observationConfig` method. With that we can add the `DefaultMeterObservationHandler` to the list of handers. With that the integration between Micrometer and publishing to JMX has been realized. What is left is to configure the `RestTemplate` to use the `ObservationRegistry` to create the metrics. For this we can simply set the `ObservationRegistry` that has been created to the `RestTemplate`. With all this in place, we can now execute requests and meanwhile gather metrics. Those metrics can be accessed through JMX (see Figure 10-9).

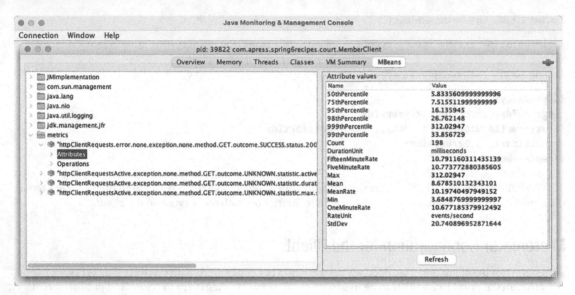

Figure 10-9. *Client metrics through JMX*

Now the metrics are published through JMX; however, the same can be applied for Prometheus, Ganglia, New Relic, etc. by providing the correct `MeterRegistry` and exposing it to the `ObservationRegistry`. You could even add multiple implementations by calling `observationHandler` multiple times. You could, for instance, combine JMX and Prometheus to expose metrics.

Micrometer Configuration for the Server

To configure the server, we need the same `MeterRegistry` and `ObservationRegistry`, but instead of adding the `ObservationRegistry` to a `RestTemplate` (unless you use one in your server application), you register a servlet filter to create metrics. The `org.springframework.web.filter.ServerHttpObservationFilter` will start creating metrics upon receiving an HTTP request.

Listing 10-90. Server metrics configuration

```
@Bean
public JmxMeterRegistry meterRegistry() {
  return new JmxMeterRegistry(JmxConfig.DEFAULT, Clock.SYSTEM);
}
```

```
@Bean
public ObservationRegistry observationRegistry(MeterRegistry meterRegistry) {
  var registry = ObservationRegistry.create();
  var handler = new DefaultMeterObservationHandler(meterRegistry);
  registry.observationConfig().observationHandler(handler);
  return registry;
}


@Bean
public ServerHttpObservationFilter metricsFilter(ObservationRegistry or) {
  return new ServerHttpObservationFilter(or);
}
```

The registration of the MeterRegistry and ObservationRegistry is exactly the same. Notice however the addition of the ServerHttpObservationFilter, which will create the HTTP metrics for the server.

As we configured the filter in our application context, this isn't directly visible to Tomcat. For this we can use the DelegatingFilterProxy. This will, as the name implies, delegate to a different filter. In this case it does a lookup for a bean in the application context with the name we pass through it, and it has to be a servlet filter. It will then delegate the calls to that Spring-managed filter. With this approach you can configure filters in your application context but still use them in your servlet container. Spring Security (see Chapter 5) uses the same approach.

In the CourtRestApplicationInitializer we need to add this DelegatingFilterProxy. This can be done by overriding the getServletFilters method.

Listing 10-91. Servlet filter configuration

```
package com.apress.spring6recipes.court.web;

import org.springframework.web.filter.DelegatingFilterProxy;
import org.springframework.web.servlet.support.
AbstractAnnotationConfigDispatcherServletInitializer;

import jakarta.servlet.Filter;

public class CourtRestApplicationInitializer extends
AbstractAnnotationConfigDispatcherServletInitializer {

  @Override
  protected Filter[] getServletFilters() {
    return new Filter[] {
            new DelegatingFilterProxy("metricsFilter")
    };
  }
}
```

After deploying the application and also launching the client (as to have some incoming and handled requests), you can connect JConsole to the Tomcat instance and view the metrics (see Figure 10-10).

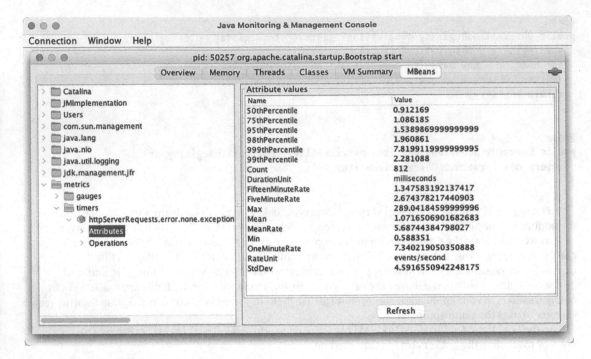

Figure 10-10. *Server metrics through JMX*

Expose Additional Metrics Through MeterBinder

Next to creating metrics through `Observations` for a `RestTemplate`, `WebClient`, or servlet filter, you can also use a `MeterBinder` to expose metrics about a certain part of your system. Think of showing metrics about your cache usage, the uptime of the JVM, or JVM memory statistics. For this purpose you can use the `MeterBinder` and implement it to expose the needed metrics.

Micrometer already ships with quite a list of `MeterBinder` implementations that you can use. Table 10-3 lists a few of them.

Table 10-3. *Micrometer MeterBinder Implementations*

Name	Description
DiskSpaceMetrics	Exposes metrics about the disk space usage on your system
HibernateMetrics	Metrics from Hibernate like query stats, entities, cache hits, etc.
JvmGcMetrics	GC metrics
JvmMemoryMetrics	Various memory metrics and buffer pools
JvmThreadMetrics	Metrics on threads, total, daemon threads, live, etc.
ProcessorMetrics	Metrics on CPU usage
TomcatMetrics	Metrics on Tomcat, like number of HTTP sessions, threads, etc.
UptimeMetrics	Timer on how long the system has been running

The easiest way to use this is to register all the MeterBinder implementations you want as beans in the application context and have an additional component retrieve all of them (see Chapter 1) from the context and iterate over all of them and call the MeterBinder.bindTo method. The bindTo method requires the previously registered MeterRegistry to function.

Using the following component, you can easily configure the MeterBinder to be used.

Listing 10-92. MeterBinderRegistrar class

```
package com.apress.spring6recipes.court;

import org.springframework.beans.factory.ObjectProvider;
import org.springframework.stereotype.Component;

import io.micrometer.core.instrument.MeterRegistry;
import io.micrometer.core.instrument.binder.MeterBinder;
import jakarta.annotation.PostConstruct;

@Component
public class MeterBinderRegistrar {

  private final MeterRegistry registry;
  private final ObjectProvider<MeterBinder> binders;

  public MeterBinderRegistrar(MeterRegistry registry,
          ObjectProvider<MeterBinder> binders) {
    this.registry = registry;
    this.binders = binders;
  }

  @PostConstruct
  public void register() {
    this.binders
        .forEach( (b) -> b.bindTo(this.registry));
  }
}
```

For each detected MeterBinder, it will, after construction, call the bindTo method. The use of the ObjectProvider is preferred here as that will delay the construction of the MeterBinder implementations. Using a collection here could force eager initialization. See Chapter 1 for more information on the core tasks and container.

Now you can have a configuration that registers some MeterBinder instances to expose metrics. Let's expose the memory, thread, and uptime metrics (see Listing 10-93).

Listing 10-93. MeterBinder configuration class

```
@Configuration
class MeterBindersConfiguration {

  @Bean
  public UptimeMetrics uptimeMetrics() {
    return new UptimeMetrics();
  }
}
```

```
@Bean
public JvmThreadMetrics jvmThreadMetrics() {
  return new JvmThreadMetrics();
}

@Bean
public JvmMemoryMetrics jvmMemoryMetrics() {
  return new JvmMemoryMetrics();
}
}
```

Now when restarting the client (or the server if you placed them in there), you can see additional metrics being exposed (see Figure 10-11).

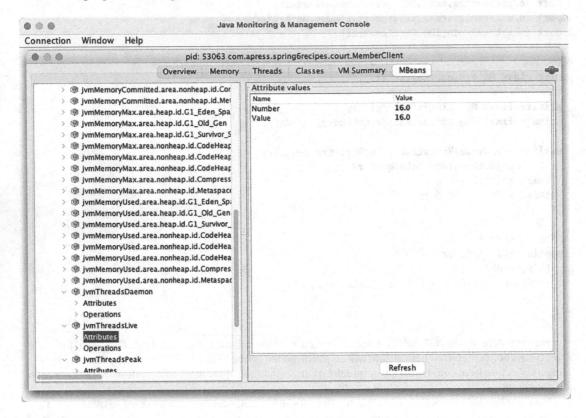

Figure 10-11. *Additional metrics through JMX*

10-12. Summary

This chapter discussed JMX and a few of the surrounding specifications. You learned how to export Spring beans as JMX MBeans and how to use those MBeans from a client, both remotely and locally by using Spring's proxies. You published and listened to notification events on a JMX server from Spring. You also learned how to do email tasks with the aid of Spring, including how to create email templates and send emails with attachments (MIME messages). You also learned how to schedule tasks using the Quartz Scheduler, as well as Spring's task namespace.

While REST has taken favor to communicate between web-based applications, SOAP is still a valid choice as well. We discussed contract-first SOAP web services and how to leverage Spring-WS to create and consume these types of services.

Finally, we looked at some of the observability support in Spring in the form of the Java Flight Recorder as well as the possibilities of the integration with the Micrometer API.

CHAPTER 11

■ ■ ■

Spring Messaging

In this chapter, you will learn about Spring's support for messaging. Messaging is a very powerful technique for scaling applications. It allows work that would otherwise overwhelm a service to be queued up. It also encourages a decoupled architecture. A component, for example, might only consume messages with a single java.util.Map-based key/value pair. This loose contract makes it a viable hub of communication for multiple, disparate systems.

In this chapter, we'll refer quite a bit to "topics" and "queues." Messaging solutions are designed to solve two types of architecture requirements: messaging from one point in an application to another known point and messaging from one point in an application to many other unknown points. These patterns are the middleware equivalents of telling somebody something face-to-face and saying something over a loud speaker to a room of people, respectively.

If you want the message sent on a message queue to be broadcast to an unknown set of clients who are "listening" for the message (as in the loud speaker analogy), send the message on a "topic." If you want the message sent to a single, known client, then you send it over a "queue."

By the end of this chapter, you will be able to create and access message-based middleware using Spring. This chapter will also provide you with a working knowledge of messaging in general, which will help you when we discuss Spring Integration in the next chapter.

We will take a look at the messaging abstraction and how to use it to work with JMS, AMQP, and Apache Kafka. For each of the technologies, Spring simplifies the usage with a template-based approach for easy message sending and receiving. Moreover, Spring enables beans declared in its IoC container to listen for messages and react to them. It takes the same approach for each of these technologies.

> **ⓘ** In the bin directory, there are several scripts for starting a Dockerized version of the different messaging providers, ActiveMQ Artemis for JMS, RabbitMQ for AMQP, and finally Apache Kafka as well.

11-1. Send and Receive JMS Messages with Spring
Problem

To send or receive a JMS message, you have to perform the following tasks:

1. Create a JMS connection factory on a message broker.

2. Create a JMS destination, which can be either a queue or a topic.

3. Open a JMS context from the connection factory.

4. Send or receive the JMS message with a message producer or consumer.

5. Handle JMSException that is a checked exception that must be handled.

6. Close the JMS connection factory and JMS context.

As you can see, a lot of coding is required to send or receive a simple JMS message. In fact, most of these tasks are boilerplate and require you to repeat them each time when dealing with JMS.

Solution

Spring offers a template-based solution to simplify JMS code. With a JMS template (Spring Framework class JmsTemplate), you can send and receive JMS messages with much less code. The template handles the boilerplate tasks and also converts the JMS API's JMSException hierarchy into Spring's runtime exception org.springframework.jms.JmsException hierarchy.

How It Works

Suppose that you are developing a post office system that includes two subsystems: the front desk subsystem and the back office subsystem. When the front desk receives mail, it passes the mail to the back office for categorizing and delivering. At the same time, the front desk subsystem sends a JMS message to the back office subsystem, notifying it of new mail. The mail information is represented by the following record.

Listing 11-1. Mail class

```
package com.apress.spring6recipes.post;

public record Mail(String mailId, String country, double weight) { }
```

The methods for sending and receiving mail information are defined in the FrontDesk and BackOffice interfaces as follows.

Listing 11-2. FrontDesk interface

```
package com.apress.spring6recipes.post;

public interface FrontDesk {

  void sendMail(Mail mail);
}
```

Listing 11-3. BackOffice interface

```
package com.apress.spring6recipes.post;

public interface BackOffice {

  Mail receiveMail();
}
```

Send and Receive Messages Without Spring's JMS Template Support

First, let's look at how to send and receive JMS messages without Spring's JMS template support. The following FrontDeskImpl class sends JMS messages with the JMS API directly.

Listing 11-4. Plain JMS FrontDesk implementation

```
package com.apress.spring6recipes.post;

import jakarta.jms.Session;
import org.apache.activemq.artemis.jms.client.ActiveMQConnectionFactory;
import org.apache.activemq.artemis.jms.client.ActiveMQQueue;

import java.util.Map;

public class FrontDeskImpl implements FrontDesk {

  public void sendMail(Mail mail) {
    try (var cf = new ActiveMQConnectionFactory("tcp://localhost:61616");
         var ctx = cf.createContext(Session.AUTO_ACKNOWLEDGE)) {
      var destination = new ActiveMQQueue("mail.queue");
      var mapContext = Map.<String, Object>of(
              "mailId", mail.mailId(),
              "country", mail.country(),
              "weight", mail.weight());
      ctx.createProducer().send(destination, mapContext);
    }
  }
}
```

In the preceding sendMail() method, you first create the JMS-specific ConnectionFactory (the ActiveMQConnectionFactory) and Destination (the ActiveMQQueue) objects with the classes provided by ActiveMQ. The message broker URL is the default for ActiveMQ if you run it on localhost. In JMS, there are two types of destinations: queue and topic.

As explained at the start of the chapter, a queue is for the point-to-point communication model, while topic is for the publish-subscribe communication model. Because you are sending JMS messages point to point from front desk to back office, you should use a message queue. You can easily create a topic as a destination using the ActiveMQTopic class.

Next, you have to create a context and message producer before you can send your message. There are several types of messages defined in the JMS API, including TextMessage, MapMessage, BytesMessage, ObjectMessage, and StreamMessage. MapMessage contains message content in key/value pairs like a map. All of them are interfaces, which all implement the Message interface. The JMSProducer has several send methods that take different types like java.util.Map, a byte[], etc. Each of these send methods corresponds with one of the message types provided by JMS. In the meantime, you sometimes have to handle JMSException, which may be thrown by the JMS API. Finally, you must remember to close the session and connection to release system resources. Using a try-with-resources helps with automatically closing it.

On the other hand, the following BackOfficeImpl class receives JMS messages with the JMS API directly.

Listing 11-5. Plain JMS BackOffice implementation

```
package com.apress.spring6recipes.post;

import jakarta.jms.JMSException;
import jakarta.jms.JMSRuntimeException;
import jakarta.jms.MapMessage;
import jakarta.jms.Message;
import jakarta.jms.Session;
import org.apache.activemq.artemis.jms.client.ActiveMQConnectionFactory;
import org.apache.activemq.artemis.jms.client.ActiveMQQueue;

public class BackOfficeImpl implements BackOffice {

  public Mail receiveMail() {
    try (var cf = new ActiveMQConnectionFactory("tcp://localhost:61616");
         var ctx = cf.createContext(Session.AUTO_ACKNOWLEDGE)) {

      var destination = new ActiveMQQueue("mail.queue");
      var consumer = ctx.createConsumer(destination);
      var message = consumer.receive();
      return convert(message);
    } catch (JMSException ex) {
      throw new RuntimeException(ex.getMessage(), ex);
    }
  }

  private Mail convert(Message msg) throws JMSException {
    var message = (MapMessage) msg;
    return new Mail(message.getString("mailId"),
            message.getString("country"),
            message.getDouble("weight"));
  }
}
```

Most of the code in this method is similar to that for sending JMS messages, except that you create a message consumer and receive a JMS message from it.

When using a JMSConsumer to receive messages, you can call one of the receive methods it provides. Some allow for specifying a timeout and others to get the specific payload (i.e., the java.util.Map, byte[], etc.) of the specific type of message. Here we expect a MapMessage, so we could directly get the payload by calling receiveBody(Map.class). Here however we chose to use the simple receive(), which would return a MapMessage.

Finally, let's create two configuration classes for the front desk subsystem (e.g., FrontOfficeConfiguration) and the back office subsystem (e.g., BackOfficeConfiguration).

Listing 11-6. FrontDesk configuration

```
package com.apress.spring6recipes.post.config;

import org.springframework.context.annotation.Bean;
import org.springframework.context.annotation.Configuration;
```

```
import com.apress.spring6recipes.post.FrontDeskImpl;

@Configuration
public class FrontOfficeConfiguration {

    @Bean
    public FrontDeskImpl frontDesk() {
        return new FrontDeskImpl();
    }
}
```

Listing 11-7. BackOffice configuration

```
package com.apress.spring6recipes.post.config;

import org.springframework.context.annotation.Bean;
import org.springframework.context.annotation.Configuration;

import com.apress.spring6recipes.post.BackOfficeImpl;

@Configuration
public class BackOfficeConfiguration {

    @Bean
    public BackOfficeImpl backOffice() {
        return new BackOfficeImpl();
    }
}
```

Now, the front desk and back office subsystems are almost ready to send and receive JMS messages. But before moving on to the final step, start up the ActiveMQ message broker (if not done already).

💡 You can easily monitor the ActiveMQ Artemis messaging broker's activity. In a default installation, you can open http://localhost:8161/console to see what's happening with mail.queue, the queue used in these examples.

Next, let's create a couple of main classes to run the message system: one for the FrontDesk subsystem—FrontDeskMain class—and another for the BackOffice subsystem, BackOfficeMain class.

Listing 11-8. Main class–FrontDesk

```
package com.apress.spring6recipes.post;

import com.apress.spring6recipes.post.config.FrontOfficeConfiguration;
import org.springframework.context.annotation.AnnotationConfigApplicationContext;
```

```
public class FrontDeskMain {

  public static void main(String[] args) {
    var cfg = FrontOfficeConfiguration.class;
    try (var context = new AnnotationConfigApplicationContext(cfg)) {
      var frontDesk = context.getBean(FrontDesk.class);
      frontDesk.sendMail(new Mail("1234", "US", 1.5));
    }
  }
}
```

Listing 11-9. Main class–BackOffice

```
package com.apress.spring6recipes.post;

import com.apress.spring6recipes.post.config.BackOfficeConfiguration;
import org.springframework.context.annotation.AnnotationConfigApplicationContext;

public class BackOfficeMain {

  public static void main(String[] args) {
    var cfg = BackOfficeConfiguration.class;
    try (var context = new AnnotationConfigApplicationContext(cfg)) {
      var backOffice = context.getBean(BackOffice.class);
      var mail = backOffice.receiveMail();
      System.out.printf("Recieved: %s%n", mail);
    }
  }
}
```

Every time you run the FrontDesk application with the preceding FrontDeskMain class, a message is sent to the broker, and every time you run the BackOffice application with the preceding BackOfficeMain class, an attempt is made pick a message from the broker.

Send and Receive Messages with Spring's JMS Template

Spring offers a JmsTemplate that can simplify your JMS code. To send a JMS message with this template, you simply call the send() method and provide a message destination, as well as a MessageCreator object, which creates the JMS message you are going to send. The MessageCreator object is usually implemented as an anonymous inner class.

Listing 11-10. JMS template FrontDesk implementation

```
package com.apress.spring6recipes.post;

import jakarta.jms.Destination;
import org.springframework.jms.core.JmsTemplate;

public class FrontDeskImpl implements FrontDesk {

  private final JmsTemplate jmsTemplate;
```

```
private final Destination destination;

public FrontDeskImpl(JmsTemplate jmsTemplate, Destination destination) {
    this.jmsTemplate = jmsTemplate;
    this.destination = destination;
}

public void sendMail(Mail mail) {
    jmsTemplate.send(destination, session -> {
        var message = session.createMapMessage();
        message.setString("mailId", mail.mailId());
        message.setString("country", mail.country());
        message.setDouble("weight", mail.weight());
        return message;
    });
}
}
```

Note that an inner class can only access arguments or variables of the enclosing method that are effectively final. The MessageCreator interface declares only a createMessage() method for you to implement. In this method, you create and return your JMS message with the provided JMS session.

A JMS template helps you obtain and release the JMS connection and session, and it sends the JMS message created by your MessageCreator object. Moreover, it converts the JMS API's JMSException hierarchy into Spring's JMS runtime exception hierarchy, whose base exception class is org.springframework.jms.JmsException. You can catch the JmsException thrown from send and the other send variants and then take action in the catch block if you want.

In the front desk subsystem's bean configuration file, you declare a JMS template that refers to the JMS connection factory for opening connections. Then, you inject this template as well as the message destination into your front desk bean.

Listing 11-11. FrontDesk configuration

```
package com.apress.spring6recipes.post.config;

import com.apress.spring6recipes.post.FrontDeskImpl;
import jakarta.jms.ConnectionFactory;
import jakarta.jms.Queue;
import org.apache.activemq.artemis.jms.client.ActiveMQConnectionFactory;
import org.apache.activemq.artemis.jms.client.ActiveMQQueue;
import org.springframework.context.annotation.Bean;
import org.springframework.context.annotation.Configuration;
import org.springframework.jms.core.JmsTemplate;

@Configuration
public class FrontOfficeConfiguration {

    @Bean
    public ConnectionFactory connectionFactory() {
        return new ActiveMQConnectionFactory("tcp://localhost:61616");
    }

    @Bean
    public Queue mailDestination() {
        return new ActiveMQQueue("mail.queue");
    }
```

```java
@Bean
public JmsTemplate jmsTemplate(ConnectionFactory cf) {
  return new JmsTemplate(cf);
}

@Bean
public FrontDeskImpl frontDesk(JmsTemplate jms, Queue destination) {
  return new FrontDeskImpl(jms, destination);
}
}
```

To receive a JMS message with a JMS template, you call the receive() method by providing a message destination. This method returns a JMS message, javax.jms.Message, whose type is the base JMS message type (i.e., an interface), so you have to cast it into a proper type before further processing.

Listing 11-12. JMS template BackOffice implementation

```java
package com.apress.spring6recipes.post;

import jakarta.jms.Destination;
import jakarta.jms.JMSException;
import jakarta.jms.MapMessage;
import jakarta.jms.Message;
import org.springframework.jms.core.JmsTemplate;
import org.springframework.jms.support.JmsUtils;

public class BackOfficeImpl implements BackOffice {

  private final JmsTemplate jmsTemplate;
  private final Destination destination;

  public BackOfficeImpl(JmsTemplate jmsTemplate, Destination destination) {
    this.jmsTemplate = jmsTemplate;
    this.destination = destination;
  }

  public Mail receiveMail() {
    var message = jmsTemplate.receive(destination);
    try {
      return message != null ? convert(message) : null;
    } catch (JMSException e) {
      throw JmsUtils.convertJmsAccessException(e);
    }
  }

  private Mail convert(Message msg) throws JMSException {
    var message = (MapMessage) msg;
    return new Mail(message.getString("mailId"),
            message.getString("country"),
            message.getDouble("weight"));
  }
}
```

However, when extracting information from the received MapMessage object, you still have to handle the JMS API's JMSException. This is in stark contrast to the default behavior of the framework, where it automatically maps exceptions for you when invoking methods on the JmsTemplate. To make the type of the exception thrown by this method consistent, you have to make a call to JmsUtils. convertJmsAccessException() to convert the JMS API's JMSException into Spring's JmsException.

In the back office subsystem's bean configuration file, you declare a JMS template and inject it together with the message destination into your back office bean.

Listing 11-13. BackOffice configuration

```
package com.apress.spring6recipes.post.config;

import com.apress.spring6recipes.post.BackOfficeImpl;
import jakarta.jms.ConnectionFactory;
import jakarta.jms.Queue;
import org.apache.activemq.artemis.jms.client.ActiveMQConnectionFactory;
import org.apache.activemq.artemis.jms.client.ActiveMQQueue;
import org.springframework.context.annotation.Bean;
import org.springframework.context.annotation.Configuration;
import org.springframework.jms.core.JmsTemplate;

@Configuration
public class BackOfficeConfiguration {

  @Bean
  public ConnectionFactory connectionFactory() {
    return new ActiveMQConnectionFactory("tcp://localhost:61616");
  }

  @Bean
  public Queue mailDestination() {
    return new ActiveMQQueue("mail.queue");
  }

  @Bean
  public JmsTemplate jmsTemplate(ConnectionFactory cf) {
    var jmsTemplate = new JmsTemplate();
    jmsTemplate.setConnectionFactory(cf);
    jmsTemplate.setReceiveTimeout(10000);
    return jmsTemplate;
  }

  @Bean
  public BackOfficeImpl backOffice(JmsTemplate jms, Queue destination) {
    return new BackOfficeImpl(jms, destination);
  }
}
```

Pay special attention to the JMS template receiveTimeout property; it specifies how long to wait in milliseconds. By default, this template waits for a JMS message at the destination forever, and the calling thread is blocked in the meantime. To avoid waiting for a message so long, you should specify a receive timeout for this template. If there's no message available at the destination in the duration, the JMS template's receive() method will return a null message.

In your applications, the main use of receiving a message might be because you're expecting a response to something or want to check for messages at an interval, handling the messages and then spinning down until the next interval. If you intend to receive messages and respond to them as a service, you're likely going to want to use the message-driven POJO functionality described later in this chapter. There, we discuss a mechanism that will constantly sit and wait for messages, handling them by calling back into your application as the messages arrive.

Send and Receive Messages to and from a Default Destination

Instead of specifying a message destination for each JMS template's send() and receive() method call, you can specify a default destination for a JMS template. Then, you no longer need to inject it into your message sender and receiver beans again. The following listing shows the modification for the FrontOfficeConfiguration; the same can be applied to the BackOfficeConfiguration.

Listing 11-14. FrontDesk configuration with a default destination

```
package com.apress.spring6recipes.post.config;

@Configuration
public class FrontOfficeConfiguration {

  @Bean
  public JmsTemplate jmsTemplate(ConnectionFactory cf, Queue destination) {
    var jmsTemplate = new JmsTemplate();
    jmsTemplate.setConnectionFactory(cf);
    jmsTemplate.setDefaultDestination(destination);
    return jmsTemplate;
  }

  @Bean
  public FrontDeskImpl frontDesk(JmsTemplate jms) {
    return new FrontDeskImpl(jms);
  }
}
```

With the default destination specified for a JMS template, you can delete the constructor argument for a message destination from your message sender and receiver classes. Now, when you call the send() and receive() methods, you no longer need to specify a message destination.

In addition, instead of specifying an instance of the Destination interface for a JMS template, you can specify the destination name to let the JMS template resolve it for you, so you can delete the destination property declaration from both bean configuration classes. This is done by setting the defaultDestinationName property.

Listing 11-15. FrontDesk configuration with a default destination name

```
package com.apress.spring6recipes.post.config;

@Configuration
public class FrontOfficeConfiguration {

  @Bean
  public JmsTemplate jmsTemplate(ConnectionFactory cf) {
    var jmsTemplate = new JmsTemplate();
    jmsTemplate.setConnectionFactory(cf);
    jmsTemplate.setDefaultDestinationName("mail.queue");
    return jmsTemplate;
  }
}
```

Extend the JmsGatewaySupport Class

JMS sender and receiver classes can also extend JmsGatewaySupport to retrieve a JMS template. You have the following two options for classes that extend JmsGatewaySupport to create their JMS template:

- Inject a JMS connection factory for JmsGatewaySupport to create a JMS template on it automatically. However, if you do it this way, you won't be able to configure the details of the JMS template.

- Inject a JMS template for JmsGatewaySupport that is created and configured by you.

Of them, the second approach is more suitable if you have to configure the JMS template yourself. You can delete the private field jmsTemplate and its constructor argument from both your sender and receiver classes. When you need access to the JMS template, you just make a call to getJmsTemplate().

Listing 11-16. FrontDesk implementation extending JmsGatewaySupport

```
package com.apress.spring6recipes.post;

import org.springframework.jms.core.support.JmsGatewaySupport;

public class FrontDeskImpl extends JmsGatewaySupport implements FrontDesk {

  public void sendMail(final Mail mail) {
    getJmsTemplate().send(session -> {
      var message = session.createMapMessage();
      message.setString("mailId", mail.mailId());
      message.setString("country", mail.country());
      message.setDouble("weight", mail.weight());
      return message;
    });
  }
}
```

Listing 11-17. BackOffice implementation extending JmsGatewaySupport

```java
package com.apress.spring6recipes.post;

import jakarta.jms.JMSException;
import jakarta.jms.MapMessage;
import jakarta.jms.Message;
import org.springframework.jms.core.support.JmsGatewaySupport;
import org.springframework.jms.support.JmsUtils;

public class BackOfficeImpl extends JmsGatewaySupport implements BackOffice {

  public Mail receiveMail() {
    var message = getJmsTemplate().receive();
    try {
      return message != null ? convert(message) : null;
    } catch (JMSException e) {
      throw JmsUtils.convertJmsAccessException(e);
    }
  }

  private Mail convert(Message msg) throws JMSException {
    var message = (MapMessage) msg;
    return new Mail(message.getString("mailId"),
            message.getString("country"),
            message.getDouble("weight"));
  }
}
```

11-2. Convert JMS Messages

Problem

Your application receives messages from your message queue but needs to transform those messages from the JMS-specific type to a business-specific class.

Solution

Spring provides an implementation of SimpleMessageConverter to handle the translation of a JMS message received to a business object and the translation of a business object to a JMS message. You can leverage the default or provide your own.

How It Works

The previous recipes handled the raw JMS messages. Spring's JMS template can help you convert JMS messages to and from Java objects using a message converter. By default, the JMS template uses SimpleMessageConverter for converting TextMessage to or from a string, BytesMessage to or from a byte array, MapMessage to or from a map, and ObjectMessage to or from a serializable object.

For the front desk and back office classes of the past recipe, you can send and receive a map using the convertAndSend() and receiveAndConvert() methods, where the map is converted to/from MapMessage.

Listing 11-18. FrontDesk using convertAndSend

```
package com.apress.spring6recipes.post;

import org.springframework.jms.core.support.JmsGatewaySupport;

import java.util.Map;

public class FrontDeskImpl extends JmsGatewaySupport implements FrontDesk {

  public void sendMail(final Mail mail) {
    var map = Map.of(
            "mailId", mail.mailId(),
            "country", mail.country(),
            "weight", mail.weight());
    getJmsTemplate().convertAndSend(map);
  }
}
```

Listing 11-19. BackOffice using receiveAndConvert

```
package com.apress.spring6recipes.post;

import jakarta.jms.JMSException;
import org.springframework.jms.core.support.JmsGatewaySupport;
import org.springframework.jms.support.JmsUtils;

import java.util.Map;

public class BackOfficeImpl extends JmsGatewaySupport implements BackOffice {

  public Mail receiveMail() {
    var message = (Map<String, ?>) getJmsTemplate().receiveAndConvert();
    try {
      return message != null ? convert(message) : null;
    } catch (JMSException e) {
      throw JmsUtils.convertJmsAccessException(e);
    }
  }

  private Mail convert(Map<String, ?> msg) throws JMSException {
    return new Mail(
            (String) msg.get("mailId"),
            (String) msg.get("country"),
            (Double) msg.get("weight"));
  }
}
```

You can also create a custom message converter by implementing the `MessageConverter` interface for converting mail objects.

Listing 11-20. MessageConverter implementation

```
package com.apress.spring6recipes.post;

import jakarta.jms.JMSException;
import jakarta.jms.MapMessage;
import jakarta.jms.Message;
import jakarta.jms.Session;
import org.springframework.jms.support.converter.MessageConversionException;
import org.springframework.jms.support.converter.MessageConverter;

public class MailMessageConverter implements MessageConverter {

  public Object fromMessage(Message message) throws JMSException,
          MessageConversionException {
    var mapMessage = (MapMessage) message;
    return new Mail(
            mapMessage.getString("mailId"),
            mapMessage.getString("country"),
            mapMessage.getDouble("weight"));
  }

  public Message toMessage(Object object, Session session) throws JMSException,
          MessageConversionException {
    var mail = (Mail) object;
    var message = session.createMapMessage();
    message.setString("mailId", mail.mailId());
    message.setString("country", mail.country());
    message.setDouble("weight", mail.weight());
    return message;
  }
}
```

To apply this message converter, you have to inject it into the JMS template.

Listing 11-21. JmsTemplate configuration with MessageConverter

```
@Configuration
public class BackOfficeConfiguration {
    ...
  @Bean
  public JmsTemplate jmsTemplate() {
    JmsTemplate jmsTemplate = new JmsTemplate();
    jmsTemplate.setMessageConverter(new MailMessageConverter());
    ...
    return jmsTemplate;
  }
}
```

When you set a message converter for a JMS template explicitly, it will override the default SimpleMessageConverter. Now, you can call the JMS template's convertAndSend() and receiveAndConvert() methods to send and receive Mail objects.

Listing 11-22. FrontDesk using convertAndSend with MessageConverter

```
package com.apress.spring6recipes.post;
...
public class FrontDeskImpl extends JmsGatewaySupport implements FrontDesk {

    public void sendMail(Mail mail) {
        getJmsTemplate().convertAndSend(mail);
    }
}
```

Listing 11-23. BackOffice using receiveAndConvert with MessageConverter

```
package com.apress.spring6recipes.post;
...
public class BackOfficeImpl extends JmsGatewaySupport implements BackOffice {

    public Mail receiveMail() {
        return (Mail) getJmsTemplate().receiveAndConvert();
    }
}
```

11-3. Manage JMS Transactions

Problem

You want to participate in transactions with JMS so that the receipt and sending of messages are transactional.

Solution

You can use the same transaction strategy as you would for any Spring component. Leverage Spring's TransactionManager implementations as needed and wire the behavior into beans.

How It Works

When producing or consuming multiple JMS messages in a single method, if an error occurs in the middle, the JMS messages produced or consumed at the destination may be left in an inconsistent state. You have to surround the method with a transaction to avoid this problem. (See Chapter 7 for more information on transactions.)

In Spring, JMS transaction management is consistent with other data access strategies. For example, you can annotate the methods that require transaction management with the @Transactional annotation.

Listing 11-24. Transactional FrontDesk implementation

```
package com.apress.spring6recipes.post;

import org.springframework.jms.core.support.JmsGatewaySupport;
import org.springframework.transaction.annotation.Transactional;

public class FrontDeskImpl extends JmsGatewaySupport implements FrontDesk {

  @Transactional
  public void sendMail(final Mail mail) {
    getJmsTemplate().convertAndSend(mail);
  }
}
```

Listing 11-25. Transactional BackOffice implementation

```
package com.apress.spring6recipes.post;

import org.springframework.jms.core.support.JmsGatewaySupport;
import org.springframework.transaction.annotation.Transactional;

public class BackOfficeImpl extends JmsGatewaySupport implements BackOffice {

  @Transactional
  public Mail receiveMail() {
    return (Mail) getJmsTemplate().receiveAndConvert();
  }
}
```

Then, in both Java configuration classes, add the @EnableTransactionManagement and declare a transaction manager. The corresponding transaction manager for local JMS transactions is JmsTransactionManager, which requires a reference to the JMS connection factory.

Listing 11-26. Transactional FrontOffice configuration

```
package com.apress.spring6recipes.post.config;

import org.springframework.jms.connection.JmsTransactionManager;
import org.springframework.transaction.annotation.EnableTransactionManagement;

@Configuration
@EnableTransactionManagement
public class FrontOfficeConfiguration {

  @Bean
  public ConnectionFactory connectionFactory() {
  }
  @Bean
  public JmsTransactionManager transactionManager(ConnectionFactory cf) {
    return new JmsTransactionManager(cf);
  }
}
```

If you require transaction management across multiple resources, such as a data source and an ORM resource factory, or if you need distributed transaction management, you have to configure JTA transaction in your app server and use JtaTransactionManager. Note that for support of multiple resource transactions, the JMS connection factory must be XA compliant (i.e., it must support distributed transactions).

11-4. Create Message-Driven POJOs in Spring
Problem

When you call the receive() method on a JMS message consumer to receive a message, the calling thread is blocked until a message is available. The thread can do nothing but wait. This type of message reception is called synchronous reception, because an application must wait for the message to arrive before it can finish its work. You can create a message-driven POJO (MDP) to support asynchronous reception of JMS messages. An MDP is decorated with the @JmsListener annotation.

ℹ️   A message-driven POJO or MDP in the context of this recipe refers to a POJO that can listen for JMS messages without any particular runtime requirements. It does not refer to message-driven beans (MDBs) aligned to the EJB specification that require an EJB container.

Solution

Spring allows beans declared in its IoC container to listen for JMS messages in the same way as MDBs, which are based on the EJB spec. Because Spring adds message listening capabilities to POJOs, they are called message-driven POJOs (MDPs).

How It Works

Suppose you want to add an electronic board to the post office's back office to display mail information in real time as it arrives from the front desk. As the front desk sends a JMS message along with mail, the back office subsystem can listen for these messages and display them on the electronic board. For better system performance, you should apply the asynchronous JMS reception approach to avoid blocking the thread that receives these JMS messages.

Listen for JMS Messages with Message Listeners

First, you create a message listener to listen for JMS messages. The message listener provides an alternative to the approach taken in BackOfficeImpl in previous recipes with the JmsTemplate. A listener can also consume messages from a broker. For example, the following MailListener listens for JMS messages that contain mail information.

Listing 11-27. Mail listener implementation

```java
package com.apress.spring6recipes.post;

import jakarta.jms.JMSException;
import jakarta.jms.MapMessage;
import jakarta.jms.Message;
import jakarta.jms.MessageListener;
import org.springframework.jms.support.JmsUtils;

public class MailListener implements MessageListener {

  public void onMessage(Message message) {
    try {
      var mail = convert(message);
      displayMail(mail);
    } catch (JMSException e) {
      throw JmsUtils.convertJmsAccessException(e);
    }
  }

  private Mail convert(Message msg) throws JMSException {
    var message = (MapMessage) msg;
    return new Mail(message.getString("mailId"),
            message.getString("country"),
            message.getDouble("weight"));
  }

  private void displayMail(Mail mail) {
    System.out.printf("Received: %s%n", mail);
  }
}
```

A message listener must implement the jakarta.jms.MessageListener interface. When a JMS message arrives, the onMessage() method will be called with the message as the method argument. In this sample, you simply display the mail information to the console. Note that when extracting message information from a MapMessage object, you need to handle the JMS API's JMSException. You can make a call to JmsUtils.convertJmsAccessException() to convert it into Spring's runtime exception JmsException.

Next, you have to configure this listener in the back office's configuration. Declaring this listener alone is not enough to listen for JMS messages. You need a message listener container to monitor JMS messages at a message destination and trigger your message listener on message arrival.

Listing 11-28. BackOffice configuration

```java
package com.apress.spring6recipes.post.config;

import com.apress.spring6recipes.post.MailListener;
import jakarta.jms.ConnectionFactory;
import org.apache.activemq.artemis.jms.client.ActiveMQConnectionFactory;
import org.springframework.context.annotation.Bean;
import org.springframework.context.annotation.Configuration;
import org.springframework.jms.listener.SimpleMessageListenerContainer;
```

```java
@Configuration
public class BackOfficeConfiguration {

    @Bean
    public ConnectionFactory connectionFactory() {
        return new ActiveMQConnectionFactory("tcp://localhost:61616");
    }

    @Bean
    public MailListener mailListener() {
        return new MailListener();
    }

    @Bean
    public Object container(ConnectionFactory cf, MailListener msgListener) {
        var smlc = new SimpleMessageListenerContainer();
        smlc.setConnectionFactory(cf);
        smlc.setDestinationName("mail.queue");
        smlc.setMessageListener(msgListener);
        return smlc;
    }
}
```

Spring provides several types of message listener containers for you to choose from in the
org.springframework.jms.listener package, of which SimpleMessageListenerContainer and
DefaultMessageListenerContainer are the most commonly used. SimpleMessageListenerContainer is the
simplest one that doesn't support transactions. If you have a transaction requirement in receiving messages,
you have to use DefaultMessageListenerContainer.

Now, you can start the message listener. Since we won't need to invoke a bean to trigger message
consumption—the listener will do it for us—the following main class, which only starts the Spring IoC
container, is enough.

Listing 11-29. BackOffice main class

```java
package com.apress.spring6recipes.post;

import com.apress.spring6recipes.post.config.BackOfficeConfiguration;
import org.springframework.context.annotation.AnnotationConfigApplicationContext;

public class BackOfficeMain {

  public static void main(String[] args) throws Exception {
    var cfg = BackOfficeConfiguration.class;
    try (var ctx = new AnnotationConfigApplicationContext(cfg)) {
      System.in.read();
    }
  }
}
```

When you start this BackOffice application, it will listen for messages on the message broker (i.e.,
ActiveMQ). As soon as the FrontDesk application sends a message to the broker, the BackOffice application
will react and display the message to the console.

Listen for JMS Messages with POJOs

While a listener that implements the MessageListener interface can listen for messages, so can an arbitrary bean declared in the Spring IoC container. Doing so means that beans are decoupled from the Spring Framework interfaces as well as the JMS MessageListener interface. For a method of this bean to be triggered on message arrival, it can use the following types as its method arguments.

Table 11-1. *Supported Method Arguments*

Type	Description
jakarta.jms.Session	Get the JMS-based session.
jakarta.jms.Message jakarta.jms.BytesMessage jakarta.jms.MapMessage jakarta.jms.ObjectMessage jakarta.jms.TextMessage	To get access to the raw JMS message.
org.springframework.messaging.Message	To get access to the Spring Messaging abstraction message.
@Payload-annotated argument	To get the payload of the message, including validation with @Valid and conversion.
@Header	To extract specific header values, including standard JMS headers.
@Headers	To extract all headers; type must be a java.util.Map.
org.springframework.messaging.MessageHeaders	To get access to all the headers.
org.springframework.messaging.support. MessageHeaderAccessor org.springframework.jms.support. JmsMessageHeaderAccessor	Convenient access to all headers in a type-safe manner.

For example, you declare a method that accepts a Map<String, ?> as its argument and annotate it with @JmsListener. This class no longer needs to implement the MessageListener interface.

Listing 11-30. Mail listener implementation with @JmsListener

```java
package com.apress.spring6recipes.post;

import org.springframework.jms.annotation.JmsListener;

import java.util.Map;

public class MailListener {

  @JmsListener(destination = "mail.queue")
  public void displayMail(Map<String, ?> map) {
```

```
    var mail = convert(map);
    displayMail(mail);
}

private Mail convert(Map<String, ?> msg) {
    return new Mail(
            (String) msg.get("mailId"),
            (String) msg.get("country"),
            (Double) msg.get("weight"));
}

private void displayMail(Mail mail) {
    System.out.printf("Received: %s%n", mail);
}
}
```

To detect the @JmsListener annotations, you need to put the @EnableJms annotation on the configuration class, and you need to register a JmsListenerContainerFactory, which by default is detected with the name jmsListenerContainerFactory.

A POJO is registered to a listener container through a JmsListenerContainerFactory. This factory creates and configures a MessageListenerContainer and registers the annotated method as a message listener to it. You could implement your own version of the JmsListenerContainerFactory, but it is generally enough to use one of the provided classes: the SimpleJmsListenerContainerFactory and DefaultJmsListenerContainerFactory. The former creates an instance of the SimpleMessageListenerContainer, whereas the latter creates a DefaultMessageListenerContainer.

For now we will use a SimpleJmsListenerContainerFactory. If the need arises, we can easily switch to a DefaultMessageListenerContainer, for instance, when transactions or async processing with a TaskExecutor is needed.

Listing 11-31. BackOffice configuration

```
package com.apress.spring6recipes.post.config;

import com.apress.spring6recipes.post.MailListener;
import jakarta.jms.ConnectionFactory;
import org.apache.activemq.artemis.jms.client.ActiveMQConnectionFactory;
import org.springframework.context.annotation.Bean;
import org.springframework.context.annotation.Configuration;
import org.springframework.jms.annotation.EnableJms;
import org.springframework.jms.config.SimpleJmsListenerContainerFactory;
import org.springframework.jms.connection.CachingConnectionFactory;

@Configuration
@EnableJms
public class BackOfficeConfiguration {

    @Bean
    public ConnectionFactory connectionFactory() {
        return new ActiveMQConnectionFactory("tcp://localhost:61616");
    }
```

```
@Bean
public MailListener mailListener() {
    return new MailListener();
}

@Bean
public SimpleJmsListenerContainerFactory jmsListenerContainerFactory(
  ConnectionFactory cf) {
    var listenerContainerFactory = new SimpleJmsListenerContainerFactory();
    listenerContainerFactory.setConnectionFactory(cf);
    return listenerContainerFactory;
}
}
```

Convert JMS Messages

You can also create a message converter for converting mail objects from JMS messages that contain mail information. Because message listeners receive messages only, the method toMessage() will not be called, so you can simply return null for it. However, if you use this message converter for sending messages too, you have to implement this method. The following example reprints the MailMessageConverter class written earlier.

Listing 11-32. MessageConverter implementation

```
package com.apress.spring6recipes.post;

import jakarta.jms.JMSException;
import jakarta.jms.MapMessage;
import jakarta.jms.Message;
import jakarta.jms.Session;
import org.springframework.jms.support.converter.MessageConversionException;
import org.springframework.jms.support.converter.MessageConverter;

public class MailMessageConverter implements MessageConverter {

  public Object fromMessage(Message message)
          throws JMSException, MessageConversionException {
    var mapMessage = (MapMessage) message;
    return new Mail(
            mapMessage.getString("mailId"),
            mapMessage.getString("country"),
            mapMessage.getDouble("weight"));
  }

  public Message toMessage(Object object, Session session)
          throws JMSException, MessageConversionException {
    var mail = (Mail) object;
    var message = session.createMapMessage();
    message.setString("mailId", mail.mailId());
    message.setString("country", mail.country());
```

```
        message.setDouble("weight", mail.weight());
        return message;
    }
}
```

A message converter should be applied to the listener container factory for it to convert messages into objects before calling your POJO's methods.

Listing 11-33. BackOffice configuration

```
package com.apress.spring6recipes.post.config;

import com.apress.spring6recipes.post.MailListener;
import com.apress.spring6recipes.post.MailMessageConverter;
import jakarta.jms.ConnectionFactory;
import org.apache.activemq.artemis.jms.client.ActiveMQConnectionFactory;
import org.springframework.context.annotation.Bean;
import org.springframework.context.annotation.Configuration;
import org.springframework.jms.annotation.EnableJms;
import org.springframework.jms.config.SimpleJmsListenerContainerFactory;

@Configuration
@EnableJms
public class BackOfficeConfiguration {

    @Bean
    public ConnectionFactory connectionFactory() {
        return new ActiveMQConnectionFactory("tcp://localhost:61616");
    }

    @Bean
    public MailListener mailListener() {
        return new MailListener();
    }

    @Bean
    public SimpleJmsListenerContainerFactory jmsListenerContainerFactory(
      ConnectionFactory cf) {
        var listenerContainerFactory = new SimpleJmsListenerContainerFactory();
        listenerContainerFactory.setConnectionFactory(cf);
        listenerContainerFactory.setMessageConverter(new MailMessageConverter());
        return listenerContainerFactory;
    }
}
```

With this message converter, the listener method of your POJO can accept a mail object as the method argument.

Listing 11-34. BackOffice configuration

```
package com.apress.spring6recipes.post;

import org.springframework.jms.annotation.JmsListener;

public class MailListener {

  @JmsListener(destination = "mail.queue")
  public void displayMail(Mail mail) {
    System.out.printf("Received: %s%n", mail);
  }
}
```

Manage JMS Transactions

As mentioned before, SimpleMessageListenerContainer doesn't support transactions. So, if you need transaction management for your message listener method, you have to use DefaultMessageListenerContainer instead. For local JMS transactions, you can simply enable its sessionTransacted property, and your listener method will run within a local JMS transaction (as opposed to XA transactions). To use a DefaultMessageListenerContainer, change the SimpleJmsListenerContainerFactory to a DefaultJmsListenerContainerFactory and configure the sessionTransacted property.

Listing 11-35. BackOffice configuration

```
@Bean
public DefaultJmsListenerContainerFactory jmsListenerContainerFactory(
  ConnectionFactory cf) {
  var listenerContainerFactory = new DefaultJmsListenerContainerFactory();
  listenerContainerFactory.setConnectionFactory(cf);
  listenerContainerFactory.setMessageConverter(new MailMessageConverter());
  listenerContainerFactory.setSessionTransacted(true);
  return listenerContainerFactory;
}
```

However, if you want your listener to participate in a JTA transaction, you need to declare a JtaTransactionManager instance and inject it into your listener container factory.

11-5. Cache and Pool JMS Connections

Problem

Throughout this chapter, for the sake of simplicity, we've explored Spring's JMS support with an instance of org.apache.activemq.artemis.jms.client.ActiveMQConnectionFactory as the connection factory. This isn't the best choice in practice. As with all things, there are performance considerations.

The crux of the issue is that the JmsTemplate closes sessions and consumers on each invocation. This means that it tears down all those objects and frees the memory. This is "safe," but not performant, as some of the objects created—like consumers—are meant to be long-lived. This behavior stems from the use of the

JmsTemplate in application server environments, where typically the application server's connection factory is used and it, internally, provides connection pooling. In this environment, restoring all the objects simply returns them to the pool, which is the desirable behavior.

Solution

There's no "one size fits all" solution to this. You need to weigh the qualities you're looking for and react appropriately.

How It Works

Generally, you want a connection factory that provides pooling and caching of some sort when publishing messages using the JmsTemplate. The first place to look for a pooled connection factory might be your application server. It may very well provide one by default.

Just like JDBC with its connection pools like HikariCP, there is also a connection pooling solution for JMS. The Pooled-JMS project, as the name implies, provides a JMS connection pool, which works regardless of the JMS implementation in use. We can use this to handle the caching of connections, sessions, consumers, and producers. The following configuration pools a connection factory in a standalone configuration. It's a drop-in replacement for the previous examples when publishing messages.

Listing 11-36. BackOffice configuration with Pooled-JMS

```
@Bean
public ConnectionFactory connectionFactory() {
    return new ActiveMQConnectionFactory("tcp://localhost:61616");
}

@Bean
@Primary
public JmsPoolConnectionFactory pooledConnectionFactory(ConnectionFactory cf) {
    var pooledCf = new JmsPoolConnectionFactory();
    pooledCf.setConnectionFactory(cf);
    return pooledCf;
}
```

ℹ️   As we declare two ConnectionFactory instances, we need to declare the one we want to use for injection as @Primary. See also Chapter 1.

If you are receiving messages, you could still stand some more efficiency, because the JmsTemplate constructs a new jakarta.jms.MessageConsumer each time as well. In this situation, you have a few alternatives: use Spring's various org.springframework.jms.listener.MessageListenerContainer implementations (MDPs), because they cache consumers correctly, or use Spring's ConnectionFactory implementations. The first implementation, org.springframework.jms.connection. SingleConnectionFactory, returns the same underlying JMS connection each time (which is thread-safe according to the JMS API) and ignores calls to the close() method.

Generally, this implementation works well with the JMS API. A newer alternative is the `org.springframework.jms.connection.CachingConnectionFactory`. First, the obvious advantage is that it provides the ability to cache multiple instances. And, second, it caches the `jakarta.jms.Session`, `jakarta.jms.MessageProducer`, and `jakarta.jms.MessageConsumer` instances used. And finally it works regardless of your JMS connection factory implementation.

Listing 11-37. CachingConnectionFactory bean

```
@Bean
@Primary
public ConnectionFactory cachingConnectionFactory(ConnectionFactory cf) {
  return new CachingConnectionFactory(cf);
}
```

11-6. Send and Receive AMQP Messages with Spring

Problem

You want to use RabbitMQ to send and receive messages.

Solution

The Spring AMQP project provides easy access and use of AMQP. It has support similar to that of Spring JMS. It comes with a `RabbitTemplate`, which provides basic send and receive options. It also comes with a `org.springframework.amqp.rabbit.listener.MessageListenerContainer` option, which mimics Spring JMS.

How It Works

First, look at how we can send a message using the `RabbitTemplate`. To get access to the `RabbitTemplate`, it is the simplest to extend `RabbitGatewaySupport`. In the following section is the `FrontDeskImpl` that uses the `RabbitTemplate`. To be able to use the classes, add the following dependencies to the classpath.

Listing 11-38. Gradle dependencies

```
implementation group: 'org.springframework.amqp', name: 'spring-rabbit', version: '3.0.0'
implementation group: 'com.rabbitmq', name: 'amqp-client', version: '5.16.0'
```

Listing 11-39. Maven dependencies

```
<dependency>
  <groupId>org.springframework.amqp</groupId>
  <artifactId>spring-rabbit</artifactId>
  <version>3.0.0</version>
</dependency>

<dependency>
  <groupId>com.rabbitmq</groupId>
  <artifactId>amqp-client</artifactId>
  <version>5.16.0</version>
</dependency>
```

Send and Receive Messages Without Spring's Template Support

First, let's look at how to send and receive messages without Spring's template support. The following
`FrontDeskImpl` class sends a message to RabbitMQ using the plain API.

Listing 11-40. Plain AMQP FrontDesk implementation

```java
package com.apress.spring6recipes.post;

import java.io.IOException;
import java.nio.charset.StandardCharsets;
import java.util.concurrent.TimeoutException;

import com.fasterxml.jackson.databind.ObjectMapper;
import com.rabbitmq.client.ConnectionFactory;

public class FrontDeskImpl implements FrontDesk {

  private static final String QUEUE_NAME = "mail.queue";

  public void sendMail(final Mail mail) {
    var connectionFactory = new ConnectionFactory();
    connectionFactory.setHost("localhost");
    connectionFactory.setUsername("guest");
    connectionFactory.setPassword("guest");
    connectionFactory.setPort(5672);

    try (var connection = connectionFactory.newConnection();
         var channel = connection.createChannel()) {
      channel.queueDeclare(QUEUE_NAME, true, false, false, null);
      var message = new ObjectMapper().writeValueAsString(mail);
      channel.basicPublish("", QUEUE_NAME, null, message.getBytes(StandardCharsets.UTF_8));
      System.out.printf("Send: %s%n", message);
    } catch (IOException | TimeoutException ex) {
      throw new RuntimeException(ex);
    }
  }
}
```

First, you create a `com.rabbitmq.client.ConnectionFactory` to obtain a `com.rabbitmq.client.`
`Connection` to RabbitMQ; we configured it for `localhost` and provided a username/password combination.
Next, you need to obtain a `com.rabbitmq.client.Channel` to finally declare a queue. Then the passed-in
`Mail` message is converted to JSON using a Jackson `ObjectMapper` and finally sent to the queue. For sending
we need to specify the exchange; we stick with the default and thus provide an empty string. For the routing
key, we use the name of the key. We don't have any additional properties to set on the message, and finally
we create a `byte[]` for the actual body of the message to be sent.

When creating connections and sending messages, we need to take care of the different exceptions that
can occur, and after sending we need to properly close and release the `Connection` again, which also can
throw an exception.

Before you can send and receive AMQP messages, you need to install a AMQP message broker.

> ℹ️   In the bin directory is a rabbitmq.sh that downloads and starts a RabbitMQ broker in a Docker container.

The following BackOfficeImpl receives messages using the plain RabbitMQ API.

Listing 11-41. Plain AMQP BackOffice implementation

```java
package com.apress.spring6recipes.post;

import com.fasterxml.jackson.databind.ObjectMapper;
import com.rabbitmq.client.AMQP;
import com.rabbitmq.client.ConnectionFactory;
import com.rabbitmq.client.DefaultConsumer;
import com.rabbitmq.client.Envelope;

import java.io.IOException;
import java.util.concurrent.TimeoutException;

public class BackOfficeImpl implements BackOffice {

  private static final String QUEUE_NAME = "mail.queue";

  private MailListener mailListener = new MailListener();

  @Override
  public Mail receiveMail() {

    var connectionFactory = new ConnectionFactory();
    connectionFactory.setHost("localhost");
    connectionFactory.setUsername("guest");
    connectionFactory.setPassword("guest");
    connectionFactory.setPort(5672);

    try (var connection = connectionFactory.newConnection();
      var channel = connection.createChannel() ) {
      channel.queueDeclare(QUEUE_NAME, true, false, false, null);

      var consumer = new DefaultConsumer(channel) {
        @Override
        public void handleDelivery(String consumerTag, Envelope envelope,
                                   AMQP.BasicProperties properties, byte[] body)
                throws IOException {
          var mail = new ObjectMapper().readValue(body, Mail.class);
          mailListener.displayMail(mail);
        }
      };
      channel.basicConsume(QUEUE_NAME, true, consumer);
```

```
    } catch (IOException | TimeoutException e) {
      throw new RuntimeException(e);
    }

    return null;
  }
}
```

This code is largely the same as the FrontDeskImpl except that we now register a com.rabbitmq.client.Consumer to retrieve the messages. Instead of implementing the full Consumer, we can leverage the com.rabbitmq.client.DefaultConsumer. In this Consumer we use Jackson to map the message to the Mail object again and pass it to the MailListener, which in turn prints the converted message to the console. When using a Channel, you can add a Consumer, which will be invoked when a message is received. The consumer will be ready as soon as it is registered with the Channel using the basicConsume method.

If you already have the FrontDeskImpl running, you will see the messages coming in quite quickly.

Send Messages with Spring's Template Support

The FrontDeskImpl class extends RabbitGatewaySupport; this class configures a RabbitTemplate based on the configuration we pass in. To send a message, we use the getRabbitOperations method to get the template. Next, to convert and send the message, we use the convertAndSend method. This method will first use a MessageConverter to convert the message into JSON and then send it to the queue we have configured.

Listing 11-42. Spring AMQP FrontDesk implementation

```
package com.apress.spring6recipes.post;

import org.springframework.amqp.rabbit.core.RabbitGatewaySupport;

public class FrontDeskImpl extends RabbitGatewaySupport implements FrontDesk {

    public void sendMail(final Mail mail) {
        getRabbitOperations().convertAndSend(mail);
    }

}
```

Let's take a look at the configuration.

Listing 11-43. Spring AMQP FrontDesk configuration

```
package com.apress.spring6recipes.post.config;

import org.springframework.amqp.rabbit.connection.CachingConnectionFactory;
import org.springframework.amqp.rabbit.connection.ConnectionFactory;
import org.springframework.amqp.rabbit.core.RabbitTemplate;
import org.springframework.amqp.support.converter.Jackson2JsonMessageConverter;
import org.springframework.context.annotation.Bean;
import org.springframework.context.annotation.Configuration;
```

```
import com.apress.spring6recipes.post.FrontDeskImpl;

@Configuration
public class FrontOfficeConfiguration {

    @Bean
    public ConnectionFactory connectionFactory() {
        var connectionFactory = new CachingConnectionFactory("127.0.0.1");
        connectionFactory.setUsername("guest");
        connectionFactory.setPassword("guest");
        connectionFactory.setPort(5672);
        return connectionFactory;
    }

    @Bean
    public RabbitTemplate rabbitTemplate(ConnectionFactory cf) {
        var rabbitTemplate = new RabbitTemplate();
        rabbitTemplate.setConnectionFactory(cf);
        rabbitTemplate.setMessageConverter(new Jackson2JsonMessageConverter());
        rabbitTemplate.setRoutingKey("mail.queue");
        return rabbitTemplate;
    }

    @Bean
    public FrontDeskImpl frontDesk(RabbitTemplate amqp) {
        var frontDesk = new FrontDeskImpl();
        frontDesk.setRabbitOperations(amqp);
        return frontDesk;
    }
}
```

The configuration is quite similar to the JMS configuration. We need a ConnectionFactory to connect to our RabbitMQ broker. We use a CachingConnectionFactory so that we can reuse our connections. Next, there is the RabbitTemplate, which uses the connection and has a MessageConverter to convert the message. The message is being converted into JSON using the Jackson2 library, hence the configuration of the Jackson2JsonMessageConverter. Finally, the RabbitTemplate is passed into the FrontDeskImpl so that it is available for usage.

ⓘ We configure a RabbitTemplate here instead of passing the ConnectionFactory to the FrontDeskImpl because we also want to modify the MessageConverter being used. The RabbitGatewaySupport only allows for a ConnectionFactory or RabbitTemplate to be injected.

Listing 11-44. FrontDesk main class

```
package com.apress.spring6recipes.post;

import com.apress.spring6recipes.post.config.FrontOfficeConfiguration;
import org.springframework.context.annotation.AnnotationConfigApplicationContext;
```

```
public class FrontDeskMain {

  public static void main(String[] args) throws Exception {
    var cfg = FrontOfficeConfiguration.class;
    try (var context = new AnnotationConfigApplicationContext(cfg)) {
      var frontDesk = context.getBean(FrontDesk.class);
      frontDesk.sendMail(new Mail("1234", "US", 1.5));
      System.in.read();
    }
  }
}
```

Listen for AMQP Messages with Message Listeners

Spring AMQP supports MessageListenerContainers for retrieving messages in the same way as Spring JMS does for JMS. Spring AMQP has the @RabbitListener annotation to indicate an AMQP-based message listener.

Let's take a look at the MessageListener that is used.

Listing 11-45. MailListener implementation

```
package com.apress.spring6recipes.post;

import org.springframework.amqp.rabbit.annotation.RabbitListener;

public class MailListener {

  @RabbitListener(queues = "mail.queue")
  public void displayMail(Mail mail) {
    System.out.printf("Received: %s%n", mail);
  }
}
```

The MailListener is almost the same as the one created in Recipe 11-4 for receiving JMS messages. This however has a @RabbitListener annotation.

Listing 11-46. Spring AMQP BackOffice configuration

```
package com.apress.spring6recipes.post.config;

import com.apress.spring6recipes.post.MailListener;
import org.springframework.amqp.rabbit.annotation.EnableRabbit;
import org.springframework.amqp.rabbit.config.SimpleRabbitListenerContainerFactory;
import org.springframework.amqp.rabbit.connection.CachingConnectionFactory;
import org.springframework.amqp.rabbit.connection.ConnectionFactory;
import org.springframework.amqp.support.converter.Jackson2JsonMessageConverter;
import org.springframework.context.annotation.Bean;
import org.springframework.context.annotation.Configuration;
```

```java
@Configuration
@EnableRabbit
public class BackOfficeConfiguration {

    @Bean
    public SimpleRabbitListenerContainerFactory rabbitListenerContainerFactory(Connection
    Factory cf) {
        var containerFactory = new SimpleRabbitListenerContainerFactory();
        containerFactory.setConnectionFactory(cf);
        containerFactory.setMessageConverter(new Jackson2JsonMessageConverter());
        return containerFactory;
    }

    @Bean
    public ConnectionFactory connectionFactory() {
        var connectionFactory = new CachingConnectionFactory("127.0.0.1");
        connectionFactory.setUsername("guest");
        connectionFactory.setPassword("guest");
        connectionFactory.setPort(5672);
        return connectionFactory;
    }

    @Bean
    public MailListener mailListener() {
        return new MailListener();
    }
}
```

To enable AMQP annotation-based listeners, the @EnableRabbit annotation is added to the configuration class. As each listener requires a MessageListenerContainer, we need to configure a RabbitListenerContainerFactory, which takes care of creating those containers. The @EnableRabbit logic will, by default, look for a bean named rabbitListenerContainerFactory.

The RabbitListenerContainerFactory needs a ConnectionFactory; for this we are using the CachingConnectionFactory. Before the MailListener.displayMail method is invoked by the MessageListenerContainer, it needs to convert the message payload, in JSON, into a Mail object using the Jackson2JsonMessageConverter.

To listen to messages, create a class with a main method that only needs to construct the application context.

Listing 11-47. BackOffice main class

```java
package com.apress.spring6recipes.post;

import com.apress.spring6recipes.post.config.BackOfficeConfiguration;
import org.springframework.context.annotation.AnnotationConfigApplicationContext;

public class BackOfficeMain {
```

```
public static void main(String[] args) throws Exception {
    var cfg = BackOfficeConfiguration.class;
    try (var context = new AnnotationConfigApplicationContext(cfg)) {
        System.in.read();
    }
}
```

11-7. Send and Receive Messages with Spring Kafka

Problem

You want to use Apache Kafka to send and receive messages.

Solution

The Spring for Apache Kafka project provides easy access and use of Apache Kafka. It has support similar to that of Spring JMS using the Spring Messaging abstraction. It comes with a KafkaTemplate, which provides basic send options. It also comes with a org.springframework.kafka.listener. MessageListenerContainer option, which mimics Spring JMS, which can be enabled by @EnableKafka.

How It Works

First, one needs to add the necessary dependencies to the project.

Listing 11-48. Gradle dependencies

```
implementation group: 'org.springframework.kafka', name: 'spring-kafka', version: '3.0.1'
implementation group: 'org.apache.kafka', name: 'kafka-clients', version: '3.3.1'
```

Listing 11-49. Maven dependencies

```
<dependency>
  <groupId>org.apache.kafka</groupId>
  <artifactId>kafka-clients</artifactId>
  <version>3.3.1</version>
</dependency>

<dependency>
  <groupId>org.apache.kafka</groupId>
  <artifactId>kafka-clients</artifactId>
  <version>3.3.1</version>
</dependency>
```

Send Messages with Spring's Template Support

Let's start by rewriting the FrontDeskImpl to use a KafkaTemplate to send a message. To do so we actually want an object that implements KafkaOperations, which is the interface implemented by the KafkaTemplate.

Listing 11-50. Kafka FrontDesk Implementation

```
package com.apress.spring6recipes.post;

import com.fasterxml.jackson.core.JsonProcessingException;
import com.fasterxml.jackson.databind.ObjectMapper;
import org.springframework.kafka.core.KafkaOperations;

public class FrontDeskImpl implements FrontDesk {

  private final KafkaOperations<Integer, String> kafkaOperations;

  public FrontDeskImpl(KafkaOperations<Integer, String> kafkaOperations) {
    this.kafkaOperations = kafkaOperations;
  }

  public void sendMail(final Mail mail) {

    var result = kafkaOperations.send("mails", convertToJson(mail));
    result.whenComplete((sendResult, ex) -> {
      if (ex == null) {
        System.out.println("Result (success): " + sendResult.getRecordMetadata());
      } else {
        ex.printStackTrace();
      }
    });
  }

  private String convertToJson(Mail mail) {
    try {
      return new ObjectMapper().writeValueAsString(mail);
    } catch (JsonProcessingException ex) {
      throw new IllegalArgumentException(ex);
    }
  }
}
```

Notice the kafkaOperations field, which takes a KafkaOperations<Integer, String>. This means we are sending a message with an Integer type as the key (generated when sending a message), and we will send a message of type String. This means we need to convert the incoming Mail instance to a String. This is taken care of by the convertToJson method using a Jackson2 ObjectMapper. The message will be sent to the mails topic, which is the first argument in the send method; the second one is the payload to send (the converted Mail message).

Sending a message using Kafka is generally an async operation, and the KafkaOperations.send methods reflect this in returning a CompletableFuture. It is a normal Future, so you could use the call to get() to make it a blocking operation or register a callback to get notified of the success or failure of the operation.

Next, we need to create a configuration class to configure the KafkaTemplate to use in the FrontDeskImpl.

Listing 11-51. FrontOffice configuration

```java
package com.apress.spring6recipes.post.config;

import com.apress.spring6recipes.post.FrontDeskImpl;
import org.apache.kafka.clients.producer.ProducerConfig;
import org.apache.kafka.common.serialization.IntegerSerializer;
import org.apache.kafka.common.serialization.StringSerializer;
import org.springframework.context.annotation.Bean;
import org.springframework.context.annotation.Configuration;
import org.springframework.kafka.core.DefaultKafkaProducerFactory;
import org.springframework.kafka.core.KafkaTemplate;
import org.springframework.kafka.core.ProducerFactory;

import java.util.Map;

@Configuration
public class FrontOfficeConfiguration {

  @Bean
  public KafkaTemplate<Integer, String> kafkaTemplate(ProducerFactory<Integer, String> pf) {
    return new KafkaTemplate<>(pf);
  }

  @Bean
  public ProducerFactory<Integer, String> producerFactory() {
    return new DefaultKafkaProducerFactory<>(producerFactoryProperties());
  }

  @Bean
  public Map<String, Object> producerFactoryProperties() {
    var properties = Map.<String, Object>of(
            ProducerConfig.BOOTSTRAP_SERVERS_CONFIG, "localhost:9092",
            ProducerConfig.KEY_SERIALIZER_CLASS_CONFIG, IntegerSerializer.class,
            ProducerConfig.VALUE_SERIALIZER_CLASS_CONFIG, StringSerializer.class);
    return properties;
  }

  @Bean
  public FrontDeskImpl frontDesk(KafkaTemplate<Integer, String> kafka) {
    return new FrontDeskImpl(kafka);
  }
}
```

The aforementioned configuration creates a basically configured KafkaTemplate. We need to configure the ProducerFactory used by the KafkaTemplate; it requires at least the URL to connect to and needs to know which key and value types we want to serialize the messages to. The URL is specified by using the ProducerConfig.BOOTSTRAP_SERVERS_CONFIG; this can take one or more servers to connect to. The ProducerConfig.KEY_SERIALIZER_CLASS_CONFIG and ProducerConfig.VALUE_SERIALIZER_CLASS_CONFIG, respectively, configure the key and value serializers used. As we want to use an Integer for the key and String for the value, those are configured with the IntegerSerializer and StringSerializer.

Finally, the constructed KafkaTemplate is passed to a FrontDeskImpl. To run the front desk application, the following main class would be all that is needed.

Listing 11-52. FrontDesk main

```
package com.apress.spring6recipes.post;

import com.apress.spring6recipes.post.config.FrontOfficeConfiguration;
import org.springframework.context.annotation.AnnotationConfigApplicationContext;

public class FrontDeskMain {

  public static void main(String[] args) throws Exception {
    var cfg = FrontOfficeConfiguration.class;
    try (var context = new AnnotationConfigApplicationContext(cfg)) {
      var frontDesk = context.getBean(FrontDesk.class);
      frontDesk.sendMail(new Mail("1234", "US", 1.5));
      System.in.read();
    }
  }
}
```

This will launch the front desk and send a message through Kafka.

Listening to Messages Using Spring Kafka

Spring Kafka also has message listener containers for listening to messages on topics just like Spring JMS and Spring AMQP. To enable the use of these containers, we need to put @EnableKafka on our configuration class and create and configure our Kafka consumer using @KafkaListener.

First, let's create the listener, which is as easy as annotating a method with a single argument with @KafkaListener.

Listing 11-53. MailListener for Kafka

```
package com.apress.spring6recipes.post;

import org.springframework.kafka.annotation.KafkaListener;

public class MailListener {

    @KafkaListener(topics = "mails")
    public void displayMail(String mail) {
        System.out.printf(" Received: %s%n", mail);
    }
}
```

For now we are interested in the raw String-based payload as that is what is being sent. Next, we need to configure the listener container.

Listing 11-54. BackOffice configuration

```java
package com.apress.spring6recipes.post.config;

import com.apress.spring6recipes.post.MailListener;
import org.apache.kafka.clients.consumer.ConsumerConfig;
import org.apache.kafka.common.serialization.IntegerDeserializer;
import org.apache.kafka.common.serialization.StringDeserializer;
import org.springframework.context.annotation.Bean;
import org.springframework.context.annotation.Configuration;
import org.springframework.kafka.annotation.EnableKafka;
import org.springframework.kafka.config.ConcurrentKafkaListenerContainerFactory;
import org.springframework.kafka.config.KafkaListenerContainerFactory;
import org.springframework.kafka.core.ConsumerFactory;
import org.springframework.kafka.core.DefaultKafkaConsumerFactory;
import org.springframework.kafka.listener.ConcurrentMessageListenerContainer;

import java.util.Map;

@Configuration
@EnableKafka
public class BackOfficeConfiguration {

  @Bean
  public KafkaListenerContainerFactory<ConcurrentMessageListenerContainer<Integer, String>>
  kafkaListenerContainerFactory(
          ConsumerFactory<Integer, String> cf) {
    var factory = new ConcurrentKafkaListenerContainerFactory<Integer, String>();
    factory.setConsumerFactory(cf);
    return factory;
  }

  @Bean
  public ConsumerFactory<Integer, String> consumerFactory() {
    return new DefaultKafkaConsumerFactory<>(consumerConfiguration());
  }

  @Bean
  public Map<String, Object> consumerConfiguration() {
    return Map.<String, Object>of(
            ConsumerConfig.BOOTSTRAP_SERVERS_CONFIG, "localhost:9092",
            ConsumerConfig.KEY_DESERIALIZER_CLASS_CONFIG, IntegerDeserializer.class,
            ConsumerConfig.VALUE_DESERIALIZER_CLASS_CONFIG, StringDeserializer.class,
            ConsumerConfig.GROUP_ID_CONFIG, "group1");
  }
```

```
@Bean
public MailListener mailListener() {
  return new MailListener();
}
}
```

The configuration is very similar to the client. We need to pass the URL(s) to connect to Apache Kafka, and as we want to deserialize messages, we need to specify a key and value deserializer. Finally, we also need to add a group ID; else, we won't be able to connect to Kafka. The URL is passed by using the ConsumerConfig.BOOTSTRAP_SERVERS_CONFIG, the key and value deserializers used are the IntegerDeserializer for the key (as that is an integer) and as the payload is a String the StringDeserializer. Finally, the group property is set.

With these properties we can configure the KafkaListenerContainerFactory, which is a factory used to create a Kafka-based MessageListenerContainer. The container is internally used by the functionality enabled by adding the @EnableKafka annotation. For each method annotated with @KafkaListener, a MessageListenerContainer is created.

To run the back office application, we would need to load this configuration and let it listen.

Listing 11-55. BackOffice main

```
package com.apress.spring6recipes.post;

import org.springframework.context.annotation.AnnotationConfigApplicationContext;

import com.apress.spring6recipes.post.config.BackOfficeConfiguration;

public class BackOfficeMain {

    public static void main(String[] args) throws Exception {
      var cfg = BackOfficeConfiguration.class;
      try (var ctx = new AnnotationConfigApplicationContext(cfg)) {
        System.in.read();
      }
    }
}
```

Now when the front desk application is started, the Mail message will be converted to a String and sent through Kafka to the back office, resulting in the following output:

```
Received: {"mailId":"1234","country":"US","weight":1.5}
```

Using a MessageConverter to Convert Payloads into Objects

Our listener now receives a String, but it would be nicer if we could automatically convert this into a Mail object again. This is quite easily done with some tweaks in the configuration. The KafkaListenerContainerFactory used here accepts a MessageConverter, and to automatically turn a String into our desired object, we can pass it a StringJsonMessageConverter. This will take the String and convert it into the object specified as an argument in the @KafkaListener-annotated method.

First, update the configuration.

CHAPTER 11 ■ SPRING MESSAGING

Listing 11-56. BackOffice configuration

```
package com.apress.spring6recipes.post.config;

import org.springframework.kafka.support.converter.StringJsonMessageConverter;

import java.util.Map;

@Configuration
@EnableKafka
public class BackOfficeConfiguration {

    @Bean
    public KafkaListenerContainerFactory<ConcurrentMessageListenerContainer<Integer, String>>
    kafkaListenerContainerFactory(
            ConsumerFactory<Integer, String> cf) {
        var factory = new ConcurrentKafkaListenerContainerFactory<Integer, String>();
        factory.setConsumerFactory(cf);
        factory.setMessageConverter(new StringJsonMessageConverter());
        return factory;
    }
}
```

Next, we need to modify our `MailListener` to use a `Mail` object instead of the plain `String`.

Listing 11-57. Modified MailListener

```
package com.apress.spring6recipes.post;

import org.springframework.kafka.annotation.KafkaListener;

public class MailListener {

    @KafkaListener(topics = "mails")
    public void displayMail(Mail mail) {
        System.out.printf(" Received: %s%n", mail);
    }
}
```

When running the back office and front desk, the message would still be sent and received.

Converting Objects to Payloads

In the front desk application, the `Mail` instance is manually being converted to a JSON string. Although not hard it would be nice if the framework could do this transparently. This is possible by configuring a `JsonSerializer` instead of a `StringSerializer`.

Listing 11-58. FrontOffice configuration

```
package com.apress.spring6recipes.post.config;

import com.apress.spring6recipes.post.FrontDeskImpl;
import org.apache.kafka.clients.producer.ProducerConfig;
import org.apache.kafka.common.serialization.IntegerSerializer;
import org.springframework.context.annotation.Bean;
import org.springframework.context.annotation.Configuration;
import org.springframework.kafka.core.DefaultKafkaProducerFactory;
import org.springframework.kafka.core.KafkaTemplate;
import org.springframework.kafka.core.ProducerFactory;
import org.springframework.kafka.support.serializer.JsonSerializer;

import java.util.Map;

@Configuration
public class FrontOfficeConfiguration {

    @Bean
    public KafkaTemplate<Integer, Object> kafkaTemplate(ProducerFactory<Integer,
    Object> pf) {
        return new KafkaTemplate<>(pf);
    }

    @Bean
    public ProducerFactory<Integer, Object> producerFactory() {
        return new DefaultKafkaProducerFactory<>(producerFactoryProperties());
    }

    @Bean
    public Map<String, Object> producerFactoryProperties() {
        var properties  = Map.<String, Object>of(
        ProducerConfig.BOOTSTRAP_SERVERS_CONFIG, "localhost:9092",
        ProducerConfig.KEY_SERIALIZER_CLASS_CONFIG, IntegerSerializer.class,
        ProducerConfig.VALUE_SERIALIZER_CLASS_CONFIG, JsonSerializer.class);
        return properties;
    }

    @Bean
    public FrontDeskImpl frontDesk(KafkaTemplate<Integer, Object> kafka) {
        return new FrontDeskImpl(kafka);
    }
}
```

Instead of a KafkaTemplate<Integer, String>, we now use a KafkaTemplate<Integer, Object> as we will now be able to send objects serialized to a String to Kafka.

The FrontDeskImpl can also be cleaned up now as conversion to JSON is now handled by the KafkaTemplate.

Listing 11-59. FrontDesk implementation

```
package com.apress.spring6recipes.post;

import org.springframework.kafka.core.KafkaOperations;

public class FrontDeskImpl implements FrontDesk {

  private final KafkaOperations<Integer, Object> kafkaOperations;

  public FrontDeskImpl(KafkaOperations<Integer, Object> kafkaOperations) {
    this.kafkaOperations = kafkaOperations;
  }

  public void sendMail(final Mail mail) {

    var result = kafkaOperations.send("mails", mail);
    result.whenComplete((sendResult, ex) -> {
      if (ex == null) {
        System.out.println("Result (success): " + sendResult.getRecordMetadata());
      } else {
        ex.printStackTrace();
      }
    });
  }
}
```

11-8. Summary

This chapter explored Spring's messaging support and how to use this to build message-oriented architectures. You learned how to produce and consume messages using different messaging solutions. For different messaging solutions, you looked at how to build message-driven POJOs using a MessageListenerContainer.

We looked at JMS and AMQP with ActiveMQ, a reliable open source message queue, and you briefly looked at Apache Kafka.

The next chapter will explore Spring Integration, which is an ESB-like framework for building application integration solutions, similar to Mule ESB. You will be able to leverage the knowledge gained in this chapter to take your message-oriented applications to new heights with Spring Integration.

CHAPTER 12

■ ■ ■

Spring Integration

In this chapter, you will learn the principles behind enterprise application integration (EAI), used by many modern applications to decouple dependencies between components. The Spring Framework provides a powerful and extensible framework called Spring Integration. Spring Integration provides the same level of decoupling for disparate systems and data that the core Spring Framework provides for components within an application. This chapter aims to give you all the required knowledge to understand the patterns involved in EAI, to understand what an enterprise service bus (ESB) is and–ultimately–how to build solutions using Spring Integration. If you've used an EAI server or an ESB, you'll find that Spring Integration is markedly simpler than anything you're likely to have used before.

After finishing this chapter, you will be able to write fairly sophisticated Spring Integration solutions to integrate applications, to let them share services and data. You will learn Spring Integration's many options for configuration too. Spring Integration can be configured entirely in a standard XML namespace, if you like, but you'll probably find that a hybrid approach, using annotations and XML, is more natural. You will also learn why Spring Integration is a very attractive alternative for people coming from a classic enterprise application integration background. If you've used an ESB before, such as Mule or ServiceMix, or a classical EAI server such as Axway Integrator or TIBCO ActiveMatrix, the idioms explained here should be familiar and the configuration refreshingly straightforward.

12-1. Integrating One System with Another Using EAI

Problem

You have two applications that need to talk to each other through external interfaces. You need to establish a connection between the applications' services and/or their data.

Solution

You need to employ EAI, which is the discipline of integrating applications and data using a set of well-known patterns. These patterns are usefully summarized and embodied in a landmark book called *Enterprise Integration Patterns*, by Gregor Hohpe, Bobby Woolf, and colleagues. Today the patterns are canonical and are the lingua franca of the modern-day ESB.

© Marten Deinum, Daniel Rubio, Josh Long 2023
M. Deinum et al., *Spring 6 Recipes*, https://doi.org/10.1007/978-1-4842-8649-4_12

How It Works

Picking an Integration Style

There are multiple integration styles, each best suited for certain types of applications and requirements. The basic premise is simple: your application can't speak directly to the other system using the native mechanism in one system. So you can devise a bridging connection, something to build on top of, abstract, or work around some characteristic about the other system in a way that's advantageous to the invoking system. What you abstract is different for each application. Sometimes it's the location, sometimes it's the synchronous or asynchronous nature of the call, and sometimes it's the messaging protocol. There are many criteria for choosing an integration style, related to how tightly coupled you want your application to be, to server affinity, to the demands of the messaging formats, and so on. In a way, TCP/IP is the most famous of all integration techniques because it decouples one application from another's server.

You have probably built applications that use some or all of the following integration styles (using Spring, no less!). Shared database, for example, is easily achieved using Spring's JDBC support.

The four integration styles are as follows:

- File transfer: Have each application produce files of shared data for others to consume and consume files that others have produced.

- Shared database: Have the applications store the data they want to share in a common database. This usually takes the form of a database to which different applications have access. This is not usually a favored approach because it means exposing your data to different clients who might not respect the constraints you have in place (but not codified). Using views and stored procedures can often make this option possible, but it's not ideal. There's no particular support for talking to a database, per se, but you can build an endpoint that deals with new results in a SQL database as message payloads. Integration with databases doesn't tend to be granular or message-oriented, but batch-oriented instead. After all, a million new rows in a database isn't an event so much as a batch! It's no surprise then that Spring Batch (discussed in Chapter 8) includes terrific support for JDBC-oriented input and output.

- Remote Procedure Invocation: Have each application expose some of its procedures so that they can be invoked remotely and have applications invoke them to initiate behavior and exchange data. There is specific support for optimizing RPC (remote procedure calls such as SOAP and RMI) exchanges using Spring Integration.

- Messaging: Have each application connect to a common messaging system and exchange data and invoke behavior using messages. This style also describes other asynchronous or multicast publish/subscribe architectures. In a way, an ESB or an EAI container such as Spring Integration lets you handle most of the other styles as though you were dealing with a messaging queue: a request comes in on a queue and is managed, responded to, or forwarded onward on another queue.

Building on an ESB Solution

Now that you know how you want to approach the integration, it's all about actually implementing it. You have many choices in today's world. If the requirement is common enough, most middleware or frameworks will accommodate it in some way. JEE, .NET, and others handle common cases very well: SOAP, XML-RPC, a binary layer such as EJB or binary remoting, JMS, or an MQ abstraction. If, however, the requirement is somewhat exotic or you have a lot of configuration to do, then perhaps an ESB is required. An ESB is middleware that provides a high-level approach to modeling integrations, in the spirit of the patterns described by EAI. The ESB provides a manageable configuration format for orchestrating the different pieces of an integration in a simple high-level format.

Spring Integration, an API in the SpringSource portfolio, provides a robust mechanism for modeling a lot of these integration scenarios that work well with Spring. Spring Integration has many advantages over a lot of other ESBs, especially the lightweight nature of the framework. The nascent ESB market is filled with choices. Some are former EAI servers, reworked to address the ESB-centric architectures. Some are genuine ESBs, built with that in mind. Some are little more than message queues with adapters.

Indeed, if you're looking for an extraordinarily powerful EAI server (with integration with the JEE platform and a very hefty price tag), you might consider Axway Integrator. There's very little it can't do. Vendors such as TIBCO and webMethods made their marks (and were subsequently acquired) because they provided excellent tools for dealing with integration in the enterprise. These options, although powerful, are usually very expensive and middleware-centric: your integrations are deployed to the middleware.

Standardization attempts, such as Java Business Integration (JBI), have proven successful to an extent, and there are good compliant ESBs based on these standards (e.g., OpenESB and ServiceMix). One of the thought leaders in the ESB market is the Mule ESB, which has a good reputation; it is free/open source, community friendly, and lightweight. These characteristics also make Spring Integration attractive. Often, you simply need to talk to another open system, and you don't want to requisition a purchase approval for middleware that's more expensive than some houses!

Each Spring Integration application is completely embedded and needs no server infrastructure. In fact, you could deploy an integration inside another application, perhaps in your web application endpoint. Spring Integration flips the deployment paradigms of most ESBs on their head: you deploy Spring Integration into your application, and you don't deploy your application into Spring Integration. There are no start and stop scripts and no ports to guard. The simplest possible working Spring Integration application is a simple Java `public static void main()` method to bootstrap a Spring context.

Listing 12-1. Main class

```
package com.apress.spring6recipes.springintegration;

import org.springframework.context.annotation.AnnotationConfigApplicationContext;

public class Main {
  public static void main(String [] args){
    var cfg = IntegrationConfiguration.class;
    try (var ctx = new AnnotationConfigApplicationContext(cfg)) {}
  }
}
```

You created a standard Spring application context and started it. The contents of the Spring application context will be discussed in subsequent recipes, but it's helpful to see how simple it is. You might decide to hoist the context up in a web application, an EJB container, or anything else you want. Indeed, you can use Spring Integration to power the email polling functionality in a Swing/JavaFX application! It's as lightweight as you want it to be.

12-2. Integrating Two Systems Using JMS

Problem

You want to build an integration to connect one application to another using JMS, which provides locational and temporal decoupling on modern middleware for Java applications. You're interested in applying more sophisticated routing and want to isolate your code from the specifics of the origin of the message (in this case, the JMS queue or topic).

Solution

While you can do this by using regular JMS code or EJB's support for message-driven beans (MDBs) or using core Spring's message-driven POJO (MDP) support, all are necessarily coded for handling messages coming specifically from JMS. Your code is tied to JMS. Using an ESB lets you hide the origin of the message from the code that's handling it. You'll use this solution as an easy way to see how a Spring Integration solution can be built. Spring Integration provides an easy way to work with JMS, just as you might using MDPs in the core Spring container. Here, however, you could conceivably replace the JMS middleware with an email, and the code that reacts to the message could stay the same.

How It Works

Building a Message-Driven POJO (MDP) Using Spring Integration

As you might recall from Chapter 11, Spring can replace message-driven bean functionality by using message-driven POJOs. This is a powerful solution for anyone wanting to build something that handles messages on a message queue. You'll build an MDP, but you will configure it using Spring Integration's more concise configuration and provide an example of a very rudimentary integration. All this integration will do is take an inbound JMS message (whose payload is of type `Map<String,Object>`) and write it to the log.

As with a standard MDP, configuration for the `ConnectionFactory` exists. Shown in the following is a configuration class. You can pass it in as a parameter to the Spring `ApplicationContext` on creation (as you did in the previous recipe, in the `Main` class).

Listing 12-2. Spring Integration configuration

```
package com.apress.spring6recipes.springintegration;

import jakarta.jms.ConnectionFactory;
import org.apache.activemq.artemis.jms.client.ActiveMQConnectionFactory;
import org.springframework.context.annotation.Bean;
import org.springframework.context.annotation.ComponentScan;
import org.springframework.context.annotation.Configuration;
import org.springframework.integration.config.EnableIntegration;
import org.springframework.integration.dsl.IntegrationFlow;
import org.springframework.integration.jms.dsl.Jms;
import org.springframework.jms.connection.CachingConnectionFactory;
import org.springframework.jms.core.JmsTemplate;

@Configuration
@EnableIntegration
public class IntegrationConfiguration {
```

```
@Bean
public CachingConnectionFactory connectionFactory() {
    var connectionFactory = new ActiveMQConnectionFactory("tcp://localhost:61616");
    return new CachingConnectionFactory(connectionFactory);
}

@Bean
public JmsTemplate jmsTemplate(ConnectionFactory connectionFactory) {
    return new JmsTemplate(connectionFactory);
}

@Bean
public InboundHelloWorldJMSMessageProcessor messageProcessor() {
    return new InboundHelloWorldJMSMessageProcessor();
}

@Bean
public IntegrationFlow jmsInbound(ConnectionFactory connectionFactory,
        InboundHelloWorldJMSMessageProcessor messageProcessor) {
    return IntegrationFlow
                .from(Jms.messageDrivenChannelAdapter(connectionFactory)
                .extractPayload(true).destination("recipe-12-2"))
                .handle(messageProcessor)
                .get();
}
}
```

Notice the @EnableIntegration; this will pull in the necessary component for Spring Integration to function and detect the needed beans and configuration in the configuration class. For the remainder it is a quite ordinary Java configuration class. You define a connectionFactory exactly as if you were configuring a standard MDP. The JmsTemplate is there, so we can use that to send a message from our main class.

Then, you define any beans specific to this solution: in this case a bean that responds to messages coming into the bus from the message queue, messageProcessor. A service activator is a generic endpoint in Spring Integration that's used to invoke functionality—whether it be an operation in a service or some routine in a regular POJO or anything you want instead—in response to a message sent in on an input channel. Although this will be covered in some detail, it's interesting here only because you are using it to respond to messages. These beans taken together are the collaborators in the solution, and this example is fairly representative of how most integrations look: you define your collaborating components, and then you define the flow using the Spring Integration Java DSL that configures the solution itself.

 There is also a Spring Integration Groovy DSL.

The configuration starts with the IntegrationFlow, which is used to define how the messages flow through the system. The flow starts with the definition of a messageDrivenChannelAdapter, which basically receives messages from the recipe-12-2 destination and passes them to a Spring Integration channel. As we only want the payload (see the next part), we specify extractPayload(true). The messageDrivenChannelAdapter is, as the name suggests, an adapter. An adapter is a component that knows how to speak to a specific type of subsystem and translate messages on that subsystem into something that can be used in the Spring Integration bus. Adapters also do the same in reverse, taking messages on the

Spring Integration bus and translating them into something a specific subsystem will understand. This is different from a service activator (covered next) in that it's meant to be a general connection between the bus and the foreign endpoint. A service activator, however, only helps you invoke your application's business logic on receipt of a message. What you do in the business logic, connecting to another system or not, is up to you.

The next component, a service activator, listens for messages coming into that channel and invokes the bean referenced through the handle method, which in this case is the messageProcessor bean defined previously. Due to the @ServiceActivator annotation on the method of the component, Spring Integration knows which method to invoke.

Listing 12-3. Service activator

```
package com.apress.spring6recipes.springintegration;

import org.slf4j.Logger;
import org.slf4j.LoggerFactory;
import org.springframework.integration.annotation.ServiceActivator;
import org.springframework.messaging.Message;

import java.util.Map;

public class InboundHelloWorldJMSMessageProcessor {

  private final Logger logger = LoggerFactory.getLogger(getClass());

  @ServiceActivator
  public void handleIncomingJmsMessage(
          Message<Map<String, Object>> inboundJmsMessage) {
    var payload = inboundJmsMessage.getPayload();
    logger.info("Received: {}", payload);
  }
}
```

Notice that there is an annotation, @ServiceActivator, that tells Spring to configure this component and this method as the recipient of the message payload from the channel, which is passed to the method as Message<Map<String, Object>> inboundJmsMessage. In the previous configuration, extractPayload(true) tells Spring Integration to take the payload of the message from the JMS queue (in this case, a Map<String,Object>) and extract it and pass that as the payload of the message that's being moved through Spring Integration's channels as a org.springframework.messaging.Message. The Spring Message is not to be confused with the JMS Message interface, although they have some similarities. Had you not specified the extractPayload option, the type of payload on the Spring Message interface would have been jakarta.jms.Message. The burden of extracting the payload would have been on you, the developer, but sometimes getting access to that information is useful. Rewritten to handle unwrapping the jakarta.jms.Message, the example would look a little different.

Listing 12-4. Service Activator - with extracted payload

```
package com.apress.spring6recipes.springintegration;

import jakarta.jms.JMSException;
import jakarta.jms.MapMessage;
import org.slf4j.Logger;
```

```
import org.slf4j.LoggerFactory;
import org.springframework.integration.annotation.ServiceActivator;
import org.springframework.messaging.Message;

import java.util.Map;

public class InboundHelloWorldJMSMessageProcessor {

  private final Logger logger = LoggerFactory.getLogger(getClass());

  @ServiceActivator
  public void handleIncomingJmsMessageWithPayloadNotExtracted(
          Message<jakarta.jms.Message> msgWithJmsMessageAsPayload) throws Throwable {
    var payload = (MapMessage) msgWithJmsMessageAsPayload.getPayload();
    logger.debug("Received: {}", convert(payload));
  }

  private Map<String, Object> convert(MapMessage msg) throws JMSException {
    return Map.of(
            "firstName", msg.getString("firstName"),
            "lastName", msg.getString("lastName"),
            "id", msg.getLong("id"));
  }
}
```

You could have specified the payload type as the type of the parameter passed into the method. If the payload of the message coming from JMS was of type Cat, for example, the method prototype could just as well have been public void handleIncomingJmsMessageWithPayloadNotExtracted(Cat inboundJmsMessage) throws Throwable. Spring Integration will figure out the right thing to do. In this case, we prefer access to the Spring Message, which has header values that can be useful to interrogate.

Also note that you don't need to specify throws Throwable. Error handling can be as generic or as specific as you want in Spring Integration.

In the example, you use the @ServiceActivator to invoke the functionality where the integration ends. However, you can forward the response from the activation on to the next channel by returning a value from the method. The type of the return value is what will be used to determine the next message sent in the system. If you return a Message, that will be sent directly. If you return something other than Message, that value will be wrapped as a payload in a Message instance, and that will become the next Message that is ultimately sent to the next component in the processing pipeline. This Message will be sent on the output channel that's configured on the service activator. There is no requirement to send a message on the output channel with the same type as the message that came on in the input channel; this is an effective way to transform the message type. A service activator is a very flexible component in which to put hooks to your system and to help mold the integration.

This solution is pretty straightforward, and in terms of configuration for one JMS queue, it's not really a win over straight MDPs because there's an extra level of indirection to overcome. The Spring Integration facilities make building complex integrations easier than Spring Core could because the configuration is centralized. You have a bird's-eye view of the entire integration, with routing and processing centralized, so you can better reposition the components in your integration. However, as you'll see, Spring Integration wasn't meant to compete with EJB and Spring Core; it shines at solutions that couldn't naturally be built using EJB3 or Spring Core.

12-3. Interrogating Spring Integration Messages for Context Information

Problem

You want more information about the message coming into the Spring Integration processing pipeline than the type of the message implicitly can give you.

Solution

Interrogate the Spring Integration `Message` for header information specific to the message. These values are enumerated as header values in a map (of type `Map<String,Object>`).

How It Works

Using MessageHeaders for Fun and Profit

The Spring `Message` interface is a generic wrapper that contains a pointer to the actual payload of the message as well as to headers that provide contextual message metadata. You can manipulate or augment this metadata to enable/enhance the functionality of components that are downstream too; for example, when sending a message through email, it's useful to specify the TO/FROM headers.

Any time you expose a class to the framework to handle some requirement (such as the logic you provide for the service activator component or a transformer component), there will be some chance to interact with the `Message` and with the message headers. Remember that Spring Integration pushes a `Message` through a processing pipeline. Each component that interfaces with the `Message` instance has to act on it, do something with it, or forward it on. One way of providing information to those components, and of getting information about what's happened in the components up until that point, is to interrogate the `MessageHeaders`.

There are several values that you should be aware of when working with Spring Integration (see Tables 12-1 and 12-2). These constants are exposed on the `org.springframework.messaging.MessageHeaders` and `org.springframework.integration.IntegrationMessageHeaderAccessor` classes.

Table 12-1. *Common Headers Found in Core Spring Messaging*

Constant	Description
ID	This is a unique value assigned to the message by the Spring Integration engine.
TIMESTAMP	Timestamp assigned to the message.
REPLY_CHANNEL	The string name of the channel to which the output of the current component should be sent. This can be overridden.
ERROR_CHANNEL	The string name of the channel to which the output of the current component should be sent if an exception bubbles up into the runtime. This can be overridden.
CONTENT_TYPE	The content type (mimetype) of the message, mainly used for websocket messages.

Next to the headers defined by Spring Messaging, there are also some commonly used headers in Spring Integration. These are defined in the `org.springframework.integration.IntegrationMessageHeaderAccessor` class (see Table 12-2).

Table 12-2. *Common Headers Found in Spring Integration*

Constant	Description
CORRELATION_ID	This is optional. It is used by some components (such as aggregators) to group messages together in some sort of processing pipeline.
EXPIRATION_DATE	Used by some components as a threshold for processing after which a component can wait no longer in processing.
PRIORITY	The priority of the message; higher numbers indicate a higher priority.
SEQUENCE_NUMBER	The order in which the message is to be sequenced, typically used with a sequencer.
SEQUENCE_SIZE	The size of the sequence so that an aggregator can know when to stop waiting for more messages and move forward. This is useful in implementing "join" functionality.
DUPLICATE_MESSAGE	true if a message was detected as being a duplicate by an idempotent receiver.
DELIVERY_ATTEMPT	When a message-driven adapter supports retrying, this header contains the current number of delivery attempts.
CLOSEABLE_RESOURCE	If the message is attached to a closable resource like an FTP session or file resource.

Some header values are specific to the type of the source message's payload; for example, payloads sourced from a file on the file system are different from those coming in from a JMS queue, which are different from messages coming from an email system. These different components are typically packaged in their own JARs, and there's usually some class that provides constants for accessing these headers. An example of component-specific headers is the constants defined for files on org.springframework. integration.file.FileHeaders: FILENAME and PREFIX. Naturally, when in doubt, you can just enumerate the values manually because the headers are just a java.util.Map instance.

Listing 12-5. Access headers through Message

```
package com.apress.spring6recipes.springintegration;

import org.slf4j.Logger;
import org.slf4j.LoggerFactory;
import org.springframework.integration.annotation.ServiceActivator;
import org.springframework.messaging.Message;

import java.io.File;

public class InboundFileMessageServiceActivator {

    private final Logger logger = LoggerFactory.getLogger(getClass());

    @ServiceActivator
    public void interrogateMessage(Message<File> message) {
        var headers = message.getHeaders();
        headers.forEach( (k,v) -> logger.debug("{} : {}", k, v));
    }
}
```

These headers let you interrogate the specific features of these messages without surfacing them as a concrete interface dependency if you don't want them. They can also be used to help processing and allow you to specify custom metadata to downstream components. The act of providing extra data for the benefit of a downstream component is called message enrichment. Message enrichment is when you take the headers of a given Message and add to them, usually to the benefit of components in the processing pipeline downstream. You might imagine processing a message to add a customer to a customer relationship management (CRM) system that makes a call to a third-party website to establish credit ratings. This credit is added to the headers so the component downstream tasked with either adding the customer or rejecting it can make its decisions.

Another way to get access to header metadata is to simply have them passed as parameters to your component's method. You simply annotate the parameter with the @Header annotation, and Spring Integration will take care of the rest.

Listing 12-6. Access single headers through @Header

```
package com.apress.spring6recipes.springintegration;

import org.slf4j.Logger;
import org.slf4j.LoggerFactory;
import org.springframework.integration.annotation.ServiceActivator;
import org.springframework.integration.file.FileHeaders;
import org.springframework.messaging.MessageHeaders;
import org.springframework.messaging.handler.annotation.Header;

import java.io.File;

public class InboundFileMessageServiceActivator {

    private final Logger logger = LoggerFactory.getLogger(getClass());

    @ServiceActivator
    public void interrogateMessage(
            @Header(MessageHeaders.ID) String uuid,
            @Header(FileHeaders.FILENAME) String fileName, File file) {
        var msg = "the id of the message is {}, and name of the file payload is {}";
        logger.debug(msg, uuid, fileName);
    }
}
```

You can also have Spring Integration pass the Map<String,Object> by annotating an argument of that type with @Headers.

Listing 12-7. Access headers through @Headers

```
package com.apress.spring6recipes.springintegration;

import org.slf4j.Logger;
import org.slf4j.LoggerFactory;
import org.springframework.integration.annotation.ServiceActivator;
import org.springframework.integration.file.FileHeaders;
import org.springframework.messaging.MessageHeaders;
import org.springframework.messaging.handler.annotation.Headers;
```

```java
import java.io.File;
import java.util.Map;

public class InboundFileMessageServiceActivator {

    private final Logger logger = LoggerFactory.getLogger(InboundFileMessageServiceActivat
    or.class);

    @ServiceActivator
    public void interrogateMessage(
            @Headers Map<String, Object> headers, File file) {
        var msg = "the id of the message is {}, and name of the file payload is {}";
        var id = headers.get(MessageHeaders.ID);
        var filename = headers.get(FileHeaders.FILENAME);
        logger.debug(msg, id, filename);
    }
}
```

12-4. Integrating Two Systems Using a File System

Problem

You want to build a solution that takes files on a well-known, shared file system and uses them as the conduit for integration with another system. An example might be that your application produces a comma-separated value (CSV) dump of all the customers added to a system every hour. The company's third-party financial system is updated with these sales by a process that checks a shared folder, mounted over a network file system, and processes the CSV records. What's required is a way to treat the presence of a new file as an event on the bus.

Solution

You have an idea of how this could be built by using standard techniques, but you want something more elegant. Let Spring Integration isolate you from the event-driven nature of the file system and from the file input/output requirements, and instead let's use it to focus on writing the code that deals with the java.io.File payload itself. With this approach, you can write unit-testable code that accepts an input and responds by adding the customers to the financial system. When the functionality is finished, you configure it in the Spring Integration pipeline and let Spring Integration invoke your functionality whenever a new file is recognized on the file system. This is an example of an event-driven architecture (EDA). EDAs let you ignore how an event was generated and focus instead on reacting to it, in much the same way that event-driven GUIs let you change the focus of your code from controlling how a user triggers an action to actually reacting to the invocation itself. Spring Integration makes it a natural approach for loosely coupled solutions. In fact, this code should look very similar to the solution you built for the JMS queue because it's just another class that takes a parameter (a Spring Integration Message<T>, a parameter of the same type as the payload of the message, etc.).

How It Works

Concerns in Dealing with a File System

Building a solution to talk to JMS is old hat. Instead, let's consider what building a solution using a shared file system might look like. Imagine how to build it without an ESB solution. You need some mechanism by which to poll the file system periodically and detect new files. Perhaps Quartz and some sort of cache? You need something to read in these files quickly and then pass the payload to your processing logic efficiently. Finally, your system needs to work with that payload.

Spring Integration frees you from all that infrastructure code; all you need to do is configure it. There are some issues with dealing with file system–based processing, however, that are up to you to resolve. Behind the scenes, Spring Integration is still dealing with polling the file system and detecting new files. It can't possibly have a semantically correct idea for your application of when a file is "completely" written, and thus providing a way around that is up to you.

Several approaches exist. You might write out a file and then write another zero-byte file. The presence of that file would mean it's safe to assume that the real payload is present. Configure Spring Integration to look for that file. If it finds it, it knows that there's another file (perhaps with the same name and a different file extension?) and that it can start reading it/working with it. Another solution along the same line is to have the client ("producer") write the file to the directory using a name that the glob pattern Spring Integration is using to poll the directory won't detect. Then, when it's finished writing, issue an mv command if you trust your file system to do the right thing there.

Let's revisit the first solution, but this time with a file-based adapter. The configuration looks conceptually the same as before, except the configuration for the adapter has changed, and with that a lot of the configuration for the JMS adapter has gone, like the connection factory. Instead, you tell Spring Integration about a different source from whence messages will come: the file system.

Listing 12-8. Integration configuration

```
package com.apress.spring6recipes.springintegration;

import org.springframework.beans.factory.annotation.Value;
import org.springframework.context.annotation.Bean;
import org.springframework.context.annotation.Configuration;
import org.springframework.integration.config.EnableIntegration;
import org.springframework.integration.dsl.IntegrationFlow;
import org.springframework.integration.dsl.Pollers;
import org.springframework.integration.file.dsl.Files;

import java.io.File;
import java.time.Duration;

@Configuration
@EnableIntegration
public class IntegrationConfiguration {

    @Bean
    public InboundHelloWorldFileMessageProcessor messageProcessor() {
        return new InboundHelloWorldFileMessageProcessor();
    }
```

```
@Bean
public IntegrationFlow inboundFileFlow(
        @Value("${user.home}/inboundFiles/new/") File directory) {
    return IntegrationFlow
            .from(
                Files.inboundAdapter(directory).patternFilter("*.csv"),
                c -> c.poller(Pollers.fixedRate(Duration.ofSeconds(10))))
            .handle(messageProcessor())
            .get();
    }
}
```

This is nothing you haven't already seen, really. The code for Files.inboundAdapter is the only new element. The code for the @ServiceActivator has changed to reflect the fact that you're expecting a message of type Message<java.io.File>.

Listing 12-9. Modified service activator

```
package com.apress.spring6recipes.springintegration;

import java.io.File;

import org.slf4j.Logger;
import org.slf4j.LoggerFactory;
import org.springframework.integration.annotation.ServiceActivator;
import org.springframework.messaging.Message;

public class InboundHelloWorldFileMessageProcessor {

    private final Logger logger = LoggerFactory.getLogger(getClass());

    @ServiceActivator
    public void handleIncomingFileMessage(Message<File> inbound) {
        var filePayload = inbound.getPayload();
        logger.debug("absolute path: {}, size: {}",
                filePayload.getAbsolutePath(), filePayload.length());
    }
}
```

12-5. Transforming a Message from One Type to Another

Problem

You want to send a message into the bus and transform it before working with it further. Usually, this is done to adapt the message to the requirements of a component downstream. You might also want to transform a message by enriching it—adding extra headers or augmenting the payload so that components downstream in the processing pipeline can benefit from it.

Solution

Use a transformer component to take a Message<T> of a payload and send the Message<T> out with a payload of a different type. You can also use the transformer to add extra headers or update the values of headers for the benefit of components downstream in the processing pipeline.

How It Works

Spring Integration provides a transformer message endpoint to permit the augmentation of the message headers or the transformation of the message itself. In Spring Integration, components are chained together, and output from one component is returned by way of the method invoked for that component. The return value of the method is passed out on the "reply channel" for the component to the next component, which receives it as an input parameter. A transformer component lets you change the type of the object being returned or add extra headers, and that updated object is what is passed to the next component in the chain.

Modifying a Message's Payload

The configuration of a transformer component is very much in keeping with everything you've seen so far.

Listing 12-10. Message transformer

```
package com.apress.spring6recipes.springintegration;

import org.springframework.integration.annotation.Transformer;
import org.springframework.messaging.Message;

import java.util.Map;

public class InboundJMSMessageToCustomerTransformer {

    @Transformer
    public Customer transformJMSMapToCustomer(Message<Map<String, Object>>
    inboundSprignIntegrationMessage) {
        var jmsPayload = inboundSprignIntegrationMessage.getPayload();
        return convert(jmsPayload);
    }

    private Customer convert(Map<String, Object> payload) {
        return new Customer(
                (Long) payload.get("id"),
                (String) payload.get("firstName"),
                (String) payload.get("lastName"),
                (String) payload.getOrDefault("telephone", null),
                (Float) payload.getOrDefault("creditScore", 0f));
    }
}
```

Nothing terribly complex is happening here: A Message with type Map<String,Object> is passed in. The values are manually extracted and used to build an object of type Customer. The Customer object is returned, which has the effect of passing it out on the reply channel for this component. The next component in the configuration will receive this object as its input Message with type Customer.

Listing 12-11. Customer class

```
package com.apress.spring6recipes.springintegration;

public record Customer(
    long id, String firstName, String lastName,
    String telephone, float creditScore) {
}
```

The solution is mostly the same as you've seen, but there is a new transformer method.

Listing 12-12. Integration configuration with a transformer

```
package com.apress.spring6recipes.springintegration;

import jakarta.jms.ConnectionFactory;
import org.apache.activemq.artemis.jms.client.ActiveMQConnectionFactory;
import org.springframework.context.annotation.Bean;
import org.springframework.context.annotation.ComponentScan;
import org.springframework.context.annotation.Configuration;
import org.springframework.integration.config.EnableIntegration;
import org.springframework.integration.dsl.IntegrationFlow;
import org.springframework.integration.jms.dsl.Jms;
import org.springframework.jms.connection.CachingConnectionFactory;
import org.springframework.jms.core.JmsTemplate;

@Configuration
@EnableIntegration
public class IntegrationConfiguration {

    @Bean
    public CachingConnectionFactory connectionFactory() {
        var connectionFactory = new ActiveMQConnectionFactory("tcp://localhost:61616");
        return new CachingConnectionFactory(connectionFactory);
    }

    @Bean
    public JmsTemplate jmsTemplate(ConnectionFactory connectionFactory) {
        return new JmsTemplate(connectionFactory);
    }

    @Bean
    public InboundJMSMessageToCustomerTransformer customerTransformer() {
        return new InboundJMSMessageToCustomerTransformer();
    }

    @Bean
    public InboundCustomerServiceActivator customerServiceActivator() {
        return new InboundCustomerServiceActivator();
    }
```

```
@Bean
public IntegrationFlow jmsInbound(ConnectionFactory connectionFactory) {
    return IntegrationFlow
            .from(Jms.messageDrivenChannelAdapter(connectionFactory)
                    .extractPayload(true).destination("recipe-12-5"))
            .transform(customerTransformer())
            .handle(customerServiceActivator())
            .get();
    }
}
```

Here, you're specifying a messageDrivenChannelAdapter, which moves the incoming content to the InboundJMSMessageToCustomerTransformer, which transforms it into a Customer. That Customer is sent to the InboundCustomerServiceActivator.

The code in the next component can now declare a dependency on the Customer class with impunity. You can, with transformers, receive messages from any number of sources and transform into a Customer so that you can reuse the InboundCustomerServiceActivator.

Listing 12-13. Service activator receiving a customer

```
package com.apress.spring6recipes.springintegration;

import org.slf4j.Logger;
import org.slf4j.LoggerFactory;
import org.springframework.integration.annotation.ServiceActivator;
import org.springframework.messaging.Message;

public class InboundCustomerServiceActivator {
    private final Logger logger = LoggerFactory.getLogger(getClass());

    @ServiceActivator
    public void doSomethingWithCustomer(Message<Customer> customerMessage) {
        var customer = customerMessage.getPayload();
        logger.debug("Received: {}", customer);
    }
}
```

Modifying a Message's Headers

Sometimes changing a message's payload isn't enough. Sometimes you want to update the payload as well as the headers. Doing this is slightly more interesting because it involves using the MessageBuilder class, which allows you to create new Message objects with any specified payload and any specified header data. The configuration is identical in this case.

Listing 12-14. Message transformer using a MessageBuilder

```
package com.apress.spring6recipes.springintegration;

import org.springframework.integration.annotation.Transformer;
import org.springframework.integration.support.MessageBuilder;
import org.springframework.messaging.Message;
```

```
import java.util.Map;

public class InboundJMSMessageToCustomerTransformer {

    @Transformer
    public Message<Customer> transformJMSMapToCustomer(
            Message<Map<String, Object>> inboundSprignIntegrationMessage) {
        var jmsPayload = inboundSprignIntegrationMessage.getPayload();
        var customer = convert(jmsPayload);
        return MessageBuilder.withPayload(customer)
                .copyHeadersIfAbsent(inboundSprignIntegrationMessage.getHeaders())
                .setHeaderIfAbsent("randomlySelectedForSurvey", Math.random() > .5)
                .build();
    }

    private Customer convert(Map<String, Object> payload) {
        return new Customer(
                (Long) payload.get("id"),
                (String) payload.get("firstName"),
                (String) payload.get("lastName"),
                (String) payload.getOrDefault("telephone", null),
                (Float) payload.getOrDefault("creditScore", 0f));
    }
}
```

As before, this code is simply a method with an input and an output. The output is constructed dynamically using MessageBuilder to create a message that has the same payload as the input message as well as copies the existing headers and adds an extra header: randomlySelectedForSurvey. We cannot reuse the existing message as messages are, by default, immutable in Spring Messaging and Spring Integration, hence the new message and copy of the headers.

12-6. Error Handling Using Spring Integration

Problem

Spring Integration brings together systems distributed across different nodes; computers; and services, protocols, and language stacks. Indeed, a Spring Integration solution might not even finish in remotely the same time period as when it started. Exception handling, then, can never be as simple as a language-level try/catch block in a single thread for any component with asynchronous behavior. This implies that many of the kinds of solutions you're likely to build, with channels and queues of any kind, need a way of signaling an error that is distributed and natural to the component that created the error. Thus, an error might get sent over a JMS queue on a different continent or in process on a queue in a different thread.

Solution

Use Spring Integration's support for an error channel, both implicitly and explicitly via code.

How It Works

Spring Integration provides the ability to catch exceptions and send them to an error channel of your choosing. By default, it's a global channel called errorChannel. By default, Spring Integration registers a LoggingHandler to this channel, which does nothing more than log the exception and stack trace. To make this work, we have to tell the message-driven channel adapter that we want the error to be sent to the errorChannel. We can do this by configuring the error channel attribute.

Listing 12-15. Integration configuration for an error channel

```
@Bean
public IntegrationFlow jmsInbound(ConnectionFactory connectionFactory) {
  return IntegrationFlow
          .from(Jms.messageDrivenChannelAdapter(connectionFactory)
                  .extractPayload(true).destination("recipe-12-6")
                  .errorChannel("errorChannel"))
          .transform(customerTransformer())
          .handle(customerServiceActivator())
          .get();
}
```

Custom Handler to Handle Exceptions

Of course you can also have components subscribe to messages from this channel to override the exception handling behavior. You can create a class that will be invoked whenever a message comes in on the errorChannel.

Listing 12-16. Integration configuration for a custom handler

```
@Bean
public DefaultErrorHandlingServiceActivator errorHandlingServiceActivator() {
    return new DefaultErrorHandlingServiceActivator();
}

@Bean
public IntegrationFlow errorFlow() {
    return IntegrationFlow
            .from("errorChannel")
            .handle(errorHandlingServiceActivator())
            .get();
}
```

The Java code is exactly as you'd expect it to be. Of course, the component that receives the error message from the errorChannel doesn't need to be a service activator. We just use it for convenience here. The code for the following service activator depicts some of the machinations you might go through to build a handler for the errorChannel.

Listing 12-17. Service activator for error handling

```
package com.apress.spring6recipes.springintegration;

import org.slf4j.Logger;
import org.slf4j.LoggerFactory;
import org.springframework.integration.annotation.ServiceActivator;
import org.springframework.messaging.Message;
import org.springframework.messaging.MessagingException;

public class DefaultErrorHandlingServiceActivator {

  private final Logger logger = LoggerFactory.getLogger(getClass());

  @ServiceActivator
  public void handleThrowable(Message<Throwable> errorMessage) {
    var throwable = errorMessage.getPayload();
    logger.error("Message: {}", throwable.getMessage(), throwable);

    if (throwable instanceof MessagingException me) {
      Message<?> failedMessage = me.getFailedMessage();

      if (failedMessage != null) {
        // do something with the original message
      }
    } else {
      // it's something that was thrown in the execution of code in some component
         you created
    }
  }
}
```

All errors thrown from Spring Integration components will be a subclass of MessagingException. MessagingException carries a pointer to the original Message that caused an error, which you can dissect for more context information. In the example, you're doing an instanceof. Clearly, being able to delegate to custom exception handlers based on the type of exception would be useful.

Routing to Custom Handlers Based on the Type of Exception

Sometimes, more specific error handling is required. In the following code, this router is configured as an exception type router, which in turn listens to errorChannel. It then splinters off, using the type of the exception as the predicate in determining which channel should get the results.

Listing 12-18. Integration configuration with exception routing

```
@Bean
public ErrorMessageExceptionTypeRouter exceptionTypeRouter() {
  var mappings = Map.of(
      MyCustomException.class.getName(), "customExceptionChannel",
      RuntimeException.class.getName(), "runtimeExceptionChannel",
      MessageHandlingException.class.getName(), "messageHandlingExceptionChannel"
  );
```

```
    var router = new ErrorMessageExceptionTypeRouter();
    router.setChannelMappings(mappings);
    return router;
}

@Bean
public IntegrationFlow errorFlow() {
    return IntegrationFlow
            .from("errorChannel")
            .route(exceptionTypeRouter())
            .get();
}
```

Building a Solution with Multiple Error Channels

The preceding example might work fine for simple cases, but often different integrations require different error handling approaches, which implies that sending all the errors to the same channel can eventually lead to a large switch-laden class that's too complex to maintain. Instead, it's better to selectively route error messages to the error channel most appropriate to each integration. This avoids centralizing all error handling. One way to do that is to explicitly specify on what channel errors for a given integration should go. The following example shows a component (service activator) that upon receiving a message, adds a header indicating the name of the error channel. Spring Integration will use that header and forward errors encountered in the processing of this message to that channel.

Listing 12-19. Service activator adding an error channel as header

```
package com.apress.springrecipes.springintegration;

import org.springframework.integration.annotation.ServiceActivator;
import org.springframework.integration.core.Message;
import org.springframework.integration.core.MessageHeaders;
import org.springframework.integration.message.MessageBuilder;

public class ServiceActivatorThatSpecifiesErrorChannel {

    @ServiceActivator
    public Message<?> startIntegrationFlow(Message<?> firstMessage)
        throws Throwable {
        return MessageBuilder.fromMessage(firstMessage).
            setHeaderIfAbsent( MessageHeaders.ERROR_CHANNEL,
                "errorChannelForMySolution").build();
    }
}
```

Thus, all errors that come from the integration in which this component is used will be directed to errorChannelForMySolution, to which you can subscribe any component you like.

12-7. Forking Integration Control: Splitters and Aggregators

Problem

You want to fork the process flow from one component to many, either all at once or to a single one based on a predicate condition.

Solution

You can use a splitter component and maybe its cohort, the aggregator component, to fork and join (respectively) control of processing.

How It Works

One of the fundamental cornerstones of an ESB is routing. You've seen how components can be chained together to create sequences in which progression is mostly linear. Some solutions require the capability to split a message into many constituent parts. One reason this might be is that some problems are parallel in nature and don't depend on each other in order to complete. You should strive to achieve the efficiencies of parallelism wherever possible.

Using a Splitter

It's often useful to divide large payloads into separate messages with separate processing flows. In Spring Integration, this is accomplished by using a splitter component. A splitter takes an input message and asks you, the user of the component, on what basis it should split the Message: you're responsible for providing the split functionality. Once you've told Spring Integration how to split a Message, it forwards each result out on the output channel of the splitter component. In a few cases, Spring Integration ships with useful splitters that require no customization. One example is the splitter provided to partition an XML payload along an XPath query, XPathMessageSplitter.

One example of a useful application of a splitter might be a text file with rows of data, each of which must be processed. Your goal is to be able to submit each row to a service that will handle the processing. What's required is a way to extract each row and forward each row as a new Message. The configuration for such a solution looks like the following.

Listing 12-20. Integration configuration

```
package com.apress.spring6recipes.springintegration;

import org.springframework.beans.factory.annotation.Value;
import org.springframework.context.annotation.Bean;
import org.springframework.context.annotation.Configuration;
import org.springframework.integration.config.EnableIntegration;
import org.springframework.integration.dsl.IntegrationFlow;
import org.springframework.integration.dsl.Pollers;
import org.springframework.integration.file.dsl.Files;

import java.io.File;
import java.time.Duration;
```

```
@Configuration
@EnableIntegration
public class IntegrationConfiguration {

    @Bean
    public CustomerBatchFileSplitter splitter() {
        return new CustomerBatchFileSplitter();
    }

    @Bean
    public CustomerDeletionServiceActivator customerDeletionServiceActivator() {
        return new CustomerDeletionServiceActivator();
    }

    @Bean
    public IntegrationFlow fileSplitAndDelete(
            @Value("file:${user.home}/customerstoremove/new/") File inputDirectory) {

        var poller = Pollers.fixedRate(Duration.ofSeconds(1));
        return IntegrationFlow.from(
                Files.inboundAdapter(inputDirectory)
                        .patternFilter("customerstoremove-*.txt"), c -> c.poller(poller))
                .split(splitter())
                .handle(customerDeletionServiceActivator())
                .get();
    }
}
```

The configuration for this is not terribly different from the previous solutions. The Java code is just about the same as well, except that the return type of the method annotated by the @Splitter annotation is of type java.util.Collection.

Listing 12-21. Splitter sample

```
package com.apress.spring6recipes.springintegration;

import org.springframework.integration.annotation.Splitter;

import java.io.File;
import java.io.IOException;
import java.nio.file.Files;
import java.util.Collection;

public class CustomerBatchFileSplitter {

    @Splitter
    public Collection<String> splitAFile(File file) throws IOException {
        System.out.printf("Reading %s....%n", file.getAbsolutePath());
        return Files.readAllLines(file.toPath());
    }
}
```

A message payload is passed in as a `java.io.File,` and the contents are read. The result (a collection or array value—in this case, a `Collection<String>`) is returned. Spring Integration executes a kind of for-each on the results, sending each value in the collection out on the output channel for the splitter (in this case an implicit channel as no channel has been explicitly provided). Often, you split messages so that the individual pieces can be forwarded to processing that's more focused. Because the message is more manageable, the processing requirements are dampened. This is true in many different architectures: in map/reduce solutions, tasks are split and then processed in parallel, and the fork/join constructs in a BPM system let control flow proceed in parallel so that the total work product can be achieved quicker.

Using Aggregators

At some point you'll need to do the reverse: combine many messages into one, and create a single result that can be returned on the output channel. An @Aggregator collects a series of messages (based on some correlation that you help Spring Integration make between the messages) and publishes a single message to the components downstream. Suppose that you know that you're expecting 22 different messages from 22 actors in the system, but you don't know when. This is similar to a company that auctions off a contract and collects all the bids from different vendors before choosing the ultimate vendor. The company can't accept a bid until all bids have been received from all companies. Otherwise, there's the risk of prematurely signing a contract that would not be in the best interest of the company. An aggregator is perfect for building this type of logic.

There are many ways for Spring Integration to correlate incoming messages. To determine how many messages to read until it can stop, it uses the `SimpleSequenceSizeReleaseStrategy` class, which reads a well-known header value (see Table 12-2) to calculate how many it should look for and to note the index of the message relative to the expected total count (e.g., 3/22). (Aggregators are often used after a splitter. Thus, the default header value is provided by the splitter, though there's nothing stopping you from creating the header parameters yourself.)

For correlation when you might not have a size but know that you're expecting messages that share a common header value within a known time, Spring Integration provides the `HeaderAttributeCorrelationStrategy`. In this way, it knows that all messages with that value are from the same group, in the same way that your last name identifies you as being part of a larger group.

Let's revisit the last example. Suppose that the file was split (by lines, each belonging to a new customer) and subsequently processed. You now want to reunite the customers and do some cleanup with everyone at the same time. In this example, you use the default completion strategy and correlation strategy, and as such you can use the default `aggregate()` in the integration flow configuration. The result is passed to another service activator, which will print a small summary.

Listing 12-22. Integration configuration

```
package com.apress.spring6recipes.springintegration;

import java.io.File;
import java.time.Duration;
import java.util.concurrent.TimeUnit;

import org.springframework.beans.factory.annotation.Value;
import org.springframework.context.annotation.Bean;
import org.springframework.context.annotation.Configuration;
import org.springframework.integration.config.EnableIntegration;
import org.springframework.integration.dsl.IntegrationFlow;
import org.springframework.integration.dsl.Pollers;
import org.springframework.integration.file.dsl.Files;
```

```
@Configuration
@EnableIntegration
public class IntegrationConfiguration {

  @Bean
  public CustomerBatchFileSplitter splitter() {
    return new CustomerBatchFileSplitter();
  }

  @Bean
  public CustomerDeletionServiceActivator customerDeletionServiceActivator() {
    return new CustomerDeletionServiceActivator();
  }

  @Bean
  public SummaryServiceActivator summaryServiceActivator() {
    return new SummaryServiceActivator();
  }

  @Bean
  public IntegrationFlow fileSplitAndDelete(
          @Value("file:${user.home}/customerstoremove/new/") File inputDirectory) throws
          Exception {
    var poller = Pollers.fixedRate(Duration.ofSeconds(1));
    return IntegrationFlow.from(
            Files.inboundAdapter(
            inputDirectory).patternFilter("customerstoremove-*.txt"),
            c -> c.poller(poller)).split(splitter())
            .handle(customerDeletionServiceActivator())
            .aggregate().handle(summaryServiceActivator()).get();
  }
}
```

The Java code for the SummaryServiceActivator is quite simple.

Listing 12-23. Summary service activator

```
package com.apress.spring6recipes.springintegration;

import org.springframework.integration.annotation.ServiceActivator;

import java.util.Collection;

public class SummaryServiceActivator {

    @ServiceActivator
    public void summary(Collection<Customer> customers) {
        System.out.printf("Removed %s customers.%n", customers.size());
    }
}
```

12-8. Conditional Routing with Routers

Problem

You want to conditionally move a message through different processes based on some criteria. This is the EAI equivalent to an if/else branch.

Solution

You can use a router component to alter the processing flow based on some predicate. You can also use a router to multicast a message to many subscribers (as you did with the splitter).

How It Works

With a router you can specify a known list of channels on which the incoming Message should be passed. This has some powerful implications. It means you can change the flow of a process conditionally, and it also means that you can forward a Message to as many (or as few) channels as you want. There are some convenient default routers available to fill common needs, such as payload type–based routing (PayloadTypeRouter) and routing to a group or list of channels (RecipientListRouter).

Imagine, for example, a processing pipeline that routes customers with high credit scores to one service and customers with lower credit scores to another process in which the information is queued up for a human audit and verification cycle. The configuration is, as usual, very straightforward. In the following example, you show the configuration. One router element, which in turn delegates the routing logic to a class, is CustomerCreditScoreRouter.

Listing 12-24. Integration configuration–inline router

```
@Bean
public IntegrationFlow fileSplitAndDelete(@Value
("file:${user.home}/customerstoimport/new/") File inputDirectory) throws Exception {

    return IntegrationFlow.from(
        Files.inboundAdapter(inputDirectory)
                .patternFilter("customers-*.txt"), c -> c.poller(Pollers.fixedRate(Duration.
                ofSeconds(1))))
            .split(splitter())
            .transform(transformer())
            .<Customer, Boolean>route(c -> c.getCreditScore() > 770,
                    m -> m
                        .channelMapping(Boolean.TRUE, "safeCustomerChannel")
                        .channelMapping(Boolean.FALSE, "riskyCustomerChannel").
                        applySequence(false)
    ).get();
}
```

Or you could use a class with a method annotated with @Router instead. It feels a lot like a workflow engine's conditional element or even a JSF backing bean method in that it extricates the routing logic into the XML configuration, away from code, delaying the decision until runtime. In the example, the strings returned are the names of the channels on which the Message should pass.

Listing 12-25. Integration configuration–dedicated router

```
package com.apress.spring6recipes.springintegration;

import org.springframework.integration.annotation.Router;

public class CustomerCreditScoreRouter {

    @Router
    public String routeByCustomerCreditScore(Customer customer) {
        if (customer.creditScore() > 770) {
            return "safeCustomerChannel";
        } else {
            return "riskyCustomerChannel";
        }
    }
}
```

If you decide that you'd rather not let the `Message` pass and want to stop processing, you can return `null` instead of a `String`.

12-9. Staging Events Using Spring Batch

Problem

You have a file with a million records in it. This file's too big to handle as one event; it's far more natural to react to each row as an event.

Solution

Spring Batch (see Chapter 8) works very well with these types of solutions. It allows you to take an input file or a payload and reliably, and systematically, decompose it into events that an ESB can work with.

How It Works

Spring Integration does support reading files into the bus, and Spring Batch does support providing custom, unique endpoints for data. However, just like Mom always says, "Just because you can doesn't mean you should." Although it seems as if there's a lot of overlap here, it turns out that there is a distinction (albeit a fine one). While both systems will work with files and message queues or anything else you could conceivably write code to talk to, Spring Integration doesn't do well with large payloads because it's hard to deal with something as large as a file with a million rows that might require hours of work as an event. That's simply too big a burden for an ESB. At that point, the term *event* has no meaning. A million records in a CSV file isn't an event on a bus; it's a file with a million records, each of which might in turn be events. It's a subtle distinction.

A file with a million rows needs to be decomposed into smaller events. Spring Batch can help here: it allows you to systematically read through, apply validations, and optionally skip and retry invalid records. The processing can begin on an ESB such as Spring Integration. Spring Batch and Spring Integration can be used together to build truly scalable decoupled systems.

Staged event-driven architecture (SEDA) is an architecture style that deals with this sort of processing situation. In SEDA, you dampen the load on components of the architecture by staging it in queues and let advance only what the components downstream can handle. Put another way, imagine video processing. If you ran a site with a million users uploading video that in turn needed to be transcoded and you only had ten servers, your system would fail if your system attempted to process each video as soon as it received the uploaded video. Transcoding can take hours and pegs a CPU (or multiple CPUs!) while it works. The most sensible thing to do would be to store the file and then, as capacity permits, process each one. In this way, the load on the nodes that handle transcoding is managed. There's always only enough work to keep the machine humming, but not overrun.

Similarly, no processing system (such as an ESB) can deal with a million records at once efficiently. Strive to decompose bigger events and messages into smaller ones. Let's imagine a hypothetical solution designed to accommodate a drop of batch files representing hourly sales destined for fulfillment. The batch files are dropped onto a mount that Spring Integration is monitoring. Spring Integration kicks off processing as soon as it sees a new file. Spring Integration tells Spring Batch about the file and launches a Spring Batch job asynchronously.

Spring Batch reads the file, transforms the records into objects, and writes the output to a JMS topic with a key correlating the original batch to the JMS message. Naturally, this takes half a day to get done, but it does get done. Spring Integration, completely unaware that the job it started half a day ago is now finished, begins popping messages off the topic, one by one. Processing to fulfill the records would begin. Simple processing involving multiple components might begin on the ESB.

If fulfillment is a long-lived process with a long-lived, conversational state involving many actors, perhaps the fulfillment for each record could be farmed to a BPM engine. The BPM engine would thread together the different actors and work lists and allow work to continue over the course of days instead of the small millisecond timeframes Spring Integration is more geared to. In this example, we talked about using Spring Batch as a springboard to dampen the load for components downstream. In this case, the component downstream was again a Spring Integration process that took the work and set it up to be funneled into a BPM engine where final processing could begin. Spring Integration could use directory polling as a trigger to start a batch job and for the start supply the name of the file to process. To launch a job from Spring Integration, Spring Batch provides the JobLaunchingMessageHandler. This class takes a JobLaunchRequest to determine which job with which parameters to start. You have to create a transformer to change the incoming Message<File> to a JobLaunchRequest.

The transformer could look like the following.

Listing 12-26. Transformer for JobLaunchRequest

```
package com.apress.spring6recipes.springintegration;

import org.springframework.batch.core.Job;
import org.springframework.batch.core.JobParametersBuilder;
import org.springframework.batch.integration.launch.JobLaunchRequest;
import org.springframework.integration.annotation.Transformer;

import java.io.File;

public class FileToJobLaunchRequestTransformer {

    private final Job job;
    private final String fileParameterName;

    public FileToJobLaunchRequestTransformer(Job job, String fileParameterName) {
        this.job=job;
        this.fileParameterName=fileParameterName;
    }
```

```
    @Transformer
    public JobLaunchRequest transform(File file) {
        var builder = new JobParametersBuilder();
        builder.addString(fileParameterName, file.getAbsolutePath());
        return new JobLaunchRequest(job, builder.toJobParameters());
    }
}
```

The transformer needs a Job and a `filename` parameter to be constructed. This parameter is used in the Spring Batch job to determine which file needs to be loaded. The incoming message is transformed into a `JobLaunchRequest` using the full name of the file as a parameter value. This request can be used to launch a batch job.

To wire everything together, the following configuration could be used (note the Spring Batch setup is missing here; see Chapter 8 for information on setting up Spring Batch).

Listing 12-27. Integration configuration–Spring Batch integration

```
package com.apress.spring6recipes.springintegration;

import org.springframework.batch.core.Job;
import org.springframework.batch.core.launch.JobLauncher;
import org.springframework.batch.integration.launch.JobLaunchingMessageHandler;
import org.springframework.beans.factory.annotation.Value;
import org.springframework.context.annotation.Bean;
import org.springframework.integration.dsl.IntegrationFlow;
import org.springframework.integration.dsl.Pollers;
import org.springframework.integration.file.dsl.Files;

import java.io.File;
import java.time.Duration;

public class IntegrationConfiguration {

  @Bean
  public FileToJobLaunchRequestTransformer transformer(Job job) {
    return new FileToJobLaunchRequestTransformer(job, "filename");
  }

  @Bean
  public JobLaunchingMessageHandler jobLaunchingMessageHandler(JobLauncher launcher) {
    return new JobLaunchingMessageHandler(launcher);
  }

  @Bean
  public IntegrationFlow fileToBatchFlow(
            @Value("file:${user.home}/customerstoimport/new/") File directory,
            FileToJobLaunchRequestTransformer transformer,
            JobLaunchingMessageHandler handler) {
    return IntegrationFlow
                .from(
                    Files.inboundAdapter(directory)
                        .patternFilter("customers-*.txt"),
```

```
                c -> c.poller(Pollers.fixedRate(Duration.ofSeconds(1))))
            .transform(transformer)
            .handle(handler)
        .get();
    }
}
```

The `FileToJobLaunchRequestTransformer` is configured, as well as the `JobLaunchingMessageHandler`. A file inbound channel adapter is used to poll for files. When a file is detected, a message is placed on a channel. A chain is configured to listen to that channel. When a message is received, it is first transformed and next passed on to the `JobLaunchingMessageHandler`.

Now a batch job will be launched to process the file. A typical job would probably use a `FlatFileItemReader` to actually read the file passed using the `filename` parameter. A `JmsItemWriter` could be used to write messages per read row on a topic. In Spring Integration a JMS inbound channel adapter could be used to receive to messages and process them.

12-10. Using Gateways

Problem

You want to expose an interface to clients of your service, without betraying the fact that your service is implemented in terms of messaging middleware.

Solution

Use a gateway—a pattern from the classic book *Enterprise Integration Patterns* by Gregor Hohpe and Bobby Woolf (Addison-Wesley, 2004)–that enjoys rich support in Spring Integration.

How It Works

A gateway is a distinct animal, similar to a lot of other patterns but ultimately different enough to warrant its own consideration. You used adapters in previous examples to enable two systems to speak in terms of foreign, loosely coupled, middleware components. This foreign component can be anything: the file system, JMS queues/topics, Twitter, and so on.

You also know what a façade is, serving to abstract away the functionality of other components in an abbreviated interface to provide courser functionality. You might use a façade to build an interface oriented around vacation planning that in turn abstracts away the minutiae of using a car rental, hotel reservation, and airline reservation system.

You build a gateway, on the other hand, to provide an interface for your system that insulates clients from the middleware or messaging in your system, so that they're not dependent on JMS or Spring Integration APIs, for example. A gateway allows you to express compile-time constraints on the inputs and outputs of your system.

There are several reasons you might want to do this. First, it's cleaner. If you have the latitude to insist that clients comply with an interface, this is a good way to provide that interface. Your use of middleware can be an implementation detail. Perhaps your architecture's messaging middleware can be to exploit the performance increases had by leveraging asynchronous messaging, but you didn't intend for those performance gains to come at the cost of a precise, explicit external-facing interface.

This feature—the capability to hide messaging behind a POJO interface—is very interesting and has been the focus of several other projects. Lingo, a project from Codehaus.org that is no longer under active development, had such a feature that was specific to JMS and the Java EE Connector Architecture (JCA—it was originally used to talk about the Java Cryptography Architecture, but is more commonly used for the Java EE Connector Architecture now). Since then, the developers have moved on to work on Apache Camel.

In this recipe, you'll explore Spring Integration's core support for messaging gateways and explore its support for message exchange patterns. Then, you'll see how to completely remove implementation details from the client-facing interface.

MessagingGatewaySupport

The most fundamental support for gateways comes from the Spring Integration class MessagingGatewaySupport. The class provides the ability to specify a channel on which requests should be sent and a channel on which responses are expected. Finally, the channel on which replies are sent can be specified. This gives you the ability to express in-out and in-only patterns on top of your existing messaging systems. This class supports working in terms of payloads, isolating you from the gory details of the messages being sent and received. This is already one level of abstraction. You could, conceivably, use the MessagingGatewaySupport and Spring Integration's concept of channels to interface with file systems, JMS, email, or any other system and deal simply with payloads and channels. There are implementations already provided for you to support some of these common endpoints such as web services and JMS.

Let's look at using a generic messaging gateway. In this example, you'll send messages to a service activator and then receive the response. You manually interface with the MessagingGatewaySupport so that you can see how convenient it is.

As MessagingGatewaySupport is an abstract class, let's define a small class so we can utilize the support provided by this class.

Listing 12-28. Simple messaging gateway

```
package com.apress.spring6recipes.springintegration;

import org.springframework.integration.gateway.MessagingGatewaySupport;

public class SimpleMessagingGateway extends MessagingGatewaySupport {

    @SuppressWarnings("unchecked")
    public <T> T convertSendAndReceive(Object payload) {
        return (T) super.sendAndReceive(payload);
    }
}
```

The class extends MessagingGatewaySupport and adds a convertSendAndReceive method, which calls the provided sendAndReceive method and converts the response to the proper type.

Listing 12-29. Main class

```
package com.apress.spring6recipes.springintegration;

import org.springframework.context.annotation.AnnotationConfigApplicationContext;
import org.springframework.integration.gateway.GatewayProxyFactoryBean;
import org.springframework.messaging.MessageChannel;
```

```java
public class Main {

    public static void main(String[] args) {
        var cfg = AdditionConfiguration.class;
        try (var ctx = new AnnotationConfigApplicationContext(cfg)) {
            var request = ctx.getBean("request", MessageChannel.class);
            var response = ctx.getBean("response", MessageChannel.class);

            var gateway = new GatewayProxyFactoryBean();
            gateway.setDefaultRequestChannel(request);
            gateway.setDefaultReplyChannel(response);
            gateway.setBeanFactory(ctx);
            gateway.afterPropertiesSet();;
            gateway.start();

            var msgGateway = new SimpleMessagingGateway();
            msgGateway.setRequestChannel(request);
            msgGateway.setReplyChannel(response);
            msgGateway.setBeanFactory(ctx);
            msgGateway.afterPropertiesSet();
            msgGateway.start();

            Number result = msgGateway.convertSendAndReceive(new Operands(22, 4));
            System.out.printf("Result: %f%n", result.floatValue());
        }
    }
}
```

The interfacing is very straightforward. The SimpleMessagingGateway needs a request and a response channel, and it coordinates the rest. In this case, you're doing nothing but forwarding the request to a service activator, which in turn adds the operands and sends them out on the reply channel. The configuration is sparse because most of the work is done in those five lines of Java code.

Listing 12-30. Integration configuration

```java
package com.apress.spring6recipes.springintegration;

import org.springframework.context.annotation.Bean;
import org.springframework.context.annotation.Configuration;
import org.springframework.integration.config.EnableIntegration;
import org.springframework.integration.dsl.IntegrationFlow;

@Configuration
@EnableIntegration
public class AdditionConfiguration {

    @Bean
    public AdditionService additionService() {
        return new AdditionService();
    }
```

```
    @Bean
    public IntegrationFlow additionFlow() {
        return IntegrationFlow.from("request")
                .handle(additionService(), "add")
                .channel("response").get();
    }
}
```

The configuration uses the request channel; anything that is received is passed on to the AdditionService while calling the add method. The result of the add method is then placed on the response channel, so that interested parties can obtain it. As our SimpleMessagingGateway puts the Operands on the request channel, it will return the result from the response channel (see the main class in Listing 12-29).

Breaking the Interface Dependency

The previous example demonstrates what's happening behind the scenes. You're dealing only with Spring Integration interfaces and are isolated from the nuances of the endpoints. However, there are still plenty of inferred constraints that a client might easily fail to comply with. The simplest solution is to hide the messaging behind an interface. Let's look at building a fictional hotel reservation search engine. Searching for a hotel might take a long time, and ideally processing should be offloaded to a separate server. An ideal solution is JMS because you could implement the aggressive consumer pattern and scale simply by adding more consumers. The client would still block waiting for the result, in this example, but the server(s) would not be overloaded or in a blocking state.

You'll build two Spring Integration solutions: one for the client (which will in turn contain the gateway) and one for the service itself, which, presumably, is on a separate host connected to the client only by way of well-known message queues.

Let's look at the client configuration first. The first thing that the client configuration does is declare a ConnectionFactory. Then you declare the flow that starts with the gateway for the VacationService interface. The gateway element simply exists to identify the component and the interface, to which the proxy is cast and made available to clients. The JMS outbound gateway is the component that does most of the work. It takes the message you created and sends it to the request JMS destination, setting up the reply headers and so on. Finally, you declare a generic gateway element, which does most of the magic.

Listing 12-31. Integration configuration–client

```
package com.apress.spring6recipes.springintegration;

import com.apress.spring6recipes.springintegration.myholiday.VacationService;
import org.apache.activemq.artemis.jms.client.ActiveMQConnectionFactory;
import org.springframework.context.annotation.Bean;
import org.springframework.context.annotation.Configuration;
import org.springframework.integration.config.EnableIntegration;
import org.springframework.integration.dsl.IntegrationFlow;
import org.springframework.integration.jms.dsl.Jms;
import org.springframework.jms.connection.CachingConnectionFactory;

@Configuration
@EnableIntegration
public class ClientIntegrationConfig {
```

```
@Bean
public CachingConnectionFactory connectionFactory() {
  var connectionFactory = new ActiveMQConnectionFactory("tcp://localhost:61616");
  return new CachingConnectionFactory(connectionFactory);
}


@Bean
public IntegrationFlow vacationGatewayFlow() {
    return IntegrationFlow
            .from(VacationService.class)
            .handle(
                Jms.outboundGateway(connectionFactory())
                        .requestDestination("inboundHotelReservationSearchDestination")
                        .replyDestination("outboundHotelReservationSearchResults
                        Destination"))
              .get();
    }
}
```

To be able to use the VacationService as a gateway itself, it needs to be annotated with the
@MessagingGateway annotation, and the method that serves as the entry point needs to be annotated
with @Gateway.

Listing 12-32. Vacation service interface

```
package com.apress.spring6recipes.springintegration.myholiday;

import org.springframework.integration.annotation.Gateway;
import org.springframework.integration.annotation.MessagingGateway;

import java.util.List;

@MessagingGateway
public interface VacationService {

    @Gateway
    List<HotelReservation> findHotels(HotelReservationSearch search);
}
```

This is the client-facing interface. There is no coupling between the client-facing interface exposed
via the gateway component and the interface of the service that ultimately handles the messages. We use
the interface for the service and the client to simplify the names needed to understand everything that's
going on. This is not like traditional, synchronous remoting in which the service interface and the client
interface match.

In this example, you're using two very simple objects for demonstration: HotelReservationSearch and
HotelReservation. There is nothing interesting about these objects in the slightest; they are simple POJOs
that implement Serializable and contain a few accessor/mutators to flesh out the example domain.

Listing 12-33. HotelReservationSearch and HotelReservation

```java
package com.apress.spring6recipes.springintegration.myholiday;

import java.io.Serializable;
import java.time.LocalDate;

public record HotelReservationSearch (
        int roomsDesired, LocalDate start,
        LocalDate stop, double maxPrice) implements Serializable {
}
```

```java
package com.apress.spring6recipes.springintegration.myholiday;

import java.io.Serializable;
import java.util.Objects;
import java.util.UUID;

public record HotelReservation(String id, String hotelName, double price)
  implements Serializable {

  public HotelReservation(String hotelName, double price) {
    this(UUID.randomUUID().toString(), hotelName, price);
  }
}
```

The client Java code demonstrates how all of this comes together:

```java
package com.apress.spring6recipes.springintegration;

import java.time.LocalDate;

import org.springframework.context.annotation.AnnotationConfigApplicationContext;

import com.apress.spring6recipes.springintegration.myholiday.HotelReservationSearch;
import com.apress.spring6recipes.springintegration.myholiday.VacationService;

public class Main {

  public static void main(String[] args) throws Throwable {
    try (var serverCtx = new AnnotationConfigApplicationContext(ServerIntegrationConte
    xt.class);
         var clientCtx = new AnnotationConfigApplicationContext(ClientIntegrationConfig.
         class)) {

      var vacationService = clientCtx.getBean(VacationService.class);

      var now = LocalDate.now();
      var start = now.plusDays(1);
      var stop = now.plusDays(8);
      var hotelReservationSearch = new HotelReservationSearch(2, start, stop, 200f);
      var results = vacationService.findHotels(hotelReservationSearch);
```

```
        System.out.printf("Found %s results.%n", results.size());
        results.forEach(r -> System.out.printf("\t%s%n", r));
    }
  }
}
```

It just doesn't get any cleaner than that! No Spring Integration interfaces whatsoever. You make a request, searching is done, and you get the result back when the processing is done. The service implementation for this setup is interesting, not because of what you've added, but because of what's not there:

```
package com.apress.spring6recipes.springintegration;

import org.apache.activemq.artemis.jms.client.ActiveMQConnectionFactory;
import org.springframework.context.annotation.Bean;
import org.springframework.context.annotation.Configuration;
import org.springframework.integration.config.EnableIntegration;
import org.springframework.integration.dsl.IntegrationFlow;
import org.springframework.integration.jms.dsl.Jms;
import org.springframework.jms.connection.CachingConnectionFactory;

import com.apress.spring6recipes.springintegration.myholiday.VacationServiceImpl;

@Configuration
@EnableIntegration
public class ServerIntegrationContext {

  @Bean
  public CachingConnectionFactory connectionFactory() {
    var url = "tcp://localhost:61616";
    var connectionFactory = new ActiveMQConnectionFactory(url);
    return new CachingConnectionFactory(connectionFactory);
  }

  @Bean
  public VacationServiceImpl vacationService() {
    return new VacationServiceImpl();
  }

  @Bean
  public IntegrationFlow serverIntegrationFlow() {
    return IntegrationFlow.from(
            Jms.inboundGateway(connectionFactory())
                    .requestDestination("inboundHotelReservationSearchDestination"))
            .handle(vacationService()).get();
  }
}
```

Here, you've defined an inbound JMS gateway. The messages from the inbound JMS gateway are put on a channel, whose messages are forwarded to a service activator, as you would expect. The service activator is what handles actual processing. What's interesting here is that there's no mention of a response channel, for either the service activator or the inbound JMS gateway. The service activator looks for, and fails to find, a reply channel and so uses the reply channel created by the inbound JMS gateway component, which in turn has created the reply channel based on the header metadata in the inbound JMS message. Thus, everything just works without specification.

The implementation is a simple useless implementation of the interface:

```
package com.apress.spring6recipes.springintegration.myholiday;

import com.apress.spring6recipes.utils.Utils;
import jakarta.annotation.PostConstruct;
import org.springframework.integration.annotation.ServiceActivator;

import java.util.List;
import java.util.concurrent.TimeUnit;

public class VacationServiceImpl implements VacationService {

    private List<HotelReservation> hotelReservations;

    @PostConstruct
    public void afterPropertiesSet() {
        hotelReservations = List.of(
                new HotelReservation("Bilton", 243.200F),
                new HotelReservation("East Western", 75.0F),
                new HotelReservation("Thairfield Inn", 70F),
                new HotelReservation("Park In The Inn", 200.00F));
    }

    @ServiceActivator
    public List<HotelReservation> findHotels(HotelReservationSearch search) {
        Utils.sleep(1, TimeUnit.SECONDS);
        return this.hotelReservations.stream()
                .filter((hr) -> hr.price() <= search.maxPrice())
                .toList();
    }
}
```

12-11. Summary

This chapter discussed building an integration solution using Spring Integration, an ESB-like framework built on top of the Spring Framework. You were introduced to the core concepts of enterprise application integration (EAI). You learned how to handle a few integration scenarios, including JMS and file polling.

In the next chapter, you will explore the capabilities of Spring in the field of testing.

CHAPTER 13

■ ■ ■

Spring Testing

In this chapter, you will learn about basic techniques you can use to test Java applications and the testing support features offered by the Spring Framework. These features can make your testing tasks easier and lead you to better application design. In general, applications developed with the Spring Framework and the dependency injection pattern are easy to test.

Testing is a key activity for ensuring quality in software development. There are many types of testing, including unit testing, integration testing, functional testing, system testing, performance testing, and acceptance testing. Spring's testing support focuses on unit and integration testing, but it can also help with other types of testing. Testing can be performed either manually or automatically. However, since automated tests can be run repeatedly and continuously at different phases of a development process, they are highly recommended, especially in Agile development processes. The Spring Framework is an Agile framework that fits these kinds of processes.

Many testing frameworks are available on the Java platform. Currently, JUnit and TestNG are the most popular. JUnit has a long history and a large user group in the Java community. TestNG is another popular Java testing framework.

Spring's testing support features have been offered by the Spring TestContext framework. This framework abstracts the underlying testing framework with the following concepts:

- Test context: This encapsulates the context of a test's execution, including the application context, test class, current test instance, current test method, and current test exception.

- Test context manager: This manages a test context for a test and triggers test execution listeners at predefined test execution points, including when preparing a test instance, before executing a test method (before any framework-specific initialization methods), and after executing a test method (after any framework-specific cleanup methods).

- Test execution listener: This defines a listener interface; by implementing this, you can listen to test execution events. The TestContext framework provides several test execution listeners for common testing features, but you are free to create your own.

Spring provides convenient TestContext support classes for JUnit, JUnit Jupiter, and TestNG, with particular test execution listeners preregistered. You can simply extend these support classes to use the TestContext framework without having to know much about the framework details.

After finishing this chapter, you will understand the basic concepts and techniques of testing and the popular Java testing frameworks JUnit and TestNG. You will also be able to create unit tests and integration tests using the Spring TestContext framework.

13-1. Creating Tests with JUnit and TestNG
Problem

You would like to create automated tests for your Java application so that they can be run repeatedly to ensure the correctness of your application.

Solution

The most popular testing frameworks on the Java platform are JUnit and TestNG. Both JUnit and TestNG allow you to annotate your test methods with a @Test annotation, so an arbitrary method can be run as a test case.

How It Works

Suppose you are going to develop a system for a bank. To ensure the system's quality, you have to test every part of it. First, let's consider an interest calculator, whose interface is defined as follows.

Listing 13-1. InterestCalculator interface

```
package com.apress.spring6recipes.bank;

public interface InterestCalculator {

  void setRate(double rate);
  double calculate(double amount, double year);
}
```

Each interest calculator requires a fixed interest rate to be set. Now, you can implement this calculator with a simple interest formula.

Listing 13-2. InterestCalculator implementation

```
package com.apress.spring6recipes.bank;

public class SimpleInterestCalculator implements InterestCalculator {

  private double rate;

  @Override
  public void setRate(double rate) {
    this.rate = rate;
  }

  @Override
  public double calculate(double amount, double year) {
    if (amount < 0 || year < 0) {
      throw new IllegalArgumentException("Amount or year must be positive");
    }
    return amount * year * rate;
  }
}
```

Next, you will test this simple interest calculator with the popular testing frameworks JUnit Jupiter and TestNG.

💡 Usually, a test and its target class are located in the same package, but the source files of tests are stored in a separate directory (e.g., test) from the source files of other classes (e.g., src).

Testing with JUnit

A test case is a method with the @Test annotation. To set up data, you can annotate a method with @BeforeEach. To clean up resources, you can annotate a method with @AfterEach. You can also annotate a static method with @BeforeAll or @AfterAll to have it run once before or after all test cases in the class.

You have to call the static assert methods declared in the org.junit.jupiter.api.Assertions class directly. However, you can import all assert methods via a static import statement. You can create the following JUnit Jupiter test cases to test your simple interest calculator.

💡 Another popular option is to use the AssertJ library to write clear and concise assertions.

ℹ️ To compile and run test cases created for JUnit Jupiter, you have to include JUnit Jupiter in your CLASSPATH. If you are using Maven, add the following dependency to your project:

```
<dependency>
  <groupId>org.junit.jupiter</groupId>
  <artifactId>junit-jupiter</artifactId>
  <version>5.9.1</version>
</dependency>
```

Or add the following for Gradle:

```
testImplementation 'org.junit.jupiter:junit-jupiter:5.9.1'
```

Listing 13-3. JUnit Jupiter InterestCalculator tests

```
package com.apress.spring6recipes.bank;

import org.junit.jupiter.api.BeforeEach;
import org.junit.jupiter.api.Test;

import static org.junit.jupiter.api.Assertions.assertEquals;
import static org.junit.jupiter.api.Assertions.assertThrows;

class SimpleInterestCalculatorTests {

  private InterestCalculator interestCalculator;
```

```
@BeforeEach
void init() {
  interestCalculator = new SimpleInterestCalculator();
  interestCalculator.setRate(0.05);
}

@Test
void calculate() {
  var interest = interestCalculator.calculate(10000, 2);
  assertEquals(1000.0, interest, 0);
}

@Test
void illegalCalculate() {
  assertThrows(IllegalArgumentException.class,
         () -> interestCalculator.calculate(-10000, 2));
}

}
```

JUnit Jupiter offers a powerful feature that allows you to expect an exception to be thrown in a test case. You can use the assertThrows method from the Assertions class to write expectations for the expected exceptional outcome.

Data-Driven Testing with JUnit

Another feature of JUnit Jupiter is that you can easily write data-driven tests. For this one needs an argument source. Several are provided out of the box with Junit Jupiter, like @CsvSource (using an inline CSV as source) and @MethodSource (using a method as source). The mechanism is extensible, so you could also write your own.

We could extend the earlier test to use a method annotated with @MethodSource to generate the arguments. The test method needs to be modified to receive those arguments so they can be used. With the changes it becomes easier to write tests for different variations of the data.

Listing 13-4. Data-driven test with @MethodSource

```
package com.apress.spring6recipes.bank;

import org.junit.jupiter.api.BeforeEach;
import org.junit.jupiter.params.ParameterizedTest;
import org.junit.jupiter.params.provider.Arguments;
import org.junit.jupiter.params.provider.MethodSource;

import java.util.stream.Stream;

import static org.junit.jupiter.api.Assertions.assertEquals;
import static org.junit.jupiter.api.Assertions.assertThrows;

class SimpleInterestCalculatorTests {

  private InterestCalculator interestCalculator;
```

```java
@BeforeEach
void init() {
  interestCalculator = new SimpleInterestCalculator();
  interestCalculator.setRate(0.05);
}

private static Stream<Arguments> calculateSource() {
  return Stream.of(
          Arguments.of(10000.0, 2, 1000.0),
          Arguments.of(10000.0, 1, 500.0)
  );
}

private static Stream<Arguments> illegalCalculateSource() {
  return Stream.of(
          Arguments.of(-10000.0, 2),
          Arguments.of(10000.0, -2),
          Arguments.of(-10000.0, -2)
  );
}

@ParameterizedTest
@MethodSource("calculateSource")
void calculate(double amount, double year, double expectedInterest) {
  var interest = interestCalculator.calculate(amount, year);
  assertEquals(expectedInterest, interest, 0);
}

@ParameterizedTest
@MethodSource("illegalCalculateSource")
void illegalCalculate(double amount, double year) {
  assertThrows(IllegalArgumentException.class,
          () -> interestCalculator.calculate(amount, year));
}

}
```

If you run this test, the `calculate` method will run twice as the `calculateSource` returns two datasets, and the `illegalCalculate` method will run three times, as there are three datasets returned by the `illegalCalculateSource`.

Testing with TestNG

A TestNG test looks very similar to a JUnit test, except that you have to use the classes and annotation types defined by the TestNG framework.

ℹ️ To compile and run test cases created for TestNG, you have to add TestNG to your CLASSPATH. If you are using Maven, add the following dependency to your project:

```
<dependency>
  <groupId>org.testng</groupId>
  <artifactId>testng</artifactId>
  <version>7.6.1</version>
</dependency>
```

Or add the following for Gradle:

```
testImplementation 'org.testng:testng:7.6.1'
```

Listing 13-5. TestNG InterestCalculator tests

```
package com.apress.spring6recipes.bank;

import org.testng.annotations.BeforeMethod;
import org.testng.annotations.Test;

import static org.testng.Assert.assertEquals;

public class SimpleInterestCalculatorTests {

  private InterestCalculator interestCalculator;

  @BeforeMethod
  public void init() {
    interestCalculator = new SimpleInterestCalculator();
    interestCalculator.setRate(0.05);
  }

  @Test
  public void calculate() {
    var interest = interestCalculator.calculate(10000, 2);
    assertEquals(interest, 1000.0);
  }

  @Test(expectedExceptions = IllegalArgumentException.class)
  public void illegalCalculate() {
    interestCalculator.calculate(-10000, 2);
  }

}
```

💡 If you are using Eclipse for development, you can download and install the TestNG Eclipse plugin from `https://testng.org/doc/eclipse.html` to run TestNG tests in Eclipse. Again, you will see a green bar if all your tests pass and a red bar otherwise.

Data-Driven Testing with TestNG

One of the powerful features of TestNG is its built-in support for data-driven testing. TestNG cleanly separates test data from test logic so that you can run a test method multiple times for different datasets. In TestNG, test datasets are provided by data providers, which are methods with the @DataProvider annotation.

Listing 13-6. Data-driven TestNG InterestCalculator tests

```
package com.apress.spring6recipes.bank;

import org.testng.annotations.BeforeMethod;
import org.testng.annotations.DataProvider;
import org.testng.annotations.Test;

import static org.testng.Assert.assertEquals;

public class SimpleInterestCalculatorTests {

  private InterestCalculator interestCalculator;

  @BeforeMethod
  public void init() {
    interestCalculator = new SimpleInterestCalculator();
    interestCalculator.setRate(0.05);
  }

  @DataProvider(name = "legal")
  public Object[][] createLegalInterestParameters() {
    return new Object[][] {
            new Object[] { 10000, 2, 1000.0 },
            new Object[] {10000.0, 1, 500.0}};
  }

  @DataProvider(name = "illegal")
  public Object[][] createIllegalInterestParameters() {
    return new Object[][] {
            new Object[] { -10000, 2 },
            new Object[] { 10000, -2 },
            new Object[] { -10000, -2 } };
  }
}
```

671

```
@Test(dataProvider = "legal")
public void calculate(double amount, double year, double result) {
  double interest = interestCalculator.calculate(amount, year);
  assertEquals(interest, result);
}

@Test(dataProvider = "illegal", expectedExceptions = IllegalArgumentException.class)
public void illegalCalculate(double amount, double year) {
  interestCalculator.calculate(amount, year);
}
}
```

If you run the preceding test with TestNG, the calculate() method will be executed twice as the legal data provider returns two datasets, while the illegalCalculate() method will be executed three times, as there are three datasets returned by the illegal data provider.

13-2. Creating Unit Tests and Integration Tests

Problem

A common testing technique is to test each module of your application in isolation and then test them in combination. You would like to apply this skill in testing your Java applications.

Solution

Unit tests are used to test a single programming unit. In object-oriented languages, a unit is usually a class or a method. The scope of a unit test is a single unit, but in the real world, most units won't work in isolation. They often need to cooperate with others to complete their tasks. When testing a unit that depends on other units, a common technique you can apply is to simulate the unit dependencies with stubs and mock objects, both of which can reduce complexity of your unit tests caused by dependencies.

A stub is an object that simulates a dependent object with the minimum number of methods required for a test. The methods are implemented in a predetermined way, usually with hard-coded data. A stub also exposes methods for a test to verify the stub's internal states. In contrast to a stub, a mock object usually knows how its methods are expected to be called in a test. The mock object then verifies the methods actually called against the expected ones. In Java, there are several libraries that can help create mock objects, like Mockito, EasyMock, and jMock. The main difference between a stub and a mock object is that a stub is usually used for state verification, while a mock object is used for behavior verification.

Integration tests, in contrast, are used to test several units in combination as a whole. They test if the integration and interaction between units are correct. Each of these units should already have been tested with unit tests, so integration testing is usually performed after unit testing.

Finally, note that applications developed using the principle of separating interface from implementation and the dependency injection pattern are easy to test, both for unit testing and integration testing. This is because that principle and pattern can reduce coupling between different units of your application.

How It Works

Creating Unit Tests for Isolated Classes

The core functions of your bank system should be designed around customer accounts. First, you create the following domain class, Account, with a custom equals() and hashCode() method.

Listing 13-7. Account class

```java
package com.apress.spring6recipes.bank;

import java.util.Objects;

public class Account {

  private final String accountNo;
  private double balance;

  public Account(String accountNo, double balance) {
    this.accountNo = accountNo;
    this.balance = balance;
  }

  public String getAccountNo() {
    return accountNo;
  }

  public double getBalance() {
    return balance;
  }

  public void setBalance(double balance) {
    this.balance = balance;
  }

  @Override
  public boolean equals(Object o) {
    if (this == o)
      return true;
    if (o instanceof Account account)
      return Objects.equals(accountNo, account.accountNo);
    return false;
  }

  @Override
  public int hashCode() {
    return Objects.hash(accountNo);
  }

  @Override
  public String toString() {
    return String.format("Account [accountNo='%s', balance=%d]", accountNo, balance);
  }
}
```

Next, you define the following DAO interface for persisting account objects in your bank system's persistence layer.

Listing 13-8. AccountDao interface

```
package com.apress.spring6recipes.bank;

public interface AccountDao {

  void createAccount(Account account);
  void updateAccount(Account account);
  void removeAccount(Account account);
  Account findAccount(String accountNo);
}
```

To demonstrate the unit testing concept, let's implement this interface by using a java.util.Map to store account objects. The AccountNotFoundException and DuplicateAccountException classes are subclasses of RuntimeException that you should be able to create yourself.

Listing 13-9. In-memory AccountDao implementation

```
package com.apress.spring6recipes.bank;

import java.util.Map;
import java.util.concurrent.ConcurrentHashMap;

class InMemoryAccountDao implements AccountDao {

  private final Map<String, Account> accounts = new ConcurrentHashMap<>();

  boolean accountExists(String accountNo) {
    return accounts.containsKey(accountNo);
  }

  @Override
  public void createAccount(Account account) {
    if (accountExists(account.getAccountNo())) {
      throw new DuplicateAccountException();
    }
    accounts.put(account.getAccountNo(), account);
  }

  @Override
  public void updateAccount(Account account) {
    if (!accountExists(account.getAccountNo())) {
      throw new AccountNotFoundException();
    }
    accounts.put(account.getAccountNo(), account);
  }

  @Override
  public void removeAccount(Account account) {
    if (!accountExists(account.getAccountNo())) {
      throw new AccountNotFoundException();
    }
```

```
      accounts.remove(account.getAccountNo());
  }

  @Override
  public Account findAccount(String accountNo) {
    var account = accounts.get(accountNo);
    if (account == null) {
      throw new AccountNotFoundException();
    }
    return account;
  }
}
```

Now, let's create unit tests for this DAO implementation with JUnit. As this class doesn't depend directly on other classes, it's easy to test. To ensure that this class works properly for exceptional cases as well as normal cases, you should also create exceptional test cases for it. Typically, exceptional test cases expect an exception to be thrown.

Listing 13-10. In-memory AccountDao JUnit Jupiter tests

```
package com.apress.spring6recipes.bank;

import org.junit.jupiter.api.BeforeEach;
import org.junit.jupiter.api.Test;

import static org.junit.jupiter.api.Assertions.*;

class InMemoryAccountDaoTests {

  private static final String EXISTING_ACCOUNT_NO = "1234";
  private static final String NEW_ACCOUNT_NO = "5678";

  private Account existingAccount;
  private Account newAccount;
  private InMemoryAccountDao accountDao;

  @BeforeEach
  void init() {
    existingAccount = new Account(EXISTING_ACCOUNT_NO, 100);
    newAccount = new Account(NEW_ACCOUNT_NO, 200);
    accountDao = new InMemoryAccountDao();
    accountDao.createAccount(existingAccount);
  }

  @Test
  void accountExists() {
    assertTrue(accountDao.accountExists(EXISTING_ACCOUNT_NO));
    assertFalse(accountDao.accountExists(NEW_ACCOUNT_NO));
  }
```

```java
@Test
void createNewAccount() {
  accountDao.createAccount(newAccount);
  assertEquals(newAccount, accountDao.findAccount(NEW_ACCOUNT_NO));
}

@Test
void createDuplicateAccount() {
  assertThrows(DuplicateAccountException.class,
          () -> accountDao.createAccount(existingAccount));
}

@Test
void updateExistedAccount() {
  existingAccount.setBalance(150);
  accountDao.updateAccount(existingAccount);
  assertEquals(existingAccount, accountDao.findAccount(EXISTING_ACCOUNT_NO));
}

@Test
void updateNotExistedAccount() {
  assertThrows(AccountNotFoundException.class,
          () ->accountDao.updateAccount(newAccount));
}

@Test
void removeExistedAccount() {
  accountDao.removeAccount(existingAccount);
  assertFalse(accountDao.accountExists(EXISTING_ACCOUNT_NO));
}

@Test
void removeNotExistedAccount() {
  assertThrows(AccountNotFoundException.class,
          () -> accountDao.removeAccount(newAccount));
}

@Test
void findExistedAccount() {
  var account = accountDao.findAccount(EXISTING_ACCOUNT_NO);
  assertEquals(existingAccount, account);
}

@Test
void findNotExistedAccount() {
  assertThrows(AccountNotFoundException.class,
          () -> accountDao.findAccount(NEW_ACCOUNT_NO));
}
}
```

Creating Unit Tests for Dependent Classes Using Stubs and Mock Objects

Testing an independent class is easy, because you needn't consider how its dependencies work and how to set them up properly. However, testing a class that depends on results of other classes or services (e.g., database services and network services) would be a little bit difficult. For example, let's consider the following AccountService interface in the service layer.

Listing 13-11. AccountService interface

```
package com.apress.spring6recipes.bank;

public interface AccountService {

  void createAccount(String accountNo);
  void removeAccount(String accountNo);
  void deposit(String accountNo, double amount);
  void withdraw(String accountNo, double amount);
  double getBalance(String accountNo);

}
```

The implementation of this service interface has to depend on an AccountDao object in the persistence layer to persist account objects. The InsufficientBalanceException class is also a subclass of RuntimeException that you have to create.

Listing 13-12. Simple AccountService implementation

```
package com.apress.spring6recipes.bank;

class SimpleAccountService implements AccountService {

  private final AccountDao accountDao;

  public SimpleAccountService(AccountDao accountDao) {
    this.accountDao = accountDao;
  }

  @Override
  public void createAccount(String accountNo) {
    accountDao.createAccount(new Account(accountNo, 0));
  }

  @Override
  public void removeAccount(String accountNo) {
    var account = accountDao.findAccount(accountNo);
    accountDao.removeAccount(account);
  }

  @Override
  public void deposit(String accountNo, double amount) {
    var account = accountDao.findAccount(accountNo);
```

```
    account.setBalance(account.getBalance() + amount);
    accountDao.updateAccount(account);
  }

  @Override
  public void withdraw(String accountNo, double amount) {
    var account = accountDao.findAccount(accountNo);
    if (account.getBalance() < amount) {
      throw new InsufficientBalanceException();
    }
    account.setBalance(account.getBalance() - amount);
    accountDao.updateAccount(account);
  }

  @Override
  public double getBalance(String accountNo) {
    return accountDao.findAccount(accountNo).getBalance();
  }
}
```

A common technique used in unit testing to reduce complexity caused by dependencies is using stubs. A stub must implement the same interface as the target object so that it can substitute for the target object. For example, you can create a stub for AccountDao that stores a single customer account and implements only the findAccount() and updateAccount() methods, as they are required for deposit() and withdraw().

Listing 13-13. AccountService JUnit Jupiter test with a test stub

```
package com.apress.spring6recipes.bank;

import org.junit.jupiter.api.BeforeEach;
import org.junit.jupiter.api.Test;

import static org.junit.jupiter.api.Assertions.assertEquals;
import static org.junit.jupiter.api.Assertions.assertThrows;

public class SimpleAccountServiceStubTests {

  private static final String TEST_ACCOUNT_NO = "1234";

  private AccountDaoStub accountDaoStub;
  private SimpleAccountService accountService;

  @BeforeEach
  public void init() {
    accountDaoStub = new AccountDaoStub();
    accountDaoStub.accountNo = TEST_ACCOUNT_NO;
    accountDaoStub.balance = 100;
    accountService = new SimpleAccountService(accountDaoStub);
  }
```

```java
@Test
void deposit() {
  accountService.deposit(TEST_ACCOUNT_NO, 50);
  assertEquals(TEST_ACCOUNT_NO, accountDaoStub.accountNo);
  assertEquals(150, accountDaoStub.balance, 0);
}

@Test
void withdrawWithSufficientBalance() {
  accountService.withdraw(TEST_ACCOUNT_NO, 50);
  assertEquals(TEST_ACCOUNT_NO, accountDaoStub.accountNo);
  assertEquals(50, accountDaoStub.balance, 0);
}

@Test
void withdrawWithInsufficientBalance() {
  assertThrows(InsufficientBalanceException.class, () ->
          accountService.withdraw(TEST_ACCOUNT_NO, 150));
}

/**
 * Partially implemented stub implementation for the {@code AccountDao}
 */
private static class AccountDaoStub implements AccountDao {

  private String accountNo;
  private double balance;

  public void createAccount(Account account) {}

  public void removeAccount(Account account) {}

  public Account findAccount(String accountNo) {
    return new Account(this.accountNo, this.balance);
  }

  public void updateAccount(Account account) {
    this.accountNo = account.getAccountNo();
    this.balance = account.getBalance();
  }
}
}
```

However, writing stubs yourself requires a lot of coding. A more efficient technique is to use mock objects. The Mockito library is able to dynamically create mock objects that work in a record/playback mechanism.

ℹ To use Mockito for testing, you have to add it to your CLASSPATH. If you are using Maven, add the following dependency to your project:

```
<dependency>
  <groupId>org.mockito</groupId>
  <artifactId>mockito-core</artifactId>
  <version>4.10.0</version>
  <scope>test</scope>
</dependency>
```

Or add the following when using Gradle:

```
testImplementation 'org.mockito:mockito-core:4.10.0'
```

Listing 13-14. AccountService JUnit Jupiter test with Mockito

```java
package com.apress.spring6recipes.bank;

import org.junit.jupiter.api.BeforeEach;
import org.junit.jupiter.api.Test;

import static org.junit.jupiter.api.Assertions.assertThrows;
import static org.mockito.Mockito.any;
import static org.mockito.Mockito.mock;
import static org.mockito.Mockito.times;
import static org.mockito.Mockito.verify;
import static org.mockito.Mockito.when;

class SimpleAccountServiceMockTests {

    private static final String TEST_ACCOUNT_NO = "1234";

    private AccountDao accountDao;
    private SimpleAccountService accountService;

    @BeforeEach
    public void init() {
        accountDao = mock(AccountDao.class);
        accountService = new SimpleAccountService(accountDao);
    }

    @Test
    void deposit() {
        var account = new Account(TEST_ACCOUNT_NO, 100);
        when(accountDao.findAccount(TEST_ACCOUNT_NO)).thenReturn(account);

        accountService.deposit(TEST_ACCOUNT_NO, 50);
```

```
      verify(accountDao, times(1)).findAccount(any(String.class));
      verify(accountDao, times(1)).updateAccount(account);
    }

    @Test
    void withdrawWithSufficientBalance() {
      var account = new Account(TEST_ACCOUNT_NO, 100);
      when(accountDao.findAccount(TEST_ACCOUNT_NO)).thenReturn(account);

      accountService.withdraw(TEST_ACCOUNT_NO, 50);

      verify(accountDao, times(1)).findAccount(any(String.class));
      verify(accountDao, times(1)).updateAccount(account);
    }

    @Test
    public void testWithdrawWithInsufficientBalance() {
      var account = new Account(TEST_ACCOUNT_NO, 100);
      when(accountDao.findAccount(TEST_ACCOUNT_NO)).thenReturn(account);

      assertThrows(InsufficientBalanceException.class, () ->
                    accountService.withdraw(TEST_ACCOUNT_NO, 150));
    }
}
```

With Mockito, you can create a mock object dynamically for an arbitrary interface or class. This mock can be instructed to have certain behavior for method calls, and you can use it to selectively verify if something has happened. In your test you want that in the findAccount method a certain Account object is returned. You use the Mockito.when method for this, and you can then either return a value, throw an exception, or do more elaborate things with an Answer. The default behavior for the mock is to return null. You use the Mockito.verify method to do selective verification of things that have happened. You want to make sure that our findAccount method is called and that the account gets updated.

Instead of manually invoking Mockito.mock to create the mocks to use, it is also possible to use the JUnit Jupiter extension for Mockito. For this you need to annotate the test class with @ExtendWith(MockitoExtension.class) and annotate the fields for the mock(s) with @Mock. The field for the class to receive the mocks can be annotated with @InjectMocks. With that in place, you can now remove the @BeforeEach method as all the setup is now done by the Mockito extension.

Listing 13-15. AccountService JUnit Jupiter test with MockitoExtension

```
package com.apress.spring6recipes.bank;

import org.junit.jupiter.api.Test;
import org.junit.jupiter.api.extension.ExtendWith;
import org.mockito.InjectMocks;
import org.mockito.Mock;
import org.mockito.junit.jupiter.MockitoExtension;

import static org.junit.jupiter.api.Assertions.assertThrows;
import static org.mockito.Mockito.any;
import static org.mockito.Mockito.times;
import static org.mockito.Mockito.verify;
import static org.mockito.Mockito.when;
```

```java
@ExtendWith(MockitoExtension.class)
class SimpleAccountServiceMockTests {

  private static final String TEST_ACCOUNT_NO = "1234";

  @Mock
  private AccountDao accountDao;
  @InjectMocks
  private SimpleAccountService accountService;

  @Test
  void deposit() {
    var account = new Account(TEST_ACCOUNT_NO, 100);
    when(accountDao.findAccount(TEST_ACCOUNT_NO)).thenReturn(account);

    accountService.deposit(TEST_ACCOUNT_NO, 50);

    verify(accountDao, times(1)).findAccount(any(String.class));
    verify(accountDao, times(1)).updateAccount(account);
  }

  @Test
  void withdrawWithSufficientBalance() {
    var account = new Account(TEST_ACCOUNT_NO, 100);
    when(accountDao.findAccount(TEST_ACCOUNT_NO)).thenReturn(account);

    accountService.withdraw(TEST_ACCOUNT_NO, 50);

    verify(accountDao, times(1)).findAccount(any(String.class));
    verify(accountDao, times(1)).updateAccount(account);
  }

  @Test
  public void testWithdrawWithInsufficientBalance() {
    var account = new Account(TEST_ACCOUNT_NO, 100);
    when(accountDao.findAccount(TEST_ACCOUNT_NO)).thenReturn(account);

    assertThrows(InsufficientBalanceException.class,
            () -> accountService.withdraw(TEST_ACCOUNT_NO, 150));
  }
}
```

Creating Integration Tests

Integration tests are used to test several units in combination to ensure that the units are properly integrated and can interact correctly. For example, you can create an integration test to test SimpleAccountService using InMemoryAccountDao as the DAO implementation.

Listing 13-16. AccountService JUnit Jupiter–based integration

```java
package com.apress.spring6recipes.bank;

import org.junit.jupiter.api.AfterEach;
import org.junit.jupiter.api.BeforeEach;
import org.junit.jupiter.api.Test;

import static org.junit.jupiter.api.Assertions.assertEquals;

public class SimpleAccountServiceTests {

  private static final String TEST_ACCOUNT_NO = "1234";

  private AccountService accountService;

  @BeforeEach
  void init() {
    accountService = new SimpleAccountService(new InMemoryAccountDao());
    accountService.createAccount(TEST_ACCOUNT_NO);
    accountService.deposit(TEST_ACCOUNT_NO, 100);
  }

  @Test
  public void deposit() {
    accountService.deposit(TEST_ACCOUNT_NO, 50);
    assertEquals(150, accountService.getBalance(TEST_ACCOUNT_NO), 0);
  }

  @Test
  public void withDraw() {
    accountService.withdraw(TEST_ACCOUNT_NO, 50);
    assertEquals(50, accountService.getBalance(TEST_ACCOUNT_NO), 0);
  }

  @AfterEach
  public void cleanup() {
    accountService.removeAccount(TEST_ACCOUNT_NO);
  }
}
```

13-3. Managing Application Contexts in Integration Tests
Problem

When creating integration tests for a Spring application, you have to access beans declared in the application context. Without Spring's testing support, you have to load the application context manually in an initialization method of your tests, a method with @BeforeEach or @BeforeAll in JUnit. However, as an initialization method is called before each test method or test class, the same application context may be reloaded many times. In a large application with many beans, loading an application context may require a lot of time, which causes your tests to run slowly.

Solution

Spring's testing support facilities can help you manage the application context for your tests, including loading it from one or more bean configuration files and caching it across multiple test executions. An application context will be cached across all tests within a single JVM, using the configuration file locations as the key. As a result, your tests can run much faster without reloading the same application context many times.

The TestContext framework provides a few test execution listeners that are registered by default (see Table 13-1).

Table 13-1. *Default Test Execution Listeners*

TestExecutionListener	Description
ApplicationEventsTestExecutionListener	Adds support for testing application events through the use of an ApplicationEvents helper. Only effective if the test class itself is annotated with @RecordApplicationEvents.
DependencyInjectionTestExecutionListener	This injects dependencies, including the managed application context, into your tests.
DirtiesContextTestExecutionListener, DirtiesContextBeforeModesTestExecutionListener	This handles the @DirtiesContext annotation and reloads the application context when necessary.
EventPublishingTestExecutionListener	Publishes events for test execution through the Spring application event infrastructure.
SqlScriptsTestExecutionListener	Detects @Sql annotations on the test and executes the SQL before the start of the test.
TransactionalTestExecutionListener	This handles the @Transactional annotation in test cases and does a rollback at the end of a test.
ServletTestExecutionListener	Handles loading of a web application context when the @WebAppConfiguration annotation is detected.

To have the TestContext framework manage the application context, your test class has to integrate with a test context manager internally. For your convenience, the TestContext framework provides support classes that do this, as shown in Table 13-2. These classes integrate with a test context manager and implement the ApplicationContextAware interface, so they can provide access to the managed application context through the protected field applicationContext.

Your test class can simply extend the corresponding TestContext support class or use the TestContext integration class for your testing framework.

Table 13-2. *TestContext Support Classes for Context Management*

Testing Framework	TestContext Support Class	TestContext Integration Class
JUnit 4	AbstractJUnit4SpringContextTests	SpringRunner
JUnit Jupiter		SpringExtension
TestNG	AbstractTestNGSpringContextTests	

If you are using JUnit or TestNG, you can integrate your test class with a test context manager by yourself and implement the ApplicationContextAware interface directly, without extending a TestContext support class. In this way, your test class doesn't bind to the TestContext framework class hierarchy, so you can extend your own base class. In JUnit Jupiter, you can simply run your test with the extension SpringExtension to have a test context manager integrated. However, in TestNG, you have to integrate with a test context manager manually.

How It Works

Start by annotating the SimpleAccountService with @Service. That way you can use component scanning to detect it. Next, create a configuration to enable that component scanning and add the InMemoryAccountDao as a @Bean method.

Listing 13-17. Configuration class

```
package com.apress.spring6recipes.bank;

import org.springframework.context.annotation.Bean;
import org.springframework.context.annotation.Configuration;

@Configuration
public class BankConfiguration {

  @Bean
  public InMemoryAccountDao accountDao() {
    return new InMemoryAccountDao();
  }

}
```

ℹ️ We create a @Bean for InMemoryAccountDao as later in the chapter we will add an additional implementation. If we would use an annotation and detect it, Spring would detect two instances and get confused, hence component scanning for the service and a bean method for the InMemoryAccountDao.

Accessing the ApplicationContext with the TestContext Framework in JUnit

If you are using JUnit to create tests with the TestContext framework, you will have two options to access the managed application context: by implementing the ApplicationContextAware interface or using @Autowired on a field of the ApplicationContext type. For the latter option, you have to explicitly specify a Spring-specific test extension for running your test, SpringExtension. You can specify this in the @ExtendWith annotation at the class level.

Listing 13-18. Spring-driven AccountService JUnit Jupiter tests

```java
package com.apress.spring6recipes.bank;

import org.junit.jupiter.api.AfterEach;
import org.junit.jupiter.api.BeforeEach;
import org.junit.jupiter.api.Test;
import org.junit.jupiter.api.extension.ExtendWith;
import org.springframework.beans.factory.annotation.Autowired;
import org.springframework.context.ApplicationContext;
import org.springframework.test.context.ContextConfiguration;
import org.springframework.test.context.junit.jupiter.SpringExtension;

import static org.junit.jupiter.api.Assertions.assertEquals;

@ExtendWith(SpringExtension.class)
@ContextConfiguration(classes = BankConfiguration.class)
class AccountServiceContextTests {

  private static final String TEST_ACCOUNT_NO = "1234";

  @Autowired
  private ApplicationContext applicationContext;
  private AccountService accountService;

  @BeforeEach
  public void init() {
    accountService = applicationContext.getBean(AccountService.class);
    accountService.createAccount(TEST_ACCOUNT_NO);
    accountService.deposit(TEST_ACCOUNT_NO, 100);
  }

  @Test
  public void deposit() {
    accountService.deposit(TEST_ACCOUNT_NO, 50);
    assertEquals(150.0, accountService.getBalance(TEST_ACCOUNT_NO), 0);
  }

  @Test
  public void withDraw() {
    accountService.withdraw(TEST_ACCOUNT_NO, 50);
    assertEquals(50, accountService.getBalance(TEST_ACCOUNT_NO), 50);
  }

  @AfterEach
  public void cleanup() {
    accountService.removeAccount(TEST_ACCOUNT_NO);
  }
}
```

Accessing the ApplicationContext with the TestContext Framework in TestNG

To access the managed application context with the TestContext framework in TestNG, you can extend the TestContext support class AbstractTestNGSpringContextTests. This class also implements the ApplicationContextAware interface.

Listing 13-19. Spring-driven AccountService TestNG tests

```
package com.apress.spring6recipes.bank;

import org.springframework.test.context.ContextConfiguration;
import org.springframework.test.context.testng.AbstractTestNGSpringContextTests;
import org.testng.annotations.AfterMethod;
import org.testng.annotations.BeforeMethod;
import org.testng.annotations.Test;

import static org.testng.Assert.assertEquals;

@ContextConfiguration(classes = BankConfiguration.class)
public class AccountServiceContextTests extends AbstractTestNGSpringContextTests {

  private static final String TEST_ACCOUNT_NO = "1234";

  private AccountService accountService;

  @BeforeMethod
  public void init() {
    accountService = applicationContext.getBean(AccountService.class);
    accountService.createAccount(TEST_ACCOUNT_NO);
    accountService.deposit(TEST_ACCOUNT_NO, 100);
  }

  @Test
  public void deposit() {
    accountService.deposit(TEST_ACCOUNT_NO, 50);
    assertEquals(accountService.getBalance(TEST_ACCOUNT_NO), 150, 0);
  }

  @Test
  public void withDraw() {
    accountService.withdraw(TEST_ACCOUNT_NO, 50);
    assertEquals(accountService.getBalance(TEST_ACCOUNT_NO), 50, 0);
  }

  @AfterMethod
  public void cleanup() {
    accountService.removeAccount(TEST_ACCOUNT_NO);
  }
}
```

Instead of manually obtaining the beans from the ApplicationContext, you could also use @Autowired to obtain the dependencies you need for the test.

If you don't want your TestNG test class to extend a TestContext support class, you can implement the ApplicationContextAware interface just as you did for JUnit. However, you have to integrate with a test context manager by yourself. Please refer to the source code of AbstractTestNGSpringContextTests for details.

13-4. Injecting Test Fixtures into Integration Tests
Problem

The test fixtures of an integration test for a Spring application are mostly beans declared in the application context. You might wish to have the test fixtures automatically injected by Spring via dependency injection, which saves you the trouble of retrieving them from the application context manually.

Solution

Spring's testing support facilities can inject beans automatically from the managed application context into your tests as test fixtures. You can simply annotate a setter method or field of your test with Spring's @Autowired annotation or JSR-250's @Resource annotation to have a fixture injected automatically. For @Autowired, the fixture will be injected by type, and for @Resource, it will be injected by name (see also Chapter 1 on dependency injection; the same applies here).

How It Works

Injecting Test Fixtures with the TestContext Framework in JUnit

When using the TestContext framework to create tests, you can have their test fixtures injected from the managed application context by annotating a field or setter method with the @Autowired or @Resource annotation. In JUnit, you can specify SpringExtesion as your test extension.

Listing 13-20. JUnit Jupiter test with injected test fixtures

```
package com.apress.spring6recipes.bank;

import org.junit.jupiter.api.AfterEach;
import org.junit.jupiter.api.BeforeEach;
import org.springframework.test.context.junit.jupiter.SpringExtension;

import static org.junit.jupiter.api.Assertions.assertEquals;

@ExtendWith(SpringExtension.class)
@ContextConfiguration(classes = BankConfiguration.class)
class AccountServiceContextTests {

  @Autowired
  private AccountService accountService;

  @BeforeEach
  void init() {
    accountService.createAccount(TEST_ACCOUNT_NO);
```

```
    accountService.deposit(TEST_ACCOUNT_NO, 100);
  }
}
```

If you annotate a field or setter method of a test with @Autowired, it will be injected using autowiring by type. You can further specify a candidate bean for autowiring by providing its name in the @Qualifier annotation. However, if you want a field or setter method to be autowired by name, you can annotate it with @Resource.

Injecting Test Fixtures with the TestContext Framework in TestNG

In TestNG, you can extend the TestContext support class AbstractTestNGSpringContextTests to have test fixtures injected from the managed application context.

Listing 13-21. TestNG test with injected test fixtures

```
package com.apress.spring6recipes.bank;

import org.springframework.beans.factory.annotation.Autowired;
import org.springframework.test.context.ContextConfiguration;
import org.springframework.test.context.testng.AbstractTestNGSpringContextTests;
import org.testng.annotations.BeforeMethod;

import static org.testng.Assert.assertEquals;

@ContextConfiguration(classes = BankConfiguration.class)
public class AccountServiceContextTests extends AbstractTestNGSpringContextTests {

  private static final String TEST_ACCOUNT_NO = "1234";

  @Autowired
  private AccountService accountService;

  @BeforeMethod
  public void init() {
    accountService.createAccount(TEST_ACCOUNT_NO);
    accountService.deposit(TEST_ACCOUNT_NO, 100);
  }
}
```

13-5. Managing Transactions in Integration Tests
Problem

When creating integration tests for an application that accesses a database, you usually prepare the test data in the initialization method. After each test method runs, it may have modified the data in the database. So you have to clean up the database to ensure that the next test method will run from a consistent state. As a result, you have to develop many database cleanup tasks.

Solution

Spring's testing support facilities can create and roll back a transaction for each test method, so the changes you make in a test method won't affect the next one. This can also save you the trouble of developing cleanup tasks to clean up the database.

The TestContext framework provides a test execution listener related to transaction management. It will be registered with a test context manager by default if you don't specify your own explicitly.

TransactionalTestExecutionListener: This handles the @Transactional annotation at the class or method level and has the methods run within transactions automatically.

Your test class can extend the corresponding TestContext support class for your testing framework, as shown in Table 13-3, to have its test methods run within transactions. These classes integrate with a test context manager and have @Transactional enabled at the class level. Note that a transaction manager is also required in the bean configuration file.

Table 13-3. *TestContext Support Classes for Transaction Management*

Testing Framework	TestContext Support Class*
JUnit	AbstractTransactionalJUnit4SpringContextTests
TestNG	AbstractTransactionalTestNGSpringContextTests

These TestContext support classes have TransactionalTestExecutionListener and SqlScriptsTestExecutionListener enabled in addition to DependencyInjectionTestExecutionListener and DirtiesContextTestExecutionListener.

In JUnit and JUnit Jupiter, you can also simply annotate @Transactional at the class level or the method level to have the test methods run within transactions, without extending a TestContext support class. However, to integrate with a test context manager, you have to run the JUnit 4 test with the test runner SpringRunner and the SpringExtension for JUnit Jupiter.

How It Works

Let's consider storing your bank system's accounts in a relational database. You can choose any JDBC-compliant database engine that supports transactions and then execute the following SQL statement on it to create the ACCOUNT table. For testing we are going to use an in-memory H2 database.

Listing 13-22. Bank SQL file

```
CREATE TABLE ACCOUNT (
    ACCOUNT_NO    VARCHAR(10)    NOT NULL,
    BALANCE       NUMERIC(20,2)  NOT NULL,
    PRIMARY KEY (ACCOUNT_NO)
);
```

Next, you create a new DAO implementation that uses JDBC to access the database. You can take advantage of the JdbcTemplate to simplify your operations. See Chapter 6 for more information on the JdbcTemplate and data access in general.

Listing 13-23. JDBC-based AccountDao implementation

```java
package com.apress.spring6recipes.bank;

import org.springframework.jdbc.core.JdbcTemplate;
import org.springframework.jdbc.core.support.JdbcDaoSupport;
import org.springframework.stereotype.Repository;

class JdbcAccountDao implements AccountDao {

  private final JdbcTemplate jdbcTemplate;

  JdbcAccountDao(JdbcTemplate jdbcTemplate) {
    this.jdbcTemplate=jdbcTemplate;
  }

  @Override
  public void createAccount(Account account) {
    var sql = "INSERT INTO ACCOUNT (ACCOUNT_NO, BALANCE) VALUES (?, ?)";
    this.jdbcTemplate.update(sql, account.getAccountNo(), account.getBalance());
  }

  @Override
  public void updateAccount(Account account) {
    var sql = "UPDATE ACCOUNT SET BALANCE = ? WHERE ACCOUNT_NO = ?";
    this.jdbcTemplate.update(sql, account.getBalance(), account.getAccountNo());
  }

  @Override
  public void removeAccount(Account account) {
    var sql = "DELETE FROM ACCOUNT WHERE ACCOUNT_NO = ?";
    this.jdbcTemplate.update(sql, account.getAccountNo());
  }

  @Override
  public Account findAccount(String accountNo) {
    var sql = "SELECT BALANCE FROM ACCOUNT WHERE ACCOUNT_NO = ?";
    var balance = this.jdbcTemplate.queryForObject(sql, Double.class, accountNo);
    return new Account(accountNo, balance);
  }
}
```

Before you create integration tests to test the AccountService instance that uses this DAO to persist account objects, you have to replace InMemoryAccountDao with this DAO in the configuration class and configure the target data source and JdbcTemplate as well:

```java
package com.apress.spring6recipes.bank;

import org.h2.Driver;
import org.springframework.context.annotation.Bean;
import org.springframework.context.annotation.ComponentScan;
import org.springframework.context.annotation.Configuration;
import org.springframework.jdbc.core.JdbcTemplate;
```

```java
import org.springframework.jdbc.datasource.DataSourceTransactionManager;
import org.springframework.jdbc.datasource.SimpleDriverDataSource;
import org.springframework.transaction.annotation.EnableTransactionManagement;

import javax.sql.DataSource;

@Configuration
@EnableTransactionManagement
@ComponentScan
public class BankConfiguration {

  @Bean
  public SimpleDriverDataSource dataSource() {
    var dataSource = new SimpleDriverDataSource();
    dataSource.setDriverClass(Driver.class);
    dataSource.setUrl("jdbc:h2:mem:bank-testing");
    dataSource.setUsername("sa");
    dataSource.setPassword("");
    return dataSource;
  }

  @Bean
  public DataSourceTransactionManager transactionManager(DataSource dataSource) {
    return new DataSourceTransactionManager(dataSource);
  }

  @Bean
  public JdbcTemplate jdbcTemplate(DataSource dataSource) {
    return new JdbcTemplate(dataSource);
  }

  @Bean
  public JdbcAccountDao accountDao(JdbcTemplate jdbcTemplate) {
    return new JdbcAccountDao(jdbcTemplate);
  }
}
```

ℹ️ To use H2 you have to add it as a dependency to your classpath.

Maven dependency for H2

```xml
<dependency>
  <groupId>com.h2database</groupId>
  <artifactId>h2</artifactId>
  <version>2.1.214</version>
</dependency>
```

Gradle dependency for H2

```
testImplementation 'com.h2database:h2:2.1.214'
```

Managing Transactions with the TestContext Framework in JUnit

When using the TestContext framework to create tests, you can have the test methods run within transactions by annotating @Transactional at the class or method level. For JUnit Jupiter, you can specify SpringExtension for your test class so that it doesn't need to extend a support class.

Listing 13-24. Transactional JUnit Jupiter AccountService test

```java
package com.apress.spring6recipes.bank;

import org.springframework.beans.factory.annotation.Autowired;
import org.springframework.test.context.ContextConfiguration;
import org.springframework.test.context.junit.jupiter.SpringExtension;
import org.springframework.transaction.annotation.Transactional;

@ExtendWith(SpringExtension.class)
@ContextConfiguration(classes = BankConfiguration.class)
@Transactional
class AccountServiceContextTests {

  private static final String TEST_ACCOUNT_NO = "1234";

  @Autowired
  private AccountService accountService;

  @BeforeEach
  void init() {
    accountService.createAccount(TEST_ACCOUNT_NO);
    accountService.deposit(TEST_ACCOUNT_NO, 100);
  }
}
```

If you annotate a test class with @Transactional, all of its test methods will run within transactions. An alternative is to annotate individual methods with @Transactional, not the entire class.

By default, transactions for test methods will be rolled back at the end. You can override this class-level rollback behavior with the @Rollback annotation, which requires a Boolean value; this can be specified either for the whole class or on a per-method basis.

ℹ️ Methods with the @BeforeEach or @AfterEach annotation will be executed within the same transactions as test methods. If you have methods that need to perform initialization or cleanup tasks before or after a transaction, you have to annotate them with @BeforeTransaction or @AfterTransaction.

Finally, you also need a transaction manager configured in the bean configuration file. By default, a bean whose type is PlatformTransactionManager will be used, but you can specify another one in the transactionManager attribute of the @Transactional annotation by giving its name.

Managing Transactions with the TestContext Framework in TestNG

To create TestNG tests that run within transactions, your test class can extend the TestContext support class `AbstractTransactionalTestNGSpringContextTests` to have its methods run within transactions.

Listing 13-25. Transactional TestNG AccountService test

```
package com.apress.spring6recipes.bank;

import org.springframework.beans.factory.annotation.Autowired;
import org.springframework.test.context.ContextConfiguration;
import org.springframework.test.context.testng.
AbstractTransactionalTestNGSpringContextTests;
import org.testng.annotations.BeforeMethod;
import org.testng.annotations.Test;

import static org.testng.Assert.assertEquals;

@ContextConfiguration(classes = BankConfiguration.class)
public class AccountServiceContextTests
        extends AbstractTransactionalTestNGSpringContextTests {

  private static final String TEST_ACCOUNT_NO = "1234";

  @Autowired
  private AccountService accountService;

  @BeforeMethod
  public void init() {
    accountService.createAccount(TEST_ACCOUNT_NO);
    accountService.deposit(TEST_ACCOUNT_NO, 100);
  }
}
```

13-6. Integration Testing Spring MVC Controllers
Problem

In a web application, you would like to integration test the web controllers developed with the Spring MVC framework.

Solution

A Spring MVC controller is invoked by `DispatcherServlet` with an HTTP request object. After processing a request, the controller returns it to `DispatcherServlet` for rendering the view. The main challenge of integration testing Spring MVC controllers, as well as web controllers in other web application frameworks, is simulating HTTP request objects and response objects in a test environment as well as setting up the mocked environment for a test. Fortunately, Spring has the mock MVC part of the Spring Test support. This allows for easy setup of a mocked servlet environment.

Spring Mock MVC will set up a `WebApplicationContext` according to your configuration. Next, you can use the `MockMvc` API to simulate HTTP requests and verify the results.

How It Works

In our banking application, we want to integration test our `DepositController` (Listing 13-26). Before we can start testing, we need to create a configuration class to configure our web-related beans (Listing 13-27).

Listing 13-26. DepositController class

```java
package com.apress.spring6recipes.bank.web;

import com.apress.spring6recipes.bank.AccountService;
import org.springframework.stereotype.Controller;
import org.springframework.ui.Model;
import org.springframework.ui.ModelMap;
import org.springframework.web.bind.annotation.PostMapping;
import org.springframework.web.bind.annotation.RequestMapping;
import org.springframework.web.bind.annotation.RequestParam;

@Controller
public class DepositController {

  private final AccountService accountService;

  public DepositController(AccountService accountService) {
    this.accountService = accountService;
  }

  @PostMapping("/deposit")
  public String deposit(@RequestParam("accountNo") String accountNo,
                        @RequestParam("amount") double amount,
                        Model model) {
    accountService.deposit(accountNo, amount);
    model.addAttribute("accountNo", accountNo);
    model.addAttribute("balance", accountService.getBalance(accountNo));
    return "success";
  }
}
```

Listing 13-27. Bank web configuration

```java
package com.apress.spring6recipes.bank.web.config;

import org.springframework.context.annotation.Bean;
import org.springframework.context.annotation.ComponentScan;
import org.springframework.context.annotation.Configuration;
import org.springframework.web.servlet.ViewResolver;
import org.springframework.web.servlet.config.annotation.EnableWebMvc;
import org.springframework.web.servlet.view.InternalResourceViewResolver;
```

```
@Configuration
@EnableWebMvc
@ComponentScan(basePackages = "com.apress.spring6recipes.bank.web")
public class BankWebConfiguration {

  @Bean
  public ViewResolver viewResolver() {
    var viewResolver = new InternalResourceViewResolver();
    viewResolver.setPrefix("/WEB-INF/views/");
    viewResolver.setSuffix(".jsp");
    return viewResolver;
  }
}
```

The configuration enables annotation-based controllers by using the @EnableWebMvc annotation.
Next, you want the @Controller-annotated beans to be picked up automatically using the @ComponentScan
annotation. Finally, there is an InternalResourceViewResolver, which turns the name of the view into a
URL that normally would be rendered by the browser, which you will now validate in the controller.

Now that the web-based configuration is in place, we can start to create our integration test. This test
has to load our BankWebConfiguration class and also has to be annotated with @WebAppConfiguration
to inform the TestContext framework we want a WebApplicationContext instead of a regular
ApplicationContext.

Integration Testing Spring MVC Controllers with JUnit

In JUnit Jupiter it is the easiest to use the SpringExtension to run the test.

Listing 13-28. JUnit Jupiter DepositController test class

```
package com.apress.spring6recipes.bank.web;

import static org.springframework.test.web.servlet.request.MockMvcRequestBuilders.post;
import static org.springframework.test.web.servlet.result.MockMvcResultMatchers.forwardedUrl;
import static org.springframework.test.web.servlet.result.MockMvcResultMatchers.status;

import org.junit.jupiter.api.BeforeEach;
import org.junit.jupiter.api.Test;
import org.junit.jupiter.api.extension.ExtendWith;
import org.springframework.beans.factory.annotation.Autowired;
import org.springframework.test.context.ContextConfiguration;
import org.springframework.test.context.junit.jupiter.SpringExtension;
import org.springframework.test.context.web.WebAppConfiguration;
import org.springframework.test.web.servlet.MockMvc;
import org.springframework.test.web.servlet.setup.MockMvcBuilders;
import org.springframework.web.context.WebApplicationContext;

import com.apress.spring6recipes.bank.Account;
import com.apress.spring6recipes.bank.AccountDao;
import com.apress.spring6recipes.bank.BankConfiguration;
import com.apress.spring6recipes.bank.web.config.BankWebConfiguration;
```

```
@ExtendWith(SpringExtension.class)
@ContextConfiguration(classes = {
        BankWebConfiguration.class,
        BankConfiguration.class })
@WebAppConfiguration
class DepositControllerContextTests {

    private static final String ACCOUNT_PARAM = "accountNo";
    private static final String AMOUNT_PARAM = "amount";
    private static final String TEST_ACCOUNT_NO = "1234";
    private static final String TEST_AMOUNT = "50.0";

    @Autowired
    private WebApplicationContext webApplicationContext;
    @Autowired
    private AccountDao accountDao;
    private MockMvc mockMvc;

    @BeforeEach
    public void init() {
        accountDao.createAccount(new Account(TEST_ACCOUNT_NO, 100));
        mockMvc = MockMvcBuilders
                .webAppContextSetup(webApplicationContext)
                .build();
    }

    @Test
    void deposit() throws Exception {
        mockMvc.perform(
                post("/deposit")
                        .param(ACCOUNT_PARAM, TEST_ACCOUNT_NO)
                        .param(AMOUNT_PARAM, TEST_AMOUNT))
            .andExpect(forwardedUrl("/WEB-INF/views/success.jsp"))
            .andExpect(status().isOk());
    }
}
```

In the init method, you prepare the MockMvc object by using the convenient MockMvcBuilders. Using the factory method webAppContextSetup, we can use the already loaded WebApplicationContext to initialize the MockMvc object. The MockMvc object basically mimics the behavior of the DispatcherServlet, which you would use in a Spring MVC–based application. It will use the passed-in WebApplicationContext to configure the handler mappings and view resolution strategies and will also apply any interceptors that are configured.

There is also some setup of a test account so that we have something to work with.

In the deposit test method, the initialized MockMvc object is used to simulate a POST request to the /deposit URL with two request parameters accountNo and amount. The MockMvcRequestBuilders.get factory method results in a RequestBuilder instance that is passed to the MockMvc.perform method.

The perform method returns a ResultActions object, which can be used to do assertions and certain actions on the return result. Finally, there are two assertions to verify that everything works as expected. The DepositController returns success as the viewname, which should lead to a forward to /WEB-INF/views/success.jsp due to the configuration of the ViewResolver. The return code of the request should be 200 (OK), which can be tested with status().isOk() or status().is(200).

Integration Testing Spring MVC Controllers with TestNG

Spring Mock MVC can also be used with TestNG. Extend the appropriate base class
AbstractTransactionalTestNGSpringContextTests and add the @WebAppConfiguration annotation.

Listing 13-29. JUnit Jupiter DepositController test class

```java
package com.apress.spring6recipes.bank.web;

import com.apress.spring6recipes.bank.Account;
import com.apress.spring6recipes.bank.AccountDao;
import com.apress.spring6recipes.bank.BankConfiguration;
import com.apress.spring6recipes.bank.web.config.BankWebConfiguration;
import org.springframework.beans.factory.annotation.Autowired;
import org.springframework.test.context.ContextConfiguration;
import org.springframework.test.context.testng.AbstractTestNGSpringContextTests;
import org.springframework.test.context.web.WebAppConfiguration;
import org.springframework.test.web.servlet.MockMvc;
import org.springframework.test.web.servlet.result.MockMvcResultMatchers;
import org.springframework.test.web.servlet.setup.MockMvcBuilders;
import org.springframework.web.context.WebApplicationContext;
import org.testng.annotations.BeforeMethod;
import org.testng.annotations.Test;

import static org.springframework.test.web.servlet.request.MockMvcRequestBuilders.get;
import static org.springframework.test.web.servlet.request.MockMvcRequestBuilders.post;
import static org.springframework.test.web.servlet.result.MockMvcResultHandlers.print;
import static org.springframework.test.web.servlet.result.MockMvcResultMatchers.forwardedUrl;
import static org.springframework.test.web.servlet.result.MockMvcResultMatchers.status;

@ContextConfiguration(classes = {
        BankWebConfiguration.class,
        BankConfiguration.class })
@WebAppConfiguration
public class DepositControllerContextTests extends AbstractTestNGSpringContextTests {

  private static final String ACCOUNT_PARAM = "accountNo";
  private static final String AMOUNT_PARAM = "amount";
  private static final String TEST_ACCOUNT_NO = "1234";
  private static final String TEST_AMOUNT = "50.0";

  @Autowired
  private WebApplicationContext webApplicationContext;
  @Autowired
  private AccountDao accountDao;
  private MockMvc mockMvc;

  @BeforeMethod
  public void init() {
    accountDao.createAccount(new Account(TEST_ACCOUNT_NO, 100));
    mockMvc = MockMvcBuilders
```

```
                    .webAppContextSetup(webApplicationContext)
                    .build();
    }

    @Test
    public void deposit() throws Exception {
      mockMvc.perform(post("/deposito")
                        .param(ACCOUNT_PARAM, TEST_ACCOUNT_NO)
                        .param(AMOUNT_PARAM, TEST_AMOUNT))
          .andExpect(forwardedUrl("/WEB-INF/views/success.jsp"))
          .andExpect(status().isOk());
    }
}
```

13-7. Integration Testing REST Clients

Problem

You want to write an integration test for a RestTemplate-based client.

Solution

When writing an integration test for a REST-based client, you don't want to rely on the availability of the external service. You can write an integration test using a mock server to return an expected result instead of calling the real endpoint.

How It Works

When working at a bank, you need to validate the account numbers people enter. You could implement your own validation, or you could reuse an existing one. You are going to implement an IBAN validation service that will use the API available at https://openiban.com.

First, you write an interface defining the contract.

Listing 13-30. IBAN validation client interface

```
package com.apress.spring6recipes.bank.web;

public interface IBANValidationClient {

  IBANValidationResult validate(String iban);

}
```

The IBANValidationResult contains the results of the call to the validation endpoint.

Listing 13-31. IBAN validation result DTO

```
package com.apress.spring6recipes.bank.web;

import java.util.ArrayList;
import java.util.HashMap;
import java.util.List;
import java.util.Map;

public record IBANValidationResult(
  boolean valid,
  List<String> messages,
  String iban,
  Map<String, String> bankData) {
}
```

Next, write the OpenIBANValidationClient, which will use a RestTemplate to communicate with the API. For easy access to a RestTemplate, you can extend RestGatewaySupport.

Listing 13-32. IBAN Validation Client RestTemplate implementation

```
package com.apress.spring6recipes.bank.web;

import org.springframework.stereotype.Service;
import org.springframework.web.client.support.RestGatewaySupport;

@Service
class OpenIBANValidationClient extends RestGatewaySupport
        implements IBANValidationClient {

  private static final String URL_TEMPLATE =
    "https://openiban.com/validate/{IBAN_NUMBER}?getBIC=true&validateBankCode=true";

  @Override
  public IBANValidationResult validate(String iban) {

    return getRestTemplate()
            .getForObject(URL_TEMPLATE, IBANValidationResult.class, iban);
  }
}
```

Next, you will create a test that will construct a MockRestServiceServer for the OpenIBANValidationClient, and you configure it to return a specific result in JSON for an expected request.

Listing 13-33. IBAN validation client test

```
package com.apress.spring6recipes.bank.web;

import org.junit.jupiter.api.BeforeEach;
import org.junit.jupiter.api.Test;
import org.springframework.core.io.ClassPathResource;
import org.springframework.http.MediaType;
import org.springframework.test.web.client.MockRestServiceServer;
```

```java
import static org.junit.jupiter.api.Assertions.assertFalse;
import static org.junit.jupiter.api.Assertions.assertTrue;
import static org.springframework.test.web.client.match.MockRestRequestMatchers.requestTo;
import static org.springframework.test.web.client.response.MockRestResponseCreators.
withSuccess;

public class OpenIBANValidationClientTest {

  private final OpenIBANValidationClient client = new OpenIBANValidationClient();

  private MockRestServiceServer mockRestServiceServer;

  @BeforeEach
  public void init() {
    mockRestServiceServer = MockRestServiceServer.createServer(client);
  }

  @Test
  public void validIban() {
    var json = new ClassPathResource("NL87TRIO0396451440-result.json");
    var expectedUri = "https://openiban.com/validate/NL87TRIO0396451440?getBIC=true&validat
    eBankCode=true";

    mockRestServiceServer
        .expect(requestTo(expectedUri))
        .andRespond(withSuccess(json, MediaType.APPLICATION_JSON));

    var result = client.validate("NL87TRIO0396451440");
    assertTrue(result.valid());
  }

  @Test
  public void invalidIban() {
    var expectedUri = "https://openiban.com/validate/NL28XXXX389242218?getBIC=true&validate
    BankCode=true";
    var json = new ClassPathResource("NL28XXXX389242218-result.json");
    mockRestServiceServer
        .expect(requestTo(expectedUri))
        .andRespond(withSuccess(json, MediaType.APPLICATION_JSON));

    var result = client.validate("NL28XXXX389242218");
    assertFalse(result.valid());
  }
}
```

The test class has two test methods, and both are quite similar. In the init method, you create a MockRestServiceServer using the OpenIBANValidationClient (this is possible because it extends RestGatewaySupport). Another option is to use the create method that takes a RestTemplate; you then pass in the RestTemplate that is being used by your client. In the test method, you set up the expectation with a URL, and now when that URL is called, a JSON response, from the classpath, will be returned as the answer (Listings 13-34 and 13-35).

Listing 13-34. JSON response file (valid)

```json
{
  "valid": true,
  "messages": [
    "Bank code valid: TRIO"
  ],
  "iban": "NL87TRIO0396451440",
  "bankData": {
    "bankCode": "TRIO",
    "name": "TRIODOS BANK NV",
    "bic": "TRIONL2U"
  },
  "checkResults": {
    "bankCode": true
  }
}
```

Listing 13-35. JSON response file (invalid)

```json
{
  "valid": false,
  "messages": [
    "Validation failed.",
    "Invalid bank code: XXXX",
    "No BIC found for bank code: XXXX"
  ],
  "iban": "NL28XXXX0389242218",
  "bankData": {
    "bankCode": "",
    "name": ""
  },
  "checkResults": {
    "bankCode": false
  }
}
```

For testing you probably want to use some well-known responses from the server, and for this you could use some recorded results from a live system, or maybe they already provide results for testing.

13-8. Integration Testing with Testcontainers
Problem

You want to use the actual database for testing instead of an in-memory one like H2.

Solution

Use Testcontainers to start a Dockerized version of the database for testing purposes.

How It Works

Recipe 13-5 explained how to do tests that rely on transactions and a database. In that recipe you used H2 as the database implementation. However, in the real world, you will probably be using a more robust database like PostgreSQL, DB2 or MySQL, etc. For most databases, there are Dockerized versions that you can use for, among other things, testing. With Testcontainers and the integration for testing libraries, it now is possible to use your actual database for testing.

Using Testcontainers with JUnit Jupiter

First, there are some dependencies that need to be added, the type of container to be used and the integration library for JUnit Jupiter.

Maven dependencies

```xml
<dependency>
  <groupId>org.testcontainers</groupId>
  <artifactId>junit-jupiter</artifactId>
  <version>1.17.3</version>
</dependency>
<dependency>
  <groupId>org.testcontainers</groupId>
  <artifactId>postgresql</artifactId>
  <version>1.17.3</version>
</dependency>
```

Gradle dependencies

```
testImplementation 'org.testcontainers:junit-jupiter:1.17.3'
testImplementation 'org.testcontainers:postgresql:1.17.3'
```

To use Testcontainers with JUnit Jupiter, there is a test extension that can be enabled by adding the @Testcontainers annotation on the test. Next, you need to specify which container to use; for this test we are using the PostgreSQLContainer as it is for a database-driven test. However, there are many more containers available for different databases, messaging implementations, etc. Or you could even specify your own containers by using a GenericContainer.

Listing 13-36. JUnit Jupiter AccountService tests with Testcontainers

```java
package com.apress.spring6recipes.bank;

import org.junit.jupiter.api.BeforeEach;
import org.junit.jupiter.api.Test;
import org.junit.jupiter.api.extension.ExtendWith;
import org.springframework.beans.factory.annotation.Autowired;
import org.springframework.test.context.ActiveProfiles;
import org.springframework.test.context.ContextConfiguration;
import org.springframework.test.context.DynamicPropertyRegistry;
import org.springframework.test.context.DynamicPropertySource;
import org.springframework.test.context.jdbc.Sql;
import org.springframework.test.context.junit.jupiter.SpringExtension;
```

```java
import org.springframework.transaction.annotation.Transactional;
import org.testcontainers.containers.PostgreSQLContainer;
import org.testcontainers.junit.jupiter.Container;
import org.testcontainers.junit.jupiter.Testcontainers;

import static org.junit.jupiter.api.Assertions.assertEquals;

@ExtendWith(SpringExtension.class)
@Testcontainers
@ContextConfiguration(classes = BankConfiguration.class)
@Transactional
@ActiveProfiles("jdbc")
@Sql(scripts = { "classpath:/bank.sql" })
class AccountServiceContextTests {

  @Container
  private static final PostgreSQLContainer<?> POSTGRES =
          new PostgreSQLContainer<>("postgres:14.5");

  private static final String TEST_ACCOUNT_NO = "1234";

  @Autowired
  private AccountService accountService;

  @DynamicPropertySource
  static void registerPgProperties(DynamicPropertyRegistry registry) {
    registry.add("jdbc.driver",   POSTGRES::getDriverClassName);
    registry.add("jdbc.url",      POSTGRES::getJdbcUrl);
    registry.add("jdbc.username", POSTGRES::getUsername);
    registry.add("jdbc.password", POSTGRES::getPassword);
  }

  @BeforeEach
  public void init() {
    accountService.createAccount(TEST_ACCOUNT_NO);
    accountService.deposit(TEST_ACCOUNT_NO, 100);
  }

  @Test
  void deposit() {
    accountService.deposit(TEST_ACCOUNT_NO, 50);
    assertEquals(150, accountService.getBalance(TEST_ACCOUNT_NO), 0);
  }

  @Test
  void withDraw() {
    accountService.withdraw(TEST_ACCOUNT_NO, 50);
    assertEquals(50, accountService.getBalance(TEST_ACCOUNT_NO), 0);
  }
}
```

Notice the `static` on the `PostgreSQLContainer`; this will start the container once for the whole test class and shut it down after all tests ran. One can also remove the `static`, and when doing so, the container will be started and stopped for each test that will be run. Which to use depends on the use case and what is being tested. Using the `static` container has the advantage of container reuse and is thus faster.

After starting the container, as the ports are dynamic, we need to supply this information to our application. The Spring TestContext framework has a dynamic property source for that. (See Chapter 1 for more information on external configuration.) To use annotate a `static` method in the test class with `@DynamicPropertySource` and register the needed config with the application (see the `registerPgProperties` method).

The properties set here will override the ones that are loaded from the regular `@PropertySource` used in the application.

The remainder of the class can remain the same as in Recipe 13-5 as the tests you are doing are the same. Now when running the test, a PostgreSQL instance will be started (first downloaded if needed), the schema is created (thanks to the `@Sql` annotation), and the tests are run.

Using Testcontainers with TestNG

Testcontainers doesn't have a support library for TestNG, and thus this will require some manual work. The container needs to be started and stopped using the TestNG life cycle methods `@BeforeSuite` and `@AfterSuite`. The `@BeforeMethod` or `@BeforeClass` won't work due to the way Spring Test needs to integrate with TestNG.

Listing 13-37. TestNG AccountService tests with Testcontainers

```
package com.apress.spring6recipes.bank;

import org.springframework.beans.factory.annotation.Autowired;
import org.springframework.test.context.ActiveProfiles;
import org.springframework.test.context.ContextConfiguration;
import org.springframework.test.context.DynamicPropertyRegistry;
import org.springframework.test.context.DynamicPropertySource;
import org.springframework.test.context.jdbc.Sql;
import org.springframework.test.context.testng.
AbstractTransactionalTestNGSpringContextTests;
import org.testcontainers.containers.PostgreSQLContainer;
import org.testng.annotations.AfterSuite;
import org.testng.annotations.BeforeMethod;
import org.testng.annotations.BeforeSuite;
import org.testng.annotations.Test;

import static org.testng.Assert.assertEquals;

@ContextConfiguration(classes = BankConfiguration.class)
@ActiveProfiles("jdbc")
@Sql(scripts = { "classpath:/bank.sql" })
public class AccountServiceContextTests extends
AbstractTransactionalTestNGSpringContextTests {

  private static final PostgreSQLContainer<?> POSTGRES =
        new PostgreSQLContainer<>("postgres:14.5");
```

```
  private static final String TEST_ACCOUNT_NO = "1234";

  @Autowired
  private AccountService accountService;

  @DynamicPropertySource
  static void registerPgProperties(DynamicPropertyRegistry registry) {
    registry.add("jdbc.driver",   POSTGRES::getDriverClassName);
    registry.add("jdbc.url",      POSTGRES::getJdbcUrl);
    registry.add("jdbc.username", POSTGRES::getUsername);
    registry.add("jdbc.password", POSTGRES::getPassword);
  }

  @BeforeSuite
  public static void start() {
    POSTGRES.start();
  }

  @AfterSuite
  public static void stop() {
    POSTGRES.stop();
  }

  @BeforeMethod
  public void init() {
    accountService.createAccount(TEST_ACCOUNT_NO);
    accountService.deposit(TEST_ACCOUNT_NO, 100);
  }

  @Test
  public void deposit() {
    accountService.deposit(TEST_ACCOUNT_NO, 50);
    assertEquals(accountService.getBalance(TEST_ACCOUNT_NO), 150, 0);
  }

  @Test
  public void withDraw() {
    accountService.withdraw(TEST_ACCOUNT_NO, 50);
    assertEquals(accountService.getBalance(TEST_ACCOUNT_NO), 50, 0);
  }
}
```

After starting the container, as the ports are dynamic, we need to supply this information to our application. The Spring TestContext framework has a dynamic property source for that. (See Chapter 1 for more information on external configuration.) To use annotate a static method with @DynamicPropertySource and register the needed config with the application (see the registerPgProperties method).

The properties set here will override the ones that are loaded from the regular @PropertySource used in the application.

The remainder of the class can remain the same as in Recipe 13-5 as the tests you are doing are the same. Now when running the test, a PostgreSQL instance will be started (first downloaded if needed), the schema is created, and the tests are run.

13-9. Summary

In this chapter, you learned about the basic concepts and techniques used in testing Java applications. JUnit Jupiter and TestNG are the most popular testing frameworks on the Java platform. Unit tests are used for testing a single programming unit, which is typically a class or a method in object-oriented languages. When testing a unit that depends on other units, you can use stubs and mock objects to simulate its dependencies, thus making the tests simpler. In contrast, integration tests are used to test several units as a whole.

In the web layer, controllers are usually hard to test. Spring offers mock objects for the Servlet API so that you can easily simulate web request and response objects to test a web controller. There is also Spring Mock MVC for easy integration testing of your controllers. What applies to controllers also applies to REST-based clients. To help you test these clients, Spring provides the MockRestServiceServer that you can use to mock an external system.

Spring's testing support facilities can manage application contexts for your tests by loading them from bean configuration files and caching them across multiple test executions. You can access the managed application context in your tests, as well as have your test fixtures injected from the application context automatically. In addition, if your tests involve database updates, Spring can manage transactions for them so that changes made in one test method will be rolled back and thus won't affect the next test method. This also applies to tests that are run with Testcontainers to use a real data store or messaging solution.

CHAPTER 14

Caching

When a heavy computation is done in a program, retrieval of data is slow, or the retrieved data hardly ever changes. It can be useful to apply caching. Caching is the ability to store and retrieve data, transparently, so that data can be served quicker to the client.

In the Java ecosystem, there are multiple cache implementations, ranging from the use of a simple Map implementation to a fully distributed cache solution (Coherence, for instance). However, there are also the proven and trusted Ehcache and Caffeine.

There is also a general caching API (JSR-107) named JCache; for this specification several implementations exists (like Apache JCS and Hazelcast). Also, Oracle Coherence is JCache compliant.

Spring provides a cache abstract to make it easier to work with any of these implementations, which makes it quite easy to add caching to your application. For testing you could use a simple map-based implementation, whereas your real system would use an Oracle Coherence cluster for caching.

In this chapter you will explore Spring's caching abstraction and will take a look at different strategies of applying caching to your application.

14-1. Caching with Caffeine
Problem

You have an application with some heavy computation tasks. You would like to cache the result and reuse it.

Solution

Use Caffeine to store the result of your computation. For each computation check if a result is already present. If it is return the cached value, or calculate and put it in the cache.

You will need to add Caffeine as a dependency to your classpath.

Listing 14-1. Gradle dependency

```
implementation group: 'com.github.ben-manes.caffeine', name: 'caffeine', version: '3.1.2'
```

Listing 14-2. Maven dependency

```
<dependency>
  <groupId>com.github.ben-manes.caffeine<groupId>
  <artifactId>caffeine<artifactId>
  <version>3.1.2<version>
</dependency>
```

How It Works

First, let's create the `CalculationService` that simulates a heavy computation by doing a sleep.

Listing 14-3. PlainCalculationService

```java
package com.apress.spring6recipes.caching;

import com.apress.spring6recipes.utils.Utils;

import java.math.BigDecimal;

class PlainCalculationService implements CalculationService {

  @Override
  public BigDecimal heavyCalculation(BigDecimal base, int power) {
    return calculate(base, power);
  }

  private BigDecimal calculate(BigDecimal base, int power) {
    Utils.sleep(500);
    return base.pow(power);
  }
}
```

As one can see, exponentiation is a very heavy computation to do. Create a `Main` class to run this program in a couple of iterations.

Listing 14-4. Main class

```java
package com.apress.spring6recipes.caching;

import java.math.BigDecimal;

public class Main {

  public static final void main(String[] args) throws Exception {

    var calculationService = new PlainCalculationService();
    for (int i = 0; i < 5; i++) {
      var start = System.currentTimeMillis();
      var result = calculationService.heavyCalculation(BigDecimal.valueOf(2L), 16);
      var duration = System.currentTimeMillis() - start;
      System.out.printf("Result: %.0f, Took: %dms%n", result, duration);
    }
  }
}
```

The main class will run the computation five times and output the results as well as the time it took to calculate the results. When running you will see that the time for each computation is around 500 milliseconds, mainly due to the `Thread.sleep()`.

Listing 14-5. Console output

```
Result: 65536, Took: 513ms
Result: 65536, Took: 504ms
Result: 65536, Took: 504ms
Result: 65536, Took: 501ms
Result: 65536, Took: 504ms
```

Using Caffeine Without Spring

Let's improve our system by introducing caching. For this you are going to use plain Caffeine. The modified service looks like the following.

Listing 14-6. PlainCalculationService with caching

```java
package com.apress.spring6recipes.caching;

import com.apress.spring6recipes.utils.Utils;
import com.github.benmanes.caffeine.cache.Cache;

import java.math.BigDecimal;

class PlainCachingCalculationService implements CalculationService {

    private final Cache<String, BigDecimal> cache;

    public PlainCachingCalculationService(Cache<String, BigDecimal> cache) {
        this.cache = cache;
    }

    @Override
    public BigDecimal heavyCalculation(BigDecimal base, int power) {
        var key = base + "^" + power;
        return cache.get(key, k -> this.calculate(base, power));
    }

    private BigDecimal calculate(BigDecimal base, int power) {
        Utils.sleep(500);
        return base.pow(power);
    }
}
```

First, notice the addition of a cache variable in the service. This cache is injected through the constructor. Let's take a look at the updated heavyCalculation method. First, it generates a unique key based on the method arguments; this key is used to look up a result from the cache. If found, it is returned. If there is no cached result, the calculation proceeds as normal, and after the calculation, the value is added to the cache, and finally it is returned. All of this is encapsulated in the cache.get method, which allows for passing a java.util.function.Function to generate the value. In this case we pass the function as a lambda expression.

Due to the need for a Caffeine cache, the `Main` class needs to be modified to bootstrap a Caffeine cache before constructing our service. The updated `Main` class looks like the following.

Listing 14-7. Main class

```
package com.apress.spring6recipes.caching;

import com.github.benmanes.caffeine.cache.Cache;
import com.github.benmanes.caffeine.cache.Caffeine;

import java.math.BigDecimal;
import java.time.Duration;

public class Main {

  public static final void main(String[] args) throws Exception {
    Cache<String, BigDecimal> cache = Caffeine.newBuilder()
            .maximumSize(1000)
            .expireAfterWrite(Duration.ofMinutes(5)).build();
    var calculationService = new PlainCachingCalculationService(cache);
    for (int i = 0; i < 5; i++) {
      var start = System.currentTimeMillis();
      var result = calculationService.heavyCalculation(BigDecimal.valueOf(2L), 16);
      var duration = System.currentTimeMillis() - start;
      System.out.printf("Result: %.0f, Took: %dms%n", result, duration);
    }
  }
}
```

We use the `Caffeine` builder to generate a cache. There are several options, but for now we create a simple cache that can hold 1000 entries (the `maximumSize`), and it will expire each entry after 5 minutes (`expireAfterWrite`). The created `Cache` is then injected into the `PlainCachingCalculationService`.

When running the main class, the first computation takes around 500 milliseconds, whereas the next computations take a lot less around 0–1 millisecond.

Listing 14-8. Console output

```
Result: 65536, Took: 529ms
Result: 65536, Took: 0ms
Result: 65536, Took: 0ms
Result: 65536, Took: 0ms
Result: 65536, Took: 0ms
```

Using Caffeine with Spring for Configuration

The application is integrated with Spring, and Spring will be leveraged for configuration of the `Cache` and constructing the service. To make this work, you need to do some Spring configuration and use an `ApplicationContext` to load everything. The configuration is the following.

Listing 14-9. Configuration

```
package com.apress.spring6recipes.caching.config;

import com.apress.spring6recipes.caching.CalculationService;
import com.apress.spring6recipes.caching.PlainCachingCalculationService;
import com.github.benmanes.caffeine.cache.Cache;
import com.github.benmanes.caffeine.cache.Caffeine;
import org.springframework.context.annotation.Bean;
import org.springframework.context.annotation.Configuration;

import java.math.BigDecimal;
import java.time.Duration;

@Configuration
public class CalculationConfiguration {

  @Bean
  public Cache<String, BigDecimal> calculationsCache() {
    return Caffeine.newBuilder()
            .maximumSize(1000)
            .expireAfterWrite(Duration.ofMinutes(5)).build();
  }

  @Bean
  public CalculationService calculationService(Cache<String, BigDecimal> cache) {
    return new PlainCachingCalculationService(cache);
  }
}
```

You also need a modified Main class that loads the configuration and obtains the CalculationService from the context.

Listing 14-10. Main class

```
package com.apress.spring6recipes.caching;

import com.apress.spring6recipes.caching.config.CalculationConfiguration;
import org.springframework.context.annotation.AnnotationConfigApplicationContext;

import java.math.BigDecimal;

public class Main {

  public static final void main(String[] args) {
    var cfg = CalculationConfiguration.class;
    try (var context = new AnnotationConfigApplicationContext(cfg)) {
      var calculationService = context.getBean(CalculationService.class);
      for (int i = 0; i < 5; i++) {
        var start = System.currentTimeMillis();
        var result = calculationService.heavyCalculation(BigDecimal.valueOf(2L), 16);
        var duration = System.currentTimeMillis() - start;
```

```
        System.out.printf("Result: %.0f, Took: %dms%n", result, duration);
    }
  }
 }
}
```

Although this reduces the direct references to Caffeine from our bootstrapping code, the implementation of the CalculationService is still riddled with references to Caffeine. Not to mention that manual caching is quite cumbersome and an erroneous task that pollutes the code. It would be nice if caching could just be applied, just like transactions, with AOP.

14-2. Caching with Spring's Cache Abstraction

Problem

You have an application with some heavy computation tasks. You would like to cache the result and reuse it, but at the same time don't want to be bound to a single cache implementation.

Solution

Use Caffeine to store the result of your computation through Spring's cache abstraction. For each computation, check if a result is already present. If it is, return the cached value; if it is not, calculate and put it in the cache.

How It Works

First, add caching to your application using Spring's Cache abstraction. Second, check if a result is already present using the get() method. If it is present, return; if it is not, continue with the program. After the calculation, the value is added to the cache.

Listing 14-11. CalculationService with the Spring cache abstraction

```java
package com.apress.spring6recipes.caching;

import com.apress.spring6recipes.utils.Utils;
import org.springframework.cache.Cache;

import java.math.BigDecimal;

public class PlainCachingCalculationService implements CalculationService {

  private final Cache cache;

  public PlainCachingCalculationService(Cache cache) {
    this.cache = cache;
  }

  @Override
  public BigDecimal heavyCalculation(BigDecimal base, int power) {
    var key = base + "^" + power;
```

```
    var result = cache.get(key, BigDecimal.class);
    if (result != null) {
      return result;
    }
    Utils.sleep(500);
    var calculatedResult = base.pow(power);
    cache.putIfAbsent(key, calculatedResult);
    return calculatedResult;
  }
}
```

Next, the CacheManager needs to be configured. First, configure a simple java.util.Map-based cache by using the ConcurrentMapCacheManager that, as the name implies, uses a java.util.concurrent.ConcurrentMap underneath for caching.

Listing 14-12. CalculationConfiguration with ConcurrentMap as a cache

```
package com.apress.spring6recipes.caching.config;

import com.apress.spring6recipes.caching.CalculationService;
import com.apress.spring6recipes.caching.PlainCachingCalculationService;
import org.springframework.cache.CacheManager;
import org.springframework.cache.concurrent.ConcurrentMapCacheManager;
import org.springframework.context.annotation.Bean;
import org.springframework.context.annotation.Configuration;

@Configuration
public class CalculationConfiguration {

  @Bean
  public CacheManager cacheManager() {
    return new ConcurrentMapCacheManager();
  }

  @Bean
  public CalculationService calculationService(CacheManager cacheManager) {
    var cache = cacheManager.getCache("calculations");
    return new PlainCachingCalculationService(cache);
  }
}
```

The PlainCachingCalculationService needs an instance of a Cache to operate. The Cache instance to use can be obtained from the CacheManager by calling the getCache method. Here, we get the cache named calculations and inject it into the PlainCachingCalculationService.

The Main class can remain unchanged.

Using Caffeine with Spring's Cache Abstraction

Although the ConcurrentMapCacheManager appears to do its job, it is not a full cache implementation. It will only add things to the cache; there is no cache eviction nor cache overflowing. Caffeine on the other hand has all of this. Using Caffeine (or another cache implementation like Ehcache or Hazelcast) is just a matter of configuration.

To use Caffeine use the `CaffeineCacheManager` to hook it up with Spring's cache abstraction. The `PlainCachingCalculationService` can remain untouched as that already uses Spring's cache abstraction to use a cache. Spring will dynamically, by default, create the caches when requested.

Listing 14-13. CalculationConfiguration with Caffeine as a cache

```java
package com.apress.spring6recipes.caching.config;

import com.apress.spring6recipes.caching.CalculationService;
import com.apress.spring6recipes.caching.PlainCachingCalculationService;
import com.github.benmanes.caffeine.cache.Caffeine;
import org.springframework.cache.CacheManager;
import org.springframework.cache.caffeine.CaffeineCacheManager;
import org.springframework.context.annotation.Bean;
import org.springframework.context.annotation.Configuration;

import java.time.Duration;

@Configuration
public class CalculationConfiguration {

  @Bean
  public CacheManager cacheManager() {
    var caffeine = Caffeine.newBuilder()
            .maximumSize(1000)
            .expireAfterWrite(Duration.ofMinutes(5));
    var cacheManager = new CaffeineCacheManager();
    cacheManager.setCaffeine(caffeine);
    return cacheManager;
  }

  @Bean
  public CalculationService calculationService(CacheManager cacheManager) {
    var cache = cacheManager.getCache("calculations");
    return new PlainCachingCalculationService(cache);
  }
}
```

14-3. Declarative Caching with AOP
Problem

Caching is a kind of crosscutting concern. Applying caching manually can be tedious and error-prone. It is simpler to specify, declaratively, what behavior you are expecting and to not prescribe how that behavior is to be achieved.

Solution

Spring offers a cache advice that can be enabled by @EnableCaching.

How It Works

To enable declarative caching, you have to add @EnableCaching to the configuration class. This will register a CacheInterceptor or AnnotationCacheAspect (depending on the mode), which will detect, among others, the @Cacheable annotation. The registered advice replaces the code used for caching, as that is mainly boilerplate and would need to be duplicated in each method in which we want to introduce caching. When the boilerplate code is removed, the following code is what would remain.

Listing 14-14. PlainCalculationService with no caching

```
@Override
public BigDecimal heavyCalculation(BigDecimal base, int power) {
  return calculate(base, power);
}

private BigDecimal calculate(BigDecimal base, int power) {
  Utils.sleep(500);
  return base.pow(power);
}
```

To enable caching for this method, you need to place a @Cacheable annotation on the method. This annotation requires the name of the cache to use to be specified (by using the value attribute of the annotation).

Listing 14-15. PlainCalculationService with @Cacheable

```
@Override
@Cacheable("calculations")
public BigDecimal heavyCalculation(BigDecimal base, int power) {
}
```

This annotation has three other attributes: key, condition, and unless. Each of these attributes takes a SpEL expression, which is evaluated at runtime. The key attribute specifies which method arguments to use to calculate the key used for caching; the default is to use all method arguments. The condition attribute can be used to define the condition for which the cache is applied; the default is to always cache and is invoked before the actual method is invoked. The unless attribute works similar to the condition attribute; however, this is used after the method invocation has been done to determine if the result should be cached or not (like skipping null values).

Using Spring AOP

The default operation mode for the @EnableCaching annotation is to use plain Spring AOP. This means a proxy will be created for the CalculationService. The configuration looks like the following.

Listing 14-16. Caching configuration

```
package com.apress.spring6recipes.caching.config;

import com.apress.spring6recipes.caching.CalculationService;
import com.apress.spring6recipes.caching.PlainCalculationService;
import com.github.benmanes.caffeine.cache.Caffeine;
import org.springframework.cache.CacheManager;
```

717

```java
import org.springframework.cache.annotation.EnableCaching;
import org.springframework.cache.caffeine.CaffeineCacheManager;
import org.springframework.context.annotation.Bean;
import org.springframework.context.annotation.Configuration;

import java.time.Duration;

@Configuration
@EnableCaching
public class CalculationConfiguration {

  @Bean
  public CacheManager cacheManager() {
    var caffeine = Caffeine.newBuilder()
            .maximumSize(1000)
            .expireAfterWrite(Duration.ofMinutes(5));
    var cacheManager = new CaffeineCacheManager();
    cacheManager.setCaffeine(caffeine);
    return cacheManager;
  }

  @Bean
  public CalculationService calculationService() {
    return new PlainCalculationService();
  }
}
```

The configuration now has a @EnableCaching annotation, and the CalculationService used only has the @Cacheable annotation, no dependency on the caching framework.

Using AspectJ

Using the AspectJ mode for caching is as easy as setting the mode attribute of the @EnableCaching annotation to ASPECTJ. Depending on whether one uses compile-time or load-time weaving, it might be necessary to add @EnableLoadTimeWeaving. For the sample it is assumed that the code uses load-time weaving. For this add the aforementioned annotation to the configuration class.

Listing 14-17. Caching configuration for load-time weaving

```java
package com.apress.spring6recipes.caching.config;

import org.springframework.cache.annotation.EnableCaching;
import org.springframework.context.annotation.AdviceMode;
import org.springframework.context.annotation.Configuration;
import org.springframework.context.annotation.EnableLoadTimeWeaving;

@Configuration
@EnableLoadTimeWeaving
@EnableCaching(mode = AdviceMode.ASPECTJ)
public class CalculationConfiguration {
}
```

More information on load-time weaving can be found in Recipe 1-20. To run the main application, you have to start it with a so-called Java agent. To run the program with load-time weaving, use
`java -javaagent:./lib/spring-instrument-6.0.3.RELEASE.jar -jar recipe_14_3_ii-6.0.0-all.jar` (from the `build/libs` directory of this recipe).

14-4. Configure a Custom KeyGenerator
Problem

The default KeyGenerator generates a key based on the method parameters. You want to modify this behavior.

Solution

Implement a custom KeyGenerator with the desired strategy and configure the caching support to use this custom KeyGenerator.

How It Works

The caching abstraction uses a KeyGenerator interface as a callback mechanism for the key generation. By default it uses the SimpleKeyGenerator class for key generation. This class takes all method arguments and calculates a hashcode for this. This hash is used as a key.

It is possible to implement your own generation strategy and use that to generate the keys. To do this create a class that implements the KeyGenerator interface and implements the generate method.

Listing 14-18. Custom key generator implementation

```
package com.apress.spring6recipes.caching;

import org.springframework.cache.interceptor.KeyGenerator;

import java.lang.reflect.Method;

public class CustomKeyGenerator implements KeyGenerator {

  @Override
  public Object generate(Object target, Method method, Object... params) {
    return params[0] + "^" + params[1];
  }
}
```

The CustomKeyGenerator takes the first and second parameters and appends them with a ^ in between (the same as was done in the samples when you generated your own key for the cache).

Next, wire up the custom implementation with the caching support in Spring. For this use the CachingConfigurer interface, which is used to further configure the caching support in Spring. You need only to implement those parts of the configuration you want to override. Here, you will override the keyGenerator and cacheManager.

ℹ️ Don't forget to put @Bean on the overridden methods; else, the created instances won't be managed by the Spring container.

Listing 14-19. Cache configuration with a custom key generator

```
package com.apress.spring6recipes.caching.config;

import com.apress.spring6recipes.caching.CalculationService;
import com.apress.spring6recipes.caching.CustomKeyGenerator;
import com.apress.spring6recipes.caching.PlainCalculationService;
import com.github.benmanes.caffeine.cache.Caffeine;
import org.springframework.cache.CacheManager;
import org.springframework.cache.annotation.CachingConfigurer;
import org.springframework.cache.annotation.EnableCaching;
import org.springframework.cache.caffeine.CaffeineCacheManager;
import org.springframework.cache.interceptor.KeyGenerator;
import org.springframework.context.annotation.Bean;
import org.springframework.context.annotation.Configuration;

import java.time.Duration;

@Configuration
@EnableCaching
public class CalculationConfiguration implements CachingConfigurer {

  @Bean
  @Override
  public CacheManager cacheManager() {
    var caffeine = Caffeine.newBuilder()
            .maximumSize(1000)
            .expireAfterWrite(Duration.ofMinutes(5));
    var cacheManager = new CaffeineCacheManager();
    cacheManager.setCaffeine(caffeine);
    return cacheManager;
  }

  @Bean
  @Override
  public KeyGenerator keyGenerator() {
    return new CustomKeyGenerator();
  }

  @Bean
  public CalculationService calculationService() {
    return new PlainCalculationService();
  }
}
```

Notice the two overridden methods from the CachingConfigurer. The first, cacheManager, is to register our CacheManager with the caching infrastructure. If not explicitly defined, the cache infrastructure will try to auto-detect a default CacheManager (a single CacheManager in the context or one marked as primary). Next, there is the keyGenerator overridden method, which will provide the KeyGenerator to use for our used cache.

14-5. Adding and Removing Objects to and from the Cache
Problem

You want to use cache eviction and cache puts when objects get created, updated, or removed.

Solution

Use the @CachePut and @CacheEvict annotations on methods that you want to update or invalidate objects in the cache.

How It Works

Next to @Cacheable Spring also has the @CachePut and @CacheEvict annotations, which, respectively, add and remove objects (or invalidate the whole cache) to/from a cache.

When using caches you don't only want your cache to fill up; you also want it to keep in sync with what is happening inside your application, including object updates and removal. For methods whose results update the cache, add a @CachePut annotation; for methods that invalidate objects inside the cache, use the @CacheEvict annotation.

There is a CustomerRepository, and obtaining the customers from the underlying data source is very time consuming. It is decided that caching is being added to the repository. First, create the CustomerRepository interface.

Listing 14-20. CustomerRepository interface

```
package com.apress.spring6recipes.caching;

public interface CustomerRepository {

  Customer find(long customerId);
  Customer create(String name);
  void update(Customer customer);
  void remove(long customerId);
}
```

There is also a need for a Customer record.

Listing 14-21. Customer class

```
package com.apress.spring6recipes.caching;

public record Customer(long id, String name) { }
```

Finally, the implementation of the `CustomerRepository` interface is based on a `ConcurrentHashMap` as it is just for testing purposes. The slow retrieval is faked with a call to `sleep()`.

Listing 14-22. Map-based CustomerRepository implementation

```java
package com.apress.spring6recipes.caching;

import com.apress.spring6recipes.utils.Utils;
import org.springframework.cache.annotation.Cacheable;

import java.util.Map;
import java.util.concurrent.ConcurrentHashMap;
import java.util.concurrent.atomic.AtomicLong;

public class MapBasedCustomerRepository implements CustomerRepository {

  private final AtomicLong idGenerator = new AtomicLong();
  private final Map<Long, Customer> customers = new ConcurrentHashMap<>();

  @Override
  @Cacheable(value = "customers")
  public Customer find(long customerId) {
    Utils.sleep(500);
    return customers.get(customerId);
  }

  @Override
  public Customer create(String name) {
    var id = idGenerator.incrementAndGet();
    return customers.computeIfAbsent(id, key -> new Customer(key, name));
  }

  @Override
  public void update(Customer customer) {
    customers.put(customer.id(), customer);
  }

  @Override
  public void remove(long customerId) {
    customers.remove(customerId);
  }
}
```

Next, everything needs to be configured with a configuration class.

Listing 14-23. Configuration class

```java
package com.apress.spring6recipes.caching.config;

import com.apress.spring6recipes.caching.CustomerRepository;
import com.apress.spring6recipes.caching.MapBasedCustomerRepository;
import com.github.benmanes.caffeine.cache.Caffeine;
```

```java
import org.springframework.cache.CacheManager;
import org.springframework.cache.annotation.EnableCaching;
import org.springframework.cache.caffeine.CaffeineCacheManager;
import org.springframework.context.annotation.Bean;
import org.springframework.context.annotation.Configuration;

import java.time.Duration;

@Configuration
@EnableCaching
public class CustomerConfiguration {

  @Bean
  public CacheManager cacheManager() {
    var caffeine = Caffeine.newBuilder()
            .maximumSize(1000)
            .expireAfterWrite(Duration.ofMinutes(5));
    var cacheManager = new CaffeineCacheManager();
    cacheManager.setCaffeine(caffeine);
    return cacheManager;
  }

  @Bean
  public CustomerRepository customerRepository() {
    return new MapBasedCustomerRepository();
  }
}
```

Last but not least, to be able to run this program, a Main class is needed.

Listing 14-24. Main class

```java
package com.apress.spring6recipes.caching;

import com.apress.spring6recipes.caching.config.CustomerConfiguration;
import org.springframework.context.annotation.AnnotationConfigApplicationContext;
import org.springframework.util.StopWatch;

public class Main {

  public static void main(String[] args) {
    var cfg = CustomerConfiguration.class;
    try (var context = new AnnotationConfigApplicationContext(cfg)) {
      var customerRepository = context.getBean(CustomerRepository.class);
      var sw = new StopWatch("Cache Evict and Put");

      sw.start("Get 'Unknown Customer'");
      var customer = customerRepository.find(System.currentTimeMillis());
      System.out.println("Get 'Unknown Customer' (result) : " + customer);
      sw.stop();
```

```java
        sw.start("Create New Customer");
        customer = customerRepository.create("Marten Deinum");
        System.out.println("Create new Customer (result) : " + customer);
        sw.stop();

        long customerId = customer.id();

        sw.start("Get 'New Customer 1'");
        customer = customerRepository.find(customerId);
        System.out.println("Get 'New Customer 1' (result) : " + customer);
        sw.stop();

        sw.start("Get 'New Customer 2'");
        customer = customerRepository.find(customerId);
        System.out.println("Get 'New Customer 2' (result) : " + customer);
        sw.stop();

        sw.start("Update Customer");
        customer = new Customer(customer.id(), "Josh Long");
        customerRepository.update(customer);
        sw.stop();

        sw.start("Get 'Updated Customer 1'");
        customer = customerRepository.find(customerId);
        System.out.println("Get 'Updated Customer 1' (result) : " + customer);
        sw.stop();

        sw.start("Get 'Updated Customer 2'");
        customer = customerRepository.find(customerId);
        System.out.println("Get 'Updated Customer 2' (result) : " + customer);
        sw.stop();

        sw.start("Remove Customer");
        customerRepository.remove(customer.id());
        sw.stop();

        sw.start("Get 'Deleted Customer 1'");
        customer = customerRepository.find(customerId);
        System.out.println("Get 'Deleted Customer 1' (result) : " + customer);
        sw.stop();

        sw.start("Get 'Deleted Customer 2'");
        customer = customerRepository.find(customerId);
        System.out.println("Get 'Deleted Customer 2' (result) : " + customer);
        sw.stop();

        System.out.println();
        System.out.println(sw.prettyPrint());
    }
  }
}
```

First thing to notice is the amount of System.out calls that use a StopWatch. These are there to show the behavior of what is happening to the program. After running this class, there should be output similar to that in Figure 14-1.

Figure 14-1. *Initial output of running main*

There are a couple of things to notice in the output of running the program. First, after removing the customer, we still get a result when trying to find the deleted customer. This is due to the fact that the object is only removed from the repository. If it still is in the cache, that is being used. Second, the first get after creating the customer is taking a long time. It would be more efficient to have the created customer cached immediately. Third, although not directly apparent from the output, is the fact that the first get after the update of the object is really fast. After updating the object, the cached instance should be removed.

Using @CacheEvict to Remove Invalid Objects

When an object is removed from the underlying repository, it has to be removed from the cache (or maybe the whole cache needs to be invalidated). To do this, add the @CacheEvict annotation to the remove method. Now when this method is called, the object with the same key will be removed from the cache.

Listing 14-25. CustomerRepository with @CacheEvict

```
package com.apress.spring6recipes.caching;

import org.springframework.cache.annotation.CacheEvict;

public class MapBasedCustomerRepository implements CustomerRepository {

  @Override
  @CacheEvict("customers")
  public void remove(long customerId) {
    customers.remove(customerId);
  }
}
```

Notice the @CacheEvict annotation on the remove method needs the name of the cache from which to remove the item. In this case the cache name is customers. It has a few other attributes that can be used (see Table 14-1).

Table 14-1. *@CacheEvict Attributes*

Attribute	Description
key	SpEL expression for computing the key. Default is to use all method arguments.
keyGenerator	The name of the bean to use for generating the key. Mutually exclusive with key.
condition	The condition on which the cache will or will not be invalidated.
allEntries	Should the whole cache be evicted; default is false.
beforeInvocation	Should the cache be invalidated before or after (the default) method invocation. When invoked before the method, the cache will invalidate regardless of the method outcome (successful or with exception).

When running the Main program again, the output has changed a little (see Figure 14-2).

Figure 14-2. *Output after adding @CacheEvict to the remove method*

Looking at the output, it is apparent that when a customer is removed, there is no more result. When retrieving the deleted customer, null is returned instead of a cached instance. Next, let's add the @CacheEvict annotation to the update method. After an update the object should be retrieved from the underlying data source again. Adding it to the update method however yields a problem. The method argument is a Customer, whereas the cache uses the id of the customer as a key. (Remember that the default key generation strategy uses all method arguments to generate the key; the find and remove methods both have a long as method argument.)

To overcome this we can write a little SpEL expression in the key attribute. We want it to use the ID property of the first argument as the key. The #customer.id expression will take care of that. It will reference the method argument named customer.

The modified update method looks like the following.

Listing 14-26. CustomerRepository with @CacheEvict on the update method

```
package com.apress.spring6recipes.caching;

import org.springframework.cache.annotation.CacheEvict;

public class MapBasedCustomerRepository implements CustomerRepository {

  @Override
  @CacheEvict(value="customers", key = "#customer.id")
  public void update(Customer customer) {
    customers.put(customer.id(), customer);
  }
}
```

After running the main, the timing information shows that the first lookup for the updated customer takes a little longer (see Figure 14-3).

Figure 14-3. *Output after adding @CacheEvict to the update method*

Using @CachePut to Place Objects in the Cache

The create method creates a Customer object based on the input at the moment. The first find for this object after the creation takes some time to finish. Although it works, it can be made faster by having the create method place the object into the cache.

To make a method put a value in the cache, there is the @CachePut annotation. The annotation requires the name of the cache to add the object to; this is done through the value attribute. Just like the other annotations, there are also the key, condition, and unless attributes.

Listing 14-27. CustomerRepository with @CachePut

```java
package com.apress.spring6recipes.caching;

import org.springframework.cache.annotation.CacheEvict;
import java.util.concurrent.atomic.AtomicLong;

public class MapBasedCustomerRepository implements CustomerRepository {

    @Override
    @CachePut(value="customers", key = "#result.id")
    public Customer create(String name) {
    }
}
```

First, notice the @CachePut annotation on the create method. It is given the name of the cache, customers, through the value attribute. The key attribute is needed because in general a method that creates an object returns the actual object to be cached. The key however is generally not the object itself, hence the need to specify a SpEL expression for the key attribute. The #result placeholder gives access to the returned object. As the id of the Customer object is the key, the expression #result.id yields the desired result.

The result of running the main program should be comparable with the one in Figure 14-4.

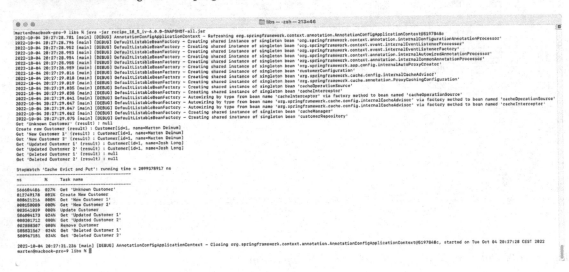

Figure 14-4. The result after adding @CachePut to the create method

The first retrieval of the newly created customer is now a lot faster as the object is returned from the cache instead of being looked up from the repository.

Vetoing Results for the @Cacheable Annotation

At the moment the find method caches all results even when the method returns null. It can be undesirable to disable caching. For certain results you can use the unless attribute on the @Cacheable annotation. When the criteria (a SpEL expression) are met, the returned object is not cached.

Listing 14-28. CustomerRepository with @Cacheable

```
package com.apress.spring6recipes.caching;

import org.springframework.cache.annotation.CacheEvict;
import java.util.concurrent.atomic.AtomicLong;

public class MapBasedCustomerRepository implements CustomerRepository {

    @Override
    @Cacheable(value = "customers", unless="#result == null")
    public Customer find(long customerId) {
    }
}
```

Notice the expression in the `unless` attribute. If the result is `null`, the caching will be vetoed. The `#result` placeholder gives one access to the object returned from the called method. This can be used to write an expression. The expression here is a simple `null` check.

Figure 14-5 shows the results after excluding null from being cached. Both lookups for the deleted customer take approximately the same amount of time.

Figure 14-5. *Results after excluding null from being cached*

14-6. Synchronize Caching with a Transactional Resource
Problem

You want your cache to be transaction aware.

Solution

Some of the Spring-provided CacheManager implementations can be made aware of the fact that they are running in a transactional context. The JCacheCacheManager is one of them. To switch on the transaction awareness, set the transactionAware property to true. For those that aren't by default aware of transactions, you can wrap them in a TransactionAwareCacheManagerProxy to make them transaction aware.

How It Works

First, create a transactional implementation of the CustomerRepository, for instance, using a JdbcTemplate (see Chapter 6 for more information).

Listing 14-29. CustomerRepository JDBC implementation

```java
package com.apress.spring6recipes.caching;

import org.springframework.cache.annotation.CacheEvict;
import org.springframework.cache.annotation.CachePut;
import org.springframework.cache.annotation.Cacheable;
import org.springframework.jdbc.core.JdbcTemplate;
import org.springframework.jdbc.support.GeneratedKeyHolder;
import org.springframework.stereotype.Repository;
import org.springframework.transaction.annotation.Transactional;

import javax.sql.DataSource;
import java.sql.Statement;

@Repository
@Transactional
public class JdbcCustomerRepository implements CustomerRepository {

  private final JdbcTemplate jdbc;

  public JdbcCustomerRepository(JdbcTemplate jdbc) {
    this.jdbc = jdbc;
  }

  @Override
  @Cacheable(value = "customers")
  public Customer find(long customerId) {
    var sql = "SELECT id, name FROM customer WHERE id=?";
    return jdbc.queryForObject(sql, (rs, rowNum) ->
            new Customer(rs.getLong(1), rs.getString(2)));
  }

  @Override
  @CachePut(value = "customers", key = "#result.id")
  public Customer create(String name) {
    var sql = "INSERT INTO customer (name) VALUES (?);";
    var keyHolder = new GeneratedKeyHolder();
    jdbc.update(con -> {
```

```
      var ps = con.prepareStatement(sql, Statement.RETURN_GENERATED_KEYS);
      ps.setString(1, name);
      return ps;
   }, keyHolder);

   return new Customer(keyHolder.getKey().longValue(), name);
}

@Override
@CacheEvict(value = "customers", key = "#customer.id")
public void update(Customer customer) {
  var sql = "UPDATE customer SET name=? WHERE id=?";
  jdbc.update(sql, customer.name(), customer.id());
}

@Override
@CacheEvict(value = "customers")
public void remove(long customerId) {
  var sql = "DELETE FROM customer WHERE id=?";
  jdbc.update(sql, customerId);
}
}
```

Now you need to add a DataSource, JdbcTemplate, and DataSourceTransactionManager and of course the JdbcCustomerRepository to your configuration.

Listing 14-30. CustomerRepository JDBC configuration

```
@Bean
public CustomerRepository customerRepository(JdbcTemplate jdbc) {
  return new JdbcCustomerRepository(jdbc);
}

@Bean
public DataSourceTransactionManager transactionManager(DataSource dataSource) {
  return new DataSourceTransactionManager(dataSource);
}

@Bean
public DataSource dataSource() {
  return new EmbeddedDatabaseBuilder()
          .setType(EmbeddedDatabaseType.H2)
          .setName("customers")
          .addScript("classpath:/schema.sql").build();
}

@Bean
public JdbcTemplate jdbcTemplate(DataSource ds) {
  return new JdbcTemplate(ds);
}
```

The CUSTOMER table is defined in the following schema.sql.

Listing 14-31. Customer table

```
CREATE TABLE customer (
  id bigint AUTO_INCREMENT PRIMARY KEY,
  name VARCHAR(255) NOT NULL
);
```

Finally, we need to wrap our `CaffeineCacheManager` in the `TransactionAwareCacheManagerProxy`. Doing so will wrap the actual `Cache` instances with a `TransactionAwareCacheDecorator` that will register the operations on the cache with the current ongoing transaction (or execute directly if no transaction is available).

Listing 14-32. CaffeineCacheManager wrapped in a transactional-aware proxy

```
@Bean
public CacheManager cacheManager() {
  var caffeine = Caffeine.newBuilder()
          .maximumSize(1000)
          .expireAfterWrite(Duration.ofMinutes(5));
  var cacheManager = new CaffeineCacheManager();
  cacheManager.setCaffeine(caffeine);
  return new TransactionAwareCacheManagerProxy(cacheManager);
}
```

Now when you run, everything should still look normal, but all caching operations are now bound to the successful execution of a transaction. So if the delete fails with an exception, the `Customer` would still be in the cache.

14-7. Using Redis as a Cache Provider
Problem

You want to use Redis as a caching provider.

Solution

Use Spring Data Redis and configure a `RedisCacheManager` to connect to a Redis instance. See also Chapter 9 for more information on Redis and Spring Data Redis.

You will need dependencies for both Redis and Spring Data Redis in your classpath.

Listing 14-33. Gradle dependencies

```
implementation group: 'redis.clients', name: 'jedis', version: '4.3.1'
implementation group: 'org.springframework.data', name: 'spring-data-redis', version: '3.0.0'
```

Listing 14-34. Maven dependencies

```
<dependency>
  <groupId>redis.clients</groupId>
  <artifactId>jedis</artifactId>
  <version>4.3.1</version>
```

```
  </dependency>
<dependency>
  <groupId>org.springframework.data</groupId>
  <artifactId>spring-data-redis</artifactId>
  <version>3.0.0</version>
</dependency>
```

How It Works

First, make sure you have Redis up and running.

 There is a `redis.sh` in the `bin` directory that starts a Dockerized version of Redis.

Configure the RedisCacheManager

To be able to use Redis for caching, you need to set up RedisCacheManager, which will delegate caching to Redis. The RedisCacheManager in turn requires a RedisConnectionFactory to use for its operations. It is also possible to change the Serializer used and for instance use Jackson to store JSON instead of a byte[].

Listing 14-35. Configuration with Redis

```java
package com.apress.spring6recipes.caching.config;

import com.apress.spring6recipes.caching.CustomerRepository;
import com.apress.spring6recipes.caching.MapBasedCustomerRepository;
import org.springframework.cache.annotation.EnableCaching;
import org.springframework.context.annotation.Bean;
import org.springframework.context.annotation.Configuration;
import org.springframework.data.redis.cache.RedisCacheManager;
import org.springframework.data.redis.connection.RedisConnectionFactory;
import org.springframework.data.redis.connection.jedis.JedisConnectionFactory;

@Configuration
@EnableCaching
public class CustomerConfiguration {

  @Bean
  public RedisCacheManager cacheManager(RedisConnectionFactory connectionFactory) {
    return RedisCacheManager.create(connectionFactory);
  }

  @Bean
  public RedisConnectionFactory redisConnectionFactory() {
    return new JedisConnectionFactory();
  }
```

```
@Bean
public CustomerRepository customerRepository() {
  return new MapBasedCustomerRepository();
}
}
```

To connect to Redis, you set up the `JedisConnectionFactory`, which itself is used to configure the `RedisCacheManager`. With the default configuration, the objects we store need to be `Serializable`, so our `Customer` record also needs to implement this interface.

The remaining code can remain untouched. When running the main program, it will show, among others things, the adding and removing of objects to and from the cache.

14-8. Summary

First, you discovered how to add caching to your application and that it is quite cumbersome to do so, especially if you want to introduce this in multiple parts of your code. You explored both the plain Caffeine Cache API and Spring's cache abstraction. After doing manual caching, you explored applying caching with AOP, both with plain Spring AOP using proxies and with AspectJ using load-time weaving.

Next, you learned about the different annotations, `@Cacheable`, `@CacheEvict`, and `@CachePut`, and how those influence the caching behavior of your application. You also learned how to use a SpEL expression to retrieve the correct key for caching or cache invalidation and how to influence the caching behavior of the `@Cacheable` annotation.

The final recipe introduced Redis as a caching solution and explored how it can be used as a local or remote caching solution.

Index

■ N

■ O

■ S

Printed in the United States
by Baker & Taylor Publisher Services